Plants and Vegetation
Origins, Processes, Consequences

Plants make up 99.9 percent of the world's living matter, provide food and shelter, and control the Earth's climate. The study of plant ecology is therefore essential to understanding the biological functions and processes of the biosphere. This vibrant new introductory textbook integrates important classical themes with recent ideas, models, and data.

The book begins with the origin of plants and their role in creating the biosphere as the context for discussing plant functional types and evolutionary patterns. The coverage continues logically through the exploration of causation with chapters, amongst others, on resources, stress, competition, herbivory, and mutualism. The book concludes with a chapter on conservation, addressing the concern that as many as one-third of all plant species are at risk of extinction.

Each chapter is enriched with striking and unusual examples of plants (e.g., stone plants, carnivorous plants) and plant habitats (e.g., isolated tropical tepui, arctic cliffs). Paul Keddy's lively and thought-provoking style will appeal to students at all levels.

PAUL KEDDY is the first holder of the Schlieder Endowed Chair for Environmental Studies at Southeastern Louisiana University. His current research explores the environmental factors that control plant communities, and how these factors can be manipulated to maintain and restore biological diversity. Dr. Keddy has published more than a hundred scholarly papers on plant ecology, and is designated a Highly Cited Researcher in Ecology and Environment by the Institute for Scientific Information. He is the author of *Wetland Ecology: Principles and Applications* (winner of the Society of Wetland Scientists' Merit Award) and *Competition* (awarded the Lawson Medal by the Canadian Botanical Association and the Gleason Prize by the New York Botanical Garden). Dr. Keddy also co-edited *The World's Largest Wetlands: Ecology and Conservation* and *Ecological Assembly Rules: Perspectives, Advances, Retreats*.

Plants and Vegetation

Origins, Processes, Consequences

Paul A. Keddy

CAMBRIDGE
UNIVERSITY PRESS

CAMBRIDGE UNIVERSITY PRESS
Cambridge, New York, Melbourne, Madrid, Cape Town, Singapore, São Paulo

Cambridge University Press
The Edinburgh Building, Cambridge CB2 8RU, UK

Published in the United States of America by Cambridge University Press, New York

www.cambridge.org
Information on this title: www.cambridge.org/9780521864800

First published 2007

Printed in the United Kingdom at the University Press, Cambridge

A catalog record for this publication is available from the British Library

ISBN-13 978-0-521-86480-0 hardback

Epigraph

The mass of vegetation on the Earth very far exceeds that of animal organisms; for what is the volume of all the large living Cetacea and Pachydermata when compared with the thickly-crowded colossal trunks of trees, of from eight to twelve feet in diameter, which fill the vast forests covering the tropical region of South America, between the Orinoco, the Amazon, and the Rio da Madeira? And although the character of different portions of the earth depends on the combination of external phenomena, as the outlines of mountains – the physiognomy of plants and animals – the azure of the sky – the forms of the clouds – and the transparency of the atmosphere – it must still be admitted that the vegetable mantle with which the earth is decked constitutes the main feature of the picture.

von Humboldt, A. 1845.

Cosmos: A Sketch of the Physical Description of the Universe.

Volume 1. Translated by E. C. Otté. Foundations of Natural History.

Baltimore: Johns Hopkins University Press. 1997.

(Originally produced in five volumes:

1845, 1847, 1850–51, 1858, and 1862.) p. 343.

Contents

Preface   *page* xvii
Acknowledgements   xxii

Chapter 1 Plants and the origin of the biosphere

1.1 Introduction   1
1.2 Energy flow and photosynthesis   4
1.3 Membranes   10
1.4 Eukaryotic cells   11
1.5 The origin of photosynthesis   15
1.6 The oxygen revolution   18
    1.6.1 Changes in ocean chemistry   18
    1.6.2 Changes in the composition of the atmosphere 20
    1.6.3 Formation of the ozone layer   20
1.7 The Cambrian explosion of multicellular life   21
1.8 Colonizing the land   21
1.9 Plants and climate   26
1.10 Sediment and ice cores: reconstructing past climates   28
1.11 Conclusion   33
    Further reading   34

Chapter 2 Description of vegetation: the search for
global patterns

2.1 Introduction   35
2.2 Phylogenetic perspectives   36
    2.2.1 Early plant classification: Linnaeus, Bentham,
        Hooker   36
    2.2.2 The discovery of evolution: Wallace, Darwin,
        Bessey   38
    2.2.3 Molecular systematics and phylogeny   41
    2.2.4 The two largest families of plants: Asteraceae
        and Orchidaceae   43
    2.2.5 World floristic regions: phylogeny and geography 46
    2.2.6 Summary and limitations   48
2.3 Functional perspectives   50
    2.3.1 von Humboldt, Raunkiaer, Küchler   51
    2.3.2 The classification of climate   56
    2.3.3 Limitations   58
2.4 Conclusion   59
    Further reading   61

Chapter 3 | Resources

3.1 Introduction   63
    3.1.1 The CHNOPS perspective   63
    3.1.2 The costs of acquisition   67
3.2 Carbon dioxide: foraging in an atmospheric reservoir   68
3.3 Light and photosynthesis: harvesting photons   70
    3.3.1 Three measures of photon harvest   70
    3.3.2 Architecture and photon harvesting   70
    3.3.3 Different photosynthetic types   73
    3.3.4 An exception to the rule: root uptake of CO_2 75
    3.3.5 Another view of photosynthetic types   76
    3.3.6 The overriding importance of height   77
    3.3.7 Ecosystem effects: net primary production changes
       with plant size   78
3.4 Below-ground resources   79
    3.4.1 Water   79
    3.4.2 Mineral nutrients: a single cell perspective   81
    3.4.3 Phosphorus   83
    3.4.4 Nitrogen   85
    3.4.5 Experimental tests for nitrogen and phosphorus
       limitation   86
    3.4.6 Other sources of evidence for nutrient limitation   91
3.5 Changing availability of resources in space and time   93
    3.5.1 Small scale heterogeneity   93
    3.5.2 Resource gradients   94
    3.5.3 Resources in transitory patches   100
3.6 Resources as a habitat template for plant populations   101
3.7 Resource fluctuations complicate short-term
    ecological studies   105
3.8 Chronic scarcity of resources and conservation   108
    3.8.1 Limitation by scarce resources   108
    3.8.2 Conservation of scarce resources   114
3.9 Soils   116
3.10 Two historical digressions   120
3.11 Humans and soil resources   121
3.12 Conclusion   123
    Further reading   125

Chapter 4 | Stress

4.1 Introduction   126
    4.1.1 Definitions   126
    4.1.2 More on terminology   127
4.2 Some general consequences of stress   128
    4.2.1 Short-term effects: stress has metabolic costs   128
    4.2.2 The costs of adaptation to stress   131

4.2.3 Growth rate   134
4.2.4 Seed size   135
4.2.5 Clonal integration   140
4.3 Habitats with drought as the predominant stress   144
4.3.1 Deserts   144
4.3.2 Mediterranean shrublands   150
4.3.3 Rock barrens   152
4.3.4 Coniferous forests   156
4.4 Unavailability of resources   159
4.5 Presence of a regulator   162
4.5.1 Salinity   162
4.5.2 Cold environments: arctic and alpine examples   167
4.5.3 Early spring photosynthesis in temperate climates   171
4.6 Extreme cases of stress tolerance   173
4.6.1 Cold and drought tolerance of lichens   173
4.6.2 Endolithic communities   174
4.6.3 Flood tolerance   176
4.7 The smoking hills: a natural occurrence of stress
     from air pollution   179
4.8 Effects of ionizing radiation upon mixed forest   180
4.9 Moisture and temperature at different scales   182
4.10 Conclusion   184
      Further reading   185

Chapter 5 | Competition

5.1 Introduction   186
5.1.1 The importance of competition   186
5.1.2 Definition of competition   187
5.1.3 Stress, strain, and the costs of competition   187
5.2 Kinds of competition   188
5.2.1 Intraspecific competition   188
5.2.2 Distinguishing between intraspecific and
       interspecific competition   190
5.2.3 Competition intensity   191
5.2.4 Competitive effect and competitive response   193
5.2.5 Competitive dominance   194
5.3 More examples of competition   197
5.3.1 Self-thinning   197
5.3.2 Dominance patterns in monocultures   198
5.3.3 Density dependence in annual plants   200
5.3.4 The relationship between intensity and asymmetry
       of competition   202
5.4 Competitive hierarchies   204
5.4.1 Establishing hierarchies   204
5.4.2 The consistency of hierarchies   206

	5.4.3 Light and shoot size	209
	5.4.4 Foraging for patches of light or soil nutrients	213
5.5	Mycorrhizae and competition	214
5.6	Competition gradients	216
	5.6.1 Measuring competition intensity	216
	5.6.2 Competition intensity gradients in an old field	217
	5.6.3 Competition and cacti	218
	5.6.4 Competition intensity along a soil depth gradient	218
	5.6.5 Competition intensity gradients in wetlands	220
	5.6.6 Competition along an altitudinal gradient	220
5.7	Conclusion	223
	Further reading	223

Chapter 6 | Disturbance

6.1	Introduction	225
6.2	Four properties of disturbance	226
	6.2.1 Duration	226
	6.2.2 Intensity	226
	6.2.3 Frequency	227
	6.2.4 Area	228
6.3	Examples of disturbance	228
	6.3.1 Fire	228
	6.3.2 Erosion	236
	6.3.3 Animals	238
	6.3.4 Burial	243
	6.3.5 Ice	249
	6.3.6 Waves	249
	6.3.7 Storms	252
6.4	Catastrophes: low frequency and high intensity	254
	6.4.1 Landslides	254
	6.4.2 Volcanic eruptions	255
	6.4.3 Meteor impacts	259
6.5	Measuring the effects of disturbance	264
	6.5.1 The Hubbard Brook study of forested watersheds	264
	6.5.2 Ottawa River marshes	268
6.6	Disturbance and gap dynamics	269
	6.6.1 Regeneration from buried seeds after disturbance	270
	6.6.2 Gap regeneration in deciduous forests	272
	6.6.3 Alluvial deposition	274
	6.6.4 Freshwater marshes	274
6.7	Synthesis: fire, flooding, and sea level in the Everglades	275
6.8	Competition, disturbance, and stress: the CSR synthesis	276
6.9	Conclusion	282
	Further reading	282

Chapter 7 | Herbivory

7.1 Introduction   284
7.2 Field observations on wildlife diets   286
    7.2.1 Herbivores in African grasslands   286
    7.2.2 Herbivorous insects in tropical forest canopies   289
    7.2.3 Giant tortoises on islands   290
    7.2.4 Herbivory in anthropogenic landscapes   292
7.3 Plant defenses   293
    7.3.1 Evolutionary context   293
    7.3.2 Structures that protect seeds: strobili and squirrels   293
    7.3.3 Secondary metabolites that protect foliage   297
    7.3.4 Two cautions when interpreting anti-herbivore traits   299
    7.3.5 Food quality and nitrogen content   300
    7.3.6 Coevolution: a brief preview   302
7.4 Field experiments   303
    7.4.1 Herbivorous insects in deciduous forest canopies   304
    7.4.2 Land crabs in tropical forest   305
    7.4.3 Herbivores in grassland: the Cape Province, the Pampas, and the Serengeti   306
    7.4.4 Effects of rhinoceroses in tropical floodplain forest   313
    7.4.5 Large mammals in deciduous forest   313
    7.4.6 Effects of an introduced species: nutria   316
7.5 Empirical relationships   318
7.6 Some theoretical context   322
    7.6.1 Top-down or bottom-up?   322
    7.6.2 Effects of selective herbivory on plant diversity   324
    7.6.3 A simple model of herbivory   325
    7.6.4 Extensions of herbivory models   327
7.7 Conclusion   332
    Further reading   334

Chapter 8 | Positive interactions: mutualism, commensalism, and symbiosis

8.1 Introduction   336
    8.1.1 Definitions   336
    8.1.2 History   337
8.2 Positive interactions between plants and plants   338
    8.2.1 Nurse plants   338
    8.2.2 Stress gradients and competition   341
    8.2.3 More cases of co-operation   342
    8.2.4 Summary   345
8.3 Positive interactions between fungi and plants   346
    8.3.1 Ectomycorrhizae and endomycorrhizae   346
    8.3.2 Ectomycorrhizae and forests   349

8.3.3 Mycorrhizae in wetlands   350

8.3.4 Costs and benefits of mycorrhizal associations   354

8.3.5 Lichens   355

8.4 Positive interactions between plants and animals   358

8.4.1 Animals and flowers   358

8.4.2 Animals and seed dispersal   365

8.4.3 The costs of sexual reproduction   379

8.4.4 Experimental tests of the value of sexuality   381

8.4.5 Animals defending plants   387

8.4.6 Microbes in animal guts   390

8.5 Mathematical models of mutualism   395

8.5.1 Population dynamics models   395

8.5.2 Cost-benefit models   396

8.6 Mutualism and apparent competition   398

8.7 Conclusion   399

Further reading   402

Chapter 9 | Time

9.1 Introduction   403

9.2 $>10^6$ years: the origin of the angiosperms and
continental drift   405

9.2.1 Temperate evergreen forests   410

9.2.2 Deserts   411

9.2.3 Tropical floras   412

9.3 $>10^4$ years: the Pleistocene glaciations   418

9.3.1 Erosion and deposition by glacial ice   419

9.3.2 Loess   419

9.3.3 Pluvial lakes   422

9.3.4 Drought and tropical forests   423

9.3.5 Sea level decrease   425

9.3.6 Migration   426

9.3.7 Hominids   428

9.3.8 Flooding   430

9.4 $>10^2$ years: plant succession   431

9.4.1 Succession   431

9.4.2 Examples of succession   432

9.4.3 Predictive models for plant succession   446

9.4.4 Synthesis   448

9.5 Conclusion   454

Further reading   455

Chapter 10 | Gradients and plant communities: description at local scales

10.1 Introduction   457

10.2 Describing pattern along obvious natural gradients   458

10.3 Multivariate methods for pattern detection   464

10.3.1 The data matrix 465
10.3.2 Measuring similarity 466
10.3.3 Ordination techniques 468
10.3.4 Ordinations based upon species data 468
10.3.5 Ordinations combining species and
environmental data 470
10.3.6 Functional simplification in ordination 471
10.4 Vegetation classification 474
10.4.1 Phytosociology 475
10.4.2 Classification and land management 476
10.5 Gradients and communities 485
10.5.1 Clements and Gleason 485
10.5.2 The temporary victory of the Gleasonian view 486
10.5.3 Null models and patterns along gradients 487
10.6 Empirical studies of pattern along gradients 491
10.7 Conclusion 500
Further Reading 501

Chapter 11 | Diversity

11.1 Introduction 502
11.2 Large areas have more plant species 502
11.3 Areas with more kinds of habitat have more species 505
11.4 Equatorial areas have more species 508
11.5 Some evolutionary context 514
11.5.1 Four key events 514
11.5.2 Some characteristics of angiosperms 515
11.5.3 Physiological constraints on diversity are
likely additive 516
11.6 Examples of plant species diversity 518
11.6.1 Mediterranean climate regions 518
11.6.2 Carnivorous plants 520
11.6.3 Deciduous forests 522
11.6.4 Diversity, biogeography, and the concept
of endemism 522
11.7 Models to describe species diversity at smaller scales 523
11.7.1 Intermediate biomass 524
11.7.2 Competitive hierarchies 526
11.7.3 Intermediate disturbance 527
11.7.4 Centrifugal organization 529
11.8 Relative abundance – dominance, diversity, and
evenness 532
11.9 Laboratory experiments on richness and diversity 539
11.10 Field experiments on richness and diversity 541
11.11 Implications for conservation 543
11.12 Conclusion 546
Further reading 547

Chapter 12 | Conservation and management

12.1 Introduction	549
12.2 Some historical context	550
12.2.1 Ancient Assyria	550
12.2.2 Deforestation in Ancient Rome and the Mediterranean	551
12.3 Vegetation types at risk	553
12.3.1 The destruction of Louisiana's alluvial forests	553
12.3.2 Islands: Easter Island and the Galapagos	564
12.3.3 Boreal forests	569
12.4 Protection of representative vegetation types	570
12.4.1 Designing reserve systems	570
12.4.2 Hot spots of biological diversity	573
12.4.3 Primary forests	574
12.4.4 Large wetlands	576
12.4.5 New discoveries of species in the Guyana highlands	578
12.4.6 Economic growth, human welfare, and wilderness	580
12.5 Fragmentation of natural landscapes	581
12.5.1 Fens in agricultural landscapes	582
12.5.2 Deciduous forests in agricultural landscapes	584
12.5.3 How much is enough?	586
12.6 Function, management, and thresholds	588
12.6.1 Two perspectives	588
12.6.2 Plant communities are dynamic	592
12.6.3 Ecological footprints for human cities	593
12.6.4 Thresholds	595
12.7 Restoration	599
12.8 Indicators	602
12.9 Conclusion	604
Further reading	608
Questions for Review	610
References	612
Index	667
Enrichment Boxes	
Box 1.1 The biosphere	3
Box 2.1 A man of his times: Alexander von Humboldt	52
Box 3.1 The composition and origin of the atmosphere	66
Box 3.2 Fritz Haber changes the global nitrogen cycle	87
Box 3.3 A Darwinian approach to plant traits	104
Box 4.1 The discovery of carnivorous plants	136
Box 5.1 Testing for higher order pattern in competitive relationships	207
Box 7.1 Experimental design	312
Box 7.2 A demographic study of the effects of deer browsing	315

Box 8.1 The discovery of mycorrhizae by Bernard Frank   348
Box 9.1 Mr. Hofmeister and the vanishing gametophyte   415
Box 10.1 Getting the history right: null models in ecology 488
Box 10.2 A possible synthesis: Gleason, Clements, and a
           community structure continuum   497
Box 11.1 Diversity indices   534
Box 11.2 Rothamsted, the Park Grass Experiment   536
Box 12.1 Conservation of tropical forest in the Carribean:
           ca. 1650–1950   583
Box 12.2 The sinking of the *Rainbow Warrior*   606

Preface

For many years it has been apparent to me that there is a need for a good textbook in plant ecology. This book is aimed at middle to senior level undergraduates. I also hope that it will serve graduate students, fellow professors, and resource managers. Since many of the topics I include were new to me, I assume that they will be new to even relatively advanced readers.

In writing this book, I made two key assumptions regarding the experience of my audience and the availability of introductory biological information. I deliberately wrote for an audience who already had some exposure to both botany and ecology – an audience having had, perhaps, a first semester course in botany and another first semester course in general ecology, or a comprehensive introductory biology course. I assumed my readers would own, or at least would have access to, a basic introductory text in biology. I have *not* tried to repeat or rewrite such texts and have taken for granted that readers will have a working familiarity with topics in plant biology such as photosynthesis, transpiration, and meiosis. I have also *not* tried to repeat basic ecological concepts such as primary production, population growth, decomposition, and nutrient cycling, nor provide a broad illustrated summary of biomes. My impression is that such topics are not only well-covered in good biology texts, but are gradually filtering their way even into the elementary school system. I do, however, revisit many basic topics from photosynthesis to nutrient cycling when important aspects need more emphasis – for example, the way early plants changed the composition of the atmosphere, or how humans have altered the nitrogen cycle with the Haber process. Similarly, while I address the general processes that unify grasslands (e.g., competition, grazing, fire, drought), anyone seeking an elementary enumeration of grassland types or basic information about the geographic distribution of individual grassland types will have to go back to an introductory text. For such background, one might choose among an introductory text in botany, an introductory text in ecology, or the outstanding *Ecology of World Vegetation* (Archibold 1995). I also do not provide a glossary as this is a standard component of introductory texts. Rather than replicating existing textbooks, I have chosen to emphasize unifying topics such as:

1. How populations of plants are assembled into communities and ecosystems.
2. How plants affect their surroundings, and how they are affected by those surroundings, at scales ranging from millimeters (the rhizosphere) to kilometers (the atmosphere).

3. How plants interact with one another, and how they interact with other species, with examples ranging from fungi and worms to tortoises and elephants.

4. How plants and plant communities are dispersed along gradients of time and space. Since so much work these days emphasizes small-scale interactions, I have tried to balance this trend with a temporal scale that includes topics often overlooked in "modern" plant ecology and consequently poorly understood by my own students, such as trends in early plant evolution, consequences of catastrophes such as meteor impacts, and responses to continental glaciations. The spatial scale is equally large, and deliberately emphasizes natural sources of variation in plant communities such as gradients of topography, flooding, fire-frequency, soil fertility, and altitude.

5. How general models and actual applications both have great value in guiding research and classifying thought. I therefore tried to provide most topics with both a theoretical context (e.g., simple mathematical models), and an applied context (e.g., examples of these ideas being applied to manage real ecosystems). These sections tend to occur toward the end of chapters. On first reading you may, if you wish, skip the sections on theory, or skip the sections on applications, or both, and still receive a workable treatment of plant ecology. I, however, would strongly encourage you to read them, at least on the second time through, as these approaches (theoretical and applied) need not be mutually exclusive, and they enrich the rest of the text.

This is explicitly a book about **plant** ecology. It draws upon and respects the variety and complexity of real plants in real plant communities (Keddy 2005b). I have gone out of my way to add examples from parts of the Earth rarely highlighted – the Guyana highlands of South America, the deserts of South Africa, and islands such as the Galapagos and New Caledonia. I have also made a point of including unusual plants – carnivorous plants, arctic-alpine plants, epiphytic plants, parasitic plants, succulent plants, and plants that attract ant colonies. I have not hesitated to include many unfamiliar plant names. As a student, I found lectures on corn and beans, or on weeds and old fields, to be boring. I wanted to learn about the full diversity of the Earth's plant types, and what determined where they were found. Some reviewers have criticized the manuscript for having insufficient examples from North America, where many college texts are marketed. This was a conscious decision on my part. *All* college students whatever their country of origin need to know about noteworthy plants and plant communities found in the rest of the world.

After choosing the audience, and deciding that I would write about real plants in real habitats, the third decision was to include the occasional opinion. I assume that by buying a book by a certain scholar (me, in this case), you wish to benefit from the experience of that scholar. It is traditional to take textbooks and rewrite them with countless referees until all traces of the writer's personality have vanished. This, indeed, was the advice given to my editor, Alan Crowden. It also was the process that another publisher tried to impose upon me. My reaction as a reader was – how boring! My reaction as a writer was – if the committee thinks they are so clever, let them write it themselves. If you want such a book go elsewhere. But before you do, be very clear on one point – all textbooks have enormous amounts of opinion in them. In most cases, that opinion is hidden – that is, the opinion is an *act of omission* – with bodies of work, ideas, and papers simply ignored. Students are unable to protect themselves from these kinds of hidden opinions (e.g., Wardle 1995, Keddy 2004, 2005a). In this book, there really are no more opinions than in any competing text – it is merely that my opinions are out in the open where you can see them; my opinions are acts of *commission*. I try to make it clear where my opinions may be particularly strong, but I am not embarrassed by them. Many papers and books in our field that pass for objective science are in fact laden with opinion, political agendas, and ignorance of history. Students using such books and papers have no way of knowing how much mere opinion they are absorbing. Here you do.

The examples I incorporate to illustrate the topics covered are drawn from work conducted over the last hundred years, including studies by long dead scholars and other scholars whom I know only from reading their work. I provide many suggestions for additional reading, including lists at the end of each chapter – I invite students to broaden their perspective and to seek out original sources. It is not a matter of who you know – it is a matter of who you have read. One referee thought that I cited too much old work – I am of the opinion that too much important old work is being ignored making students (and their professors) vulnerable to false claims of novelty. I would like nothing more than to stimulate a student to go to the library and read old and new work by other scholars. Trust no one, and certainly not me. Read it for yourself.

If there is one other philosophy that guides this book, it is the need to seek general relationships while respecting the details (Keddy 1987, 1994, 2005b). In any field there is a risk that one may become so fascinated by detail that one is unable to relate to any coherent set of principles for summarizing the detail, or for extending them to new situations. At the other extreme, there are monographs written by physicists or zoologists regarding computer models – treatises that are so far removed from botanical reality that they mislead students into thinking that superficial assumptions are a substitute for knowledge about plants. I have tried to ride the razor's edge (or perhaps the enormous valley) between the two – combining respect for the detail (e.g., Figures 4.31, 5.2, 7.11, 8.11) with respect for scientific generalities (e.g., Figures 3.5, 6.3, 7.23, 12.26).

One obstacle to the synthesis of general relationships in ecology is the development of myriad factions, each emphasizing a different view of the discipline. For example, there is a school of phytosociology, a school of plant demography, a school exploring the multivariate techniques of ordination and classification, a school focussed upon mineral nutrition, a school that uses molecular techniques to explore phylogenetic patterns, a school that emphasizes field experiments, and a school studying theoretical models. Superimposed upon this are the schools that organize themselves by habitat, such as wetland ecologists, foresters, desert ecologists, grassland ecologists, and agronomists. Given all these subdivisions of plant ecology, finding generality is challenging. Indeed, any attempt at unification seems to be interpreted as a threat to the importance of each school.

My scientific philosophy is rooted in the pragmatic tradition (e.g., James 1907, Keddy 2001, 2005b). I strove to find unifying principles that organize the mass of botanical data that exist today. Some principles may be well-established, others may be more speculative, and I hope that I have made this distinction clear. Further, I try to emphasize that the search for general principles and their strict testing provide both a unifying framework for the discipline and a means of scientific progress. Without a unifying framework, and without an emphasis upon the experimental testing of hypotheses, plant ecology will stagnate (perhaps wither is a better term). We will then lose the best minds to other *apparently* more exciting fields and be left with second-rate minds recycling second-rate ideas.

My objective is to write a text that provides a unified perspective of plant ecology, while including a variety of frames of reference and taking the best from each. No doubt experienced scholars will find inadequacies in their focal areas. I ask them to consider the scope of the discipline that I have covered. Further, anticipating such views, let me suggest that the balance provided is a strength of this book – I do not belong to any one school (I have worked in a range of them), I do not identify with a single habitat (although I confess to having written a book on wetland ecology), and I do not have a small circle of friends whom I intend to cultivate by citing their work to the exclusion of others. Indeed, chronic illness has tended to isolate me for the past 15 years, and from such isolation comes a certain distance and therefore perhaps, a clearer perspective. Hermits and monks have even been thought to obtain wisdom from such isolation.

Will instructors want to use this book in their courses? Or, as some referees suggested, is it too demanding for undergraduates? I am of the opinion that students come to university to learn topics in depth and breadth, and therefore we short-change them when we fail to challenge them sufficiently. If you believe your class to be insufficiently versed in topics such as photosynthesis, transpiration, meiosis or biomes, include these topics in your lectures and guide students through the chapters they find more difficult. Other instructors using this book may prefer to work through chapter by chapter, having students read one chapter each week, and perhaps requiring extra reading for each chapter from the current literature and from papers prior to 1970. Students should be encouraged to visit the library in addition to using the internet to obtain literature. To assist with this process, I have included a set of recommended readings at the end of each chapter. I further suggest instructors add a personal perspective, drawing upon their own experiences in plant ecology. Encourage students to get out in the field and to identify local plants. Emphasize the importance of clear testing of conflicting hypotheses. Raise the topic of the enormous number of plants facing extinction. Remind students that this is a living discipline where bright young minds can make a difference.

My message to students is straightforward: get on with the development of plant ecology. Learn something about the history of your discipline. Learn to identify plants. Buy a good field guide and a magnifying glass. Travel to wild places. Learn about the areas you visit. Find a good ecologist to train you. Do not get involved in political games or one-upmanship. Show respect for those who have gone before by reading their work and thinking about their ideas. Enjoy yourselves. Contribute something to society.

Acknowledgements

I thank the many colleagues who contributed the original research that I have drawn upon for this book. Some of you I still know only from your writing, but that perhaps is the way it should be. I have greatly appreciated the many permissions to reproduce drawings and photographs, and authors' efforts to send originals and notify me of changes. Not every contributor is mentioned here, but the origins of each drawing and photo are clearly stated. Ian Keddy provided considerable assistance, manipulating files in multiple formats to create and adjust illustrations. In addition, line drawings by Howard Coneybeare appear courtesy of Friends of Algonquin Park, line drawings by Rochelle Lawson were borrowed from *Wetland Ecology: Principles and Conservation*, and Betsy Brigham contributed several new illustrations. Cheryl Cundell greatly assisted with compiling the first version of the manuscript. Jennifer Tynes helped with updating permissions. Over the years I have talked with many colleagues about this project, and may not always be aware of important ideas borrowed from them. Early input from Evan Weiher was most helpful. Sara Tenney and Alan Crowden provided solid editorial advice. Recent input from the following was much appreciated: Peter Bellingham, Walter Judd, Walter Larcher, Craig Loehle, Tiffany McFalls, Rick Miller, and Susan Wiser. The librarians at Southeastern Louisiana University provided steady support with many interlibrary loans. Throughout this lengthy process, Cathy Keddy provided encouragement and editorial services beyond compare.

Chapter 1

Plants and the origin of the biosphere

Energy flow and molecular complexity. Membranes. The serial endosymbiosis hypothesis for the origin of eukaryotes. Photosynthesis. The oxygen revolution. The ozone layer. Respiration. Multicellular life. Plant life moves onto land. Evolution and diversification of land plants. Plants, coal, and climate.

1.1 | Introduction

Plants occur in almost every conceivable habitat on Earth – submerged on lake bottoms, exposed on wind-swept mountain tops, hidden within polar rocks, or perched perilously on branches in the rain forest canopy. They can be microscopic (oceanic plankton) or enormous like sequoias and eucalypts that may tower more than a hundred meters tall. Their flowers may span nearly a meter across (*Rafflesia arnoldii*) or extend the height of a human (*Amorphophallus titanum*), and be almost any color of the rainbow. Moreover, plants comprise *more than 99 percent* of all the Earth's living matter! We can also say with confidence that the history of the biosphere is largely the history of the origin and diversification of plants. Without plants, conditions on Earth – including temperature, types of rocks, the composition of the atmosphere, and even the chemical composition of the oceans – would be vastly different.

While plant ecology is generally defined as "the study of relationships between plants and the environment," plants do not, as this definition implies, merely inhabit environments. Plants also modify the environments, and they may even control them. Where, then, should one begin a book on plant ecology? The answer is clearly genesis – the origin of plants and the processes that created the current biosphere.

As we all learned in our first biology course, plants live by capturing sunlight. The first chemical process we were expected to memorize may well have been photosynthesis. This was a world-changing process. Yet by even this early phase in education, too many students are already convinced that plants are boring and can be ignored. Without them, however, none of us would exist. One of my objectives in writing this text was to try to recapture an appreciation of plants and basic botany, while also illustrating the importance of studying plants and their environments.

The world will always need botanists and plant ecologists. Many of the students in my courses seem to want to use their skills to protect wild species and improve the human condition, but I often find it necessary to explain that it is rarely possible to be effective at these tasks without some understanding of botany and ecology. If you want to contribute to ecology, or to conservation, or to many kinds of human welfare, you have to know something about plants first.

Since plants have a broad impact, those of you planning to work in fields including forestry, zoology, fisheries management, geography, planning, or environmental studies (not to mention molecular biology and medicine), may find it helpful, if not absolutely necessary, to know something about plant ecology. Indeed, one could suggest further that there is little point in going on a tropical holiday if you are unable to appreciate the remarkable plants and vegetation. If this book inspires you to continue with the study of plant ecology, and provides some resources to guide you in doing so, it will have succeeded. Equally, however, if it enriches another scholarly discipline that you intend to follow, or at least helps you better appreciate parts of the world that you one day visit, then it will have succeeded.

Before we examine the details of individual plants and types of vegetation, it seems essential that we begin by considering them as a unified whole – as a part of the biosphere. Hence this first chapter. Most newer students that I teach appear to know relatively little about global processes and geological time scales. I will therefore start with the story of plants and the origin of the biosphere in a quite general way, emphasizing long-term consequences for the atmosphere, the oceans and the land. The list of readings will allow you to pursue a deeper understanding of the impacts of plants on biogeochemical cycles, energy flow and the greenhouse effect. In Chapter 2 we will examine global patterns in plant distribution, and some of the explorers who made these important discoveries, which might inspire you to visit new areas of Earth and explore them yourself. Then and only then will we encounter the material with which most text books begin: resources and plant growth. In Chapters 4 to 8 we will work our way through the processes by which plants interact with other plants, fungi, and animals (including competition, herbivory, and mutualism), and the ecological consequences of these interactions. In Chapter 9, we will return to time, including the impacts of meteor collisions and ice ages upon plants and vegetation. Chapters 10 and 11 have more advanced work on patterns in vegetation and how they are studied. We will conclude, in Chapter 12, with the large scale again: the growth of human populations, and its consequences for the biosphere and the Earth's 300 000 plant species.

The word **biosphere**, which refers to that relatively thin layer on the surface of the Earth within which life exists, is now rather familiar to students. Yet the concept, according to Hutchinson (1970), was introduced into science rather casually by the Australian geologist, Eduard Suess in 1875. The idea was largely overlooked until the Russian mineralogist, Vladimir Vernadsky, published *La Biosphère* in 1929 (Box 1.1). The word has now attained a general usage and significance that Vernadsky probably could not have imagined.

Box 1.1 | The biosphere

La Biosphère by Vladimir Vernadsky (1863–1945, Figure B1.1) was published in 1929, based upon a Russian edition in 1926. In this slim book, Vernadsky publicised the term biosphere, which he attributes to E. Suess, a professor at the University of Vienna, an eminent nineteenth century geologist, who introduced the term in 1875. Vernadsky then lays out some basic principles that would become important themes in ecology as the century progressed. These included:

1. That the rates of reproduction of organisms such as termites will lead to geometric rates of increase in population size. A queen termite, for example, produces 60 eggs per minute, or 86 400 in 24 h, in which case in a few years they could cover the entire surface of the Earth, which he estimates at 5.10065×10^8 square kilometres (pp. 39–41). (Darwin, of course, used this observation in formulating the principles of natural selection and evolution.)
2. That, as all organisms could multiply to this extent, an external force (obstacle extérieur) sets an upper limit to their population size. There must be, he adds, some maximum numbers for different life forms, and these abundances, N_{max}, are characteristics of different species (pp. 46–48). (Today this upper limit is termed the carrying capacity, and finds its way into the Lotka-Volterra equations as K.)
3. That the gases of the atmosphere are identical to those created by the gaseous exchange of living organisms. These are oxygen, nitrogen, carbon dioxide, water,

Figure B1.1 Nataliia and Vladimir Vernadsky, 1910 (from Bailes 1990).

hydrogen, methane, and ammonia. This, he adds, is not accident (ne peut être accidentel). The amount of oxygen produced by plants, some 1.5×10^{21} g, corresponds to the amount of living matter that has been produced by plants (p. 57). (The origin of life on Earth is now traced back to gases such as these, leading Morowitz to observe that life is not an accident but an inevitable outcome of energy flow through the atmosphere. In spite of this, too many people, scholars and creationists, insist that life arose by accident.)

Of course, Vernadsky was not always correct. For example, he asserts on p. 63 that:

The green micro-organisms in the ocean are the principal transformers of solar energy to chemical energy on the planet.

(While promises of oceans feeding the world persisted into the late twentieth century, better measures of production revealed that most of the oceans are unproductive, with pockets of high production along coasts, in estuaries, and where upwellings are produced by ocean currents.) None-the-less, one can see in this book an attempt to chart the major processes on Earth in terms of chemical and biological process calculated for the entire planet. The extensive literature on biogeochemical cycles can be traced back to early work such as this.

The biosphere has conditions that are rare in the universe as a whole – liquid water in substantial quantities, an external energy source (the Sun), and temperatures at which there are interfaces between solid, liquid, and gaseous forms of water. Liquid water exists under a rather narrow range of conditions of temperature and pressure. It was once abundant present on Mars and may still occur beneath the ice on Jupiter's moon Europa. New information is continually emerging from interplanetary space probes. At one end of the galactic temperature gradient there are temperatures of trillions of degrees inside stars, and, at the other end, there are conditions near absolute zero in the vastness of space. Neither extreme provides the conditions where biological chemistry, at least as humans understand it, can occur. The Earth offers an intermediate set of environmental conditions, and if it did not, we would not be here to write or to read this book.

1.2 | Energy flow and photosynthesis

For life to exist, energy flow is required. Such a requirement is met when a planet is situated near enough to a star for sufficient energy released by solar fusion to pass the planet before dissipating into outer space. This is the case for our particular planet, situated near a star we know as the Sun. While it is not known how often life occurs, it may not be infrequent, given the enormous size of the universe – our own galaxy has some 100 billion suns, and there now appears to be convincing evidence that some of these suns have their own solar

Table 1.1. | *The early atmosphere of Earth probably resembled the composition of gases produced by volcanoes such as these two on Hawaii (from Strahler 1971).*

Volcanic gases from basaltic lava of Mauna Loa and Kilauea	Percent composition
Water, H_2O	57.8
Total carbon, as CO_2	23.5
Sulfur, S_2	12.6
Nitrogen, N_2	5.7
Argon, A	0.3
Chlorine, Cl_2	0.1
Fluorine, F_2	—
Hydrogen, H_2	0.04

systems. This provides many opportunities for other possible planets to be affected by flowing energy. Proximity to a source of solar energy is essential for life because that energy flow, by itself, organizes matter. Life, at least as it is presently understood, is matter that has been organized by energy flow. Morowitz (1968) has examined the relationships among energy flow, thermodynamics, and life asserting that in order to properly understand life, one must look at the relationship between physical laws and biological systems. He demonstrates that flowing energy can create complexity out of simplicity.

Once the requirement for energy is met, life then requires resources. This begs the question of what those early resources might have been. One way to answer such a question is to ask what conditions would have existed in the early Earth's atmosphere before there was life, since the early atmosphere would likely have been one source of resources for the precursors of living cells. Determining what the early atmosphere was like, however, requires considerable detective work (e.g., Oparin 1938, Strahler 1971, Levin 1994). It seems that this atmosphere would have come, in part, from volcanic out-gassings. For clues about its composition one can measure the current composition of volcanic gases. Table 1.1 shows that the early atmosphere would likely have been composed of water, carbon dioxide, and sulfur. It was an atmosphere rather different from that of today. Yet, some billions of years later, these basic molecules remain as the principal constituents of cellulose, the dominant structural molecule of plants, and the most abundant (by mass) molecule in the biosphere (Duchesne and Larson 1989).

Morowitz (1968) presents thermodynamic calculations illustrating how energy flow stimulates chemical interactions and creates molecules with higher potential energy. From chemical interactions taking place within the volcanic gas mixture given in Table 1.1, molecules such as methane and ammonia will result. These molecules are thought to have been major constituents of the early atmosphere. Morowitz demonstrates mathematically that, with energy flow

Table 1.2. *The equilibrium concentration of chemical compounds formed in the mixed gas with the composition $C_2H_{10}NO_8$ at 1 atm and 500 °C (from Morowitz 1968).*

Compound	Equilibrium concentration	Compound	Equilibrium concentration
Water	2.24	Glycine	0.48×10^{-21}
Carbon dioxide	0.88	Acetylene	0.11×10^{-22}
Nitrogen	0.50	Lactic acid	0.20×10^{-23}
Methane	0.12	Acetamide	0.11×10^{-23}
Hydrogen	0.18×10^{-1}	Ethylene glycol	0.62×10^{-24}
Ammonia	0.15×10^{-3}	Benzene	0.52×10^{-25}
Carbon monoxide	0.54×10^{-4}	Alanine	0.97×10^{-27}
Ethane	0.34×10^{-7}	Furan	0.14×10^{-28}
Formic acid	0.93×10^{-9}	Pyrrole	0.31×10^{-30}
Acetic acid	0.25×10^{-9}	Pyridine	0.16×10^{-30}
Methanol	0.73×10^{-11}	Cyanogen	0.77×10^{-31}
Formaldehyde	0.13×10^{-11}	Benzoic acid	0.65×10^{-31}
Ethylene	0.88×10^{-13}	Pyruvic acid	0.31×10^{-31}
Hydrogen cyanide	0.73×10^{-13}	Pyrimidine	0.13×10^{-31}
Methylamine	0.64×10^{-13}	Phenol	0.10×10^{-31}
Acetaldehyde	0.81×10^{-14}	Xylene	0.17×10^{-33}
Ethanol	0.49×10^{-15}	Benzaldehyde	0.12×10^{-35}
Acetone	0.92×10^{-17}	Naphthalene	$<10^{-38}$
Ketone	0.19×10^{-17}	Anthracene	$<10^{-38}$
Methyl ether	0.30×10^{-19}	Asphalt	$<10^{-38}$
Formamide	0.24×10^{-20}	Oxygen	$<10^{-38}$

and simple mixtures of gases, increasingly complex molecules are formed. For example, a gaseous mixture of carbon, hydrogen, nitrogen, and oxygen at 500 °C yields mostly water and CO_2 with smaller amounts of other molecules, such as methane and ethane, which have higher potential energy (Table 1.2). The latter molecules are less likely to form because they are larger and therefore more energy is required to create them. As energy flows through the molecular system, however, the energy distribution shifts upward toward more and more complicated molecules.

Morowitz postulates that energy flow through the early atmosphere yielded similar results: starting off with simple low energy molecules such as water, CO_2, and nitrogen, more complex molecules were produced. The production of molecules was driven by the external energy source, which on Earth is the Sun. While some authors suggest that the origin of life by such means contradicts the second law of thermodynamics, what they fail to appreciate is that the second law applies to closed systems. The biosphere is an open system where, so long as energy flow occurs, organization will increase.

Another important physical condition of the early environment on Earth was the abundance of water. It is not surprising that water is still a major constituent of the bodies of living organisms. Given the probable temperatures on Earth at that time, water would be evaporating from some areas, condensing in the atmosphere, and then falling as rain. As it flowed back into the sea, water would dissolve elements from the rocks – elements that would rise in concentration as water evaporated from the ocean again. These elements could interact in solution, and concentrate in locations where seawater was evaporating most rapidly.

Of course, while energy flow tends to produce larger and more complex molecules, there is a natural countervailing tendency – complex molecules will also tend to fall apart into simpler molecules. But here is the crucial point – some molecules will be more stable than others. These stable ones will tend to persist and accumulate. They will steadily become more common than those other molecules that are unstable. It does not require any great scientific insight to appreciate this, nor does it require us to imagine any sort of magical complexity or life force – this process is simply a logical consequence of what we mean by the terms "stable" and "unstable." Nothing lasts forever. Some things fall apart quickly, some things fall apart slowly. So long as both kinds of things are being steadily built by energy flow, the long-lived ones will tend to become more common than the short-lived ones. It is so very simple – yet note that even at the chemical level, long before there is anything that one might be tempted to call life, there is a crude process of natural selection. Some things are surviving longer than others, and hence are becoming more common. Ammonia and methane are two such molecules that likely accumulated in the Earth's early atmosphere.

Once a reservoir of larger and more stable molecules forms, these molecules can in turn interact with each other, yielding molecules with greater complexity and higher levels of potential energy. Like the simpler molecules, these more complex molecules will have varying degrees of stability. Again, molecules that are unstable will fall apart and those that are stable will accumulate. Imagine this process continuing, with increasingly complex molecules forming as a consequence of external energy flow. In this simple scenario, there is ongoing natural selection for stability and persistence, even at the molecular level (Figure 1.1).

Such ideas are based upon thermodynamic calculations, simple chemistry, and logic. Experimental work nicely complements them. In an early experiment, Miller and Urey (Miller 1953) set up a simple atmospheric system with a hydrological cycle (Figure 1.2). Water was evaporated and then cooled and condensed while sealed within glass tubes. Miller and Urey then let the hydrological cycle run, created electrical sparks to simulate lightning (the electrical sparks were used as an alternative to sunlight as a possible external energy source), and found that primitive amino acids formed. This classic

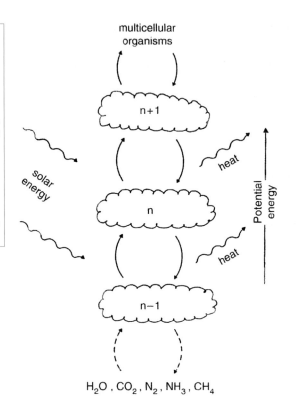

Figure 1.1 Solar energy creates high-energy molecules out of simpler low-energy molecules. Complex molecules and multicellular organisms are inevitable thermodynamic consequences of energy flow in the biosphere. For any arbitrary level of potential energy there is a restricted pool of substrate molecules at the next-lower level, so that even in simple molecular systems a form of resource competition can be observed (from Keddy 2001).

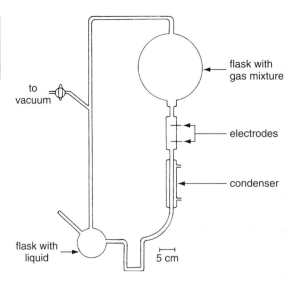

Figure 1.2 The original illustration of the apparatus used in the classic Miller and Urey experiment (from Miller 1953).

piece of work was done in the early 1950s, and it is worth emphasizing that it was done by a graduate student. Miller was fishing around for a research project to do for graduate work and had already tried one project that did not work. Then he and his advisor heard a seminar about early conditions on Earth that stimulated them to try their experiment. This single study led to a large series of experiments wherein researchers created all manner of artificial atmospheres and utilized different types of energy flow to explore what kinds of molecules could be produced.

One could ask what factors might allow complex molecules to further increase in stability and further accumulate. Such factors would likely include: (1) protective walls, (2) the direct use of sources of energy such as sunlight, and (3) the ability to form larger aggregations to buffer against short-term periods of unsuitable conditions. Consciousness would be another step, but this is not a step that plants have taken. In *The Selfish Gene*, Dawkins (1976) argues that consciousness can be thought of as the ability to develop predictive models for future events. For example, if an organism knows that certain conditions are likely to bring winter, then it can store up food. Such ideas will not be explored further here, but Dawkins does raise other issues, one of them being the way in which molecules that copy themselves will proliferate.

Returning to Figure 1.1, let us try to mentally reconstruct the circumstances on Earth some 4 billion years ago. Pools of increasingly complex molecules are accumulating as water evaporates and energy flow stimulates chemical interactions. Molecules that are stable are accumulating, those that are unstable are falling apart. Now consider the possibility of replication. Any molecule that tends to create copies of itself will accumulate more rapidly than other molecules. Dawkins suggests that the occurrence of such replicators was a critical event in the origin of life. Although he uses the word "replication," "reproduction" is the analogous biological term. From this perspective, then, molecular stability is survival, and molecular replication is reproduction. Thus, in a very basic and non-living molecular system, it is possible to find the sorts of ecological and evolutionary processes that occur in whole organisms. Further, one can also find larger ecological processes such as competition and predation (Keddy 1989).

Margulis and Sagan (1986) describe the circumstances on Earth at this time:

> The ponds, lakes and warm shallow seas of the early Earth, exposed as they were to cycles of heat and cold, ultraviolet light and darkness, evaporation and rain, harbored their chemical ingredients through the gamut of energy states. Combinations of molecules formed, broke up, and reformed, their molecular links forged by the constant energy input of sunlight. As the Earth's various microenvironments settled into more stable states, more complex molecule chains formed, and remained intact for longer periods. By connecting to itself five times, for example, hydrogen cyanide (HCN), a molecule created in interstellar space and a deadly poison to modern oxygen-breathing life, becomes adenine ($H_5C_5N_5$), the main part of one of the universal nucleotides which make up DNA, RNA and ATP.
>
> (p. 52)

Now we will turn from this very general discussion of the origin of life and look at more specific issues such as the origin of cellular envelopes, mitochondria, and chloroplasts.

1.3 | Membranes

Membranes are essential to all life as we know it, and it seems probable that they originated rather early in the history of life. In the most basic way, there is no life without a membrane to divide the world into inside (living organism) and outside (environment). The importance of membranes is emphasized by Day (1984) in his book *Genesis on Planet Earth*. One line of inquiry into the origin of membranes has examined various colloids, mixtures of finely dispersed organic matter suspended in water. Depending upon the composition and concentration, small droplets called coacervates appear.

Coacervates appear prominently in *The Origin of Life*, published in 1938 by another Russian scientist, Aleksandr Oparin. He too emphasized how energy flow drove the assembly of molecules from elements in the early biosphere, and, like Morowitz, emphasized that life did not arise by chance, but as a consequence of the principles of physics and chemistry. He stresses that "...the formation of complex coacervates ... was unavoidable because their formation requires very simple conditions, merely the mixture of two or more high-molecular organic substances ...." (p. 159)

A good deal of later research examines what kinds of circumstances create coacervate droplets. In some cases, coacervate droplets actually have the ability to grow by absorbing from solutions around them. Under other conditions, coacervate droplets start dividing thereby simulating a simple form of cellular replication. They also have the ability to protect their contents from ultraviolet light irradiation (Okihana and Ponnamperuma 1982). Day argues that coacervates are only pseudo cells, that they look cell-like under the microscope, but that the walls around these coacervate droplets do not behave like or have the structure of the membranes cells have today. He concludes that one must look to other examples for origins of the cellular envelope.

On natural freshwater bodies such as lakes, one finds a surface film that tends to accumulate organic matter; this occurs because of the presence of proteins. Proteins have hydrophobic and hydrophilic components and will orient with the hydrophilic end in the water and the hydrophobic end pointing out. A thin type of membrane results. Day offers a model wherein four steps produce the modern membrane (Figure 1.3): (1) first a surface film forms with the lipid facing the atmosphere and with the protein in the water, (2) turbulence from wind causes the film to buckle, (3) eventually the film buckles so much that the edges of the film touch each other, and (4) finally the air dissolves into the water, leaving a vesicle with lipids inside and proteins outside. This lipid bilayer membrane is one of the most basic structures of life. These lipid bilayers have now been experimentally produced in laboratories and have demonstrated the ability to selectively accumulate certain substances in the

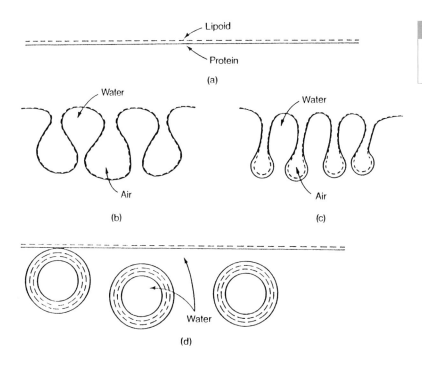

(a)

(b)

(c)

(d)

Figure 1.3 Proposed model for the formation of membranes by wave action on surface films (from Day 1984).

surrounding water. Once membranes exist, they provide the opportunity for a powerful form of natural selection to operate, as stable entities will tend to accumulate at the expense of those that are less stable.

As an alternative hypothesis, Cairns-Smith (1985) observes that clay particles also appear to be self-organizing; they are capable of growing in size, and, as they break apart, they also exhibit simple replication. At the mouths of rivers, where clay particles are carried into the sea, crystals are constantly forming and falling apart. Early mineral organisms, if they existed, might at some point have begun using organic matter, which eventually would have replaced the clay based forms.

1.4 | Eukaryotic cells

Prokaryotic cells (Figure 1.4) are probably rather good examples of what some of the earliest cells were like. There was considerable excitement at the discovery of possible 3.1-billion-year-old fossils of prokaryotic cells in South Africa (Schopf and Barghoorn 1967), and the fossil record for early one-celled organisms is steadily accumulating (Figure 1.5), although caution is necessary to distinguish between real fossils and microstructures that are non-biological in origin (Cloud 1976). The oldest eukaryote fossils, discovered in China, appear to date from 1.8–1.9 billion years BP, a date roughly consistent with that obtained from molecular clock estimates (Knoll 1992). It appears that the most primitive living eukaryotes are aerotolerant

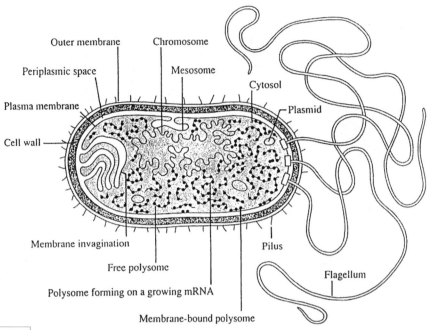

Figure 1.4   The main structural features of a Gram-negative bacterial cell (from de Duve 1991).

anaerobes, most of which live parasitically within animal hosts. These organisms have a well-defined nucleus and flagella but relatively simple cytoskeletons and no mitochondria or chloroplasts (Knoll 1992). Despite the apparent simplicity of these primitive eukaryotes, one is still faced with the thorny problem of an apparent leap of complexity from prokaryotes to eukaryotes. How did one arise from the other?

Evolution does not appear to involve spectacular leaps in complexity. As so often happens, what initially appears to be a sudden step actually involves a number of unexpected intermediaries. One hypothesis for the origin of eukaryotes can be traced back to Lynn Margulis, who in 1970 proposed that eukaryotes are in fact symbiotic associations of several prokaryotes (the serial endosymbiosis hypothesis, Figure 1.6). Earlier still, in the 1920s, an American physician I. E. Wallin raised this possibility, and even published a book entitled *Symbioticism and the Origin of Species*, but his enthusiasm for the concept was far ahead of the quality of his data (Wallin 1927). It is now thought that at least three structures in the eukaryotic cell had a symbiotic origin: the mitochondrion, the chloroplast, and the flagellum. If an early prokaryote was invaded by a non-photosynthetic bacterium, a cyanobacterium, and a spirochete, the result would be rather similar to a modern eukaryotic cell (Figure 1.6). There is a good deal of evidence accumulating to support the serial endosymbiosis hypothesis (Margulis and Sagan 1986, Smith and Douglas 1987, de Duve 1991, Margulis 1993, Roger 1999), although sceptics remain (Cloud 1976). The following sections

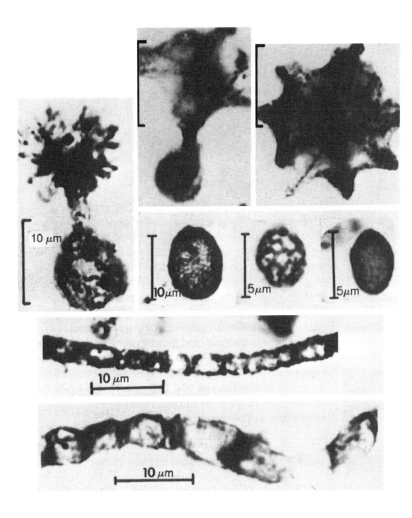

Figure 1.5 Fossil remains of microorganisms from the Gunflint chert. The three specimens across the top with umbrella-like crowns are *Kakebekian umbellata*. The three subspherical fossils are species of *Huroniospora*. The filamentous microorganisms with cells separated by septa are species of *Gunflintia* (from Levin 1994).

outline some ideas about the enodsymbiotic origin of mitochondria, chloroplasts, and flagella.

Mitochondria are ubiquitous organelles and are extremely important to cells because they are the sites where organic substances are oxidized and where energy is released. The serial endosymbiosis hypothesis suggests that an early prokaryote invaded another cell and that the mitochondrion is really the remains of the prokaryote. Some of the evidence for this is that mitochondria are similar in size to bacteria, they have their own DNA, and they replicate independently of the nucleus. Ribosomes in the mitochondria of a cell appear more similar to those of bacteria than to ribosomes in the cytoplasm of the cell. Also, certain antibiotics will block the function of ribosomes both in bacteria and mitochondria but not of those ribosomes in the cytoplasm, providing further evidence that the ribosomes in the mitochondria are more like those of bacteria than those of the cytoplasm that they invaded. In some experiments, where amoebae are infected with bacteria, the strain of infected amoebae is initially weakened by the bacteria, but after only five generations, the amoebae

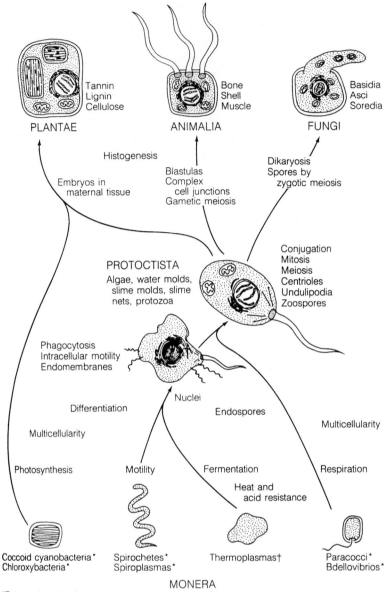

Figure 1.6 The serial endosymbiosis hypothesis for the origin of eukaryotic cells (from Margulis 1993).

evolve a certain amount of dependence on the bacteria. Further, some aerobic bacteria such as *Paracoccus denitrificans* have a metabolism nearly identical to that of mitochondria.

Chloroplasts are an absolutely fundamental part of plant cells; they are the site of photosynthesis. Again there is some evidence to support the serial endosymbiosis hypothesis, which suggests that chloroplasts are derived from an ancestral type of cyanobacteria that invaded an early cell. First, chloroplasts have their own DNA. Second, they are similar in size to cyanobacteria. Third, chloroplast DNA is different from the DNA in the nucleus of the cell and much more similar to that of cyanobacteria. Molecular data suggest that chloroplasts have arisen independently six times, with separate symbioses giving rise to the rhodophytes, chlorophytes, chromophytes, cryptophytes, photosynthetic euglenids, and photosynthetic dinoflagellates (Knoll 1992).

Flagella are cell appendages responsible for movement. The structure of the flagellum seems to be consistent throughout the plant and animal kingdoms. Even the flagella of green algae and human sperm are remarkably similar, which suggests that they have a common origin. Support for the serial endosymbiosis hypothesis, as regards flagella, comes from the fact that, in some circumstances, free-living spirochetes will attach themselves to other cells and move these cells around. This fact, combined with the constant structure of flagella, suggests that flagellar endosymbiosis occurred early in the evolution of life.

Finally, there is a marvellous living example of endosymbiosis: the organism is called *Myxotricha paradoxa* and it lives in the guts of termites (Smith and Douglas 1987). Why would one look for an example of an early endosymbiotic organism in animal guts? The reason is simple: guts are anaerobic, and thus like the early protoatmosphere. *Myxotricha paradoxa* has three symbionts. There are no mitochondria in *Myxotricha*, instead, there are endosymbiotic bacteria. *M. paradoxa* is moved around by spirochetes, and associated with each of these spirochetes is a mitochondrion-like bacterium (Figure 1.7). The serial endosymbiosis hypothesis proposes that by mixing nonphotosynthetic bacteria, spirochetes, or cyanobacteria one can derive most of the kinds of cells there are on the Earth today. Even cells in our bodies are symbioses of other living organisms.

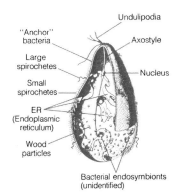

Figure 1.7 *Myxotricha paradoxa*, an endosymbiotic organism of termite guts (from Margulis 1993).

1.5 | The origin of photosynthesis

The oxygen revolution was probably the most important event in the history of life on this planet. One reads a great deal about the meteors that allegedly caused the extinction of the dinosaurs (Section 6.4.3), but the extinction of the dinosaurs pales in significance to the origin of photosynthesis. To fully comprehend the significance of the origin of photosynthesis, one must remember that Earth's earliest cells were dependent upon anaerobic metabolic processes for survival. There was no oxygen in the early atmosphere, so these cells were dependent upon breaking down the chemicals that had been created by the flow of solar energy. Neither was there an ozone layer, which, like oxygen, is a product of life, so there would have been much more intense bombardment of the planet by solar energy than there is now. The complex molecules that accumulated, as a result of chemical interactions driven by solar energy, were scavenged and broken down by early organisms in the absence of oxygen. This process, called fermentation, is the basic metabolic pathway upon which other, more elaborate, metabolic pathways have been superimposed.

Imagine protocells scavenging for large molecules in solution. Large molecules would be selectively absorbed and the high energy of these molecules would be used to make other needed molecules. Thus protocells would be limited in growth by the scarcity of large molecules. Over time, large molecules would probably become increasingly rare because many other protocells would also be absorbing them. One way to avoid competition with other cells, then, would be to make the large molecules internally. Thus there would be a strong selective advantage for any cell line able to use sunlight to convert raw materials into larger molecules, particularly as conversion could occur within a membrane, thus within the control of the cellular environment. As well, the membrane would shield end products from neighbors. Thus cells developed internalized processes of chemical synthesis instead of simply absorbing products formed by chemical reactions that took place outside of their membranes.

How might such a transformation have occurred? Was it some chance event? Probably not; the transformation may have, in fact, been quite deterministic. Examine the early conditions of Earth from the point of view of physics. Is it possible to determine what type of chemical process might arise and then be selected for in order that the efficiency of early cells would be enhanced? To put the question another way, assuming that energy synthesis, of some form, must occur, is it possible to predict what kind of energy synthesis early cells would be most likely to employ? Would it be radiosynthesis, electrosynthesis, thermosynthesis, magnosynthesis, photosynthesis ...?

In order to determine what type of chemical process might arise and then be selected for in early cells, three basic questions must be asked. The first and most basic is, "What type of energy has the greatest flow in the atmosphere of the Earth?" The source of energy that life might exploit would likely be abundantly available. Consider the possible terrestrial energy sources. There is sunlight, electric discharges, cosmic rays, radioactivity, and volcanic energy (Table 1.3). In terms of calories per square centimetre per year, sunlight would likely be the source of energy used by organisms on this planet, not radioactivity or volcanic energy. Simply based on the energy flux, one can predict that *photo*synthesis would be likely to arise.

The second question that one must ask is, "Given that sunlight would be an obvious source of energy for early organisms to utilize, is there a particular section of the electromagnetic spectrum most likely be exploited?" Table 1.4 shows a breakdown of energy versus wavelength for each part of the spectrum. Note that wavelength increases toward the infrared and energy increases toward the ultraviolet. Consider what the different wavelengths of solar energy do. Along the entire electromagnetic spectrum, from x-rays on the left to radiowaves on the right (Figure 1.8), there is only one small portion of the entire spectrum that can cause electron orbital changes and therefore actually be directly involved in chemical interactions: that is, the visible range. At the ultraviolet end of the spectrum, the effects of

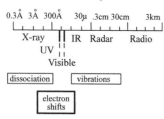

Figure 1.8 The electromagnetic spectrum, showing the narrow range of wavelengths causing electron shifts that is used in photosynthesis and vision.

Table 1.3. *Possible sources of energy for life to exploit (from Morowitz 1968).*

Source	Energy (cal cm^{-2} year^{-1})
Sunlight (all wavelengths)	260 000
<2500 Å	570
<2000 Å	85
<1500 Å	3.5
Electric discharges	4
Cosmic rays	0.0015
Radioactivity (to 1.0 km depth)	0.8
Volcanoes	0.13

Note:
1 Å = 0.1 nm.

Table 1.4. *The characteristics of some regions of the electromagnetic spectrum (from Morowitz 1968).*

Region	Wavelength range (μm)	Energy range (kcal/Einstein)	Fraction of solar spectrum (%)	Molecular changes
Far ultraviolet	0.1–0.2	152.2–304.4	0.02	Ionization
Ultraviolet	0.2–0.38	75.3–152.2	7.27	Electronic transitions and ionizations
Visible	0.38–0.78	36.7–75.3	51.73	Electronic transitions
Near infrared	0.78–3	9.5–36.7	38.90	Electronic and vibrational transitions
Middle infrared	3–30	0.95–9.5	2.10	Rotational and vibrational transitions

electromagnetic energy tend to break molecules apart. At the infrared end, the energy generates heat: that is, it causes the molecules to vibrate. Only in a narrow "visible" range does light interact with chemistry. Natural selection would therefore tend to favor cells that had internal chemistry that responded to the visible light spectrum.

Questions remain. Why are metal molecules in both chlorophyll and hemoglobin? Why do plants absorb nearly the same wavelengths that animals can see? Why do plants look green? The answers to such questions have broad implications for the early steps in the evolution of life.

The origin of chlorophyll is obviously closely related to the origin of photosynthesis. Within the photosynthetic pathway, there are a number of different molecules that are sensitive to solar energy, and chlorophyll appears to be a relatively recent addition to the light trapping system. The earlier molecules sensitive to sunlight were probably much simpler in structure and yielded a rather crude form of working photosynthesis. It seems probable that some cells synthesized porphyrins, which fortuitously had the property of absorbing sunlight in the visible wavelengths. This step probably led to bacterial photosynthesis, which requires an external source of hydrogen such as hydrogen sulfide. One group of bacteria, known as desulfovibrios, absorbs sulfate and emits sulfurous gases as waste products. During the conversion of sulfate to sulfide, ATP is generated; to carry out this conversion a porphyrin ring is used (Margulis and Sagan 1986). (The resulting hydrogen sulfide is what gives some marshes their smell of rotten eggs.)

At first, molecules such as hydrogen (H_2), hydrogen sulfide (H_2S), or simple organic molecules (CH_2O) might have provided the source of hydrogen for constructing more complex organic molecules, which are, after all, chains of carbon and hydrogen. As such sources of hydrogen were scavenged by more and more microorganisms, the increasing scarcity of hydrogen would have strongly selected against organisms that were unable to exploit other hydrogen sources. The chemical bond holding hydrogen to oxygen in water is much stronger than the bonds holding hydrogen in the above molecules; nonetheless it seems likely that an early photosynthetic organism acquired a means to use light to split water molecules into hydrogen and oxygen. The separated hydrogen could then be added onto carbon from the atmosphere and organic matter thus synthesized. Cells with the ability to split water molecules would then have been able to extract hydrogen from a nearly inexhaustible pool. With photosynthesis achieved via hydrolysis, water and sunshine could be converted into living material. As Hutchinson (1970) describes, "The overall geochemical result [was] to produce a more oxidised part of the biosphere, namely the atmosphere and most of the free water in which oxygen is dissolved, and a more reduced part, namely the bodies of organisms and their organic decomposition products in litter, soils and aquatic sediments." Chlorophyll might then have been added to the far more ancient photosynthetic pathways.

1.6 | The oxygen revolution

Photosynthesis via hydrolysis shaped the biosphere, for while it enabled cells to synthesize organic matter from abundantly available water and solar energy, it also produced a by-product – oxygen. This gas, that was dangerously unstable and tended to react violently with other organic compounds, was released into the atmosphere. Thus the consequences of a more efficient form of photosynthesis were catastrophic for many early life forms. Three important consequences of photosynthesis are considered below (Mains 1972, Margulis and Sagan 1986, Levin 1994).

1.6.1 Changes in ocean chemistry

Since the first photosynthetic organisms were aquatic, the oxygen released by photosynthesis entered seawater, and began to rust metals present in the oceans. Up until this point there were many metal ions dissolved in seawater; with the appearance of oxygen, the metal ions were oxidized and precipitated. This process of oxidation formed enormous beds of sedimentary rocks that contain rusted metal ions, particularly iron oxide. Often these rocks have alternating layers of silica and iron oxide (banded iron formations) that suggests that there was some periodicity in iron precipitation (Figure 1.9). So long as iron oxide formation used up the supplies of oxygen, however, oxygen could not accumulate in appreciable quantities.

Figure 1.9 Banded iron formations. (a) This formation is exposed at Jasper Knob in Michigan's Upper Peninsula. (b) Banded iron formations occur worldwide in Proterozoic rocks, as suggested by these at Wadi Kareim, Egypt (from Levin 1994). The Gunflint Chert deposits around Lake Superior in Canada include banded iron deposits, some of which are over 1000 m thick and extend over 100 km.

1.6.2 Changes in the composition of the atmosphere

Once the oceans of the world rusted (Section 1.6.1), oxygen began leaking out into the atmosphere. Here the oxygen reacted with methane and ammonia, which were broken down and stripped from the atmosphere by rainfall. Once oxygen began to accumulate, there was, necessarily, a growing selection for cells with cell walls that provided protection from the oxidative effects of oxygen. In the absence of a sufficiently resistant cell wall, the interior contents of a cell would oxidize. Early oxygen concentrations were initially quite low, perhaps 1 percent of contemporary concentrations, but for the first time the atmosphere assumed some of the properties associated with it today. For example, it oxidized metals. The type of erosion changed with the presence of oxygen in the atmosphere. The whole physical and chemical nature of the planet changed.

Until this period, various kinds of fermentation had probably fuelled the cellular machinery. Now it became possible for several kinds of respiration to arise. It is interesting to note that the chemical pathways in respiration appear to have been built upon an older system that used fermentation. So respiration did not suddenly appear but was slowly modified from the existing biosynthetic pathways in fermentation. Chemical evolution, like the evolution of skeletons, is conservative and slowly modifies existing structures rather than suddenly building new ones. For example, modern terrestrial plants can use two sources of nitrogen: ammonia and nitrate. Ammonia was widely available early in the Earth's history, whereas nitrate is an oxidized form that would have been another by-product of the oxygen revolution.

1.6.3 Formation of the ozone layer

As oxygen levels in the atmosphere continued to increase, oxygen in the upper atmosphere would have been exposed to bombardment by ultraviolet light, resulting in the production of ozone. The accumulating ozone would gradually have begun to absorb ultraviolet light. It was as if a giant window blind were slowly being pulled over the Earth. Ultraviolet light may even have produced some of the larger molecules that early microbes fed on; any such organisms would then have starved. Waves of extinction in primitive microorganisms were likely associated with these events, just as waves of diversification were a likely consequence of the new conditions. All this raises an important question: when did this most significant event in the Earth's history happen?

The answer seems to be – at least 2 billion years ago (Mains 1972, Levin 1994). There are two sources of evidence. Uranium dioxide, uraninite, is deposited in sedimentary rocks only under low oxygen conditions, and the last major deposits are about this age. Extensive deposits of banded iron (Figure 1.9) also indicated early oxygen production. Different layers, sometimes only microns thick, of oxidized hematite and less oxidized magnetite may indicate seasonal cycles of photosynthesis. Oxygen-producing photosynthetic bacteria, living in warm volcanic pools in iron-rich water, may have been responsible for seasonal surges of oxygen waste. There was a surge of banded iron formation between 2.2 and 1.8 billion years BP, but some banded formations in Labrador and Greenland appear to be as ancient as 3 billion years old. These banded iron formations provide something like 90 percent of the world's sources of extractable iron (Margulis and Sagan 1986).

The presence of photosynthetic cells and an oxidising atmosphere bring us to a situation where we can see, at least in outline, the processes we study in the field of plant ecology. Yet there are at least two more important evolutionary events from the perspective of plants. The first is the colonization of land; the second is the origin of flowers and seeds. The former is examined here, while the latter is deferred to Chapters 8 and 9.

1.7 | The Cambrian explosion of multicellular life

Near the beginning of the Cambrian era, about 700 million years ago, there was apparently an explosion of multicellular life. Exactly when this happened is still somewhat unclear (Day 1984), but the timing will no doubt be better defined as more enthusiastic students work in the area of paleoecology. Why did it take so long for multicellular life to form? There are many competing hypotheses (Gould 1977). One suggestion is that it took that long for there to be sufficient oxygen in the atmosphere for respiration to evolve, and from this perspective, multicellularity is a consequence of aerobic respiration. Another suggestion is that multicellular organisms lived in shallow water and that it took that much time for there to be sufficient ozone to shield the shallow water from ultraviolet bombardment. Another more interesting suggestion is that the fossil record may be somewhat misleading, and perhaps earlier multicellular life was abundant but did not have any skeletons that would fossilize. There may have been a change in oceanic chemistry, near the beginning of the Cambrian era, which permitted the deposition of calcium carbonate required to make preservable skeletons. The real explanation for the sudden diversification of life remains a puzzle, perhaps one that a student reading this book will one day solve.

1.8 | Colonizing the land

The land was apparently colonized about 400 million years ago (Niklas et al. 1985, Taylor 1988, Stewart and Rothwell 1993). So far as one can infer from the known fossil record, both plants and animals colonized the land at about the same time, give or take

50 million years. Terrestrial plants may have originated from a green algal ancestor similar to living members of the genus *Coleochaete*. *Coleochaete* is the only known green alga in which the zygote remains attached to the parent plant and undergoes cell division there (Taylor 1988). The attachment of sporophyte to gametophyte appears to be a common trait in primitive land plants. As with the Cambrian explosion of multicellular life, it is not clear why there was a long delay before life forms were able to colonize terrestrial habitats. One hypothesis is that it took that long for there to be sufficient oxygen in the atmosphere for respiration. Another suggestion is that it took that long for ozone to accumulate and shield the Earth's surface. A further suggestion is that sexuality arose making it possible for rates of evolution to increase. Perhaps the acquisition of chloroplasts led to an explosive radiation of new groups of organisms. The origins of terrestrial plants are still under study; the interpretation of microfossils of early terrestrial plants, particularly spores, fragments of cuticle, and tracheid-like cells, is particularly difficult but ongoing (Kenrick and Crane 1977, Taylor et al. 2005).

If, in fact, the formation of the ozone layer was the main factor that made life on land possible, there is good evidence that the actual colonization of the land also required the evolution of symbiosis between plants and fungi. Much of the nutrient uptake by terrestrial plants is still accomplished by a mere 130 species of fungi in the relatively ancient genus *Zygomycotina* in the Order Glomerales (Peat and Fitter 1993, Simon et al. 1993). Re-examination of fossil plants from the Devonian suggests that mycorrhizal fungi were associated with plant roots as early as some 400 million years BP (Pirozynski and Dalpé 1989, Taylor 1990).

Turning to molecular data, and using substitution rates to date evolutionary events (Berbee and Taylor 1993, Simon et al. 1993, Heckman et al. 2001), it appears that both the fungi and the eukaryotic plants originated some 1 billion years ago. Mycorrhizal fungi in the Glomerales originated between 462 and 353 million years ago. The latter date is remarkably similar to the appearance of early land plants around 400 million years ago. The fact that mycorrhizae are now found worldwide, and in groups including ferns, gymnosperms, and angiosperms, is further evidence of their early origin. The fungi therefore appear to have diversified along with the vascular flora, and molecular clock data suggest that the basidiomycetes appeared in the Jurassic (Figure 1.10).

Interestingly, the colonization of land by plants was probably disastrous for oceanic life. Up until that point there would have been very rapid rates of erosion as material washed off the naked land into the oceans. Once plants occupied the land, large amounts of nutrients would have been retained, both in tissues and in the soil that formed from decaying organic remains. Those organisms in the ocean that were accustomed to vast amounts of eroded material might have starved.

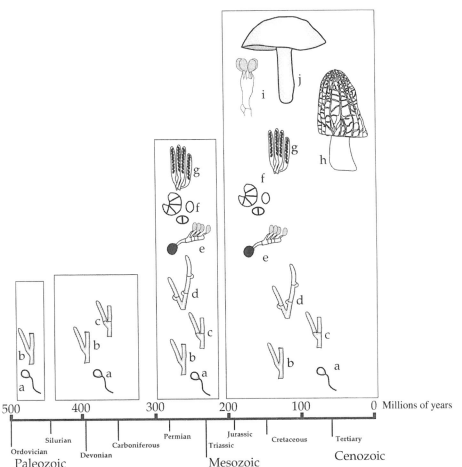

500   400   300   200   100   0 Millions of years

Silurian   Permian   Jurassic   Cretaceous   Tertiary
                    Carboniferous   Triassic
Ordovician   Devonian
        Paleozoic   Mesozoic   Cenozoic

The land produced intense selection upon plants. A whole new suite of traits, including a cuticle to reduce desiccation, stomata to control water loss but admit CO_2, sclerenchyma to strengthen stems for vertical growth, and water conducting tissues, arose out of the strong natural selection to cope with desiccation. Early land plants still betrayed their aquatic origins by having free-living sperm that swam from male to female organs. This is obviously workable in the ocean but not a terribly good trait for dry conditions (we return to this topic in Box 9.1). In fact, a recurring theme in many discussions of plant evolution is the way that terrestrial environments have driven modifications to plant reproductive systems to get around the constraints imposed by a terrestrial habitat (Raven et al. 2005). The gymnosperms appear to have been one of the first groups in which selection eliminated motile sperm and produced the pollen tube (although free water is still required for the pollination droplets that capture the pollen). Further, the cycads, alone among the gymnosperms, still have sperm cells that swim down pollen tubes to fertilize the egg. The rest of the gymnosperms, and all of the

Figure 1.10 Some milestones in the evolution of fungi. Branching, aseptate fungal filaments (b) originated after terrestrial higher fungi diverged from water molds (a). Septate filaments (c) evolved after the pre-basidiomycetes-ascomycetes diverged from the Glomaceae. Clamp connections (d) mark early basidiomycetes. Sexual structures, asci (g) and basidia (e), probably evolved before ascomycetes and basiodiomycetes radiated. Asexual spores (f) and complex fruiting bodies (h) probably increased as filamentous ascomycetes radiated. Mushrooms (j), sharing basidial type (i) and other morphological features with *Athelia* and *Spongipellis*, probably radiated about 130 Ma ago (from Berbee and Taylor 1993).

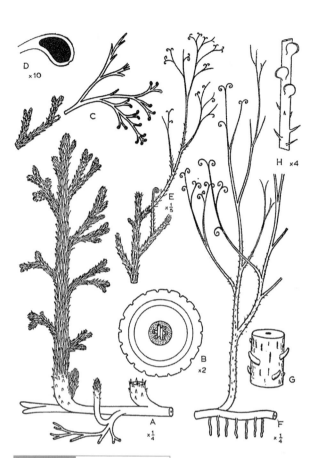

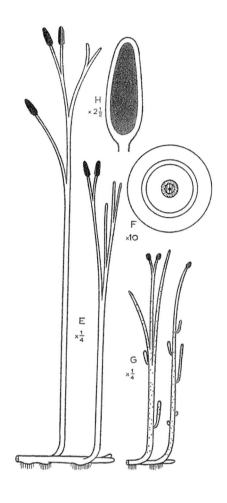

Figure 1.11 Reconstruction of some early fossil plants discovered in the Rhynie chert in Scotland including *Asteroxylon* species (left A–E), *Psilophyton princeps* (left F–H) and *Rhynia* species (right E–H) (from Sporne 1970).

angiosperms, have lost even this vestige of their aquatic origin; only nuclei move down the pollen tube.

The earliest land plants are increasingly well understood (Stewart and Rothwell 1993, Kenrick and Crane 1997) and include genera such as *Asteroxylon* and *Rhynia* (Figure 1.11), first described from Rhynie chert found in Scotland by Kidston and Lang (1921). Some similar genera still alive today include *Psilotum* (Psilotophyta), *Lycopodium*, and *Selaginella* (Lycopodiophyta). Plant height increased steadily through geological time, presumably as a consequence of increasing competition for light (Figure 1.12). For a period of time trees, such as *Lepidodendron* (Lycopodiophyta), were the dominant form of life on Earth (Figure 1.13). The light provided by most light bulbs is generated in part by burning coal, which is the remains of such species. This period was followed by a time when ferns (Pteridophytes) and seed ferns (Pteridosperms) dominated the Earth. These were in turn replaced by conifers, and there was a long period when conifers and cycads dominated the Earth (Figure 1.14). Then, just over

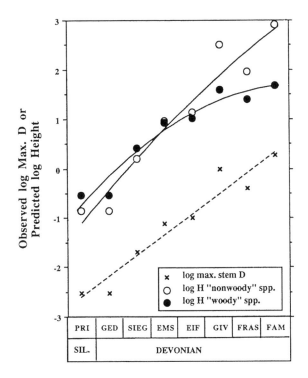

Figure 1.12 Predicted $\log_{10}$ transformed plant height based upon maximum stem diameters of early Paleozoic vascular plants and allometric equations for non-woody and woody species (from Niklas 1994).

Legend (within plot):
- ×   log max. stem D
- ○   log H "nonwoody" spp.
- ●   log H "woody" spp.

Time axis: PRI | GED | SIEG | EMS | EIF | GIV | FRAS | FAM
SIL. | DEVONIAN

Y-axis: Observed log Max. D or Predicted log Height

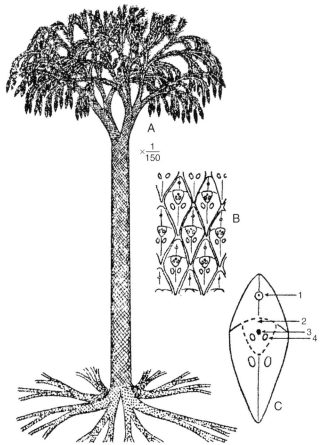

$\times\frac{1}{150}$

Figure 1.13 Reconstructions of *Lepidodendron* trees (A whole plant, B, C leaf base: 1 ligule pit, 2 area of leaf base, 3 vascular bundle, 4 parichnos scars) (from Sporne 1970).

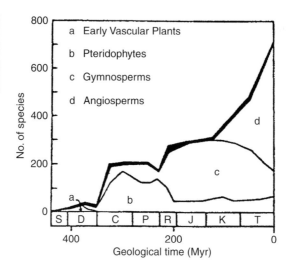

Figure 1.14 Trends in vascular plant diversity illustrated by the estimated number of fossil species in four major plant groups (from Niklas et al. 1983).

100 million years ago, angiosperms arose – a topic further explored in Section 9.2.

Humans now occupy a planet with an oxygenated atmosphere, an ozone layer, and a plant layer, but the story of plants and the biosphere is not yet complete, for there was (and is) one more activity by which plants further transformed the Earth: the storage of carbon.

1.9 | Plants and climate

The early atmosphere appears to have had vast amounts of CO_2. Carbon dioxide is a greenhouse gas – that is, it absorbs infrared radiation and reradiates it as heat, raising the temperature of the atmosphere. Space probes that have visited our nearest neighbor toward the Sun, Venus, have discovered an inhospitable planet with a surface temperature of 750 K and a pressure of 90 Earth atmospheres. At least 500 K of this temperature has been calculated to be the effects of the high CO_2 concentrations of the atmosphere. This could be described as runaway greenhouse effect. Our other near neighbor, Mars, has a thin atmosphere, and the concentration of CO_2 in its atmosphere is sufficient to raise the surface temperature by only 10 K, for a chilly 220 K. Earth is somewhere in between; the minor CO_2 concentration in the atmosphere is enough to produce a greenhouse effect of 35 K and a mean surface temperature of 290 K (Table 1.5). Yet the early atmosphere on Earth almost certainly had more CO_2 (Table 1.1), enough to produce much warmer conditions.

Plants use carbon as their main structural molecule, and now large amounts of CO_2 are stored in plant tissues. Further, when plants in the past died, their organic remains sometimes did not decay but instead formed thick seams of organic carbon now called coal. Ocean life forms also died and did not fully decay, which contributed to organic shales and oil-bearing rocks. Because of their organic origins,

Table 1.5. *The Earth in context: basic comparisons with Venus and Mars (from MacDonald 1989).*

	Venus	Earth	Mars
Main gas	CO_2	N_2	CO_2
Atmospheric pressure (atm)	90	1.0	0.01
Mean surface temp. (K)	750	290	220
Greenhouse effect (K)	500	35	10
Δ Temp. poles to equator (percent)	2	16	40

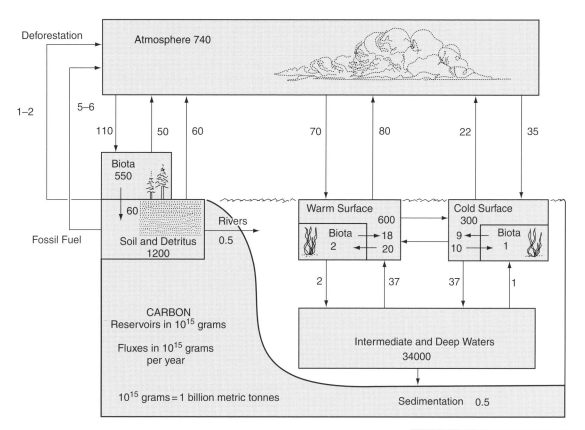

Figure 1.15 The carbon cycle showing storage in living plants, soils, and fossil fuels (from Moore and Bolin 1987).

these modern fuels are called fossil fuels, and together they store vast amounts of organic carbon (Figure 1.15). While there is some CO_2 in the atmosphere of Earth, most is now trapped in living plants and fossil fuels, so temperature is moderated.

How is it that vast amounts of carbon have been stored as coal and oil? The ecological reasons are still unclear. With coal, it is clear from the fossil plants and the associated sediment that ancient swamps were important sites for coal deposition. If one assumes that then, as now, inundation played an important role in reducing rates of decomposition (Stewart and Rothwell 1993, Keddy 2000), perhaps the periods of coal deposition had unusually large areas of wetland. Higher CO_2 levels in the atmosphere may have stimulated rapid plant growth, while simultaneously causing warm climates that melted glaciers and inundated coastal areas.

The rates at which organic carbon was buried at different periods in the Earth's history can be estimated from the chemical composition and volume of sedimentary rock of different ages. These estimates show a dramatic peak at some 300 million years BP (Figure 1.16). Moreover, deposition conditions can be estimated by ratios of pyrite sulfur to organic carbon, with lower ratios indicating that deposition took place on land. Robinson (1990) attributes the peak in coal deposition to the evolution of lignin, which is not only difficult to degrade but inhibits the decay of associated materials. Only the recently evolved basidiomycete fungi can degrade lignin, and this process is inhibited at the low oxygen levels that are typically found in flooded soils. Robinson estimates that in the Pennsylvanian, the lignin content of plants was 40 percent or higher. Her interpretation of Figure 1.16 is that, "Paleozoic forests had limited geographic extent and contained less biomass than modern forests. By providing a rich source of lignin in an environment where lignolytic organisms were rare or absent, however, they greatly increased the C_{org} content of the infill of subsiding basins and caused the greatest bulge in terrigenous C_{org} burial in Earth history" (Robinson 1990, p. 609). This would be consistent with current understanding of the evolution of fungi, particularly the relatively recent origin of the lignin-consuming basidiomycetes (recall Figure 1.10).

Southwood (1985) offers a complementary interpretation. He notes the following: (1) plants produce structural molecules (cellulose, lignin) that "are powerful obstacles to the digestive juices of animals," (2) these structural molecules are well defended by secondary metabolites (phenolics, terpenoids), and (3) there is a major biochemical difference between the biochemical composition of plants and animals. He suggests that there was a period of 60–70 million years when plants were comparatively free from herbivores – and consequently coal accumulated. Both Robinson's and Southwood's interpretations, however, suffer from the supposition that insects and fungi evolved their biochemical abilities slowly, whereas most insects, and many fungi, have generation times much shorter than trees. As a consequence, their rates of evolution might well be expected to match if not exceed those of woody plants.

1.10 | Sediment and ice cores: reconstructing past climates

Let us now turn to two much shorter time periods: the past 65 million years, and the past half million years. Both are merely the very tail end of the lengthy period shown at the bottom of Figure 1.16, but

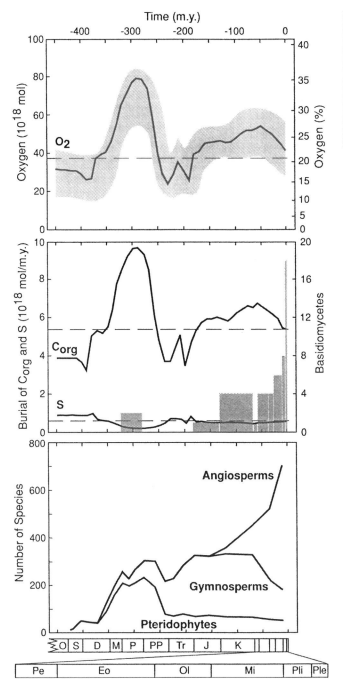

Figure 1.16 Chronology of oxygen production, carbon burial, reduced sulfur deposition, and plant life forms through geological history. Lower ratios of reduced sulfur (pyrite sulfur) to organic carbon indicate deposition in terrestrial conditions (from Robinson 1990).

both are natural time periods for plant ecologists to consider. It was 65 million years ago that an enormous meteor hit the earth, triggering the end of the dinosaurs, and the rise of mammals and flowering plants (the K/T extinctions, Section 6.4.3). And it was the past half million years that has seen plant communities exposed to at least

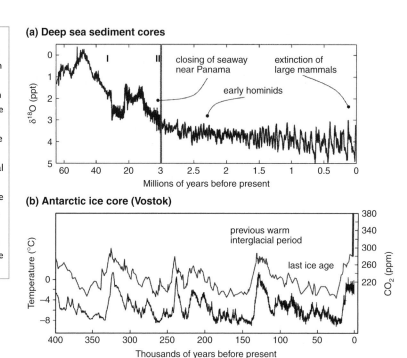

Figure 1.17 Changes in global climate over two time scales from two sources of data (adapted from Fedorov et al. 2006). (a) Global temperature for the last 65 million years inferred from oxygen isotope ratios in deep sea sediment cores. **I** marks the onset of glaciers at the south pole, and **II** the onset of glaciers at the north pole. (b) Global temperature for the past 400 000 years inferred from oxygen isotope ratios in an ice core (bottom line), and associated CO_2 levels measured from bubbles (top line). Vertical bar denotes change in time scale.

four major ice advances (Section 9.3). Since you will read more on the K/T extinctions and ice ages in these later sections, let us focus here upon the theme of climate change and CO_2.

The two time scales are studied with different sources of evidence. For the 65 million year time scale, scientists have drilled many sediment cores in the deep ocean floor (Zachos et al. 2001). These record the history of the Earth as measured by debris that settled out of the sea water. As Figure 1.17(a) shows, temperature (as measured by oxygen isotope ratios) has declined more or less steadily over this period. Note that as the Earth has cooled, the temperature has also shown more striking fluctuations. These are thought to be caused by cyclical changes in characteristics of the Earth's orbit (precession, obliquity and eccentricity), termed Milankovitch cycles (Imbrie et al. 1992, Muller and MacDonald 1997), named for the Serbian mathematician and engineer Milutin Milankovitch (1979–1958), who proposed their relationship with ice ages. This era has seen several major changes in plants and climate. These include the gradual rise in dominance of the flowering plants (Figure 1.16 bottom), the expansion of C_4 grasses, the development of ice sheets first in Antarctica (**I**) and then the north (**II**), the diversification of grazing animals (e.g., horses), the closing of the isthmus of Panama, and the appearance of hominids. Overall, it has been a period of steady cooling.

Ice cores drilled from glaciers provide more detailed information on the past half million years, the Pleistocene. Ice cores also contain small bubbles that hold actual samples of the previous atmosphere. This allows scientists to track changes in greenhouse gases like CO_2 and methane. An ice core taken from Vostok (Antarctica) reached a depth of 3623 m and provides a vivid picture of climate change over the past 400 000 years (Petit et al. 1999). It shows that major cool periods have occurred about every 100 000 years (Figure 1.17(b)). This cycle is approximately consistent with that predicted by Milankovitch; evidence can also be found for shorter cycles of 41, 23 and 19 thousand years (Petit et al. 1999). Alternating with these ice advances were warmer interglacial periods, which are closely correlated with peaks in CO_2 concentration (as shown by the top line of Figure 1.17(b) and methane (not shown)). We are currently in a prolonged interglacial period.

The linkages among plants, atmosphere, and climate are both simple and complex. Simply, plants can control the composition of the atmosphere, including global CO_2 levels, and thereby affect climate. The complexity arises because they are not acting alone. The Earth has been through a prolonged cooling period over the past 60 million years, variation in the Earth's orbit having become increasingly influential in driving cycles of glaciation (Figure 1.17(a)). Milankovitch cycles were not so important in the warmer past, but appear now to be driving the onset and conclusion of ice ages. Other factors amplify this pattern (Fedorov et al. 2006). Rising levels of greenhouse gases near the end of glacial periods (Figure 1.17(b)) appear to accelerate the rate at which ice melts. As the ice melts, the albedo (reflectivity) of the Earth falls, white snow and ice being replaced by darker colored earth and vegetation that absorb more heat. Changes in cloud cover over the ocean may simultaneously alter albedo. Changes in ocean circulation and surface temperate may further amplify changing climate, but this change depends in part upon the configuration of continents. Plant communities are affected by, and yet also affect, these patterns. The vast peatlands of the northern hemisphere arose after the last glacial period, and now continue to store organic debris from plants, particularly *Sphagnum* moss (Figure 4.21), thereby having a cooling effect. They also emit methane, a greenhouse gas. Peatlands now cover some 500 million ha, nearly 4 percent of the Earth's ice-free land area (Gorham 1990). Should they cease to grow, or should they burn during droughts, CO_2 levels would increase further.

Here we have focused upon ocean sediment cores and ice cores to address the history of the Earth at the global scale. You should be aware that sediment cores taken from lakes and peat bogs record many other more local features of the Earth's history. Such sediment cores contain many kinds of organic debris: pollen grains record past vegetation types (Moore et al. 1991), charcoal fragments record past fires (Section 6.3.1), while phytoplankton remains record aquatic events (Smol and Cumming 2000).

Let us end with the shortest time scale, the past century, where we have various direct measurements of CO_2 levels in the atmosphere. If you examine the far right hand side of the ice core record in

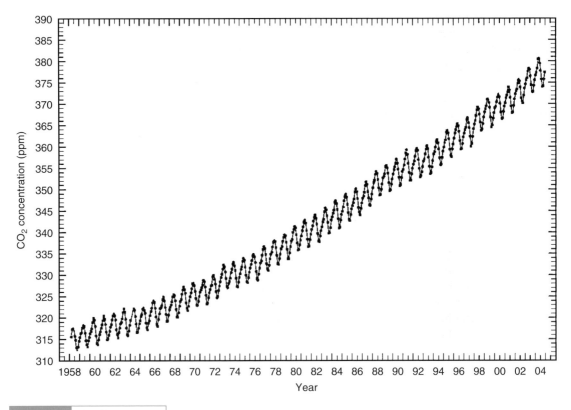

Figure 1.18 Monthly average concentrations of atmospheric CO_2 measured at Mauna Loa Observatory, Hawaii (from Keeling and Whorf 2005).

Figure 1.17(b), you can see a sudden spike in CO_2 levels that corresponds with humans clearing forests and burning fossil fuels. On a geological time scale, this is a sudden event; from the short term perspective of humans, it has seemed gradual. Over the last century, CO_2 levels have been rising steadily (Figure 1.18).

The study of past climate may provide important information about future climates. During the warm period 40 to 60 million years ago, there were no glaciers in the northern hemisphere, and sea level was about 25 m higher than today (Fedorov et al. 2006). The last four interglacial periods have all been relatively short, and the current interglacial in which we live, the Holocene, is already the longest of the four. Thus we know that it is possible for the Earth to be both much warmer or much colder than present with relatively small changes in solar input. Moreover, the current atmosphere takes humans into unknown territory, since atmospheric CO_2 levels are not only strikingly higher than in previous interglacial periods, they are well above any level recorded in the past half million years (Figure 1.17(b)), and they continue to rise (Figure 1.18). There is therefore ample reason to suspect that rising global temperatures will have a significant effect on plant distributions in the coming century, a topic explored further in Flannery (2005) and Gore (2006).

Finally, note that the trend in CO_2 with time measured at Mauna Loa itself shows a cycle. This brings us back to plants. Each year the rapid growth of plants in the northern hemisphere draws down the pool of atmospheric CO_2 and each winter as the organic matter decays and organisms respire, that carbon is returned to the atmosphere. Figure 1.18 thus illustrates the overall theme of this chapter: that plants are not only influenced by the atmosphere, but they can change the atmosphere.

1.11 | Conclusion

The series of events outlined in this chapter formed and transformed the physical and chemical nature of the biosphere (Table 1.6). Each event was driven by the one group of organisms able to intercept solar energy and store organic carbon – plants. Consider for a moment those first early cells with their crude forms of photosynthesis: who would have predicted their eventual ability to multiply, alter, and then dominate the biosphere? The great communities of plants that rule the world are the topic of the remainder of this book.

Table 1.6. *Some of the major effects of plants in creating life on Earth.*

Stage of plant evolution	Some principal effects

Origin of photosynthesis	1. Increased amounts of biological matter
	2. Oxidation of oceans
	    a. Precipitation of metal ions
	    b. Respiration
	    c. Eukaryotic cells
	3. Oxidation of atmosphere
	    a. Ammonia and methane removed
	    b. Ozone layer formed
	    c. Nitrates replace ammonia
	    d. Oxidative weathering of rocks

Invasion of land	1. Reduced rates of erosion and sedimentation 2. Removal of atmospheric CO_2 and cooling of Earth 3. Production of coal 4. Formation of soils 5. Food and shelter for terrestrial animals
Origin of angiosperms	1. Flowers lead to insect diversification 2. Fruits provide food for birds, mammals, and insects

Further reading

Lavoisier, A. L. 1789. Elements of Chemistry. Translated by R. Kerr and reprinted. pp. xii and 1–60. In M. J. Adler (ed.). 1990. *Great Books of the Western World*, 2nd edn., Vol. 42. Encyclopaedia Britannica in collaboration with the University of Chicago, IL.

Morowitz, H. J. 1968. *Energy Flow in Biology: Biological Organization as a Problem in Thermal Physics*. New York, NY: Academic Press.

Margulis, L. 1993. *Symbiosis in Cell Evolution*. 2nd edn. New York: W. H. Freeman.

Mains, G. 1972. *The Oxygen Revolution*. Newton Abbot: David and Charles.

Niklas, K. J., B. H. Tiffney and A. H. Knoll. 1983. Patterns in vascular land plant diversification. *Nature* **303**: 614–616.

Day, W. 1984. *Genesis on Planet Earth*, 2nd edn. New Haven, CT: Yale University Press.

Ferris, T. 1988. *Coming of Age in the Milky Way*. Anchor Books edition 1989. New York, NY: Doubleday.

Robinson, J. M. 1990. Lignin, land plants, and fungi: biological evolution affecting phanerozoic oxygen balance. *Geology* **18**: 607–610.

Moore, P. D., J. A. Webb and M. E. Collinson. 1991. *Pollen Analysis*, 2nd edn. London: Blackwell Scientific.

Knoll, A. H. 1992. The early evolution of eukaryotes: a geological perspective. *Science* **256**: 622–627.

Schopf, J. W. and C. Klein (eds.). 1992. *Evolution of the Proterozoic Biosphere – A Multidisciplinary Study*. New York, NY: Cambridge University Press.

Levin, H. L. 1994. *The Earth Through Time*, 4th edn., updated. Fort Worth, TX: Saunders College Publishing; Harcourt Brace College Publishers.

Vernadsky, V. I. 1998. *The Biosphere*. New York, NY: Copernicus (Springer-Verlag). Translated by D. B. Langmuir, revised and annotated by M. A. S. McMenamin.

Petit, J. R. et al. 1999. Climate and atmospheric history of the past 420 000 years from the Vostok ice core, Antarctica. *Nature* **399**: 429–436.

Flannery, T. 2005. *The Weather Makers: How Man is Changing the Climate and What it Means for Life on Earth*. New York, NY: Atlantic Monthly Press.

Chapter 2

Description of vegetation:
the search for global patterns

Two ways of sorting plants into groups: phylogeny and function. Phylogenetic classification: Linnaeus, Bentham, Hooker, Wallace, Darwin, Bessey. Molecular systematics. Asteraceae, Orchidaceae. Takhtajan. Functional classification: von Humboldt, Raunkiaer, Küchler. Classification of climate: the Köppen system. Synthesis: ecoregions.

2.1 | Introduction

Some 2 billion years of plant life have made the Earth what it is today: a planet with an atmosphere composed largely of nitrogen and oxygen. Only trace amounts of carbon dioxide remain. Most carbon is now locked into organic molecules in living organisms (mainly plants, mostly cellulose) or as part of the liquid or solid remains of earlier life forms (petroleum and coal, respectively). Of all of the above-ground organic carbon present in living organisms, 99.9 percent is stored in plants (Whittaker 1975). The rest of the Earth's biota, including insects, birds, reptiles, amphibians, and mammals, comprises a mere 0.1 percent of the carbon pool. This living organic carbon is spread in a thin layer over the Earth's surface – thinnest in deserts and thickest in forests.

To proceed further with the scientific analysis of vegetation, it is necessary to subdivide this vast pool of organic carbon into categories. Two basic approaches for subdivision exist, the phylogenetic and the functional, and they can be both contradictory and complimentary. The phylogenetic approach aims to sort plants into groups sharing a common evolutionary history – early work used traits such as floral morphology, more recent work uses direct measurement of similarity in gene structure. The functional approach aims to sort plants into groups sharing common physiology, form and life history – early work used morphological traits such as leaf shape, more recent work includes physiological and chemical characteristics. A well-trained plant ecologist should be familiar with both approaches. Too often, however, practitioners become stuck on one view, unwilling to appreciate the value of the other. These two approaches have entangled historical roots going back several centuries; in presenting them, however, I shall focus largely on our current understanding of each view.

2.2 | Phylogenetic perspectives

2.2.1 Early plant classification: Linnaeus, Bentham, Hooker

One way of organizing the study of organic biomass is to divide it into individuals. This is, in fact, rather arbitrary but nonetheless convenient. Individuals can be grouped into local populations, and these in turn can be grouped into species. Since the pioneering work of Carolus Linnaeus (1707–1778) and his treatises including *Systema Naturae* (1735) and *Genera Plantarum* (1737), botanists have invested three centuries exploring the world and sorting organisms into named species (Figure 2.1). Even so, there are still many species of plants unknown to science and as yet unnamed. Earlier systems of classification existed, of course, as far back as Theophrastus, but the foundation of our modern classification is essentially Linnaean (Benson 1959, Porter 1967, Mayr 1982). By 1764 Linnaeus had listed 1239 genera of plants.

To put Linnaeus in context, it may be helpful to remember that at the time of his birth, Sweden was a European power; its territory extended to Finland, part of northwestern Russia, Estonia, Latvia, and part of northern Germany. The Swedish monarch, Carl XII, fought

Figure 2.1 Historical outline of some of the attempts toward the development of a natural system of flowering plant classification (from Benson 1959).

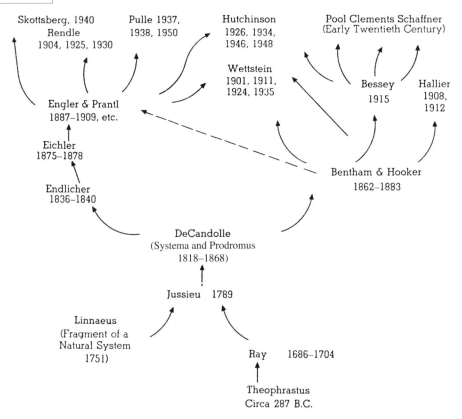

ceaselessly against his neighbors from 1699 to 1718, but after Carl XII's death, in 1718, the impoverishing effects of warfare were evident. Linnaeus was born in 1707, in the midst of the war campaigns, and named for the monarch (Black 1979). He is best known for his work in establishing the binomial system of nomenclature for species, and his books addressing both plants (*Species Plantarum*, 1753 and *Genera Plantarum*, 5th edition, 1754) and animals (*Systema Naturae*, 10th edition, 1758) have been internationally accepted as the starting point for biological nomenclature. Hence, Linnaeus marks the start of the modern taxonomic era, and no names published before Linneaus are accepted, unless they were adopted by him or by subsequent authors. Botanists and zoologists concerned with European, North American, and Indian plants and animals have continually referred to Linnaeus when checking the validity of names.

While his name is now associated with a strong sense of the order in nature, during his time Linnaeus was accused of being a botanical pornographer and of introducing lewd methods into classification (Stearn 1979). These criticisms arose because of his emphasis upon using the male and female characteristics of plants as a means of classification. It probably did not help his cause that his early identification keys referred not to stamens and pistils *per se* but rather to characteristics (and terms) including the visibility of flowers (public as opposed to clandestine marriages), bisexual or unisexual flowers (husband and wife in the same bed or separate beds), and the number of stamens (one male, two males up to many males). Critics were outraged; one (J. G. Sigesbeck) stated in 1737 that "such loathsome harlotry" as several males to one female would never have been permitted in the vegetable kingdom by the Creator. Linneaus obtained revenge by naming an unpleasant, small-flowered weed after him, *Sigesbeckia*.

It is important to remember that Linnaeus' travels were confined to northern Europe, Lapland in particular, although he did encounter tropical plants later in his career when he visited Holland. Stearn (1979) observes of Linnaeus: "His own system thus rested in the first place upon an intimate acquaintance with the comparatively limited flora of a Swedish parish" (p. 98). As the flood of plant material from global explorers washed over Europe, it became clear that the 1239 genera recognized by Linnaeus were vastly insufficient for describing the diversity of the plant kingdom. New workers rose to the challenge. George Bentham (1800–1884) and Sir Joseph Hooker (1817–1911) were both British botanists who developed a system of classification "based upon an unexcelled study of a great section of the world's flora by detailed research upon families, genera, and species" (Benson 1959, p. 464). Together they published *Genera Plantarum* (3 Vols., 1862–1883). Hooker also went on expeditions to New Zealand, Antarctica, and India, and had a special interest in Asia. In 1849, while returning from Tibet, he was seized, along with the government agent to Sikkim, by a local anti-British ruler. Hooker was, however, allowed to collect rhododendron seeds even as they were marched south in captivity: "To stop such banditry and show – in Hooker's words – that the rajahs 'could not play fast and loose with a British subject,' southern Sikkim was promptly annexed for the Crown, with Hooker advising the expeditionary forces" (Desmond and Moore 1991, p. 370).

Hooker also became a close advisor to Charles Darwin. He was invited to examine Darwin's plants from the Beagle voyage "which were still lying unstudied in a room at Cambridge" (Browne 1995, p. 452). In 1844 Darwin wrote to Hooker of his ideas on the transmutation of species. The reply was positive, for which Darwin was "overwhelmingly grateful. He felt sure Hooker would be one of the best and most erudite sounding boards for his theories . . ." (p. 453). Hooker was in attendance, with Charles Lyell, to present Wallace's paper, along with Darwin's 1844 essay, to the Linnaean Society in 1858. In 1876 he was put forward for a knighthood and a very specific additional honor, the Star of India, in acknowledgement of his decades-long work on the Himalayan flora: "Hooker told Darwin that he 'would rather go down to posterity as one of the 'Star of India' than as of any other dignity whatever that the crown can offer' " (Desmond and Moore 1991, p. 626). Hooker also served as pall-bearer at Darwin's funeral at Westminster Abbey in 1882.

2.2.2 The discovery of evolution: Wallace, Darwin, Bessey

Alfred Wallace (1823–1913) explored the Amazon in 1848, and published *A Narrative of Travels on the Amazon and Rio Negro* in 1853. Money was a constant problem. His companion in the Amazon, Henry Bates, had an agent who gave him fourpence a specimen (from which he took 20 percent commission) so that Bates received a mere £27 for 20 months work (Edmonds 1997). In the end, Wallace did not even have this to fall back on: "Wallace on his return to England, was struck by catastrophe. The ship on which he travelled caught fire (August 6, 1852) and sank, with his entire magnificent collection and most of his journals, notes and sketches" (Mayr 1982, p. 418).

From 1854 to 1862 Wallace explored the islands linking Australia to Asia and during this period, while staying at Sarawak in Borneo, wrote an explicit essay on evolution, "*On the Law Which Has Regulated the Introduction of New Species*" (1855). He became ill again from malaria in 1858, and, while in a fever, connected his ideas to those of Malthus: "There suddenly flashed upon me the *idea* of the survival of the fittest." It is well known that he sent a manuscript to Darwin, who immediately recognized the similarities to his own work. On the advice of Lyell and Hooker, Wallace's essay along with Darwin's own was read to the Linnean Society on July 1, 1858. A new era of science had begun.

Darwin seems to have received a preponderance of the credit for the discovery of evolution. It may be worth noting that Wallace was a man of modest means, while the Darwins were well-established and well-connected within English society:

> In most respects, both men were about as different as two people can be: Darwin, the wealthy gentleman, with many years of college education, a private scholar, able to devote all of his time to research; Wallace, a poor man's son with only a lower middle-class background (a very important factor in Victorian England), without any higher education, never particularly well-to-do, always having to work for a living, for the longest time in the exceedingly dangerous profession of a collector of birds and insects in fever-ridden tropical countries. But they agreed in some decisive points. Both of them were British, both had read Lyell and Malthus, both were naturalists, and both had made natural-history collections in tropical archipelagos.
>
> (Mayr 1982)

Darwin also had powerful friends in his circle of Cambridge gentlemen, friends who defended and propagated his ideas. The image remains of Darwin living in comfort, with servants on his estate, while Wallace lies sick in the Moluccas. Given that Wallace published his ideas first, it seems remarkable how much he has been eclipsed by the Darwin industry. Tangentially but amusingly, the President of the Linnaean Society, in his annual report for 1858, stated: "The year … has not, indeed, been marked by any of those striking discoveries which at once revolutionise, so to speak, the department of science on which they bear" (Mayr 1982).

The unifying framework of evolution stimulated the search for natural systems of plant classification. Bessey (1845–1915) extended Bentham's and Hooker's work; he postulated that the order Ranales (most closely related to the current Magnoliid complex, Figure 2.4) represented the most primitive flowering plants. This group, he suspected, had ancestors with bisexual strobili in which the sterile bracts became a perianth, the microsporophylls became stamens, and the megasporophylls became carpels. His entire flowering plant phylogeny, then, rests on such ancestors (Figure 2.2). The five genera and 90 species in the Winteraceae of the southwestern Pacific, Australia, Madagascar, South America and Mexico appear to possess a particularly large number of primitive angiosperm traits. The genus *Drimys* typifies a primitive type of ovary in which the margins of the carpel are not yet fused into a cylinder. The genus *Magnolia* is a better-known representative (Figure 2.3), and the basis of the name for the complex.

Adolf Engler (1844–1930) and Karl Prantl (1849–1893), in contrast, were taken by the similarity between the catkins of those angiosperms in the Amentiferae and the strobili of gymnosperms. If one regards catkins as primitive flowers, one derives a very different phylogenetic tree from that of Bessey. The preponderance of

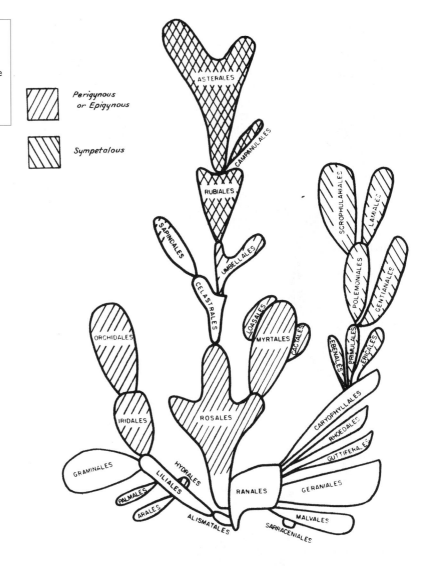

Figure 2.2 Origin and relationships of the orders of flowering plants. The areas are approximately proportional to the number of species in the orders (from Benson 1959 after Bessey 1915).

evidence no longer supports this reconstruction, and while the origin of catkins remains unclear (are they greatly reduced from more elaborate inflorescences?; do they represent an independent lineage within the angiosperms?).

The fossil record also shows that the early angiosperms had mono-sulcate pollen grains and simple, entire leaves with poorly organized pinnate venation. The modern families in the order Magnoliales have retained this type of pollen and primitive vessels. Thus the derivation of angiosperms from ancestors in this order has often been considered (Sporne 1956, Benson 1959, Thorne 1963, Cronquist 1993). The class Liliopsida (monocots), within the angiosperms, includes groups such as the palms (Arecaceae), grasses (Poaceae), orchids (Orchidaceae), and sedges (Cyperaceae), and appears to be derived from aquatic ancestors. This is indicated by the absence of three key traits

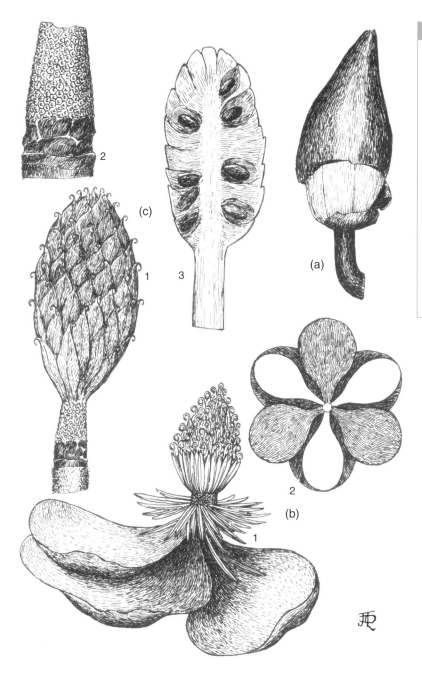

Figure 2.3 The strobilus-like flower of an angiosperm in the Magnoliales (Magnoliaceae: *Magnolia grandiflora*) showing primitive characteristics. (a) Flower bud opening, the sepals being ruptured; (b) flower, 1 anthesis, the upper stamens having fallen, 2 arrangement of sepals and petals in cycles of three; (c) head of fruits, each formed from a single carpel, these obscurely coalescent at the bases, 1 side view, 2 enlargement of a portion of the receptacle showing the scars at the points of attachment of the three sepals, the six petals (in two series), and the numerous spirally arranged stamens, 3 longitudinal section (from Benson 1959).

typically found in the class Magnoliopsida (dicots): well-developed xylem, a branching arborescent growth form, and woodiness.

2.2.3 Molecular systematics and phylogeny

In the late twentieth century it became possible to determine the sequences of amino acids in proteins and of nucleotides in DNA. This opened a vast new realm of information on plant evolution.

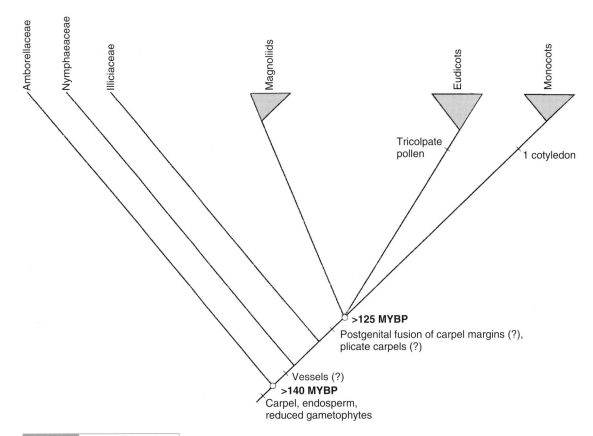

Figure 2.4 A cladogram showing the presumed phylogenetic relationships of the angiosperms. It was constructed using both morphological and molecular data. Question mark (?) means the position of the character is uncertain. MYBP, million years before present (derived from Judd et al. 2002).

New statistical techniques were developed to sort this sequence data and create evolutionary trees called **cladograms** (an example appears in Figure 2.4). While many of the fundamentals of the early classification schemes remained intact, this new source of information shows that some earlier ideas of phylogeny had to be revised.

Chloroplast DNA is abundant in cells, and plant systematists have collaborated to build a large database of sequences of the chloroplast gene *rbcL*. This gene codes for a large subunit of a photosynthetic enzyme called RuBisCO (ribulose-1,5-bis-phosphate carboxylase/oxygenase). More than 2000 species have been sequenced, and phylogenetic relationships mapped (Judd et al. 2002). The cladogram in Figure 2.4 summarizes the current phylogeny of flowering plants with this input of molecular data.

Figure 2.4 shows a set of three primitive "basal groups", the Amborellaceae, Nymphaeaceae, and Illiciaceae. The Amborellaceae is represented only by a small evergreen tree called *Amborella trichopoda*, endemic to New Caledonia (note that Takhtajan (1986) made New Caledonia, a small fragment of former Gondwana, a separate floristic region, Figure 2.7). A data set combining five gene sequences from 51 taxa indicated that *Amborella* was a basal taxon (Parkinson et al. 1999), but a complete sequence of the chloroplast genome of this plant brings this into question (Goremykin et al. 2003). The Nymphaeaceae are represented by the more familiar and widespread white water lily (Figure 2.5) and include the genera *Nymphaea*, *Nuphar*, *Victoria*, and *Camboba*. The Illiciaceae (Figure 2.6) contains one genus, *Illicium*, with 37 species of small trees and shrubs that occur mainly in southeastern Asia and the southeastern USA. Once these three basal families are delineated, the Magnoliids can be treated as one large monophyletic group containing families such as Magnoliaceae, Annonaceae (e.g., pawpaw), Myristicaceae (e.g., nutmeg), and Lauraceae (e.g., sassafras). The remaining flowering plants fall into two evolutionary groups: the traditional Monocots and what are now called the Eudicots (true dicots) (Figure 2.4).

Other more traditional methods of research continue. In China, from rocks aged at 125 million years, paleobotanists have found roots, leaves, reproductive organs, and pollen of an aquatic plant representing a new basal angiosperm family, the (now extinct) Archaefructaceae (Sun 2002). In Australia, an entirely new genus of conifer (*Wollemia*, Araucariaceae) was discovered clinging to the ledges in a deep sandstone gorge in Wollemi National Park in 1994 (Jones et al. 1995). Only 40 adult plants are known (National Parks and Wildlife Service 1998).

2.2.4 The two largest families of plants: Asteraceae and Orchidaceae

Phylogenetic classification of the families within the Magnoliid complex in Figure 2.4 is hindered by the large gaps among families resulting from extinction. "These families have the appearance of being 'old groups', in which evolution is proceeding at a leisurely pace and extinction has greatly affected the pattern of variation" (Dodson 1991, p. 745). In contrast, the Asteraceae and Orchidaceae are two relatively homogeneous families that have recently diversified in the eudicots and monocots, respectively. Owing to their vast size (Asteraceae 23 000 species; Orchidaceae 19 500 species, Judd et al. 2002) something more should be said about each of these two major angiosperm groups.

The Asteraceae are sharply defined by having flowers grouped into compact inflorescences surrounded by bracts, hence the older name of Compositae. This trait is so clear that there is no species where there is doubt as to whether or not it is properly included within the Asteraceae (Cronquist 1991). Further, the species within the Asteraceae are so similar to one another that most could be placed in a single genus – partly explaining the challenges posed by this group when learning plant identification. One genus, however, would be impractical, and botanists have found it necessary to recognize subfamilies, tribes, and genera to convey a sense of order. Three of the many tribes (Eupatorieae, Senecioneae, and Veronieae)

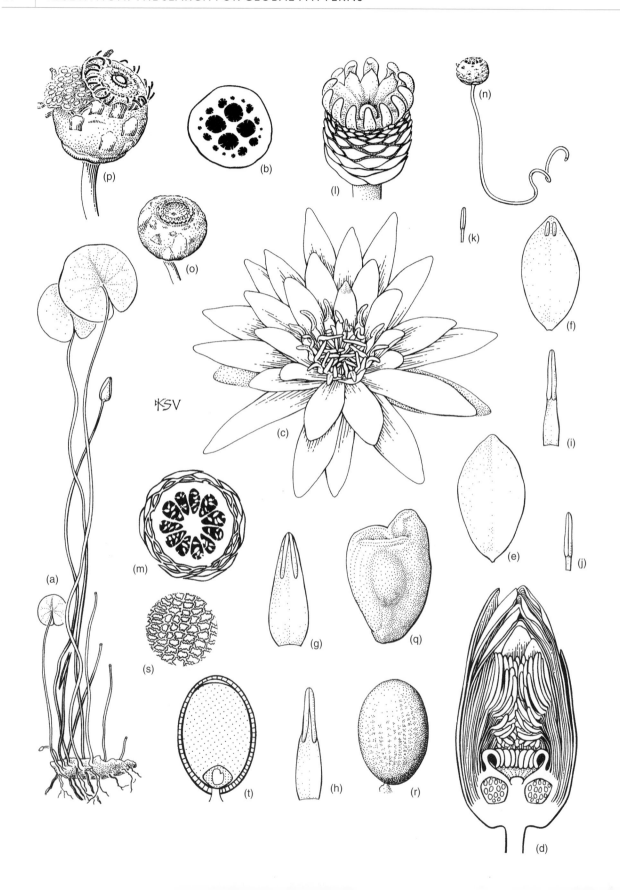

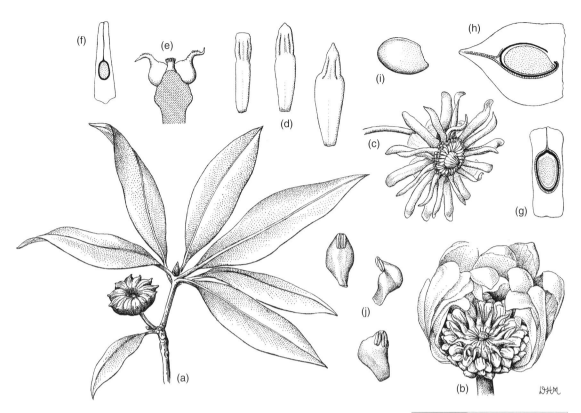

are dominated by a single very large genus and other small satellite genera.

The progenitor of the Asteraceae is likely to have been a small tree species from the dry highlands of Mexico (Cronquist 1991). It probably had a well-developed resin system and opposite, simple leaves. There were likely a few terminal inflorescences arranged as a cyme, each yellow flower in the head being subtended by a bract. The Asteraceae are not well-represented in the fossil record until the early Pleistocene, about 2 million years ago, at which time climatic change may have stimulated dispersal and adaptive radiation. There is still no satisfactory explanation for the significance of the inflorescence, or other traits, in the rapid diversification of this group. The Asteraceae are common in sunny places including fields associated with human agricultural activity, and indeed, the presence of pollen from the genus *Ambrosia* (ragweed) is used as a marker of European agriculture when interpreting sediment cores from lakes and peat

Figure 2.6 Illiciaceae. *Illicium floridanum*: (a) fruiting branch (× 0.4); (b) opening flower bud with receptive carpels (× 3.2); (c) flower, later stage at shedding of pollen (× 1.2); (d) stamens, inner, outer, and an unusual subpetaloid form (× 5.6); (e) two carpels on receptacle (× 3.2); (f) carpel in cross section; note single ovule (× 12); (g) mature fruit, with single seed, endosperm stippled (× 2.4); (h) mature fruit in longitudinal section (× 2.4); (i) seed (× 2.4); (j) *I. parviflorum*: stamens (× 2.4) (illustration by Dorothy H. Marsh, from Judd et al. 2002).

Figure 2.5 Nymphaeaceae. *Nymphaea odorata*: (a) habit (× 0.3); (b) petiole, in cross section (× 5); (c) flower (× 1); (d) flower, in longitudinal section (× 1.5); (e) petal (× 1.5); (f–h) petal-like stamens (× 1.5); (i–k) inner stamens (× 1.5); (l) gynoecium showing numerous carpels (× 2); (m) gynoecium in cross section (× 1.5); (n) fruit, with coiled floral peduncle (× 0.5); (o) fruit (× 1); (p) dehiscing fruit (× 1.5); (q) seed, with aril (× 15); (r) seed (× 30); (s) seed coat (greatly magnified); (t) longitudinal section of seed, with embryo, endosperm, and perisperm (× 30) (illustration by Karen Stoutsenberger Velmure, from Judd et al. 2002).

cores. The family is now widespread, but still particularly common in open habitats of arid regions in North America, the Near East and South Africa. Primitive woody forms still occur in the dry highlands of Mexico.

The Orchidaceae may have even more species than the Asteraceae, but exact numbers will remain unknown until further work is completed in tropical regions. Orchids possess three sets of distinctive traits: (1) the pollen stays in masses called pollinia, (2) the stamens and pistil are fused into one structure called the column, and (3) the tiny seeds lack endosperm and so require fungi for germination. Pollination by bees, moths, butterflies, birds, and flies has been documented and the group is well-known for close co-evolution between flower and pollinator. Many orchids also have a drought-tolerant type of photosynthesis known as CAM photosynthesis (Section 3.3.3).

Similar to the Asteraceae, there is thought to have been rapid diversification of orchids in geologically recent time, making it difficult to delineate genera or higher categories. The reasons for this rapid diversification are unclear and remain a challenging question with both ecological and evolutionary components. One hypothesis could invoke the significance of pollinia in producing multiple matings with one pollinator visit. Another might emphasize the significance of the distinctive seed dispersal syndrome – minute wind-borne seeds allowing the production of vast numbers of seeds with long distance dispersal. Perhaps like the Asteraceae, it is possible to invoke climate change. Even though many orchids are found in tropical regions, seemingly far-removed from the effects of glaciation, alternating periods of aridity have been postulated as a mechanism for fragmenting tropical forests and creating refugia (Section 9.3.4). Comparison with the Bromeliaceae, another member of the monocots that has diversified to some 2000 species in the New World, might be instructive, particularly as the epiphytic habit is predominant in both orchids and bromeliads.

2.2.5 World floristic regions: phylogeny and geography

While biogeographic representations (e.g., Figure 2.10) provide a useful synthesis of zoology and botany, they also obscure many of the details of plant evolution. Figure 2.7 therefore presents the floristic regions of the world according to the classification provided by the Russian botanist, Takhtajan (1969, 1986). Each region of the figure is mapped based on floristic similarities. To illustrate Takhtajan's regional classification, consider two examples, one from North America and the other from Africa. The North American Atlantic Region (3) is described as follows:

> Endemic families Hydrastidaceae and Leitneriaceae, no fewer than a hundred endemic genera (including *Sanguinaria, Sarracenia, Dirca, Neviusia, Hudsonia, Dionaea, Yeatesia, Pleea, Uvularia*) and numerous endemic species.

(Takhtajan 1969, p. 244)

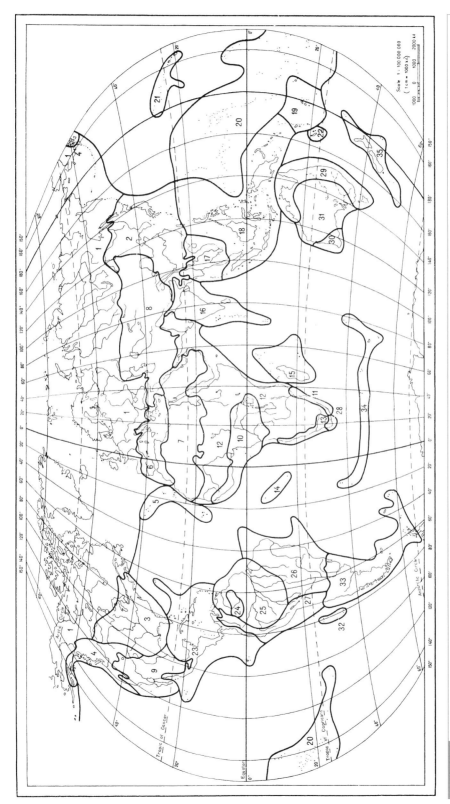

Figure 2.7 The 35 floristic regions of the world (from Takhtajan 1986). See Table 2.1 for region names. Note that an earlier version (Takhtajan 1969) recognised 37 regions.

Table 2.1. | *The 35 floristic regions of the world mapped in Figure 2.7 following Takhtajan (1986).*

I. Holarctic Kingdom
  A. Boreal Subkingdom
    1. Circumboreal
    2. Eastern Asiatic
    3. North American Atlantic
    4. Rocky Mountain
  B. Tethyan Subkingdom
    5. Macaronesian
    6. Mediterranean
    7. Saharo-Arabian
    8. Irano-Turanian
  C. Madrean Subkingdom
    9. Madrean

II. Paleotropical Kingdom
  A. African Subkingdom
    10. Guineo-congolian
    11. Uzambara-Zululand
    12. Sudano-Zambezian
    13. Karroo-Namib
    14. St. Helena and Ascension
  B. Madagascan Subkingdom
    15. Madagascan
  C. Indo-Malesian Subkingdom
    16. Indian
    17. Indochinese
    18. Malesian
    19. Fijian

  D. Polynesian Subkingdom
    20. Polynesian
    21. Hawaiian
  E. Neocaledonian Subkingdom
    22. Neocaledonian

III. Neotropical Kingdom
    23. Caribbean
    24. Guayana Highlands
    25. Amazonian
    26. Brazilian
    27. Andean

IV. Cape Kingdom
    28. Cape

V. Australian Kingdom
    29. Northeast Australian
    30. Southwest Australian
    31. Central Australian
      (Eremaean)

VI. Antarctic Kingdom
    32. Fernándezian
    33. Chile-Patagonian
    34. South Subantarctic
      Islands
    35. Neozeylandic

Similarly, the Karroo-Namib Region (13) is described as having:

> Very many endemic species; *Mesembryanthemum* and allied genera, *Tetragonia, Pelargonium, Rhigozum, Pentzia, Pteronia* and other shrubby Asteraceae are especially characteristic; in the northern parts of the Namib *Welwitschia* and *Acanthosicyos horridus* are endemic.
>
> (Takhtajan 1969, p. 248)

Takhtajan's entire classification of regions is presented in Table 2.1. For the descriptions of the other 33 regions, his works should be consulted. You should be aware too, that a related system exists that combines plants and animals (Udvardy 1975).

2.2.6 Summary and limitations

In the phylogenetic lineage of classification, the goal is to arrange species according to their relatedness. This perspective places a great deal of emphasis upon conserved characters, particularly those of reproductive systems, which make it possible to retrace the evolution

Table 2.2. *The major taxonomic groups of land plants. The four divisions of non-flowering seed plants are collectively called gymnosperms.*

Kingdom Plantae	Bryophytes	Division Marchantiophyta (liverworts)
		Division Anthocerophyta (hornworts)
		Division Bryophyta (mosses)
	Vascular plants	
	Seedless plants	Division Lycopodiophyta (clubmosses)
		Division Equisetophyta (horsetails)
		Division Pteridophyta (true ferns)
		Division Psilotophyta (whisk ferns)
	Seed plants	Division Cycadophyta (cycads)
		Division Ginkgophyta (ginkgo)
		Division Pinophyta (conifers)
		Division Gnetophyta (gnetae)
		Division Magnoliophyta (flowering plants)
		Class Magnoliopsida (dicots)
		Class Liliopsida (monocots)

and diversification of plants. Thus, for example, species with free-living gametophytes (e.g., Pteridophyta) are classified as entirely separate groups from those with gametophytes that are retained upon the sporophytes (e.g., Magnoliophyta) (Table 2.2). Further, the latter groups are considered to be more recently evolved because the life cycle has been abbreviated, simplified, and made less dependent upon rainfall. We will return to the evolutionary basis of Table 2.2 in Box 9.1.

So many species of plants have now been identified and cataloged that no single worker can be familiar with more than a subset. The subset might be defined by taxonomic boundaries (e.g., the palm family) or geographic boundaries (e.g., the flora of the Galapagos). One of the first duties for a plant ecologist is to master the flora of the particular region to be studied; this, in itself, is no easy task. In the long run, teams of scientists may need to collaborate to ensure that the full range of necessary expertise is brought to a study.

While a phylogenetic approach is useful for subdividing the vast plant kingdom, there are at least five problems created by phylogenetic classifications:

1. Some groups of plants, in some geographic regions, particularly those from the tropics, are still poorly understood and may even be unnamed. Ecologists, however, cannot cease to study tropical areas until such time as complete classifications and phylogenetic reconstructions are available.
2. Even if the flora of an area is well-studied, the flora may be so large as to present an obstacle to field identification. Further, while classification usually assumes knowledge of reproductive traits, plant ecologists often encounter large numbers of pre-reproductive individuals, and even the mature individuals may lack the

required structures for identification. In the case of tropical trees, reproductive features that may be found only in the canopy create a further obstacle.

3. Even if the flora of an area is well-known, small enough for easy identification, and consists of individuals easily assigned to species, the enumeration of species names does not necessarily convey useful information to other ecologists. Papers using nomenclature from a different biogeographic region may be nearly indecipherable to those unfamiliar with that region's flora. The names, then, do not necessarily enhance communication among scientists but may even subdivide them into geographic cliques.

4. Even if the above obstacles are surmounted, the taxonomic and phylogenetic status of an individual may tell a great deal about evolutionary relationships but very little about its ecological function. In temperate climates, the Lily family may be represented by spring ephemerals of deciduous forests (e.g., *Erythronium* spp.), in boreal regions the Lily family may be found in *Sphagnum* bogs (*Smilacina* spp.), and in arid regions the representatives of the Lily family may be evergreen succulents (*Aloe* spp.) (Benson 1959). While all these species may share an evolutionary heritage, as illustrated by similarities in floral structure, and similarities in chloroplast DNA, they now occupy entirely different habitats and have different functional traits.

5. For some scientific purposes, there simply may be "too many" species in nature. For studies of biodiversity or evolutionary diversification, the detail provided by thorough taxonomic subdivisions may be necessary, but for vegetation mapping, extreme simplification is necessary.

Those familiar with paleobotany, molecular systematics, and the task of phylogenetic reconstruction will no doubt be frustrated by the few paragraphs allocated to these important tasks, as well as annoyed by the lengthy list of limitations. More thorough treatments of these topics can be found in Benson (1959), Mayr (1982), Foster and Gifford (1974), Stewart and Rothwell (1993), and Judd et al. (2002). For the task at hand – an introduction to plant ecology – it is the products of such studies that are of importance. The regional floras of the world provide vital tools for research in plant ecology.

2.3 | Functional perspectives

If it is any consolation, the following treatment of plant functional classifications will be equally brief. Here again the roots of the discipline lie in the 1700s, but this text will focus largely upon the present. The concern of functional classification is quite different from that of phylogenetic classification; one is interested, not in constructing groups that reflect evolutionary relationships, but rather in constructing groups that reflect evolutionary convergence

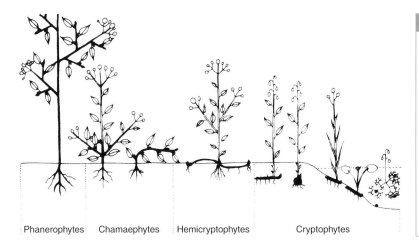

Phanerophytes Chamaephytes Hemicryptophytes Cryptophytes

irrespective of origin. Succulents, for example, are associated with arid climates, but they are drawn from a wide array of plant families. The physiognomic similarities amongst succulents are the consequence of natural selection, which drives organisms to adopt similar physical forms in spite of their different origins. It is possible, however, to deduce differences in origin among species that share similar functional traits by examining conservative traits, largely those of floral structure, which enable one to construct phylogenetic relationships.

2.3.1 von Humboldt, Raunkiaer, Küchler

One of the earliest functional classifications, by von Humboldt (Box 2.1), recognized 19 *Hauptformen*. Most were named after a typical genus or family, such as Palmen-form, Cactus-form, and Gras-form. As with many systems that are initially simple, Humboldt's was expanded to accommodate diversity and apparent exceptions. By 1872 Grisebach's work, *Die Vegetation der Erde*, published in Leipzig, yielded some 60 physiognomic types. These were, however, grouped into seven main categories (Shimwell 1971, p. 67):

Holzgewächse – woody plants
Succulente Gewächse – succulents
Schlinnggewächse – climbing plants
Epiphyten – epiphytes
Kräuter – herbs
Gräser – grasses
Zellenpflanzen – lower plants (cryptogams).

In 1903 Raunkiaer first presented his influential system of functional classification, which is based largely upon the location of perennating meristems (Figure 2.8, Table 2.3). He emphasized that the location of perennating meristems was closely connected to climate, easily recognizable in the field, and a single characteristic

Box 2.1 | A man of his times: Alexander von Humboldt

The great era of global exploration in the 1800s has passed. In today's era of satellite imagery, robot explorers on distant planets, and near-instantaneous electronic communication around the world, it may be difficult to appreciate the tasks that faced early global explorers and scientists a little over a century ago. Of early scientific expeditions, Darwin's voyage of the Beagle down the east coast of South America and up the west coast to the Galapagos is perhaps the best known. Countless other names are less-appreciated: Stanley (1874–1889, Africa), Livingstone (1849–1864, Africa), Przhevalsky (1870–1880, Mongolia and Tibet), Cook (1768–1779, Pacific Ocean and Western Coast of North America), Mackenzie (1789–1793, north western North America), Younghusband (1887–1891, Tibet). This list does not include the names of explorers of infamy who used the force of arms in their search for land or gold (e.g., Cortez, Pizzaro) and who destroyed what they found and enslaved the native inhabitants of the places that they reached; nor does it include missionaries who sought to change what they found. The names that deserve recognition are those who made contributions to humanity through their attempts to expand the frontiers of human understanding. Perhaps the greatest of these was the German naturalist Alexander von Humboldt (1769–1859, Figure B2.1a).

Humboldt's family were Huguenots (French Protestants) who had fled Catholic France after Louis XIV revoked religious freedom. Humboldt initially thought of joining the army, began futile studies in economics, and then developed a passionate interest in botany. Between 1799 and 1803 he explored the northern areas of South America, from the rain forests of present day Venezuela to the Andes

Figure B2.1(a) Portrait in 1814 of Alexander von Humboldt (1769–1859), a naturalist explorer, scientist, and model for aspiring plant ecologists (from Kellner 1963).

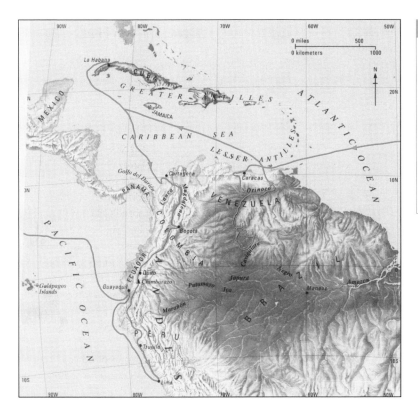

Figure B2.1(b) The voyage of Humboldt 1799–1803 took him from flood plain forests to deserts and mountain peaks. All the while he collected plants, made careful notes, measured temperature and barometric pressure, and later on the trip even collected data on social and economic conditions in Mexico. On the way home, he visited President Jefferson in the United States (from Edmonds 1997).

(Figure B2.1b). He even set the world altitude limit for mountain climbing while ascending Mount Chimborazo, although altitude sickness and bad weather prevented him from reaching the peak. The years 1804 to 1827 were spent in Paris where he published the results of this expedition.

His fame was such that he was compared at the time with Napoleon, but in addition to being a determined explorer and an accomplished scientist, he was also a decent human being. He sought out promising students and personally supported them in spite of his precarious finances; Justus von Liebig and Louis Agassiz were both launched by him. He encouraged the young Charles Darwin. Like Darwin, he denounced slavery and forced labor, but, unlike Darwin, he freely mixed with society and appeared regularly in the salons of Paris. His enthusiasm for the popularization of science led him to publish *Kosmos*, an overview of the structure of the universe, and he gave public lectures to audiences of a thousand at a time. He died at 90 while still working on the fifth volume of *Kosmos* (von Humboldt 1845–1862).

In 1831 Darwin was inspired by von Humboldt's seven-volume, 3754-page account of his trip to South America. He is said to have read out long passages to his friend John Stevens Henslow in order to encourage a joint trip to Tenerife, but before arrangements for the trip could be made, he received a letter (29 August 1831) offering him passage on the Beagle in the role of a well-bred gentleman to ease the isolation of Fitzroy's command (Desmond and Moore 1991). Darwin sent Humboldt a complimentary copy of his book on the voyages of the Beagle. Humboldt, says Darwin's biographer, was a figure of "almost mythic proportions in Darwin's mind . . . Humboldt's highly laudatory reply consequently electrified him. The grand old man behaved just as grand old men were expected to behave, and warm congratulations poured from his pen like honey, praising Darwin's 'excellent and admirable book' " (Browne 1995, p. 416).

Here is a potential model for young plant ecologists, a man brave and determined, accomplished in botany, yet compassionate and awake to the needs of his world. Compare his personality with that of Galileo, who denied Kepler a badly-needed telescope out of fear of what he might discover, or of Newton, who huddled in his office at Cambridge completely cut off from the rest of the world, unwilling to share his discoveries. Perhaps even Darwin fares badly by comparison. He was reclusive and, it appears, feared the negative publicity that would arise if he published his ideas; he spent 8 years studying barnacles rather than publicizing his views on topics such as slavery. Indeed, says a biographer (Browne 1995), Darwin turned his house into the Beagle, "self contained" and "safely isolated from the concerns of the world" (p. 530).

Table 2.3. *Raunkiaer's life-form classification system slightly expanded from Figure 2.8 to correspond with Table 2.4 (Raunkiaer 1934).*

Stem succulents		S
Epiphytes		E
Phanerophytes:		
Megaphanerophytes	>30 m ⎫	
Mesophanerophytes	8–30 m ⎬	MM
Microphanerophytes	2–8 m	M
Nanophanerophytes	<2 m	N
Chamaephytes		Ch
Hemicryptophytes		H
Geophytes		G
Helophytes	⎫	
Hydrophytes (protected by flooding)	⎬	HH
Therophytes (annuals)		Th

that could be enumerated for statistical comparisons of regions (Raunkiaer 1907, 1908). The location of meristems was considered a fundamental trait associated with adaptation to adverse conditions. Raunkiaer was also astute enough to recognize the need for a null model against which world floras could be compared on the basis of meristem location (see Box 10.1). Thus he objectively selected 1000 species from around the world to provide a random sample of life-forms. It was therefore possible to use his life-form spectra not only to compare specific sites with different climates but also to compare each site to a standard, worldwide reference spectrum (Table 2.4).

Although many other functional classification systems exist, most involve various elaborations and expansions of the Raunkiaer

Table 2.4. | *Selected life-form spectra (after Raunkiaer 1908). See Figure 2.8 and Table 2.3.*

Region		No. species	Percentage distribution of species among life-forms									
			S	E	MM	M	N	Ch	H	G	HH	Th
Franz Josef Land, Russia	82°N, 55°E	25	—	—	—	—	—	32	60	8	—	—
Iceland	65°N, 19°W	329	—	—	—	—	2	13	54	10	10	11
Sitka, Alaska	57°N, 9°E	222	—	—	3	3	5	7	60	10	7	5
Death Valley, California	36°N, 117°W	294	3	—	—	2	21	7	18	2	5	42
Ghardaïa, Algeria	32°N, 4°E	300	0.3	—	—	—	3	16	20	3	—	58
Aden, Yemen	13°N, 45°E	176	1	—	—	7	26	27	19	3	—	17
Seychelles	5°S, 56E	258	1	3	10	23	24	6	12	3	2	16
Normal spectrum		1000	1	3	6	17	20	9	27	3	1	13

Table 2.5. | *Seven life forms of plants in tropical rain forests (from Richards 1952).*

A. Autotrophic plants (with chlorophyll)
  1. Mechanically independent plants
    a. Trees and "shrubs" ⎫
                 ⎬ arranged in a number of strata (layers)
    b. Herbs ⎭
  2. Mechanically dependent plants
    a. Climbers
    b. Stranglers
    c. Epiphytes (including semi-parasitic epiphytes)
B. Heterotrophic plants (without chlorophyll)
  1. Saprophytes
  2. Parasites

system. At finer scales, where larger geographic and climatic gradients are not involved, this system may lack discrimination: that is, sites that vary in ecological attributes may not vary according to the Raunkiaer system (e.g., Westoby 1998, Weiher et al. 1999). As well, complex vegetation structure, such as that within stands of tropical rain forest, may require a different system. In his monograph on the tropical rain forest, Richards (1952) introduces a classification of life forms with seven categories (Table 2.5). The inclusion of parasitic and saprophytic plants is a noteworthy feature of this system and a discrimination that may be necessary in other vegetation types. Küchler has also devised a system for classifying vegetation with particular emphasis upon a scheme that can be used to produce vegetation maps (Table 2.6). "Unfortunately," says Shimwell (1971 p. 180), "like many other investigators before him, Küchler (1966)

Table 2.6. *Vegetation structure classification of Küchler (from Shimwell 1971).*

Life form categories

Basic life forms	1949	1966	Special life forms	1949	1966
Broadleaf evergreen	B	B	Epiphytes	e	X
Broadleaf deciduous	D	D	Lianas	j	C
Needleleaf evergreen	E	E	Stem succulents	k	K
Needleleaf deciduous	N	N	Tuft plant	y	T
Aphyllous	O	O	Bamboos	v	V
Semi-deciduous (B + D)	–	S	Cushion plants	q	–
Mixed (D + E)	–	M	Palms	u	–
			Aquatic vegetation	w	–

Herbaceous plants			*Leaf characteristics*		
Graminoids	G	G	Hard	–	h
Forbs	H	H	Soft	–	w
Lichens, mosses	L	L	Succulent	–	k
			Large (400 cm^2)	–	l
			Small (4 cm^2)	–	s

Structural categories

Height (stratification)	1966	1949	
>35 m	8	t	tall: minimum tree height 25 m
20–35	7		minimum herbaceous height 2 m
10–12	6	m	medium: trees 10–25 m
5–10	5		herbs 0.5–2 m
2–5	4	l	low: trees to 10 m
0.5–2	3		herbs to 0.5 m
0.1–0.5	2	s	shrubs, minimum height 1 m
<0.1	1	z	dwarf shrubs, maximum height 1 m

Coverage (1967)	1949	1966
Density (1949)		
continuous (>75%)	c	c
interrupted (50–75%)	i	i
parklike, patchy (25–50%)	p	p
rare (6–25%)	r	r
barely present (1–5%)	b	b
almost absent (<1%)	–	a

falls foul of the revision trend so that his early scheme (1949) becomes considerably altered in his 1966 paper" (Table 2.6 attempts to reconcile these schemes).

2.3.2   The classification of climate

Integral to a study of global vegetation patterns is an understanding of climate. Earth, like most planets, has strong temperature gradients, as illustrated by the accumulation of ice at the poles. Modifying this latitudinal temperature gradient are other factors such as winds, mountains, and large water bodies. All of these factors also influence precipitation patterns. The kinds of plants and plant communities that arise in any area are strongly controlled by temperature and precipitation, so that the search for patterns of plant form and vegetation type has occurred in parallel with the search for a simple method of classifying the world's climates.

Daubenmire (1978) traces the links of vegetation classification and mapping to climatic classification and mapping but buries his useful overview on pages 280–285, in between "Tropical Alpine Region" and "Marine Vegetation." He credits von Humboldt with first plotting isotherms of mean annual temperature and relating these to vegetation (the thermometer having been invented in 1714). In 1836, Meyen added to the relationships established by von Humboldt by showing that annual variation in temperature was important as well as the mean. Precipitation too was important, but its quantification remained problematic.

In 1869 Lisser proposed evaluating the effectivity of precipitation by calculating the ratio of monthly precipitation to monthly temperature: "This concept of discounting precipitation in proportion to temperature was so far ahead of its time that its significance was overlooked for several decades. In fact, his contribution seems never to have been acknowledged by subsequent workers in the field" (Daubenmuire 1978, p. 282). In 1874 Alphonse de Candolle (son of the famous taxonomist Augustin de Candolle) published a classification of five major types of plants, in relationship to both temperature and moisture, but he "either did not know of Lisser's contribution or did not appreciate its significance. Neither did he grasp the importance of seasonal differences in temperature as Meyen had pointed out" (Daubenmuire 1978, pp. 282–283).

Such early work led to the classification systems proposed by Köppen in 1900, and Thornthwaite in 1948. The latter included the use of "potential" evapotranspiration and soil moisture storage, but Dansereau concludes that in spite of the added sophistication, the climatic types do not correspond to vegetation any better than those of Köppen's system. Indeed, Köppen's system (Figure 2.9) is still widely used and is the system adopted both by the *Encyclopaedia Britannica* (1991a) and the *Oxford Atlas of the World* (1997). In fact, the *Britannica* summary of climate and weather (vol. 16, pp. 436–522) is essential and entertaining reading. Köppen's system, particularly, will appeal to plant ecologists because of his search for critical climatic factors that would coincide with the boundaries of world vegetation types.

The Köppen system (still named for him, but refined by later scholars) has only five main climate types: tropical rainy (A), dry (B), warm temperate rainy (C), cold temperate rainy (D), and polar (E). A highland category (H) was later added to address the variation of climatic zones in high mountains. Small letters are used as modifiers. One set addresses rainfall properties; for example, f denotes rainfall throughout the year, m denotes monsoon rains, s denotes a dry

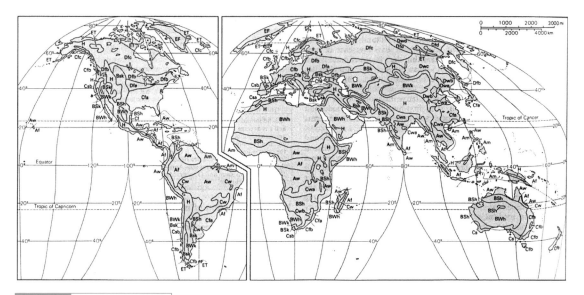

Figure 2.9 The Köppen system of climate classification (from *Encyclopaedia Britannica* 1991a).

summer, and w, a dry winter. The Amazon River basin, for example, can thus be divided into Af, Am, and Aw regions. Most of Europe, in contrast, has a Cf or Cs climate.

Another set of small letters (a,b,c,d,h, and k) addresses special characteristics of temperature:

a   hot summer
b   warm summer
c   cool, short summer
d   cool, short summer and cold winter
h   hot dry climate
k   cool dry climate.

2.3.3 Limitations

While classifying plants according to functional type is useful for scientific purposes, there are certain problems with any system of functional classification:

1. The categories provided may be of too coarse a scale to describe many kinds of patterns, yet when the schemes are expanded they often become too complicated to be easily or usefully applied.
2. The traits used to construct the systems have to be easily assessed in the field; this, however, constrains any system to a small set of morphological attributes. Many other characteristics of plants such as physiology, anatomy, and ecology cannot be included; therefore, the system may be both unrealistic and unable to adequately cover the array of plant types that occurs.
3. There is no obvious way to test which system is best and therefore no way to end the proliferation of classification systems.

All of the systems of plant classification that are described in this chapter assign individual plants to categories, be they phylogenetic or functional. When it comes to classifying local vegetation, as opposed to individual species, however, neither a phylogenetic nor a functional classification system is particularly appropriate. One general solution is often to select a few species that are dominant and use their names to designate the vegetation type. The phylogenetic system might then yield designations such as "*Podocarpus* forest," "*Acer-Fagus* forest," "Ericaceous shrubs," or "*Andropogon* prairie." The functional system would yield more general descriptions such as "evergreen phaneropytes," "deciduous phanerophytes," "nanophanerophytes," and "hemicryptophytes and geophytes." Sometimes these two types of classification are mixed. Thus Daubenmire's (1978) description of plant geography in North America includes "The *Quercus falcata* Province within the Temperate Mesophytic Forest Region" or "The *Agropyron spicatum* Province in the Steppe Region." The description of vegetation is discussed at length in Chapter 10.

2.4 | Conclusion

The culmination of two centuries of field exploration and laboratory examination is shown in two maps. The first map (Figure 2.10) uses a phylogenetic classification and presents eight biogeographic regions based upon the evolutionary history of the world's biota. The second map (Figure 2.11) employs a functional classification system and presents 17 biomes based upon dominant plant growth forms. These two figures summarize what is known about the large-scale distribution of terrestrial organic matter.

Since the science of plant ecology is rather young, both the phylogenetic and functional systems of plant classification are actively evolving. Each system has its strengths, weaknesses, and value. For studies that aim to preserve the genetic diversity of the Earth's biota, the phylogenetic system would receive priority. For studies that aim to predict the consequences of climate change, the functional system would be most useful.

Figure 2.10 The eight biogeographic regions of the world compiled by Pielou (1979) to reconcile zoogeographical and phytogeographical systems. The stippling indicates those regions that separated as Gondwana from Laurasia about 200 million years BP (see Figure 9.6). The line north-south through the Atlantic Ocean marks the location of its origin some 100 million years ago. Such barriers allowed the floras to evolve largely in isolation from one another. The line between the Australasian and Indo-Malay regions is often called "Wallace's line" (adapted from Pielou 1979 by Olson et al. 2001).

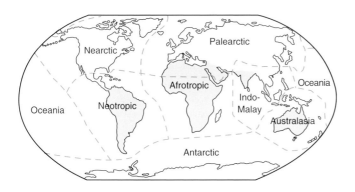

1	Temperate deciduous forests
2	Temperate mixed forests
3	Subtropical mixed forests
4	Taiga
4	Northwestern coniferous forest
5	Alpine tundra and mountain forests
6	Mixed west-coast forests
7	Arctic tundra
8	Ice desert
9	Grasslands
10	Savannas
11	Mediterranean scrub
12	Deserts and semideserts
13	Juniper savanna
14	Southern woodland and scrub
15	Tropical mixed forests
16	Monsoon forests
17	Rainforests

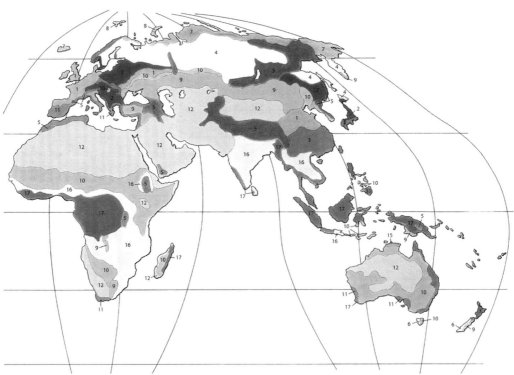

Figure 2.11   Küchler's map of world biomes (from Raven et al. 1999).

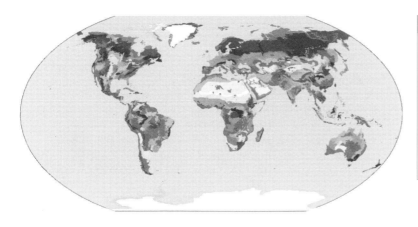

Figure 2.12 The map of world ecoregions identifies 867 areas containing distinct natural communities and species. It combines the phylogenetic perspective (Figure 2.10) and the functional perspective (Figure 2.11) to provide a foundation for conservation planning and ecological research (from Olson et al. 2001).

It may be possible to combine the phylogenetic and functional systems into one system using the concept of an ecoregion. Olson et al. (2001) define ecoregions as "relatively large units of land containing a distinct assemblage of natural communities and species, with boundaries that approximate the original extent of natural communities prior to major land-use change." Their map (Figure 2.12) recognizes a total of 867 ecoregions, nested within 14 biomes and 8 biogeographic realms (Figure 2.10). Maps of ecoregions are now used by many agencies for planning reserve systems to protect ecological communities.

There may be merits to simultaneously keeping two separate systems. Carpentry projects, for example, can require both a saw and a hammer. If one asked a carpenter "Is the hammer or the saw the best tool?" one would reveal only one's ignorance of carpentry. A combination of the two is also likely to have its limitations. A plant ecologist must therefore be adept at using multiple systems of classification for describing global patterns in plant distribution.

Further reading

Raunkiaer, C. 1908. The statistics of life-forms as a basis for biological plant geography. pp. 111–147. In C. Raunkiaer. 1934. *The Life Forms of Plants and Statistical Plant Geography: Being the Collected Papers of Raunkiaer*. Oxford: Clarendon Press.

Küchler, A. W. 1949. A physiognomic classification of vegetation. *Annals of the Association of American Geographers* **39**: 201–210.

Udvardy, M. D. F. 1975. A classification of the biogeographical provinces of the World. IUCN Occasional Paper No. 18, International Union for the Conservation of Nature and Natural Resources, Morges, Switzerland.

Takhtajan, A. 1986. *Floristic Regions of the World*. Tanslated by T. J. Crovello. Berkeley, CA: University of California Press.

Woodward, F. I. 1987. *Climate and Plant Distribution*. Cambridge: Cambridge University Press.

Archibold, O. W. 1995. *Ecology of World Vegetation*. London: Chapman and Hall.

Browne, J. 1995. *Charles Darwin: Voyaging*. Princeton, NJ: Princeton University Press.

Edmonds, J. (ed.). 1997. *Oxford Atlas of Exploration*. New York, NY: Oxford University Press.

Weiher, E., A. van der Werf, K. Thompson, M. Roderick, E. Garnier, and O. Eriksson. 1999. Challenging Theophrastus: a common core list of plant traits for functional ecology. *Journal of Vegetation Science* **10**: 609–620.

Gaston, K. J. 2000. Global patterns in biodiversity. *Nature* **405**: 220–227.

Camerini, J. R. (ed.). 2002. *The Alfred Russel Wallace Reader. A Selection of Writings from the Field*. Baltimore, MD: The Johns Hopkins University Press.

Chapter 3

Resources

Resource acquisition as one logical starting point for plant ecology. The CHNOPS perspective. Costs of acquisition. The global carbon pool. Harvesting photons. Canopy architecture. Photosynthetic types (C_3, C_4, CAM). Height. The search for below-ground resources. Water. Algae in fresh water. Phosphorus. Nitrogen. Fertilization experiments. Resources in space and time. Gradients and patches. Conceptual classification of resources. Complications of resource fluctuation. Chronic scarcity of resources. Stress tolerance. Plants in tropical canopies, succulents, carnivorous plants, parasitic plants. Nutrient conservation. Soils. Some history. Humans and soil resources. Synthesis.

3.1 | Introduction

3.1.1 The CHNOPS perspective

Plants, like all living organisms, comprise relatively few elements (Table 3.1). Morowitz (1968) has therefore described the Earth-based life forms as CHNOPS organisms. These six elements could thus be considered the fundamental resources for ecologists to study. Organisms do not use these elements in equal amounts. Table 3.2 shows that oxygen and carbon predominate, whereas sulfur and phosphorus make up less than 1 percent of organisms.

These elements are not equally available in time or space. In order to grow and reproduce, plants must forage for, absorb, and internally transport such resources before being able to construct new tissues. They also face the challenges of conserving such resources when they are in short supply. While it is true that all life forms must go through similar steps, vascular plants face a situation very different from most other life forms. Since plants occupy the narrow interface between the atmosphere and the soil, plants must forage simultaneously in two different environments for two different sets of resources. Plants must forage in the atmosphere for carbon dioxide and light, and forage in the soil for water and mineral nutrients. Hence, plants have a distinctively dual nature, possessing two kinds of architecture, morphology, anatomy, and physiology. (There are partial exceptions to this specific duality, such as carnivorous plants and epiphytes that forage for nutrients with their leaves (Section 3.8.1), but these are noteworthy precisely because they deviate from the norm.) Since photosynthesis is a defining characteristic of plants, the capture and processing of light energy is normally a major part of any book on plant ecology. As I noted in the

Table 3.1. *Major elements required by living organisms and their functions (from Morowitz 1968).*

Element	Function
C	Structure; energy storage in lipids and carbohydrates
H	Structure; energy storage in lipids and carbohydrates
N	Structure of proteins
O	Structure; aerobic respiration for energy release
P	Structure of nucleic acids and skeletons; energy transfer within cells
S	Structure of proteins

Table 3.2. *Atomic composition of four typical CHNOPS organisms – [a]humans, [b]alfalfa, [c]copepods, [d]bacteria (from Morowitz 1968).*

Element	Mammal[a]	Vascular plant[b]	Arthropod[c]	Moneran[d]
C	19.37	11.34	6.10	12.14
H	9.31	8.72	10.21	9.94
N	5.14	0.83	1.50	3.04
O	62.81	77.90	79.99	73.68
P	0.63	0.71	0.13	0.60
S	0.64	0.10	0.14	0.32
Total	97.90	99.60	98.07	99.72

Preface (p. xvii), I assume in writing this book that you have already had introductory courses in botany and ecology. It would be presumptuous of me, and a waste of your time, to repeat lengthy treatments of photosynthesis and plant nutrition already written by far more qualified authors. My approach here is to: (1) remind you of some basic principles, (2) tie these basic principles clearly to processes in plant populations and communities, and (3) introduce you to some important topics that are often overlooked in more basic books (e.g., the CHNOPS perspective, gradients and their consequences, nutrient conservation in infertile habitats, and foraging). My intention is to lay the groundwork for future chapters without repeating too much that has already been well-covered elsewhere.

Before continuing with the problem of foraging for resources, however, let us continue by briefly exploring the CHNOPS resources themselves. Figure 3.1 shows that these elements share two chemical properties. First, all have relatively low atomic numbers (<20). Thus they are among the most common elements, since abundance varies inversely with atomic number. Further, they all have a first ionization energy between 10 and 15 eV, lower than that of the noble gases (which have low chemical reactivity) and higher than that for most other elements. Such similarities suggest that early in the history of life there was natural selection for those molecules that were relatively common and had intermediate levels of reactivity.

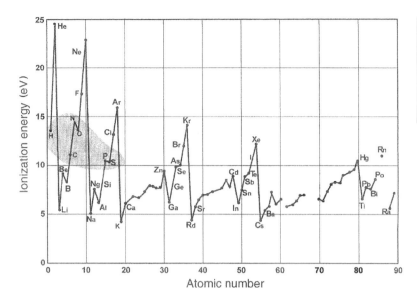

Figure 3.1 The first ionization energy I_1 of the elements as a function of atomic number. The stippled region encloses the basic elements of CHNOPS life forms (after Brackenridge and Rosenberg 1970).

This seems inherently reasonable. Life would be formed from the most common building blocks available. If these building blocks had too little reactivity, chemical interactions could not occur, and they would rarely be incorporated into molecules. If these building blocks were too reactive, reactions would be very frequent and molecules would be easily established by small amounts of energy.

The repetitive simplicity and similarity of the basic building blocks of living organisms is illustrated by the structure of a typical amino acid in Figure 3.2. Although there are more than 100 kinds of amino acids in nature, only 20 are common, and they differ in the chemical structures attached at the R position in the molecule. In glycine, R represents merely a hydrogen atom, H; in aniline R represents CH_3, and, in serine, CH_2–OH. Proteins, the basic structural matter of life, are composed of chains of these different amino acids, but the similarity of their elemental composition, largely C, H, O, and N, reflects the elements that were available in the Earth's atmosphere (Table 1.1, Box 3.1).

The NH_2 in each amino acid sets the stage for a recurring issue in the struggle for survival and reproduction by plants: how to obtain those critical nitrogen atoms for protein synthesis. Every amino acid requires a nitrogen atom. On a planet with an atmosphere that is practically three-quarters nitrogen, the acquisition of nitrogen may seem to be relatively straightforward. Yet, it is not, because plants cannot use gaseous nitrogen. One of the remarkable physiological puzzles of botany is the dependence of all plants upon a relatively small subset of microorganisms that are still able to transform gaseous nitrogen into its biologically useful forms. The relative abundance of this element, and yet its great scarcity from the perspective of plants, is an over-riding theme of plant ecology, and one that quite likely spills over into the animal kingdom as well (White 1993).

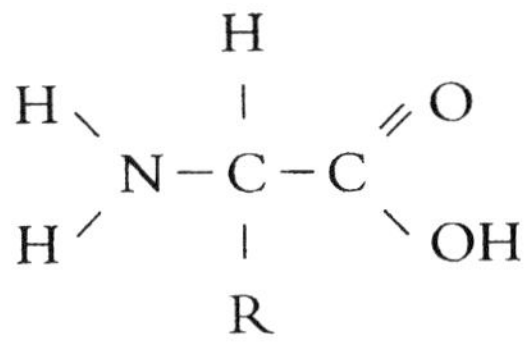

$$
\begin{array}{c}
H \\
| \\
H\diagdown\diagup O \\
N-C-C \\
H\diagup|\diagdown OH \\
R
\end{array}
$$

Figure 3.2 Every amino acid requires four elements: carbon, hydrogen, nitrogen, and oxygen. They differ only in the chemical structure appended at the R position.

Box 3.1 | The composition and origin of the atmosphere

The composition and origin of the atmosphere was already a matter of systematic enquiry when Antoine Lavoisier (1743–1794, Figure B3.1) prepared *Elements of Chemistry (Traité Elémentaire de Chimie)* in 1789. He begins Chapter III:

> From what has been premised, it follows that our atmosphere is composed of a mixture of every substance capable of retaining the gaseous or aeriform state in the common temperature, and under the usual pressure which it experiences.
>
> (p. 16)

Not only does Lavoisier present experimental methods for determining the composition of the atmosphere, but he concludes that the atmosphere is composed of two gases, one of which supports respiration (oxygen) and the other which does not (nitrogen). (Although Lavoisier states a preference for the terms *azote* and *azotic gas* which expresses " that property . . . of depriving such animals as breathe it of their lives.") He even speculates upon possible changes in atmosphere composition if the Earth's temperature were to be greatly increased by being transported into the region of the planet Mercury. Previously solid materials

> . . . would be changed into permanent aeriform fluids or gases, which would become part of the new atmosphere. These new species of airs or gases would mix with those already existing, and certain reciprocal decompositions and new combinations would take place, until such time as all the elective attractions or affinities subsisting amongst all these new and old gaseous substances had operated fully; after which, the elementary principles composing these gases, being saturated would remain at rest.
>
> (p. 15)

He further speculates upon changes to be expected in the case of extreme cold, in which case "the water which at present composes our seas, rivers, and springs"

Figure B3.1 Portrait in 1788 of Antoine-Laurent Lavoisier (1743–1794), a chemist and revolutionary who explored the properties of the Earth's atmosphere (from Guerlac 1975).

would become mixed with foreign substances and become "opaque stones of various colours." New liquids would also form, ". . . whose properties we cannot, at present, form the most distant idea." (p. 16)

One of his contemporaries, Jean Paul Marat (1743–1793), also wrote several scientific works. His contribution in 1789 was not a chemistry book, but rather a radical newspaper, *L'ami du peuple*, inciting the poor to violence. These were the turbulent years of the French Revolution. After narrow escapes from the police (including a well-known escape through the sewers of Paris which left him with an agonizing skin infection from which he never recovered and which forced him to spend most of his life in a bath), Marat was elected to the Convention as a deputy for Paris. In 1791 Marat began denouncing Lavoisier for his associations with, and employment by, the former government, and in 1794 Lavoisier was tried and convicted by the Revolutionary Tribunal. On May 8, 1794 he was guillotined, his body being thrown into a nameless grave in the cemetery of La Madeleine. All the same, he outlived Marat, who was assassinated in his bath by Charlotte Corday on 13 July 1793.

Phosphorus is unusual in the CHNOPS list precisely because, unlike nitrogen, it is a comparatively rare element. Phosphorus is a constituent of nucleic acids, the phospholipids of biological membranes, and the phosphate esters that provide the metabolic machinery of cells (Marschner 1995). In particular it is an integral part of the citric acid cycle that extracts chemical energy from large molecules; ATP being used to store the resulting chemical energy. Each ATP molecule requires three phosphorus atoms (as well as five nitrogen atoms). Phosphorus appears to be useful because, relative to most elements, there are quite large bond energies (Dickerson 1969). This requirement for large numbers of phosphorus atoms to complete a fundamental metabolic process allows one to predict that phosphorus would be an important resource for plants.

Nitrogen and phosphorus, along with sulfur (also potassium, calcium, magnesium), are usually termed *macronutrients* because they are required in considerable amounts. A large number of other rare elements are required in much smaller amounts and are hence termed *micronutrients*; these include many metals (iron, manganese, zinc, copper, molybdenum) and two non-metals (boron and chlorine) (Larcher 2003). While a treatise on plant nutrition must address each of these elements in turn, it is reasonable to ask how many of them need to be considered for a general knowledge of plant growth and vegetation development. Is there some minimum number of resources that, by themselves, enables one to make useful predictions about the structure and function of plants and their communities? Keep this question in mind for the remainder of the chapter.

3.1.2 The costs of acquisition

Resources are not just of interest to ecologists. In the very first paragraph of *Das Capital*, Marx (1867) introduces the concept of commodity. A commodity, he says, "is an object outside us, a thing that by its properties satisfies human wants of some sort or another" (p. 13). In other words, it is a resource. The value of a commodity, he continues, following from Smith (1776), is determined by the amount of labor required to produce a unit of it: "If we could succeed at a small expenditure of labor in converting carbon into diamonds, their value might fall below that of bricks" (p. 15). Commodities that appear to be very different (say, a coat, tea, gold) can be exchanged once we agree upon such a measure of value.

The energetic costs for acquisition of each resource may be one useful way of measuring their value to plants. For example, van der Werf et al. (1988) measured the respiratory energy costs of ion uptake in a species of sedge (*Carex diandra*) and reported that the proportion of total ATP demand for ion uptake ranged from 10 to 36 percent. Neighbors will tend to reduce the availability of resources, and thereby increase the cost of acquisition. Any study of a plant population or community should probably begin by explicitly considering resources. Resources will always play a role in organizing communities, whereas other factors like weather or herbivores, although they may sometimes be important, are not inevitably significant (Price 1984). Since the above-ground organs of a plant are the most obvious to humans, we will first examine foraging for resources in the atmosphere and then turn to foraging in the soil. This should not, however, lead to the supposition that the below-ground nutrients are less important.

3.2 | Carbon dioxide: foraging in an atmospheric reservoir

Carbon is first on the CHNOPS list. Nearly all life forms are constructed from gaseous atmospheric carbon and CO_2. Plants must forage for this atmospheric carbon in the same way they forage for water and mineral nutrients; a fact sometimes overlooked, perhaps because CO_2 is an odorless, colorless gas. The task of locating and assimilating CO_2 might at first seem to be a relatively simple task, since the distribution of CO_2 would appear to be quite homogenous and constant. As Harper (1977) puts it: "The concentration of CO_2 in the atmosphere away from a photosynthetic surface is about 300 parts per million and shows only a slight variation from place to place" (p. 323). True, it is widespread and fairly homogenous, but then it is also scarce everywhere. Stems and leaves are frequently viewed as organs for intercepting light when in fact they function equally in removing CO_2 from the atmosphere.

The steps for extracting CO_2 from the atmosphere evolved early in the history of life; the biochemical steps known as the Calvin Benson cycle being ubiquitous in plants (Keeley and Rundel 2003). Foraging for CO_2 is a costly process, particularly in dry environments, because the stomata that admit CO_2 from the atmosphere into plants also allow another important resource, water, to escape. Moreover, global CO_2 levels are much lower now than during the Earth's early history (recall the immense stores of carbon removed from the atmosphere and stored as coal, e.g., Figure 1.15). Some of the inefficiencies inherent in the photosynthetic process may well have arisen at this time when CO_2 levels were higher – the consequence for the present being "suboptimal performance under contemporary atmospheric gas composition" (Keeley and Rundel 2003, p. S55). In general, the more CO_2 absorbed, the more water lost – a pattern to keep in mind when we discuss the C_4 photosynthetic pathway below. Moreover, all terrestrial plants, and many aquatic plants, withdraw CO_2 from one common atmospheric pool, allowing for plant–plant inter- actions over large distances. Further, this widespread gaseous resource can be locally depleted. Figure 1.18 shows how the levels of CO_2 in the atmosphere decline about 6 ppm during each growing season as plants remove CO_2 by photosynthesis; the CO_2 levels then increase throughout the winter as a consequence of respiration. It is also known that these depleted CO_2 levels reduce plant perform- ance; experiments show that plants can grow as much as 50 percent faster when CO_2 levels are increased and that the largest increases in growth occur at relatively low levels of augmentation (Hunt et al. 1991, Woodward 1992).

The importance of carbon sources for photosynthesis is illus- trated by studies in which plants are grown under elevated CO_2 levels to study the possible effects of increased CO_2 in the Earth's atmos- phere (e.g., Mooney et al. 1991, Porter 1993, Loehle 1995). Most plants show a surge in growth when CO_2 supplies increase (Table 3.3), although plants from infertile habitats, and plants with CAM photo- synthesis, respond less than others. The overall response to CO_2 suggests that one of the most dramatic and overlooked examples of diffuse competition occurs when plants around the world draw down the CO_2 level of the atmosphere. We will continue with the problem of carbon uptake in the next section.

Table 3.3. *Responses of plants to elevated CO_2 levels. Mean weight ratio is the ratio of weight at the end of an experiment at high vs. low CO_2 levels (from Loehle 1995).*

Group	Weight ratio	Number of species
Crops	1.58	19
Wild C_3 non-woody plants	1.35	62
Fast growing	1.54	18
Slow growing	1.23	20
Woody plants	1.41	50
Fast growing	1.73	13
Other	1.31	37
CAM	1.15	6

3.3 | Light and photosynthesis: harvesting photons

3.3.1 Three measures of photon harvest

Rates of CO_2 uptake by plants are closely tied to light availability. The foliage of plants must intercept photons that were generated far away by the fusion of elements within stars. Increased photon flux (light supply) will promote increased photosynthesis until a certain threshold is reached. At this point, I_s (irradiance saturation), the photosynthetic process is said to be light-saturated. The CO_2 uptake rate, maximized at this threshold, provides one useful way of describing a plant's photosynthetic character.

Another useful trait of a photosynthetic organism is its light compensation point, I_c, which is the level of irradiance at which photosynthetic CO_2 uptake and respiratory CO_2 production are in equilibrium. Plants that respire rapidly, then, require more light to achieve compensation. Once I_c has been exceeded, there is a linear relationship between irradiation and CO_2 uptake until I_s is reached.

A third measure of photon harvest is the quantum yield, Φ_A. It measures the inherent efficiency of the photosynthetic system. The greater the quantum yield, the greater the slope of the curve of CO_2 uptake plotted as a function of irradiation. These three measurable attributes of photosynthetic systems summarize essential aspects of the capture of plant resources in the atmosphere (for further details, see Marschner 1995, Larcher 2003, Raven et al. 2005). Some details for light compensation and light saturation for plants are given in Table 3.4.

3.3.2 Architecture and photon harvesting

A tree can be thought of as an array of solar panels on stalks (Colinvaux 1993). Using this analogy, he challenges us to consider the way in which plants are actually constructed (multiple repetitions of small leaves on twigs) in comparison with a mechanical ideal: a large flat solar collector (Figure 3.3). Following an analysis of leaf size and shape offered by Horn (1971), Colinvaux argues that the primary advantage of many small leaves is as follows. In the monolayer designs one huge leaf traps all incident sunlight. But in bright sunlight, photosynthesis would rapidly become saturated. In contrast, if the panel were subdivided so that the upper layers shaded the lower layers, then the lower layers would receive diffuse light. A three-layered device (shown in Figure 3.3) would outperform a single-layer device, and, of course, plant canopies usually consist of many more than three layers. "The payoff is increased photosynthesis in bright light" (p. 46). In such a design, the shape of the upper panels will affect the kind of shade cast upon lower panels. Irregular shapes reduce effective diameter. This may explain why so many trees have deeply notched leaves: notches increase light transmission to lower

Table 3.4. *Light response of net photosynthesis of single leaves, under conditions of ambient CO_2 and optimal temperature (from Larcher 2003).*

Plant group	Light compensation I_c (μmol photons$\cdot$m$^{-2}\cdot$s^{-1})	Light saturation I_s (μmol photons$\cdot$m$^{-2}\cdot$s^{-1})
Terrestrial plants		
Herbaceous flowering plants		
C$_4$ plants	20–50	>1500
C$_3$ desert plants		>1500
Agricultural C$_3$ plants	20–40	1000–1500
Heliophytes	20–40	1000–1500
Spring geophytes	10–20	300–1000
Sciophytes	5–10	100–200
Epiphytes	6–15	200–500
Woody plants		
Tropical forest trees		
Sun leaves	15–25	600–1500
Shade leaves	ca. 10	200–300
Young plants	2–5	50–150
Deciduous broadleaved trees		
Sun leaves	20–50 (100)	600–>800
Shade leaves	10–15	200–500
Evergreen broadleaved trees		
Sun leaves	10–30	600–800
Shade leaves	2–10	100–150
Sclerophylls of regions with high light intensity	20–40	600–1200
Coniferous trees		
Sun shoots	30–40	800–1000
Shade shoots	2–10	150–200
Ferns		
Sunny habitats	ca. 50	400–600 (800)
Shade ferns	1–5	50–150
Mosses	ca. 50	200–500
Lichens	50–100	700–1000 (1500)
Aquatic plants		
Planktonic algae		200–500
Intertidal-zone seaweeds	5–8	200–500
Deep-water algae	2	150–400
Submersed vascular plants	8–20 (30)	(60) 100–200 (400)

layers of leaves. Such ideas suggest testable hypotheses; for example, upperstorey trees should have leaves arranged in multiple layers, whereas understorey trees should have leaves arranged in a monolayer.

An ideal mechanical model, such as that in Figure 3.3(a), certainly stimulates thought. However, precisely because reality is contrasted

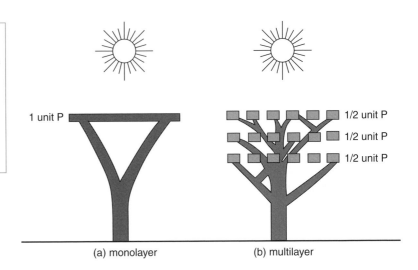

Figure 3.3 The tree on the left has a single huge leaf, whereas the one on the right has multiple leaves with multiple layers. What are the relative photosynthetic efficiencies of these two growth forms? Does this explain why most trees have many small leaves arrayed in multiple layers? (after Colinvaux 1993).

1 unit P

1/2 unit P
1/2 unit P
1/2 unit P

(a) monolayer   (b) multilayer

with such an ideal model, there are many other hypotheses that might be equally tenable. Several come to mind; you may be able to think of others:

1. First is the issue of redundancy. In case (a) (one large layer), damage from a storm might disrupt photosynthesis in a significant portion of the leaf. In case (b) (many smaller leaves), those that are damaged are unlikely to influence those that remain intact. Think of it this way. If a brick is thrown at a window, which will be more damaged: a window with one large sheet of plate glass, or a window with 100 independent sub-panes? Almost certainly the former, and this may be why sessile organisms, such as plants and corals, that cannot move to safety are constructed on a modular basis. Indeed, Harper (1977) has challenged botanists to think of plants as colonies of independent meristems. Given that nature is full of forces that will damage leaves (wind, rain, hail, herbivores, falling branches) there is likely strong selection against investing too much tissue in any large leaf. Thus canopy trees that are most exposed to storm and wind shear will have multiple small leaves, whereas more protected understorey trees can have larger leaves (a monolayer).

2. Perhaps it works this way. In one large monolayer the surface area is minimal. As the solar panel is subdivided into progressively smaller units, the surface area increases. Since CO_2 uptake is likely a function of surface area, selection for many subdivided units would enhance CO_2 uptake.

3. Nature is not perfect. Evolution by natural selection does not produce the best of all possible worlds (although it is frequently misunderstood in this way), it merely tends to select the best of available options. There are, at very least, strict biomechanical limits on the shape and size that plants can take. It is unlikely that any evolutionary pressure would be capable of producing,

say, large diameter trunks at the ends of small twigs. Similarly, leaves are produced by individual meristems. It is possible that the monolayer in Figure 3.3(a) could be produced by reducing the number of meristems and increasing the amount of leaf tissue produced by each meristem, the limiting case being a single large leaf on one stalk (a structure we might think we can see in leaves of genera such as *Podophyllum* or *Nymphaea*). But if branches and twigs are lost in this process, greatly strengthened veins within the leaf must replace them. In the case of *Podophyllum*, the leaf requires reinforced veins; in *Nymphaea* the round leaf floats on water. Even in these cases, there is not really a single monolayer leaf; while each shoot may appear to be a single solar panel, these shoots are attached to one another underground by way of rhizomes. Thus there are likely many biomechanical restraints upon the form of plants. Natural selection does not produce optimal shapes and sizes; it merely tends to perpetuate the best available options under the multiple constraints faced by many living organisms.

The issue of leaf size and shape will arise in several other contexts, including the relationship between leaf shape and climate (Figures 4.10, 4.32) and the effect of leaf shape upon early-spring photosynthesis (Figure 4.34). If we are as yet unable to answer simple questions concerning why leaves are the shapes and sizes they are, it is no wonder that answers to more complex questions continue to elude us.

3.3.3 Different photosynthetic types

The three attributes of photosynthesis previously described (I_s, I_c, Φ_A, Section 3.3.1) vary among plant functional types. We will look at two classifications.

One fundamental dichotomy is C_3 and C_4 photosynthesis. (Here I assume that you already know something about the fundamental process of photosynthesis, since this is taught in all introductory biology courses). Recall that C_4 photosynthesis is the more recent modification, and has an added energetic cost. The primary benefit of C_4 photosynthesis is low rates of photorespiration, thereby yielding higher rates of photosynthetic energy fixation. A second advantage is higher water use efficiency (Keeley and Rundel 2003). C_4 plants are most common in environments where light and temperature do not limit carbon uptake, that is sunny habitats with higher growing season temperatures. Tropical and subtropical grasslands are dominated, therefore, by C_4 grasses and sedges. The grasses (Poaceae) are the dominant C_4 family. They appear to have originated during the Cretaceous era in either South America or Australia, and have since dispersed to a global distribution. Widespread C_4 genera include *Andropogon*, *Chloris*, *Muhlenbergia*, *Paspalum*, and *Sporobolus*. Other examples of C_4 plants include annual plants in deserts, and certain shrubs of arid areas. This type of photosynthesis is rare in trees, which is to be expected since their growth form is ultimately a response to light competition (Keeley and Rundel 2003). One exception occurs in the Hawaiian Islands where ancient colonization by a C_4 member of the Euphorbiaceae started an evolutionary lineage of C_4 shrubs and a C_4 tree, *Euphorbia forbesii*; even so, this tree occurs in relatively open habitats.

Let us return to the important trade-off between CO_2 uptake and water loss. Higher levels of CO_2 in the atmosphere would reduce rates of water loss from plants. Hence, periods with higher CO_2 would appear, from a plant's perspective, to be wetter. Conversely, as CO_2 levels in the atmosphere fall, drought becomes an increasingly important constraint upon plants. The spread of grasslands in the late Miocene (about 15 million years ago) might therefore have been triggered in part by declining levels of atmospheric CO_2 which made plants more sensitive to reduced rainfall (Keeley and Rundel 2003). Other factors such as changing climate or increased frequency of fire are competing hypotheses for the appearance of C_4 plants. This may have implications for future changes in plant communities: higher levels of CO_2 (recall Figures 1.17, 1.18) may not only increase plant growth rates overall, but may reduce the impacts of drought and reduce the competitive advantage of C_4 growth forms. Such predictions are, however, complicated by the fact that the C_4 pathway is more successful under higher temperatures.

CAM photosynthesis is a modification of the C_4 system. The term CAM (Crassulacean Acid Metabolism) originated with succulents in the family Crassulaceae in which the process was first found, but it has since been documented in 33 plant families, and seems to have evolved independently on a number of occasions (Keeley and Rundel 2003). Since CO_2 uptake normally leads to water loss, any photosynthetic modifications that reduce such losses may be advantageous in dry environments. In CAM photosynthesis, CO_2 is absorbed at night for use in photosynthesis during the day. Hence, the stomata are open when rates of water loss are likely to be lowest. CAM photosynthesis is found in many desert plants such as the Cactaceae (Nobel 1985). It is also found in other groups where drought may be an issue, such as in epiphytes (Moffett 1994, Lowman and Rinker 2004) – in both the Bromeliaceae and the Orchidaceae, which are prominent in epiphytic communities, more than half of the species have CAM photosynthesis. Some cacti, such as the popular Christmas cactus (*Schlumbergera* spp.), are also epiphytes. The Asclepiadaceae, also common in deserts, has many CAM species.

Although in terrestrial plants C_4 is thought to be a relatively recent modification (albeit one that has evolved in multiple ways and places), it also occurs in ancient plants such as *Isoëtes*, and in aquatic plants. How does this fit into the above understanding of photosynthesis, C_4, and CAM? The answer seems to be that CAM photosynthesis is an advantage in other kinds of habitats with very low CO_2 levels (Keeley 1998, Keeley and Rundel 2003). Since gases such as CO_2 dissolve poorly in water, CO_2 levels will tend to be low, and these will be further reduced by photosynthesis. Hence, CO_2 can be critically low in aquatic habitats, in which case it may be selectively advantageous to absorb CO_2 during the night when levels are higher due to respiration of surrounding aquatic organisms and the lack of photosynthesis which would remove CO_2 from the water.

In conclusion, foraging for atmospheric carbon has several features that distinguish it from foraging for most other resources. First, it is the only resource that occurs in a gaseous form. Second, there is a fairly well-mixed global pool of CO_2, for which plants in very different localities compete. Third, while temporary depletion zones form, they are far more transitory than depletion zones for water and soil nutrients. Finally, the absorption of atmospheric carbon has important consequences for global temperature. Were it not for plants, the Earth might have conditions like those on Venus, with CO_2 comprising some 96% of the atmosphere and a mean temperature of 750 K, 500 K of which is attributed to a greenhouse effect (MacDonald 1989).

3.3.4 An exception to the rule: root uptake of CO_2

The genus *Isoëtes* is an obscure group of herbaceous plants thought to be evolutionary relics related to *Lycopodium* and *Selaginella*. These latter genera represent a form of plant life that once produced tree-like forms and dominated Earth. Many of the beds of coal burned today in electricity generating plants are derived from the remains of these plants. *Isoëtes* look rather like small pincushions and grow mostly in shallow water in oligotrophic lakes, although some species grow in temporary pools and a few are terrestrial. One member of this group grows at high altitudes (usually >4000 m) in the Peruvian Andes, and the following account of the species comes from work by Keeley et al. (1994). At one time this plant was considered so distinct that it was put in its own genus (*Stylites*), but it is now considered to be more appropriately classified as *Isoëtes andicola*. This bizarre plant not only has an unusual reproductive system (heterospory with free-living gametophytes), but also, over half its biomass is tied up in roots, and only the tips of the leaves emerge above ground and have chlorophyll (4 percent of total biomass).

Studies with $^{14}CO_2$ demonstrated that the bulk of the carbon that *Isoëtes andicola* uses for photosynthesis is obtained through the root system. There are no stomata in the leaves, and the plant has a CAM photosynthetic system. Since the partial pressure of CO_2 decreases with altitude, these may be an adaptations to its highland habitat. Further studies of carbon isotopes were carried out to explore the source of carbon. Here some background is necessary. In the early 1960s, atomic bomb testing contaminated the entire atmosphere with new carbon isotopes. Studies of isotope ratios in tree rings, for example, show dramatic increases in certain carbon isotopes after the 1960s, but Keeley et al. (1994) report that the levels of CO_2 isotopes in the *Isoëtes* are far below current levels and conclude that the plant is growing by fixing CO_2 from decaying peat – peat that was formed from other plants that grew long before the atmospheric testing of nuclear weapons.

The adaptive significance of this source of carbon is not immediately clear, although the lack of above-ground sources seems an inviting hypothesis. Certainly, there is an entire group of evergreen rosette-type plants called, because of their superficial resemblance to *Isoëtes*, isoetids, and these plants are restricted to oligotrophic lakes where inorganic carbon levels in the water are very low. Some of these (e.g., *Lobelia dortmanna*) are also known to use their roots to take up CO_2 from sediments (Wium-Anderson 1971), and some have CAM photosynthesis (Boston 1986, Boston and Adams 1986), which indicates that isoetids have physiological as well as morphological similarities. Keeley et al. (1994) report that, in one small lake in Columbia, the CO_2 level in the sediment was $1.7 \, mol \cdot m^{-3}$, whereas that in the water column was only $0.20 \, mol \cdot m^{-3}$.

3.3.5 Another view of photosynthetic types

Larcher (2003) recognizes four distinctive functional types: C_4 plants, C_3 heliophytic herbs, trees, and sciophytes (Figure 3.4). We have already noted (Section 3.3.3) that trees are almost exclusively C_3 plants. Sciophytes are plants that typically grow under a forest canopy and have adapted to cope with shade. Passing clouds may have little effect on heliophytes, but when intermittent sunflecks strike the leaves of sciophytes, photosynthetic activities are triggered if the intensity of the sunflecks reaches ten times that of average incident radiation (Larcher 1995). In this way, the leaves can exploit even very brief phases of strong light. The cost of shade tolerance is that these plants rapidly reach light saturation (Figure 3.4), and their saturation

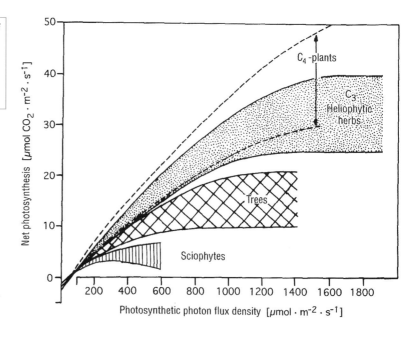

Figure 3.4 Light–effect curves of net photosynthesis for plants of different functional groups at optimal temperature and with the natural CO_2 supply (from Larcher 1995).

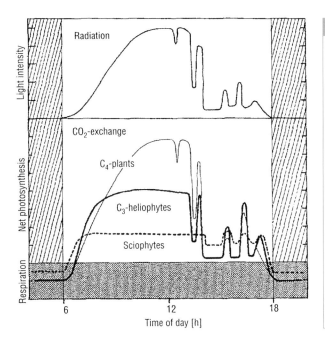

Figure 3.5 Schematic diagram of the daily fluctuation in CO_2 exchange as a function of the available radiation. C_4 plants can utilize even the most intense illumination for photosynthesis, and their CO_2 uptake follows closely the changes in radiation intensity. In C_3 plants photosynthesis becomes light-saturated sooner, so that strong light is not completely utilized. Sciophytes, adapted to using dim light, take up more CO_2 than heliophytes in the early morning and late evening, as well as during periods when they receive little light due to cloud cover or shade from the tree canopy, but they cannot utilize bright light as efficiently as the heliophytes (from Larcher 1995).

rates are a fraction of those of the heliophytic herbs and C_4 plants. In contrast, C_4 grasses such as *Sorghum* and *Zea* do not reach light saturation, and even at moderate irradiation levels assimilate at higher rates than C_3 plants.

Another way of viewing these differences in photosynthetic response is to picture rates of CO_2 uptake during a typical day for different types of photosynthetic systems (Figure 3.5). While the heliophytes and C_4 plants steadily outperform sciophytes, during brief periods of light the latter briefly exceed the performance of the other type. Each of these light-uptake systems can often be related to the type of habitat in which these plants occur.

3.3.6 The overriding importance of height

Life forms on land have added problems to contend with, such as preventing desiccation and providing support to remain erect. These themes are often dealt with in introductory botany books. But there is one other consequence to living on land with a self-supported shoot: the acquisition of light now has a cost, at least when there are neighbors. This cost is incurred in constructing and maintaining the aerial shoot and leaves. In early land plants both the gametophytes and sporophytes were probably photosynthetic (as in modern day ferns and fern allies), but as the density of plants on land increased, neighbors became more abundant, reducing the light availability to aerial shoots. As a consequence, increased height was selected for in plants (Niklas 1994), and tree-like forms arose in a number of lineages (recall Figures 1.12, 1.13) including the Lycopodiophyta, Pterospermatophyta and Pinophyta.

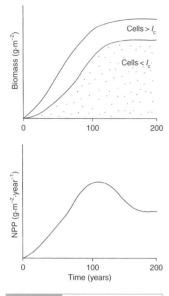

Figure 3.6 Biomass and net primary productivity change through successional time as a consequence of the relative numbers of cells above and below the compensation point, I_c, where rates of photosynthesis are balanced by rates of respiration.

Secondary growth can therefore be seen as an evolutionary response to light shortages attributable to neighbors. Since the gametophyte phase in the life cycle of each plant produces antheridia and archegonia, and since a film of free water is required for sperm to swim from the antheridium to the egg in the archegonium, there may have been selection against increased size in this life cycle phase. This constraint upon gametophytes may explain why, in terrestrial plants, the gametophyte stage has been reduced in time, while the sporophytes have become dominant (Keddy 1981a).

The benefits from increased height are most evident when neighbors are present (Givnish 1982). Since light comes from one direction, the taller plant is always at an advantage over the shorter. This may have important implications for the nature of competition; the tall plant can shade the short one, but the short one cannot shade the tall one. As a consequence, competition for light may be strongly asymmetric, and this may in turn explain why strong competitive hierarchies occur in plant communities (Chapter 5).

3.3.7 Ecosystem effects: net primary production changes with plant size

The balance between respiration and photosynthesis in leaves or shoots can have large-scale effects on entire ecosystems. For example, plant ecologists have often documented the progressive increase in plant biomass that occurs after a disturbance (Figure 3.6); this increase in biomass is one of the key features of plant succession (Section 9.4). It is widely observed that net primary production, that is the rate of accumulation of biomass, reaches a maximum early in succession and then declines. This is one reason why foresters prefer to keep forests at a relatively early stage in succession; they know that at this stage they can maximize the rates at which stands of trees produce commercially valuable wood or fiber. The basis of both theories of succession and practical management of forests can be traced back to changes in compensation points for individual leaves or even cells. Early in succession, almost all cells will be exposed to periods of intense light ($I_c \gg 0$).

Over time, competition among plants results in larger species replacing smaller ones. This has two consequences. First, some leaves (generally those of small plants or the lower leaves of larger plants) are shaded. For increasing numbers of cells in increasingly more leaves, rates of respiration then exceed rates of photosynthesis ($I_c < 0$). Further, larger plants must allocate progressively more tissues to support functions. Woody stems and branches do not photosynthesize, but they do respire. For support tissues, respiration exceeds photosynthesis, ($I_c \ll 0$). Thus, as time passes, the number of cells with $I_c < 0$ increases absolutely and as a proportion of the cells present in the forest. Production begins to fall. The objective of commercial forest management then is to increase the proportion of photosynthesizing cells relative to respiring cells. In short, there is a cascade of relationships from physiological parameters up to competitive interactions among populations of plants right through to the management of landscapes, and I encourage you to think through these hierarchical relationships as you proceed through this book.

3.4 | Below-ground resources

3.4.1 Water

The second major constituent of CHNOPS life forms (Section 3.1.1) is hydrogen. Water is an abundant source of this element. Photosynthesis is the name of the process in which oxidized carbon from the atmosphere and oxidized hydrogen from water are reduced and combined to construct organic compounds of carbon and hydrogen. In most cases, water for the process is removed from soil, often from meters below the surface; hence, the investment in large root systems to locate and then transport this water to shoots.

In the absence of any life at all, water would still flow within the soil from wetter areas (high water concentration) to drier areas (low water concentration), and water would still evaporate from the surface of the soil into the atmosphere. Evapotranspiration by plants, then, is not so much a new evolutionary process as a simple harnessing of the natural physical process of diffusion. That is, the soil, plants, and water are three parts of one continuum (Kramer 1983). Plants exploit and enhance this natural process in at least two ways. First, the vascular system of the plant provides a more or less continuous path for the diffusion of water from the soil into the atmosphere. Second, the shoots and leaves of plants enlarge the surface area available for the evaporation of water. This combination of enhanced transport and enlarged surface area explains why evapotranspiration rates are so much higher than rates at which water would otherwise evaporate passively from a relatively flat soil surface. As water passes into roots and evaporates from shoots, it simultaneously provides a medium for the transport of other soil resources into plant tissues.

The transport of water can be described by a simple equation, the flow of water being a consequence of the driving force divided by the resistance (Kramer 1983). The driving force is the difference in water potential between the soil and the atmosphere. The resistance arises from obstacles to diffusion such as cell walls. Through evolutionary time, the numerator in this equation (difference in water potential) has increased as leaves have become elevated further away from the soil surface. Simultaneously, the denominator of the equation (resistance) has decreased through the evolution of multicellular roots, and the change in xylem cells from thin tracheids to wide vessel elements. The rate of movement of water through the plant is controlled primarily by the resistance to flow imposed by the cuticle and the stomata of leaves. In summary: (1) water flow is primarily controlled by the evaporation surfaces of the plant, (2) the stomata

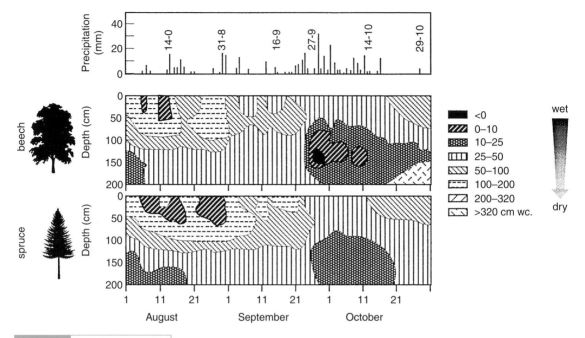

Figure 3.7 Changes in soil moisture tension beneath beech and spruce woodland. Rainfall is shown above (after Benecke and Mayer 1971).

are the principal regulators of water movement, and (3) increased resistance elsewhere in the soil or roots reduces water flow indirectly by reducing leaf turgor enough to cause the stomata to close (Kramer 1983).

Water is far from homogeneously distributed in soils (Figure 3.7); its availability varies with depth, time of year, and vegetation type. As this figure illustrates, tree roots must actively forage for reservoirs of water. Since a tree can transpire 200 liters of water in a single hour (King 1997), patches of water can be quickly depleted by the transpiring canopy. Two kinds of forces cause water movement into roots from the soil: osmotic movement (in slowly transpiring plants) and mass flow (in rapidly transpiring plants). In the first case, the accumulation of solutes in the xylem of the root lowers the water potential of the root below that of the soil; water then diffuses inward and root pressure develops in the xylem. As the rate of transpiration increases, the mass flow of water dilutes the root xylem sap, reducing osmotic flow. Reduced water pressure in the root from transpiration produces a steep gradient in water potential between the roots and soil.

Many plants regularly can lose from 25 to 75 percent of their saturation water content under conditions of "normal" water supply. As water content falls, stomata close, but this has significant negative consequences for growth, since photosynthesis is dependent upon the unimpeded flow of oxygen and CO_2, and since evapotranspiration is necessary for the uptake and transport of dissolved minerals. Thus, any loss of turgor will reduce rates of foraging and growth. In many, if not most, natural environments there are periods with insufficient water for plant growth. The consequences of shortages will be explored further in the following chapter on stress.

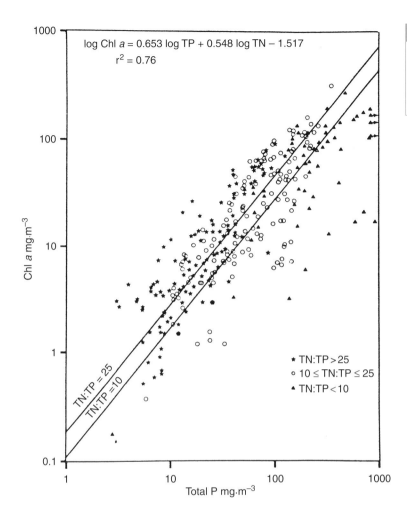

Figure 3.8 Total dissolved phosphorus is an important predictor of the abundance of phytoplankton as measured by the concentration of chlorophyll *a* (from Smith 1982).

3.4.2 Mineral nutrients: a single cell perspective

Phytoplankton provide a useful model for studying mineral nutrients, in part because, at least in fresh water, they usually comprise single cells. Further, they represent a form of plant life that was common early in the history of the Earth. Single cells floating near the surface of an aqueous medium are unlikely to be limited by any of the three resources mentioned so far: light, water, or CO_2. As a result, there is a striking linear relationship between the abundance of phyto-plankton in lakes and the concentration of phosphorus (Figure 3.8). As well, some of the remaining variance that is unaccounted for by phosphorus concentration can be dealt with by incorporating the concentration of nitrogen. For phytoplankton, the ratio of nitrogen to phosphorus determines the degree to which cyanobacteria (for-merly called blue–green algae) dominate the community (Figure 3.9). This result is hardly surprising if one knows something about cyano-bacteria. (Yes, it really was important to pay attention to introductory botany!) Not only are they regarded as a particularly ancient form of

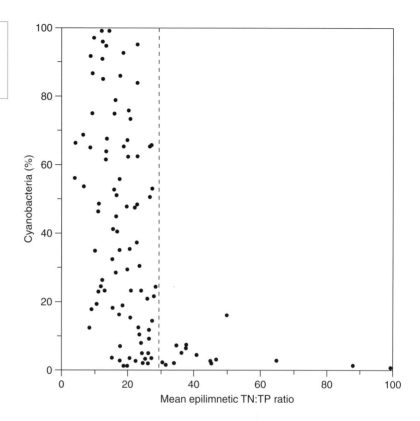

Figure 3.9 At N:P ratios lower than 29, cyanobacteria (formerly called blue–green algae) can become dominant in lakes (from Smith 1983).

photosynthetic life, but they also have a structure, called a hetero-cyst, that provides anaerobic conditions for the fixation of atmospheric nitrogen.

Presumably the heterocyst provides similar conditions to the early Earth's atmosphere for nitrogen fixation to occur. Since the construction of heterocysts and the conversion of atmospheric nitrogen to ammonia is energetically costly, one may assume that cyanobacteria are only at an advantage when dissolved nitrogen is in scarce supply. If nitrogen is abundant, other types of algae can simply take it up directly from the water. Based upon this knowledge of phytoplankton, one could predict that at low N:P ratios, cyanobacteria would predominate, and this is exactly the case. Such generalizations are essential in science. One is, after all, looking for the minimum number of factors one must explore and measure to understand the nature of the living world.

Other nutrients can also occasionally control the distribution and abundance of plant species. In the oceans, for example, there can be relatively high concentrations of nitrogen and phosphorus yet low phytoplankton biomass. To test whether dissolved iron might be limiting growth, it was added to an unenclosed 64-km^2 patch of ocean, which was then tracked with a buoy while an inert tracer was used to monitor the shape of the patch (Martin et al. 1994, Carpenter et al. 1995). Photosynthetic efficiency increased within

Table 3.5. *The three components of nutrient uptake (interception, mass flow, and diffusion) in a crop of* Zea mays *(from Marschner 1995).*

Nutrient	Demand $(kg \cdot ha^{-1})$	Estimates on amounts $(kg \cdot ha^{-1})$ supplied by		
		Interception	Mass flow	Diffusion
Potassium	195	4	35	156
Nitrogen	190	2	150	38
Phosphorus	40	1	2	37
Magnesium	45	15	100	0

the first 24 h, and by the third day, chlorophyll concentrations had tripled. This was enough to cause a reduction in CO_2 of the surface waters, but there were no detectable reductions in nitrogen or phosphorus.

3.4.3 Phosphorus

For terrestrial plants, as opposed to phytoplankton, the necessary phosphorus must be obtained from the soil (except in the case of some tropical rain forest plants which use phosphorus in rainfall; Section 3.8.1). There are three components of foraging by roots: (1) direct interception by roots, (2) mass flow, and (3) diffusion. For (1), as roots grow, their surfaces will naturally expand in area and encounter nutrient ions. For (2), as transpiration by shoots causes mass flow of water toward the roots, dissolved nutrients are transported. For (3), nutrients can diffuse through water in the soil to replace ions extracted by roots. Measurements of these three components of nutrient uptake (Table 3.5) show that interception is of minor importance and that the relative importance of mass flow and diffusion varies by nutrient. Phosphorus stands out because of its low values for both interception and mass flow, with nearly the entire demand being met by diffusion. The driving force of diffusion is a concentration gradient, and this gradient is produced and maintained as roots deplete the soil of phosphorus. This requires the presence of water in the soil pores. In practice, the depletion zones around plants are measured in mm (Figure 3.10).

The degree to which plant growth is limited by problems with phosphorus uptake is best illustrated by the exceptional means used to acquire it. Limited access to soil phosphorus has resulted in symbiotic relationships between plants and fungi, in the form of mycorrhizae (Lewis 1987, Wardle et al. 2004). The hyphae of the symbiotic fungi can absorb and translocate phosphorus to the plant from soil outside the depletion zone, increasing by 2–3 times the phosphorus uptake per unit of root length (Tinker et al. 1992). "Land plants need to grow towards phosphate rather than wait for it to diffuse to them" (Lewis 1987, p. 165). A remarkable experiment by Li et al. (1991)

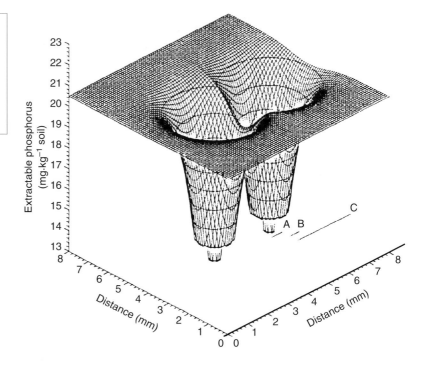

Figure 3.10 Profile of extractable phosphorus around two individual maize roots with overlapping depletion zones. A = root cylinder; B = root hair cylinder; C = maximal depletion zone (adapted from Marschner 1995).

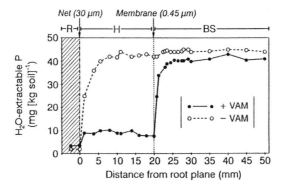

Figure 3.11 Depletion profile of water-extractable phosphorus in the root (R), hyphal (H), and bulk soil (BS) compartments of non-mycorrhizal (−VAM) and mycorrhizal (*Glomus mosseae* = VAM) white clover plants (from Li et al. 1991).

measured the importance of roots and mycorrhizae in phosphorus uptake by using netting to exclude roots, and a membrane to exclude hyphae, from experimental containers (Figure 3.11). It is clear that the mycorrhizae increased the distance over which phosphorus could be extracted from the soil and therefore the total amount of phosphorus available to the plant.

In conclusion, phosphorus limitation must be an important problem for plants if it is necessary to incur the energy costs of supporting mycorrhizae. It is logical to assume that evolutionary solutions arise only in response to a pressing problem in survival. Increasingly it appears that the symbiotic relationship between plants and fungi is not some bizarre aberration but rather a general phenomenon. Terrestrial plants with mycorrhizae might be viewed as large lichens in which the single-celled alga has been replaced by a multicellular plant. It is even possible that the association between algae and fungi was essential for the earliest invasion of land; this is supported not only by the ubiquity of the alga–fungus relationship but by the presence of apparent fossilized mycorrhizae in early land plants such as *Rhynia* (Figure 1.11), as well as the mycorrhizal gametophytes of fern allies today.

3.4.4 Nitrogen

Each amino acid contains an atom of nitrogen as NH_2. Hence, nitrogen is essential for plant and animal growth. Since the atmosphere is 78 percent nitrogen, plants are bathed in atmospheric nitrogen – yet nitrogen availability is one of the most important factors limiting plant growth and reproduction. How can this be? The principle reason is the structural stability of atmospheric nitrogen, that is, the strength of the bond that links the two atoms that make the molecule N_2.

The main forms of nitrogen which plants can use are ammonium and nitrate. Ammonium and its counterpart, ammonia, are toxic at quite low concentrations; they are therefore usually absorbed and incorporated into organic compounds in the roots. In contrast, nitrate is easily transported in the xylem and can be stored in vacuoles of roots, shoots, or storage organs. The cost of nitrate use lies in the necessity of reducing it back to ammonium to enable it to be further used in metabolic processes; this process consumes energy and is analogous to the process of reduction and assimilation of CO_2 in photosynthesis (Marschner 1995). These processes of nitrogen uptake are essential to our understanding of plants and plant communities, not only because nitrogen is a key resource for plants, but because it is equally the key resource for animals (White 1993).

Until the industrial revolution, plants and plant communities depended upon two natural sources of nitrogen (Vitousek et al. 1997). The first source was biologically fixed nitrogen from free-living organisms (e.g., cyanobacteria such as *Anabaena*), and some symbiotic organisms (e.g., bacteria such as *Rhizobium*). These organisms produce the enzyme nitrogenase, and under appropriate (usually anaerobic) conditions they can extract nitrogen from the atmosphere and incorporate it into their tissues, thereby making it available eventually to other living organisms. The second, smaller source was atmospheric fixation. The enormous energy of lightning discharges is able to catalyze the production of ammonia from atmospheric nitrogen. Biological fixation greatly exceeds atmospheric fixation – fixation on land alone is in the order of $100 \text{ Tg} \cdot \text{year}^{-1}$, whereas atmospheric fixation is probably less than $10 \text{ Tg} \cdot \text{year}^{-1}$ (a teragram, Tg, is a million metric tonnes of nitrogen).

All natural plant communities, and all agricultural systems, were once dependent upon only these two sources of nitrogen. As nitrogen was depleted from European fields, it had to be augmented locally (by growing legumes and by recycling animal waste) or by importation.

Ships transported sea bird excrement (guano) from islands off the coast of Chile to supplement nitrogen supplies for European agriculture.

All this changed with the discovery of industrial methods for transforming atmospheric nitrogen into biologically usable forms (see Box 3.2). The rate of industrial fixation was 80 Tg · year^{-1} in the 1990s, and continues to grow (Vitousek et al. 1997, Matson et al. 2002). Eutrophication by surplus nitrogen is now an emerging problem for the Earth's plant communities (Ellenberg 1988a, Keddy 2000). Rainfall in industrial areas of Europe, North America, and Asia now contains significant concentrations of nitrogen, and plants that normally inhabit infertile communities are disappearing as the habitats become more fertile and are invaded by species that exploit fertile soils. These topics will be explored further in Chapter 11.

3.4.5 Experimental tests for nitrogen and phosphorus limitation

One direct way to assess the relative importance of a mineral element in controlling plant growth is to supplement nutrient supplies and see which ones cause an increase in growth (Chapin et al. 1986). Such field experiments suggest that a simple dichotomy between nitrogen and phosphorus does not exist. In an early study of fertilization, Willis (1963) examined the effects of adding N, P, K, and NPK fertilizer to the vegetation of wet areas among sand dunes. These areas had sparse vegetation, in which the dominant species were *Agrostis stolonifera*, *Anagallis tenella*, *Bellis perennis*, and three species of *Carex*. In field trials, the addition of complete nutrients led to the production of three times as much biomass and reduced the number of plant species, after only 3 years. When the effects of nutrients were examined individually, the greatest response was produced by added nitrogen, with phosphorus of secondary importance. Willis then transplanted pieces of turf to the greenhouse and subjected them to different fertilization treatments. The results were similar to his field trials: complete nutrient treatment yielded 151 g of shoots (fresh weight), whereas nitrogen-deficient treatments produced 34 g, and phosphorus-deficient treatments produced 44 g. He concludes: "the sparse growth and open character of the vegetation of the Burrows are brought about mainly by the low levels of nitrogen and phosphorus in the sand." It is also noteworthy that complete nutrients resulted in grasses becoming dominant, a pattern since observed in many other fertilization experiments. He suggests that increased fertility causes declines in diversity because grasses stifle species intolerant of competition from them, particularly rosette plants, annuals, and bryophytes. Willis further observed that sedges and rushes appeared to be particularly successful in areas of phosphorus deficiency, suggesting that the ratio of nitrogen to phosphorus may control which particular plant group dominates a site, as Smith observed with algae (Figure 3.9).

Hayati and Proctor (1991) did a similar fertilization study involving mires in southern England, using sites including a dry *Calluna*

Box 3.2 | Fritz Haber changes the global nitrogen cycle

Until the end of the industrial revolution, plants and plant communities depended upon two natural sources of nitrogen: biologically fixed nitrogen and nitrogen fixed by lightning discharges. All of this changed in the early 1900s. The first driving factor was gunpowder, the production of which also required nitrogen. The Germans knew that in the case of war, access to the rich beds of guano in Chile would be cut off by the British navy. The second driving factor was also related to military matters. In the case of war, German supplies of fertilizer (and hence food) would also be at risk. There had to be a way to extract nitrogen directly from the atmosphere.

This process was discovered by a German chemist named Fritz Haber (Figure B3.2a) in 1909, and it is still named the Haber process in his honor (Oakes 2002). At high temperature and pressure, a metal catalyst is used in converting nitrogen to ammonia. So long as there are sufficient supplies of fuel, such as natural gas, the supplies of nitrogen are now nearly endless.

At very least, Dr Haber prolonged the cataclysmic First World War by ensuring that both gunpowder and food would be amply available for the German war machine. Sadly, Haber was unable to stop there. To prove his loyalty to Germany, he became further involved with chemical warfare, and introduced poison gas attacks, personally supervising them and refining the methods (Figure B3.2b).

(a)

Figure B3.2(a) Fritz Haber was awarded the 1918 Nobel Prize for chemistry for the synthesis of ammonia from its elements (courtesy Edgar Fahs Smith Memorial Collection, University of Pennsylvania Library).

Figure B3.2(b) A poison gas attack on the eastern front during the First World War. As the gas drifts downwind to the left, the shadows of advancing German troops can seen on the right. Fritz Haber helped develop and refine methods of gas warfare that killed or injured more than a million soldiers (www.ga.k12.pa.us, accessed 15/2/05).

Hundreds of thousands of soldiers from Russia, France, Britain and Canada, among others, were blinded, crippled or killed (Haber 1986, Stoltzenberg 2004). Haber married in 1901, his wife Clara being the first woman in Germany to have earned a PhD in chemistry. Horrified by his involvement in chemical warfare, she shot herself in 1915. Haber continued his poison gas research, and married an apparently less squeamish woman in 1917.

The year after the end of the war, even at the time he was considered a war criminal, Haber received his Nobel Prize in chemistry (Oakes 2002). He was, however, eventually forced to leave Germany because of his Jewish ancestry, and died of a heart attack in Switzerland in 1934. The poison gas research at his institute led to the Zyklon process (Stoltzenberg 2004) which was used to produce Zyklon B, the poisonous gas used to murder Jews, political dissidents, homosexuals, gypsies and other "undesirables" in their millions in concentration camps such as Auschwitz and Birkenau.

Quite apart from the dark history of chemical warfare, his other legacy, the Haber process, continues to alter the world's nitrogen cycle. The rate of industrial fixation was 80 Tg per year in the 1990s, and continues to grow (Vitousek et al. 1997). Eutrophication by surplus nitrogen (Figure B3.2c) is now an emerging problem for the Earth's plant communities (Ellenberg 1988a, Keddy 2000).

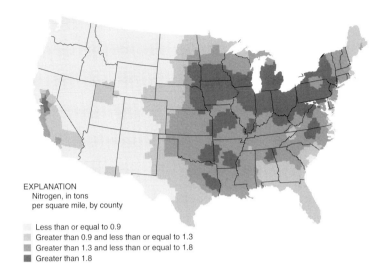

EXPLANATION
Nitrogen, in tons
per square mile, by county

- Less than or equal to 0.9
- Greater than 0.9 and less than or equal to 1.3
- Greater than 1.3 and less than or equal to 1.8
- Greater than 1.8

Figure B3.2(c) The production of ammonia for agriculture by means of the Haber process has grown throughout the last century. The consequences are illustrated by these maps from the United States of America showing atmospheric deposition of nitrogen (top) and nitrogen applied in commercial fertilizer (bottom) (from Puckett 1994).

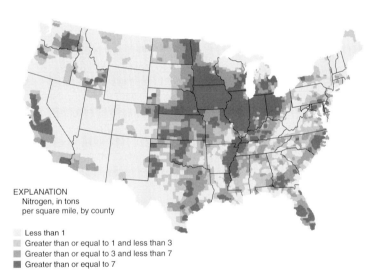

EXPLANATION
Nitrogen, in tons
per square mile, by county

- Less than 1
- Greater than or equal to 1 and less than 3
- Greater than or equal to 3 and less than 7
- Greater than or equal to 7

blanket bog, a valley bog with *Sphagnum* and *Erica tetralix*, and an acid mire with *Sphagnum* and *Carex echinata*. Fertilizer application to *C. echinata* grown in pots of peat from each site produced growth attributable to three main effects: nitrogen, phosphorus, and between-site differences. Nitrogen was more limiting on the wet heath peats, whereas phosphorus was more limiting on the blanket bog. There was a minor effect of potassium, suggesting that it was present in adequate supply everywhere except in the blanket bog. The use of peat in pots may have increased experimental control, but it is vulnerable to the criticism that it does not necessarily show that the same nutrients are important under more natural field conditions. Sediments collected from waterways and put into pots suggest too that nitrogen rather than phosphorus usually limits plant growth (Smart and Barko 1978, Barko and Smart 1978, 1979).

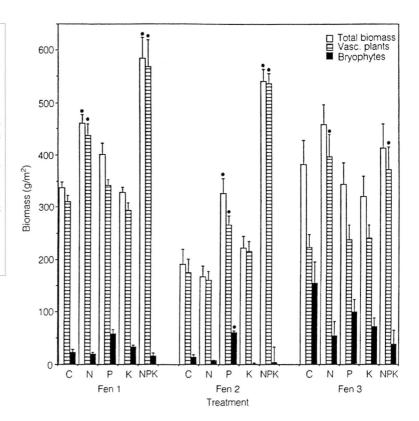

Figure 3.12 Response of aboveground biomass (harvested in August) to fertilization with N, P, K and all three of these elements compared to a control in three fens. Values significantly different from the control are indicated by a black dot ● (after Verhoeven and Schmitz 1991). Fen 1: fen in groundwater discharge area terrestrialized in the 1940s and harvested since the 1960s; fen 2: fen in groundwater discharge area terrestrialized about 1990 and harvested since the 1930s; fen 3: as fen 1 but in groundwater recharge area (from Verhoeven et al. 1993).

Let us look at one more example. Verhoeven et al. (1993) fertilized three fens with three essential nutrients (N, P, K) and a combination treatment (N + P + K). Figure 3.12 shows that the results varied among sites and plants. In fen 1, the addition of nitrogen and NPK produced significant increases in the biomass of vascular plants. In fen 2, the addition of phosphorus produced significant increases in the vascular plant and bryophyte biomass, while the addition of NPK increased only the vascular plant biomass. Fen 3 was similar to fen 1, except that the significant increase for vascular plants was accompanied by a decline for bryophytes so that total biomass was unchanged. These sorts of results might appear discouraging because each study site appears to be unique.

In a review of 45 studies of fertilization of herbaceous wetlands, Koerselman and Meulman (1996) found an almost even split between nitrogen-limited sites and phosphorus-limited sites (Table 3.6). Co-limitation, that is, a response only to combined fertilizations, was rare. Wet heathlands all had growth limited by phosphorus, whereas fens and dune slacks could be limited by either nitrogen or phosphorus. The wet grasslands were the most complicated, with cases of nitrogen, potassium, and nitrogen plus potassium limitation.

How can we explain such patterns? Verhoeven et al. (1996) emphasize differences between the two nutrients. For phosphorus, the main source is weathering from rocks, and the main input to

Table 3.6. *Limiting factors in seven habitat types, as determined by biomass response in fertilization experiments. Figures indicate number of cases in which the element was shown to be limiting (from Verhoeven et al. 1996).*

Habitat	N	P	K	N+P	N+K	P+K
Wet grassland	3	0	2	0	4	0
Wet heath	0	3	0	0	0	0
Rich fen	7	5	0	0	0	0
Poor fen	2	1	0	0	0	0
Litter fen	1	2	0	1	0	0
Bog	1	3	1	0	0	0
Dune slack	5	2	0	2	0	0
Total (45 cases)	19	16	3	3	4	0

wetlands is from water flow. In contrast, the main source of nitrogen is fixation from atmospheric nitrogen (and increasingly, deposition of pollutants in precipitation, Box 3.2). Thus, there is likely to be a shift from nitrogen to phosphorus limitation during succession, since early in succession phosphorus is available in ground water and there is little nitrogen stored in organic matter. Consistent with this view, Table 3.6 shows that early-successional rich fens are generally nitrogen limited, while late-successional bogs and moist heaths are phosphorus limited.

3.4.6 Other sources of evidence for nutrient limitation

The concentrations of nutrients in plant tissues seem to be obvious measures of resource requirements. High concentrations of nutrients may be difficult to interpret, since they might mean that the nutrient is available in excess and is being easily taken up in luxury for future use, or that the nutrient is scarce and is being stored for future use. This is particularly problematic in infertile soils, where nutrient uptake may be entirely uncoupled from periods of growth (Grime 1977). While such nutrient data must be viewed with caution, the ratio of nitrogen to phosphorus in tissues may still be informative about the relative importance of these elements. Returning to the wetlands described in Section 3.4.5, Verhoeven et al. (1996) examined tissue nutrient concentrations for the same set of studies. The N:P ratio of 15:1 (as measured in plants from control sites) clearly separated N-limited from P-limited situations: "It can be concluded the N:P ratio of above-ground biomass at the end of the growing season (August) provides a reliable indicator of the degree to which each of these elements has been limiting plant growth in herbaceous mires." They conclude that N:P ratios greater than 16 indicate phosphorus limitation, and N:P ratios less than 14 indicate nitrogen limitation.

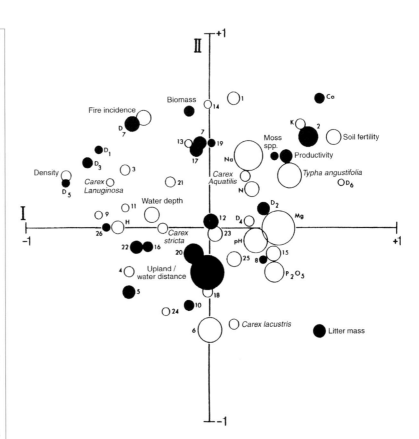

Figure 3.13 Interrelationships of fertility and productivity in a riparian wetland in eastern Canada (using a factor analysis model). The first and second components are shown on the horizontal and vertical axes, respectively. Factor loadings on the third component are represented by circle diameters (open = negative, closed = positive). D1–D7 are species diversity indices. Coded variables include: 1 soil organic matter, 2 soil (Ca + Mg)/(K + Na), 3 date since 1 May, 4 tussock incidence, 5 distance to upland, 6 distance to water, 7 biomass, 8 average stem height, 9 *Equisetum fluviatile*, 10 *Onoclea sensibilis*, 11 *Thelypteris palustris*, 12 *Potentilla palustris*, 12 *Viola pallens*, 13 *Hypericum virginicum*, 15 *Galium palustre*, 16 *Lysimachia thyrsiflora*, 17 *Lythrum salicaria*, 18 *Cicuta bulbifera*, 19 *Utricularia vulgaris*, 20 *Impatiens capensis*, 21 *Lycopus uniflorus*, 22 *Campanula aparinoides*, 23 *Carex diandra*, 24 *Calamagrostis canadensis*, 25 *Sparganium eurycarpum*, 26 *Sagittaria latifolia* (from Auclair et al. 1976a).

Many other field studies have tried to understand nutrients and plants by seeking relationships between soil nutrient levels and plant abundance or growth. Often the results suggest important roles for both nitrogen and phosphorus. Figure 3.13 shows the interrelationships of soil nutrients, biomass, and primary productivity in one riparian wetland (Auclair et al. 1976a). In this case, biomass and productivity are positively correlated with nitrogen ($r = 0.38$, 0.39) but negatively correlated with phosphorus ($r = -0.29$, -0.23). Yet in a similar geographic region, but in a *Carex*-dominated ecosystem, there were no significant correlations between production and either nitrogen or phosphorus (Auclair et al. 1976b). At a slightly larger scale, but still within the same region, Wisheu et al. (1991) found a positive correlation between biomass and soil phosphorus in three different wetlands (Figure 3.14), although in each case, soil phosphorus accounted for only about 50 percent of the variation.

The evolution of plants may also reveal something of the importance of nutrient limitation. It may explain in part why cellulose rather than chitin is the main structural molecule in plants. Using data on the above-ground biomass of ecosystems (Whittaker 1975), and knowing that plants are 40 to 60 percent cellulose, we can calculate that the existing global pool of cellulose is some 9.2×10^{11} tons, with a production rate of 0.85×10^{11} tons per year (Duchesne and Larson 1989). Cellulose consists of repeating molecules of

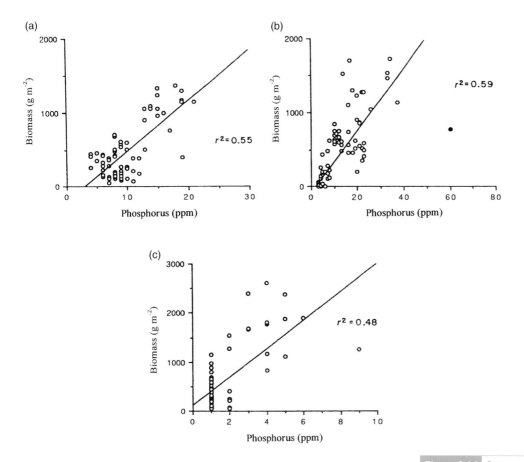

Figure 3.14 Biomass as a function of soil phosphorus in three temperate zone marshes: (a) Luskville, Quebec, (b) Westmeath, Ontario (solid outlier not included in analysis), (c) Presqu'ile Provincial Park, Ontario (from Wisheu et al. 1991).

glucose ($C_6H_{12}O_6$) attached end to end; these thin molecules are then united into microfibrils about 10–25 nm wide and wound together like strands in a cable to form macrofibrils. These fibrils are as strong as an equivalent thickness of steel. Chitin, a structural molecule still found in arthropods, some algae, some diatoms, and most fungi, has a tensile strength half that of cellulose. Chitin also requires nitrogen. Duchesne and Larson (1989) estimate that if plants used chitin as opposed to cellulose, the nitrogen content of wood would increase 12-fold, from the current 0.33% to approximately 4%. Not only would this greatly increase demand for a critically limited resource, it would also make plants much more palatable to herbivores.

3.5 | Changing availability of resources in space and time

3.5.1 Small scale heterogeneity

We have already seen that water is far from homogenously distributed in soils (Figure 3.7), and the same is true of other below-ground resources. Figure 3.15 depicts a small tract of prairie; even at this very

Figure 3.15 Spatial heterogeneity of soil nitrogen in a 12 × 12 m plot of sandy soil in a Minnesota prairie (after Tilman 1982).

restricted scale, nutrients such as nitrogen occur in patches. Further, these nutrient patches can be expected to move in time and space as a consequence of processes such as fire, and with animals adding patchiness through grazing, defecation, burrowing, and death. Even if the latter four processes were eliminated, say by removing all animals from experimental plots of prairie, other processes such as growth, death, decay, and changing rainfall and temperature would continue to alter the size, shape, and duration of nutrient patches. At this scale, the essential questions may involve how organisms can best acquire and sequester nutrients when they are disturbed as short-lived patches.

3.5.2 Resource gradients

Erosion by running water is one of the dominant features shaping the surface of the Earth. As water moves from highlands to lowlands, it dissolves minerals from rocks and erodes soil. In some world drainage basins, the mass of eroded sediments exceeds 1 tonne per km^2 per year (Milliman and Meade 1983). The yield of sediment varies with annual precipitation and land use (Judson 1968). As a consequence of steady erosion and deposition, depressions in the landscape are repositories of accumulated organic matter and mineral nutrients. Deposition rates in the order of 20 to 3000 cm per 1000 years are suggested by palynological studies of English landscapes, with some of this being peat produced *in situ* (Walker 1970). Rozan et al. (1994) suggest that rates of deposition in a floodplain in eastern North America were below 10 cm per 1000 years prior to this century but increased to nearly 1 m per 1000 years as humans modified the landscape. This is close to the range of deposition rates reported for coastal deltas (Boesch et al. 1994).

Erosion and deposition produce gradients at a wide range of scales. In the Great Smoky Mountains, for example, rich deciduous forests develop in fertile valleys called coves, while open oak and pine forests establish on dry ridges (Whittaker 1956). Sediments from uplands are deposited in valleys to form the rich soils associated with alluvial wet prairies, marshland, and swamps (e.g., Sioli 1964, Davies and Walker 1986). In peatlands, strong fertility gradients are associated with the degree to which running water, as opposed to rainwater, maintains the water table, and this gradient produces striking changes in the species found. The peatlands fed by groundwater (fens) have higher pH and nutrient concentrations than those fed by rainwater (raised bogs) (Gorham 1953, Glaser et al. 1990, Glaser 1992). At even more local scales, depressions in old fields contain soil with more water and nutrients than the ridges between them (Reader and Best 1989). Gradients of soil fertility typify a wide range of habitats from montane forests to wetlands to old fields. To focus upon small resource patches, or to assume environmental homogeneity, denies one of the most natural aspects of landscapes. Therefore, more attention needs to be placed upon gradients and the way in which resources and organisms become distributed along them.

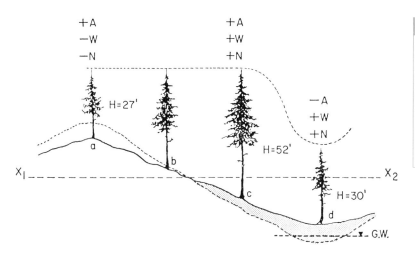

Figure 3.16 Effects of topography on moisture (W), aeration (A), and nutrient content (N) of soil and the resulting growth of trees. Line X1–X2 delineates positive topography, subject to denudation, and negative topography, subject to deposition of eroded materials (from Wilde 1958).

The following illustrates the wisdom on resource gradients available in a traditional forestry source such as Wilde's (1958) treatise on forest soils:

The modifying influence of the local physiographic conditions deserves particular attention in classification of forested soils in rolling or hilly topography. Such soils usually provide striking illustrations of the effects of the three major edaphic factors: water, aeration, and nutrients [Figure 3.16].

The top and upper slopes of a ridge or a mound represent elements of so-called positive topography. Soils overlying this portion of the relief receive the least rain water and are subject to denudation, which decreases the supply of available nutrients. Consequently, such soils often support forest stands of low rate of growth. On the other hand, the negative topography of lower slopes receives run-off water and fertilizing products of erosion – mineral colloids, humus, and soluble salts. As the result of this enrichment of the soil, forest stands increase their height growth, or, as foresters say, "Trees level the relief with their crowns." With the descent to a depression the water accumulates in excess, and the growth of trees drops abruptly in accordance with the rapidly decreasing soil aeration.

(p. 248)

In heavily developed landscapes, where pastures have replaced forests, similar resource gradients can be found. Again, erosion from upper slopes produces a soil resource gradient (Figure 3.17). Superimposed upon this, however, are grazing pressures that are most intense in the valleys. At a finer scale, local sites of erosion (eroded pasture) produce adjacent sites with deposition (very oligotrophic pasture). These local gradients are also superimposed upon the longer gradient running down the elevation gradient.

Overlaid upon such erosional patterns are changes in soil organic matter and types of mycorrhizal associations. Figure 3.18 shows some of the major types of mycorrhizae, and Figure 3.19 summarizes their distributions along elevation gradients. Regrettably,

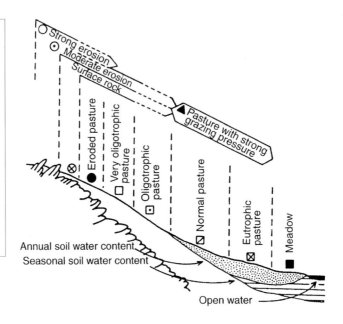

Figure 3.17 Typical sequence of grassland communities on a slope. Community names are vernacular and based on nutrient status and grazing intensity. The main sequence runs from "Meadow" in the bottom of valleys to "Eroded pasture" higher up the slope. The distribution patterns of the types "Strong grazing," "Moderate erosion," and "Strong erosion" are superimposed on the main sequence, or occur occasionally; here arrows indicate the intervals where they usually appear (from Puerto et al. 1990).

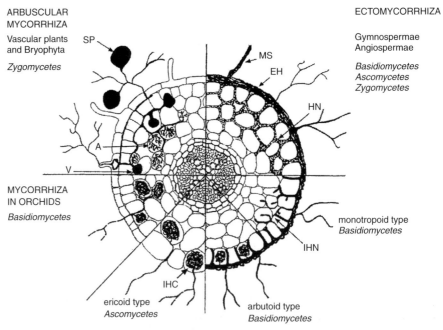

Figure 3.18 A schematic overview of the different forms of mycorrhizae and their symbiotic partners. MS, Mycelial strands; EH, external hyphal mantle; HN, Hartig net; IHN, intercellular hyphal net; IHC, intracellular hyphal complexes; V, fungal vesicle; A, arbuscule; SP, spore (from Larcher 2003).

the wetland habitats in valley bottoms are not included in this figure, but evidence to date suggests that flooding reduces both the abundance of soil fungi (Kalamees 1982) and the occurrence of mycorrhizae (Rickerl et al. 1994).

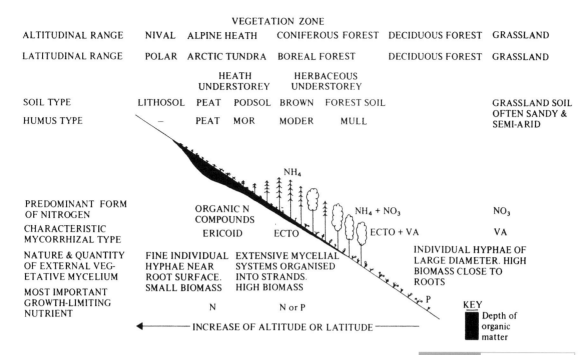

Figure 3.19 Diagrammatic presentation of the postulated relationship between latitude or altitude, climate, soil and mycorrhizal type, and development of the vegetative mycelium associated with mycorrhizae (from Lewis 1987).

The following resource gradient data come from a slightly specialized example of the foregoing general pattern. Even in wetlands, which may seem to have relatively uniform topography, one can find similar gradients. They stretch from infertile sandy shores, from which waves are eroding nutrients, to sheltered fertile bays, where silt, organic matter, and nutrients accumulate (Figure 6.26). At this large scale (illustrated by, but not restricted to, wetlands), one can reasonably discuss resource gradients, because all major resources (N, P, K, Mg) are distributed along a common gradient. They are in low availability on sandy or eroding shorelines; they are in high availability wherever sediments accumulate. In other cases, vast sand plains create extensive areas of wet but infertile conditions (Figure 3.20).

What happens if one examines resource patterns progressing from a large (landscape sized) scale to a small (quadrat sized) scale? Table 3.7 provides the opportunity to move down this scale, from the top matrix (marshes in eastern North America) to the bottom matrix (a single sedge meadow). In the top matrix, the soil samples are from wetlands ranging from the highly fertile (e.g., *Typha* marshes and floodplains) to highly infertile sand or gravel shorelines where insectivorous genera such as *Drosera* and *Utricularia* are common. As well, both organic matter and silt and clay content of the soil were positively correlated with nitrogen and phosphorus levels. Similar patterns occur within a single wetland (Table 3.7(b)). At the lower-most scale (Table 3.7(d)), still larger than the small piece

Figure 3.20 Infertile habitats. (a) Wave washed shorelines like this one in Axe Lake, Ontario, are similar to hill tops in that they are habitats from which nutrients are eroded. The fine particles with attached nutrients are deposited elsewhere, thereby creating the strong resource gradients typical of terrestrial and wetland vegetation (Keddy 1981b); (b) sand plains in the southeastern United States have been leached by winter rainfall for millions of years and support vegetation such as this pitcher plant bog (from Peet and Allard 1993).

of prairie shown in Figure 3.15, many of the correlations among resources have become negligible.

As it shall become evident, assumptions about the appropriate scale of enquiry have a big impact upon one's view of competition. The assumption of nearly homogeneous environments and trade-offs among resources (e.g., Tilman 1982) may be quite appropriate for a patch such as Figure 3.15 or perhaps a single sedge meadow, whereas the assumption of resource gradients and trade-offs between stress tolerance and resource competition (e.g., Keddy 1989) seem more appropriate to larger scales of enquiry. Further, these different scales treat resources in entirely different ways. At the small scale, resource availability is seen to be under biological control, with plants creating

Table 3.7. *Resource gradients in wetlands from the large scale (top) to the small scale (bottom). Note that patterns (as indicated by the size of correlation coefficients) fade as the scale becomes smaller (after Keddy 2001).*

(a) Marshes in north eastern North America (Gaudet 1993, her Table 1.2)

	% Organic	P	N	K	Mg	pH
Standing crop	0.77	0.76	0.66	0.58	0.67	−0.28
% Organic		0.77	0.57	0.50	0.51	−0.47
P			0.72	0.56	0.66	−0.13
N				0.53	0.63	−0.02
K					0.70	−0.28
Mg						−0.14

(b) One wetland complex in the Ottawa River watershed (Gaudet 1993, her Table 1.4)

	% Organic	P	N	K	Mg	pH
Standing crop	0.74	0.80	0.69	0.76	0.69	−0.45
% Organic		0.80	0.61	0.66	0.62	−0.61
P			0.62	0.82	0.59	−0.46
N				0.68	0.53	−0.18
K					0.64	−0.35
Mg						−0.72

(c) One vegetation zone of the St. Lawrence River (Auclair et al. 1976a, their Table 1)

	% Organic	P	N	K	Mg	pH
Standing crop	0.34	−0.29	0.38	0.49	0.17	0.21
% Organic		−0.27	0.37	0.75	0.59	0.18
P			−0.01	−0.48	0.33	−0.55
N				0.39	0.32	0.14
K					0.43	0.38
Mg						0.12

(d) Carex meadow, St. Lawrence River (Auclair et al. 1976b, their Table 1)

	% Organic	P	N	K	Mg	pH
Standing crop	0.13	−0.02	−0.02	−0.22	−0.23	−0.11
% Organic		−0.39	0.30	0.52	0.17	−0.14
P			−0.26	0.18	−0.21	0.03
N				0.24	0.26	0.04
K					0.16	−0.01
Mg						0.52

depletion zones around their roots. At the large scale, resource availability is viewed as a consequence of erosion and topography, with plants interacting with one another for access to different sections of this resource gradient. Perhaps greater attention to the distribution of resources in nature would allow one to better decide which scale of investigation is appropriate to a particular set of circumstances.

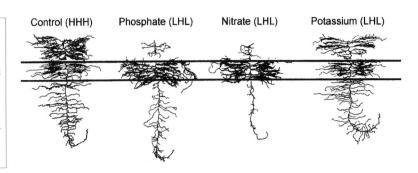

Control (HHH)   Phosphate (LHL)   Nitrate (LHL)   Potassium (LHL)

Figure 3.21 Responses of barley root systems to different nutrient supplies. The plants were grown in a three-chambered flowing nutrient system with the central chamber having the relevant ion at a concentration 100-fold that in the other two chambers. H, high; L, low (from Leyser and Fitter 1998 after Drew 1975).

3.5.3 Resources in transitory patches

Soil resources are not only distributed unequally in space, but patches themselves may be transitory in time. Nutrients may be available only after a transitory event such as a pulse of rainfall. Alternatively, the roots of neighbors may intercept and deplete pockets of resources. When a neighbor dies, or when surrounding biomass is damaged by an event such as freezing, the nutrients from those neighbors may also be re-released in a pulse creating a transitory patch of nutrients. Plant roots must locate such patches. While the primary root is unaffected by nitrate, the activity of lateral root primordia is strongly influenced by the nitrate (and phosphate) concentration in the substrate (Figure 3.21). At low nutrient levels, a localized region of high nitrate will stimulate lateral root growth (Drew 1975). This root proliferation should help capture ions that have very limited mobility in the soil, such as NH^{4+} and inorganic phosphate. In contrast, there might be rather little advantage to root proliferation in response to highly mobile ions such as NO^{3-} (Robinson 1996).

However reasonable such logic may seem, apparently some species such as *Arabidopsis* have a mechanism for detecting NO^{3-} rather than NH^{4+} (Forde and Zhang 1998). The possible explanation lies in the relative rates of diffusion of theses two ions in the soil. Under aerobic conditions, decaying organic matter will release both ions, but the relative immobility of NH^{4+} means that it is likely to be the NO^{3-} ion that is the first to reach nearby roots. NO^{3-} may therefore signal the presence of a nearby nitrogen source, allowing a plant detecting NO^{3-} to respond before one detecting NH^{4+}.

In another series of experiments (Campbell et al. 1991), two plants contrasting ecologically were exposed to resource pulses of widely different durations (from 1 min to 100 h out of every 6 days). The relatively slow-growing *Festuca ovina* showed increased relative growth rates as the length of pulse increased (Figure 3.22, solid dots). Now consider a second species, *Arrhenatherum elatius*, which has the potential to be a fast-growing species in fertile habitats. Note the top of Figure 3.22; when pluses were of short duration this species actually grew more slowly than *F. ovina*. It was apparently inferior in ability to exploit temporary pulses of nutrients, an interpretation strengthened by measurements of nitrogen absorption rates (Figure 3.22(b)). Once pulses lasted longer than 10 h, the

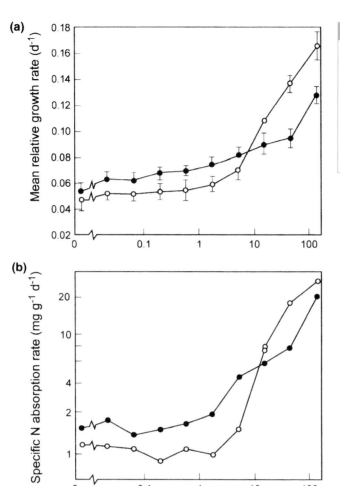

Figure 3.22 (a) Mean relative growth rate ($\pm$ 95% CI) and (b) mean specific nitrogen absorption rate of potentially rapid-growing *Arrhenatherum elatius* ($\circ$) and slow-growing *Festuca ovina* ($\bullet$) plants plotted against the duration of pulses of nutrient enrichment. Pulses occurred once every 6 days (after Grime 1994).

growth rate of *A. elatius* nearly doubled and exceeded that of the other species.

It is clear that the ability of plants to capture soil resources can be dramatically affected by the duration of resource pulses. Figure 3.22 does not show the consequences for competition, but it does suggest that infertile habitats with short pulses of resource might provide a refuge for the slower growing species. One can imagine that similar patterns might be found in other circumstances; say, birds exploiting nectar with different pulses of availability, or fungi exploiting detritus with different decay rates.

3.6 | Resources as a habitat template for plant populations

In order to relate the resources in a habitat to the kinds of plants found there, we might try to recognize a few fundamental types of

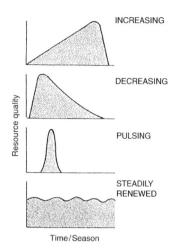

Figure 3.23 labels: INCREASING, DECREASING, PULSING, STEADILY RENEWED. Y-axis: Resource quality. X-axis: Time/Season.

Figure 3.23 Four kinds of resources classified by pattern of temporal variation (after Price 1984). This scheme does not consider spatial variation or chronically low resource availability.

patterns in resources (Grime 1977, Southwood 1977). Price (1984) recognized five kinds. Four of these are shown in Figure 3.23. Increasing resources are those which increase and then suddenly decline. Decreasing resources are produced suddenly at the beginning of a season, and they gradually decline. Pulsing or ephemeral resources increase rapidly and then decline rapidly. Steadily renewed resources are continuously renewed over long periods. Continuous resources, not shown in Figure 3.23, are physical in nature and are largely unaffected by seasonal change. Price uses this last category to deal with space as a resource for sessile organisms. Since disturbance and death continually create new spaces for colonists, space can be treated as another example of a continually renewed resource. Price's five resource types can therefore be reduced to four.

If uniform and patchy distributions of each kind of resource are recognized, then the number of kinds of resources based on Price's scheme can be doubled. Southwood (1977) produced a more elaborate classification, which included both spatial and temporal variation. He recognized four temporal categories and three spatial categories. Combining the two produced 12 different resource types (Figure 3.24).

Life span is one important plant trait that varies among habitats, depending upon the resource types present. Short-lived plants germinate and produce seeds within a few months while long-lived plants survive and produce seeds over centuries. Let us consider these two extremes in more detail.

Short-lived plants, often called **ruderals**, or **annuals**, allocate all of their reproductive energy to seeds. They typically occupy habitats in which resources are freely available, but the probability of surviving to reproduce in future years is small, usually as a result of recurring disturbance (a "seasonal" or "ephemeral" habitat in Figure 3.24). Consider some examples. Some annual plants occur on sandy coastal beaches that are fertilized by rotting seaweed in the summer but churned by winter waves (Keddy 1982). Many occur as weeds in agricultural fields (Harper 1977). A more unusual case is the annual plants that occur in deserts, where the plants exploit short wet periods between long droughts (Venable and Pake 1999). At the other extreme from deserts, some annual plants also occur in wetlands during temporary periods of low water (van der Valk and Davis 1978). In general, any short-lived habitat selects for plants with short life spans and relatively rapid growth rates (Grime 1977, 1979). Ruderals often produce large numbers of relatively small seeds. These seeds may remain dormant in the soil, producing large concentrations of buried seeds known as **seed banks** (Leck et al. 1989). (Table 6.6 shows some examples of densities of buried seeds in flooded habitats.)

Long-lived plants, usually called **perennials**, delay reproduction until they achieve relatively larger sizes, a process that may take many years. Trees are the most common example. Sequoia trees (*Sequoia sempervirens*), for example, can live over 1000 years, and at maturity can produce 4.5×10^6 seeds per year (Harper and White

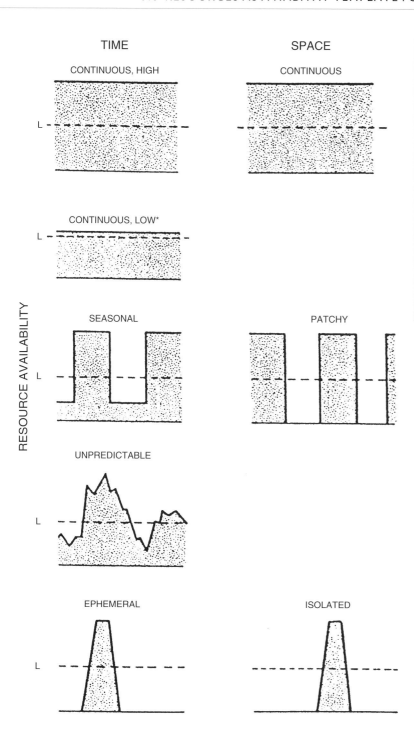

Figure 3.24 A more elaborate classification of resource types, based upon variation in resource availability in time and space. Five temporal distributions can be combined with three spatial distributions for a total of 15 possible resource types. L indicates the level of resource necessary for reproduction. This is after Southwood (1977) by the addition of the "continuous, low" category marked with an asterisk. For simplicity, scaling terms such as generation time and foraging range have been left off the figure; more complete accounts of scaling are given in Southwood (1977, 1988) and Begon and Mortimer (1981).

1974). Long-lived plants occupy habitats with continuous or patchy resources where adult mortality is low enough that reproduction can be safely postponed. Resources that are not allocated to reproduction (Box 3.3) can then be allocated to stems, leaves and shoots. This may allow these plants to compete with neighbors for access to light and

Box 3.3 | A Darwinian approach to plant traits

"Plant ecologists," say Harper and White (1974, p. 419), "have concentrated on the physiology, structure and taxonomy of vegetation, while largely ignoring the population phenomena that constitute the underlying flux." Harper (1967) advocated that plant ecologists should adopt the perspective of zoologists, and focus upon the quantitative study of single populations of species of plants. This approach, sometimes called the Darwinian approach (Harper 1967) or plant demography (Harper and White 1974), explores how life history characteristics such as birth and death rates interact to influence the abundance of plants in specific habitats. Each population of plants exists, after all, only so long as its rate of reproduction exceeds, in the long run, its rate of mortality.

Population ecologists study how characteristics such as rates of flowering, seed production, seed dispersal, germination, and survival vary among habitats (Harper 1977, Silvertown and Charlesworth 2001). They also explore the trade-offs that drive the evolution of different life history traits. A plant can allocate only so much energy or nutrients to reproduction. What are the relative costs and benefits of allocating scarce resources to seeds as opposed to new shoots? What are the costs and benefits of producing a few seeds when a plant is young as opposed to delaying reproduction and producing more seeds in the future? What are the relative costs and benefits of producing a few large seeds as opposed to many small seeds? Figure B3.3a shows how seed production increases with plant size. Figure B3.3b shows the trade-off between the number of seeds a plant produces and the size of those seeds.

Figure B3.3(a) The number of seeds a plant produces is positively correlated with plant size ($r = 0.62$). In this example plant size is expressed as ramet (shoot) weight; these data represent 285 ramets from 57 species from habitats including wetlands, old fields and woodlands in the vicinity of Montreal, Canada (from Shipley and Dion 1992).

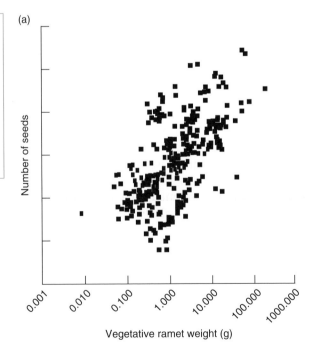

(b)

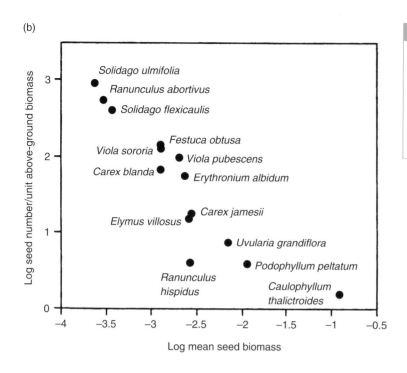

Figure B3.3(b) The number of seeds a plant produces is negatively correlated with the investment in each seed. The data are from 14 species of herbaceous woodland plants, including many spring wildflowers, sampled in upland forest of central Iowa (from Mabry 2004).

nutrients (Harper 1977, Keddy 2001). Longer-lived plants usually produce fewer, but larger, seeds – think for example of the size of acorns and walnuts. Such large seeds are easily found and damaged by seed-eating herbivores, and hence tend not to accumulate in the soil. Most perennial plants are iteroparous, reproducing for many years upon reaching adulthood, but one small sub-set flowers and reproduces only once before dying (semelparous plants). The latter group includes foxgloves (*Digitalis purpurea*, Sletvold 2002), bamboos (Janzen 1976), and yuccas (Young and Augspruger 1991). There are conflicting views of the forces that select for this "big-bang" mode of reproduction. Hypotheses include the possibility that producing large numbers of seeds in one burst will satiate and overwhelm seed predators, or that the large inflorescences attract pollinating insects with greater success (Young and Augspruger 1991). The precise age of reproduction for semelparous plants often varies with the conditions of the habitat, but those that normally take only two years to reproduce (e.g., *Beta vulgaris, Campanula medium, Daucus carota, Digitalis purpurea, Echium vulgaris, Verbascum thapsus*) are termed biennials.

3.7 | Resource fluctuations complicate short-term ecological studies

Resource levels (and all other environmental constraints) present two further perplexing problems. First, they fluctuate, and, frustrating as

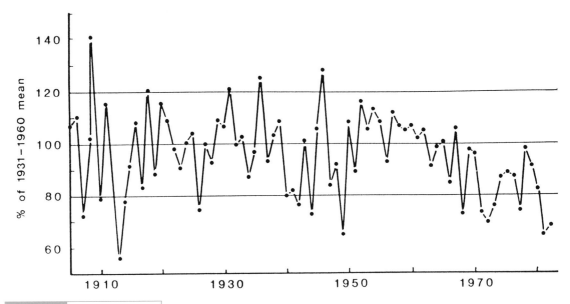

Figure 3.25 Annual rainfall from five stations in the Sahel expressed as a percentage of the 1931–1960 mean. Years that fall 20% above or below the mean indicate extreme events. The years of 1912 and 1949 were years of drought similar to those of 1981. These periodic droughts may have far more effect upon ecological communities than the mean value, particularly if overgrazing is an ongoing pressure (from Sinclair and Fryxell 1985).

it may be, may change over a wide array of time spans, from the hourly changes in soil moisture after a heavy rainfall in a forest, to the changes in rainfall patterns that occur over millennia. Such constant change is difficult enough to accommodate in ecological studies, but it is accentuated by a second problem; it may be the extreme events rather than the average conditions that control the properties observed. For example, it may not be the mean annual rainfall over the last century, but one period of drought 50 or 100 years ago that produced the mixture of species observed today (Figure 3.25). It is readily apparent that a short-term field experiment is not well suited to address causal processes in ecological systems that are largely the result of long-term fluctuations and periodic extreme events. Moreover, even if one happens to encounter an apparent extreme event during an experiment, it is unlikely that one will then simultaneously obtain the necessary comparative results from the long-term average to put the apparent extreme in an ecological context.

This conundrum apparently led MacArthur (1972) to propose that the best evidence for the existence of competition has to come from biogeographers who are accustomed to dealing with long time scales. Further, he suggested that the evolutionary responses of species, that is their ecomorphological properties (e.g., bill size and diet in birds) and geographical distributions, are the most appropriate kind of data for the study of competition. This opinion was echoed by Wiens (1977), who suggested that traits of organisms may reflect short periods of intense selection (bottlenecks) interspersed with much longer periods of weaker selection. Expanding upon this, one can imagine that any property of a species or community may be the product of short periods when resources crash below a critical level. Of course, convincing theories built upon extreme events are much

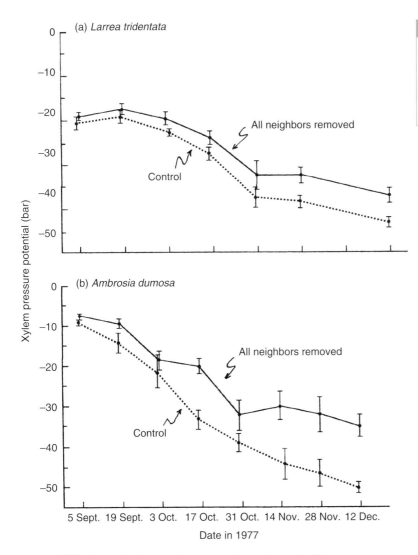

(a) *Larrea tridentata*

All neighbors removed

Control

(b) *Ambrosia dumosa*

All neighbors removed

Control

Xylem pressure potential (bar)

5 Sept. 19 Sept. 3 Oct. 17 Oct. 31 Oct. 14 Nov. 28 Nov. 12 Dec.

Date in 1977

Figure 3.26 Declines in water potential of two desert shrubs after an August rainfall. The performance of each species is shown for control plots and for plots with neighboring plants removed (after Fonteyn and Mahall 1981).

more difficult to derive and to test than those built upon means. Extreme events are, by definition, relatively rare. Further, one may be accustomed to looking for relationships among means rather than among extremes. A compensating factor may be that at least the effect of extreme events such as fire, flood, or drought may be so clear that the link between the environment and its effects is not subtle but self-evident.

The effects of fluctuating resource levels are well-illustrated by the effects of drought upon two species of desert shrubs. The water potential (xylem pressure potential) of both species was measured immediately after a rainfall, and then re-measured approximately every two weeks as the soil dried (Figure 3.26). Further, some of the shrubs had neighbors, whereas other shrubs did not, the neighboring plants having been removed as a part of the experiment. Shortly after a 60-mm rainfall in mid August (the far left side of Figure 3.26), the water potential of each species was relatively high, and little-affected by neighbors. Over the next three months, as the soil dried, water potential fell steadily. Moreover, water potential fell more rapidly in those shrubs with neighbors (dashed lines), showing that the consumption of water by neighboring plants increased the physiological effects of the drought. This experiment has several important lessons. It shows from direct physiological measurements how plants are affected by a fluctuating resource. It also shows how neighbors can amplify the impacts of scarce resources, illustrating the effects of competition, which is the theme of Chapter 5 (Section 5.2.2). The experiment also shows how the results of field experiments can change with time – this case, the impacts of drought, and the effects of neighbors, only became apparent after months of measurement. Had the experiment stopped earlier, the effects of neighbors might not have been detected.

Water is an obvious resource that fluctuates over time, and rainfall data like those in Figure 3.25 are useful because they have been routinely collected for many years. Other examples of fluctuating resources or resource patches include nectar (Feinsinger 1976), seeds in desert soils (Price and Reichman 1987), carcasses (Corfield 1973), grazing lands (Sinclair and Fryxell 1985), marshes (Keddy and Reznicek 1986), freshwater periods in saline marshes (Zedler and Beare 1986), light gaps in vegetation (Grubb 1977), and bare areas on submerged stones (Hemphill and Cooper 1983). It would appear that relatively constant environments, or continually available resources, are exceptions and that one of the major problems faced by all organisms is coping with constantly changing environmental conditions (Levins 1968).

3.8 | Chronic scarcity of resources and conservation

3.8.1 Limitation by scarce resources

Resource acquisition is a problem that faces all plants. We have even borrowed a term from zoology, and considered it as a problem of foraging – that is, of finding and exploiting patches where resources are locally abundant. There may, however, be situations where resource levels are so low that the investment in foraging does not yield a positive return. What if there are no patches to be found or if their quality is so low that the cost of finding them exceeds the benefits obtained? Habitats with chronically low supply rates of resources may well be a distinctive category (for example Grime 1977, 1979, Greenslade 1983, Southwood 1988). The classification of resources in Figure 3.24 anticipated this problem by including a category for resources that have a constant but chronically low supply rate ("continuous, low"). Grime (1977, 1979) has argued that such circumstances lead to an evolutionary strategy he terms "stress tolerance" (see Section 4.1.2). Under such circumstances, he argues, there is strong selection for the conservation of resources. Conservation is accomplished both by storing excess resources

Table 3.8. *Some attributes of stress-tolerant plants from chronically resource-limited habitats (in part from Grime 1977, Givnish 1988).*

Attribute	Presumed selective advantage
Inherently slow growth rates	Reduced demands upon resources
Evergreen foliage, long-lived organs	Reduced loss of resources
Storage of water and nutrients	Uncoupling of resource supplies from plant growth
Investment in anti-herbivore defenses	Costly replacement minimized
Symbioses	Alternative paths for uptake or storage of resources
Carnivory	Alternative source of nutrients
Reduction in size	Reduced demands upon resources, low above-ground competition
Low allocation to seeds	Limited expenditure of resources, resources available for asexual reproduction

within the tissues of the organism and by minimizing losses (Table 3.8). This is often associated with reduction in the size and growth rate of the organism concerned. These kinds of adaptations are well-known in plants from arctic and alpine habitats, arid habitats, and an array of nutrient-deficient habitats such as sandy soils, serpentine soils, tree canopies, and peatlands.

We will devote the entire next chapter to these types of extreme habitats, but to make this chapter on resources complete, we will continue here with plants adapted to chronically low supplies of one or more resources: epiphytes, succulents, carnivorous plants, parasites.

Epiphytes

Let us begin with an unusual example from a newly-emerging field of plant ecology known as canopy ecology (Moffett 1994, Lowman and Rinker 2004). The canopy of tropical forests supports more than 2500 species of Pteridophytes and 20 000 species of flowering plants (Benzing 1990). Such epiphytic plants lack any access to mineral soil, yet must still acquire resources such as nitrogen and phosphorus.

Some epiphytic bromeliads have a bowl-like shape that traps both water and detritus, including animal excrement and dust. These plants still possess roots that securely grip the substratum, but these roots are essentially non-absorptive (Benzing 1990). The efficiency of this kind of nutrient capture is illustrated by a study in Venezuela, where the annual input of phosphorus in rainfall was 28.4 $kg \cdot ha^{-1} \cdot year^{-1}$. Of this input, 21.7 $kg \cdot ha^{-1} \cdot year^{-1}$ was absorbed by the forest canopy, leaving only 6.7 $kg \cdot ha^{-1} \cdot year^{-1}$ to reach the forest floor (Jordan et al. 1980). Africa may actually provide phosphorus for neotropical bromeliads and forests, with dust from the Sahara Desert being transported across the Atlantic Ocean (Jickells et al. 1998). The presence of animal remains has led to claims that certain bromeliads are carnivorous, but Benzing concludes that these claims are not convincing.

Other epiphytes in tropical canopies gather nutrients by housing ant colonies, and may provide specialized organs called **domatia** to

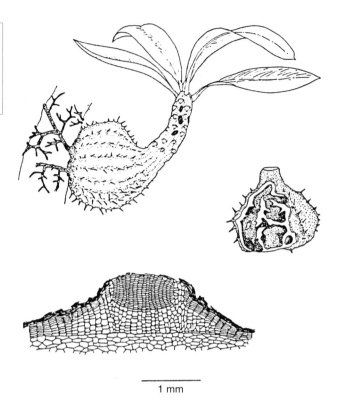

Figure 3.27 A tropical ant-fed, ant-house epiphyte: *Myrmecodia tuberosa*; habit, tuber chambers, and transverse section through absorptive papillae (from Benzing 1990).

1 mm

accommodate them. Detritus carried back to the domatia provides an important source of mineral nutrients. Some such plants will produce roots within their own domatia, in which case they are literally rooting within their own self-contained flowerpots. *Myrmecodia tuberosa* (Figure 3.27) has a chambered tuber that houses ants and absorptive papillae for nutrient uptake. Similarly, *Dischidia rafflesiana* has flask-shaped leaves that collect rainwater as well as detritus that is transported by the ants that live in the flasks. At least seven families of plants (Asclepiadaceae, Bromeliaceae, Melastomataceae, Nepenthaceae, Orchidaceae, Piperaceae, and Polypodiaceae) produce domatia that are occupied by ants (Janzen 1974, Huxley 1980, Benzing 1990). Less specialized cases include members of the Araceae, Bromeliaceae, Gesneriaceae, Orchidaceae, and Piperaceae that root in arboreal ant nests.

Succulents

Although shortages of two essential elements, nitrogen and phosphorus, are implicated in many examples of stress tolerance, shortages of water in deserts cause some equally remarkable responses in plants. The typical barrel shape of many cacti not only allows for water storage within their tissues, but reduces surface to volume ratios to minimize water losses from evapotranspiration (Figure 3.28). Other factors may also contribute to this growth form such as shortages of resources for constructing leaves and the inevitable losses of nitrogen

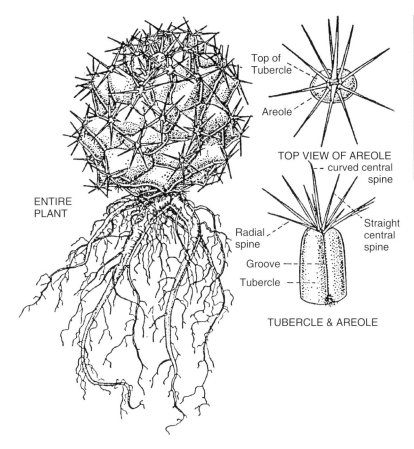

Top of
Tubercle

Areole

TOP VIEW OF AREOLE

curved central
spine

ENTIRE
PLANT

Radial
spine

Straight
central
spine

Groove

Tubercle

TUBERCLE & AREOLE

Figure 3.28 The barrel cactus has many features of a stress tolerator including tissues for storing water and a reduced surface to volume ratio to minimize losses from evapotranspiration. Secondary characteristics include the array of spines to protect the resources that have been acquired and an inherently slow growth rate (from Benson 1950).

and phosphorus when the leaves are shed. Reduction in leaf area and increase in leaf longevity are well-illustrated by succulents, but the argument is not restricted to this growth form. The presence of evergreen leaves in chronically infertile habitats, such as tropical sand plains and temperate peat bogs, suggests that the pressures to conserve nitrogen and phosphorus are sufficient to produce evergreen plants even when water is freely available (Wardle et al. 2004). Many succulents have dense arrays of spines to protect the stored water and nutrients from being consumed by herbivores.

Carnivorous plants

In some habitats with low nitrogen and phosphorus availability, carnivorous plants exploit animal bodies as a supplementary source of nutrients (Givnish 1988). Worldwide, approximately 538 species of carnivorous plants have been described and classified in 18 genera and 8 families. Darwin appears to be the first to have realized that carnivorous plants are largely restricted to areas of infertile soils (Box 4.1). Some of the better-known genera are sundews (*Drosera* spp.), pitcher plants (*Sarracenia* spp.) and bladderworts (*Utricularia* spp.). In some sterile sites of South America and tropical Africa, the genus *Genlisea* (Lentibulariaceae) actually consumes soil protozoa.

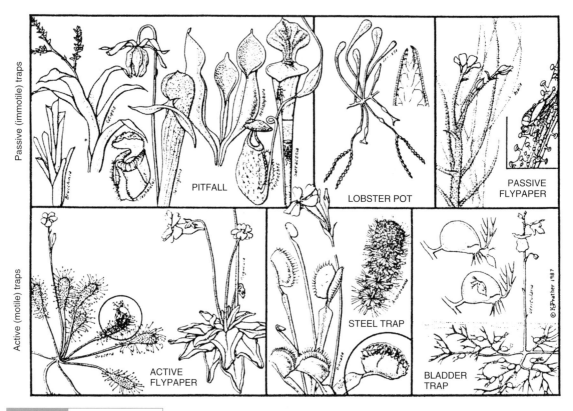

Passive (immotile) traps

Active (motile) traps

PITFALL

LOBSTER POT

PASSIVE FLYPAPER

ACTIVE FLYPAPER

STEEL TRAP

BLADDER TRAP

Figure 3.29 Carnivorous plants have evolved on at least six independent occasions as a response to chronic shortages of nitrogen and phosphorus (from Givnish 1988).

These plants have no roots, and produce only a small rosette of linear leaves above ground. Below ground are bundles of hollow subterranean leaves that chemically attract, entrap and then dissolve ciliates (Barthlott et al. 1998). The intensity of the pressure to acquire nitrogen and phosphorus is illustrated by evidence that carnivory seems to have arisen independently at least six times (Figure 3.29) (Givnish 1988).

Parasites

In deeply shaded habitats, there may be no source of energy save for that captured by taller neighbors. Parasitism could provide a plant with resources without necessitating light capture. Over 4500 species of vascular plants in 19 families are parasitic upon other plants (Nickrent 2006) from which they may take water and nutrients, and possibly photosynthates. Many parasitic plants have greatly-reduced leaves and root systems since they do not need to gather resources with these organs (Figure 3.30). Among the known parasitic plants, according to Kuijt (1969), there are no vascular cryptogams, one gymnosperm (*Parasitaxus ustus*) in New Caledonia (its host is also a member of the Podocarpaceae, Farjon 1998), and no monocots: "It is a startling and unexplained fact that the known parasitic vascular plants are limited to the dicotyledons" (p. 3). He suggests that parasitism has evolved independently at least eight times, five times in relatively

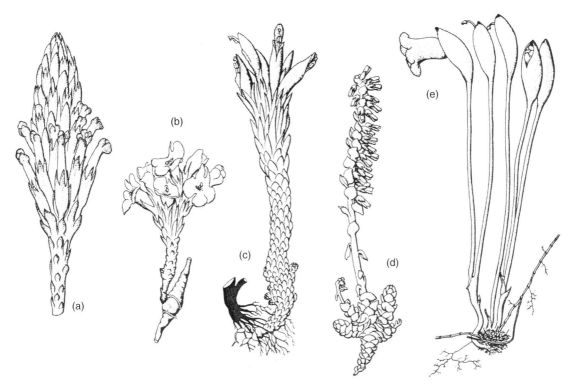

Figure 3.30 The broomrapes (Orobanchaceae) are most common in temperate or Mediterranean climates, and generally absent from tropical regions. These five examples lack chlorophyll and show the typical parasitic growth form with greatly reduced leaves and root systems. Indeed, such plants could be described as little more than parasitic inflorescences. (a) *Harveya squamosa*, slightly less than natural size, (b) *H. purpurea* on root of *Roella ciliata*, (c) *Hyobanche glabrata*, (d) *Lathraea squamaria*, and (e) *Aeginetia japonica* on *Miscanthus sinensis* (from Kuijt 1969).

large groups – Santalales, Scrophulariaceae and Orobanchaceae, Rafflesiaceae and Hydnoraceae, Balanophoraceae, Lennoaceae, and three times in isolated genera – *Cuscuta*, *Cassytha*, and *Krameria*. Evolutionary relationships of parasites are further addressed by Press and Graves 1995, Moreno et al. 1996, and Nickrent 2006.

The occurrence of parasitic plants has been documented for centuries. The large fleshy shoots of the Balanophoraceae appear superficially like a large fungus, but as early as 1729 Micheli reported in *Nova Plantarium Genera* that it was an actual vascular plant parasitic upon other plants. Similarly, the parasitic habit of the Rafflesiaceae was described in 1822 in the *Transactions of the Linnaean Society of London*. In spite of this, when Kuijt produced *The Biology of Parasitic Flowering Plants* in 1969, he was able to begin with the observation that no treatise on parasitic plants was yet available.

There is considerable variation in degree and nature of parasitism. Some species, termed **hemiparasites**, retain most of their photosynthetic ability and apparently take only water and mineral nutrients from hosts (e.g., some members of the Santalaceae, Loranthaceae and Scrophulariaceae). In more extreme cases, termed **holoparasites**, species may have no chlorophyll and be totally dependent upon their hosts for water, minerals, and photosynthetic products. This is the case in some members of the Orobanchaceae, Rafflesiaceae, and Balanophoraceae. Other species of plants, such as the ghostly white Indian pipe (*Montropa uniflora*), may superficially appear to be parasites, with reduced leaves and the absence of chlorophyll. Some of these plants (e.g., *Sarcodes, Monotropa, Corallorhiza*) instead are associated with fungi that are saprophytic or mycorrhizal. While most parasites attach to the roots of host plants, aerial parasites occur in three families: Cuscutaceae, Lauraceae, and Lornathaceae. The mechanism of parasitism is, however, similar across all groups: contact is made with the host through a **haustorium**, a specialized root that forms a connection between the vascular systems of the host and the parasite.

Although the novelty of this mode of existence is undeniable, its significance in actual plant communities is less clear. There are undoubtedly certain cases of host plants being damaged by parasites; certainly, some parasitic plants are thought to reduce growth of trees in commercial plantations (Musselman and Mann 1978). In most natural communities, it would appear that parasitism has a minor effect upon vegetation, particularly when compared with relatively strong factors such as competition and grazing. However, generalizations are still risky when there have been so few experiments with parasites in natural vegetation. Consider two examples.

Rhinanthus minor is a hemiparasite found in herbaceous vegetation of temperate areas. When it was experimentally removed from four different vegetation types in England, diversity increased in three of them (Watkinson and Gibson 1988). Preferred hosts such as *Koeleria macrantha* increased when the parasite was removed, while neighboring species such as *Festuca rubra* and *Carex arenaria* declined. In the one case where diversity declined, removal of the parasite apparently allowed the favored host plant, *Koeleria*, to increase and suppress neighboring species. *Cuscuta salina* is a parasitic twining plant on *Salicornia virginica* in the salt marshes of California. It damages *S. virginica*, thereby indirectly facilitating growth of two other marsh plants, *Limonium californicum* and *Frankenia salina* (Pennings and Callaway 1996). These presumed facilitative effects, however, vary with elevation.

In summary, parasitism is a distinctive method of resource acquisition often associated with traits including reduced leaves, lowered production of chlorophyll, and haustoria. In some circumstances, parasitic plants can influence the abundance of other plants – either their hosts or neighbors of their hosts. Because of the relative rarity of parasitic plants, however, their significance as factors controlling vegetation will probably always be rather low.

3.8.2 Conservation of scarce resources

Evergreen plants tend to have much lower tissue nutrient concentrations than deciduous plants (Aerts 1996). Evergreen leaves contain 14 percent nitrogen, compared to 22 percent in deciduous leaves. Evergreen leaves contain 1 percent phosphorus, compared to 1.6 percent in deciduous leaves. Thus, from the perspective of the plant, the construction costs of leaves (measured in terms of nutrients invested per unit weight of leaf tissue) is lower for evergreen than for deciduous leaves. Evergreen plants may therefore have an advantage in infertile habitats (Grime 1977, Wardle 2002). Further, evergreen plants will tend, in the longer run, to produce impoverished soils (Wardle et al. 2004).

But costs of construction are less than half the story. Ecologists, like economists (and like mining companies), often tend to emphasize extraction costs – the foraging and harvesting of resources needed for building new structures. This perspective omits the issues of conservation and recycling. Plants can recycle nutrients by removing elements from leaves before the leaves senesce and fall. This process of recycling is known as **resorption**. Completely wasteful plants would discard tissues without removing any nitrogen or phosphorus; completely conserving plants would remove all the nitrogen and phosphorus before senescence. What is the case with real plants? The proportion of nitrogen and phosphorus recovered from discarded leaves, termed **resorption efficiency**, is a measure of nutrient conservation (Killingbeck 1996). A survey of published studies on nutrient resorption in more than 200 species of plants (Aerts 1996) found that resorption efficiency differed little between nitrogen and phosphorus, or between deciduous and evergreen leaves – in all cases 50 percent resorption was a good first approximation. More precisely, nitrogen resorption efficiency was slightly lower in evergreen plants (47 percent) than in deciduous plants (54 percent), and phosphorus resorption efficiency was not significantly different between the two. The benefits of evergreen leaves would thus seem to arise from the low cost of construction rather than efficiencies of resorption.

Instead of measuring resorption efficiency (percent removal of nutrients) it is also possible to measure **resorption proficiency** (minimum concentration of nutrients in discarded leaves). In the case of proficiency, there are chemical limits on the amounts of nitrogen and phosphorus that can be extracted from discarded leaves, the lower limit being about 0.3 percent for nitrogen and 0.01 for phosphorus (Killingbeck 1996). In a study of resorption proficiency in 77 species of woody plants, Killingbeck found that evergreen and deciduous plants did not differ with respect to nitrogen whereas evergreen plants were significantly more proficient in resorbing phosphorus. Five species of evergreen plants were able to extract nitrogen and phosphorus to the lowest recorded levels of less than 0.3 percent for nitrogen and 0.01 for phosphorus: *Banksia grandis* (Australia), two species of *Eucalyptus* (Australia), *Lyonia lucida* (North America), and *Pinus rigida* (North America). Plant species that have leaves with leaf nutrient levels higher than these values, then, are not fully conserving foliar nutrients.

There are some discrepancies between the two foregoing studies, probably the result of measuring resorption efficiency (percent removal) as opposed to resorption proficiency (terminal concentration). Aerts's data showed that evergreen plants had greater efficiency of nitrogen removal, whereas Killingbeck's data showed that evergreen plants had greater proficiency of phosphorus removal. At the present, it is probably best to accept that both nutrients are

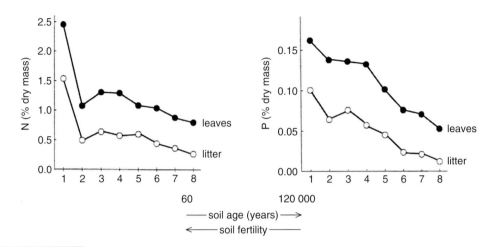

Figure 3.31 Concentrations of nitrogen and phosphorus in plant leaves decline along a gradient from young fertile soils (left) to old infertile soils (right). The concentrations in leaf litter (resorption proficiency) also decline. The numbers 1–8 indicate the rank order of site soil age from 60 to 120 000 years (after Richardson et al. 2005).

essential to plants, and that efficiency and proficiency are important but different measures of conservation ability in plants.

One way to measure the relationships between soil nutrients and plant responses exploits natural nutrient gradients. Relatively large-scale gradients are provided by retreating glaciers. The youngest soils occur where the ice has most recently melted. Some classic studies of ecological succession have used such circumstances (Section 9.4.2). A series of differently aged soils is sometimes called a chronosequence, from the word *khronos*, Greek for time. One such sequence in New Zealand provides a gradient of soils ranging from 60 to ca. 120 000 years old. The older soils are more infertile – available soil phosphorus declines from $5 \, mg \cdot kg^{-1}$ to $1 \, mg \cdot kg^{-1}$, while available nitrogen falls from $110 \, mg \cdot kg^{-1}$ to $15 \, mg \cdot kg^{-1}$. Richardson et al. (2005) collected leaves and recently fallen litter from eight communities arranged along this gradient. Figure 3.31 shows that nutrient concentrations in leaves declined along this gradient. It also shows that the resorption proficiency decreased with declining nutrient availability in soils, with the communities on the oldest soils having litter that approaches the minimum values previously described, 0.3 percent for nitrogen and 0.01 for phosphorus.

3.9 | Soils

Soils provide the large-scale template for patterns of nutrient availability and for plant distribution. At the same time, plant activities contribute to soil production. There is thus an ongoing set of complicated feedbacks between plants and soils, as well as among other components of ecosystems such as fungi and grazing animals. Here we will look at some of the basic processes that produce different soil types, and some of the procedures used in classifying them.

Soils vary across many scales, ranging from the local scale of meters (e.g., topographic scale, Figure 3.16) to the global scale of hundreds of kilometers (e.g., ecoregion scale, Figure 2.12). Without fertile soils to support farming, human civilization might never have progressed beyond the hunter-gatherer stage. It is no coincidence that two major centers of human culture developed on the fertile valley soils of the Middle East and Asia.

A few soil-forming processes can occur without living plants. Oxidation, for example, changes soil minerals such as iron, sulfur, uranium, and manganese into oxidized forms such as hematite, pyrite, uraninite, and manganese dioxide. Oxidation itself would not occur, however, without plants to produce oxygen (Section 1.6). Soils would not have formed, at least not in the conventional sense of the word, until plants invaded the land and provided a steady input of organic matter.

To start simply, the type of soil at a site can be attributed to just two causal factors, water and organic matter, with each of these being further divided between inputs and losses. This yields the following four factors that drive soil formation:

1. Rate of water infiltration
2. Rate of evapotranspiration
3. Rate of input of organic matter
4. Rate of decay of organic matter.

These factors drive processes at very small scales (centimeters of depth in the soil column) and at very large scales (thousands of kilometers across continents). At the very small scale, as water and minerals move through the soil column, and organic matter accumulates, distinctive regions form at different depths. These are known as soil horizons, and are often used in classifying soils. Some examples are shown in Figure 3.32. At the large scale, the very same factors produce major soil types in response to two basic climatic variables: temperature and rainfall. Rates of chemical processes, such as oxidation, are largely dependent upon temperature, and rates of leaching are largely determined by rainfall. Superimposed upon these are biological factors: rates of production generally increase with rainfall and temperature but so do rates of decomposition.

Although the above system provides a simple, mechanistic perspective, it largely ignores geology, topography, and time. Faulkner and Richardson (1989) use a five-parted definition and explanation regarding soil formation, observing that soil arising in any particular location is a function of (1) the parent material that (2) has been acted upon by organisms and (3) climate, and (4) conditioned by relief (5) over time. Further, the capacity of a soil to hold nutrients until captured by plants is determined by surface area and the surface charge of soil particles. Surface area, in turn, is determined by the fraction of clay-sized particles as well as by the content of organic matter. The electrical charge of the soil is also important. In most temperate zone soils, the soil particles have a net negative charge, thereby providing electrostatic bonding sites for positively charged

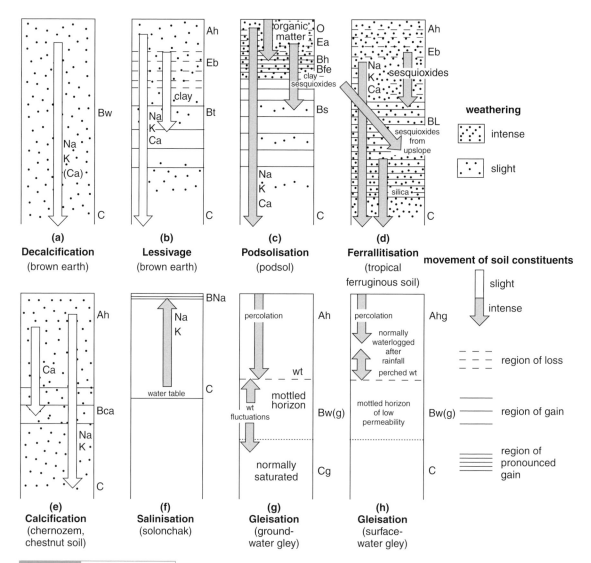

Figure 3.32 The basic processes of soil formation and the types produced (from White et al. 1992).

cations. These cations, ionically bound on the surface of soil particles, can exchange with other cations that are in solution. The cation exchange capacity measures the capacity of soil to hold cations on soil particles. Metal ions (Ca^{2+}, Mg^{2+}, Na^+) dominate in mineral soils, whereas hydrogen ions (H^+) dominate in areas with high organic content, such as peatlands.

Good soil maps are vital for studying plant distributions and vegetation types in landscapes. There are, however, multiple systems for soil classification and mapping. While no single system is yet universally accepted, the World Reference Base provides a harmonized global system (Deckers et al. 1998, Bridges et al. 1998). This system recognises 30 soil reference groups. Depending upon where you live, and the scale at which you work, you may also need to learn a local or regional system until there is global consensus. (As but one example of possible confusion, heavily weathered tropical soils can be called ferruginous soils or ferralsols.)

There is little point in listing all 30 types and their characteristics here: they are described and mapped in Deckers et al. (1998) and Bridges et al. (1998). The origins of these soil types lie largely in the climate and the vegetation types mapped in Chapter 2. The many different types of soils are, however, produced principally by the four factors listed on page 117 – the effects of water and organic matter. These effects can be expanded into eight categories of process, such as decalcification and levissage (Figure 3.32) to produce the major soil types of the world. For a much simpler view than the eight processes and 30 soil types, we can focus on just leaching by water and the accumulation of organic matter. Five common soil types then naturally arise: podsols, ferralsols, solonchaks, chernozems and histosols.

Certain soils are leached by excess rainfall. The typical **podsol** of northern forests has a relatively high organic content in part because of relatively low rates of decomposition. Clay particles and ions are leached by rainfall to accumulate in different soil horizons. This is very different from the typical **ferralsol** beneath tropical forests. Here high rates of decomposition produce soils with little organic matter, and heavy rainfall, in combination with the lack of organic matter, results in intense leaching. In arid climates, organic content tends to be low because primary production is low. High rates of evapotranspiration produce the opposite of leaching; ions such as Na^+ and K^+ are carried upward and deposited near the surface by evaporating water, producing a saline soil or **solonchak**. As rainfall increases, primary production increases and salinization decreases so that **chernozems** with high organic content form. Rainfall is neither so low that salinization occurs nor so high that leaching removes ions, and this balance results in soils highly productive for agriculture. **Histosols** occur where organic matter has accumulated as peat, and are commonly used in delineating wetlands.

In the United States of America, the soil classification system emphasizes amounts of weathering, and draws upon Latin and Greek terminology to designate ten soil orders (U.S.D.A. 1975, Steila 1993). Let us consider five of these. The most recently deposited soils, called **entisols**, lack any diagnostic horizons and include young sand dunes and recent delta sediments. **Aridisols** form where conditions are warm enough for plant growth, but where a lack of moisture constrains weathering. In such soils, calcification (the accumulation of calcium carbonate) or salinization (the accumulation of mineral salts) occurs. **Mollisols** are typical of grasslands. These fertile, dark-colored soils are thought to be formed primarily by the underground decomposition of the roots of grasses. **Spodosols** tend to form in cooler climates where conifers or ericaceous plants are found. Here, precipitation filtered through organic litter forms acids, which eventually allow clays to move downward, resulting in surface soils dominated by silicate minerals. **Ultisols** are deeply weathered acid soils formed in temperate landscapes that were not disturbed during the recent glaciations. Extremely long periods of weathering have leached soluble bases and allowed oxidation of iron and magnesium compounds.

Apart from plants and microscopic decomposers, invertebrates also play an important role in soil formation (Wardle 2002, Wardle et al. 2004). Chief among these are earthworms, of which there are some 3000 species. Their activities include dragging plant litter down their borrows into the soil, ingesting and macerating plant litter, producing fecal material, releasing urine and glandular secretions, increasing porosity, and supporting soil micro-organisms (including nitrogen-fixing micro-organisms) in their guts (Lee 1985). Although some earthworms in forests are confined to leaf litter or rotting logs, most excavate burrows. Up to half of the upper layers of forest soils consist of earthworm fecal material, and annual rates of production reach as high as $25 \text{ kg} \cdot \text{m}^{-2}$, in which case nearly one-quarter of the upper soil horizons are consumed and overturned each year. In his extensive studies on earthworms, Darwin (1881) documented how such activity results in the burial of stones and cinders at a rate of 0.25 to $0.5 \text{ mm} \cdot \text{year}^{-1}$. Lee suggests that earthworms are among the most ancient of terrestrial animal groups, which seems reasonable given that a subterranean habit would allow them to tolerate two stresses that would have faced early life on land: desiccation and high levels of ultraviolet radiation. Earthworms were once uncommon in some habitats, such as the eastern deciduous forests of North America, and their introduction is now having a major effect upon soils and vegetation (Bohlen et al. 2004).

3.10 | Two historical digressions

Only a few hundred years ago, it was still assumed that plants grow by feeding upon the soil, with roots acting in a manner similar to the stomachs of animals. Lieth (1975) observes that this hypothesis, advanced by Aristotle (384–322 BC) persisted until Jean Baptiste von Helmont (1579–1644) demolished it with an elegant experiment in the early 1600s. In Lieth's words:

> Von Helmont, besides performing odd experiments to find methods of obtaining mice from junk and sawdust, did one rather intelligent experiment. He grew a willow twig weighing 5 lb. in a large clay pot containing 300 lb. of soil, and irrigated it with rainwater. After 5 years, he harvested a willow tree of 16 lb. with a loss of only 2 oz of soil. Von Helmont concluded from this that water was condensed to form plants.
>
> (p. 8)

A more charitable overview of von Helmont (Magnusson 1990) notes that he showed the indestructibility of matter in chemical changes, invented the word gas, and was the first to take the melting point of ice and the boiling point of water as standards for temperature. His critical work in plant nutrition, which laid the foundation for modern studies of biogeochemical cycles, is underappreciated – a statement that can easily be confirmed by seeking his name in the indices of ecology texts such as McIntosh's (1985) history of ecology, or Marschner's (1995) treatise on mineral nutrition of plants. Von Helmont's willow experiment also laid the foundation for later research in agriculture, particularly Justus von Liebig's research on minerals in plant nutrition. According to Lieth, Liebig had to fight intensely against the still widely accepted view in the mid 1800s that plants lived by extracting humus from the soil.

Now to the New World. Gorham (1953) recounts early research by Titus Smith, Jr. (1768–1850), a native of New England who traveled with his father to Nova Scotia in 1783. Smith was commissioned by the governor of the colony to survey "the unfrequented areas of Nova Scotia, for the purpose of describing their natural resources, agricultural potentials, and suitability for settlement." The unpublished journals of these tours are deposited in the public Archives of Nova Scotia, but Smith's ecological ideas were also published in 1835 in the *Magazine of Natural History*, a report which Gorham suggests may well be the first major contribution to plant ecology in North America. This paper strongly emphasizes the contrast between vegetation of fertile and infertile habitats (an emphasis that would not surprise a visitor today interested in farming or plant ecology):

> Upon the fertile soils the vegetation is composed of hardwood, and succulent plants with annual leaves. Their growth is rapid, and the outer bark is extremely thin … Upon a barren soil the trees are evergreen, except the hacmetac: the greater parts of the shrubs and plants are evergreens. Their leaves contain more resinous and more woody matter, than the plants of fertile soils: they also have a strong thick epidermis. The trees on this soil grow slowly, the unusual quantity of epidermis increases in an inverse proportion to the growth of the tree.
>
> (p. 120)

3.11 Humans and soil resources

Soil resources are the basis of prosperity and power in agricultural societies. Here we will consider the impact of soil quality upon the Carthaginians and Mayans in turn; in Section 12.2.2 we will return to the larger issues of deforestation in ancient Rome and the Mediterranean. Rome and Carthage fought several wars. The Roman leader and former soldier, Cato, advocated a policy of justice and non-intervention with all foreign states – with one exception – Carthage (Durant 1944). Sent to Carthage on an official mission in

175 BC, he had been shocked by the rapid recovery of the city from the effects of preceding wars: "the fruitful orchards and vineyards, the wealth that poured in from revived commerce, the arms that mounted in the arsenals. On his return he held up before the Senate a bundle of fresh figs that he had plucked in Carthage three days before, as an ominous symbol of her prosperity and her nearness to Rome" (p. 105). In 150 BC the Roman fleet arrived offshore at Carthage. The Senate promised that if Carthage turned over 300 children of the noblest families as hostages, Carthage would remain free. Once this was done, the Romans demanded "the surrender of remaining ships, a great quantity of grain and all her engines and weapons of war." When these conditions too were met, the Romans insisted that the Carthaginians should leave their city and stay ten miles away while it was burned to the ground. The city revolted against its own leaders. Public buildings were demolished to provide metal and timber, statues were melted to make swords, and even the hair of women was collected to make ropes: "In two months the beleaguered city produced 8000 shields, 18 000 swords, 30 000 spears, 60 000 catapult missiles, and built in its inner harbor a fleet of 120 ships" (pp. 106–107). They withstood siege by land and sea for three years, but in 147 BC, the walls were breached. The Carthaginians fought on street by street. When the survivors were reduced from 500 000 to only 55 000, they surrendered; they were sold as slaves, and the city was turned over to the legions for pillage. The Roman Senate ordered that all of her allies were to be destroyed and, finally, that the soil should be ploughed with salt. The latter decision may be regarded as an early example of chemical warfare, since in a semi-arid climate it would be many years before more crops would grow.

In contrast to the Carthaginians, the Mayans may have been architects of their own demise for failing to conserve their soil resources. Binford et al. (1987) describe how, over a period of some 1000 years, the Mayan population of the Americas grew rapidly. The vegetation was gradually shifted from forest to grassland, and phosphorus was leached from the soils into water bodies (Figure 3.33). Binford et al. (1987) attribute the precipitous decline in the Mayan population in part to over exploitation of the land and the exhaustion of soils.

Over human history, at least three phases of soil erosion are recognized (McNeill and Winiwarter 2004). First, around 2000 BC, soil erosion accelerated as early river-basin civilizations expanded and ascended nearby forest slopes. Second, in the sixteenth to nineteenth centuries, stronger and sharper plowshares allowed agriculture to expand into the Eurasian steppe, the North American prairies and the South American pampas. Third, in the mid twentieth century, the combined effects of agricultural machinery, industrial nitrogen fixation (Box 3.2) and exponential human population growth began driving soil erosion.

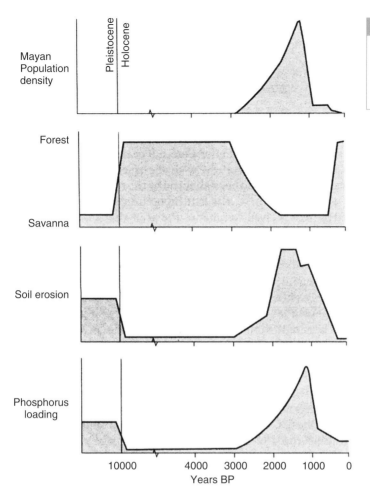

Figure 3.33 Mayan population density related to changes in vegetation, soil erosion, and phosphorus loading in sediments (from Keddy 2000 after Binford et al. 1987).

3.12 | Conclusion

Plants and animals share a need for the same set of resources, CHNOPS. Shortages of water, nitrogen or phosphorus frequently limit plant growth in natural habitats. There are often strong natural gradients in the availability of these resources, and they determine the distribution of plant species and the traits of these species. Figure 3.34 summarizes our understanding of differences between plant communities that contrast in resource availability. With this context, you may benefit from re-reading a more thorough treatment of the physiological processes involved in photosynthesis and nutrient uptake offered in introductory biology textbooks.

The way in which plants forage for resources is not well understood. Part of the problem may be that most of these processes occur underground. Other factors such as competition or herbivory may override natural selection for differing modes of resource

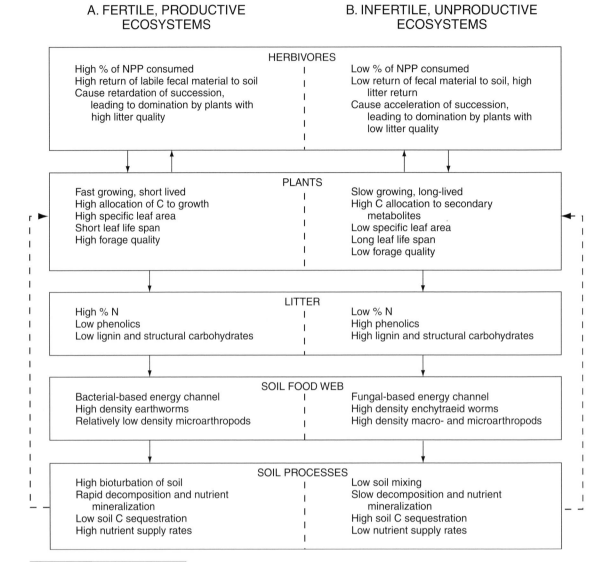

A. FERTILE, PRODUCTIVE
ECOSYSTEMS

B. INFERTILE, UNPRODUCTIVE
ECOSYSTEMS

HERBIVORES

High % of NPP consumed
High return of labile fecal material to soil
Cause retardation of succession,
    leading to domination by plants with
    high litter quality

Low % of NPP consumed
Low return of fecal material to soil, high
    litter return
Cause acceleration of succession,
    leading to domination by plants with
    low litter quality

PLANTS

Fast growing, short lived
High allocation of C to growth
High specific leaf area
Short leaf life span
High forage quality

Slow growing, long-lived
High C allocation to secondary
    metabolites
Low specific leaf area
Long leaf life span
Low forage quality

LITTER

High % N
Low phenolics
Low lignin and structural carbohydrates

Low % N
High phenolics
High lignin and structural carbohydrates

SOIL FOOD WEB

Bacterial-based energy channel
High density earthworms
Relatively low density microarthropods

Fungal-based energy channel
High density enchytraeid worms
High density macro- and microarthropods

SOIL PROCESSES

High bioturbation of soil
Rapid decomposition and nutrient
    mineralization
Low soil C sequestration
High nutrient supply rates

Low soil mixing
Slow decomposition and nutrient
    mineralization
High soil C sequestration
Low nutrient supply rates

Figure 3.34 A comparison of the effects of soils having high (left) and low (right) mineral resources. Low levels of resources produce plants that conserve resources, being slow-growing and long-lived. Such plants tend to support lower populations of herbivores. These plants also drop litter that decomposes slowly, reducing soil fertility, and producing microbial food webs dominated by fungi rather than bacteria (adapted from Wardle et al. 2004).

acquisition. Theoretical classifications of resource patterns (Figure 3.24) provide a system of organization, but few plant habitats can be accurately assigned to such categories. It may be that past work has overemphasized acquisition, while conservation of resources has been largely overlooked.

Ultimately it seems necessary to measure certain resource properties such as abundance, patchiness, or predictability, and then relate these to the ecological properties of plant communities. We may learn from other disciplines. Lavoisier observed in his treatise, *Elements of Chemistry*, in 1789 (Box 3.1) that, "We must trust to nothing but facts: these are presented to us by nature and cannot deceive" (p. 2). In resource acquisition and foraging, the transition from ideas to measurable properties, to quantitative relationships, and to experiments, still largely remains to be made. Perhaps this reflects a number of historical tendencies in ecology. Since many ecologists are initially attracted by organisms themselves, the study of plant ecology naturally begins with the distribution of the organisms rather than the distribution of their resources. Resources are generally more difficult to measure than plant distributions. Much of the scientific study of plants and resources comes from relatively fertile agricultural soils. Finally, ecologists have tended to seek out homogeneous environments where patterns in resource distribution are minimized. Seeking out situations with the least possible variation, and then expecting to find general scientific relationships, is not unlike going to the bookshelves in a convenience store to uncover the great trends in literature. Future research might benefit from two perspectives. Since so much of our knowledge comes from agricultural soils, much may be learned by the study of more extreme habitats and the novel ways in which plants cope with them. At the same time, the CHNOPS perspective reminds us that all life shares the need for but a few common resources, and hence there may be remarkable similarities among very different species. Finding the right trade-off between natural historical detail and broad scale generality is always a challenge in ecology.

Further reading

Harper, J. L. 1967. A Darwinian approach to plant ecology. *Journal of Ecology* **55**: 247–270.

Southwood, T. R. E. 1977. Habitat, the templet for ecological strategies? *Journal of Animal Ecology* **46**: 337–365.

Grime, J. P. 1977. Evidence for the existence of three primary strategies in plants and its relevance to ecological and evolutionary theory. *The American Naturalist* **111**: 1169–1194.

Chapin, III, F. S. 1980. The mineral nutrition of wild plants. *Annual Review of Ecology and Systematics* **11**: 233–260.

Smith, V. H. 1982. The nitrogen and phosphorus dependence of algal biomass in lakes: an empirical and theoretical analysis. *Limnology and Oceanography* **27**: 1101–1112.

Young, T. P. and C. K. Augspruger. 1991. Ecology and evolution of long-lived semelparous plants. *Trends in Ecology and Evolution* **6**: 285–289.

White, T. C. R. 1993. *The Inadequate Environment: Nitrogen and the Abundance of Animals*. Berlin: Springer-Verlag.

Marschner, H. 1995. *Mineral Nutrition of Plants*, 2nd edn. London: Academic Press.

Larcher, W. 2003. *Physiological Plant Ecology. Ecophysiology and Stress Physiology of Functional Groups*, 4th edn. Berlin: Springer.

Vitousek, P. M., J. Aber, R. W. Howarth *et al.* 1997. Human alteration of the global nitrogen cycle: causes and consequences. *Ecological Applications* **7**: 737–750.

Wardle, D. A., R. D. Bardgett, J. N. Klironomos, H. Setälä, W. H. van der Putten, and D. H. Wall. 2004. Ecological linkages between aboveground and belowground biota. *Science* **304**: 1629–1633.

Chapter 4

Stress

Definitions. Avoidance and tolerance. Stress as a metabolic cost. Measurement of stress in experiments. Evolution in stressed habitats. Plant traits and stress (low growth rate, seed size, clonal integration). Drought: deserts, Mediterranean shrublands (maquis, kwongan, fynbos), rock barrens (rock domes, tepui, alvars, serpentine), conifer forests. Resource unavailability (peat bogs). Regulators: salt marshes and mangal, Arctic and alpine plants, early spring leaves. Extremes: lichens on and in rocks, wetland plants. Acid precipitation in the Smoking Hills. Radiation. The issue of scale.

4.1 | Introduction

4.1.1 Definitions

Resources such as C, H, N, O, P, and S are essential for the construction of new plant tissues. We have just seen in Chapter 3 that habitats with a chronic scarcity of such resources tend to have plants that differ from those in habitats in which resources are more freely available. Shortages of resources will tend to reduce rates of growth, thereby reducing attributes such as shoot size, root length, and allocation to flowers and seeds (Levitt 1980, Grime 1979, Larcher 2003). **Stress** is therefore defined as *any factor that reduces the rate of production of biomass*. It is important to understand that stress is different from disturbance, because disturbance, as we shall see in Chapter 6, removes only biomass that has already been produced.

Like any word, the term stress can be used carelessly. Too often, as Harper (1982) observes, it has meant "little more than the observer judging what I don't think I'd like if I was a buttercup, kangaroo, flea, beetle, etc." Careless use of this word can have at least three serious consequences for the development of plant ecology. If one cannot measure the degree of unsuitability of a habitat:

1. One cannot predict the probable consequences for the characteristics of plant communities.
2. One cannot compare published studies.
3. One cannot test many hypotheses that use the word stress.

The careless use of a term, however, need not render it valueless; it may simply emphasize the need for a more discerning application. Because the term stress is frequently misunderstood, Section 4.1.2 will examine its use in more depth.

There is a vast and growing scientific literature describing the physiological mechanisms by which plants respond to stress, and it would be possible to devote a life time to the study of how selected species respond to selected environmental constraints. Levitt (1980), for example, has written a two-volume review on environmental constraints, excluding nutrient deficiencies, the latter being covered in Marschner (1995). Further, Larcher (2003) has provided an overview of physiological ecology. This chapter draws upon these three sources where necessary. The emphasis in this chapter is, however, upon general principles that apply to a broad array of types of plants and plant communities. The intention is to describe the evolutionary consequences of survival under conditions that continually constrain growth, and the types of vegetation that arise under such conditions. Given the vast number of plant species in the biosphere and the large number of constraints that can affect them, some such generalizations must be made. The mechanisms by which such effects arise at the molecular, cellular, and tissue levels are not addressed in depth here, since fine texts by better-qualified authors are already available. It would still be helpful (although not strictly necessary) to have some basic understanding of how stress acts at the lower levels of organization such as cells and tissues, and those wishing to pursue this knowledge can consult the above three sources.

4.1.2 More on terminology

Although we will use the definition of stress in Section 4.1.1, you should know that other books (e.g., Levitt 1980, Larcher 2003) use the term differently. Larcher (2003) warns against its careless use, "In order to avoid any misunderstanding, the meaning of the term stress must in every case be well defined and unambiguous: *stress factor* (or *stressor*) indicates the stress stimulus, and *stress response* or *state of stress* denotes the response to the stimulus as well as the ensuing state of adaptation" (p. 346).

Levitt (1977, 1980) uses two terms, stress and strain. **Stress** is the external pressures put on an organism by its environment, and **strain** is the degree to which the physiology of the organism is damaged by that stress. An organism can therefore adapt to a stress by either (1) increasing the stress necessary to produce a specific strain or (2) decreasing the strain produced by a specific stress (Levitt 1980). In the first case, while the organism cannot alter the external stress, it can prevent the penetration of the stress into its tissues; this is called **stress avoidance**. Some kind of barrier is generally used to prevent the stress from causing strain. Alternatively the organism may allow the stress to enter its tissues but all the same avoid the internal damage. An organism with **stress tolerance** is able to prevent, decrease, or repair the injurious strain induced by the stress. In the case of flooding, for example, the strategy of stress avoidance supplies oxygen to the tissues; the strategy of stress tolerance adapts a metabolism to withstand low oxygen concentrations (Section 4.6.3).

4.2 | Some general consequences of stress

4.2.1 Short-term effects: stress has metabolic costs

In Chapter 3 we saw that foraging for resources incurs costs. These costs might be measured as the energy expended to transport ions across root membranes, as the energy invested in constructing roots to forage for nutrients, or as the nitrogen invested in constructing new leaves to forage for light. The general effect of stress is to reduce the return per unit of investment. This generalization applies to all plants (and all living organisms) whether typical of stressed or productive habitats. The lower the availability of resources, the lower the return for any investment, and the higher the cost of survival. Recall from the previous chapter that the respiratory energy costs of ion uptake in a species of sedge (*Carex diandra*) was as high as 36% of available ATP (van der Werf et al. 1988).

To survive, any individual must maintain a positive energy balance; that is, the rate of photosynthesis must exceed the rate of respiration. Shortages of resources tend to simultaneously reduce rates of photosynthesis and increase rates of respiration. Consider a plant growing in a productive site that is temporarily droughted. Closed stomata will reduce the rate of water loss, but will simultaneously inhibit rates of photosynthesis. Since living cells continue to respire, the ratio of respiration to photosynthesis climbs. If respiration exceeds photosynthesis, the plant is living on stored resources, and if this continues for sufficient time, the plant will exhaust these stored reserves and die. Further, in order to obtain water, particularly if neighbors are present depleting the same scarce water, energy must be expended to build new roots to forage for water. Hence, just when respiration rates are already high, and photosynthesis rates are already low, added resources may have to be expended for survival.

The first definition of stress (Section 4.1.1) may therefore be rephrased: **stress** *is any factor that increases the metabolic costs of survival, and the intensity of the stress is measurable by the amount of energy consumed to deal with it.* This accords nicely with the view that energy is the common currency with which to measure the ecological consequences of various phenomena.

One general experimental procedure for examining stress would be to grow individuals along a gradient of resource availability and measure their performance under different conditions. A physiologist might measure metabolic effort as, say, grams CO_2 emitted per unit of time, at each position along the gradient. A less elegant, but usually satisfactory alternative is to use biomass as an indicator of performance. Reductions in biomass represent the net costs imposed by each set of conditions. It would also be possible to measure the relative growth rates for each treatment as the difference in biomass per unit time. If we designate the best observed growth in the most benign treatments as P_0, and growth in a particular less suitable treatment as P_i, the intensity of stress would therefore be calculated as $[(P_0 - P_i)/P_0] \times 100$ for any point P_i along the gradient. Relationships like these, between performance and resources, are commonly seen in experiments. What is less appreciated is that they equally provide a means to estimate the metabolic costs of stress.

Grasses along a resource gradient

Austin and Austin (1980) created a nutrient gradient using from $\frac{1}{64}$ to 16 times the recommended concentration of a nutrient solution and grew 10 species of grass along it. The plants were grown alone and in both 5- and 10-species mixtures.

First consider the response of these species when grown alone; that is, their physiological response to the gradient. All 10 had similar patterns of performance, with maximum biomass being reached in the 4 to 8 × concentrations (the 16 × concentration appeared slightly toxic). There was a geometric increase in growth, from less than a gram per pot at $\frac{1}{64}$ concentration to as high as 100–200 g per pot in the 4 to 8 × concentrations. This result – that plants grew bigger when fertilized – is not in itself surprising, but given that these grasses occupied different habitats in the field, their uniform response in the lab is noteworthy. The fact that species with different field distributions have similar experimental responses had been described before by Ellenberg (Austin and Austin 1980), who proposed the terms "ecological response" to describe field distributions and "physiological response" to describe lab performance patterns. (Zoologists have since invented the terms "fundamental niche" and "realized niche" to describe the same phenomenon.) Ellenberg attributed the differences between physiological and ecological responses to competition, with weaker competitors being displaced from their preferred habitat by better competitors. [Similar patterns in the zoological realm were documented by Miller (1967) and Colwell and Fuentes (1975), with competition again being offered as the cause.] Ernst (1978) challenged the role of competition in explaining the discrepancy, rightly pointing out that in comparing lab gradients with field gradients, there were many differences between them besides the presence of competition.

There is often difficulty in comparing lab and field experiments. If Austin and Austin had shown that plants with different field distributions had identical physiological responses, one would have been left unable to invoke competition with any confidence, but they also grew the species in mixture. Figure 4.1 shows that in mixture, the shapes of the response curves were very different from one another. Species such as *Festuca ovina*, *Vulpia membranacea*, and *Poa annua* (which had all reached maximum biomass in the 4 to 8 × concentrations when grown alone) now declined in relative importance as nutrient levels increased. Their actual biomass still increased in a similar manner, but their proportional contribution

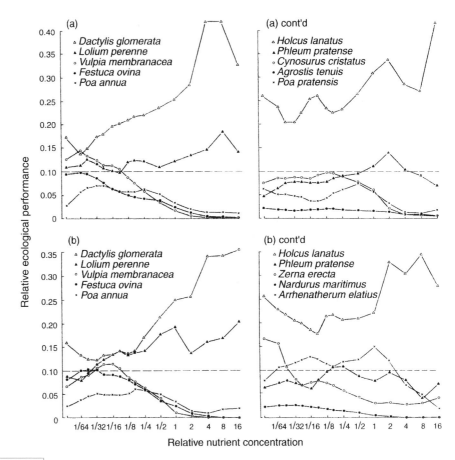

Figure 4.1 Relative ecological performance (proportion that a species forms of the yield of all species in that pot) of species in two 10-species mixtures (a, b) along a nutrient gradient. Sum of all species in a treatment is 1.0. Dashed line shows expected value if all species had the same performance (from Austin and Austin 1980).

did not. The discrepancy between the two curves (grown alone and in mixture) was clearly attributable to competition from neighboring grasses. The shift from physiological response to ecological response can be explained by two factors. The first is competitive displacement. The second is the tendency for the competitive dominants at the fertile end (e.g., *Dactylis glomerata, Holcus lanatus*) to also be the largest plants under fertile conditions. In other words, the species growing fastest and largest in monoculture also tended to grow fastest and largest in mixture, thereby monopolizing the fertile end of the gradient.

Austin (1982) suggested that these results could be better understood by dividing the nutrient gradient into five zones. At the extreme left end (tap water only), there was "extreme nutrient deficiency." From $\frac{1}{64}$ to $\frac{1}{6} \times$ there was "nutrient limited performance." From ¼ to 2 × the canopy closed, so that there was "nutrient/shading interaction determining performance." From 4 to 8 ×, shading and nutrient toxicity predominated and at 16 × there was extreme nutrient toxicity. This suggests an interpretation where competition intensity increases from $\frac{1}{64}$ to 8 ×, with competition for light predominating from 4 to 8 ×. Regrettably, calculations of these effects are not reported.

Wetland plants along a resource gradient

To pursue these questions further, let us explore the responses of 11 wetland plants to a fertility gradient similar to that used by Austin and Austin (1980). Biomass of both individual species and of the mixture increased exponentially along the gradients; the mixture, for example, ranged from <5 g per pot to >50 g per pot. All species tested grew best at the higher fertilities; that is, low nutrient availability was a stress for all species tested. Thus far, the experiment repeats Austin and Austin's results, except that in this case there was little evidence of toxicity.

Mean competition intensity was then determined for each fertility level. This was calculated from the sum of the differences between the performance with and without neighbors over all species. The very lowest fertility level had a significantly lower intensity of competition (0.6) than all the others, which were very similar at 0.8; that is, irrespective of fertility, neighbors reduced plant performance on average by some 80 percent, except at the lowest fertility level where it was only a 60 percent reduction. Clearly, competition had a major effect upon performance, but there was little evidence for change in competition intensity along the gradient.

Performance was actually simultaneously reduced by two factors: low fertility and neighbors. The relative importance of these factors can be compared. Total strain (effects of nutrient stress and competition) can be calculated for each level by comparing plant performance in mixture to the best performance when grown alone (usually growth at the highest fertility level). Total strain minus performance reduction due to competition (as determined above) gives strain due to low fertility. Figure 4.2 shows that the contribution of strain from competition to total strain showed a major shift. At the infertile end of the gradient, plant performance was reduced almost entirely by physiological stress from lack of nutrients. At the fertile end of the gradient, plant performance was reduced almost entirely by competition.

4.2.2 The costs of adaptation to stress

It is imperative to separate in one's mind the short-term consequences of stress, that is reduced photosynthesis and increased respiration, from the long-term consequences that result from natural selection (evolutionary adaptation). Confusion can arise because of language; stress can be short-term or chronic, adaptation is used to describe short-term physiological changes (e.g., closure of stomata, wilting) or long-term genetic changes (e.g., reduction in the number of stomata). All plants must experience periods of stress, and natural selection continually eliminates those least able to tolerate the stress. But in some habitats, the effects of stress have been so extreme that the plants show particularly dramatic changes in physiology, anatomy, or growth form. Early classifications of plant form, such as that of Raunkiaer (Figure 2.8), recognized those changes in

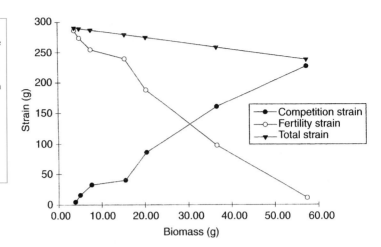

Figure 4.2 Competition and fertility strain change in importance along an experimental nutrient gradient. Total strain is the sum of the differences in biomass between optimum growth and growth in a competition treatment for all species. Fertility is represented by biomass (mean total for a competition treatment) (from Keddy 2001).

morphology that were related to stress from extremes of climate. Raunkiaer wrote:

> I have ... chosen the adaptation of the plant to survive the unfavourable season, having special regard to the protection of the surviving buds or shoot-apices. The continued existence of the individual depends upon the preservation of the buds ... if the plant survives the unfavourable season it will manage without difficulty to get through the favourable season.
>
> (Raunkiaer 1908, pp. 112–113)

It is traditional to cover the topic of adaptations to stress by reviewing either the kinds of factors that produce stress (e.g., drought, cold, infertility), or else by reviewing the kinds of habitats that illustrate stress (e.g., deserts, tundra, sand dunes). Before reviewing such examples, here are two themes to keep in mind during this chapter.

1. Adaptation to stress incurs evolutionary costs, usually with the primary consequence of slower growth, often with further secondary consequences for processes such as herbivory and competition.
2. Stressed habitats need careful consideration in planning the selection and management of natural areas.

Let us examine these themes further. First, adaptation to stress always involves costs. For every benefit accrued, there is also a cost incurred. The most obvious costs can be measured as the energy or nutrient investment in traits such as spines or thick layers of wax. Other adaptations incur more subtle costs, what we might call the costs of forgone opportunities. Generally, this involves the loss of the ability to exploit better conditions. Natural selection for reduced density of stomata in desert plants, for example, may have enhanced survival in extremely dry climates. If, however, there are short-term improvements in water availability, such drought-resistant plants may be unable to transpire rapidly enough to take full advantage of pulses of water and nutrients. That is, the adaptation to the stress involves a trade-off, usually some loss of some ability to exploit good conditions fully. If the benign conditions persist, the plants that are capable of tolerating adverse conditions may actually be replaced by species better able to exploit the improved conditions.

There is now good evidence that adaptation to extreme conditions frequently incurs reductions in inherent growth rates (Grime 1977, 1979, Loehle 1998a). The previous example of reduction in density of stomata illustrates how natural selection can produce traits that adapt a plant to stress but simultaneously limit growth rates under better conditions. More generally, it seems that there are at least three potential causes of low growth rates in plants tolerant of stress. These are better understood in the case of cold tolerance, so let us digress and briefly consider some of the inherent costs of adaptation to cold (Larcher 2003, Loehle 1998a).

1. *Higher production costs.* Plants from cold regions have thicker leaves, cell walls, and cuticles. The increased strength of leaves likely reduces deformation when the leaf is frozen. The cost of this tolerance to freezing is incurred in the added costs of energy and nutrients needed to produce such strongly lignified leaves.

2. *Higher operating costs.* Many northern leaves contain a variety of chemical compounds including lipids and sugars that act as anti-freeze, allowing leaves to reach lower temperatures without physical damage from frozen and ruptured cells. Anti-freeze compounds, however, not only have production costs, but high concentrations may interfere with other aspects of cellular metabolism. Such interference is likely to reduce growth rates.

3. *Selection for risk aversion.* Periods of extreme stress are likely to select for traits that minimize risk rather than traits that maximize growth. That is, even if production costs and operating costs were zero, there might still be selection for cautious growth. A northern plant that produces shoots rapidly in early spring may be killed by a late frost. The advantage of growing earlier than most neighbors would seem to be substantial, but this advantage may be balanced by the high costs of damage during unfavorable years. Hence, the logic goes, plants from stressful habitats minimize risk by cautiously investing in production of new roots and shoots. To draw upon a human analogy, this is equivalent to investing one's retirement money in low yielding bonds, rather than putting it all in the stock market. True, the stock market can produce much greater returns – but it simultaneously increases the risk of catastrophic losses. In plant communities, catastrophic loss usually means death and a failure to contribute to future generations. Those plants present today are the progeny of the cautious investors, since the risk-takers have died during bad periods.

The net result of these factors is a conservative growth strategy that tracks the long-term average or the worst conditions and fails to respond to enrichment or favorable growing conditions.

(Loehle 1998a, p. 736)

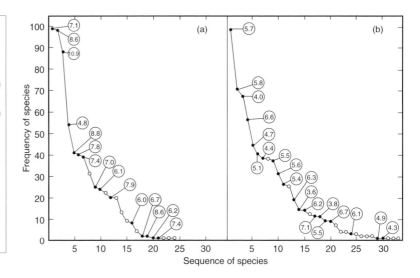

Figure 4.3 Comparison of two one-square-meter samples of vegetation showing the degree of dominance (frequency) and the relative growth rate (value in circle) for each species. (a) a productive meadow (Coombsdale, Derbyshire) and (b) an ancient limestone pasture (Cressbrookdale, Derbyshire). Solid dots show the species for which estimates of maximum relative growth rate (RGR $_{(max)}$ in mg·g^{-1}·h^{-1}) had been determined under controlled laboratory conditions (after Grime 1973a).

Hence, the relative growth rates of species in stressful habitats tend to be measurably lower than those from other habitats, even when they are grown in experimental conditions where the stress no longer occurs (Grime and Hunt 1975, Grime 1977, 1979). Figure 4.3 illustrates this with a comparison of the plant species in two British habitats: a productive grassland and an ancient limestone pasture (Grime 1973a). The numbers in the large open circles give the maximum relative growth rates (RGR $_{(max)}$ in mg·g^{-1}h^{-1}) measured under conditions with freely available water, light, and nutrients. It is apparent that the species found in ancient limestone pasture tend to grow more slowly than those in productive grassland. These differences in relative growth rates are all the more noteworthy, since they occur in relatively similar floras within the same region of England. Comparisons among regions with greater stress differences have yet to be made, but the differences would likely be much larger.

4.2.3 Growth rate

The inherently low growth rates in stressed habitats, then, arise not only because resources for growth are in short supply, but because natural selection has consequently shaped species in such habitats to be inherently conservative and slow-growing. This has important implications for both plant ecology and resource management, many of which will be encountered later in this book. Let us briefly list some of them here:

1. Stressed habitats will, in general, recover more slowly from disturbance. Hence, grazing, logging, or the use of off-road vehicles may have to be strictly controlled or entirely prohibited in stressed vegetation types.
2. Since the balance between disturbance rates and recovery rates likely determines plant diversity (Section 11.7.3), slow recovery rates might lead to higher plant diversity in areas with inherently

low rates of disturbance. But in contrast, when disturbance is higher still, stressed areas may be unable to support vegetation at all.

3. When a stressed site is fertilized, plants with inherently low growth rates will likely be displaced by species with higher growth rates. In many cases, this results in rare plant species such as those of pine barrens or chalk grassland being replaced by widespread and common species (Section 11.11).

4. Owing to the high costs of producing leaves, plants of stressed conditions may also have higher investments in anti-herbivore protection (Figure 3.34, Section 7.3.3).

Stressed sites also tend to have other distinctive botanical characteristics that may be unrelated to slow growth rates:

5. Some sites with chronic stress seem to accumulate large numbers of plant species. The fynbos of South Africa (Section 11.6.1) and the tepui of the Guyana highlands (Section 12.4.5) are apparently inhospitable habitats, yet areas with extremely high plant diversity.

6. Most stressed sites seem to have higher below-ground competition than above-ground competition (Section 5.6.5, Figure 9.35).

7. Wet areas with low nutrient availability often have carnivorous plants (Box 4.1, Section 11.6.2).

8. The kinds of mycorrhizae change with the intensity of stress (Figures 3.19 and 8.6).

9. Stressed conditions also seem to increase the likelihood of positive interactions among plants (Section 8.2).

Note that few of these effects are direct – many stressed habitats reveal their unusual characteristics only when disturbance or eutrophication occur, or when herbivory or competition is also examined. Owing to their suite of distinctive species and communities, however, stressed communities are of considerable interest to plant ecologists. Many even have distinctive names such as alvars, maquis, fynbos, and kwongan. What they all share is one or more environmental conditions that strongly constrain the growth of plants.

4.2.4 Seed size

There is enormous variation in seed size among plants, some of the smallest being the dust-like seeds of orchids (ca. 0.0001 mg) to the 20-kg seeds of the double coconut (Figure 4.4). In the preceding chapter we saw that there is an inherent trade-off in allocating resources to reproduction: the production of many small seeds as opposed to the production of a few large seeds. Other factors that likely influence seed size include the mode of dispersal used, coevolution with herbivores that disperse seeds, adaptations to specific germination conditions, and the ability to form long-lived seed banks (Section 6.6.1). There is a growing consensus that plants with seedlings that establish under stressful conditions will allocate more

Box 4.1 | The discovery of carnivorous plants

The discovery of carnivorous plants and of the relationship between carnivory and infertile soils were other contributions made to science by Charles Darwin. Before an introduction to his monumental treatise on Sundews, consider the times in which he worked. Despite his wealth and privilege – as described by Desmond and Moore (1991), two of Darwin's many biographers – the productive period of Darwin's writing life (ca. 1840–1880) was a time of both political and personal turmoil. It is true that the British Empire was near the peak of power and prestige, and that Darwin himself was wealthy, but Europe was in chaos. There was, for example, famine in Ireland, and falling corn prices hit farm incomes, including those of Darwin's own tenants; Darwin was forced to reduce rents. At the same time, his "old sickness was as virulent as ever . . .. Friends thought him a hypochondriac, because he routinely trotted it out as an excuse . . .. But he was no malingerer. The sickness was real and distressing, although no one knew what caused it" (p. 335).

In 1848 an insurrection swept Italy. Barricades went up in Paris at the same time, protesters were shot, the troops mutinied, and the French King abdicated; 30 000 communists were said to be planning revolution. Panic spread among the wealthy, even in England, where 150 000 Chartists were expected to converge in London to support their demands for land taxes, property taxes, and wealth taxes – all of which would have hit Darwin hard. Eighty-five thousand special constables were sworn in "to quell the insurrection by force" (p. 353).

His health continued to fail. "Nine months of nagging fears and obsessive work had taken their toll, leaving Charles chronically depressed. Waves of dizziness and despondency swept over him. Through the winter he suffered dreadful vomiting fits every week. His hands started trembling and he was 'not able to do anything one day out of three.' There were disquieting new symptoms: involuntary twitching, fainting feelings, and black spots before his eyes" (p. 361). He was convinced that death was approaching.

There was carnage in Crimea. By 1871 Paris was under siege. "Dogs and cats were being eaten, and rats brought a franc each in the starving streets" (p. 578). The city then fell to Prussian troops.

The *Origin of Species*, published in 1859, had been a great success, but by 1871 Darwin had become an invalid, impeded by the chronic illness that frequently left him unable to work at all, or a best an hour or two a day. Even the news that *Expression of the Emotions* had sold over 5000 copies failed to inspire him. Not only had his beloved daughter Annie died in 1851 at the age of ten, baby Charles was retarded, Henrietta was already an invalid and George and Horace were ill and home for nursing. His close friend and supporter, Hooker, was being broken by court action, and Darwin took up a collection for him, raising £2000. The local vicar was scheming and imposing his plans upon projects such as a public reading room supported by the Darwins. In spite or perhaps because of these distractions, Darwin focused his remaining energy upon his sundews:

Darwin sprinted on with *Insectivorous Plants*, plagued by the interminable manuscript. The prose was muddy, and by February he was bogged down and gasping. He hardly helped George's low spirits by commiserating, "I know well the feeling of life being objectless & all being vanity of vanities." He was even "ready to commit

suicide," a startled Hooker heard, and the death of an old, sad Lyell on the 22nd
[of February] left him feeling "as if we were all soon to go."

(p. 613)

Insectivorous Plants appeared that year and sold out quickly; "in July a 1000 copy
reprint vanished within a fortnight. The name Darwin was a draw now however odd
the subject. Who could imagine a 450-page catalogue of plant experiments selling
faster than the *Origin of Species*?" (p. 616).

Let us now leave his biographers, and let him speak for himself. The book
begins:

> During the summer of 1860, I was surprised by finding how large a number of
> insects were caught by the leaves of the common sun-dew (*Drosera rotundifolia*) on
> a heath in Sussex.
>
> (p. 1)

In his memoirs, edited by his son Francis (Darwin 1950), he describes it thus:

> In the summer of 1860 I was idling and resting near Hartfield where two species of
> *Drosera* abound; and I noticed that numerous insects had been entrapped by the
> leaves. I carried home some plants, and on giving them insects saw the movements
> of the tentacles, and this made me think it probable that the insects were caught for
> a special purpose. Fortunately a crucial test occurred to me, that of placing a large
> number of leaves in various nitrogenous and non-nitrogenous fluids of equal
> density; and as soon as I found that the former alone excited energetic movements,
> it was obvious that here was a fine new field for investigation.
>
> During subsequent years, whenever I had leisure, I pursued my experiments,
> and my book *Insectivorous Plants* was published in July 1875 – that is, sixteen years
> after my first observations.
>
> (p. 62)

Returning to *Insectivorous Plants*, Charles Darwin summarizes the benefits arising
from carnivory:

> The absorption of animal matter from captured insects explains how *Drosera* can
> flourish in extremely poor peaty soil, – in some cases where nothing but sphagnum
> moss grows, and mosses depend altogether on the atmosphere for their
> nourishment.
>
> (p. 14)

The mechanism is relatively simple. The leaves of *Drosera* are round and
covered in gland-bearing tentacles that secrete a sticky fluid (Figure B4.1):

> When an insect alights on the central disc, it is instantly entangled by the viscid
> secretion, and the surrounding tentacles after a time begin to bend, and ultimately
> clasp it on all sides. Insects are generally killed, according to Dr. Nitschke, in about a
> quarter of an hour, owing to their trachea being closed by the secretion.
>
> (p. 13)

In the second edition of *Insectivorous Plants* completed by his son, Francis
Darwin, in 1888, we find the description of additional experiments carried out by
Francis (pp. 15–16):

> My experiments were begun in June 1877, when the plants were collected and
> planted in six ordinary soup-plates. Each plate was divided by a low partition into
> two sets, and the *least* flourishing half of each culture was selected to be 'fed'. While

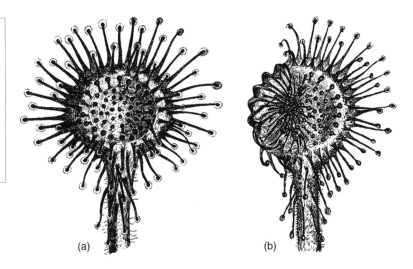

Figure B4.1 The upper surface of the leaves of *Drosera rotundifolia* (round-leaved sundew), Charles Darwin (1809–1882) determined, is covered by an average of 192 tentacles (a). When he placed a piece of meat on the disc, the tentacles on that side inflected over it as they would with an insect (b). These drawings were made by his son, George (from Darwin 1888).

(a)   (b)

the rest of the plants were destined to be 'starved'. The plants were prevented from catching insects for themselves by means of a covering of fine gauze, so that the only animal food they obtained was supplied in very minute pieces of roast meet given to the 'fed' plants but withheld from the 'starved' ones. After only 10 days the difference between the fed and starved plants was clearly visible: the fed plants were of brighter green and the tentacles of a more lively red. At the end of August the plants were compared by number, weight, and measurement, with the following striking results:

	Starved	Fed
Weight (without flower-stems)	100	121.5
Number of flower-stems	100	164.9
Weight of stems	100	231.9
Number of capsules	100	194.4
Total calculated weight of seed	100	379.7
Total calculated number of seeds	100	241.5

These results show clearly enough that insectivorous plants derive great advantage from animal food. It is of interest to note that the most striking difference between the two sets of plants is seen in what relates to reproduction – i.e. in the flower-stems, the capsules, and the seeds.

energy to individual seeds to better support the early establishment phase of the seedling (Westoby et al. 1997). Figure 4.5 shows evidence consistent with this view. Nine woody plant species with an array of seed sizes were established in shade and their death rates then monitored (Grime and Jeffrey 1965). The trees with the larger seeds (e.g., *Quercus rubra*, *Castanea mollissima*) had much lower death rates than those with smaller seeds (*Betula lenta*, *B. populifolia*).

By contrast, Salisbury (1942), after making an exhaustive study of seed production, observed that several groups of plants occurring in

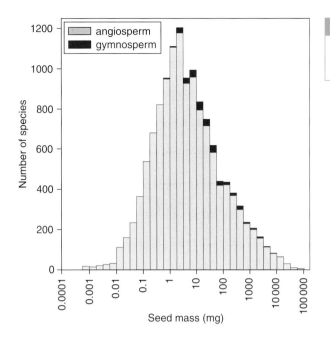

Figure 4.4 Frequency distribution for seed mass across 12 987 seed plant species (Moles et al. 2005).

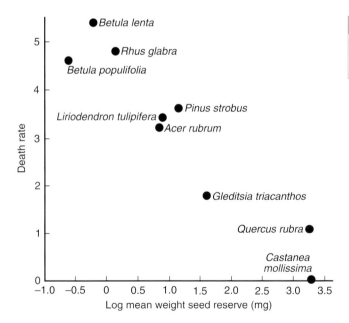

Figure 4.5 The relationship between death rate in shade and seed size for nine tree species (from Grime and Jeffrey 1965).

stressed habitats have extremely small seeds (Figure 4.6) in which "the food provision for the germinating seedling is meagre in the extreme" (p. 5). This is particularly characteristic of the families Orchidaceae, Pyrolaceae, and Ericaceae. "[I]t may be as an epiphyte, in the dim light of a tropical rain forest; as a terrestrial orchid, in the close turf of a chalk down; or as a pyrola in the dull illumination of a calluna heath or a pine wood" (p. 5), but the seedling is able to capture

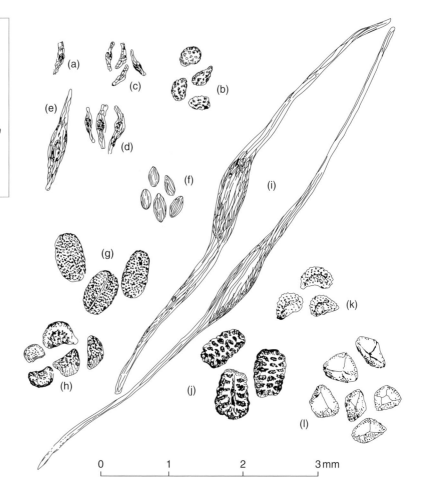

Figure 4.6 A selection of dust-sized seeds found in the British flora. (a) *Gymnadenia conpsea* (an orchid), (b) *Orobanche elatior* (parasitic), (c) *Pyrola secunda*, (d) *Pyrola media*, (e) *Drosera anglica*, (f) *Crassula tillaea*, (g) *Digitalis purpurea*, (h) *Polycarpon tetraphyllum*, (i) *Narthecium ossifragum*, (j) *Scrophularia nodosa*, (k) *Spergularia rubra*, (l) *Samolus valerandi* (from Salisbury 1942).

sufficient resources through mycorrhizal fungi (Section 8.3). Two other plant groups also have extremely small seeds, saprophytic plants (Section 8.3.4) and parasitic plants (Figure 3.30). The former also have fungal associates, while the latter are directly attached to neighboring plants.

4.2.5 Clonal integration

Plants need not produce seed at all. One of the remarkable features of plants is their capacity for clonal growth – growth without sexual reproduction. The bodies of mammals reach a certain size and stop growing; then they require sexual activity for reproduction. Most plants, in contrast, have multiple growing points called meristems, and if some meristems are damaged, the others will continue growth. Plants can therefore grow to indeterminately large sizes – either in height, as in trees, or laterally, as in many herbaceous plants.

Clonal reproduction appears to be particularly common in stressful habitats (Grime 1977) such as deserts (Gibson and Nobel 1986), tundra (Savile 1972), freshwater wetlands (Sculthorpe 1967) and salt

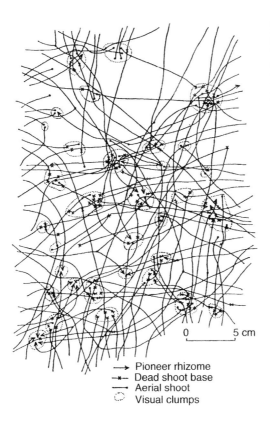

Figure 4.7 The arrangement of aerial shoots and rhizomes in an established sward of *Calamagrostis neglecta* in Iceland (from Kershaw 1962).

0   5 cm

→ Pioneer rhizome
–×– Dead shoot base
— Aerial shoot
⌣ Visual clumps

marshes (Adam 1990). In these habitats, the aerial shoots of each clone are interconnected by a dense interwoven mass of rhizomes (Figure 4.7). Clones can be extensive. In the common bracken fern (*Pteridium aquilinum*), clones may exceed 1000 m in diameter (Parks and Werth 1993). The world's largest plant (by mass) is a single clone of aspen (*Populus tremuloides*) with 47 000 stems connected below-ground, and covering more than 42 ha (Grant 1993).

Why do plants have this clonal capacity? Stress may limit the resources needed to construct flowers, it may reduce the availability of pollinators, but most often it likely reduces the probability of regeneration from seed. There is a clear evolutionary trade-off: produce large numbers of small seeds, each with a low probability of establishment, or allocate the same resources to fewer larger clonal offspring, each having a higher probability of establishment.

Considerable effort has gone into unravelling the advantages and disadvantages of clonal growth (e.g., Jackson et al. 1985, Harper et al. 1986), but three older models (Williams 1975) still retain their value. The names used for Williams's models include animals, and I have not tried to rename them in strictly botanical terms, although you may find this a useful, if challenging, exercise. Here are his three models that address clonal growth, sexual reproduction, and environmental conditions.

1. The Aphid-rotifer model

The model name refers to the life cycle of aphids and rotifers. Both cycle between periods of asexual reproduction in the summer and periods of sexual reproduction toward the autumn. Clonal reproduction may be advantageous during periods with relatively stable environmental conditions, whereas sexual reproduction may be reserved for times when the environment begins to change. Future environmental conditions that will arise from the change are unknown. Sexual reproduction, which results in greater variation among offspring, increases the likelihood that some will be better adapted to surviving under the new conditions. Continued clonal reproduction would produce only individuals adapted to the environment before the change occurred.

2. The strawberry-coral model

Strawberries and corals both produce colonies by clonal reproduction, but can also produce large numbers of small, sexual offspring. Clonal reproduction may be advantageous within relatively desirable patches of habitat, whereas sexual reproduction may be reserved largely for dispersal among patches.

When a young strawberry seedling first becomes established, it develops stolons that asexually produce new individuals. This process could continue without limit – as long as the favorable patch is very large. Yet the more the plant expands, the greater the number of shoots that will arise ever further from the location where the plant first established as a seedling. Hence, as the plant expands, the odds increase that a shoot will encounter less favorable conditions. At some point, further allocation of resources to new shoots at the edge of the clone will not result in more offspring. At this point, sexual reproduction allows dispersal to new sites.

Occasional sexual reproduction is also advantageous when patch characteristics change as described for the previous model. No patch will survive forever. The change may be physical, such as a drought or fire that erases the patch and replaces it with a different set of conditions. The change may also be biological, since new genotypes and species are continually dispersing seeds into the patch. The bigger the clone, the more reproductive propagules it can produce, and so there may be a selective advantage to those clones that delay sexual reproduction until the local patch is filled. The strawberry-coral model is similar to the aphid-rotifer model, but it address the trade-offs created by environmental conditions that change in space rather than in time.

3. The elm-oyster model

In some cases, clonal reproduction is unlikely to be advantageous and there may be strong selection for sexual reproduction. The model name refers to those species, like elm trees and oysters, that can be thought of as having no clonal reproduction – single individuals hold one small piece of space and flood adjoining areas with sexually produced offspring. Elms produce vast numbers of seeds, and it should be readily apparent that one elm tree can produce vastly more seedlings than can possibly establish as adult trees. The space occupied by each adult elm tree is not unlike the single patch occupied by the clone of a strawberry. Large numbers of seedlings may colonize a patch, but owing to intense competition among them, a site will tend to be occupied by the one individual that is marginally better at exploiting resources, suppressing neighbors, and minimizing losses to pathogens and herbivores. Over evolutionary time, those trees that survived were not those most successful at making more copies of the same genotype, but rather those producing offspring with many different genotypes with differing competitive abilities.

In addition to the potential importance of clonal growth as a reproductive strategy discussed above, it has other advantages, particularly in areas where water or nutrients are in very low supply. The interwoven webs of rhizomes (Figure 4.7) may permit shoots to share resources. Shoots that are located in stressful patches may be able to use resources transferred from adjoining shoots in richer patches. The branching pattern of a plant may reflect its style of foraging in an array of such patches (Bell 1984, Huber et al. 1999), and we have already seen an example of grasses foraging in patches of nitrogen (Section 3.5.3).

This proposition can be experimentally tested. For example, Salzman and Parker (1985) experimentally evaluated the physiological connection among shoots of the herbaceous perennial *Ambrosia psilostachya*. Pairs of shoots connected by a section of rhizome were grown in partitioned pots that were watered with either freshwater, saltwater (the stress condition), or a split environment with half of each. Shoots in the saline treatments produced only 34 percent of the biomass of those in the freshwater treatments, illustrating the negative effects of salinity on plant growth. If, however, shoots in saline soil were connected to shoots in fresh water treatments, they then reached 74 percent of the biomass of fresh water treatments: "thus, connection to a stem in a non-saline soil greatly ameliorated the harmful effects of salt." Moreover, they add: "rhizome connections among plants in contrasting environments do not result in a simple averaging of the effects of the two environments; the benefits received by plants in a stressful environment outweighed the costs incurred by their connected neighbors in a favorable environment."

A similarly designed experiment (Slade and Hutchings 1987) used another herbaceous perennial, *Glechoma hederacea*, in three soil nutrient regimes: nutrient rich, nutrient poor (the stress), and split treatments. Although growth was more vigorous in the fertile treatments, the results for split treatments were intermediate between the pure treatments. Hence the conclusion that there was "no integration between primary stolons subjected to different nutrient levels." *Glechoma hederacea* is, however, a common species in woods, grasslands, and disturbed sites; it is not normally found in sites that would be called stressed so much as disturbed. The ability to endure stressful patches may not be the causal factor for clonal growth of *G. hederacea*.

A further complication in such experiments is the likelihood that plants differ greatly in the rate of transport along connecting rhizomes. In some cases, the shoots may be all but independent. In other cases, there may be rapid exchange between individuals and the entire set of interconnected shoots may be functioning more like an integrated unit.

In summary, it is likely that there is more than one set of environmental conditions determining the balance between clonal and sexual reproduction. The general tendency for clonal offspring to be relatively large suggests that they provide an alternative to the production of large numbers of small offspring, and are selected for under conditions that prevent or inhibit sexual modes of reproduction. Williams's three models provide a useful template for thinking about the advantages of clonal reproduction. However, further work suggests other possibilities (e.g., Jackson et al. 1985, Harper et al. 1986). In addition to the advantages of clonal offspring discussed here, the avoidance of what is known as "the cost of meiosis" is also an hypothesis and we will consider it in Chapter 8.

4.3 | Habitats with drought as the predominant stress

4.3.1 Deserts

Water is an essential constituent of life. A good place to begin the exploration of stress is in habitats that lack water. Shortages of water have been a constant stress on plants ever since their ancestors first occupied terrestrial environments more than a quarter of a billion years ago. There are environmental factors other than drought that constrain plant growth. Shortages of nutrients, for example, are almost as ubiquitous as shortages of water. And then there are habitats that have the potential to be fertile, were it not for an environmental factor such as temperature or salinity that regulates the availability of essential resources. After exploring such examples, we will look at a few others that could be considered classics in the study of how plants and plant communities react to stress.

The absence of water is the key factor that produces the world's deserts (Figure 4.8). These occupy 26–35 percent of the land surface of the Earth; the largest example is the Sahara, which covers some 9 million km^2 of North Africa (Archibold 1995). In deserts rainfall is often less than 100 mm per year, although it can be much lower or higher. The coastal Atacama Desert in Chile averages only 0.7 mm per year, and several years can pass with no measurable precipitation. In other cases, areas in South Africa and Australia may receive more than 500 mm per year yet be classed as deserts because the rain falls over such short periods that organisms still face long periods of drought (Archibold 1995).

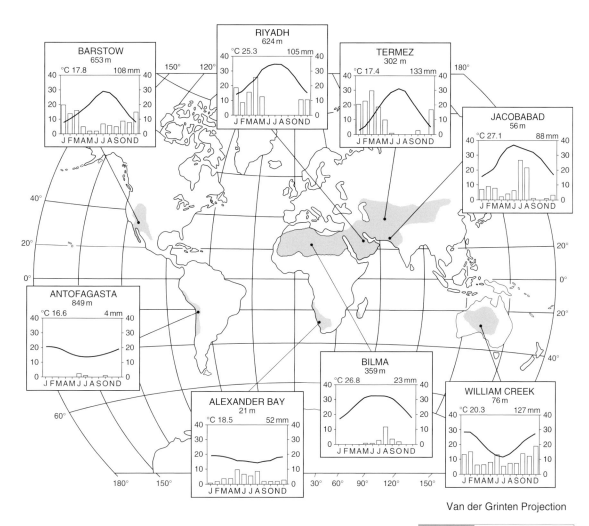

Figure 4.8 Distribution of arid regions and representative climatic conditions. Mean monthly temperatures are indicated by the line and mean precipitation for each month is shown by the bars. Station elevation, mean annual temperature, and mean annual precipitation appear at the top of each climograph (from Archibold 1995).

Van der Grinten Projection

Plants that tolerate these environments must have a suite of traits that reduce strain from water loss. To maintain internal water concentrations that allow chemical processes to occur, plants must take up water when it is available and reduce rates of loss when it is not. Even small losses in water potential, a few bars (8–10 percent of saturation) is sufficient to decrease rates of cell division. Since most water arrives in short bursts of precipitation (Noy-Meir 1973), desert plants must either absorb water from brief surface pulses or else construct deep roots (Schwinning and Sala 2004).

Desert plants provide crisp examples of traits that reduce water loss. An early classification of desert plants developed by Kearney and Shantz (1912) divided them into drought-escaping, drought-evading, and drought-enduring species. Drought-escaping plants are largely annuals that remain as buried seeds until stimulated to germinate by rainfall. Drought-evading plants are perennials that remain dormant during dry periods but rapidly produce shoots during short-lived wet

Table 4.1. *Traits associated with plants tolerant of drought (from Gibson and Nobel 1986 and Archibold 1995).*

Relative importance	Trait
Primary	Reduced surface to volume ratio
	Wax coating
	Reduced density of stomata
	Spines/hairs (for shading)
	CAM photosynthesis
Secondary	Spines (defense against herbivores)
	Secondary metabolites (defense against herbivores)
	Camouflage (defense against herbivores)

Figure 4.9 Some examples of different growth forms allowing plants to survive drought. (a) Deciduous "bottle" trees with water-storing trunks (*Adansonia/Chorisa* type); (b) succulents storing water in the stem (Cacti/*Euphorbia* type); (c) succulents with water-storing leaves (*Agave*/Crassulaceae type); (d) evergreen trees and shrubs with deep tap root systems (sclerophyll type); (e) deciduous, often thorny shrubs (*Capparis* type); (f) chlorophyllous-stemmed shrubs (*Retama* type); (g) tussock grasses with renewal buds protected by leaf sheaths, and with wide-ranging root systems (*Aristida* type); (h) cushion plants (*Anabasis* type); (i) geophytes with storage roots (*Citrullus* type); (j) bulb and tuber geophytes; (k) pluviotherophytes (annual plants); (l) desiccation-tolerant plants (poikilohydric type) (from Larcher 1995).

periods. The best-known desert plants are, however, the drought-enduring plants, long-lived perennials in which photosynthesis continues for much of the year in spite of severe water shortages (Figure 4.9). Some of the typical traits of these species are shown in Table 4.1.

Since water loss occurs through the epidermis, and in particular through stomata, desert plants have a thick layer of wax covering the epidermis and greatly reduced numbers of stomata. In non-desert

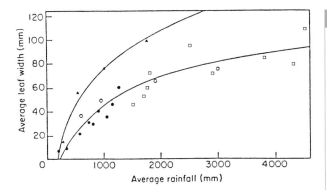

Figure 4.10 Average leaf width at low elevations as a function of annual rainfall in tropical regions (after Givnish 1984). Curves represent the relationships $y = 32.7 \ln (x/244.5)$ for sites in southern South America, Central America, and Australia ($r^2 = 0.82$, $P < 0.001$, df = 20), and $y = 45.0 \ln (x/188.6)$ for sites in northern South America with a less marked dry season ($r^2 = 0.98$, $P > 0.01$, df = 2). The less seasonal sites in South America support broader leaves at a given rainfall. ▲ northern South America; ● southern South America; ○ Australia; □ Central America (from Givnish 1987).

species the number of stomata per square millimeter of leaf surface ranges from 800 in some trees to 100–200 in most annuals, but in desert succulents there are only about 20 (Marschner 1995). Further, surface to volume ratios are dramatically reduced by eliminating (or at least reducing) leaf surface area (Figure 4.10). Consider three examples. *Pachypodium namaquanum* has tree-like trunks, but the leaves are reduced to small tufts at the summit of the plant (Figure 4.11). Many members of the Cactaceae are reduced to cylinders or globes in order to bring surface to volume ratios to an absolute minimum (recall Figure 3.28). The stone plant, *Lithops salicola*, can be considered to have taken this "minimum" to a further extreme, reducing its exposed surface area further by being entirely buried except for two flattened leaves at the soil surface (Figure 4.12).

If evapotranspiration were entirely prevented, however, photosynthesis would also cease. Many desert plants therefore have a distinctive type of photosynthesis called CAM (Crassulacean Acid Metabolism) photosynthesis. Stomata open only during the night, when rates of water loss from evapotranspiration are at their lowest (Figure 4.13). Carbon dioxide is absorbed and then stored in vacuoles as malate. (Photosynthesis, of course, cannot occur during the night.) During the following day, the stomata close to conserve water, but photosynthesis can proceed using the stored carbon (Figure 4.14). As a consequence, desert succulents such as *Agave deserti* transpire only 25 g of water for each gram of CO_2 taken up by leaves, and the barrel cactus *(Ferocactus acanthodes)* loses 70 g (Nobel 1976). Equivalent values for C_3 and C_4 plants are 450–600 and 250–350 g water/g CO_2, respectively (Szarek and Ting 1975).

Preventing water loss is only half the equation. Equally, water is taken up rapidly after rainstorms. During dry periods roots have few, if any, lateral branches, but upon wetting rain roots rapidly form. By the time the soil is dried again, these rain roots have been shed, and the main roots become sealed for the drought (Gibson and Nobel 1986). Once absorbed, the water can be stored for long periods in the spongy tissues of cacti. In the barrel cactus (*F. acanthodes*), stored water can extend photosynthesis for up to 50 days (Nobel 1977). A specimen of *Opuntia* cactus (*O. bigelovii*) was still alive after three

Figure 4.11 *Pachypodium namaquanum* (Apocynaceae) growing on a steep south-facing slope in Richtersveld National Park, South Africa. It typically occurs in colonies of 30 to 1000 on steep granite slopes. For an unknown reason, the apices of the plants face north toward the sun (from Rundel et al. 1995).

years of being completely severed from its roots and suspended on a post in the desert (Gibson and Nobel 1986).

The presence of spines is also characteristic of desert plants, but why should this be the case? What do spines have to do with water retention or uptake? Some spines may indeed minimize the direct effects of drought – spines can provide shade to the plant and reduce heat loading and evapotranspiration. In most cases, however, spines are probably best understood as a secondary adaptation to drought; their main function appears to be protection against herbivores

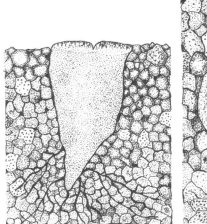
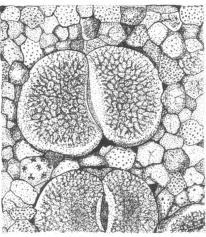

Figure 4.12 Stone plants such as *Lithops salicola* (Aizoaceae) reduce the surface area for water loss by means of burial. This habit may also reduce exposure to herbivores, since the two leaves may mimic the color and even the texture of surrounding stones. Left, growth form; right, surface view of expanded leaves (from Cloudsley-Thompson 1996).

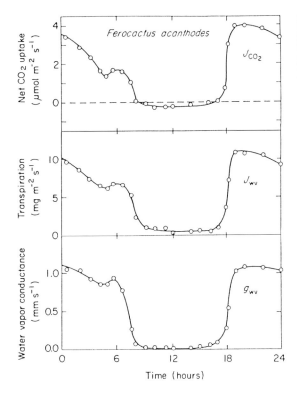

Figure 4.13 Gas exchange measured in the field for *Ferocactus acanthodes* over a 24-h period (from Gibson and Nobel 1986).

(Gibson and Nobel 1986). The logic assumes that the costs of producing plant tissue in the desert are so high that extreme measures are called for to protect tissues from animals. Spines are often supplemented by a variety of secondary metabolites, of which the alkaloid mescaline in the peyote cactus (*Lophophora williamsii*) is perhaps the best known. Some succulents seem to have cryptic shapes and colors to avoid detection by herbivores – *Lithops salicola* in the Aizoaceae (Figure 4.12) resembles the small stones in the surrounding desert.

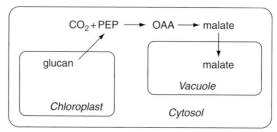

Figure 4.14 Schematic summary of CAM biochemistry during (a) night-time and (b) daytime, indicating the cellular components and overall reactions involved for chlorenchyma cells. PEP, phosphoenolpyruvate; OAA, oxaloacetate. (From Gibson and Nobel 1986.)

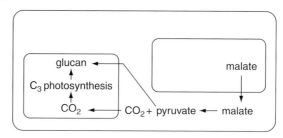

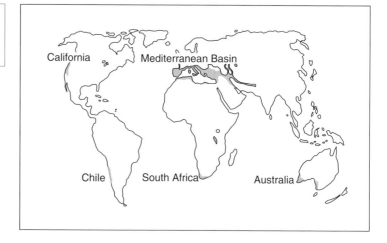

Figure 4.15 The five mediterranean-climate regions of the world (from Cowling et al. 1996).

4.3.2 Mediterranean shrublands

Water shortages are an obvious feature of deserts, but many other parts of the world have vegetation limited by water deficits in a less conspicuous manner. For example, regions of Mediterranean climate have warm dry summers that alternate with cool moist winters (Archibold 1995, Cowling et al. 1996). These conditions occur in five widely separated geographic regions totaling about $1.8\,km^2$ (Figure 4.15). In order of decreasing size these are the Mediterranean basin, coastal California, southwestern Australia (kwongan), central Chile, and the cape of South Africa (fynbos).

Table 4.2. *Life-form spectra (recall Figure 2.8, Table 2.3) for various Mediterranean shrub communities. Ph, Phanerophyte; Ch, chamaephyte; H, hemicryptophyte; C, cryptophyte; Th, therophyte (after Archibold 1995).*

Location	No. species	Life forms (%)				
		Ph	Ch	H	C	Th
California						
Chaparral	44	41	16	18	11	14
Coastal scrub	65	17	19	20	3	41
Chile						
Matorral	108	24	14	20	6	36
Coastal matorral	109	12	15	17	9	46
Southern Africa						
Fynbos	448	34	31	16	15	4
Coastal renosterveld	127	12	14	19	45	10
Australia						
Mallee-broombush	288	57	19	9	8	7
E. diversifolia heath	274	56	19	10	7	8
E. behriana-herb alliance	50	48	24	12	2	14
Israel						
Quercus-Pistachia association	206	47	14	20	8	11
Pinus-Juniperus association	73	8	37	20	15	20
Arbutus-Helianthemum association	138	20	23	28	17	12

Many of the plant species in these areas are sclerophyllous shrubs that are resistant to both recurring fire and drought; the life form spectra are shown in Table 4.2. These shrubs have many traits associated with drought tolerance (Mooney and Dunn 1970, Archibold 1995): (1) small heavily cutinized leaves, (2) small stomata (although relatively large numbers of them, up to $1000/mm^2$, roughly ten times that of succulents), (3) vertically oriented leaves to reduce heat loading and promote stem flow when rain occurs, and (4) vigorous resprouting after fire. In the Mediterranean basin, the effects of drought have been increased by centuries of forest clearance and overgrazing, and have produced dense shrub communities known as "maquis" or "garrigue." The Southern Hemisphere family Proteaceae is very well represented in both the fynbos and kwongan. Other genera have rapidly diversified into this habitat including *Eucalyptus* (>300 species), *Acacia* (>400 species), and *Erica* (>500 species). Altogether, however, these shrubs show a large number of similar traits associated with drought and fire tolerance (Figure 4.16).

Switching our frame of reference from functional types to phylogenetic diversification, the flora of the fynbos has a pool of more than 8500 species, with a species density greater than 95 per 1000 km^2, a value exceeded only by tropical rain forests with >100 per 1000 km^2 (Bond 1997). This distinctive flora occurs in a particularly adverse environment: one of drought combined with infertile soils and

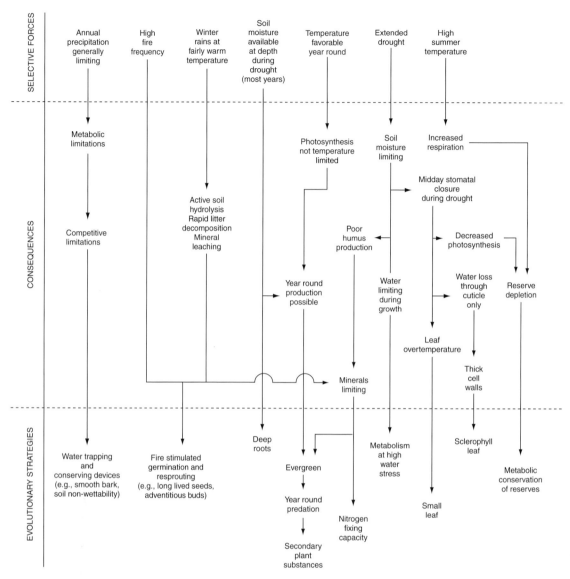

Figure 4.16 An evolutionary model for the Mediterranean-climate shrub form (from Archibold 1995 after Mooney and Dunn 1970).

frequent fire (Cowling 1990, Bond 1997). Table 4.3 illustrates some examples of this globally significant vegetation type.

4.3.3   Rock barrens

Wherever there is shallow soil, it is likely that plants will be under stress. Shallow soil stores less water, thereby increasing the probability, intensity, and duration of drought. As well, essential nutrients will be in short supply since the volume of soil available to any plant is a function of soil depth. Consequently, areas with rock near the surface tend to have distinctive vegetation, including plant species tolerant of infertility and drought (McVaugh 1943, Anderson et al. 1999). Since dry vegetation burns easily, recurring fire is also often associated with such conditions.

Table 4.3. *Plant community and soil characteristics of fynbos vegetation on the Agulhas Plain, South Africa (from Cowling 1990).*

Site community	Dominant species	Soil (parent material)	Soil fertility index[b]
Geelrug transect			
G1 Proteoid Fynbos[1][a]	*Protea compacta, Elegia filiacea*	Deep, colluvial podzol (TMG sandstone)	−0.25
G2 Proteoid Fynbos[2]	*Leucadendron platyspermum, Restio similis*	Gravelly, leached lithosol (TMG sandstone)	−0.19
G3 Proteoid Fynbos[3]	*Leucadendron elimense, Blaeria klotzschii*	Lithosol (Sil-ferricrete)	0.17
G4 Asteraceous Fynbos[4]	*Disparago anomala, Thoracosperma interruptum*	Duplex-loam on clay with ferricrete sandstone (Bokkeveld shale)	0.59
G5 Renoster shrubland[5]	*Elytropappus rhinocerotis, Ischyrolepis caespitosa*	Alluvial sand over transported clay	0.36
Hagelkraal transect			
H1 Proteoid Fynbos[1]	*Protea compacta, Willdenowia glomerata*	Deep, colluvial podzol (TMG sandstone)	−0.22
H2 Proteoid Fynbos[6]	*Protea susannae, Euchaetes burchellii*	Deep, colluvial podzol (Bredasdorp limestone)	−0.14
H3 Proteoid Fynbos[7]	*Leucadendron meridianum, Phylica sp. nov.*	Calcareous lithosol (Bredasdorp limestone)	0
H4 Asteraceous Fynbos[8]	*Passerina paleacea, Euclea racemosa*	Deep, calcareous dune sand	0.16
H5 Forest[9]	*Sideroxylon inerme, Stipa dregeana*	Deep, colluvial, calcareous sand (Bredasdorp limestone)	0.69
Soetanysberg transect			
S1 Proteoid Fynbos[1]	*Protea compacta, Staavia radiata*	Deep, colluvial podzol (TMG sandstone)	−0.23
S2 Ericaceous Fynbos[10]	*Syndesmanthus globiceps, Erica coccinea*	Leached lithosol (TMG sandstone)	−0.12
S3 Restiod Fynbos[11]	*Leucadendron linifolium, Chondropetalum deustum*	Shallow, calcareous sand (TMG sandstone)	−0.05
S4 Asteraceous Fynbos[8]	*Agathosma collina, Ischyrolepis eleocharis*	Deep, calcareous dune sand	−0.03
S5 Thicket[12]	*Olea exasperata, Euclea racemosa*	Deep, calcareous dune sand	0.31
Miscellaneous plots			
HN1 Proteoid Fynbos[7]	*Leucadendron meridianum, Thamnochortus paniculatus*	Calcareous lithosol (Bredasdorp limestone)	0.02
S6 Ericaceous Fynbos[10]	*Blaeria ericoides, Thamnochortus lucens*	Leached lithosol (TMG sandstone)	−0.09

Notes:
[a] Sites with the same superscript numeral belong to the same community.
[b] Derived from covariance biplot analysis of soil data.

Rock barrens are common at high latitudes or altitudes where glaciers have removed most of the surface soil. Other conspicuous examples of rock barrens can be found outside glaciated regions. In the southern Appalachians, outcrops of metamorphic rocks can form smooth domes rising as much as 200 m above the surrounding terrain. Rainfall drains off such domes, and may also carry away organic matter that might otherwise form soil. McVaugh (1943) described a series of such outcrops, and their distinctive flora and vegetation. Amidst expanses of bare rock, small depressions accumulate water and organic matter, and thereby support islands of vegetation. Each depression develops a series of distinctive vegetation zones. At the very margin are crustose lichens or mosses (*Grimmia* spp.); these give way in turn to fruticose lichens (*Cladonia* spp.) or fern allies (*Selaginella* spp.), then large mosses (*Polytrichum* spp.) and finally, near the very center, vascular plants including grasses (*Andropogon* spp., *Panicum* spp.), rushes (*Juncus* spp.), and sedges (*Rhynchospora* spp.). These domes have presumably been isolated from the surrounding forest vegetation for considerable time since, in the southern USA, at least 12 plant species are endemic to such outcrops (Shure 1999).

In equatorial regions, rock outcrops can have a remarkably rich flora. One of the best examples is the tepui (or "inselbergs") of the Guyana highlands in northern South America. Here rock outcrops rise steeply from amidst tropical forest. The flora on these outcrops tends to be dominated by four families: Rubiaceae, Melastomataceae, Orchidaceae, and Cyperaceae (Prance and Johnson 1991). Many plants have a bizarre growth form characterized by "thick, sclerophyllous, highly reduced, glossy, waxy or revolute leaves, often crowded into tufts of rosettes or covered by a sericeous, gray, white or brown tomentum. Frequently the stem becomes conspicuously shortened or elongated, simple and virgate producing a weird appearance in the landscape" (Steyermark 1982, p. 205). Owing to their unique vegetation and rich flora, we shall return to a consideration of tepui in Section 12.4.5, but if you wish, you may flip ahead to Figure 12.16 to see a photograph.

Returning to northern areas, alvars are a special kind of rock barren formed over limestone (Figure 4.17). Alvars are a globally restricted habitat, being common only in the Baltic areas of northern Europe and in the area north of the Great Lakes (Petterson 1965, Catling and Brownell 1995). Soil depth and vegetation biomass are the primary gradients that produce different vegetation types (Belcher et al. 1992), and in those sites studied to date, below-ground competition exceeds above-ground competition (Belcher et al. 1995). In Europe, grazing has been an important historic factor in alvars, whereas in North America there is evidence that fires were important (Catling and Brownell 1998). Periodic drought may also greatly inhibit invasion by forest, mortality of rates of 60 to 100 percent having been observed in woody plants during one dry summer (Stephenson and Herendeen 1986).

Figure 4.17 Limestone pavement in the Misery Bay alvar on the south coast of Manitoulin Island. *Sporobolus heterolepis*, *Deschampsia caespitosa* and *Potentilla fruticosa* grow in the cracks between the pavement blocks. Some of the world's largest alvars occur on this island and the Bruce Peninsula (from Catling and Brownell 1995).

Certain rock outcrops impose further constraints upon plant growth through the lack of major nutrients or the presence of higher than normal concentrations of elements such as nickel or chromium. In ultramafic rocks, low silica content (45 percent) is often accompanied by dark-colored ferromagnesian minerals (Coleman and Jove 1992). These rocks are collectively known as serpentine. They are widespread, with significant outcrops in locations including California, Newfoundland, central Europe, Scandinavia, Russia, Tibet, China, Japan, Brazil, Zimbabwe, New Zealand, and Australia (Whittaker 1954a, b, Coleman and Jove 1992). Although the composition of serpentine rocks is variable, leading some to conclude that the term is of doubtful value, the recurring themes of inadequate soil nutrients and high concentrations of metals lend credence to the recognition of a class of rock types distinctively inhospitable to plants. Further, there is now evidence that serpentine rocks have a distinctive geological origin (Coleman and Jove 1992, Roberts 1992). They appear to form when slabs of seabed are lifted onto continental margins instead of being subducted and destroyed along the margins of oceanic plates. Thus, the regions of serpentine are associated with the margins of ancient oceans.

Part of the difficulty in drawing generalizations about the ecological consequences of ultramafic rocks lies in the interaction of stress effects with climate. The major recurring stresses irrespective of climate likely include: (1) low essential macronutrients and micronutrients, particularly calcium, and (2) toxic amounts of magnesium, nickel, or chromium. In northern areas, such as Newfoundland, superimposed upon these are: (1) drought, (2) wind, (3) erosion from lack of vegetative cover, and (4) cryoturbation (disturbance by recurring freeze–thaw cycles). Here, serpentine rocks therefore support arctic-alpine plant communities in exposed locations, peatlands and sedge meadows in less exposed sites, and occasionally trees and shrubs in sheltered areas. In tropical areas, cryoturbation is not an issue, but leaching may increase the deficiency of nutrients. In Brazil, for example, such rocks yield sparsely vegetated domes covered in *cerrado* (grasses, shrubs, and low trees) giving way to *campo rupestre* (grasses and shrubs) (Brooks et al. 1992). In serpentine areas of Cuba, the vegetation is physiognomically distinct, being characterized by sclerophylly, microphylly, and spinosity (Borhidi 1992).

Experiments provide some better understanding of the stresses created by serpentine. Most such experiments compare endemic ecotypes (those races adapted to serpentine) to similar ecotypes or species that do not occur on serpentine. Simple pot experiments using serpentine soil (Kruckeberg 1954) showed that fertilization with NPK increased the growth of plants in serpentine but only if the plants already possessed the ability to grow on serpentine. Non-serpentine plants did not respond to NPK, which indicates that some other factor was limiting their growth in these soils. Only the serpentine plants could grow on serpentine soil alone, but if calcium was added as gypsum, then both serpentine and non-serpentine plants were able to grow.

Such experiments suggest that it is the low calcium level rather than absence of the macronutrients NPK that prevents many plants from growing on serpentine. Of course, increasing the soil pH will also reduce the solubility of possibly toxic metal ions such as nickel and aluminum. This also implies the importance of competition. Serpentine ecotypes cannot spread to sites with normal soils because other plants are better able to exploit these soils. This appears to be another case where stress-tolerant species are competitively excluded to inferior habitats. Serpentine vegetation contains large numbers of endemic species and thus is of some conservation significance. Further, because the vegetation is slow to regenerate after disturbance, barrens of all kinds are particularly vulnerable to human disturbance.

4.3.4 Coniferous forests

There are many more subtle effects of water shortages. Early biogeographers were aware that transitions between major vegetation types, such as grassland to forest, or broadleaved to evergreen forest, were in some way linked to differences in temperature and rainfall patterns (recall Section 2.3). The connection between temperature and water may be particularly significant:

> For a plant to use energy for growth, water must be available; otherwise, the energy acts only to heat and stress the plant. Similarly, for a plant to use water for growth, energy must be available; otherwise, water simply percolates through the soil or runs off, unused. The effects of climate on plants, therefore, are determined by the interactions of energy and water.
>
> (Stephenson 1990, p. 649)

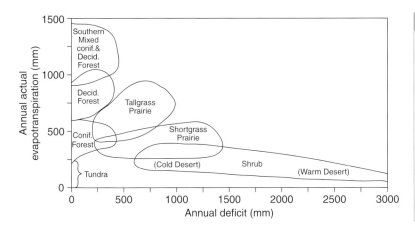

Figure 4.18 Mean annual evapotranspiration and deficit of the major North American plant formations. For clarity, the three transition formations (northern mixed forest, woodland and savanna, and shrub steppe) were not plotted. Values of actual evapotranspiration and deficit for the transition formations usually fell within the range of the formations that the transition formations physiognomically bridged (from Stephenson 1990).

The interactions between energy and water are described by the climatic water balance. The factors in water balance address how much energy and water are available to plants, how much evaporative demand is not met by available water, and how much excess water exists. These can be described in two equations, $W = E_A + S$ and $E_P = E_A + D$, where W is available water, E_A is actual evapotranspiration, S is surplus, E_P is potential evapotranspiration and D is the water deficit (Stephenson 1990).

Actual evapotranspiration and deficit measure aspects of climate that are of direct physiological importance to plants. Actual evapotranspiration measures the simultaneous availability of water and the energy to evaporate it; there is a good correlation between E_A and net primary productivity. Deficit is perhaps best understood as an evaporative demand that is not met by available water. This includes heating that cannot be regulated by transpiration as well as, indirectly, metabolic costs that cannot be met by active photosynthesis. There is some evidence that net primary productivity is negatively correlated with water deficit. Surplus measures water available for leaching nutrients on well-drained soils or water available for flooding and the creation of anoxic conditions on poorly drained soils. Both of these might be expected to reduce primary production.

How is vegetation related to these factors? Figure 4.18 shows E_A plotted against D for a series of North American vegetation types. While the gross patterns are of obvious interest, they are also somewhat self-explanatory, so let us turn our attention to a more subtle pattern, the shift from deciduous to coniferous forest. This shift, after all, is not only one of physiognomy but also of evolutionary lineage (angiosperms to gymnosperms). Stephenson says that for a region to support deciduous forest, three climatic conditions must be met:

1. Annual precipitation (water supply) must be >600 mm.
2. Annual potential evapotranspiration (energy supply) must be >600 mm.

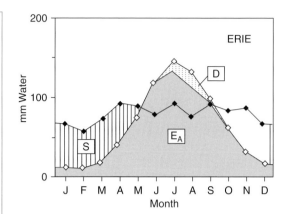

Figure 4.19 The water balance of Erie, Pennsylvania (42°N 80°W), a locality supporting deciduous forest. From October through May, water supply (estimated from precipitation ◆) exceeds potential evapotranspiration (◇); during this period, actual evapotranspiration (E_A, gray) equals potential evapotranspiration. From October to December, excess water replaces soil water used during the summer: the white area between precipitation and potential evapotranspiration curves represents soil–water recharge. From December to May, after soil water has been replenished, the difference between precipitation and potential evapotranspiration is surplus (S, stripes). From June through September, potential evapotranspiration exceeds precipitation. During this period, actual evapotranspiration equals available water, precipitation plus water extracted from the soil (which is shown as the curve between the precipitation and potential evapotranspiration curves). Deficit (D, stippling) is the difference between potential evapotranspiration and available water (from Stephenson 1990).

3. The seasonal timing of available water and potential evapotranspiration must be such that at least 600 mm of both occur simultaneously.

These conditions are met in Erie, Pennsylvania (Figure 4.19) where deciduous forest occurs, but they are violated in three other regions where conifer forests occur (Figure 4.20):

1. Flagstaff, Arizona is forested, but lacks sufficient water to support deciduous forests. Although the energy supply is adequate, rainfall is only 470 mm so criterion 1 is not met. Many coniferous montane forests may be produced by such circumstances.
2. Moosonee, Ontario is forested, but deficient in energy. Water supply is adequate but potential evapotranspiration is only 345 mm. Moosonee typifies the vast areas of boreal forest that stretch across the Northern Hemisphere. It may be noteworthy that further south, conifers are often restricted to north facing slopes, and further north, hardwoods are often found on south facing slopes; in such cases topography may be shifting the energy balance sufficiently to alter canopy types.
3. Portland, Oregon has sufficient precipitation and energy supplies to support deciduous forests, but the bulk of the rainfall comes in the winter when there is insufficient energy for plants to use it. It therefore runs off as surplus. This seasonally asynchronous energy and water combination yields too little potential evapotranspiration (only 560 mm) for deciduous forest to occur.

These sorts of correlations provide valuable insights into the constraints upon the distribution of plants and vegetation types. They also have limitations. Further discrimination among vegetation types, for example, might be provided by considering the manner in which deficits are distributed over the year. An annual deficit spread over the entire year is likely to have different consequences than one concentrated in a few summer months. At the same time, the data above draw upon 30-year averages, and conditions over shorter periods of time may have important effects. One might also wish to

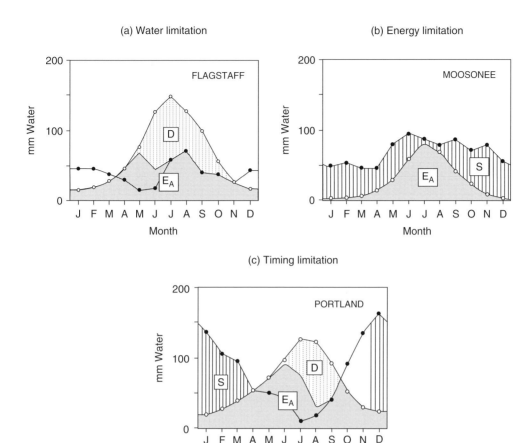

(a) Water limitation

(b) Energy limitation

(c) Timing limitation

Figure 4.20 The water balances of three North American localities supporting coniferous forest. Annual actual evapotranspiration (E_A, gray) is less than 600 mm because of (a) water limitation (Flagstaff, Arizona, 35°N 112°W), (b) energy limitation (Moosonee, Ontario, 51°N 81°W), (c) asynchronous timing of the energy and water supplies (Portland, Oregon, 46°N 126°W). ● precipitation, ○ potential evapotranspiration (see Figure 4.19 for additional explanation) (from Stephenson 1990).

explore physiological mechanisms in more detail. The presence of sclerophyllous foliage, evergreen leaves, and a hypodermis around vascular bundles in the needles might all provide mechanistic explanations for tolerance to environmental stress, but even were such linkages to be found, they would not explain why conifers did not occur in the site (Figure 4.19) where growing conditions are better. Some experiments implicate competition as an important mechanism preventing conifers from inhabiting sites with better growing conditions (Goldberg 1982a,b). The logic would appear to be that the traits that provide the ability to tolerate stressful climatic conditions simultaneously reduce competitive performance on better quality sites (Keddy 1989).

4.4 | Unavailability of resources

In some habitats, the resources are physically present, but stored in a form that plants cannot use. From the perspective of the plant, strain is again induced, but the cause is subtly different, in which case natural selection may have produced different adaptations for coping with the strain. A particularly good example of this is provided by peat bogs, where the plants grow in a matrix of organic matter, but because of low decay rates, the essential elements such as nitrogen and phosphorus remain chemically bound within partially decayed plant remains. In extreme cases, such as ombrotrophic peat bogs, the vegetation depends upon the dilute nutrient solution provided by rainwater.

Peatlands are flooded more or less permanently, but the water table is at or near the soil surface. Under these conditions decomposition rates are reduced, and since there are no waves, flowing water, or tides to carry away debris, the organic matter accumulates. Once organic matter has accumulated to a depth of about 10 cm, plant roots are increasingly isolated from access to the mineral soils beneath the peat. The plants therefore become more dependent upon dilute nutrients deposited in rainwater (Gorham 1957, van Breemen 1995) and have distributions strongly related to nutrient levels in the groundwater (e.g., Gore 1983, Glaser et al. 1990, Vitt and Chee 1990). Fertilization experiments have shown an array of types of limitation involving nitrogen, phosphorus and potassium (Section 3.4.5).

Adaptation to these infertile conditions requires a variety of unusual plant traits. The most visible is the tendency toward leathery and evergreen (sclerophyllous) foliage; although the cause of sclerophylly in wet peatlands was at first unclear and thought to be a consequence of physiological drought (Small 1972a, b, Richardson 1981), it is now thought that it is an adaptation to infertile conditions. Deciduous leaves require conditions of relative fertility, since a plant must continually replace the nitrogen and phosphorus lost in deciduous foliage (Grime 1977, 1979, Chapin 1980, Vitousek 1982). Thus evergreen shrubs in the Ericaceae and evergreen trees in the Pinaceae dominate peatlands. A secondary consequence of evergreen foliage is recurring disturbance by fire (Christensen et al. 1981).

Peatlands are also distinctive in the abundance of bryophytes, and one genus, *Sphagnum* (Figure 4.21), is dominant in bogs. This single genus of moss is largely responsible for the creation of peatlands; indeed, there may be more carbon incorporated in *Sphagnum*, dead and alive, than in any other genus of plant (Clymo and Hayward 1982). The success of *Sphagnum* in dominating large areas has been attributed to at least three characteristics (Clymo and Hayward 1982, van Breemen 1995, Verhoeven and Liefveld 1997). First, the morphology and anatomy ensure that *Sphagnum* carpets act like sponges to create permanently wet conditions; about 98 percent of a living *Sphagnum* carpet is pore space, 10–20 percent in the hyaline cells of the moss tissue, and the rest on the outside of the plant (van Breemen 1995). Second, the cell walls have a high cation exchange capacity that both acidifies the local environment and retains nutrients. Third, organochemical compounds such as phenolics and uronic acids may contribute to suppressing the growth of vascular plants. Measured accumulation rates of peat range from $40 \, \mathrm{g \, m^{-2} \, yr^{-1}}$ in boreal bogs of Russia to $450 \, \mathrm{g \, m^{-2} \, yr^{-1}}$ in subtropical

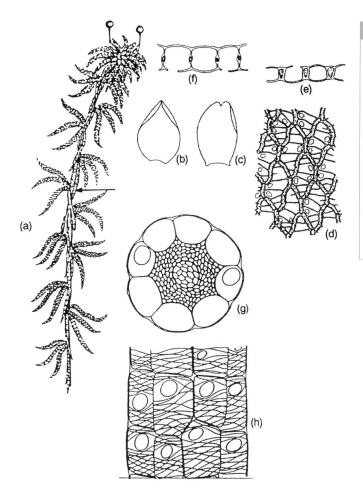

Figure 4.21 Morphology and anatomy of *Sphagnum*. (a)–(e) *S. papillosum*: (a) sporophyte-bearing shoot (with pendent branches; see arrow); (b) branch leaf; (c) stem leaf; (d) network of chlorophyllose (stippled) leaf cells, surrounded by porose hyaline cells; (e) cross-section of leaf; (f) same for *S. magellancium*; (g) and (h) cross section and external view of stem of *S. papillosum*, showing the large, porose hyaline cells, with fibril thickenings of cell walls at the outside (from van Breemen 1995).

fens of Florida (Bakker et al. 1997), so that over time, peat can accumulate to a depth of many meters, gradually transforming the landscape (Dansereau and Segadas-Vianna 1952, Gorham 1953). As peat accumulates and absorbs water, the diminutive *Sphagnum* moss can actually flood and kill forests, a process known as paludification (van Breemen 1995).

Many studies have explored changes in vegetation along gradients in peatlands. Glaser et al. (1990), for example, studied a large mire in northern Minnesota, where it was possible to identify an array of vegetation types and a chemical gradient that covered the entire range reported for boreal peatlands. For example, the rich fens had a pH above 7 and calcium concentrations ranged from 20 to 45 mg/l. In contrast, the raised bog had a pH below 4 and a calcium concentration below 1.1 mg/l. Species composition changed dramatically along this gradient; species richness tended to increase with rising pH and calcium concentrations. A stratigraphic exploration of the raised bog showed that under the roughly 3 m of accumulated peat were the remains of a sedge fen under a swamp forest, confirming the successional trend associated with peat accumulation.

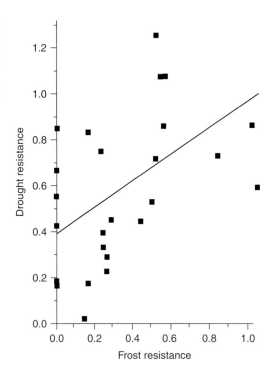

Figure 4.22 Relationship between drought resistance and frost resistance in 26 grassland plants ($P < 0.005$, df $= 24$) (from MacGillivray et al. 1995).

Tolerance to mineral nutrient stress may be a trait with general predictive ability. In extremely infertile soils, carnivory may supplement nutrient supplies (Section 11.6.2). Other traits that promote the tolerance of mineral nutrient stress include long-lived organs, low rates of nutrient turnover, and growth uncoupled from periods of nutrient uptake (Grime 1977). These are likely to be associated with both low growth rates and low rates of recovery from disturbance. MacGillivray et al. (1995) tested for correlations with resistance to two kinds of stress by subjecting pieces of turf to freezing conditions and to drought and then returning them to the field where performance was later assessed. The drought resistance and frost resistance of species was positively correlated with their ability to tolerate low nitrogen, phosphorus, and calcium. As well, the index of drought resistance was positively correlated with the index of frost resistance (Figure 4.22). Growth rates of species are generally inversely related to their ability to tolerate nutrient stress, so screening for relative growth rates (Grime and Hunt 1975, Shipley and Peters 1990) may provide a trait with great simplifying value.

4.5 | Presence of a regulator

4.5.1 Salinity

An environmental factor that is not itself a resource, but which reduces the rates of acquisition of a resource, can be called a regulator. Cold, salinity, and acidity are all examples of regulators. In salt marshes and

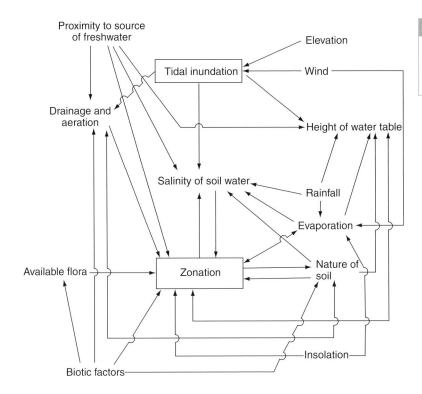

Figure 4.23 Environmental factors influencing salt marsh zonation (modified from Adam 1990 after Clarke and Hannon 1969).

mangal, salinity and flooding act as regulators (Frey and Basan 1978, Niering and Warren 1980) (Figure 4.23). Plants therefore occur in discrete zones associated with specific elevations and salinity (e.g., Poljakoff-Mayber and Gale 1975, Tomlinson 1986, Adam 1990).

To understand how salinity creates a form of drought, one must appreciate that evapotranspiration creates osmotic gradients within plant tissues. The water deficit in the leaves is transmitted down the plant through the xylem, thereby causing water to diffuse into roots (Salisbury and Ross 1988). The greater the salinity, the stronger this osmotic gradient must be to extract water from the soil. Water deficits in photosynthetic tissues can be measured with a pressure bomb, and Figure 4.24 shows that plants growing in salt water have much greater negative tension in their xylem. Other consequences of elevated salinity are shown in Figure 4.25.

The distribution of species in zoned wetlands (whether freshwater or saltwater) might be solely a consequence of each species' ability to cope with the physical constraints associated with flooding and salinity. A sober second thought, however, might be less encouraging. While data such as Figure 4.24 show that plants respond, for example, to flooding or salinity, this sort of data is insufficient to draw firm conclusions about the causes of plant distributions. Rarely does such research proceed to the logical next step, and test for a significant correlation between physiological properties and distribution in the field. Even if such correlations exist, the pattern does not prove that distributions are controlled by physiological

Figure 4.24 Xylem tension in plants of two contrasting wetland habitats (after Scholander et al. 1965).

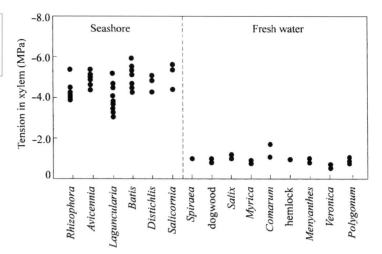

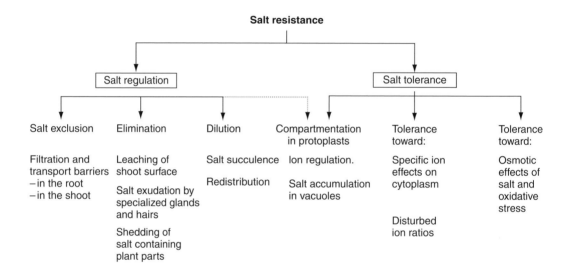

Figure 4.25 Components of the resistance of halophytes to salt stress (from Larcher 2003).

responses. Can you think of an alternative explanation for such correlations?

Perhaps it is possible to entirely reverse the suggested cause and effect and argue that a completely independent factor, such as grazing, produces vegetation patterns and that the observed physiological properties are simply pragmatic evolutionary responses to the conditions that are present. While few ecologists would deny that the physiological traits of organisms represent evolutionary responses to stress, these traits still do not demonstrate whether physiological differences are the cause of zonation or merely an effect. Field experiments are required for this. In saline plant communities, several such experiments have now been conducted.

In Alaskan salt marshes there are four zones that can be delineated as elevation increases (Jefferies 1977, Vince and Snow

1984): outer mud flat, (*Puccinellia nutkaensis*), inner mud flat (*Triglochin maritima*), outer sedge marsh (*Carex ramenski*), and inner sedge marsh (*C. lyngbyaei*). At one extreme, the outer mud flat with *P. nutkaensis* is flooded some 15 times per summer for periods of 2–5 days each, creating soil water salinity of 15–35 percent. The inner sedge marsh with *C. lyngbyaei* is flooded only twice per summer, when a new or full moon coincides with the perigee (although this single flood may last more than 5 days), and soil salinity is only 6–11 percent, slightly below the 12 percent of flooding sea water.

Reciprocal transplant experiments (with the addition of a fifth habitat, riverbank levees occupied by *Poa eminens*) showed that all species could grow in all habitats so long as neighboring plants were removed (Snow and Vince 1984). Further, the *P. nutkaensis* from the outer mud flats actually grew nearly four times larger when transplanted upslope to the inner mud flat than when transplanted within its own zone. The two species from the highest elevations (*C. lyngbyaei* and *P. eminens*) did, however, show reduced growth when transplanted to the outer mud flats. When the same five species were grown at different salinities in pots, all grew best in waterlogged but low salinity conditions. Thus, in spite of conspicuous zonation, the limited distributions of these species cannot be accounted for simply by narrow physiological tolerances to stress from salinity and flooding. Zonation must be partly produced by biological interactions; in general, Snow and Vince (1984) suggest that "species occurring in zones along a physical gradient are often limited by physiological tolerance toward one end of the gradient, and by competitive ability towards the other."

Zedler and Beare (1986) describe a quite different process in salt marshes in southwestern North America, where Mediterranean-type rainfall patterns (wet winters, dry summers) occur. There are also substantial year-to-year differences in stream flow. During dry years, hypersaline conditions develop; marsh species such as *Spartina foliosa* and *Typha domingensis* cannot tolerate these conditions and are slowly replaced by salt-tolerant species such as *Salicornia virginica*. This process is reversed during abnormally wet years when higher stream flows and longer rainfalls flush accumulated salt from the soil. If the wet period is short (3–6 weeks), only halophytic species such as *S. foliosa* can re-establish, but if it is extended, brackish and fresh-water marsh species can re-establish as well. Rare events appear to be particularly important in both destroying vegetation and allowing the establishment of new plants. The duration and intensity of fresh-water periods determine which species can regenerate. The duration and intensity of hypersaline periods act as a filter to determine which species persist. There is thus a constant cycling through different vegetation types driven by changes in moisture supply (Figure 4.26). This example illustrates another important principle regarding stress: the patterns that one observes at any particular point in time can often be interpreted only by understanding how stress changes with time.

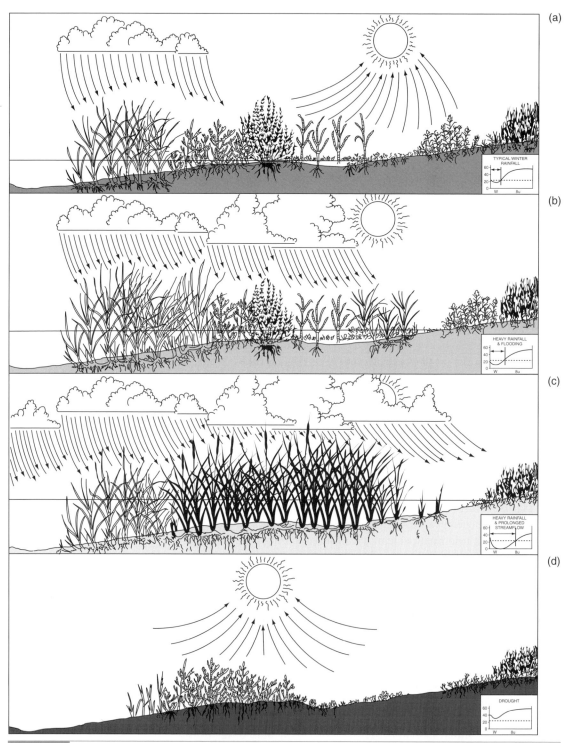

Figure 4.26 Cyclical changes of salt marsh vegetation in arid climates. (a) Typical situation where brief periods of low salinity allow salt marsh species to germinate and establish. (b) Floods reduce salinity and allow expansion of *Spartina foliosa*. (c) Prolonged flooding eliminates salt marsh vegetation and allows brackish marsh species to establish. (d) Periods without rainfall or flooding create hypersaline conditions which kill all but a few highly salt-tolerant species such as *Salicornia virginica* (from Zedler and Beare 1986).

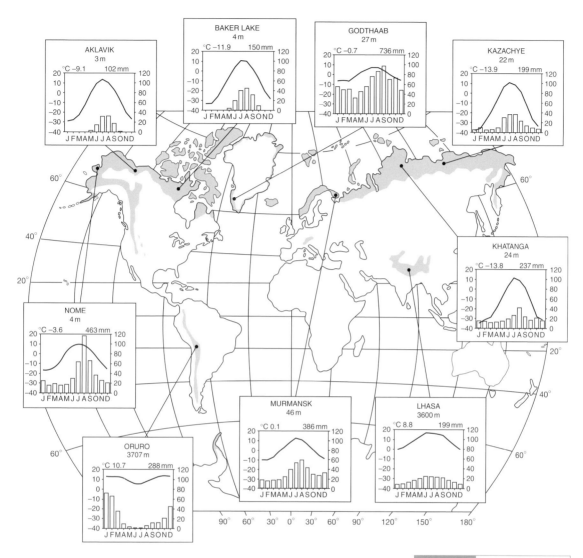

Figure 4.27 Distribution of polar and high mountain tundra ecosystems and representative climatic conditions. Mean monthly temperatures are indicated by the line and mean precipitation for each month is shown by the bars. Station elevation, mean annual temperature, and mean precipitation appear at the top of each climograph (from Archibold 1995).

4.5.2 Cold environments: arctic and alpine examples

Temperature gradients are found on all known planets. Earth and Mars both have ice caps at the poles, although Earth has only water ice, whereas Mars appears to have both water ice and carbon dioxide ice. High mountain tops have similar extremes of cold, and so the vegetation of arctic and alpine regions is usually treated jointly as arctic–alpine vegetation (Figure 4.27). These environments share a number of environmental characteristics that put stress on plants (Billings and Mooney 1968, Savile 1972): (1) low winter temperature, (2) low summer temperature, (3) short growing season, (4) strong winds, (5) long photoperiod, (6) low light intensity, (7) low soil nitrogen, and (8) low precipitation. The flora of the arctic and alpine regions is drawn from many different plant families, but all species must be able to cope with these environmental conditions.

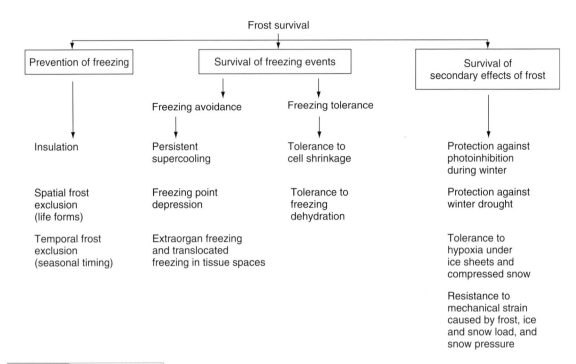

Frost survival

Prevention of freezing | Survival of freezing events | Survival of secondary effects of frost

Freezing avoidance | Freezing tolerance

Insulation | Persistent supercooling | Tolerance to cell shrinkage | Protection against photoinhibition during winter

Spatial frost exclusion (life forms) | Freezing point depression | Tolerance to freezing dehydration | Protection against winter drought

Temporal frost exclusion (seasonal timing) | Extraorgan freezing and translocated freezing in tissue spaces | | Tolerance to hypoxia under ice sheets and compressed snow

Resistance to mechanical strain caused by frost, ice and snow load, and snow pressure

Figure 4.28 How plants survive frost events and winter stress (from Larcher 2003).

Low temperatures appear to be the overriding factor. Life as we know it requires liquid water and, if the water is frozen, metabolic processes cannot occur. Further, when ice crystals form in tissues, cell walls and membranes are ruptured (for a graphic demonstration, take a piece of soft plant tissue like a fruit, freeze it, thaw it, and note how the tissues are softened and how much water leaks out). The exact temperature at which the liquid content of cells will freeze depends upon the concentration of solutes. In some cases cell fluids may be supercooled, meaning that they can be cooled to a temperature below freezing without ice crystals forming. Solute concentrations can be increased by the accumulation of soluble carbohydrates, polyols, amino acids, polyamines, and water-soluble proteins (Larcher 2003). These and other aspects of cold tolerance are summarized in Figure 4.28.

The predominant effect of low temperature is the reduction in acquisition of resources through lower rates of photosynthesis and nutrient uptake (Woodward and Kelly 1997) – this is why cold is considered a regulator. While the exact mechanisms will vary, it should again be evident that chemical reactions, in general, are a function of temperature and, furthermore, that most enzymes have certain temperature ranges within which they function most efficiently. While the cold conditions can be modified by increasing the temperature of tissues, or reducing the temperature of optimum enzyme function, there is no way to avoid the basic laws of chemistry. Plants can avoid cold stress by growing only during warm conditions, or they can tolerate cold, say, by increasing the concentrations of compounds within cells that act as anti-freeze, but both of these strategies have costs.

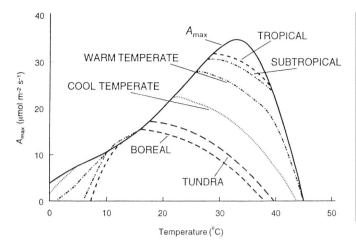

Figure 4.29 Temperature response of the maximum photosynthetic rate by biome. A_{max} is a general maximum photosynthetic rate that cannot be exceeded in any climate and has been defined from the temperature responses of CO_2 fixation, O_2 fixation, and high-temperature enzyme inactivation. The rates for biomes were derived from data referenced in Woodward and Smith 1994 (from Woodward and Kelly 1997).

Stress avoidance usually incurs the high costs of a greatly reduced growing season. Even brief cold periods can damage new shoots. "During the most intensive phase of elongation growth, most plants can scarcely become hardened at all, and are therefore extremely sensitive to low temperatures" (Larcher 2003, p. 387). The shoots of arctic and alpine plants must therefore be able to tolerate frosts even in the summer. Creeping and rosette growth forms are less exposed to damage from cold; their meristems are protected in at least three ways: they remain close to ground that is heated by the sun, they are less exposed to wind, and the dense (and often hairy) foliage may trap warm air (Archibold 1995). Some arctic plants also have deep anthocyanin pigmentation, which appears to increase rates of absorption and therefore the temperatures of tissues. Savile (1972) suggests that deeply pigmented plants can even extend the growing season by absorbing enough light to commence growth while still buried under snow in the spring. A few arctic and alpine plants also have flowers that track the sun and are shaped like parabolic reflectors (e.g., *Dryas integrifolia, Papaver radicatum*). The higher temperatures that are produced by this combination are thought to both attract pollinating insects and enhance maturation of the seeds by maintaining higher temperatures in the tissues of the ovary (Kevan 1975). Although many arctic plants have vivid flowers, nearly all have vigorous means for vegetative reproduction to maintain growth when the seed set is unreliable.

Stress tolerance incurs the cost of constructing anti-freezing compounds, and their possible interference with other aspects of cellular metabolism (Loehle 1998a). As a consequence of such constraints, the maximum photosynthetic rates of arctic and alpine plants are at best only a half of those of plants in warmer areas (Figure 4.29).

Woodward (1987) recognized five temperature limits for survival of different physiognomic classes of vegetation: evergreen broadleaf (chilling sensitive, 10 °C), evergreen broadleaf (frost sensitive, 0 °C), evergreen broadleaf survival (−15 °C), deciduous broadleaf survival

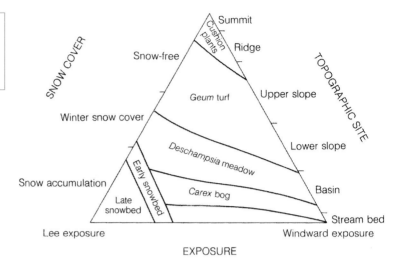

Figure 4.30 Alpine vegetation patterns associated with environmental gradients in the Rocky Mountains (from Archibold 1995).

($-40\,^{\circ}\text{C}$) and boreal ($<-40\,^{\circ}\text{C}$). Some species can withstand temperatures in excess of $-50\,^{\circ}\text{C}$.

Abrasion may be a less-appreciated consequence of cold. Savile (1972) observes that: "The most serious form of winter injury to arctic plants is unquestionably that due to abrasion by wind-driven snow particles" (p. 15). Rather than the large soft flakes of snow typical of the temperate zone, much of the arctic snow consists of small, hard, and sharp crystals which, when driven by winter gales, are strongly abrasive. Valleys and the lees of hills provide shelter where dwarf phanaerophytes are found, but each winter the new shoots may be trimmed back by winter gales. Woody plants may be abraded an entire meter above the snow.

These effects of wind abrasion may further illustrate why Raunkiaer placed emphasis upon the location of meristems in his physiognomic classification of plants (recall Figure 2.8). Traits that are interpreted as adaptations to cold may in fact be adaptations specifically to reduce abrasion. Many genera of arctic plants (e.g., *Empetrum*, *Salix*, *Vaccinium*, *Arctostaphylos*) have a prostrate, creeping growth form in spite of being woody plants. Others (e.g., *Draba*, *Diapensia*, *Cassiope*, *Saxifraga*) form densely packed shoots. Grasses and sedges tend to grow in tussocks where dead tissue provides protection to new shoots. Any variation in topography will modify exposure to wind speed and snow depth (Johnson and Billings 1962, del Moral 1983) with consequent changes in species composition (Figure 4.30). While areas that are buried by snow are protected from abrasion, they also have a very short growing season, and tend to have very few species (e.g., *Viola glabella*, *Luzula campestris*, *Ranunculus eschscholzii*, and *Carex spectabilis* in the Olympic Peninsula of western North America (del Moral 1983)).

Extreme environments such as cliffs may have arctic plants beyond what is considered their normal geographic range. These disjunct species presumably reflect distributions that were once

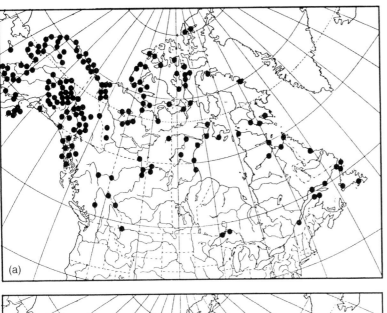

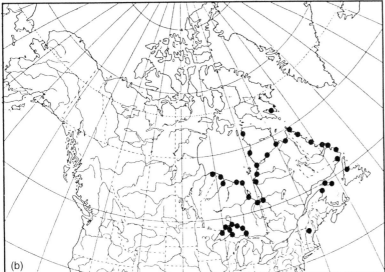

Figure 4.31 North American examples of arctic–alpine plant distributions: (a) *Cerastium alpinum* (s. *l.*); (b) *Castilleja septentrionalis* (from Given and Soper 1981).

more extensive during the ice age. The cliff creates a cold and wet environment that simulates some arctic conditions. It may also simply provide a refuge from competition with better-adapted temperate zone species. In eastern North America, for example, disjunct populations of arctic and alpine plants are found along the north shore of Lake Superior (Figure 4.31) and on sea cliffs in Nova Scotia.

4.5.3 Early spring photosynthesis in temperate climates

Botanists have long noticed that leaf shape varies with latitude: tropical plants tend to have comparatively large leaves with entire margins, but as mean annual temperature drops, the proportion of species with toothed or lobed leaves increases (Figure 4.32). Entire

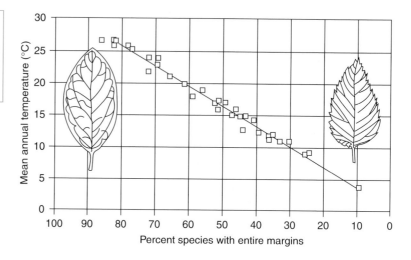

Figure 4.32 Correlation between the percentage of species in a local flora with entire-margined leaves (leaf on left) and mean annual temperature for mesic East Asian forests (from Wing 1997).

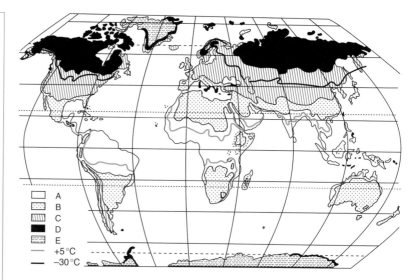

Figure 4.33 Occurrence of low temperature and frost on the Earth. zone A: Frost-free zone; zone B: episodic frosts down to −10 °C; zone C: regions with a cold winter and average annual minimum temperature between −10 and −40 °C; zone D: average annual minimum below −40 °C; zone E: polar ice and permafrost; —— −30 °C minimum isotherm; —— +5 °C minimum isotherm. The zones above correspond to the areas of distribution of species with different degrees of frost resistance. *Chilling-sensitive plants*: equatorial zone with minima not below +5 °C; *freezing-sensitive plants*: zone A; plants protected by *freezing point depression and effective supercooling*: zone B; plants with *limited freezing tolerance* and trees with wood capable of *deep supercooling*: zone C; completely *freezing-tolerant plants*: zone D (from Larcher and Bauer 1981).

leaves are also negatively correlated with mean annual temperature range (Pielou 1979). (This makes it somewhat easier to identify temperate zone trees, and explains why many temperate zone ecologists may be bewildered by tropical forests. How do you tell trees apart when their leaves are so similar?) This difference in leaf shapes is so well documented that paleo-ecologists use the nature of leaf margins on fossil plants to infer past climates (Wing 1997). The distribution of the world's principal forest types is closely related to a few key low-temperature isotherms (Figure 4.33). While the pattern is clear, the causal mechanism has, however, remained elusive.

Since early angiosperm forests were moist and tropical with largely entire leaves (Axelrod 1970, Niklas et al. 1985), one might ask whether the radiation of angiosperms into more extreme climates might have had something to do with leaf lobing. Here one must carefully consider the constraints acting upon temperate zone

 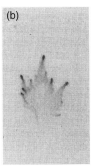  

5 mm

Figure 4.34 Autoradiography of immature leaves. The dark regions indicate ^{14}C assimilation due to heightened photosynthetic activity in the marginal teeth and lobes. (a) *Liquidambar styraciflua*; (b) *Acer rubrum*; (c) *Carya alba*; (d) *Ulmus alata* (from Baker-Brosh and Peet 1997).

trees, particularly the annual loss of leaves, an obvious example of stress avoidance. Leafless trees, however, cannot photosynthesize, and in the northern temperate zones, new leaves may not be fully expanded until early June, by which time it is nearly the summer solstice. It is hardly an exaggeration to say that by the time trees have opened their leaves, fully half the year's sunlight has already been received, and days are starting to shorten.

But this still leaves the unanswered question of why it should matter whether leaves are lobed. To explore a possible function of lobed leaves, Baker-Brosh and Peet (1997) used radioactive-labelled carbon to measure sites of photosynthetic activity in the juvenile leaves of 18 woody plants from temperate deciduous forests. Radiography showed that marginal teeth were far more photosynthetically active than the rest of the leaves (Figure 4.34): "Our data indicate that leaf teeth and lobe tips of some species mature early, producing swollen and photosynthetically active tissue while the leaf is quite young and otherwise not photosynthetically active .... The deciduous nature of temperate forests creates a situation where precocious photosynthetic structures may be beneficial to trees" (pp. 1253–1254). Lobes and teeth, then, may be leaf organs that mature early to take advantage of the precious long days of sunlight in the spring and help balance the inevitable costs of stress avoidance.

4.6 | Extreme cases of stress tolerance

4.6.1 Cold and drought tolerance of lichens

Lichens have long been regarded as one of the groups of macroscopic organisms most tolerant of cold, heat, drought, and radiation. To illustrate this hardiness, and the laminations upon it, consider one study on five species of *Umbilicaria*, frozen dry and stored in the dark at $-20\,°C$ for 10 years (Larson 1989). When thawed and placed in a controlled environment growth chamber, one species, *U. vellea*, showed an immediate return to normal rates of gas exchange.

Such hardiness, however, is less evident when the lichens are frozen wet. In any study of damage to lichens, it is essential to recall that lichens consist of two symbiotic organisms, an alga and a fungus, and either or both may be damaged independently. By

Table 4.4. *Responses of five species of* Umbilicaria *lichen after 10 years of storage at −20 °C (− no respiration, * respiration low, ** respiration high) (after Larson 1989).*

		Storage conditions			
		Frozen dry		Frozen wet	
Lichen	Habitat	Alga	Fungus	Alga	Fungus
U. vellea	Exposed cliffs	**	**	−	−
U. mammulata	Shaded cliffs	**	**	−	*
U. papulosa	Boulders and small cliff faces	*	**	−	*
U. muhlenbergii	Boulders and small cliff faces	−	*	−	*
U. deusta	Level snow-covered ground	**	**	**	**

measuring respiration rates in both the light and the dark, Larson was able to distinguish respiration by the fungal component alone. Four out of five species were damaged when frozen wet (Table 4.4). Photosynthesis was entirely absent, indicating the death of the alga, although some dark respiration showed that the fungal component was alive, if impaired, in three of these species. The one exception was *U. deusta*, which is found in sites that are sheltered, and which therefore may naturally be exposed to freezing when wet. Further, if a species from exposed cliffs, *U. vellea*, is experimentally moved to sheltered sites normally dominated by *U. deusta* (Scott and Larson 1985), it does not survive. Although sheltered sites might be thought to be more favorable to plant growth, it may be that the combination of freezing and wetness is unsuitable to most lichens.

4.6.2 Endolithic communities

Some plants may even grow within rocks. Extreme temperatures and wide temperature fluctuations are thought to be the principal factors rendering rock surfaces uninhabitable by plants (Bell 1993). Endolithic floras have been reported from sites in Europe, North America, South Africa, Australia, and Antarctica. Consider the last case. Some areas of the Antarctic continent are ice-free deserts; temperatures range from −15° to 0 °C in the summer to as low as −60 °C in winter. There is no visible plant or animal life, and even lichens are rare. A flora, including lichens and cyanobacteria, is found growing either in cracks (chasmoendoliths) or structural cavities in porous rocks (cryptoendoliths). Only translucent rocks can provide a habitat for such species. Figure 4.35 shows a cross-section through such rocks and a diagramatic interpretation of growth and exfoliation.

Rock-inhabiting species have been thoroughly studied on the limestone escarpment in southern Canada by measuring photosynthesis and respiration of rock fragments, assaying ground rock samples for chlorophyll, and using randomly located microscope fields to

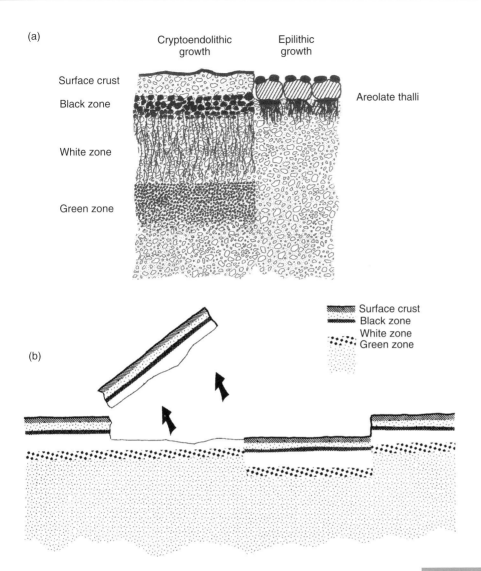

(a)

Cryptoendolithic growth

Epilithic growth

Surface crust

Black zone

Areolate thalli

White zone

Green zone

(b)

Surface crust
Black zone
White zone
Green zone

Figure 4.35 Lichens in Antarctic sandstone with (a) cryptoendolithic and epilithic growth contrasted and (b) exfoliation and regeneration (from Friedmann 1982).

count visible organisms (Matthes-Sears et al. 1997). To put the results of this study in context, the surface of the rocks showed cover of 26 percent by cyanobacteria, 20 percent by lichens, and 3 percent by green algae. In the endolithic samples, 50 percent of the random microscope fields contained fungi, 4 percent contained green algae, and 1 percent cyanobacteria. The abundance of fungi is noteworthy, since their source of carbon is unknown, and no other studies of endolithic communities mention fungi.

In this experiment, each square meter of rock sampled contained a mean of 73.0 mg of chlorophyll a and 19.8 mg of chlorophyll b, a majority of this in the surface dwelling (epilithic) species. All rock samples had high rates of respiration in the dark, but as light was raised to high levels (700 μmol $\cdot$ m^{-2} $\cdot$ s^{-1}), there was a net uptake of carbon. Given, however, that rates of dark respiration were five times higher than maximum net photosynthesis even under bright light, Matthes-Sears et al. (1997) concluded that the organisms on cliff faces were net consumers rather than producers of organic carbon.

4.6.3 Flood tolerance

Both too little water and too much water can be stresses. Some wetlands rival deserts in the severity of constraints imposed upon plant growth. The roots of actively growing plants require oxygen, and in well-drained soils, aerobic respiration of plant roots and soil microorganisms typically consumes 5 to 24 g oxygen per square meter (Jackson and Drew 1984). When the soil is flooded, pore spaces become filled, and gas exchange between the soil and the atmosphere is virtually eliminated. Micro-organisms and roots consume any remaining oxygen. Toxic compounds such as ammonia, ethylene, hydrogen sulfide, acetone, and acetic acid are then formed from the anaerobic decomposition of organic matter (Ponnamperuma 1984). Hence, an excess of water acts as a regulator. Flood tolerance has been dealt with extensively (e.g., Crawford 1982, Kozlowski 1984) and particularly in books on aquatic plants (Sculthorpe 1967, Hutchinson 1975).

The principal mechanism of stress avoidance is air spaces, lacunae, which may extend as aerenchyma tissue, from the leaf parenchyma through the petiole into the stem and into the buried rhizome or root. The continuity of these air spaces was (according to Hutchinson 1975) illustrated by Barthelemy, who, in 1874, found that when a leaf was placed under reduced pressure, air could be drawn upward from the rhizome. The presence of aerenchyma is one of the most obvious characteristics of wetland plants. In some cases, it appears that the roots of aerenchyma-bearing plants can oxidize their surroundings (Hook 1984) and even provide oxygen for the respiration of roots by neighboring plants (Callaway and King 1996).

In the absence of other evidence, it is assumed that oxygen diffuses down aerenchyma. But in water lilies, and perhaps in other species as well, there is an internal pressure gradient that causes mass flow. Gases are pressurized in young leaves, thereby forcing air down through the petiole into the rhizome, back up old petioles, and finally escaping through older leaves (Figure 4.36). As much as 22 l of air a day can enter a single floating leaf and flow to the rhizome (Dacey 1980, Dacey in Salisbury and Ross 1988, pp. 68–70). Most trees do not show such obvious features for withstanding flooding, but there is one conspicuous exception. Some woody plants produce above-ground extensions of their roots called pneumatophores (Figure 4.37). Although it has been suggested that this allows roots direct access to atmospheric gases, the function has yet to be convincingly demonstrated. It may simply be that pneumatophores vent toxic gases from the flooded soil. Since pneumatophores occur in both major groups of woody plants, gymnosperms (e.g., *Taxodium*) and angiosperms

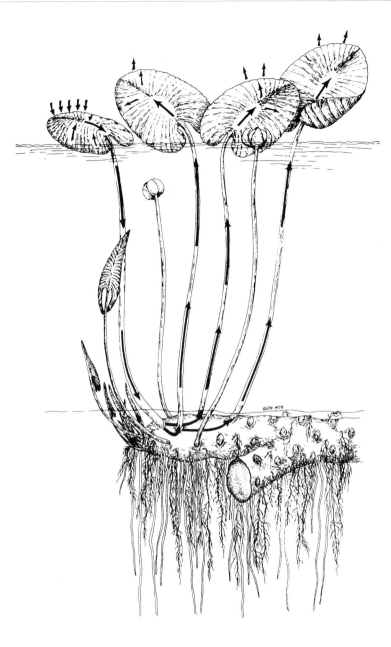

Figure 4.36 The movement of air through aerenchyma in water lilies (*Nuphar luteum*) (from Dacey 1981).

(e.g., *Avicennia*), there would seem to be some consistent evolutionary advantage to their possession.

Within a plant, flooding "usually sets in motion a sequential and complicated series of metabolic disturbances" (Kozlowski and Pallardy 1984). Stomata close, the rates of transpiration and photosynthesis decline, and the nitrogen and phosphorus contents of tissues decrease. Roots cease extending apical meristems and begin to degenerate. Ethylene levels in the tissues also increase (Reid and Bradford 1984), and this is implicated in stimulating the development of aerenchyma.

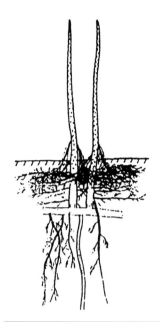

Figure 4.37 The rooting system of the mangrove *Avicennia nitida* under conditions of peat formation showing pneumatophores which may assist with aeration of the roots (from Chapman 1940).

Besides avoiding stress through the development of aerenchyma, there is also good evidence for tolerance to lack of oxygen in some aquatic plants. It has long been known that some contain ethanol and that the rhizomes of plants such as *Nymphaea tuberosa*, *Sagittaria latifolia*, and *Typha latifolia* can live anaerobically for extended periods (Hutchinson 1975). This remarkable tolerance of rhizomes to anaerobic conditions was demonstrated by Laing (1940, 1941), who grew rhizomes from genera including *Acorus*, *Nuphar*, *Peltandra*, and *Scirpus* in water through which nitrogen was bubbled. The rhizomes were able to respire anaerobically, producing ethanol, with 3 percent or less of oxygen. Both *Pontederia* and *Typha* showed long persistence even in pure nitrogen. In Laing's words:

> The presence of alcohol in the rhizome but not in the aerial leaf shows that anaerobic respiration or fermentation had undoubtedly occurred in the submerged portion of the plant. Rhizomes of *Nuphar advenum* dug from under the ice of a frozen lake in mid-winter possessed the usual terminal cluster of coiled young leaves commonly noticed in very early spring, thus showing that growth is practically continuous excepting during extremely low temperatures. These rhizomes contained an abundance of food reserves, as evidenced by the starch-filled cells of the uniseriate reticulum that makes up the bulk of the tissue, and they were practically comparable to those dug in mid-summer insofar as their respiration was concerned. This abundance of food and the ability to tolerate the by-products of fermentation help to explain how these plants can endure the anaerobic conditions of their habitat . . . .
>
> Although the amount of CO$_2$ produced aerobically was greater than that produced anaerobically, nevertheless it was seldom three times as much. If respiration in terms of the amount of carbon dioxide produced is taken as the criterion, then respiration in air is greater than that in the absence of oxygen, but if the amount of respirable material used is the criterion, then it is probable that respiration is greater in the absence of oxygen. This is according to the equation for aerobic and anaerobic respiration which states that only one-third as much carbon dioxide is produced anaerobically as aerobically from one molecule of glucose assuming that 2 molecules of alcohol are formed for each 2 molecules of CO$_2$. It is therefore evident that because of the lack of oxygen and consequent anaerobic respiration in these plants, more food material is utilized in respiration than would be utilized if the plants had access to more oxygen. Hence, while life in the water has some advantages such as more uniform temperature and freedom from drouth, nevertheless growth may be reduced due to excessive utilization of food in anaerobic respiration.

(Laing 1940, p. 580)

More recent work has expanded the list of species that grow apparently unimpeded by lack of oxygen (Spencer and Ksander 1997). Crawford (1982) proposes that some flood-tolerant species can also produce malate rather than ethanol. Moreover, the malate is available for aerobic respiration when inundation ceases, leading Hutchinson to suggest that this characteristic may be more typical of frequently flooded rather than permanently immersed species. Jackson and Drew (1984), however, are of the opinion that some of the evidence for metabolic stress tolerance in these latter species is still equivocal.

4.7 | The smoking hills: a natural occurrence of stress from air pollution

East of the delta of the Mackenzie River in the Northwest Territories of Canada, bituminous shale in 100-m-high sea cliffs has ignited naturally (Figure 4.38). Explorers document burning as early as 1826, but large piles of ash and oxidized shale at the base of the cliffs suggest that burning has occurred for a much longer period. The prevailing wind carries sulfurous plumes inland where the tundra is fumigated with sulfuric acid mists. Along a gradient of increasing exposure to smoke, concentrations of soil contaminants rise and the number of plant species declines (Freedman et al. 1990). In the most intensely affected sites, all terrestrial vegetation has been killed. Near the cliffs are pollution-tolerant species including *Artemisia tilesii*, the grasses, *Arctagrostis latifolia* and *Phippsia algida*, and lichens such as *Cladonia bellidiflora*. These species are rarely found elsewhere, except at sites where disturbance by erosion is frequent. The least polluted sites have typical tundra vegetation

Figure 4.38 Smoke rises from smouldering bituminous shale on the shores of the Beaufort Sea east of the Mackenzie River delta (from Freedman et al. 1990).

including lichens, bryophytes, *Carex* spp., *Eriophorum* spp., *Dryas integrifolia*, *Luzula arctica*, and *Salix glauca*. These effects rival the worst anthropogenic cases of ecological damage in the vicinity of metal smelters.

4.8 | Effects of ionizing radiation upon mixed forest

Long Island lies on the eastern coast of North America near New York, and is covered with oak-pine forest with *Quercus alba*, *Q. coccinea*, and *Pinus rigida* as the principal tree species (Figure 4.39). During the Cold War that followed the Second World War, in the 1950s and 1960s, there was great concern about the effects of the fallout that might occur after a nuclear war. These worries were amplified by the frequent testing of atomic bombs in the atmosphere, and by the growing risks posed by commercial nuclear reactors. To study the effects of radiation, a source of caesium 137 was exposed on a post in a stand of Long Island forest (Woodwell 1962, 1963). Rates of exposure varied from several thousand roentgens per day, within a few meters of the post, to about 2 R per day at a distance of 130 m. After 6 months of irradiation, effects were obvious as far as 40 m from the source, where exposure rates were approximately 40 R per day. Figure 4.40 shows the resulting vegetation zonation. Six zones could be delineated, ranging from total kill of all higher plants to intact oak-pine forest:

1. Devastated zone (>360 R·day^{-1}) where all woody and higher herbaceous plants were killed, leaving mosses and lichens.
2. Sedge zone (150–360 R·day^{-1}) where all woody plants were killed and the sedge *Carex pennsylvanica* increased in cover.

Figure 4.39 A devastated region of forest produced by six months exposure to gamma radiation shows up as a circular bare patch near the center of this aerial photograph. The forest is on the property of the Brookhaven National Library on Long Island, NY (from Woodwell 1963).

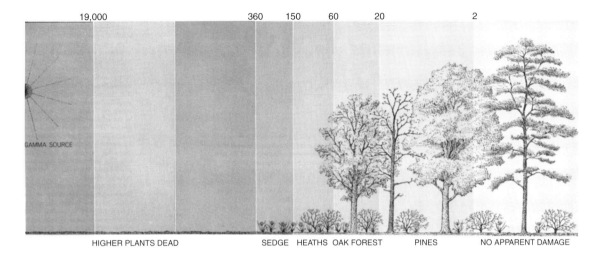

HIGHER PLANTS DEAD   SEDGE HEATHS OAK FOREST   PINES   NO APPARENT DAMAGE

Figure 4.40 The effects of chronic irradiation upon species composition and physiognomy of oak-pine forest on Long Island, NY. Numbers indicate radiation level (R·day^{-1}) (from Woodwell 1963).

3. Heath zone (60–150 R · day^{-1}) where the trees were killed and ericaceous shrubs were the dominant plants.
4. Oak forest (20–60 R · day^{-1}) where the pines were killed leaving an oak canopy.
5. Pine zone (2–20 R · day^{-1}) where pine shoot expansion was greatly reduced.
6. Oak-pine forest zone (<2 R · day^{-1}) where there was no apparent damage, although reduction in pine shoot elongation occurred at exposures as low as 1 R · day^{-1}.

Individual tree trunks provided sufficient shielding to produce green "shadows" of living *Carex* where most other vascular plants were killed. Lichens were most resistant to radiation, 11 species surviving on trees at exposures exceeding 2200 R·day^{-1} after 32 months. Pine trees were more sensitive than oaks. It appears that larger plants were more sensitive than small ones. Further, the relative sensitivities of tree species were inversely correlated with the mean volume of chromosomes at interphase. The diversity of plant species also decreased with increasing radiation.

Overall, there is a notable similarity in the response of the vegetation to stress from radiation and stress from natural gradients of soil depth or exposure. In all cases, woody plants are replaced by ericaceous shrubs, which in turn are replaced by grasses and sedges, with lichens in the most exposed sites. This suggests that responses of ecosystems to stress can be compared across different kinds of stress although, of course, details of species' responses will likely vary from one kind of stress to the next depending upon peculiarities of the autecology of the species (Rapport et al. 1985). Woodwell's experiment on Long Island provided early evidence of the severe ecological effects to be expected from nuclear war. In popular terms, it led to predictions that the post-nuclear world would be a "republic of insects and grass" (Schell 1982). Combined with other impacts such as those of nuclear winter, scientists concluded that any large-scale nuclear exchange would probably damage the victor nearly as much as the country that was defeated. Such experiments may have contributed to the ending of atmospheric testing of weapons, to nuclear non-proliferation agreements, and even to treaties that have reduced the risk of nuclear war.

4.9 | Moisture and temperature at different scales

Major biomes such as desert, rain forest, and boreal forest can be understood and explained by different amounts of rainfall and different minimum temperatures (Chapter 2). The distributions of species at more local scales can also be determined by differences in moisture and temperature. In the Great Smoky Mountains, for example (Whittaker 1956), the gradients of exposure and altitude that control tree distributions can be regarded as surrogates for moisture and temperature, respectively (see Figure 10.4). Similarly, differences in topography and snow accumulation will control moisture and temperature in alpine vegetation (Figure 4.30) and on cliffs (Figure 5.17). Studies that seek to explain such patterns by invoking stress (or, more precisely, strain caused by the physical environment) have to consider the many scales at which species are distributed and the many ways in which moisture and temperature can affect plants. To emphasize this obvious point, Figure 4.41 shows the hierarchical distribution of a moss, *Tetraphis pellucida*, from its global distribution at the upper left to its distribution on a single stump at the lower right. There is still not a single species of plant for which the causal factors of distribution, at each of these scales, are yet understood.

Although the mechanisms are likely complicated in their details, in the most general way, it seems reasonable that temperature and moisture are implicated for most species at each scale. Forman (1964) used 504 different experimental environments to measure growth of several life history stages of *T. pellucida*. The purpose of the experiment was to determine the environmental factors that limit growth of this species: "the distribution pattern at each level in the hierarchy," says Forman, "is explained by applying the experimental limits to known field conditions" (p. 24). At the continental scale, there was some similarity between experimentally predicted tolerance limits and the distribution of *T. pellucida*. Of ten transplant sites, growth occurred at three where it was predicted and did not occur at two where conditions were predicted to be unsuitable. The other five sites, however, gave ambiguous results, possibly due to other climatic factors or lack of adequate climatic data from weather stations.

In comparison with this study, most physiological studies are accompanied only by "explanations" for how the physiological traits adapt a species to its environment and control its distribution. Not

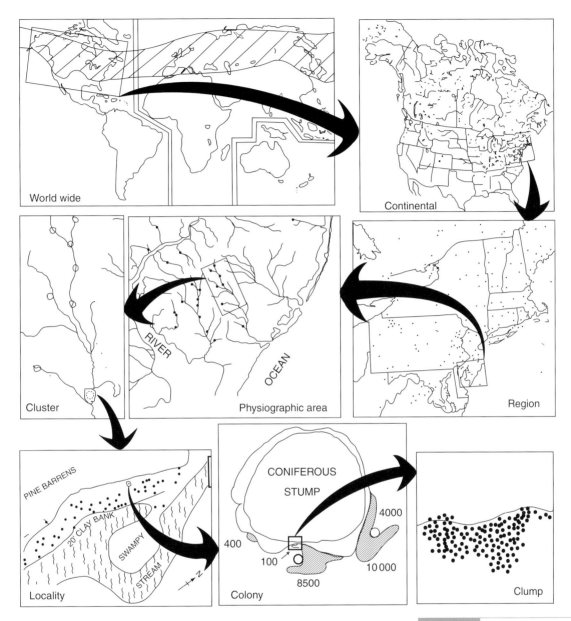

Figure 4.41 The hierarchy of distribution of the moss *Tetraphis pellucida*. Each map is a magnification of the square in the preceding map (from Forman 1964).

surprisingly, few workers have concluded that the physiology of their organism was *not* related to its environment! Nor is it typical to specify in advance what might constitute lack of fit. As a consequence, one could argue that much of the work written on stress consists of little more than physiological studies combined with entertaining stories about how the data show adaptation in nature. Forman's study was prescient in that in 1964 he had the courage to both make predictions from his physiological measurements and to admit failure when the predictions failed.

4.10 | Conclusion

The acquisition of resources is a basic task for all organisms. The study of stress is the study of those conditions that interfere with acquisition of resources. Stress is usually measured as the costs it imposes upon plants for the acquisition of resources, and while these costs can be measured at many levels of organization, reduced growth rates and reduced biomass are the most visible consequences. These can be experimentally studied by creating gradients of resource availability.

Many plants of stressed habitats have inherently low growth rates that remain even when moved to better growing conditions. Owing to their suite of distinctive species and communities, many stressed communities have special names such as alvar, maquis, fynbos, and kwongan. These often have rare or endemic plant species, and require special attention when considering conservation or management of unique habitats.

There is no entirely successful categorization of kinds of stress. The three-category classification used in this chapter (absence of resources, unavailability of resources, presence of a regulator) is artificial and not very satisfying – a conclusion you may already have reached from the selection of examples. Consider the limitations. The distinction between absence and unavailability is somewhat artificial since, from the plant's perspective, the situation is the same: a shortage of a resource is preventing growth. From an agricultural perspective, the distinction may retain its utility. In the first case, "absence of resources," one can increase productivity just by supplying the necessary resource – irrigation of deserts being an obvious example. In the case of "unavailability of resources," one needs instead to modify the environment in order to release the resource from its chemical bonds – afforestation is often accomplished by draining peatlands thereby allowing decomposition to occur and releasing nutrients for tree growth. The category of "regulators" is also problematic. Salinity is primarily a stress on plants, to be sure, yet seawater does contain many minerals essential for plant growth (Na, K, Mg, Cl); it is only the high concentrations of the minerals that create stress. In the case of flooding, a major part of the stress is caused by depletion of oxygen, which is a resource. Yet even if one were to somehow provide the roots of submersed plants with oxygen, the physical damage from moving water and the filtration of sunlight by water would remain as stresses (Larson 2001).

These three categories of stress are helpful if they illustrate the array of ways in which stress can occur; the same classification, however, can become an obstacle if one applies it mindlessly or if one attempts to fit every example encountered into a single neat category. Perhaps some bright young reader will produce a better system. Meanwhile, stressed vegetation types provide a natural experiment where ecologists can study the evolutionary consequences of chronic shortages of resources. These consequences can include evergreen foliage, low growth rates, high below-ground competition, carnivory, and communalism. Further, as humans continue to exploit and damage the biosphere, it appears that there will always be work for ecologists willing to study stress in ecological communities.

Further reading

Woodwell, G. M. 1962. Effects of ionizing radation on terrestrial ecosystems. *Science* **138**: 572–577.

Grime, J. P. and R. Hunt. 1975. Relative growth-rate: its range and adaptive significance in a local flora. *Journal of Ecology* **63**: 393–422.

Levitt, J. 1980. *Responses of Plants to Environmental Stresses*, Vols. I and II, 2nd edn. New York, NY: Academic Press.

Grime, J. P. 1979. *Plant Strategies and Vegetation Processes*. Chichester, UK: John Wiley.

Dacey, J. W. H. 1981. Pressurized ventilation in the yellow water lily. *Ecology* **62**: 1137–1147.

Friedmann, E. I. 1982. Endolithic microorganisms in the Antarctic cold desert. *Science* **215**: 1045–1053.

Rapport D. J., C. Thorpe and T. C. Hutchinson. 1985. Ecosystem behaviour under stress. *The American Naturalist* **125**: 617–640.

Givnish, T. J. 1988. Ecology and evolution of carnivorous plants. pp. 243–290. In W. B. Abrahamson (ed.) *Plant-Animal Interactions*. New York, NY: McGraw-Hill.

Keeley, J. E. and P. W. Rundel. 2003. Evolution of CAM and C_4 carbon-concentrating mechanisms. *International Journal of Plant Science* **164** (Supplement): S55–S77.

Larcher, W. 2003. *Physiological Plant Ecology: Ecophysiology and Stress Physiology of Functional Groups*. 4th edn. Berlin: Springer.

Richardson, S. J., D. A. Peltzer, R. B. Allen and M. S. McGlone. 2005. Resorption proficiency along a chronosequence: responses among communities and within species. *Ecology* **80**: 20–25.

Chapter 5

Competition

Brief history. Definition. Costs of competition: stress and strain. Intra-and interspecific competition. Competition intensity. Effect and response. Dominance. Monocultures. Asymmetry. Hierarchies. Mycorrhizae. Competition gradients. Old fields, prairies, alvars, wetlands, and mountainsides.

5.1 | Introduction

5.1.1 The importance of competition

More than a century ago, Malthus and Darwin both appreciated the intrinsic nature of organisms to multiply exponentially against limits set by resources and saw that this produced a struggle for survival. Thomas Malthus (1766–1834) was an English economist and clergyman; Charles Darwin (1809–1882) was, of course, the English naturalist who, along with Alfred Wallace, proposed the theory of evolution through natural selection. The capacity for exponential growth means that both houseflies and elephants, given sufficient time, could multiply rapidly enough to entirely cover the land area of Earth. Given a few more generations, a ball of flies or elephants would then expand outward from the Earth's surface and eventually reach light speed; the flies, being more fecund than the elephants, would, of course, have a head start. Darwin used a human example in *The Descent of Man and Selection in Relation to Sex* (1871):

> Civilised populations have been known under favourable conditions, as in the United States, to double their numbers in twenty-five years; . . . the present population of the United States (thirty millions), would in 657 years cover the whole terraqueous globe so thickly, that four men would have to stand on each square yard of surface. The primary or fundamental check to the continued increase of man is the difficulty of gaining subsistence [resources].
>
> (pp. 275–276)

Malthus and Darwin both saw that this did not happen because some other factor, usually a shortage of resources, prevented most young from surviving. Although each elm tree in a forest may produce millions of seeds, only one need reach adulthood for each tree to be replaced and for the forest to remain intact. The other millions of young must perish. Darwin reported that he saw, "on reading Malthus 'On Population' that natural selection was the inevitable result of the rapid increase of all organic beings." Malthus published

An Essay on the Principle of Population in 1798; even in the early 1800s, then, ecological similarities between humans and other "organic beings" were appreciated.

5.1.2 Definition of competition

While competition has long been important to humans, it has really been only during the last century that science has sought a precise definition. The right definition is like a sword that will clearly cleave nature into pieces that can be understood; the wrong definition is like a blunt instrument that only mashes the object of inquiry into more confusion. This is why scientists seem to spend so much time arguing about definitions. It may be difficult to find a definition of competition that will encompass the full array of possibilities in nature while simultaneously being precise enough to clarify every particular circumstance where it is applied. Further, one may look for a definition that emphasizes the mechanisms of competition, its measurement by means of experiment, or its long-term evolutionary consequences. Recent textbooks of ecology reveal a wide variety of attempts to satisfy these conflicting objectives. Some authors even advocate that the term no longer be used. In this chapter **competition** is defined as:

> the negative effects that one organism has upon another by consuming, or controlling, access to a resource that is limited in availability.

5.1.3 Stress, strain, and the costs of competition

One important feature of the definition of competition above is its emphasis upon the measurable costs of competition to the individuals experiencing it. While there are many possible long-term consequences of competition, which range from extinction to coevolution, one must begin with a clear understanding of the short-term effects of competition upon organisms. Recall from Section 4.2 that any stress has costs for an individual plant. These costs might be immediate (the need for increased root construction to locate water), or they might be longer term (the energy required to produce bark to reduce evaporation). Some environments are so far removed from an organism's requirements that they are lethal. One can measure the degree to which any environment departs from the optimum conditions by measuring what it costs the organism to survive under these suboptimal conditions.

If one begins with a situation in which abiotic conditions themselves already impose some metabolic strain (Section 4.1.2) upon individuals (Figure 5.1, lower curve), the presence of neighbors will increase the strain by further reducing resource levels. The strain of competition is therefore superimposed upon the strain already present from abiotic circumstances (Figure 5.1 top curve). Weldon and Slauson (1986) propose that competition should be defined as: "The induction of strain in one organism as a direct result of the use of resource items by another organism." While this definition

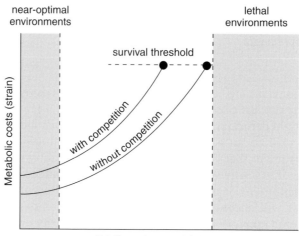

Figure 5.1 Suboptimal environments produce strain within organisms. At some extreme combination of conditions, the plant can no longer maintain homeostasis and it dies (●). Competition increases the abiotic stress by reducing resource supplies. This can be thought of as pushing habitats to greater extremes along the stress axis (from Keddy 2001).

places slightly greater emphasis upon mechanism, by introducing the concept of strain, it is very similar in intent to the definition used in this chapter.

5.2 | Kinds of competition

Let us continue the investigation of competition by examining the kinds of competition that occur.

5.2.1 Intraspecific competition

Plants require basic resources such as nitrogen, phosphorus, water, and carbon dioxide to construct their tissues (Chapter 3). As the number of plants in a unit area increases, the per-capita supply of resources declines; therefore, as plant density increases, the mean plant size declines. The relationship between plant density and plant size has been extensively studied because agriculture requires some understanding of the effects of sowing density upon crop yield. Even the backyard gardener thinning a patch of radishes or peas understands intuitively that reducing the density of plants will enhance the performance of remaining individuals. Ecologists have also studied the effects of density on plants because it is relatively easy to manipulate sowing density (much easier, say, than manipulating the density of bears, birds, or fungi) and thereby explore the effects of intraspecific competition. Figure 5.2 shows that eight different plant species all exhibit declining performance with increasing density. The steepness of the slope indicates how intense intraspecific competition is; the steeper the slope, the greater the effect each added individual has upon its neighbors (note the vertical scale is logarithmic).

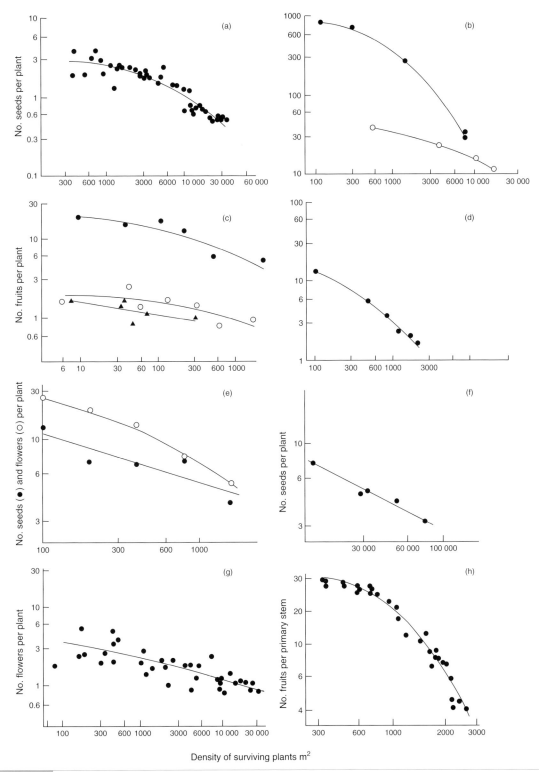

Figure 5.2 The relationship between reproductive output per plant and plant density at maturity. (a) *Vulpia fasciculata*, (b) *Salicornia europaea* in a high (○) and low (●) marsh. (c) *Cakile edentula* on the seaward (●), middle (○), and landward (▲) portions of a sand dune. (d) *Rhinanthus angustifolius*, (e) *Floerkea proserpinacoides*, (f) *Polygonum confertiflorum*, (g) *Diamorpha smallii*, (h) *Androsace septentrionalis* (from Watkinson 1985a).

The lines in Figure 5.2 are fit by an equation of the form:

$$w = w_m(1 + aN)^{-b}$$

where w is the weight of individual plants, N is density, and w_m, a, and b are parameters (Watkinson 1985a). The form of this equation is of some interest because w_m can be interpreted as the weight a plant will attain if grown in isolation – where intraspecific competition is zero. The area required to supply the resources to achieve w_m is then a: a is the minimum area, or the neighborhood, that a plant requires to find the resources necessary to achieve maximum growth. Finally, b can be considered a measure of the effectiveness with which resources are extracted from an area. Therefore, the actual yield of an individual plant, w, will decrease as N (density) increases, as a (minimum required area) increases, or as b (effectiveness of resource extraction) decreases.

The decline in reproductive output that occurs with increasing plant density is usually the result of individual plants being smaller and therefore yielding fewer seeds. In addition, the proportion of resources allocated to reproduction within an individual plant may decline with increasing density or decreasing resource supplies (Harper and Ogden 1970, Abrahamson and Gadgil 1973). To examine this experimentally, Snell and Burch (1975) grew *Chamaesyce hirta*, an annual member of the Euphorbiaceae, at four different densities combined with four levels of fertilization. Not surprisingly, mean plant size increased with fertilization and decreased with density, from a maximum size of 10 g at high fertility and low density to a minimum of <0.5 g at high density and low fertility. Over this extreme range of size variation, reproductive allocation declined from 26 to 7 percent (Figure 5.3). From one perspective, this testifies to the degree to which plants are able to maintain internal homeostasis and regulate biomass allocation in spite of an order of magnitude variation in size. From another perspective, it also appears that when resources are less freely available, a smaller proportion of them is invested in reproduction. Presumably this occurs because under stressful conditions of high density and low fertility, a greater proportion of the resources must be spent in building roots and leaves. Burch and Snell also expressed their results in calories as well as grams, although the actual limiting resources being partitioned may in fact be nitrogen or phosphorus rather than grams or calories of tissue. The actual currency by which one measures the costs of competition is still unclear.

5.2.2 Distinguishing between intraspecific and interspecific competition

The relative importance of intra- and interspecific competition can be measured using simple removal experiments. Consider the example of two desert shrubs, *Larrea tridentata* (creosote bush) and *Ambrosia dumosa* (burbage), which dominate some 70 percent of the Mojave

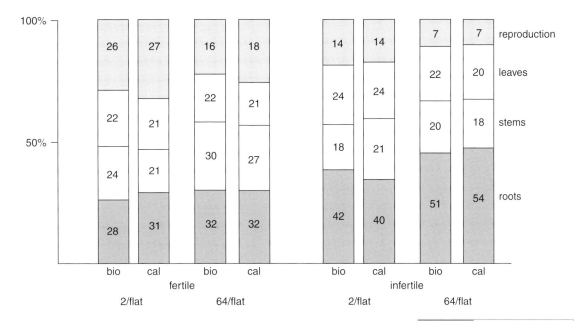

Figure 5.3 Allocation to reproduction is reduced by competition. Tissue allocation for the annual plant *Chamaesyce hirta* at two densities and two levels of fertility. bio, biomass; cal, calories (after Snell and Burch 1975).

Desert in the southwestern USA (Fonteyn and Mahall 1978). An advantage to studying desert plants is that the limiting resource is almost certainly water, and the water status of the test plants can be determined. By clipping off a branch and inserting it in a pressure bomb, one can measure how much of a water deficit exists in the branch, providing a nearly instantaneous measurement of how plants are being affected by neighbors. The lower the pressure, the greater the effect. The experiment had control plots and three different removal treatments for each of the two test species (Figure 5.4). Xylem pressure potentials were determined every two weeks through three consecutive wetting and drying cycles. Figure 5.5 shows that for both species, water potential was lowered by intra-specific neighbors (that is, the same species – histogram labelled intra) and by interspecific neighbors (histogram labelled inter). In *A. dumosa*, interspecific competition reduced water potential more than did intraspecific competition. In *L. tridentata* the two types of competition had similar effects on water potential.

5.2.3 Competition intensity

Competition intensity, or total competition, refers to the effects of all neighbors upon the performance of a population or an individual. This can be detected by removing all neighbors, and measuring the release, if any, of the remaining population or individual relative to control plots (for example, Putwain and Harper 1970, Fowler 1981). The individuals of the test species remaining in the treatment plots serve as a "bioassay" of competition intensity (del Moral 1983,

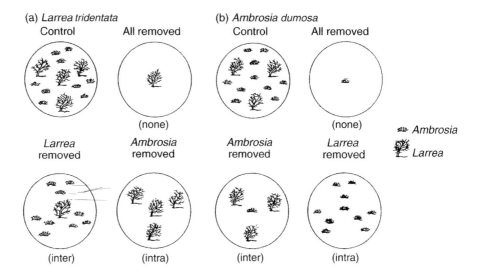

A removal experiment to measure intra- and interspecific competition in desert shrubs. In one treatment, both types of competition were removed (none) (from Fonteyn and Mahall 1981).

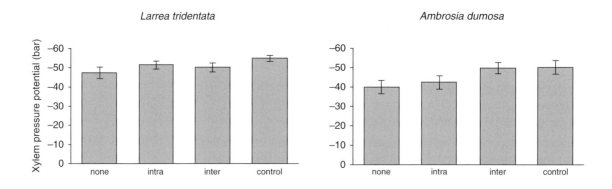

Effects of three kinds of experimental removals (see Figure 5.4) upon the xylem pressure potential ($\pm$ SE) of two desert plants at the end of July; these data could be re-scaled as percent reduction in performance relative to plants experiencing no competition (none) (after Fonteyn and Mahall 1981).

Wilson and Keddy 1986a). The difference between the performance of test individuals in treatment plots and in intact vegetation (control) measures competition intensity. Weldon and Slauson (1986) propose that competition intensity can also be measured by comparing the physiological state of organisms in plots with and without neighbors.

Shipley et al. (1991) assessed the mean intensity of competition faced by plant shoots in a large marsh along the Ottawa River, Canada. Ramets of three dominant plants (a sedge – *Carex crinita*, sweeet flag – *Acorus calamus*, cattail – *Typha angustifolia*) were placed in cleared plots (Table 5.1, cleared) and in intact vegetation (Table 5.1, control). The clearings were maintained by weeding and by the use of plastic barriers to prevent roots or rhizomes from re-invading below ground. Further, the experiment was repeated at three elevations to test for possible changes in competition intensity with flooding. After

Table 5.1. *Relative competitive intensity (RCI) in a riverine wetland measured over two years by the performance (proportional decrease in plant dry weight) of three plant species at three elevations (after Keddy 2001 after Shipley et al. 1991).*

Species	Elevation	Cleared (g)	Control (g)	CI[a]	RCI[b]
Acorus calamus	High	12.81	7.46	5.35	42
	Medium	12.18	11.13	1.05	9
	Low	7.77	2.59	5.18	67
Carex crinita	High	21.76	11.47	10.29	47
	Medium	16.44	8.85	7.59	46
	Low	23.34	19.89	3.45	15
Typha angustifolia	High	18.17	20.09	−1.92	−11
	Medium	51.42	27.66	23.76	46
	Low	22.20	26.05	−3.85	−17

Notes:
[a] CI = (cleared − control) (g).
[b] RCI = [(cleared − control)/cleared] × 100.

two growing seasons the transplanted shoots were harvested, dried, and weighed. The difference in weight between the transplanted shoots in cleared and uncleared plots provided the measure of competition intensity (CI). To correct for differences in test plant size, the absolute difference in weight was divided by the weight in the cleared plot, yielding relative competition intensity (Table 5.1, RCI). This shows that competition intensity was sometimes in excess of 50 percent (*A. calamus* on flooded sites low on the shore) and often greater than 30 percent (5/9 cases).

Surprisingly, there was no evidence of a change in competition intensity with test species or elevation. The data in Table 5.1 also suggest that species in some habitats (e.g, *T. angustifolia* at low elevation) might be entirely unaffected, or even assisted by the presence of neighbors.

5.2.4 Competitive effect and competitive response

When referring to the "competitive ability" of a species growing in mixture, one is actually describing something that has two separate components (Goldberg and Werner 1983, Goldberg 1990). The first is competitive **effect**: that is, the damage that each species can do to its neighbors. The second is competitive **response**: that is, the ability of each species to withstand the effects of competition from neighbors. In general use, it appears that the term "competitive ability" is frequently used as a synonym for "competitive effect"; more precision is needed.

The distinction between these components may be important in two ways (Goldberg and Werner 1983). First, competitive effects may be relatively similar among species, whereas responses may not. For example, a seedling growing in the shade is inhibited by lack of light and may be relatively insensitive to which species is actually intercepting the light. The competitive effects of all neighbors, then, may be similar. In contrast, each species of seedling might have different means to tolerate lack of light, so perhaps competitive response could be quite different. Recent experimental work, however, fails to support this suggestion; hierarchies of competitive response appear similar regardless of neighbor species (Goldberg and Landa 1991).

The categories above do not exhaust the possibilities for recognizing different kinds of competition and competitive interactions. Two others deserve consideration. First, Arthur (1982, 1987) has emphasized competition between different genotypes within populations and the evolutionary consequences of such interactions. This presents competition within the conceptual framework of ecology. Second, Buss (1988) has explored competition among different cell lines within individuals and its implications for the evolution of development. Although investigations of intra- and interspecific competition dominate the current literature, future progress may lie along research paths that explore higher levels of organization (e.g., competition intensity gradients) and lower levels of organization (e.g., intra-organismal competition).

5.2.5 Competitive dominance

Competitive dominance is an outcome of interactions where one species suppresses another through exploitation and/or interference competition. It is driven by **asymmetric competition**, which occurs when two competing plant species have different competitive abilities. In other words, competition is asymmetric when the effect of species A upon species B is large, while the effect of species B upon species A is small (Keddy 2001). Hence, one can usefully refer to one species as dominant and the other as subordinate. Asymmetric competition is probably widespread in nature. The effects of the dominant upon the subordinate increase through time by means of two positive-feedback loops (Figure 5.6). First, there is exploitation competition. The dominant lowers the resource levels for the subordinate and is simultaneously better able to forage for additional resources itself by reinvesting the newly captured resources in further growth. This foraging and growth lowers further the resources available to the subordinate. Second, there may be direct interference with neighbors to reduce their foraging and growth. The relative importance of these two positive-feedback loops is likely to vary from situation to situation, and in some cases effects may be separated into exploitation and interference only with difficulty. With plants, exploitation competition for light, water, and nutrients is well-documented. Interference competition is probably less important, but might involve plants poisoning their neighbors. This possibility has long

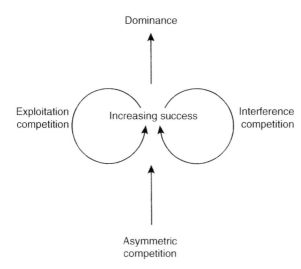

Dominance

Exploitation competition

Increasing success

Interference competition

Asymmetric competition

Figure 5.6 The positive-feedback loops that generate dominance. Success at exploitation competition increases the resources available to forage for new resources, and simultaneously reduces the resource supply for neighbors. Increased availability of resources allows some to be channeled to interference competition, damaging neighbors and leaving more resources available for exploitation by the dominant (from Keddy 2001).

been suspected (e.g., Molisch 1937, Muller 1966, 1969, Gopal and Goel 1993). Muller (1969) noted that biochemical interactions among plants had been reviewed 13 times between 1939 and 1960, yet the role of allelopathy is still contentious (Williamson 1990). The end-result of competitive dominance, however, is that one species suppresses another or excludes it from a given community. This is not a new idea. In 1929, Weaver and Clements wrote:

> The plants may be so nearly of the same height that the difference is only a millimeter. Yet this may be decisive, since one leaf overlaps the other. It continues to receive light and make photosynthate, while the shaded one can not. A difference of 2 or 3 days with full or reduced photosynthetic activity is quickly shown in difference in growth. The second pair of leaves of the fully lighted plant develops earlier, the stem is thicker and can better transport food to the rapidly growing roots. These, because of their greater food supply, penetrate a little deeper, spread farther laterally, and have a few more branches than those of their competitor. The increase in leaf surface not only reduces the amount of light for the plant beneath it, but it also renders necessary the absorption of more water and nutrient salts and correspondingly decreases the amount available. New soil areas are drawn upon for water and nutrients, and the less vigorous competitor must absorb in the area already occupied. The result is that the successful individual prospers more and more and becomes dominant.
>
> (p. 127)

One of the difficulties encountered when discussing dominance arises from the tendency to assume that competitive interactions are symmetric and to talk loosely about "competition" between two species. As soon as there is asymmetric competition, the experiences of the dominants and subordinates diverge. It becomes essential to

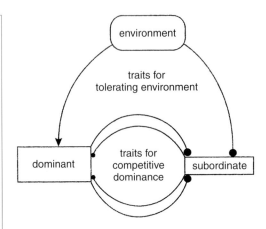

Figure 5.7 The possible interactions between the dominant, the subordinate, and the environment. Arrows are positive effects, solid circles are negative effects. Competitive dominance refers solely to the direct links between the dominant and the subordinate (bottom). The environment (top) may independently determine which species dominates a site. In this example the environment is enhancing the effects produced by asymmetric competition, so dominance is only partly attributable to competition (from Keddy 2001).

specify whether competition is being viewed from the perspective of the dominant or the subordinate. The analysis of such interactions is clarified by considering that in any competitive interaction there are both effects and responses (Section 5.2.4). The subordinate may be killed and disappear. The subordinate may tolerate the impact of the dominant, in which case it remains present, albeit at a low level. The subordinate may escape from the competition by dispersing in space or time to another site (ruderal or fugitive species). The analysis of asymmetric interactions requires explicit consideration of the effects of the dominant and of the responses of the subordinate organisms. These issues are discussed further in Section 5.4, which looks at hierarchically structured communities.

It is important here to clarify the distinctions between competitive dominance and dominance. The word dominant is sometimes used to describe any organism that is abundant in a community. This use is misleading; abundance need not be the result of competitive dominance. Competitive dominance is abundance achieved as a consequence of exploitation of, and interference competition for, resources; that is, there is an active process of suppressing neighbors (Figure 5.7, bottom). Grime (1979) describes dominance as a process whereby one species achieves numerical dominance and suppresses others. His use of dominance is not equivalent to the term competitive dominance used here, since Grime includes a second group of effects: a species may become dominant because of inherently better abilities to withstand environmental effects such as fire, infertility, or grazing. This added group of effects is shown in the upper portion of Figure 5.7. It seems useful to distinguish between situations where a species is dominant simply because of the inherent traits it has for tolerating the environment and situations where a species is dominant because it has traits for suppressing neighbors. The former type of dominance could occur in the absence of any competition. Experiments in which possible dominants are removed and the responses of subordinates observed are necessary to determine the kind of dominance present in a habitat or vegetation type. In this book competitive dominance is emphasized, but it is important to recognize that both forms of dominance occur in nature and that competitive dominance is a subset of dominance as used by Grime (1979).

5.3 | More examples of competition

5.3.1 Self-thinning

One of the simplest methods for detecting intraspecific competition is to test for a negative relationship between performance and population density. Performance (or fitness) can be measured in many ways, depending upon the organism and the circumstances; it can be determined by examining correlations between density and measures of growth rate, survival rate, and reproductive output. If the correlation is negative (higher density leading to lower performance) there is evidence for intraspecific competition. Figure 5.8 illustrates the possible relationships between performance and density and emphasizes that for any species there may be a different performance-density relationship for each habitat. Also, only a portion of the line shown in Figure 5.8 may be found in nature; experimental manipulation may be necessary to observe the dashed sections.

The relationship between the size of individuals and density has been extensively studied in plant populations, partly because of the obvious agricultural implications (recall Figure 5.2). Further, there is a well-established relationship, or "self-thinning line," between the mean mass of individuals and the density at which they are grown (Yoda et al. 1963, Harper 1977, Westoby 1984, Weller 1990), with a slope of $3/2$. Most of the data regarding plant–density relationships come from the experimental study of plants in **monoculture** (coexisting individuals of a single species); Gorham (1979), however, has shown that there is a strong relationship between shoot weight and shoot density across 29 different plant species (Figure 5.9) ranging in size from trees (upper left) to a moss (lower right).

Such descriptive approaches have three weaknesses which, depending upon the particular system, may be fatal flaws:

1. The most obvious is that correlation does not demonstrate cause and effect. Since different habitats, years, or quadrats provide each datum point, it is possible that the correlation is spurious. If, for example, habitats providing the most nitrogen were also most exposed to grazing or pathogens, high individual performance and low survival could be correlated in the complete absence of intraspecific competition.
2. A second, related, weakness is that such studies assume that only population density measures are needed to describe a particular habitat. Given the range of habitats that most species occupy, the performance–density relationship is likely to differ among them. Species may occur in habitats where populations have density-dependent relationships, and others where these are absent. Most species will therefore be represented by a family

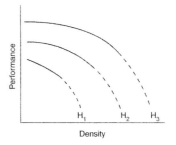

Figure 5.8 Hypothetical relationships between performance and density, which are consistent with intraspecific competition. Measures of performance may include survival, fecundity, or size. Each line represents a different habitat, emphasizing that performance–density relationships may differ with environmental conditions. In this case both the intercepts and shapes of the curves vary among habitats (see Keddy 1981c for other possible situations). The dashed sections of the lines represent situations not normally found in nature, which can only be observed by experimentally increasing population density (from Keddy 2001).

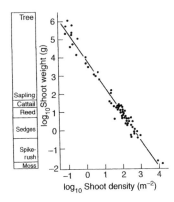

Figure 5.9 The relationship between performance (shoot weight) and density for 65 stands of plants representing 29 species from trees (upper left) to a moss (lower right). Intraspecific competition appears to set an upper limit to the number of shoots of a specific size that can coexist (after Gorham 1979).

of performance–density response curves (Keddy 1981c, Morris and Myerscough 1991).

3. A third potential problem is that a species may have the same density in two habitats, but in one there may be a positive population growth rate and in the other a negative growth rate. The equivalence of density may therefore be transitory and misleading.

5.3.2 Dominance patterns in monocultures

Although it is rare in natural communities, in agricultural situations monocultures are common; cotton and wheat fields offer two examples. In a monoculture, there is no interspecific competition. Since most of the individuals are fairly similar in relative competitive ability, one might expect that the plants would all grow to be nearly the same size. This is not the case. In fact, one often finds enormous differences in size developing. It seems that small differences in initial advantages, such as slightly earlier germination or a slightly better location, multiply up to enormous differences in outcome. To study this phenomenon, one can borrow from economists who have studied income disparity in human societies.

The basic experiment is as follows. One grows a monoculture of a selected species and measures the size of each plant. The dependent variable of the experiment is size variability, which could be measured by the standard deviation or coefficient of variation in size. The usual measure of size variation is the Gini coefficient, which varies from 0 (all plants identical) to 1 (plants maximally different in performance). Weiner (1985, 1986) has examined patterns in the Gini coefficient in groups of plants grown at different densities and at different fertility levels.

In theory, plants grown in monoculture might all be the same size. Weiner sets out to test this theory. He begins by contrasting two models that might cause departures from size equality. The first is an exponential resource depletion model (Koyama and Kira 1956). Consider a population of seedlings that are equivalent in size or normally distributed. Allow each seedling to grow in size exponentially. The final size distribution will be a function of several variables, but the important thing is that if initial sizes are equal and relative growth rates are normally distributed, a log-normal size distribution should develop. If both the initial sizes and relative growth rates are normally distributed, a log-normal distribution will still develop (Weiner 1986). Thus even if there is no interaction at all among seedlings, a log-normal size distribution can be expected. In contrast to this exponential resource depletion model are resource pre-emption models of competition: "Such models assume that larger individuals are able to get more than their proportional share of resources," and thereby grow at the expense of smaller individuals (Harper 1977, Weiner 1986, p. 215). There are various approaches for incorporating this sort of "one sided" or "asymmetric" aspect of competition, but it is what the model predicts that is of interest. The essential point of difference between these two types of models is that resource pre-emption models all predict higher size inequality at higher densities.

Instead of comparing the results of simulation models, Weiner compared data from published studies and then did some simple but compelling experimental studies. The comparison of published studies was clear: of 16 experiments, 14 supported the hypothesis of asymmetric competition (Weiner 1986). Then, in a series of experiments, Weiner manipulated density to explicitly test between the resource depletion model and the resource pre-emption model. The latter model predicts that size asymmetry (measured, in this case, by the Gini coefficient) will increase with density. Figure 5.10 shows the size distributions of a common herbaceous species, when grown alone, at low density and at high density, and at two different levels of soil fertility.

The results of Weiner's experiments are clear. Inequality increased from low to high density. These results contradict the resource

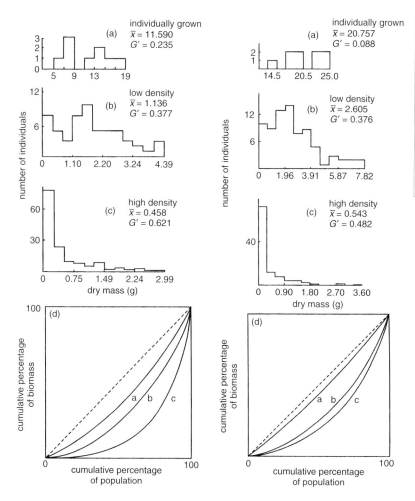

Figure 5.10 Dry mass distributions (with inequality measured by the unbiased Gini coefficient G') and Lorenz curves for monospecific populations of *Trifolium incarnatum* grown in low-fertility soil (left) and high-fertility soil (right). (a) individually grown, (b) low density (200 individuals/m^2), (c) high density (1200 individuals/m^2), (d) Lorenz curves for a, b, and c (from Weiner 1985).

depletion model. Finally, while both models predict increased plant-size inequality with increased soil fertility, the resource depletion model predicts that inequality should be greatest in plants grown individually, and this is what occurred with *Trifolium*. Weiner concludes that size differences are continually generated by dominance and suppression but are simultaneously reduced by mortality of the smallest individuals. He suggests that the mechanism for size hierarchies is asymmetric competition for light:

> ... a plant's ability to take up water or nutrients is a function of the surface area of its roots. A small plant with relatively little root surface area will not be able to absorb as much of the soil nutrients as a large plant, but it may be able to take up an amount proportionate to its root surface area, and accordingly to reduce the nutrients available to its large neighbour. However, when competition for light is intense, the effects of interference are not shared in proportion to size; a small plant will not be able to get its share of this resource, and its growth will be reduced disproportionately. Thus, if plants do not grow to the point at which the canopy becomes closed and competition for light is important, we would not expect to see dominance and suppression.
>
> (p. 748)

The development of dominance hierarchies among plants as a result of asymmetric competition is clearly demonstrated by Weiner's work on monocultures. If such size irregularities and suppression can arise in simple experimental monocultures, it becomes easier to see how they can arise in mixtures of species. In mixtures one can expect species to differ both in relative growth rates and ability to suppress neighbors. These differences can be expected to generate size inequalities even greater than those found in monocultures.

5.3.3 Density dependence in annual plants

The first two weaknesses of descriptive approaches in density dependence studies (Section 5.3.1) were addressed in a field study of an annual plant, *Cakile edentula*, which grows on sand dunes along the coast (Keddy 1981c, 1982). The third weakness was addressed in a re-analysis of these data (Watkinson 1985b). *Cakile edentula* can be found in a wide range of habitats and shows corresponding changes in plant size, reproductive output, survival, and population density (Keddy 1981c, 1982). These habitats are arranged along a gradient. At one end one can find large plants with thousands of seeds growing amidst decaying seaweeds on open sand beaches. At the other end tiny plants with but one or two seeds can be found beneath a canopy of dune grasses.

Density dependence was tested for by sowing a range of seed densities, allowing germination and growth to occur for one summer, and then testing whether performance was negatively correlated with sowing density. Two measures of performance were used: percentage of seeds sown that produced reproductive plants and mean number of fruits produced per plant. The principal results are shown in Figure 5.11. Density dependence clearly varied among the three

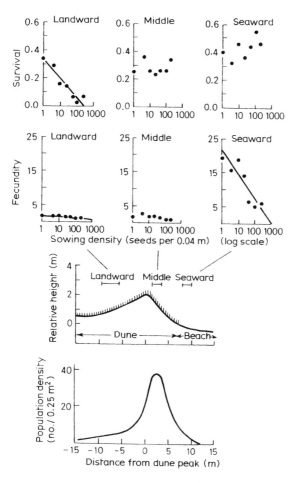

Figure 5.11 A study of an annual plant, *Cakile edentula*, growing on sand dunes, which shows that the effects of density upon survival and fecundity vary among habitats. The two measures of performance – survival and reproduction – had very different responses to habitat and density. Thus the habitat and the performance measure selected may determine whether a researcher detects competition in the field. For example, if the study had been conducted measuring only reproductive output in the middle section of the dune, which is where most of the plants are found, then no evidence for competition would have been detected (after Keddy 1981c, 1982, Silvertown 1987).

habitats. In the middle of the gradient there was no evidence for it. At the seaward end extreme crowding significantly reduced only reproductive output, whereas at the landward end both reproductive output and survival declined with density. Survival reduction was the predominant effect at the landward end.

There are two general conclusions for studies of intraspecific competition. First, the relationship between performance and density is not a trait of a species, or a population alone, but is strongly dependent upon the environment itself. Second, the dependent variable selected is extremely important: if only survival or reproductive output had been used, then entirely different conclusions would have been reached about the magnitude of intraspecific competition in different habitats. The problem with this experimental approach is that it does not yield unequivocal statements about the actual intensity of intraspecific competition in real populations unless the usual range of population density in the habitat is known. If, for example, seaward populations usually have low densities (and they do), then the intensity of intraspecific competition shown in the seaward site is a potential that is rarely realized. Thus, such experimental data need to be combined with measures of population density.

One problem of interpretation still has not been removed: how is one to know that the density dependence is attributable to intraspecific competition? Many potentially confounding effects of temporal or spatial variation have been eliminated by using experimentally produced densities, so that a large number of potential alternative hypotheses have been eliminated; others, however, remain. If predation were density dependent, then the density dependence of survival could be attributed to predation, not competition. In fact, epidemics of damping-off disease (Burdon 1982) do occur in *C. edentula* populations, although there was no evidence for it in the year in which this study was conducted. Mixed strategies can even be imagined where intraspecific competition weakens individuals that then fall prey to pathogens or are buried by drifting sand because of their small stature. One source of evidence for competition would be to augment the supply of a resource that is postulated to be limiting. By running a series of treatments with nitrogen fertilization, Keddy (1981c) showed that reproductive output of low-density landward plants (but not their survival) increased when this potential resource was supplied. This is additional evidence that intraspecific competition for nitrogen limited plant size. Since there were no effects on survival, one may postulate that an independent factor (perhaps competition for another resource, or predation) controlled survival.

The greatest weakness in this sort of experimental study is the absence of information on year-to-year variation. If storms destroy seaward populations in most years, then intraspecific competition may be much less important than the data in Figure 5.11 suggest. This criticism could only be answered by repeating the study in several years with very different weather conditions.

5.3.4 The relationship between intensity and asymmetry of competition

There are relatively few studies of asymmetry and intensity, and even fewer where both are measured simultaneously. Johansson and Keddy (1991) therefore grew six species of wetland plants in an additive pairwise design, so that asymmetry and intensity could be measured in each pairwise interaction. An additive design is one in which plants are grown singly to measure their potential performance and then grown with a series of neighbors to measure how each neighbor suppresses performance. Based upon a survey of traits in 43 species of wetland plants (Boutin and Keddy 1993), six species were selected for testing: three were obligate annuals and three were facultative annuals. These represent only two of a much larger number of functional groups found in wetland plants, but all of the plants selected were capable of completing their life cycle within a single growing season. Each species was grown alone to measure, Y, the yield of one individual. To assess the effects of neighbors, relative yield per plant (RYP) was calculated. When species i was grown with species j, performance in mixture (Y_{ij}) was divided by performance when grown alone (Y_i) to measure the reduction in performance from the neighboring plant. For example, when a relatively weak competitor, *Mimulus ringens*, was grown with a relatively strong competitor, *Lythrum sali-caria*, its biomass declined by 0.86 compared to its biomass when grown alone; that is, RYP = 0.14. Conversely, when the strong competitor *L. salicaria* was grown with *M. ringens*, its performance declined by only 0.24; that is, RYP was 0.76. Therefore, two RYP values are obtained for each mixture, since each species in mixture can be compared to its growth alone.

To estimate the intensity of competition in any pot, one sums the declines in performance observed for each species. In the example above, the intensity of competition in mixture was the sum of 0.86 (the decline of *M. ringens* owing to *L. salicaria*) and 0.24 (the decline of *L. salicaria* owing to *M. ringens*). For any pair of species, intensity was measured as $I = [(1 - RYP_{ij}) + (1 - RYP_{ji})]$. If both species are little reduced in mixture, I is near zero, whereas if both species are greatly reduced, I approaches 2.

Asymmetry can be measured by comparing the relative decline of species' performance in mixture. If both species decline the same amount in mixture, irrespective of whether it is a large or small decline, then the interaction is symmetric. In the example above, *M. ringens* declined 0.86 in mixture, whereas *L. salicaria* declined only 0.24; this is a relatively asymmetric interaction. One measure of asymmetry is $A = [(1 - RYP_{ij}) - (1 - RYP_{ji})]$; A can range from 0, where the species suppress each other equally, to 1, where one species eliminates the other. These two measurements, I and A, produce a phase space where intensity can range from 0 to 2 and asymmetry can range from 0 to 1. The 36 pairwise interactions measured by Johansson and Keddy (1991) occupied a small region of this space (Figure 5.12). Asymmetry values ranged from approximately 0.1 to 0.7, while intensity values ranged between 0.6 and 1.1.

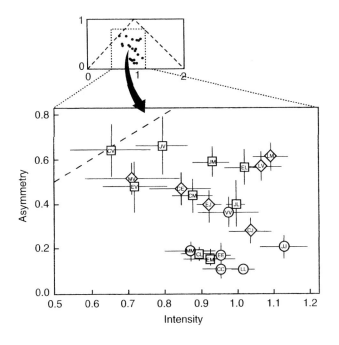

Figure 5.12 Phase-space diagram of asymmetry and intensity of competition for interactions between two plants of different species, where ○ = intraspecific, ◇ = intra-guild and □ = inter-guild interactions. Species names are abbreviated as follows: C, *Cyperus rivularis*; E, *Eleocharis obtusa*; J, *Juncus bufonius*; L, *Lythrum salicaria*; M, *Mimulus ringens*; V, *Verbena hastata*. For clarity, the upper small diagram shows the whole area of possible value ranges for asymmetry and intensity in a competitive interaction, with the dashed lines indicating the theoretical limits. In the lower diagram the area, which covers intensity and asymmetry values from this experiment, is enlarged. Note that, for visual expression, the intensity axis is disproportionately enlarged (from Johansson and Keddy 1991).

5.4 | Competitive hierarchies

5.4.1 Establishing hierarchies

Plant communities usually contain many kinds of species mixed together. It is not uncommon to find from 10 to 25 species in one small plot of grassland or wetland. How do all these species interact with one another? Why are some relatively common and others relatively rare? To explore completive interactions in the community, one could simply choose two species and measure their relative competitive ability. But which two species should you choose? If you choose the two commonest ones, it is possible, perhaps even probable, that you will also select two competitive dominants. You thereby lose information on the effects of these two dominants upon all the other plant species in the community. Arbitrarily choosing two species is clearly not a good way to study competitive interactions within a community.

One alternative is to include all the species in one large experiment. In such an experiment, each species is grown with every other species. There are some problems with this approach. The first is the sheer size of the experiment – if there are n species you wish to study, there are $(n^2/2)$-n possible pairs of plants to grow in mixture. (The term n^2 is divided by two because when you grow species A with species B, you simultaneously grow species B with species A.) The second issue is a technical one. You must also grow plants of each species without interspecific competition, in **monoculture**, to use as reference plants for assessing the effects of interspecific competition. Do you grow the monoculture plants singly (without any competition), or do you grow the monoculture plants paired with a second individual of the same species (with intraspecific competition)? The first case is known as an **additive** design, whereas the second case is known as a **substitutive** design. Each has its strengths. Most studies use the substitutive design, sometimes termed 'deWit replacement series' or 'diallele' (de Wit 1960, Harper 1977), although it is possible that the additive design is preferable (Firbank and Watkinson 1985, Connolly 1986, Keddy 2001).

You should know how to interpret such experiments. Let us consider an example from a wetland plant community where seven species of plants were grown in all possible pairwise combinations using a substitutive design (Table 5.2). The table contains values of RIP$_{ij}$ (relative increase in biomass per plant compared to biomass in monoculture) for target species (i) grown with neighbor species (j). The RIP for each species grown with itself (monoculture value; often referred to as RYP$_{ii}$ or relative yield per plant) is assigned a score of 1.0, forming the diagonal of the matrix. The first column, Dul, shows how *all target species* respond to being grown with *one* neighbor species, *Dulichium arundinaceum*, a shoreline sedge. Two species are strongly inhibited by *D. arundinaceum*, Jun (*Juncus pelocarpus*) with an

Table 5.2. *Pairwise interactions among seven wetland plants. RIP is the relative increase in biomass per plant of species i when grown with species j. A row shows the effects of all neighbors on one target species and a column shows the effects of one neighbor on all target species (from Wilson and Keddy 1986b).*

Target species*	Neighbor species							Target score**
	Dul	Jun	Lys	Hyp	Rhy	Dro	Eri	
Dul	1.00	1.33	1.18	1.17	1.25	1.18	1.34	1.20^{ab}
Jun	0.63	1.00	1.34	1.46	1.46	1.52	1.49	1.28^{a}
Lys	0.88	0.87	1.00	1.63	1.63	1.78	1.57	1.31^{a}
Hyp	1.09	0.99	0.91	1.00	1.22	1.29	1.23	1.11^{abc}
Rhy	1.05	0.73	0.93	0.91	1.00	1.21	1.36	1.03^{bc}
Dro	0.98	0.91	0.93	1.02	1.02	1.00	1.11	0.98^{bc}
Eri	0.65	0.71	0.88	0.89	0.87	1.48	1.00	0.93^{c}
Neighbor score	0.89^{a}	0.93^{ab}	1.03^{abc}	1.15^{bcd}	1.21^{cd}	1.35^{d}	1.30^{d}	

Notes:
* Dul = *Dulichium arundinaceum*, Jun = *Juncus pelocarpus*, Lys = *Lysimachia terrestris*, Hyp = *Hypericum ellipticum*, Rhy = *Rhynchospora fusca*, Dro = *Drosera intermedia*, Eri = *Eriocaulon septangulare*
** Target and neighbor scores not significantly different from one another (Tukey's studentized range test, p < 0.05) are denoted by common superscripts.

RIP of 0.63 and Eri (*Eriocaulon septangulare*) with a RIP of 0.65. Two others species are less negatively affected (RIPs of 0.88, 0.98). Two species grow slightly better with *D. arundinaceum* than in monoculture, Hyp (*Hypericum ellipticum*) with a RIP of 1.09 and Rhy (*Rhynchospora fusca*) with a RIP of 1.05. The same sort of species by species analysis can be done with each column. In the last column, for example, all species grow better (RIP > 1) with *E. septangulare* as a neighbor than when grown with their own species. In contrast to a column in the table, a row shows how *one* target species responds to *all neighbor species*.

The table thus gives the results of all possible pairwise interactions among these plants. Now let us try to sort the species from strongest to weakest competitor. One way to do this is to compare the RIPs of target species (ie., compare rows in the table). The greater the competitive ability of a target species, the fewer neighbors will suppress it (ie., the higher the number of RIPs >1). For target species suppressed by the same number of neighbor species (e.g., Lys and Hyp, each suppressed by two neighbor species), the mean RIP (target score) is used to determine competitive strength (Lys is stronger than Hyp). These two criteria were used to order the species in Table 5.2 from strongest (*D. arundinaceum*, not suppressed by any neighbors, all RIPs > 1) to weakest competitor (*E. septangulare*, suppressed by five neighbor species). In a similar way, competitive ability could be determined by the ability of a species to suppress other species (the greater the number of RIPs in a neighbor column that are <1, the greater the ability of the species to suppress other species). Further, species could also be ordered from most to least competitive by target score (mean amount of suppression) or neighbor score (mean ability to suppress). In the first case, *Lyssimachia terrestris* (highest target score) would be the strongest and *E. septangulare* (lowest target score) the weakest. In the second case, *D. arundinaceum* would be the strongest (lowest neighbor score) and *D. intermedia* (highest neighbor score) the weakest.

Such tables provide important information about the multiple competitive interactions that can organize plant communities. At a minimum, they allow us to picture how each species affects the other species. These sorts of tables also provide a basis for further questions. One can test for hierarchies of sets of species, and compare one matrix to another (Box 5.1). One can ask whether the hierarchies change if you change the growing conditions (Section. 5.4.2). One can ask what plant characteristics might determine position in the hierarchy (Section 5.4.3).

5.4.2 The consistency of hierarchies

If communities are composed of species with relatively similar competitive abilities and contingent competitive interactions, reversals of position in competitive hierarchies should be commonplace. But if species differ in their relative competitive abilities, if interactions are asymmetric, and if competition is relatively less contingent, one may expect reversals of positions in competitive hierarchies to be relatively less common. There is a good deal of evidence to suggest that the latter situation seems more typical of real communities. Yet, in spite of the evidence of hierarchies, the view of symmetric interactions and contingent competition is firmly entrenched. In addressing the defenders of contingency and symmetry, Shipley and Keddy (1994) noted the marked tendency of the critics to prefer opinions over data.

The following examples examine three explicit tests for consistency in relative competitive ability. The first test used 23 species of wetland plants transplanted into two contrasting environments: fertile and infertile (Gaudet 1993). Relative competitive effect was measured by the ability of each species to suppress the growth of a reference species, *Lythrum salicaria*. Figure 5.13 shows that after two growing seasons, the competitive effect of species in fertile conditions is strongly correlated with competitive performance in infertile conditions. At the same time, the relationship is imperfect ($r^2 = 0.58$); it appears that changing the environment may allow a species to slightly improve its performance relative to that of a neighbor in a similar position in the hierarchy but not significantly change its position in the hierarchy. (That is to say, an apprentice may become a journeyman, or a duke or earl, but there is no evidence that an apprentice suddenly rises to become king.)

Box 5.1 | Testing for higher order pattern in competitive relationships

Experimentally derived competition matrices may contain important information about the nature of plant interactions. Keddy and Shipley (1989) explored such matrices for two properties: (1) the degree of asymmetry (non-reciprocity) of pairwise interactions, and (2) the degree to which species are arranged in competitive hierarchies (transitive networks).

Let Y_{ii} be the yield of an average individual (ramet) of species i grown in monoculture and Y_{ij} be the yield of an average individual of species i when grown in mixture with species j. A common measure of competitive ability of species i relative to species j is its relative yield per plant:

$$RYP_{ij} = Y_{ij} / Y_{ii}.$$

An RYP_{ij} value greater than 1 means that species i grows better in mixture with species j than it does in monoculture. If n species are grown in all pairwise combinations then an $n \times n$ matrix of RYP values is obtained. A binary matrix A can be constructed in the following way:

$$a_{ij} = \{1 \text{ if } RYP_{ij} > 1, 0 \text{ if } RYP_{ij} < 1\}.$$

Such a matrix records which species are competitively superior to other species. Using graph theory, one can construct paths of increasing length; the length of a path is one less than the number of species included within it. Figure B5.1(a) shows a transitive path with three species. The path begins with species 1, passes through species 2, and ends at species 3. The path is transitive because knowledge that species 1 competitively excludes species 2, and that species 2 competitively excludes species 3, implies that species 1 also competitively excludes species 3. Thus the species can be ranked in a hierarchy from species 1, which is capable of excluding other species, to species 3, which is capable of excluding neither of the other two species.

Note that there are also three transitive paths of length one, corresponding to the three cases of pairwise interactions. Figure B5.1(b) also shows a path of length two, but this time the path is intransitive, since although species 1 excludes species 2, and species 2 excludes species 3, species 1 does not exclude species 3. Table B5.1 summarizes the competitive hierarchies detected in nine published experiments using this technique. In every case except the last one (Harper 1965) the matrices show strong evidence of transitive competitive hierarchies.

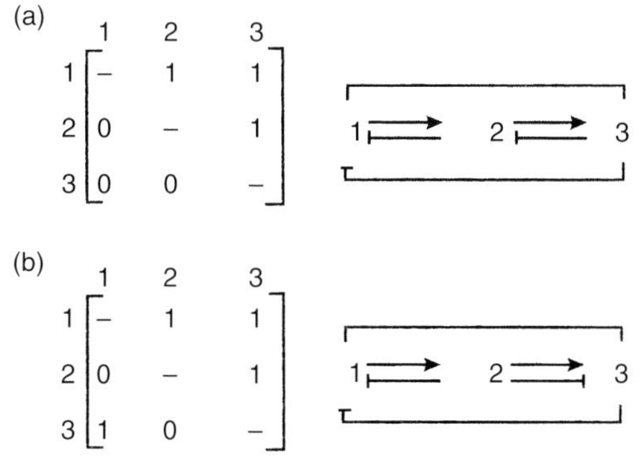

Figure B5.1 Representation of competitive hierarchies as graphs. (a) Transitive: a binary matrix and digraph with a transitive path of length two; (b) intransitive: a binary matrix and digraph with an intransitive path of length two (from Keddy and Shipley 1989).

Table B5.1. *The total number of transitive paths of various lengths (L) in the binary matrices of eight published competitive diallele experiments. T (L), The total possible number of transitive paths of various lengths in each matrix; p, the binomial probability of "success"; μ, the number expected; m(L), the number observed, and the probability of at least m(L) transitive paths occurring under the null hypothesis; S, the number of species (or varieties) in the matrix; θ, the frequency of 1's in the binary matrix (from Keddy 2001 after Keddy and Shipley 1989).*

L	T(L)	p	μ	m(L)	Probability ($\geq m(L)$)
Wilson and Keddy (1986b): $S = 7$, $\theta = 26/42$					
1	21	4.8×10^{-1}	4.95	16	6.6×10^{-3}
2	35	2.6×10^{-2}	0.46	16	1.3×10^{-16}
3	35	6.3×10^{-3}	0.11	7	2.0×10^{-9}
4	21	1.5×10^{-3}	0.02	1	3.0×10^{-2}
Mitchley and Grubb (1986): $S = 6$, $\theta = 19/30$					
1	15	4.6×10^{-1}	3.48	11	3.3×10^{-2}
2	20	2.6×10^{-2}	0.25	5	1.1×10^{-4}
3	15	5.8×10^{-3}	0.04	1	8.4×10^{-2}
Goldsmith (1978): $S = 13$, $\theta = 86/156$					
1	78	5.0×10^{-1}	19.29	56	$<5.0 \times 10^{-7}$
2	286	3.0×10^{-2}	4.33	90	$<5.0 \times 10^{-7}$
3	715	7.4×10^{-3}	2.68	98	$<5.0 \times 10^{-7}$
4	1287	1.9×10^{-3}	1.19	60	$<5.0 \times 10^{-7}$
5	1716	4.6×10^{-4}	0.39	19	$<5.0 \times 10^{-7}$
6	1716	1.1×10^{-4}	0.10	2	1.6×10^{-4}
Caputa (1948), year 1944: $S = 9$, $\theta = 34/72$					
1	36	5.0×10^{-1}	18.0	32	8.9×10^{-7}
2	84	3.1×10^{-2}	2.60	50	4.5×10^{-53}
3	126	7.7×10^{-3}	0.97	47	2.9×10^{-64}
4	126	1.9×10^{-3}	0.24	26	1.3×10^{-43}
5	84	4.8×10^{-4}	0.04	8	1.2×10^{-15}
6	36	1.2×10^{-4}	0.00	1	4.3×10^{-3}
Caputa (1948), year 1945: $S = 9$, $\theta = 39/72$					
1	36	5.0×10^{-1}	18.0	27	1.7×10^{-3}
2	84	3.1×10^{-2}	2.57	31	2.2×10^{-24}
3	126	7.6×10^{-3}	0.96	17	2.0×10^{-15}
4	126	1.9×10^{-3}	0.24	3	1.8×10^{-3}
Caputa (1948), year 1946: $S = 9$, $\theta = 31/72$					
1	36	4.9×10^{-1}	17.65	27	1.4×10^{-3}
2	84	2.9×10^{-2}	2.48	26	1.1×10^{-18}
3	126	7.2×10^{-3}	0.91	18	3.9×10^{-17}
4	126	1.8×10^{-3}	0.22	7	3.9×10^{-8}
5	84	4.3×10^{-4}	0.04	1	3.6×10^{-2}
Williams (1962): $S = 7$, $\theta = 24/42$					
1	21	4.9×10^{-1}	10.29	16	1.0×10^{-2}
2	35	2.9×10^{-2}	1.03	16	1.9×10^{-14}
3	35	7.2×10^{-3}	0.25	5	5.2×10^{-6}
Harper (1965), low density: $S = 6$, $\theta = 17/30$					
1	15	4.9×10^{-1}	7.37	11	5.2×10^{-2}
2	20	3.0×10^{-2}	0.59	6	1.8×10^{-5}
Harper (1965), high density: $S = 6$, $\theta = 17/30$					
1	15	4.9×10^{-1}	7.73	7	6.7×10^{-1}
2	20	3.0×10^{-2}	0.59	2	1.2×10^{-1}

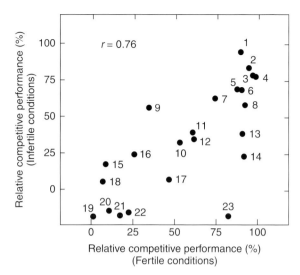

Figure 5.13 Competitive performance of 23 wetland plant species under low nutrient conditions plotted against competitive performance under high nutrient conditions. Adult plants were collected and grown together for two growing seasons. 1, *Lythrum salicaria*; 2, *Phalaris arundinacea*; 3, *Phragmites communis*; 4, *Typha xglauca*; 5, *Euthamia galetorum*; 6, *Mentha arvensis*; 7, *Acorus calamus*; 8, *Spartina pectinata*; 9, *Juncus filiformis*; 10, *Lysimachia terrestris*; 11, *Eleocharis palustris*; 12, *Eleocharis calva*; 13, *Sparganium eurycarpum*; 14, *Scirpus fluviatilis*; 15, *Triadenum fraseri*; 16, *Dulichium arundinaceum*; 17, *Carex crinita*; 18, *Viola lanceolata*; 19, *Scirpus torreyi*; 20, *Juncus pelocarpus*; 21, *Eleocharis acicularis*; 22, *Hypericum ellipticum*; 23, *Rumex verticillatus* (from Keddy 2001 after Gaudet 1993).

The second test involved 20 species of wetland plants, grown from seed, which interacted for one growing season. The species again ranged from large aggressive species (e.g., *Typha angustifolia*) to small, rare rosette species (e.g., *Sabatia kennedyana*). Performance in infertile conditions was again strongly correlated with performance in fertile conditions (Figure 5.14).

A third test used species from different terrestrial habitats: 63 species of herbaceous plants from old fields, rock barrens, and alvars in eastern Ontario (Keddy et al. 2002). In this case, the reference species was an annual plant typical of disturbed habitats. The plant species chosen were differently distributed along a gradient of soil depth and water availability, and the experimental treatments consisted of large, well-watered versus small, droughted pots. The relative competitive performance of the plants was based on their ability to suppress the reference species. Figure 5.15 shows that competitive performance in large and small pots was strongly correlated.

5.4.3 Light and shoot size

One of the basic characteristics of plants is their dependence upon sunlight. If two plants are neighbors and one plant is slightly taller than the other, then there are immediate consequences. The taller plant intercepts more light, as a consequence of its height, and is thereby further enabled to grow; simultaneously, it deprives the shorter plant of some photons and thus inhibits the growth of the shorter plant. This sets up two positive-feedback loops (Figure 5.6) that can often lead to increased success for the large plant and declining success for the small one. Short plants simply do not shade tall ones to the same extent that tall ones shade short ones. Competitive hierarchies may therefore be inevitable consequences of differences in size (Weaver and Clements 1929, Weiner and Thomas 1986, Keddy and Shipley 1989). Interestingly, allometric studies of fossils reveal an

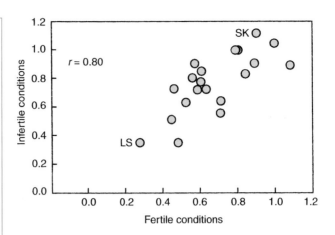

Figure 5.14 Competitive performance of 20 species of wetland plants grown in infertile conditions plotted against their competitive performance in fertile conditions. Note that the greater the competitive effect, the lower the position on the axes, since these values reflect the size of the three indicator species grown with each of the 20 test species. At the bottom left is *Lythrum salicaria* (LS), a fast-growing invasive species, and at the very top is *Sabatia kennedyana* (SK), a rare species that in Canada is restricted to a few lakes in a single river valley of Nova Scotia (from Keddy et al. 1994).

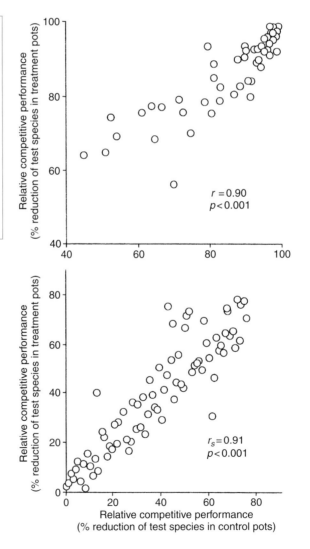

Figure 5.15 Competitive performance of 63 species from old fields, alvars and rock barrens of eastern Ontario in a stress treatment (small pots, drought) plotted against competitive performance in the control treatment (large pots, well watered). The top figure shows competitive performance measured as actual percentage reduction in the phytometer and the bottom figure shows only rank order (position in competitive hierarchy) (from Keddy et al. 2002).

exponential rate of increase in plant height during the Devonian era (Niklas 1994). This exponential rate of increase would be consistent with increasing competition for light as a result of increased terrestrial plant biomass.

Of course, plants do not compete only for light; nor do they interact only by shading. Access to light, however, can control a plant's ability to acquire other resources. Light is necessary both for constructing roots and for the physiological processes of nutrient uptake. Plants with more access to light will therefore be better able to forage for nutrients than plants with less access to light. Plants that are shaded are not only denied the photons necessary for constructing above-ground parts, but, simultaneously, their access to other raw materials is reduced, and their growth is further restricted. Minor differences in height, amongst plants, can have a major effect on both the quantity and quality of the light available. Fitter and Hay (1983) have shown that light availability declines exponentially with distance below the top of the canopy; also, the red to far-red ratio declines below the canopy. Aware that light is an essential resource for plants, Weiner (1986) designed an elegant experiment to compare above- and below-ground competition: he found that competition for light was asymmetric, whereas competition for nutrients was symmetric. Other relevant examples are discussed in Keddy and Shipley (1989).

If asymmetric interactions for light determine a plant's position in a competitive hierarchy, then plant height should be significantly correlated with position in the hierarchy. Clements (1933) summarized the results of hundreds of transplant and removal experiments done with prairie vegetation (for example, Weaver and Clements 1929, Clements et al. 1929) and concluded that, in general, "the taller grasses enjoyed a decisive advantage over the shorter." Goldsmith (1978) studied sea-cliff plants and showed that the larger species suppressed the smaller (Figure 5.16). Wilson and Keddy (1986a) experimentally derived a competitive hierarchy for seven shoreline species. The dominants were tall species, whereas the subordinate was a small, rosette species. Keddy and Shipley (1989) showed that more than one-third of the competitive ability of these species, when grown in mixture, could be predicted based on knowledge of their heights ($r^2 = 0.37$). Similarly, in a chalk grassland study, Mitchley and Grubb (1986) derived a dominance hierarchy for six plant species. They found a significant correlation between position in the hierarchy and mean turf height of the species in monoculture; they noted that "the plants with the tallest leaves were the most effective interference." Mitchley (1988) has since shown that there is a positive correlation between the height of grassland species and their relative abundance.

Since diallele designs increase in size by the square of the number of species examined, there are upper limits upon the number of species that can be studied if one wishes to relate traits to competitive ability. To overcome this problem, Gaudet and Keddy (1988) used a modified

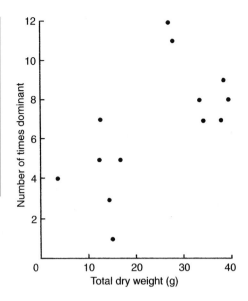

Figure 5.16 The relationship between position in the competitive hierarchy (measured as number of times dominant) plotted against plant size in monoculture for sea-cliff plants (data from Goldsmith 1978). Large plants suppress small ones, but the relationship is less clear for plants that are very similar in size ($r = 0.61$; $P < 0.05$) (from Keddy 2001).

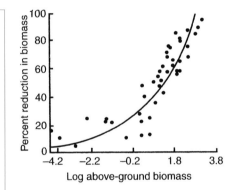

Figure 5.17 Screening for competitive ability in wetland plants. Percentage reduction in the biomass of *Lythrum salicaria* (when grown with different neighbors) plotted against the mean above-ground biomass of each of the neighbors [44 species, $n = 5$ replicates, $y = \exp(3.34 + 0.44x)$, $r^2 = 0.69$]. The points on the left represent small evergreen species such as *Ranunculus reptans* and *Lobelia dortmanna* whereas points on the right represent large, leafy species such as *Typha latifolia* and *Lythrum salicaria* (data from Gaudet and Keddy 1988).

additive design that incorporated 44 wetland plant species that differed greatly in size, morphology, and other traits. To measure competitive ability, each plant species was grown with a reference species or phytometer (*Lythrum salicaria*), and competitive ability was measured as the ability to suppress this phytometer. They showed that simple traits such as biomass, height, and canopy diameter could account for 74 percent of the measured competitive ability. Above-ground biomass was the best predictor ($r^2 = 0.43$). A subset of the species was tested against a different phytometer and similar results were obtained. Figure 5.17 shows the relationship between the percentage reduction in the phytometer and above-ground biomass for the 44 species.

The importance of size in determining competitive ability is well established, but what other traits might control the competitive success of plants? One might ask whether a plant's ability to forage for resources is important. Early studies of resource uptake focused upon measures of the gross uptake of nutrients, as estimated by

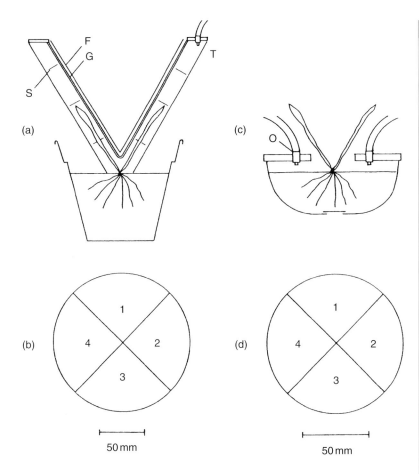

Figure 5.18 Two techniques to assay the "resource-foraging" attributes of the leaf canopy and root system of individual plants. Plants are presented with standardized patches of resource depletion created without the use of partitions or barriers that could impede growth between patches. Light patches (a, b). (a) Section through cone-shaped chamber for imposing partial shading on developing shoot system. A transparent glass upper surface (G) is covered with filters (F) to produce standardized patches of shade. Fine struts (S) support leaves and the chamber is supplied with compressed air (T). (b) View from above of shading pattern. Quadrants 1 and 3 are fully illuminated and quadrants 2 and 4 are shaded filters. Nutrient patches (c, d). (c) Section through bowl used to impose patches of nutrient depletion on developing root system. Nutrient solution fed by peristaltic pumps is dripped continuously onto the surface at symmetrically arranged outlets (O). (d) View from above of nutrient distribution pattern. Quadrants 1 and 3 are supplied with nutrient-rich solution and quadrants 2 and 4 are supplied with nutrient-poor solution (from Grime 1994).

the relative growth rates of seedlings grown under standardized conditions (e.g., Grime and Hunt 1975, Grime 1979). Other studies of resource uptake have emphasized various factors thought to be significant in nutrient uptake such as early germination (Wilson 1988), root morphology (Boot 1989), and shoot thrust (Campbell et al. 1992). Recently emphasis has turned to the ability to forage for nutrients in patchy environments. While many pot experiments provide relatively homogeneous water and nutrient conditions, in the field these resources occur, at least at the small scale affecting single plants, as ephemeral patches.

5.4.4 Foraging for patches of light or soil nutrients

We do not know what other plant traits may determine competitive ability. We need more systematic measurements of plant traits. Campbell et al. (1991) introduced two new techniques to investigate the efficiency with which different plant species were able to exploit patches of light or nutrients (Figure 5.18). Using their procedure, one can measure the partitioning of dry matter – the investment the plant makes in either shoots or roots – between depleted and undepleted sectors. In the studies examined here, several different species of

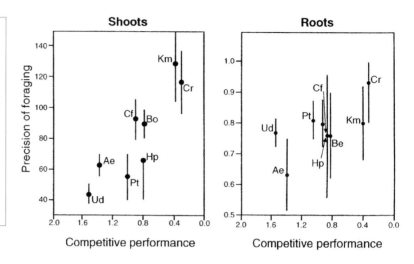

Figure 5.19 The relationship between precision of foraging and competitive performance for eight herbaceous plant species from Britain. Precision is measured as percentage of either shoot or root biomass allocated to resource-rich quadrants. Competitive performance is measured as log relative percentage of shoot biomass after growing in mixture for 16 weeks (note reversal of horizontal axis!) (after Grime 1994).

plants were first grown in a uniform productive environment; resource patchiness was then imposed upon them. These same species were also grown together in an equiproportional mixture in a greenhouse in order to assess their relative competitive performance. The question that such an experiment is designed to answer is whether the precision with which plants can exploit resource patches is a predictor of their performance when in competition with neighbors. Figure 5.19 shows that the species with the best performance in mixture (Ud, *Urtica dioica*, and Ae, *Arrhenatherum elatius*) showed low precision in foraging ability. While the results are interesting, there are several limitations in this work, notably the small number of species and the large confidence limits upon the measure of precision. Further, plant performance in mixture is based upon only 16 weeks of growth. Nonetheless, this study illustrates the benefits that can be obtained from systematic measurement of ecological and physiological attributes under standardized conditions – if the trouble is taken to relate these to other attributes such as competitive performance.

5.5 | Mycorrhizae and competition

It is important, when studying plant competition, to consider mycorrhizae and the role that they play in resource uptake by plants (Section 3.4.3). Might mycorrhizae influence the relative competitive ability of plants? Mycorrhizae could modify competitive interactions amongst plants by transferring either soil resources or carbohydrates from dominant plants to subordinate ones (Newman 1988, Allen and Allen 1990). The ubiquity of networks of fungal hyphae linking plants is now well appreciated, and plant mycorrhizal associations are widespread, except in certain narrow sets of conditions (e.g., flooding) and in certain plant families (e.g., Cyperaceae, Proteaceae).

Eissenstat and Newman (1990) tested the possibility that mycorrhizae influence competitive relationships by growing seedlings of plantain (*Plantago lanceolata*) alone and with older plantain plants, and with and without mycorrhizae. The expectation was that the seedlings would suffer asymmetric competition when grown with the larger adults, and the issue to be tested was whether these effects would be ameliorated if the seedlings were infected with mycorrhizal fungi. To measure competitive performance, three characteristics of seedlings were measured: biomass, phosphorus content, and nitrogen content. There were no significant benefits to seedlings when infected with fungi (Figure 5.20). In fact, Eissenstat and Newman noted that "the concentration of nitrogen and phosphorus was higher in the seedlings than the large plants ... so that net transport of nitrogen and phosphorus from large to small plants seems unlikely." Similar results, reported by Ocampo (1986), were achieved when *Sorghum* was used as a test species.

While the work of Eissenstat and Newman and Ocampo focused on the possible amelioration of intraspecific competition, Grime et al. (1987) tested the possible effects of mycorrhizae on interspecific competition. They grew seedlings of 20 grassland plants in mixture with larger *Festuca ovina* plants, with and without mycorrhizae. Although the mycorrhizae had little impact on the performance of *F. ovina* seedlings competing with larger plants of the same species, the balance between *F. ovina* and seedlings of other species was affected. Thus, mycorrhizae may play a role in interspecific competition, but a minor role that does not change the relative position in a hierarchy. Similarly, when two species of grass (*Holcus lanatus*, *Dactylus glomerata*) were grown in competition both with and without infection by arbuscular mycorrhizae, infection was found to increase plant weight, but any increases were offset by the higher intra- and interspecific competition that resulted from the plants being larger. As a consequence, when mycorrhizal and non-mycorrhizal treatments were compared, the benefits of mycorrhizal infection declined with increasing density (Watkinson and Freckleton 1997).

While mycorrhizae do not appear to change the relative competitive ability of plants, further work to examine the role of mycorrhizal networks in allowing subordinates to persist in the presence of competition seems worthy (Allen and Allen 1990). Any work will, however, need to clearly distinguish between mycorrhizae as agents of persistence as opposed to agents that can shift competitive relationships. To use an analogy from economics, mycorrhizae may act as a kind of welfare, but they do not so far appear able to alter class structure. Some studies suggest that fungi infecting the aerial portions of plants (mycophylla *sensu* Lewis 1987) have an important role in plant growth, from grasslands to tropical rain forest canopies (Carroll 1988). Compared to mycorrhizae, mycophylla have received very little attention, although there is evidence that they too can affect the relative competitive abilities of individual plants (Clay 1990).

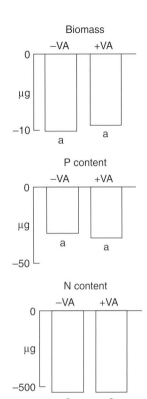

Figure 5.20 The reduction in biomass and nutrient content of shoots of plantain seedlings, grown with (+VA) and without (−VA) mycorrhizae, caused by competition with large plants. Means followed by the same letter are not significantly different at $P < 0.05$ (determined by competition × mycorrhizal interaction in a two-way ANOVA) (from Eissenstat and Newman 1990).

5.6 | Competition gradients

5.6.1 Measuring competition intensity

The intensity of competition may be one of the most fundamental properties of a community. Techniques for measuring competition intensity have tended to view vegetation as aggregations of populations and consequently have tried to dissect these communities by studying pairwise interactions among species. In natural plant and animal communities, however, each species present experiences the cumulative effects of all neighbors more or less simultaneously (Keddy 1989, Grace 1993). In such cases, each species is said to be experiencing "diffuse competition." I prefer, and use in this section, the broader term "competition intensity" for the combined effects of neighbors; diffuse competition and predominant competition are then two ends of a continuum (Keddy 2001).

Competition intensity is measured by comparing the performance of a control organism (all neighbours present) with that of a treatment (all neighbours absent) (Figure 5.21). If the removal of all neighbors has no effect on performance, competition intensity is not detectable. The greater the difference between treatment and control, the greater the intensity of competition. This technique borrows from Clements's early work on phytometers (Weaver and Clements 1929, Clements 1935). Transplanted test individuals, he argued, were more sensitive than any environmental measurements taken at a site. Of course, it is probable that the removal of neighbors from plant communities will lead to measurable increases in light, soil moisture, and nitrogen and phosphorus levels. While measurement of these factors would be helpful for developing an understanding of the possible mechanisms of competition, it is only by allowing one or more test plants to consume these resources that one can determine just how much performance has been reduced by surrounding neighbors. If the experimental design in Figure 5.21 is repeated in a series

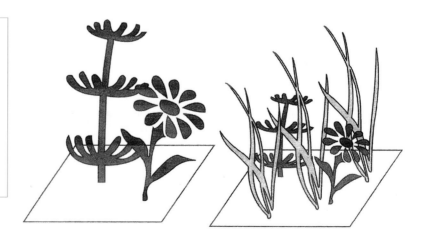

Figure 5.21 The use of two indicator species to measure competition intensity at one point along a gradient. The test species are transplanted into a clearing (left) and intact vegetation (right). The difference in biomass of the test species after a period of time is directly proportional to the intensity of competition in the intact vegetation (courtesy of C. Gaudet).

of habitats, it then becomes possible to test whether there is a gradient of competition intensity along the series of habitats.

5.6.2 Competition intensity gradients in an old field

Most natural gradients include a set of correlated environmental factors. In old fields, for example, depressions accumulate water and nutrients while ridges tend, by comparison, to be dry and infertile. Hawkweed (*Hieracium floribundum*) is a rosette plant that is frequently found in dry and infertile fields and pastures. Reader and Best (1989) studied the performance of this plant using demographic variables: survival, recruitment, and population growth. Rather than studying a series of sites along the topographic gradient, they examined the extremes of the gradient, the tops and bottoms of depressions. Depression bottoms had deeper soil, more nitrogen and phosphorus, higher above-ground biomass and lower light levels. In each habitat, the performance of *H. floribundum* was measured with and without neighbors. Only in the bottoms of depressions did competition have a significant effect on performance (Figure 5.22). Another element of this experiment was the addition of water to increase the availability of a possibly limiting resource (watered treatments are designated "wet" in Figure 5.22). Watering increased recruitment of rosettes significantly only in the bottoms of depressions. In contrast, watering had no effect on mortality.

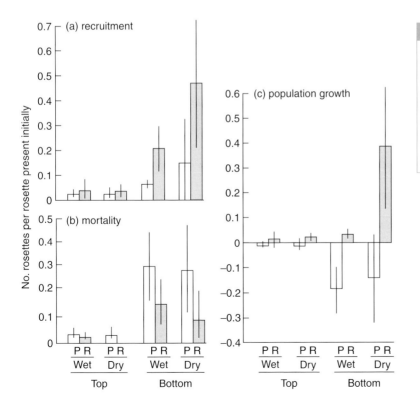

Figure 5.22 Mean (± 1 SD) of (a) recruitment, (b) mortality, and (c) population growth (i.e., recruitment minus mortality) for *Hieracium floribundum* with neighbors present (P) or removed (R) in subplots watered frequently (wet) or infrequently (dry) at the top or bottom of depressions (after Reader and Best 1989).

Overall, population growth was affected directly only in depression bottoms by removing neighbors and by increasing the availability of water.

Reader and Best conclude that the prostrate growth form of *H. floribundum* makes it particularly sensitive to shading. The sensitivity of rosette species to environmental gradients has been documented in habitats ranging from British grasslands (e.g., Grime 1973a,b) to North American wetlands (e.g., Keddy 1983). The study by Reader and Best illustrates several distinctive approaches to the study of competition. It used demographic variables rather than biomass to measure performance, contrasted two sites rather than a complete gradient of sites, experimentally supplemented a resource, used existing plants rather than transplanted individuals, and used a test species with a distinctive and widespread growth form.

5.6.3   Competition and cacti

Cacti can occur in grasslands as well as deserts, particularly in arid, exposed sites with low plant cover. Burger and Louda (1995) used a factorial design experiment to test whether competition with grasses is a factor controlling the distribution of *Opuntia fragilis*, in the Sandhills prairie of western Nebraska. The experiment had plots with and without neighbor vegetation that were watered and unwatered. In each plot the performance of *O. fragilis* and damage from insects were assessed for two years. Performance of the cactus was measured by counting the number of cladodes, or pads, that comprise a plant. Cactus plants without neighbors had nearly three times the number of cladodes, which shows clearly the effects of competition, but the addition of water did not have an effect on competition. Finally, herbivore loading was higher with neighbors. Larvae of the stem-feeding moth, *Melitara dentate*, and the weevil, *Gerstaeckeria* sp., were the major causes of cladode death, and these higher death rates may also exclude *O. fragilis* from areas of dense grass. In this case, then, the effect of herbivores appears to enhance rather than counteract those of competition with grasses in restricting the distribution of *O. fragilis*.

5.6.4   Competition intensity along a soil depth gradient

Soil depth is a useful natural gradient on which to base a study of plant communities. Not only is soil depth easily measured, but all major soil resources (e.g., water, nutrients) are correlated with soil volume. This simplifies the complexity of multiple measurements of soil resources. Belcher et al. (1995) therefore sought out a plant community in an area where shallow soil was a predominant factor limiting growth – an alvar. An alvar is a terrestrial vegetation type that forms on thin soil over limestone (Petterson 1965, Catling et al. 1975). Alvars are similar to the cedar glades of the United States (Baskin and Baskin 1985) and are most abundant in the Baltic area of Europe and the Great Lakes basin of North America. Along the soil

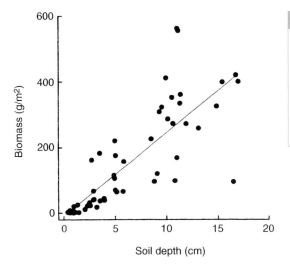

Figure 5.23 The relationship between above-ground biomass and soil depth within experimental plots in alvar vegetation. The relationship is described by the linear equation: biomass $= 9.85 + 25.29$ (soil depth) ($r^2 = 0.65$, $P \ll 0.001$, $n = 55$) (from Belcher et al. 1995).

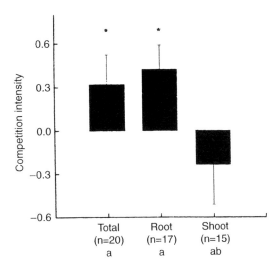

Figure 5.24 Mean competition intensity measured by phytometer performance for total, root and shoot competition in an alvar plant community. Bars indicate $+1$ SE (sample sizes are shown in brackets). *Competition intensity was greater than 0 ($P < 0.05$). Means sharing the same letter are not significantly different ($P > 0.05$) (from Belcher et al. 1995).

depth gradient of an alvar, one may find bare limestone with shallow soil-filled depressions, grassy meadows, and even mixed forest. The meadows and depressions support a rich and varied flora.

In an experiment on competition in alvar vegetation, Belcher et al. (1995) examined the intensity of total, root, and shoot competition along the soil depth gradient. Figure 5.23 shows that aboveground biomass was strongly correlated with soil depth ($r^2 = 0.65$, $P < 0.001$) which indicates that as soil resources increased, light availability decreased. Phytometers (the annual plant, *Trichostemma brachiatum*, in the mint family) were transplanted into areas without neighbors, with neighbors' roots only (the neighbor shoots were held aside by netting), and with neighbors' roots and shoots, in order to determine competition intensity. Figure 5.24 shows that the intensity of both total and root competition were significantly greater than zero ($P < 0.05$); intensity of shoot competition was not.

Competition in this system was primarily below-ground. Moreover, competition intensity did not vary significantly along the soil depth gradient.

5.6.5 Competition intensity gradients in wetlands

Soil fertility and primary production are closely linked in plant communities, and resource gradients are of broad interest to community ecologists. Some vegetation types may have only narrow fertility gradients, and may therefore not be suitable for experiments involving competition intensity gradients. In wetlands, where sand dunes or sand bars grade into sediment-rich bays, a rare opportunity exists to study long, natural resource gradients. Twolan-Strutt and Keddy (1996) measured total competition intensity and its above- and below-ground components in two wetlands that represented extremes in habitat productivity: an infertile sandy shoreline and a fertile bay. Transplants of *Lythrum salicaria* and *Carex critina* were grown with no neighbors, with roots of neighbors only, and with roots and shoots of neighbors; their growth rates during the study were used to measure competition intensity. The experiment was carried out to answer the following main questions:

1. Is there a difference in total, above- or below-ground competition intensity in two wetlands that differ in standing crop?
2. Does standing crop have an effect on total, above- or below-ground competition intensity when the data from the two wetlands are combined?

Results using both transplanted species show that total and above-ground competition intensity were greater in the high standing crop wetland, but below-ground competition did not differ between wetlands (Figure 5.25). Moreover, when all experimental plots were examined independently, the two study sites overlapped enough to construct a resource gradient. In Figure 5.25 standing crop is used as the measure of site fertility, but independent measurements of soil nitrogen and phosphorus confirm this pattern. The top graph shows a marked gradient of competition intensity; results are near zero on sandy sites (left) and reach a maximum of about 0.6 in fertile bays (right): in fertile bays, there is a 60% reduction in growth rate owing to the presence of neighbors.

5.6.6 Competition along an altitudinal gradient

Although some terrestrial experiments appear to contradict results from wetlands, a potential problem with most terrestrial experiments is that old fields are used as an experimental system. Old fields are a relatively new type of habitat created, in many cases, only a few hundred years ago and containing a mixture of native and exotic plants. Old fields might therefore not exhibit patterns found in native plant communities where species may have coevolved for thousands or even millions of years. Further, the patterns in such communities are largely ones of small-scale heterogeneity rather than of longer

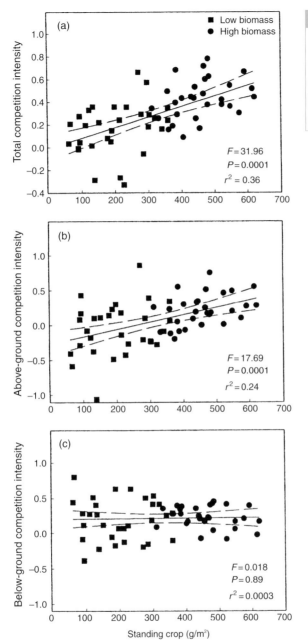

Figure 5.25 The relationship between standing crop and (a) total competition intensity, (b) above-ground competition intensity, and (c) below-ground competition intensity for a marsh. Broken lines give 95% confidence bands (from Twolan-Strutt and Keddy 1996).

environmental gradients. The following example is of a study of competition intensity that avoids such problems – a study of altitudinal zonation in the Snowy Mountains of Australia. These mountains have a zonation pattern typical of many altitudinal gradients: trees giving way to heathland giving way to grassland and alpine meadows. In the specific case of the Snowy Mountains, the tree line is formed by *Eucalyptus pauciflora*, which gives way to 1-m-tall heathland dominated

Figure 5.26 Growth rates of transplants of three species grown in alpine grassland and heath in three competition treatments: no neighbors present (NN), only roots of neighbors present (RN) and all neighbors present (AN). The results of two-factor ANOVA are shown for each species with vegetation type (V) and competition treatment (C) as main effects (*$P < 0.05$, **$P < 0.01$, ***$P < 0.001$). Means with different lower-case letters are significantly different ($P < 0.05$) among competition treatments within each vegetation type for each species. Means with different upper-case letters are significantly different among competition treatments across both vegetation types for each species (from S. D. Wilson 1993).

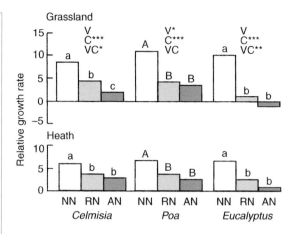

by *Phebalium ovatifolium*, and at still higher altitudes is replaced by tall alpine herbfield, a grassland dominated by *Poa costiniana*.

S. D. Wilson (1993) measured competition intensity in the two higher elevation zones using three different species: the tree *E. pauciflora*, the grass *P. costiniana*, and a rosette composite that is abundant at higher altitudes, *Celmisia longifolia*. Each species was grown in both vegetation zones under three conditions: plots entirely cleared with herbicide (NN, no neighbors), plots where neighbors were present but the above-ground parts were tied back so that only roots could interact (RN, roots of neighbors present), and natural vegetation (AN, all neighbors present). After two growing seasons, the transplanted individuals were harvested and above-ground growth rate was calculated. The effects of above-ground competition (the difference between treatments RN and AN) were typically small and did not vary between vegetation types (Figure 5.26). In contrast, below-ground competition (the difference between treatments NN and RN) was always significant and differed among the three species and between the two vegetation types.

The rosette plant, *Celmisia*, was least suppressed, and the woody plant, *Eucalyptus*, most suppressed by below-ground competition. Wilson concluded that, in these habitats, below-ground competition was more important than above-ground and that it was greater in the higher elevation grassland. Further, the ability of species to compete for below-ground resources (*Celmisia* > *Poa* > *Eucalyptus*) was the same as their distribution along the altitudinal gradient. Thus, as in Twolan-Strutt and Keddy (1996), competition intensity differed between the two vegetation types. In the mountain vegetation, above-ground competition was constant and below-ground competition increased, whereas in the wetland, it was below-ground competition that was constant and the above-ground component that changed. Measurements of soil resources along the altitudinal gradient in the Snowy Mountains showed that although the grassland had intense below-ground competition, it had higher soil nitrogen levels, higher soil water levels, and higher plant growth rates than the adjacent heathland.

Wilson's experiment is a model of the way in which competition experiments can be executed: it used a natural habitat, compared two major zones of an altitudinal gradient, incorporated three plant species of widely contrasting autecology, lasted two full growing seasons, partitioned competition into above- and below-ground components, and measured resources available to the organisms. There is but one limitation, and this is a feature of the analysis. Like so many competition studies, the effects of competition are partitioned into effects on a species-by-species basis. At no point does Wilson ask whether competition varies between the two zones irrespective of the test species used; note that in every case, the effects of competition seem slightly higher in grassland but that breaking the data down into three species has two important consequences. First, it focuses one's attention upon the response of test species rather than the overall intensity of competition in a particular habitat. Second and more importantly, it significantly reduces the number of degrees of freedom in the analysis and greatly reduces its power by splitting the data for between-habitat comparison into three groups. It is difficult to break free from a species-oriented view of nature.

5.7 | Conclusion

Given that populations can grow exponentially, whereas resources do not, most individuals are likely to be inhibited by shortages of resources. Neighbors will usually further reduce resource levels and may also directly interfere with resource acquisition or growth. While competition for resources may be ubiquitous, the actual nature of competition (e.g., exploitation versus interference, intra-specific versus interspecific, monopolistic versus diffuse, above-ground versus below-ground) probably changes dramatically from site to site. Too many ecologists have asked "is there competition?" between a pair of selected species rather than asking what the nature of the competition is and how it varies along gradients (Keddy 1989). Soil resource gradients are widespread, in which case gradients in competition intensity, and gradients in the relative importance of above- and below-ground competition, are likely common. There was insufficient space in this chapter to introduce the models used to study competition, but these are surveyed in Keddy (2001) and Grace and Tilman (1990).

Further reading

Clements, F. E., J. E. Weaver, and H. C. Hanson. 1929. *Plant Competition*. Washington, D. C.: Carnegie Institution of Washington.

Tilman, D. 1982. *Resource Competition and Community Structure*. Princeton: Princeton University Press.

Silander, J. A. and J. Antonovics. 1982. Analysis of interspecific interactions in a coastal plant community – a perturbation approach. *Nature* **298**: 557–560.

Snow, A. A. and S. W. Vince. 1984. Plant zonation in an Alaskan salt marsh II: an experimental study of the role of edaphic conditions. *Journal of Ecology* **72**: 669–684.

Watkinson, A. R. 1985. Plant responses to crowding. pp. 275–298. In J. White (ed.) *Studies in Plant Demography: A Festschrift for John L. Harper*. London: Academic Press.

Underwood, T. 1986. The analysis of competition by field experiments. pp. 240–268. In J. Kikkawa and D. J Anderson (eds.) *Community Ecology. Pattern and Process*. Melbourne: Blackwell.

Gaudet, C. L. and P. A. Keddy. 1988. A comparative approach to predicting competitive ability from plant traits. *Nature* **334**: 242–43.

Reader, R. J. and B. J. Best. 1989. Variation in competition along an environmental gradient: *Hieracium floribundum* in an abandoned pasture. *Journal of Ecology* **77**: 673–84.

Keddy, P. A. and B. Shipley. 1989. Competitive hierarchies in plant communities. *Oikos* **49**: 234–241.

Grace J. B. and D. Tilman (eds.). 1990. *Perspectives on Plant Competition*. San Diego: Academic Press.

Wilson, S. D. 1993. Competition and resource availability in heath and grassland in the Snowy Mountains of Australia. *Journal of Ecology* **81**: 445–451.

Keddy, P. A. 2001. *Competition*, 2nd edn. Dordrecht: Kluwer.

Chapter 6

Disturbance

Definitions. Properties: duration, intensity, frequency, area. Fire. Erosion and deposition. Animals: beaver ponds and 'gator holes. Burial by rivers. Flooding. Ice damage. Exposure to waves: chronic low level disturbance. Catastrophic events: landslides, volcanoes, and meteors. Comparing disturbance effects. Gaps and gap dynamics. Buried seeds. Mosaics for duck production. A synthetic view: fire, drought and flooding in the Everglades. Broad scale comparisons.

6.1 Introduction

Disturbance is an all pervasive process in communities and ecosystems (e.g., Huston 1979, Sousa 1984, Pickett and White 1985, Botkin 1990), but disturbance is perhaps a dangerous concept in ecology. It is dangerous precisely because the word is non-technical; therefore, many people assume they understand it when they do not. Moreover, in popular use, the word disturbance includes so many effects that it hardly excludes anything in nature. It may encompass everything from a deer walking across a peatland, to a meteor colliding with the Earth. It may include everything from a botanist collecting plant specimens to an all-out nuclear war followed by nuclear winter. Words that mean everything end up meaning nothing. **Disturbance** shall be defined here as a short-lived event that causes a measurable change in the properties of an ecological community.

This at first may seem vague. What is short-lived? Southwood (1977, 1988) suggests measuring duration in terms of organisms' life spans. Short-lived can be defined as an event that occurs as a pulse with duration much shorter than the life span of the dominant species in the community. According to this definition, a fire or 1-year drought would be a disturbance; a slow and long-term climate change would not. Insisting upon measurable change further requires that the user of the word identifies at least one property that is measurable (e.g., biomass, diversity, species composition) and shows that it changes. No change, no disturbance (see Cairns 1980).

Grime (1977, 1979) has suggested defining disturbance as a factor that removes biomass. White (1994) explains, "When the structural resistance and physiological tolerance of the vegetation is exceeded, substantial and sudden destruction of living biomass occurs; hence the recognition of … events as disturbances." Disturbances such as fire, sudden freezes, or floods tend to be discrete events in time, and infrequent. In general, destruction is fast and recovery is slow. Time lags are therefore important.

6.2 | Four properties of disturbance

Using the working definition of disturbance in 6.1, the next step is to consider some of the properties it possesses. These would include: (1) duration, (2) intensity, (3) frequency, and (4) area (Sousa 1984, Pickett and White 1985). Each of these is measurable. To some extent they are self-explanatory, but let us briefly consider them in turn.

6.2.1 Duration
Duration refers to how long the event lasts. A frost, fire, or lava flow may last only hours; floods or herbivory may continue for years. For example, flooding for three years can all but eliminate emergent wetland plants from marshes (Figure 6.1). A pulse of flooding is therefore a disturbance. The duration of an event may be expressed in terms of the life spans of the organisms of concern (Southwood 1977, 1988).

6.2.2 Intensity
The intensity of a disturbance is best judged by the severity of its effects upon a community. The simplest measure of intensity would be the proportion of biomass at a site that is killed or removed. A factor that disturbs one group (e.g., plants) might not disturb another (e.g., insects), so the change in abundance of several groups might be measured simultaneously. Change in species composition would be an alternative measure of intensity. There is a wide range of measures of similarity between samples (Legendre and Legendre 1983). Using a standard measure of ecological similarity, one could define a range of disturbance intensities from 0 (the community is the same before and after the disturbance) to 1 (the community is completely different after disturbance). Figure 6.1 shows that the

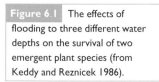

Figure 6.1 The effects of flooding to three different water depths on the survival of two emergent plant species (from Keddy and Reznicek 1986).

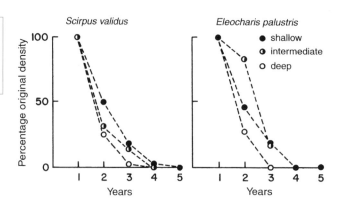

deeper the flooding of a wetland, the more rapid the decline in abundance of two emergent plants. Were one to measure the degree of similarity each year, through time it would decrease most rapidly with the deepest flooding (most intense disturbance). Similar effects would be observed if, instead of using composition, biomass had been measured.

6.2.3 Frequency

Some events, such as hurricanes or spring floods, happen on a yearly basis. Others, such as ice storms or asteroid collisions, happen rarely. Historical data for water levels in the Great Lakes (Figure 6.2) illustrate the frequency with which different degrees of low water occur. In general, the greater the intensity of disturbance (extreme high or low water periods), the lower the frequency. It seems reasonable to argue that the more frequent an event is, the more likely organisms are to develop resistance to it. In the short term, frequency can be expressed in years; in the long term ecologists will probably find it necessary to translate this into the lifetimes of dominant organisms.

Figure 6.2 Changes in water levels of the Great Lakes (from Environment Canada 1976).

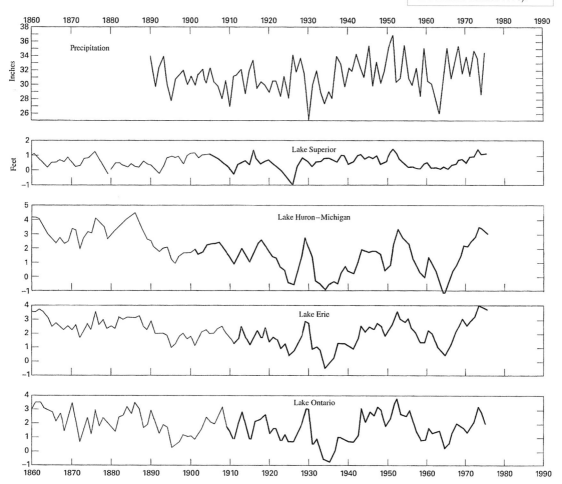

6.2.4 Area

This is self-explanatory, but it bears mention because it reminds one of at least one way to rank disturbances in terms of their ecological significance. Disturbances that affect huge areas will usually demand more attention than those influencing smaller areas. Hurricanes, for example, are large-scale disturbances that are also intense. They may kill between 25 and 75 percent, and as much as 90 percent of low lying mangal, leading Lugo and Snedaker (1974) to suggest that "hurricanes may have a very large role in determining the ratios of species within vegetation types over large areas."

6.3 | Examples of disturbance

The generalizations above may seem to belabor the obvious, but as long as the word "disturbance" is used in a careless manner, confusion results. The following provide concrete examples of studies that have explicitly explored disturbance in different plant communities.

6.3.1 Fire

Fires are a frequent event in an array of vegetation types from prairie through to evergreen forests (Heinselman 1981, Wright and Bailey 1982, Whelan 1995) and even, in some cases, wetlands (Smith and Kadlec 1985a,b, Kuhry 1994, White 1994). The effects of heat include alteration of chemical reaction rates, dissociation of molecules, and rupturing of cells by steam through to outright combustion of the tissues (Figure 6.3). In woody plants, one of the most conspicuous impacts of fire is death of the cambium, the thin layer of cells that produce both the woody tissues and the bark. When heat is applied to the surface of the bark, it is transmitted inward and the cambium temperature rises. An exposure to at least 60 °C for a duration of 60 seconds or longer is usually sufficient to cause death in vascular plant tissue (Wright and Bailey 1982, Whelan 1995). Insulation by bark helps protect the cambium from reaching this temperature (Figure 6.4).

Uhl and Kauffman (1990) compared the fire resistance of different trees in rain forest just south of the equator in Para State, Brazil. A cotton rope saturated with kerosene was attached to the trunk of trees and temperature of the cambium was monitored with thermocouples inserted 10 cm above the point of attachment of the rope. The length of rope used was one half the diameter of each tree to ensure a standard level of heat exposure per unit area. In *Jacaranda copaia* (Figure 6.5), the temperature reached by the cambium exceeded the critical exposure level if the bark was less than 6 mm thick: bark greater than 10 mm thick provided good defence of the cambium.

Bark thickness varies among species. In the case of Amazonia, Uhl and Kauffman (1990) found that bark thickness usually ranged between 3 and 20 mm. Eleven taxa, however, had bark thickness less

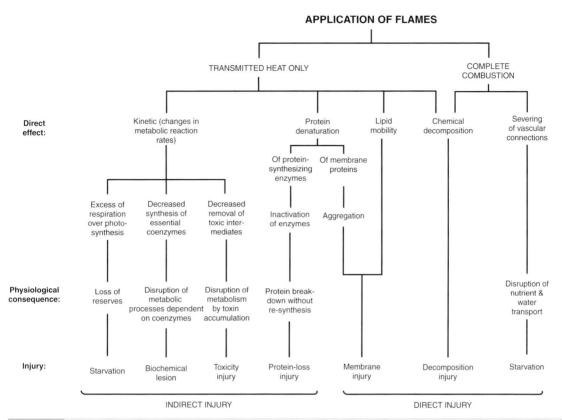

Figure 6.3 Range of pathways through which the application of heat to plants causes direct and indirect damage (after Whelan 1995).

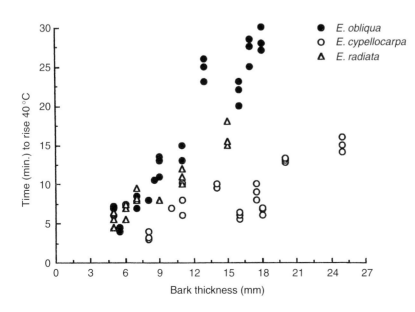

Figure 6.4 The influence of bark as an insulator of the cambium in Australian *Eucalyptus* species. For a given bark thickness, *E. obliqua* takes longer to heat up than either *E. cypellocarpa* or *E. radiata* (from Whelan 1995).

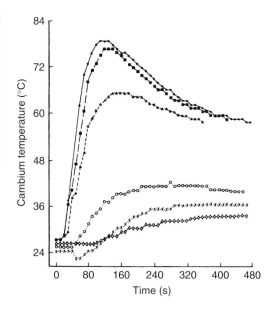

Figure 6.5 Temperature of cambium surface during wick (experimental, tree surface) fires for individuals of *Jacaranda copaia* with bark thickness of 4 mm (●), 5 mm (■), 6 mm (▲), 10 mm (○), 14 mm (×), and 15 mm (◇) at Victoria Ranch near Paragominas, Para, Brazil (from Uhl and Kauffman 1990).

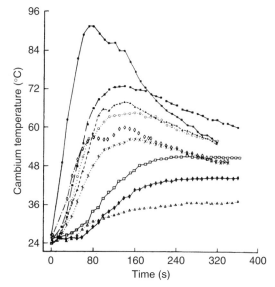

Figure 6.6 Mean temperature flux at the cambium surface during wick (experimental, tree surface) fires for two individuals (between 20 and 30 cm dbh) in each of nine taxa: *Ecclinusa* sp. (●), *Jacaranda copaia* (■), *Metrodorea flavida* (▲), *Pourouma guianensis* (○), *Inga alba* (◇), *Cercropia sciandaphylla* (×), *Lecythis idatimon* (□), *Lecythis lurida* (◆), and *Manilkara huberi* (△) at Victoria Ranch near Paragominas, Para, Brazil (from Uhl and Kauffman 1990).

than 3 mm; these included a species of *Ecclinusa*, *Apeiba echinata*, *Pterocarpus shorii*, and *Dialium guianensi*. In contrast, five species had bark greater than 20 mm thick, including *Cecropia obtusa*, *Caryocar villosum*, and *Laetia procera*. When an array of species was exposed to fire, there were substantial differences in the temperature reached by the cambium (Figure 6.6), and this temperature was closely related to bark thickness (Figure 6.7). In the event of large fires, one can expect substantial mortality of trees and predictable changes in species composition.

In areas that are frequently burned, woody plants may be unable to survive to reproductive age. In such cases, prairie or savanna vegetation may result. Soil, like bark, is a good insulator. Many

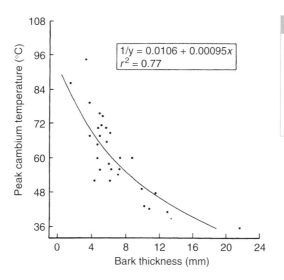

$$1/y = 0.0106 + 0.00095x$$
$$r^2 = 0.77$$

Figure 6.7 The relationship between bark thickness and peak temperature of the cambium during wick fires for 30 individuals distributed among 15 species at Victoria Ranch near Paragominas, Para, Brazil (from Uhl and Kauffman 1990).

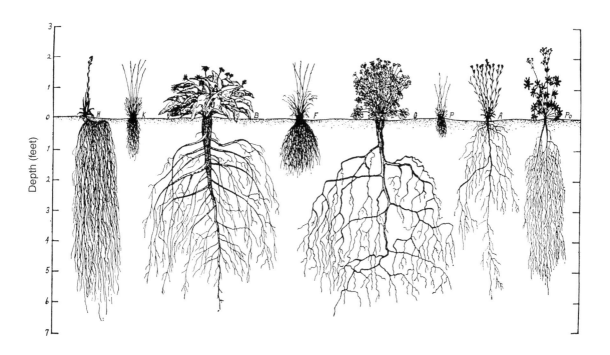

prairie plants therefore have deeply buried rhizomes, tubers, or bulbs (Figure 6.8). Fire may destroy the above-ground portions of the plant, but these are quickly replaced by new shoots produced by the buried portions of the plant. The importance of fire in maintaining prairie is illustrated by problems in prairie nature reserves from which fire is often excluded, either because natural prairie fires no longer occur or because of deliberate suppression of fire owing to the proximity of crops and houses. In such cases, woody plants often

Figure 6.8 Root systems of prairie plants illustrating some adaptations to fire such as rhizomes and burried root crowns (from Weaver and Clements 1938).

invade and begin to replace the native prairie flora; vegetation managers then have to re-introduce fire to re-establish and maintain the herbaceous prairie vegetation. The boreal forests of northern latitudes are as fire-dependent as prairies, but a discussion of disturbance by fire in boreal forests will be deferred to Section 9.4.2.

Even some kinds of wetlands do indeed burn during dry years. Sutter and Kral (1994) (Table 6.1) postulate that fire frequency, along with hydrology, is the principal factor determining the kinds of wetland communities formed in the southeastern United States. Fire is regarded as a major controller of plant diversity in both pocosin peatlands (Christensen et al. 1981) and the Everglades (Loveless 1959). Loveless concludes: "The importance of fire and its influence on the vegetation of the Everglades can hardly be over-emphasized." Fire becomes important during prolonged periods of drought. Low-intensity fires can simply remove existing vegetation, shift the composition of plant species from woody to herbaceous, and increase plant diversity (Christensen et al. 1981, Thompson and Shay 1988). Figure 6.9 shows the effect of fire incidence on both litter accumulation and plant diversity in *Carex*-dominated wetlands along the St. Lawrence River in eastern North America. Hogenbirk and Wein (1991) have measured responses to fire in two vegetation types of the Peace-Athabasca delta (Figure 6.10). Fire reduced both the height and density of the dominant species. But although the number of dicots increased, there was little effect upon total species richness. During the longer droughts, however, more intensive fires can burn the organic matter in the soil and create new depressions and pools (e.g., Loveless 1959, Vogl 1969).

Peatlands are particularly useful for the study of fire because, under certain circumstances, charcoal layers and macrofossils record both the fire history and the vegetation responses to the fire. *Sphagnum*-dominated peatlands are probably the most abundant peatland type in western boreal North America. Kuhry (1994) studied a series of peat cores to reconstruct fire and vegetation histories. He found that these peatlands had many macroscopic charcoal layers as a consequence of past fires. In the eight studied peat deposits, he estimated there had been one local surface fire approximately every 1150 years. While this may be a surprisingly high rate of fire frequency, it is still an order of magnitude less frequent than estimates of fire frequency in coniferous forests in western boreal Canada (e.g., Ritchie 1987). During the hypsithermal, a period of warmer and drier climate about 7000 years ago, fire frequencies in peatlands appear to have been twice as high as in the past 2500 years. These fires not only burned the vegetation, but they also burnt the superficial peat deposits. In spite of this, the cores suggest that the effect of peat surface fires on vegetation was short lived. This is apparently also the case in contemporary reports of peat fires. An interesting natural history story complements these findings; *Sphagnum* can apparently regenerate from stems at depths of 30 cm in the peat deposit (estimated to be 25–60 years old) (Clymo and Duckett 1986).

Table 6.1. *Description of non-alluvial wetland communities of the southeastern United States (after Sutter and Kral 1994).*

Community	Canopy dominants	Soil	Hydroperiod/water source	Fire frequency
Forested wetlands in basins				
Pond cypress pond forest	*Taxodium ascendens*	Mineral to organic	6–12 months/rainfall	Infrequent, 20–50 years
Swamp tupelo pond forest	*Nyssa biflora*	Organic to peat	6–12 months/rainfall	Rare, one fire per century
Cypress dome	*Taxodium ascendens*	Peat	6–9 months/rainfall	20+ years
Basin swamp forest	*Nyssa biflora, Acer rubrum, Liquidambar styraciflua*	Organic	6–9 months/groundwater	Infrequent, 20–50 years
Wetland complexes in basins				
Limestone pond complex (karst ponds)		Mineral	Deep groundwater	1–10 years/yellow sand, 36–60 years/white sand
Coastal plain small depression pond		Mineral	Variable	Dependent on surrounding forests
Coastal plain lakeshore complex		Mineral	Variable	Rare, one fire per century
Okefenokee swamp wetland mosaic		Mineral-peat	Variable	Infrequent, 20–50 years
Woodlands and savannas in basins				
Pond cypress savanna	*Taxodium ascendens*	Mineral	6–9 months/rainfall	20+ years
Pond pine woodland	*Pinus serotina, Cyrilla racemiflora*	Shallow organics and peats	6–9 months/rainfall	10–20 years
Woodlands and savannas on flat coastal terraces				
Slash pine flatwoods	*Pinus serotina*	Mineral	<3 months/groundwater	3–10 years
Wet longleaf pine flatwoods	*Pinus palustris*	Mineral	<3 months/groundwater	3–10 years
Wet longleaf pine-slash pine flatwoods	*Pinus palustris, Pinus serotina*	Mineral	<3 months/groundwater	3–10 years

Table 6.1. (cont.)

Community	Canopy dominants	Soil	Hydroperiod/water source	Fire frequency
Woodlands and savannas on flat coastal terraces (continued)				
Longleaf pine savanna	Pinus palustris	Mineral	3–6 months/groundwater	1–5 years
Coastal plain pitcher plant flat	A diversity of graminoid and herbaceous species including Sarracenia spp.	Mineral	6 months/groundwater	1–5 years
Evergreen shrub wetlands				
Low pocosin	Pinus serotina, Cyrilla racemiflora, Zenobia pulverulenta	Deep peat >0.5 m	6–9 months/rainfall	15–30 years
High pocosin	Pinus serotina, Cyrilla racemiflora, Lyonia lucida	Shallow peat <0.5 m	6–9 months/rainfall	15–10 years
Small depression pocosin	Pinus serotina, Cyrilla racemiflora, Lyonia lucida	Shallow peat <0.5 m	6–9 months/rainfall	15–30 years

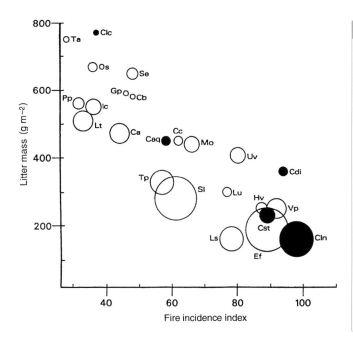

Figure 6.9 Litter mass and species diversity are related to a fire incidence index in a riparian wetland. Circle diameter is proportional to diversity (range 0.86–1.61). Principal *Carex* species shown in solid circles include: Caq, *C. aquatilis*; Cdi, *C. diandra*; Clc, *C. lacustris*; Cln, *C. lanuginosa*; Cst, *C. stricta*. Other species include: Ef, *Equisetum fluviatile*; Gp, *Galium palustre*; Hv, *Hypericum virginicum*; Ic, *Impatiens capensis*; Ls, *Lythrum salicaria*; Lt, *Lysimachia thyrsiflora*; Lu, *Lycopus uniflorus*; Mo, moss species; Os, *Onoclea sensibilis*; Pp, *Potentilla palustris*; Se, *Sparganium eurycarpum*; Sl, *Sagittaria latifolia*; Ta, *Typha angustifolia*; Tp, *Thelypteris palustris*; Uv, *Utricularia vulgaris*; Vp, *Viola pallens* (from Auclair et al. 1976b).

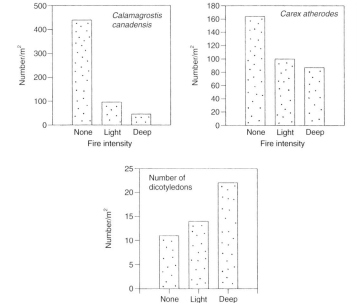

Figure 6.10 Effects of three fire intensities upon three properties of wetlands in the Peace-Athabasca delta (from data in Hogenbirk and Wein 1991).

Kuhry (1994) could have stopped with his pictures of peat profiles, but in addition to these qualitative observations, he went on to test for quantitative relationships among rates of peat accumulation and fire frequency. Fire frequency was estimated as the number of macroscopic charcoal layers per 1000 years, and peat accumulation rates were determined from radiocarbon dating. There was a negative relationship between peat accumulation rates and fire frequency

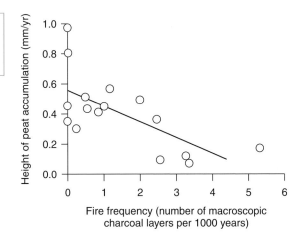

Figure 6.11 Peat accumulation as a function of fire frequency in western boreal Canada (from Kuhry 1994).

(Figure 6.11). It appears, then, that the flush of nutrient-rich ash released by burning (and the presumed higher plant growth rates) does not compensate for the loss of peat consumed by the fire. Thus fires significantly retard the growth of peatlands. This has important consequences for global warming because peatlands are an important reservoir for carbon storage. An increase in temperature would presumably lead to higher frequencies of burning, which in turn would lead to further releases of carbon stored in the peatlands (Gorham 1991, Hogg et al. 1992). This would then act as a positive feedback loop to increase rates of global warming (Section 1.10).

6.3.2 Erosion

Running water can create many kinds of disturbance in watersheds; these disturbances can range from splash erosion caused by individual rain drops, through soil wash on valley slopes, to bank erosion and slumping in valley bottoms (Strahler 1971, Rosgen 1995). The latter are certainly predominant disturbances in the lower reaches of watersheds, where rivers flow through valleys filled with alluvial sediments; these areas often have extensive floodplain forests (swamps) and, to a lesser degree, marshes. Alluvial sediments are continually reworked by the river, thereby destroying established vegetation and exposing new substrates for succession. The dynamics of meanders have received a good deal of attention from geologists (e.g., Strahler 1971). Meanders originate from the enlargement of bends in the course of a river. As the river undercuts and erodes a bank at one point, the material from this bank is carried down stream and deposited as a point bar; the point bar deflects the current to the other side of the river, where the force of the water cuts into the bank, further producing another point bar on the opposite side. Once a bend is produced, centrifugal forces thrust the river flow toward the outside of bends, increasing rates of erosion until a meander loop is formed (Figure 6.12). Meanders in floodplains take on a characteristic geometric form in which meander wavelength is linearly related

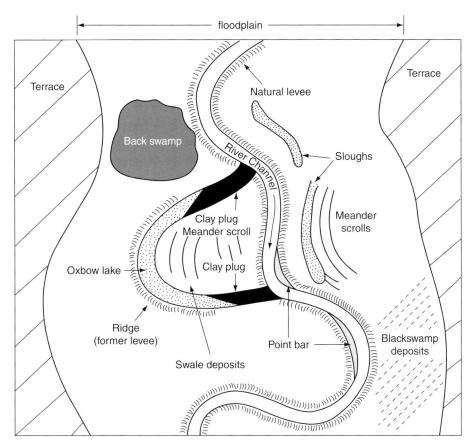

Figure 6.12 Dynamic processes create the wide array of wetland habitats along a water course. These habitats comprise the template upon which hydrological variation and ecological communities are superimposed (from Mitsch and Gosselink 2000).

to the mean annual discharge. Once these meanders are formed, there is a gradual movement downstream ("down valley sweep") so that over time all the alluvial sediments are eroded and reworked between the limits set by river bluffs.

These processes have important effects on vegetation because they continually remove established communities and allow the process of succession to begin anew. The result is a mosaic of vegetation types of different ages and species composition. Such processes have been described from lowland podocarp forests in New Zealand (Duncan 1993). These forests are dominated by conifers in the Podocarpaceae, along with the angiosperm *Weinmannia racemosa*. Two species of podocarp, *Dacrycarpus dacrydiodes* and *D. cupressinum*, establish in large openings created by floods. In the absence of further flooding, species composition shifts toward the latter species. Over longer periods yet, the more shade-tolerant *W. racemosa* would be expected to dominate, but stands of this tree are absent from this region of New Zealand due to the frequency of disturbance. Duncan concludes that podocarp forests occur largely because of recurring disturbance.

In an area one-half million square kilometers of the Peruvian Amazon, Salo et al. (1986) report that 26.6 percent of the modern lowland forest shows characteristics of recent erosion and deposition and that fully 12 percent of the Peruvian lowland forest is in successional stages along rivers. During one 13-year period, Landsat images showed that the mean lateral erosion rate of meander bends was $12\,\text{m}\cdot\text{year}^{-1}$. The total area of newly created land available for primary succession was $12\,\text{km}^2$, representing nearly 4 percent of the present floodplain area. The new substrates were first colonized by herbaceous species in genera such as *Tessaria*, *Cyperus*, *Ipomoea*, and *Panicum*; smaller trees in the genera *Cecropia*, *Ficus*, and *Cedrela* gradually formed a closed canopy, and eventually these became mixed with later successional species. Kalliola et al. (1991) have described the successional processes in more detail, documenting a pioneer flora of 125 plant species. Salo et al. (1986) conclude:

> According to the repetitive nature of river dynamics, the migration of the river channel course creates a mosaic of successional forests within the present meander plain. The mosaic forest is composed of patches of differentially aged sequential successional forest and patches of forests originating from a succession on the sites of former oxbow lakes. The annual floods further modify the mosaic pattern.

While the numbers are impressive, they do not convey the breadth of this phenomenon as powerfully as do aerial photographs (Figure 6.13). Although studies of rain forests have tended to emphasize gap dynamics, that is the regeneration of individual trees within light gaps created by fallen trees (Grubb 1977, Connell 1978), Salo et al. (1986) point out that the regeneration in floodplains is fundamentally different, since it is a more intense kind of disturbance, with entirely new substrates for colonization. The heterogeneity of the substrate, and its continual disturbance, may partly account for the very high plant species diversity of tropical floodplain forests.

6.3.3 Animals

An entire chapter on herbivory follows this one. The general conclusion from that chapter is that herbivory can have major effects on vegetation, but the size of the area affected appears limited. Such cases include mega-herbivores grazing in the African grasslands and crabs feeding in salt marshes. Animals can also create entirely new patches of habitat. Consider two conspicuous examples, beavers and alligators.

Beaver ponds

Beavers obstruct water flow in streams thereby flooding forest and creating small ponds (Figure 6.14). Occasionally, under the right physical conditions, they can also regulate the water levels of lakes. Before the arrival of Europeans, the beaver population of North America was estimated to be 60 to 400 million individuals, with a range stretching from arctic tundra to the deserts of northern Mexico. The ponds that beavers create cause changes in forest structure, nutrient cycling, decomposition rates, and the properties of water downstream (Naiman et al. 1988) as well as plant and animal diversity (Grover and Baldassarre 1995, Wright et al. 2002). Jones et al. (1994)

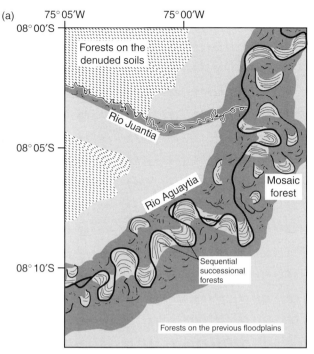

(a)

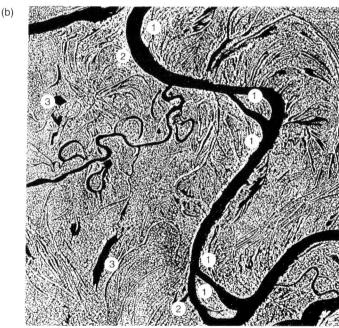

(b)

Figure 6.13 Evidence for lateral erosion and channel migration in Amazonian lowland forest from Landsat multi-spectral scanner images. (a) A simplified map of a meander system in a white water river (the Ucayali at Pucallpa, Peru). (b) A detailed map of forests along a meander system downstream from top figure, showing (1) areas of intense primary succession, (2) eroding forest at outer edges of meanders and (3) isolated oxbow lakes (from Salo et al. 1986).

point out that beavers are only one of many organisms that create, modify, or maintain natural habitats. They propose that we recognize a class of organism called ecosystem engineers. In wetlands, these would include beavers building ponds, alligators excavating wallows, and *Sphagnum* mosses building peat bogs. Other examples would include coral reefs, termite mounds, and prairie dog colonies.

Figure 6.14 Beavers can produce water level fluctuations by building dams that periodically break or are abandoned (courtesy of Friends of Algonquin Park).

Beavers create cyclical disturbance and succession in the landscape with two different frequencies. The short-term cycle is one of dam destruction and repair. Dams may be washed out during floods, holes may be punched in dams by mammals such as otters, or predators may kill the beavers maintaining the dam. In such cases, water levels suddenly fall and many plant species regenerate from buried seeds. Although nearly 40 species of plants are known from beaver pond seed banks (Le Page and Keddy 1998), Table 6.2 shows that a few genera of moncotyledons (e.g., *Juncus*, *Leersia*, *Scirpus*) are most common. A surge of regeneration of these marsh and wet meadow species will occur unless the dam is repaired. The short duration of these low-water periods probably explains the abundance of annuals and facultative annuals.

A long-term cycle occurs when beaver populations colonize and then abandon sites (Figure 6.15). Building a dam changes forest to open water and wetland. Abandonment of the dam results in a short-lived mud flat, a longer period of marsh formation, and then, as the

Table 6.2. *The 10 most common species that germinated from the mud in beaver ponds in central Canada (from Le Page and Keddy 1998).*

Species	Number of seedlings
Juncus effusus	388
Leersia oryzoides	355
Scirpus cyperinus	224
Juncus brevicaudatus	155
Ludwigia palustris	89
Hypericum boreale	87
Unknown dicot	66
Eleocharis obtusa	57
Galium palustre	56
Hypericum majus	49

Beaver pond cycle

1.

2.

3.

4.

Forest succession

Figure 6.15 The beaver pond cycle is one kind of natural disturbance that can generate plant diversity in landscapes. It begins with a forest and a stream (1). When beavers build a dam, the site first becomes a pond with dead standing trees (2), which eventually becomes open water surrounded by wetland vegetation (3). When the food supply diminishes (as indicated by the predominance of conifers in the forest), the beavers decline and the dam deteriorates, leaving a wet meadow (4). Over time, forest succession will occur and forest will re-establish (illustration by B. Brigham).

beaver meadow gradually dries, woody plants will re-invade. This longer cycle of beaver ponds alternating with swamp forest probably has a frequency of centuries rather than decades.

Aerial photographs might provide one method to quantify rates of pond formation and abandonment by beavers. In much of eastern North America, beaver populations were very low at the turn of century and then expanded rapidly after 1940. Johnston and Naiman (1990) examined six sets of aerial photographs (covering 1940 to 1986) from the Kabetogama Peninsula of Voyageurs National Park in northern Michigan and found that the number of pond sites increased from 71 to 835. The mean area was 4 ha (range from <1 to 45 ha) and decreased over time, which suggests that later ponds were established in less suitable areas. During the first half of the period (1940 to 1961), ponds were created at the rate of 25 year^{-1}, but later (from 1961 to 1986) the rate declined to 10 year^{-1}. These figures, however, include all areas with vegetation altered by past or present ponds, both active ponds and beaver meadows covered in grasses and sedges. The sequence of events they describe is thus a progressive increase in the area of patches influenced by beavers, to some 3000 ha by 1986. Since over the 40-year period no patches were lost, it is not possible to calculate what rates of pond abandonment might result from food shortages or what the equilibrium patch densities might be. The rapid spread of beavers in this region is in part explained by their biology: the average litter size is 3–4 kits year^{-1}, and at the age of two years kits generally disperse within a 16-km radius, so that over a 46-year period it would be possible for them to colonize areas more than 700 km from an initial nucleus.

Beaver ponds provide important habitat for wetland species including amphibians, mammals, and birds. In a sample of 70 wetlands representing three classes of beaver activity Grover and Baldassarre (1995) found a total of 106 species of spring birds, with between nine and 39 species per wetland. Larger wetlands had more species, as did wetlands with active beaver colonies. Active ponds had more open water, more dead standing trees, more flooded emergents, and a higher habitat diversity index. Nineteen obligate wetland species were found in active ponds compared with 12 in the inactive ones, and there were 18 facultative wetland species that used cavities in the standing dead trees. Grover and Baldassarre conclude that beaver ponds provide habitat for more than half of the regional avifauna.

Alligator holes

The southern equivalent of the beaver pond may be the 'gator hole (Figure 6.16). These are depressions that are either made or maintained by alligators. During winter dry periods, these holes may be the only ponds remaining in a wetland (Loveless 1959, Craighead 1968). The alligator maintains ponds by pulling loose plants and dragging them out of the pool. Thicker muck is either pushed or carried to the edges of the pond.

Figure 6.16 A 'gator hole in the Florida Everglades. The soil the alligator deposits around the edge of the pool it creates becomes habitat for a wide variety of plants such as pickerel weed, cocoplum, red bay, and sweet bay. Aquatic plants such as alligator flag, arrow arum, and arrowhead emerge from the water around the edges of the hole.

'Gator holes were once a predominant feature of wetlands in South Florida. Craighead concludes that "in the first two decades of this century every inland pond, lake, and river held its quota of alligators." He suggests that a density approaching one alligator per acre existed in some regions. Historical records are always suspect, but the naturalist William Bartram, who traveled the St. Johns River in 1774–1776, described alligators massed around his boat. He reported that when camping on beaches, it was necessary to keep a large fire burning all night for protection. 'Gator holes are "reservoirs for an amazing biological assemblage." Within them live "diatoms, algae, ferns, flowering plants, protozoans, crustaceans, amphibians, reptiles and fish" (Craighead 1968). The productivity of these ponds is enhanced by uneaten food. Larger animals, such as hogs and deer, are killed by drowning but may be left for several days for ripening. The aquatic flora includes widespread genera such as *Myriophyllum*, *Utricularia*, *Potamogeton*, *Nymphoides*, and *Naias*. The shallow water near the banks has marsh genera such as *Peltandra*, *Pontederia*, and *Sagittaria*. Indeed, the description of this flora is remarkably reminiscent of beaver ponds. Connecting the 'gator holes are well-developed trail systems. Heavy 'gators may erode the trails into troughs that are 15 cm deep and 60 cm wide.

6.3.4 Burial

Terrestrial communities are rarely subject to burial, an exception being catastrophic events such as volcanic eruptions or landslides (e.g., Guariguata 1990, del Moral et al. 1995) (Section 6.4), or burial by wind-deposited sand (e.g., Maun and Lapierre 1986, Brown 1997). Such events may be dramatic and conspicuous, but they are also infrequent enough that they are rarely significant factors in controlling community structure over large areas. In contrast, rivers continually erode the land's surface and carry sediments that are deposited in wetlands as water movement slows. It is estimated that the world's

(a)

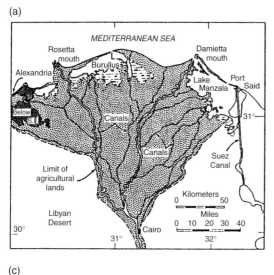

(b)

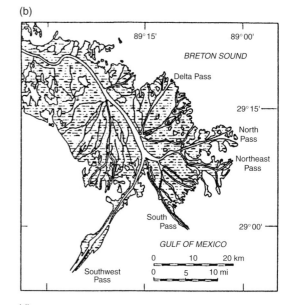

(c)

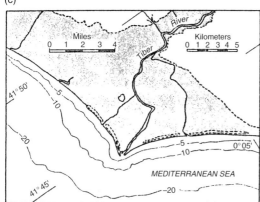

(d)

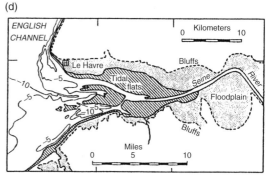

Figure 6.17 The world's large deltas illustrate the amounts of sediment transported and deposited by rivers. (a) Nile, (b) Mississippi, (c) Tiber, (d) Seine (from Strahler 1971).

rivers deliver in the order of 10^{10} tons of sediment per year to their mouths, which leads to the formation of large floodplains and deltas (Figure 6.17). Burial is clearly a routine experience for riparian vegetation.

The importance of sedimentation as an ecological factor varies among watersheds (Figure 6.18). The Ganges-Brahmaputra River apparently carries the largest load of sediment in the world (Milliman and Meade 1983). In fact, southeastern Asian rivers, in general, are among the most prodigious transporters of sediment. Taiwan, for example, an island of 36 000 km^2 (roughly half the size of Ireland or the same size as Indiana), produces nearly as much sediment as the entire coterminous United States (Milliman and Meade 1983). The Yellow, Ganges-Brahmaputra, and Amazon have the highest annual suspended sediment loads in the world (Figure 6.19).

It is frequently useful to distinguish between **autogenic** burial (burial by locally produced organic matter such as occurs in peat bogs, Section 9.4.2) and **allogenic** burial (burial by externally

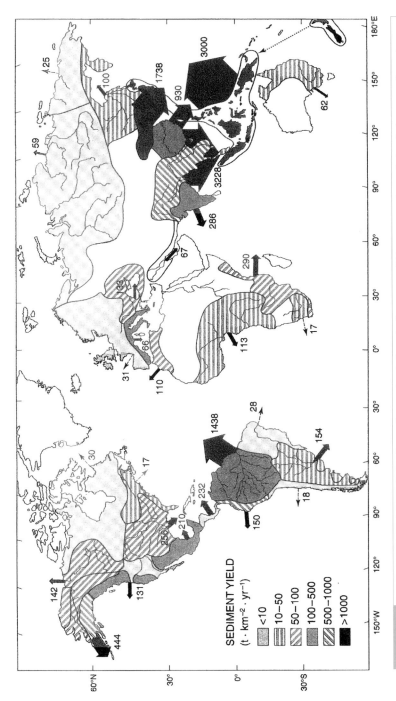

Figure 6.18 Annual discharge of suspended sediment from major drainage basins; arrow width corresponds to relative discharge, numbers give average annual input in millions of tons (after Milliman and Meade 1983).

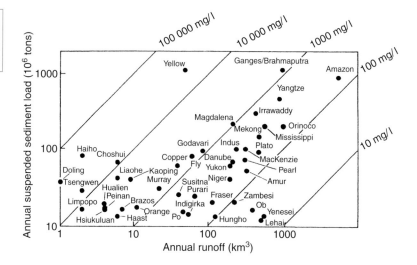

Figure 6.19 Annual suspended sediment load as a function of annual runoff in major rivers (from Milliman and Meade 1983).

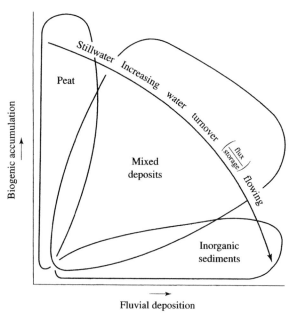

Figure 6.20 Biogenic accumulation and fluvial deposition are the two causes of burial in wetlands. These orthogonal axes may be represented (and caused) by one gradient – water transfer (from Brinson 1993b).

produced sediment or organic matter such as occurs in river deltas). Both kinds of burial can cause changes in plant communities. This chapter is concerned with allogenic burial, because rates of burial are generally much higher in this category. Allogenic burial typically occurs over 10^0 to 10^2 years, but autogenic burial occurs on timescales of 10^3 to 10^4 years and thus would not be considered a disturbance. Brinson (1993a,b) uses the terms *biogenic accumulation* and *fluvial deposition* to distinguish between these two types of burial. He proposes that both types are controlled by one gradient, water turnover (as measured by the ratio of flux to storage) (Figure 6.20).

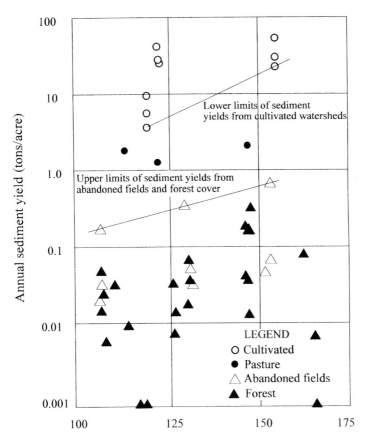

Figure 6.21 Annual sediment yield is a function of annual precipitation and land use (after Judson 1968).

Deposition rates on the shores of lakes in the order of 0.2–3 mm·year^{-1} (2–30 cm·100 years^{-1}), with the majority in the lower part of the range, are suggested by palynological studies in the English landscape (e.g., Walker 1970). Data compiled from boreal and subarctic peatlands yield peat accumulation rates in the range of 0.3–0.8 mm·year^{-1} (Gorham 1991). Higher rates of deposition, some 3–6 mm·year^{-1}, appear to be more typical of salt marshes (Niering and Warren 1980, Stevenson et al. 1986, Orson et al. 1990) and mangrove swamps (Ellison and Farnsworth 1996). Rozan et al. (1994) suggest that the annual rates of deposition in a floodplain in eastern North America were below 0.1 mm prior to this century but then accelerated to approximately 1 cm·year^{-1}. Deposition rates closer to 1 cm·year^{-1} appear more typical in coastal deltas (Boesch et al. 1994). In contrast with the figures above, floods or storms can deposit 10 cm or more of sediment in a single year (e.g., Robinson 1973, Zedler and Onuf 1984, Rybicki and Carter 1986).

In general, sediment loads in rivers are determined by rainfall and vegetation cover; cultivated watersheds have sediment loading rates orders of magnitude higher than forested watersheds (Figure 6.21). Similarly, the clay content of the soil and the amount of land in row crops are the best predictors of phosphorus loadings to water courses. Although larger rivers can be expected to carry larger volumes of

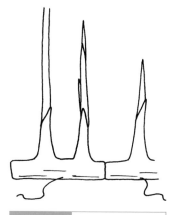

Figure 6.22 Rhizomes and pointed shoots allow buried plants to re-emerge (from Keddy 2000).

sediment, rainfall and human disturbance to vegetation can play equally important roles in determining sedimentation rates in watersheds.

Many wetland plants have well-developed rhizomes and pointed shoots (Figure 6.22). Examples include genera such as *Typha*, *Juncus*, *Scirpus*, and *Carex*. Pointed shoots and underground storage structures are considered to be adaptations for penetrating accumulations of leaf litter (Grime 1979), and it is likely that the same traits also are adaptations for penetrating sediment. In contrast, evergreen rosette life forms would likely be extremely intolerant of burial, and this may be one reason why they are largely restricted to eroding shorelines (Pearsall 1920). At a larger scale, this may also explain partly why such plants are often restricted to oligotrophic lakes. Eutrophic lakes and bays with high sedimentation rates are generally occupied by larger rhizomatous plants. While one can explain some of this pattern by differences in relative competitive abilities (Chapter 5), differing tolerances to burial may also play a role.

Although tubers and rhizomes provide reserves for shoots to re-emerge after burial, an actual experiment showed that as little as 15 cm of sediment can kill half of the tubers of *Valisneria* (Figure 6.23). Burial by sand was more damaging than burial by silty clay; only 15 cm of sand caused as much mortality as 20 cm of silty clay. Rybicki and Carter (1986) conclude that since *Valisneria* tubers are already covered by 10 cm of sediment under field conditions, deposition of as little as 10 cm of additional sediment from storms can damage stands of aquatic plants.

Allison (1995) covered salt marsh vegetation near San Francisco with 10 cm of sediment dug out of nearby tidal channels. He then followed the recovery of the plots for four years. For all species combined, vegetation cover returned to control values after only two years. Species such as *Salicornia virginica* and *Distichlis spicata* recovered quickly; other species such as *Frankenia grandifolia* and *Jaumea carnosa* recovered only when the disturbances occurred early in the growing season. In general, plots were revegetated by ingrowth

Figure 6.23 Number of viable *Valisneria* plants in relation to depth of burial (from data in Rybicki and Carter 1986).

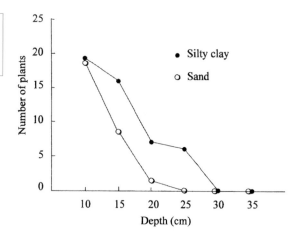

from adjoining plants, or else from buried rhizomes. There was very little seedling establishment. Recovery was relatively rapid because the disturbed areas were only 1-m^2 circular plots; since most recovery was from adjoining areas, larger areas of spoil or sediment would presumably take much longer to recover. In contrast with fresh water wetlands, it would seem that seed banks play a minor role in recolonizing disturbed areas in salt marshes (Hartman 1988, Allison 1995).

6.3.5   Ice

Anyone who has watched great cakes of ice grind against a shoreline during spring flooding will be impressed by the power of ice scour to modify vegetation. In salt marshes or large lakes, one can find entire meter square pieces of marsh with 20 cm or more of substrate chopped out of the ground and moved many meters. At a smaller scale, there is the constant grinding of freshwater shorelines by the movement of ice as water levels rise and fall. Although the effects of ice cakes grinding on shorelines are visible (and audible) during spring thaw, the processes beneath ice and snow during long winters are more difficult to study. Geis (1985) described how ice freezes onto the shoreline of lakes, forming an "ice foot." Sediments can become incorporated into this ice foot. Entire sections of shoreline are torn out of place when ice is lifted by rising water levels. According to Geis, plant biomass and diversity are reduced in the zone affected by the ice foot. Further north, ice pushing can create ridges, which produce a distinctive undulating topography along shorelines (e.g., Bliss and Gold 1994). As salinity declines and nutrient levels increase in meadows between the ridges, there is a transition from brackish wetlands with *Puccinellia* to freshwater wetlands with *Carex*.

One possible way to study ice damage is to put wooden pegs in a wetland substrate and measure the amount of damage accumulated over different periods of time. Figure 6.24 shows a typical vertical profile of ice damage. Note that the effects vary between an exposed shore and a sheltered bay. This technique could be extended to examine how ice damage is related to other habitat and vegetation properties. Wisheu and Keddy (1989a) found loss on ignition and silt/clay content were both negatively correlated with ice damage (Table 6.3). Moreover, woody plants grew closer to the water on shores protected from ice damage.

Given the importance of ice scour on shorelines, it seems that there is much more that could be done with such simple techniques. For example, entire beds of pegs of different sizes could be used to map both the intensity and area of winter disturbance. These could be compared to known water levels during the winter. Both could be tested for their ability to predict vegetation patterns.

6.3.6   Waves

Waves illustrate events of very short duration and high frequency, almost exactly the opposite kind of disturbance from meteor impacts

Table 6.3. *Correlations among four environmental factors on a temperate zone lakeshore (n = 121). This lake is frozen for approximately half of each year (after Wisheu and Keddy 1989a).*

	Loss on ignition	Silt/clay	Ice[a]	Soil
Silt/clay	0.78	–	–	–
Ice	−0.47	−0.37	–	–
Soil	ns[b]	ns	ns	–
Shrubs	−0.37	−0.43	0.31	ns

Notes:
[a] Ice damage in each plot was measured with 10 wooden pegs; intensity of ice damage could range from 0 (no damage) to 20 (all pegs sheared off or removed).
[b] $p > 0.001$.

Figure 6.24 Number of ice-damaged pegs as a function of elevation on two contrasting shorelines; elevation 0 corresponds to the typical late summer water level ($n = 25$). 1.25-cm-diameter wooden pegs, each 20 cm long, were pounded 10 cm into the ground in the summer of 1980 and damage was assessed the following spring. The study site is described in Keddy (1981b).

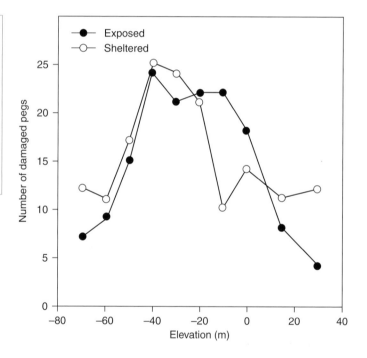

or volcanoes. Waves provide an opportunity for the study of the effects of chronic disturbance. It has long been observed that vegetation varies with exposure to waves, and sketches such as Figure 6.25 are typical of those in many books on aquatic botany. The effects of chronic exposure to waves are complex. Pearsall (1920) noted that there were both direct effects (e.g., biomass removal from plants, uprooting, seed dispersal) and indirect effects (e.g., erosion of nutrients, sorting of substrates, litter transport). The indirect effects create fertility gradients, so as disturbance from waves increases, fertility decreases.

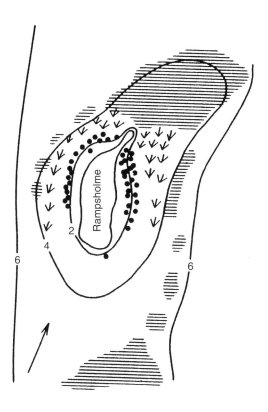

Figure 6.25 Distribution of rooted plants around a small island in Derwentwater. Note that *Nitella* grows in the lee of the island where it is assumed that sedimentation is more rapid (from Hutchinson 1975).

≡≡≡ *Nitella opaca*

↓ ↯ *Isoetes lacustris*

•⦂• *Litorella lacustris*

Since many models (e.g., Southwood 1977, Grime 1977) assume that fertility and disturbance are the two fundamental axes that control life history evolution, the fact that both occur on shorelines, and that they are arranged in opposition to one another, makes this a particularly useful situation. In order to move from sketch maps to science, it is necessary to find ways to measure exposure gradients.

Here one is aided by the long history of waves having an impact on humans. Storms destroyed much of the Spanish Armada and thereby changed European history (Fernández-Armesto 1989). They also badly damaged artificial channel ports constructed for the Normandy landings in the Second World War, which nearly changed European history again (Blizard 1993). It is therefore natural that much of the work on waves can be found in manuals published by engineering agencies (e.g., U.S. Army Coastal Engineering Research Centre 1977). Their equations have been adapted for use by aquatic ecologists (e.g., Keddy 1982, 1983, Weisner 1990).

Using data on fetch and wind directions, one can calculate indices of wave energy expected at shorelines. These indices can be used to rank

Figure 6.26 A wet meadow on a shoreline sheltered from waves on Long Point, Lake Erie (courtesy A. Reznicek).

areas of shoreline in terms of exposure, which is negatively correlated with the proportion of silt and clay in sediments. The depth ranges occupied by species such as *Eriocaulon septangulare* and *Lobelia dortmanna* increase with exposure to waves, whereas the depth range occupied by shrubs decreases with exposure to waves (Keddy 1983). Weisner used similar methods and showed that the lower limits of emergent plants exhibit a striking pattern: as exposure increased, the lower limits of marsh plants extended into deeper water. In combination, the results of these two studies suggest that exposure to waves seems to expand vegetation zones by simultaneously increasing both the landward and waterward (upper and lower) limits of emergent marsh plants. Wet meadows and marshes may then be widest on shores with moderate levels of exposure to waves. Species composition also changes with exposure to waves; Figure 3.20(a) showed the type of vegetation that develops on a shoreline chronically exposed to small waves. Contrast that with the vegetation that develops in a sheltered, bay where silt and organic matter accumulate (Figure 6.26).

Similar processes have been reported from Australian floodplains (Roberts and Ludwig 1991). Four main vegetation types were found along the River Murray: (1) riparian grasses (*Cynodon dactylon*, *Paspalidium jubiflorum*), (2) *Cyperus gymnocaulos* and riparian grasses, (3) *Eucalyptus camaldulensis* (river redgum) with sedges and grasses, and (4) *Eucalyptus* with *Phragmites australis*. These vegetation types were thought to result as a consequence of current speed and wave action. The riparian grasses, for example, occurred on steep banks with the swiftest currents.

6.3.7 Storms

The ubiquity of storm damage is now widely recognized in both temperate and tropical forests (e.g., Denslow 1987, Dirzo et al. 1992, Merrens and Peart 1992). Hurricanes and typhoons (Figure 6.27) are

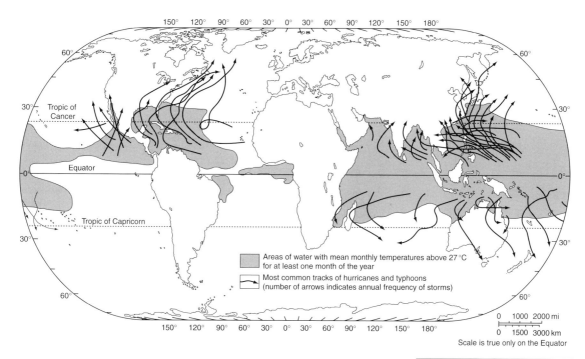

Figure 6.27 Major tracks and frequency of hurricanes and typhoons (*Encyclopaedia Britannica* 1991c).

frequent enough that their effects can be expected to have a recurring influence upon forests by breaking open the forest canopy and thereby allowing growth of seedlings. While there is now little doubt that storms play a role in most natural forest communities, as with most studies of disturbance, the relative importance of storm disturbance, compared to other kinds of disturbance and ecological processes, needs to be better understood. Frequently this is not possible because accurate information on the frequency, intensity, or proportional area of disturbance is not available to put these events into a proper context. For example, there are likely important differences between those communities formed in gaps created by the infrequent windthrow of canopy-forming dominants and those formed through mass re-colonization after frequent, intense fires. Frequencies of these two types of disturbance, for example, will vary. Fire return times in forests can vary from 80 years in *Pinus banksiana* forests to 1200 years for *Tsuga canadensis-Pinus strobus* forests (Seischab and Orwig 1991). To assess where communities fall along this continuum, one needs data on the area and frequency of disturbance by storms.

A good example of a study of systematic disturbance properties used early surveyors' records of two large tracts of forest in western New York State south of lakes Ontario and Erie (Seischab and Orwig 1991). Here a total of some $25\,000\,\text{km}^2$ was surveyed beginning in 1788. Surveyors often made notes of tree types, burns, dead trees, windthrows, and old fields, and if one knows both the linear distances walked and the proportion of these lines falling into the above categories, one can reconstruct both early vegetation cover and disturbances. In a total area of $>25\,000\,\text{km}^2$, there were $140\,\text{km}^2$ of

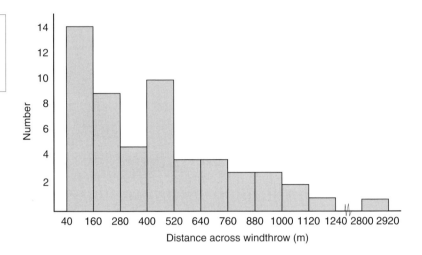

Figure 6.28 Size-class distribution of windthrows in presettlement forests of western New York in 1788 (from Seischab and Orwig 1991).

windthrows, $25 \, km^2$ of agricultural fields (possibly aboriginal), $15 \, km^2$ of dead trees, and $5 \, km^2$ of burn. The great majority of the windthrows occurred on dissected landscapes with steep slopes or ravines. The size class distribution of windthrows (Figure 6.28) shows that the majority were less than 500 m across. Further, this comprised less than 1 percent of the study area. If one assumes that surveyors could recognize windthrows for about 15 years after the event, this yields a return time of 1720 years. Seischab and Orwig conclude that "only a small percentage of the western New York forests were subject to windthrow" (p. 119) and in general "natural disturbances were infrequent in the northern hardwood forests ... steady state communities dominated the presettlement landscape" (p. 121).

6.4 | Catastrophes: low frequency and high intensity

Disturbance can often be studied in the present using properly designed field experiments. Unfortunately for ecologists, certain events that are important in the structure of ecological communities have two frustrating properties. First, they are infrequent and unlikely to occur during the life span of an ecologist, or, if and when they do occur, it is unlikely that an ecologist will be there to see them. Second, when they do occur, they have a massive effect upon ecosystem structure and therefore cannot be ignored. The two most obvious examples are volcanic eruptions and meteor impacts. What is one to do with phenomena that are rarely witnessed and yet cannot be ignored?

6.4.1 Landslides

Landslides might be thought of as a relatively infrequent form of disturbance. Guariguata (1990) measured the frequency and area of landslides within $44 \, km^2$ of lower montane wet forest in the Luquillo Mountains of Puerto Rico. On average, all months receive at least

200 mm of rain, but intense rains, associated with hurricanes, can deliver up to 500 mm in a day and trigger major landslides. Between 1936 and 1988, 46 landslides occurred. The most frequent size class (ca. 40%) was from 200 to 400 m^2, but large infrequent landslides >1800 m^2 created almost 40 percent of the area disturbed (Figure 6.29). On average, minima of 0.3 percent and 0.08 percent of the forest area are disturbed each century, on slopes underlain by intrusive and volcaniclastic rocks, respectively. Studies of the landslide vegetation showed that some species that apparently do not colonize small, tree-sized gaps benefit almost exclusively from landslide openings. These include light-demanding ferns (*Dicranopteris pectinata, Gleichenia bifida*), herbs (*Phytolacca rivinoides, Isachne angustifolia*), and one tree species characteristic of mature forests (*Cyrilla racemiflora*). Almost pure stands of *Gleichenia* and *Dicranopteris* ferns have also been reported on landscape scans in other tropical forests; both species spread by rhizomes and form thick canopies up to 1.5 m tall. Mature forests on landslides are dominated by *Calycogonium squamulosum* (Melastomataceae), *C. racemiflora* (Cyrillaceae), and *Micropholis garciniaefolia* (Sapotaceae), interspersed with patches of an emergent palm, *Prestoea montana*.

6.4.2 Volcanic eruptions

Volcanic eruptions are less frequent than landslides, but enough have occurred in the last century (publications include the Galapagos, Hawaii, New Zealand, Japan, Russia, and the United States (del Moral and Grishin 1999)) that data on their ecological effects are accumulating. Vegetation can be disrupted by lava, mud flows (lahars) and air-borne pyroclastic materials (tephra). Tephra deposits tend to sort by size; the fine materials are called ash, the intermediate ones lapilli, and large blocks breccia or bombs. Small particulates, of course, are distributed the farthest by air currents and may spread over many square kilometers. If ejected high into the atmosphere, volcanic dust can be spread around the world. Figure 6.30 shows the distribution of volcanoes in the western United States and the results of an eruption 7000 years BP that distributed ash over some 2500 km^2 and blanketed the hatched area with pumice more than 15 cm deep.

In the Kamchatka Peninsula of Russia there was a violent eruption of the Ksudach Volcano on March 28, 1907. Between one and two cubic kilometers of tephra was ejected, spreading pumice over more than 8500 km^2, with deposits over a meter deep over some 50 km^2 (Table 6.4). This table illustrates the sort of good quantitative data one needs to record for both the intensity and area of different kinds of ecological disturbance. Three different impact zones can be recognized (Grishin et al. 1996). The first received pumice deposits deeper than 100 cm. No vegetation survived. Trees still have not re-established in this zone; it remains lichen-covered with sparse herbs and shrubs. The second zone received deposits of 30–100 cm. Occasional trees survived this disturbance and provided seed sources

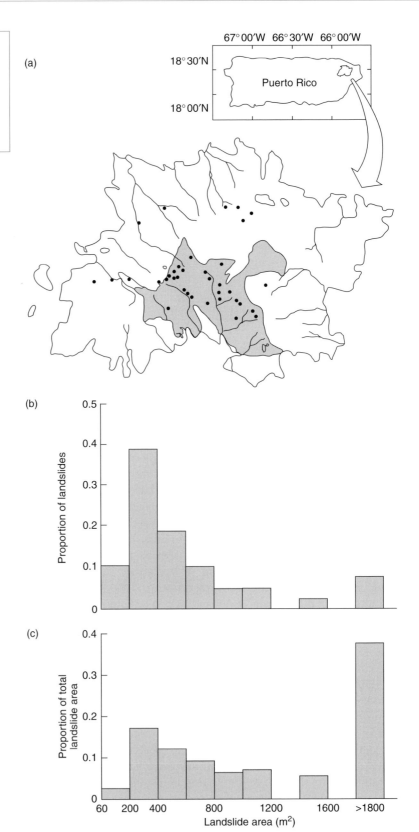

Figure 6.29 Location of the Luquillo experimental forest in Puerto Rico and 46 landslides (a). The shaded area is underlain by intrusive rocks. The frequency plots (b, c) summarize the characteristics of the landslides (from Guariguata 1990).

Table 6.4. *The relationship between pumice depth and degree of vegetation destruction (from Grishin et al. 1996).*

Deposit thickness (cm)	Deposit area (km²)	Nature of destruction
1–5	8460	Destruction of some mosses, lichens, herbs and dwarf shrub; minor damage to taller plants
5–10	1458	Substantial destruction of some species in moss-lichen, herb and dwarf shrub layers; damage to taller plants
10–20	954	Loss of lichen-moss layer, significant destruction to herb and dwarf shrub layer; some trees die slowly by drying
20–30	228	Total destruction of lichen-moss layer, herb layer; most of shrub layer lost; significant die back of trees
30–70	484	Destruction of all layers of vegetation and tree layer; isolated trees survive
70–100	62	Total destruction of all vegetation; reinvasion of vascular plants
Over 100	54	Total destruction of all vegetation; lichen desert persists

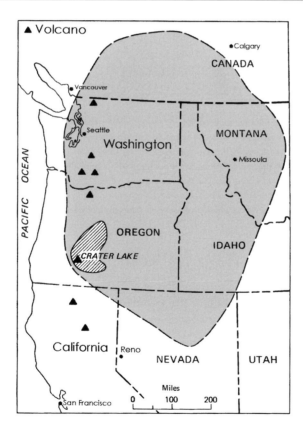

Figure 6.30 The area covered by pumice eruption at Crater Lake about 7000 years ago. The shaded area shows maximum limits of ash fall and the hatched area indicates coverage by pumice of 15 cm or more (from Crandell and Waldron 1969).

for re-colonization. Further, dead snags attracted birds that facilitated seed dispersal. Once plants established, their roots could reach buried soils. As a consequence, primary succession occurred more rapidly and smaller areas had secondary succession. In the areas that received less than 30 cm of volcanic deposits, there was substantial

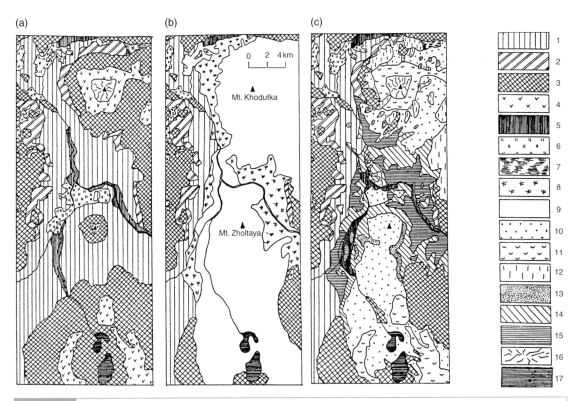

Figure 6.31 Portions of vegetation maps of the Ksudach Volcano study area. (a) Potential vegetation (before the 1907 eruption); (b) disturbed vegetation (a few years after eruption); (c) modern vegetation. 1, *Betula ermanii* forest; 2, *B. ermanii* – *Alnus kamtschatica* subalpine complex; 3, *A. kamtschatica* thickets; 4, high-mountain vegetation; 5, river valley forest; 6, meadows with shrubs on level sites in the forest belt; 7, moist *Calamagrostis* – *Carex* spp. meadow; 8, pumice desert; 9, pumice desert with scattered surviving trees; 10, pumice desert with lichen cover; 11, pumice desert sparse sub-alpine plants; 12, complex of mountain meadows with *A. kamtschatica* thickets; 13, pumice desert with lichen cover and isolated birches; 14, open young *B. ermanii* forest with dwarf shrubs-lichen cover; 15, closed young *B. ermanii* forest with isolated mature trees that survived the eruption; 16, nival belt; 17, lakes (from Grishin et al. 1996).

survival, and secondary succession was sufficiently rapid that there are now well-developed forests similar to those nearby that were less disturbed. Where the pumice was sufficiently thin, it may be more appropriate to describe changes as vegetation recovery rather than succession. Figure 6.31 summarizes the changes in vegetation resulting from this eruption.

The eruption of Mount St. Helens in the United States provided a fine opportunity for ecologists to study the effects of volcanoes (del Moral and Bliss 1993, del Moral et al. 1995). Having been dormant for 130 years, Mount St. Helens erupted on 18 May 1980 when a lateral burst levelled trees up to 20 km distant. Tephra was spewn over thousands of square kilometers, with the largest deposits on the northern slopes. Melting glaciers produced mudslides that swept downstream channels. Fine materials coated forests. Figure 6.32 shows the results. In spite of the publicity that this eruption has received, it was relatively small compared to other eruptions; the

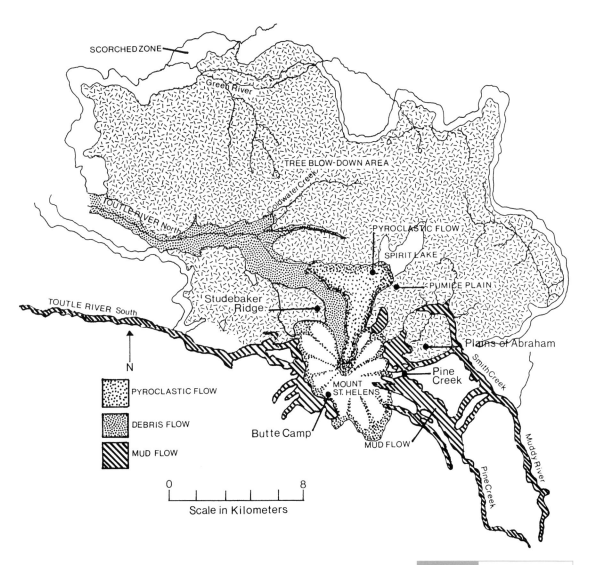

Figure 6.32 Mount St. Helens volcanic impact area (from del Moral and Wood 1993).

volume of ejecta, was for example less than 5 percent of Krakatoa, which erupted in Indonesia in 1883 and 1930 (del Moral and Bliss 1993).

Coarse tephra is particularly inhospitable to plants because it has little water-holding capacity, is extremely nutrient poor, and is unstable (del Moral and Grishin 1999). Since many deposits also occur at higher altitudes, climatic stress may further inhibit the re-establishment of plants. Because the dates of tephra deposits and volcanic flows can often be precisely established, eruptions, like landslides, may provide a valuable opportunity to study ecological succession.

6.4.3 Meteor impacts

One only has to look at the surface of the Moon to realize that collisions among astronomical objects occur. It is easy to forget this because such events are rare (from the perspective of an ape's life

Figure 6.33 The K/T boundary interval at the Starkville North site near Trinidad, Colorado. The fossil-pollen-defined boundary is at the top of a white-weathering, kaolinitic claystone bed beneath the dark coal layer. The claystone consists of finely crystalline to amorphous kaolinite with scattered fragments of quartz and feldspar. It contains abundance anomalies of Ir ($6\,ng \cdot g^{-1}$) and other elements, including Sc, Ti, V, Cr, and Sb, that distinguish it from other non-boundary kaolinitic clay beds that occur in coaly sequences. A thin, flaky, dark shale separates the kaolinitic claystone from the overlying thin coal bed (from Tschudy et al. 1984).

span) and because erosion obliterates the effects of such collisions on Earth. Each day as the Moon rises, however, one should be reminded that catastrophes can and must have occurred on Earth too. How is one to study them?

One way is to look for discontinuities in the geological record. Geologists have long recognized that a major change in the Earth's biota occurred at the Cretaceous/Tertiary boundary; indeed, the dramatic change in the fossil record defines the transition between these geological periods. The Cretaceous Period marks the end of the Mesozoic Era, known as the Age of Reptiles. The vegetation was dominated by cone-bearing tress (gymnosperms), although early flowering plants (angiosperms) were also present. It was the period of some dramatic forms of reptilian life such as Ornithopods, Stegosaurs, and Ankylosaurs. Some of these were herbivores with dentition well suited for cutting and chewing plants. Others were some of the largest carnivores to have occupied Earth. It has been suggested that angiosperms evolved in part as a response to the pressure of herbivory from low grazing ornithischians (Bakker 1978). Such gradual changes, however, give way to an abrupt transition. Dinosaurs disappear; mammals become abundant. Angiosperms radiate and become the dominant plant forms. We now live in the Age of Mammals and Angiosperms. What event triggered this sudden change from the Mesozoic (gymnosperm/reptile) biota to the Cenozoic (angiosperm/mammal) biota?

There are various theories ranging from gradual climate change (perhaps associated with drifting continents) to competition with, or predation by, mammals. The geological record, however, suggests something slightly more abrupt. Figure 6.33 shows a cross-section of bedrock representing the transition from Mesozoic to Cenozoic. Recent studies have shown some unusual features of this transition. Anomalously high iridium concentrations have been found at over

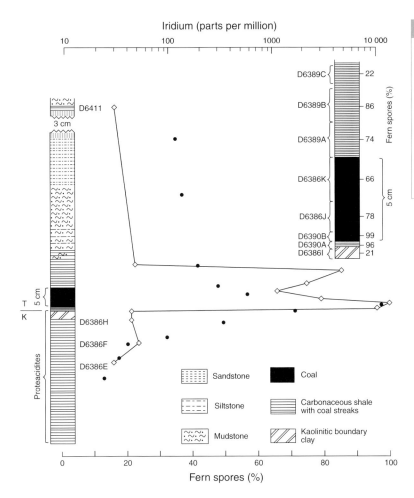

Figure 6.34 Diagram of the lithology of the K/T boundary interval at the Starkville North site, near Trinidad, Colorado. The large black dots show the variation in Ir concentration, the solid line and diamonds show the fern-spore percentages, and the inset shows the detail of the boundary interval. The USGS locality numbers are shown adjacent to the columns (from Tschudy et al. 1984).

50 sites around the world. Iridium is a rare element on Earth, although common in meteors. This transition is now widely believed to record the effects of a meteorite, some 10 km in diameter, that collided with Earth (Tschudy et al. 1984, Wolbach et al. 1985).

Paleobotanical work has now uncovered events during this transition (Tschudy et al. 1984, Wolfe 1991). Take a closer look at Figure 6.33. Just beneath the dark coal layer in this picture is a bed of rock derived from clay. This rock contains anomalously high concentrations of iridium, as well as other uncommon elements such as Sc, It, V, and Cr. Fossil pollen has been used to study floristic changes across this boundary (Tschudy et al. 1984). The cretaceous *Proteacidites* species occur only below this boundary (Figure 6.34). Immediately above this layer, fern spores become abundant and then, within a few centimeters, decline relative to angiosperms. Organic materials such as fusinite are present. They interpret this to mean that some major catastrophic event at the end of the Cretaceous was responsible for massive destruction of the vegetation. The presence of fusinite suggests that fire also was involved. The Chicxulub crater on the

Table 6.5. *Characteristics of the 10 largest terrestrial impact structures on Earth (from Earth Impact Database 2006).*

Crater name	Location	Diameter (km)	Age (Ma)
Vredefort	South Africa	300	2023 ± 4
Sudbury	Ontario, Canada	250	1850 ± 3
Chicxulub	Yucatan, Mexico	170	64.98 ± 0.05
Popigai	Russia	100	35.7 ± 0.2
Manicouagan	Quebec, Canada	100	214 ± 1
Acraman	South Australia	90	~ 590
Chesapeake Bay	Virginia, USA	90	35.5 ± 0.3
Puchezh-Katunki	Russia	80	167 ± 3
Morokweng	South Africa	70	145.0 ± 0.8
Kara	Russia	65	70.3 ± 2.2

Yucatan Peninsula is likely the product of a collision with an asteroid or comet, and is widely thought to have been the event that caused the K/T boundary (Kyte 1998, Flannery 2001). Other work, however, suggests that the Chicxulub crater was formed nearly 300 000 years before the end of the Cretaceous (Keller et al. 2004).

Wolbach et al. (1985) specifically sought out evidence on the nature of the postulated fires. They collected samples from the K/T boundary in both the northern and southern hemispheres and found 0.36–0.58 percent graphitic carbon, indicating a world-wide layer of soot. This corresponds to a volume of soot equal to 10 percent of the present biomass of the Earth! This implies either that much of the Earth's vegetation burned or that substantial amounts of fossil fuels were also ignited. This soot would have had at least three effects (e.g., Wolbach et al. 1985, Alvarez 1998, Flannery 2001). First, it would have blocked virtually all light reaching Earth and thereby prevented photosynthesis. Second, the pyrotoxins formed during combustion would have harmed most land life. Carbon monoxide alone, if produced in the same amount as soot, would have reached a toxic level of 50 ppm (Wolbach et al. 1985). Third, the Earth would have cooled as soot blocked out sunlight.

Specific events, such as the Cretaceous/Tertiary boundary shown in Figure 6.34, indicate the kind of major impacts a single meteor collision could have. Is it possible to generalize further? A single case is interesting, but, after all, science deals in general principles. Table 6.5 shows that the Chicxulub crater is not an isolated case, while Figure 6.35 shows the distribution of known craters and their diameters. These data are complicated by at least three constraints: (1) only larger objects make it through the atmosphere without burning up, (2) erosion buries or erases older craters, and (3) many craters likely remain undiscovered. Still, these data, combined with the crater-scarred surfaces of the Moon and other planets, provide vivid evidence that such collisions are not uncommon and that

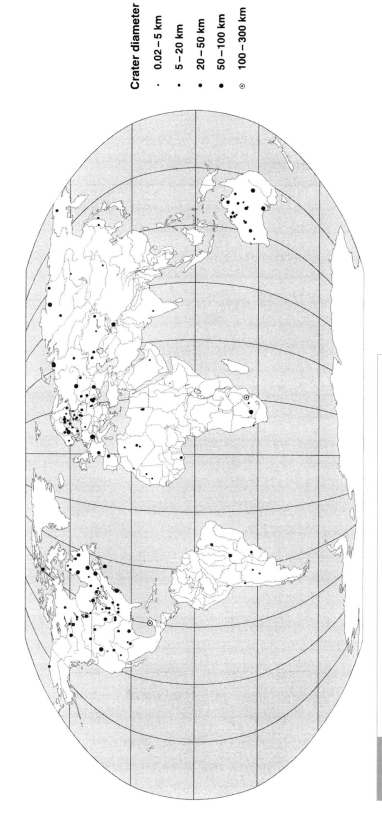

Crater diameter

· 0.02 – 5 km

• 5 – 20 km

● 20 – 50 km

⬤ 50 – 100 km

⊙ 100 – 300 km

Figure 6.35 The distribution and size of terrestrial impact structures on Earth (from French 1998).

meteoric impacts provide a recurring, if little understood, perturbation of the biosphere.

There is one historical example, but alas, it occurred in an isolated area far removed from scientific observation and enquiry. This "near-collision", called the Tunguska event, occurred in 1908 in central Siberia and was recorded by seismographs as far away as western Europe. It has been estimated that the object weighed between 10^5 and 10^6 tons and arrived at a speed of 100 000 km · h^{-1}. Because of the remoteness of the site, it was not investigated scientifically until 1927. The Russian scientist L. A. Kulik found that an area of pine forest was flattened; around the epicenter everything was scorched, and very little was growing two decades later. The felled trees all pointed away from the epicenter. The absence of any object or crater suggests that the object, possibly a comet fragment, disintegrated in the atmosphere (Encyclopaedia Britannica 1991b).

The effects of meteor collisions are of interest not only to paleo-ecologists. There is growing evidence that a moderate-scale nuclear exchange would generate these sorts of effects, producing the so-called nuclear winter. Wolbach et al. (1985) suggest that the commonly used nuclear winter models may significantly underestimate the efficiency with which soot is carried into the atmosphere by fires. On the other hand, they also suggest that the effects on the biosphere "though disastrous, were not apocalyptic." About half the known genera survived, although the impact, at 10^{30} ergs, far exceeded the total explosive power of 3×10^{26} ergs assumed for nuclear winter. Even the strongest voices against nuclear war have not suggested that life itself would be extinguished, rather, as Schell (1982) put it, a post nuclear world would be "a republic of insects and grass."

6.5 | Measuring the effects of disturbance

To better understand the effects of disturbance on vegetation, one must more precisely define, and then measure, the relative effects of disturbance upon community properties. Consider two examples.

6.5.1 The Hubbard Brook study of forested watersheds

The Hubbard Brook valley in the White Mountains of northern New Hampshire is covered by second-growth Northern Hardwood Forest growing in shallow soil over gneiss bedrock (Figure 6.36). Principal plant species of the area include sugar maple (*Acer saccharum*), beech (*Fagus grandifolia*), basswood (*Tilia americana*), hemlock (*Tsuga canadensis*), and white pine (*Pinus strobus*). Variants of this type of forest stretch from Nova Scotia in the east, to Minnesota in the west, and south in the Appalachians to Virginia and North Carolina. In the White Mountains there is also altitudinal variation; deciduous forests are replaced by coniferous forest at higher altitudes (ca. 760 m) and then by tundra (ca. 1500 m).

Figure 6.36 A young, second-growth northern hardwood forest at about 600 m elevation on Mount Moosilauke, Warren, New Hampshire. The forest was heavily cut about 65 years prior to the photograph (from Bormann and Likens 1981).

The experimental forest covers approximately 3000 ha and has a range of altitude from 200 to 1000 m. A series of adjoining watersheds was identified, and near the base of each, a weir was constructed to monitor stream flow and water chemistry (Figure 6.37). In this way, nutrient outputs for an entire watershed could be monitored by sampling at a single point. One watershed, (W6) served as a reference system; another (W2) was experimentally deforested and maintained bare for three years before vegetation was allowed to regrow, while another (W4) was clear-cut in strips over a four-year period (Figure 6.38). Comparisons among these watersheds provided a great deal of data on the way in which forests cycle nutrients. The results of this work were published in a series of scientific papers

Figure 6.37 The weir at Watershed 4 (Hubbard Brook Experimental Forest, New Hampshire) showing a flow of 0.6 l·s^{-1}. Average annual flow of W4 is 9.2 l·s^{-1} (from Bormann and Likens 1981).

Figure 6.38 The Hubbard Brook Experimental Forest showing monitored watersheds w-1, w-3, w-5, w-6 and experimentally manipulated watersheds w-2 (deforested), w-4 (strip-cut), and w-101 (commercially clear-cut). Note elevational gradient with northern hardwoods giving way to spruce-fir forest at higher elevations and on knobs (Bormann and Likens 1981).

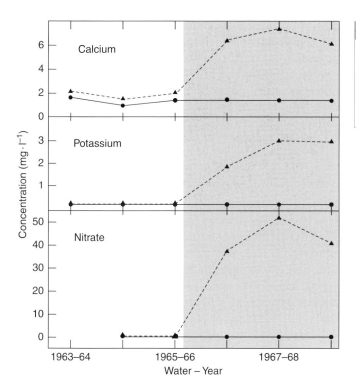

Figure 6.39 Annual weighted average of dissolved ions in stream water: ●, watershed 6; ▲, watershed 2. Shaded area represents period when watershed was devegetated (Bormann and Likens 1981).

during the 1970s and were summarized in Likens et al. (1977) and Bormann and Likens (1981).

In the deforested watershed, annual run-off increased by some 30 percent and storm peaks were accentuated; this was the result of transpiration being all but eliminated. Loss of soil particulates increased by about a factor of ten, from 1491 to 8834 kg · ha^{-1}. The concentration of most dissolved nutrients in run-off increased several fold after cutting (Figure 6.39) and produced net losses of soil nutrients including nitrate (>114 kg · ha^{-1}), calcium (>77 kg · ha^{-1}), and potassium (>30 kg · ha^{-1}). These nutrient losses reached a maximum after two years of devegetation, although the treatment continued for a further year, presumably the result of "progressive exhaustion of the supply of easily decomposable substrate present in the ecosystem" (Likens et al., p. 88) at the start of the experiment. This series of experiments showed the degree to which plants are able to exercise biotic control of watersheds: "These processes, integrated within limits set by climate, geology, topography, biota and level of ecosystem development, determine the size of nutrient reservoirs and produce nutrient cycles typified by minimum outputs of dissolved substances and particulate matter and by maximum resistance to erosion" (Likens et al., p. 78).

The Hubbard Brook study emphasized that ecosystems tend to protect and recycle their nutrient capital, and one of the important detrimental effects of human disturbance is to increase the rate of leakage of nutrients. Leakage of nutrients is now widely regarded as a symptom of an ecosystem that is undergoing stress. This work also emphasized the importance of declining soil fertility as a potential constraint on sustainability; that is, landscapes may be unable to withstand repeated logging due to the combination of nutrient losses from the biomass that is removed and from erosion and leaching of the soil. Species that grow rapidly after disturbance may be particularly important for reducing leakiness since they recover and retain nutrients for later stages of forest succession.

6.5.2 Ottawa River marshes

Herbaceous vegetation forms along temperate zone rivers where flooding or ice damage prevents woody plants from establishing. The Ottawa River in southern Canada is typical of many temperate zone rivers, with wet meadows dominated by *Carex* spp., *Eleocharis* spp., and *Lythrum salicaria* high on the shore; emergent marshes with *Scirpus* spp., *Typha* spp., and *Sparganium* spp. in shallow water; and aquatic vegetation with *Nymphaea odorata*, *Potamogeton* spp., and *Valisneria americana* in deeper water. The vegetation also changes with increased exposure to flowing water (Section 6.3.6) and the disturbance caused by ice cakes that are carried by the water in the spring (Section 6.3.5). This gradient, from sheltered bays to exposed headlands, is a natural gradient of disturbance.

Moore (1990, 1998) artificially created bare patches in five different vegetation types along an exposure gradient. At each site, above-ground biomass was removed from 1-m² plots and the vegetation in them repeatedly compared with undisturbed controls over two growing seasons. There were two questions: (1) did the measured disturbance effects change among the particular ecological properties measured? and (2) did the effects vary among the five wetland types? The properties measured included both community-level properties (e.g., biomass, evenness) and lower-order properties (the abundance of selected species). Moore found that a single growing season was sufficient for community-level properties such as biomass, richness, and evenness to return to control levels. The dominants removed at each site tended to remain depressed for the first growing season, although by the second year effects were negligible. At the guild level, recovery was also rapid, although there were minor changes, such as a modest increase in facultative annuals. The species level of organization tended to be the most sensitive to disturbance. Overall, it appeared that removing above-ground biomass had a marginal effect on this vegetation type; this may not be a great surprise, given the dynamic nature of riparian wetlands.

Moore also tested whether effects of disturbance varied among the five wetland vegetation types by measuring the magnitude of disturbance effects for several ecological properties. Since biomass removal was proposed as a measure of disturbance in the introduction to this chapter, Moore's calculation of disturbance effects is worth examining more closely. For any property

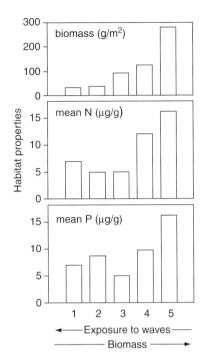

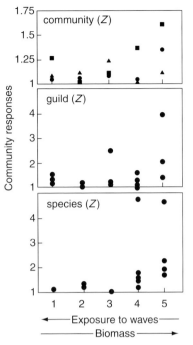

Figure 6.40 Effects of experimental disturbance (removal of all above-ground biomass) upon five different wetland communities. Z is a measure of departure from control plot values, and is scaled so all change is greater than 1. The greater Z, the greater the departure from control values. Effects had largely disappeared by year two, and so are not included in the figure (after Moore 1998).

(e.g., biomass, diversity) the magnitude of disturbance effects was determined as Z, where

$$\frac{x_0}{x_t} \times \frac{y_t}{y_0} = Z$$

and x_0 is the mean value before treatment in the control sites, x_t is the mean value after treatment in the control sites, y_0 is the mean value before treatment in the disturbance sites, and y_t is the mean value after treatment in the disturbance sites (see Ravera 1989). The value of Z is independent of initial levels of the properties and is also independent of any ongoing temporal trends in the community. A Z of 1.0 indicates no treatment effects, while values above or below 1 indicate increase or decrease. Figure 6.40 shows that, in each case, the experimental disturbance had the greatest effects in sheltered bays. That is, sites with higher biomass and higher fertility tended to show the most response to disturbance. Perhaps this is because these are the riparian communities where disturbance is normally most infrequent.

6.6 | Disturbance and gap dynamics

The effects of disturbance can be studied from two different viewpoints. Many of the examples above have discussed disturbance gradients. In some situations disturbance occurs, instead, as discrete patches (Sousa 1984, Pickett and White 1985). Much of the work on patch dynamics is concentrated in forests where the effects of storms (Section 6.3.7) can create patches ranging from the size of a single fallen tree to entire stands (Urban and Shugart 1992). There are rather fewer studies of patch dynamics in wetlands, yet one might reasonably expect this process to be important. Examples might include patches burned by fire, eaten by muskrats, cut out by ice cakes (vegetation is frozen into the ice, and uprooted and moved during spring breakup), killed by floating mats of litter, or buried by alluvial deposits.

6.6.1 Regeneration from buried seeds after disturbance

The episodic destruction of biomass in vegetation can be caused by many factors including fire, flooding, ice scour, and herbivory. When biomass is removed, resources such as light and nitrogen become available. Many plant species have traits that enable them to exploit these temporary patches of resources. Buried reserves of viable seeds, often called seed banks, allow plants to rapidly exploit disturbed patches. This phenomenon is well studied in wetlands, where seed densities in excess of a thousand seeds per square meter are common in both prairie marshes and freshwater coastal marshes, and densities in excess of ten thousand per square meter are common in wet meadows (Table 6.6). These high densities of buried seeds provide evidence of the importance of disturbance. Possibly the most familiar example is the regeneration of wetland vegetation after disturbance by flooding and drying, well documented in both prairie wetlands (e.g., van der Valk and Davis 1976, 1978) and lakeshores (Keddy and Reznicek 1982, 1986).

For many marsh and wet meadow species, regeneration in gaps provides the only opportunity for establishment from seed. Grubb (1977) coined the term "regeneration niche" to describe the many ways in which plant seedlings and juveniles can exploit the different kinds of natural disturbance. Buried seeds appear to detect natural disturbances as a result of three factors: increased fluctuations in soil temperature, increased quantity of light, and changes in the quality of light (Grime 1979). Thus most plants adapted to exploit natural disturbances are stimulated to germinate by a combination of high light levels and fluctuating temperatures (Grime et al. 1981).

Colonization of gaps by buried seeds appears to be infrequent in saline environments, where seed densities are often low (<50 m^{-2}) (Hartman 1988) and a majority of the revegetation occurs by expansion of plants bordering the gap (Hartman 1988, Allison 1995). This exception is probably a consequence of the constraints that salinity places on the establishment of seedlings; periodic flooding with fresh water may provide the only opportunity for some salt marsh species to establish from buried seeds (Zedler and Beare 1986). The large viviparous seedlings found on some mangrove species (Tomlinson 1986) may also provide a means of circumventing constraints imposed by salinity. Mangrove seedlings are thought to play an

Table 6.6 | *Reserves of buried seeds are an important feature of wet meadows and marshes (adapted from Keddy and Reznicek 1986).*

Study	Site	Seedlings m^{-2}
Prairie marshes		
Smith and Kadlec (1983)	*Typha* spp.	2 682
	Scirpus acutus	6 536
	S. maritimus	2 194
	Phragmites australis	2 398
	Distichlis spicata	850
	Open water	70
Van der Valk and Davis (1978)	Open water	3 549
	Scirpus validus	7 246
	Sparganium eurycarpum	2 175
	Typha glauca	5 447
	Scirpus fluviatilis	2 247
	Carex spp.	3 254
Van der Valk and Davis (1976)	Open water	2 900
	Typha glauca	3 016
	Wet meadow	826
	Scirpus fluviatilis	319
Freshwater coastal marshes		
Moore and Wein (1977)	*Typha latifolia*	14 768
	Former hayfield	7 232
	Myrica gale	4 496
Leck and Graveline (1979)	Streambank	11 295
	Mixed annuals	6 405
	Ambrosia spp.	9 810
	Typha spp.	13 670
	Zizania spp.	12 955
Lakeshore marshes		
Nicholson and Keddy (1983)	Lakeshore, 75 cm water	38 259
Keddy and Reznicek (1982)	Waterline of lake	1 862
	30 cm below waterline	7 543
	60 cm below waterline	19 798
	90 cm below waterline	18 696
	120 cm below waterline	7 467
	150 cm below waterline	5 168
Wisheu and Keddy (1991)	Wilson's Lake	8 511
McCarthy (1987)	Hirst Lake	24 430
	Hirst Lake	16 626
	Goose Lake	11 455
	Goose Lake	3 743
Beaver ponds		
Le Page and Keddy (1988)	Canadian Shield	2 324

important role in regeneration after damage by storms (Lugo and Snedaker 1974).

6.6.2 Gap regeneration in deciduous forests

The southern regions of the Appalachian Mountains in eastern North America have one of the world's richest deciduous forests. There are five species of magnolia, 10 species of oaks, seven species of hickory, along with a rich array of other woody plants (Stupka 1964). The other two principal areas of deciduous forests are in western Europe and Eastern Asia. Once these forest areas were contiguous, as illustrated by the species and genera that these three regions share, but continental drift and climate change have now isolated them from one another (Braun 1950, Pielou 1979). All three areas also have dense human populations, and therefore the protected Great Smoky Mountains area is probably of global significance.

The large number of tree species in the southern Appalachian forests can be accounted for by a number of factors. History is probably important. During the ice age, tree species were able to migrate southward along the mountains; in contrast, trees in Europe may have been trapped by the Alps and driven to extinction. As a result, species known from past interglacial eras no longer occur in Europe. The high number of tree species presently found is also probably due to the variation in topography. Differences in slope, aspect, altitude, and exposure provide habitat for different species of trees (Whittaker 1956). In addition, the extreme sites provide refuge from competition illustrated by the centrifugal organization model (Keddy and MacLellan 1990). Within homogeneous areas, there is also evidence that tree species alternate with one another, saplings of one species establishing under the canopy of another (Fox 1977, Woods and Whittaker 1981). Another important factor, however, is gap regeneration. There is constant disturbance within deciduous forests, from relatively large gaps carved out by severe storms to individual trees falling. This creates an array of different gap sizes with different light regimes. Depending upon their light requirements, different tree species may come to occupy the clearings (Grubb 1977). Thus even where sites are relatively homogeneous at first, the tree canopy and different gap sizes create a form of biological heterogeneity.

To experimentally study the role of gap regeneration in maintaining the diversity of tree species, Phillips and Shure (1990) censused an area to determine the relative abundance of tree species, six of which are shown in Figure 6.41. They then cut gaps of four different sizes: 0.016, 0.08, 0.4, and 2.0 ha, and monitored regeneration in these gaps. Two years after cutting there were marked differences. *Liriodendron tulipifera* (a member of the magnolia family) had highest regeneration in the smallest gaps but was able to colonize most sizes. *Robinia pseudoacacia* (a member of the pea family) showed a striking preference for the largest clearings. *Quercus rubra*, like *Liriodendron*, grew best in the smallest gaps but, unlike *Liriodendron*, did not establish well in the larger gaps. *Quercus prinus* and *Carya* species showed very low

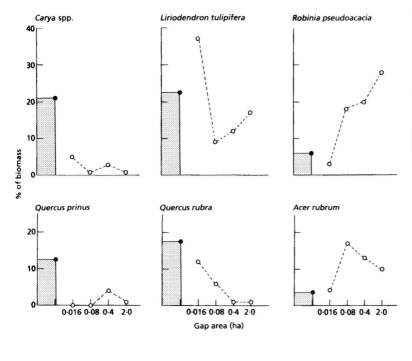

Figure 6.41 Regeneration of principal tree species in artificially created gaps of four sizes in mixed-species deciduous forest in North Carolina. The abundance of each species is expressed as a percentage of the total biomass. Mean value before cutting (●), second year after cutting (○) (after Newman 1993).

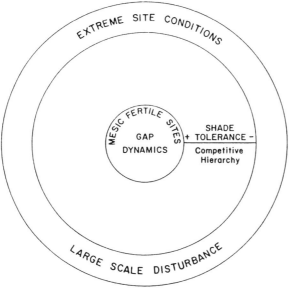

Figure 6.42 Three mechanisms for producing tree diversity in landscapes (gap dynamics when the canopy is dense, relative tolerance to shade in intermediate habitats, and tolerance of extreme site conditions) can be summarized in a centrifugal model.

regeneration in the gaps, which possibly reflected a requirement for fire to remove leaf litter. These patterns of gap regeneration can be combined with differential distributions along competition gradients to account for the overall high tree diversity in the area (Figure 6.42).

In the centrifugal model shown in this figure, the core region contains mesic, fertile sites with high biomass, while the peripheral region contains unproductive and/or highly disturbed sites. Three biological consequences arise. In the core region, the canopy is dense, and species can escape from shade only by establishing in small clearings created by gap dynamics. In the peripheral region, extreme site conditions such as rock outcrops, cliffs, fire barrens and alvars allow a different suite of trees to occur. In the middle region, species composition is determined by relative shade tolerance. Centrifugal models are discussed further in Section 11.7.4.

6.6.3 Alluvial deposition

Patches are also formed where rivers deposit sediments. Natural processes of erosion and deposition still occur in the valleys of some rivers such as the Amazon (Salo et al. 1986) and northern North American rivers (Nanson and Beach 1977), but overall they have been greatly reduced around the world (Dynesius and Nilsson 1994). The Rhine River, for example, has been markedly manipulated with dams, dikes, and channels, whereas there were once extensive alluvial forests associated with water level fluctuations of 2–3 m (Schnitzler 1995). These forests were of two main types: a "softwood" type (alder/poplar/willow) and a "hardwood" type (maple/ash/oak/elm). Newly deposited alluvial sediments are generally colonized by the softwood group, but after a period of 20–30 years, the hardwood species begin to establish. The change humans have made to the Rhine make it difficult to sort out the natural processes that would once have predominated; there are, for example, two distinctive classes of trees (120–150 years, 30–40 years) that correspond to the two eras of canalization.

The overall diversity of plant communities along the Rhine can apparently be explained by two factors. First, there is the continual creation of new patches of alluvial deposits and successional development through time. From this perspective, the Rhine forests, like most alluvial forests (Chapter 14 in Mitsch and Gosselink 1986, Salo et al. 1986), are a mosaic of different aged stands of forest on alluvial deposits. A second source of variation is superimposed upon this dynamic landscape because all patches are not the same. Depending upon the environmental conditions in the patch, a different community develops. For example, along the Rhine, wet clay may stay vegetated by willow and poplar, whereas drier gravels will become dominated by oak and elm. Much of the richness of alluvial plant communities can be explained by gaps with different characteristics that allow a variety of plant species to regenerate (Grubb 1977, Salo et al. 1986).

6.6.4 Freshwater marshes

In freshwater marshes, patches can be formed by flooding, fire, or herbivores (e.g., Weller 1978, 1994, van der Valk 1981, Ball and Nudds 1989). Figure 6.1 showed that as little as three years of flooding can kill stands of emergent plants. Such disturbances create a mosaic of different vegetation types; the simplest example may be dense stands of cattails interspersed with patches of open water (Figure 6.43). Experimental studies have shown that breeding ducks select a 1:1

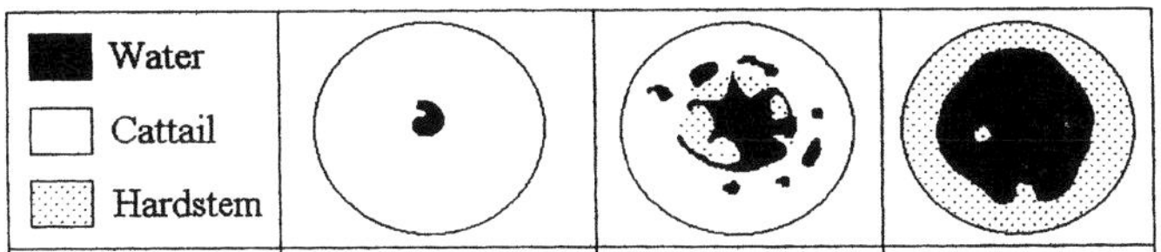

■ Water □ Cattail ▦ Hardstem			
Water depth	Shallow	Medium	Deep
Vegetation	Dense	Moderate	Sparse
Size of bird populations	Medium	Large	Small
Bird species richness	Low	High	Low
Number of muskrats	Few	Many	Few

Figure 6.43 Gaps create habitat interspersion in freshwater marshes (after Weller 1994).

ratio of these two patch types (e.g., Kaminski and Prince 1981). Since many shallow water marshes are slowly dominated by cattails, mosaics can easily be created by human manipulation. Ball and Nudds (1989) describe an experiment in which circular patches of 0.02, 0.09, and 0.15 ha were either cut or burned into cattail stands around Lake St. Clair in Canada. They observed that gaps created by mowing lasted longer that those produced by burning.

6.7 | Synthesis: fire, flooding, and sea level in the Everglades

White (1994) has synthesized the many kinds of disturbance active in the Everglades. This area has "a great deal of structural and compositional variation, from open water sloughs with sparse macrophytes to sedge- and grass-dominated freshwater marshes, open pine stands and dense broad-leaved evergreen forest." Nine physical driving forces are superimposed on this mosaic; they range from those that show gradual change (e.g., climate change, sea level rise, for which change is measured on time scales greater than 10^2 years) to those disturbances for which change is measured on scales of less than 10^2 years, (e.g., flood, drought, fire, storms, freezing temperatures). These latter natural disturbances tend to be short-lived events, but the communities recover from them slowly. Hence there is a basic asymmetry: disturbance is fast, recovery is slow. These recovery lags mean that periodic disturbances can generate a mosaic representing a particular degree of recovery from the last disturbance. The rates of recovery will depend upon the amount of vegetation (if any) that persists through the disturbance, the influx of new propagules from adjoining areas, and the productivity of the site.

In the Everglades, 11 of the 15 plant community types depend upon two key factors: hydrology and fire. Both of these factors are in

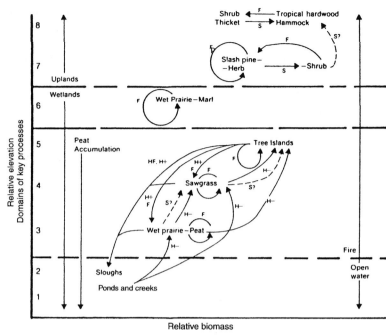

Figure 6.44 Plant communities of the central freshwater Everglades and the processes that produce them (from White 1994).

F = Fire HF = Hot fire (peat consuming)
H+ = Increased hydroperiod H− = Decreased hydroperiod
S = Succession (peat accumulation)
S? Uncertain succession

turn connected to relative elevation. In general, as peat accumulates, there is a succession from sloughs to treed islands (the main sequence in Figure 6.44). Light fires will create patches in the vegetation, but severe fires can consume peat, thereby lowering the relative elevation of the site and returning it to a much earlier successional stage. The more intense the fire, the longer will be the recovery time. Intense fire and alligators (Section 6.3.3) are apparently the only processes that can actually increase the hydroperiod of a site.

Since the mid 1980s, approximately 25 percent of the wet prairie and slough in the Everglades has been replaced by stands of sawgrass, probably as a consequence of reduced flooding and decreased fire frequency. Wet prairies and sloughs have higher plant diversity, are major sites of periphyton production, and are important habitats for crustaceans and fish. Drainage and fire control, therefore, has not only changed the vegetation but also the capacity of the area to produce and support other organisms. Restoration of the Everglades will require restoration of flooding and fire as natural disturbances.

6.8 | Competition, disturbance, and stress: the CSR synthesis

At this point some synthesis may be desirable, if not absolutely necessary. The origin and classification of plant communities was examined in Chapters 1 and 2; then, in four successive chapters, the major factors that control their distribution and abundance were examined: resources, stress, competition, and disturbance. The large number of examples may already be difficult to mentally absorb and organize. The synthesis that follows was initially developed to examine the evolutionary strategies that might occur in different types of living organisms. This framework can also be used to describe the processes that predominate in creating different plant communities.

The CSR scheme was developed in the early 1970s by Phil Grime, a plant ecologist at the University of Sheffield; for historical accuracy, however, it is noteworthy that a nearly identical scheme was presented at almost the same time by an animal ecologist, Richard Southwood (1977, 1988). Grime's logic, to summarize a large volume of work (e.g., 1973a,b, 1974, 1977, 1979) in a few sentences, can be expressed as follows. Plants require resources to grow. In the absence of external environmental constraints, plants will interact strongly with one another for access to these resources. Roots and shoots will grow rapidly so that a plant may acquire resources; simultaneously these resources will be denied to neighboring plants. Plants that possess traits that confer success in this active contest for resources are considered to be competitors. If, however, there is frequent disturbance, these sorts of intense interactions will be prevented. Instead, there will simply be a race to capture as many resources as possible before the next disturbance kills the members of the community. Under these conditions, short-lived and fast-growing species will occur, a group called ruderals. Those familiar with the r-K continuum will recognize ruderals as being the typical r-selected species and competitors as more like the K-selected species.

Grime's contribution was to recognize that there is another possibility, and one that is orthogonal to the former axis of variation. If resources are scarce, rapid growth will be prevented, in which case ruderals will not occur. Active foraging and intense interspecific competition will also be unlikely because there will be insufficient resources to permit that style of growth: the returns from active foraging will be minimal and quite possibly well below the costs of building elaborate roots and shoots. Instead, there will be slow growth and, in particular, growth will be uncoupled from periods of resource availability. This will produce a conservation strategy rather than an exploitation strategy and stress tolerators will occur. The characteristics of these three functional types of plants are summarized in Table 6.7.

The three groups of species, suggested Grime, can be positioned along two axes, disturbance and stress, and yield C (competitor), S (stress tolerator), and R (ruderal) strategies (Figure 6.45). The fourth possibility is not possible because the combination of disturbance and stress has no viable evolutionary solution; such habitats remain unvegetated. Southwood presented a very similar analysis of life

Table 6.7. *Some characteristics of competitive, stress-tolerant, and ruderal plants (from Grime 1977).*

Characteristic	Competitive	Stress tolerant	Ruderal
Morphology of shoot	High dense canopy of leaves; extensive lateral spread above and below ground	Extremely wide range of growth forms	Small stature, limited lateral spread
Leaf form	Robust, often mesomorphic	Often small or leathery, or needle-like	Various, often mesomorphic
Litter	Copious, often persistent	Sparse, sometimes persistent	Sparse, not usually persistent
Maximum potential relative growth rate	Rapid	Slow	Rapid
Life forms	Perennial herbs, shrubs, and trees	Lichens, perennial herbs, shrubs, and trees (often very long lived)	Annual herbs
Longevity of leaves	Relatively short	Long	Short
Phenology of leaf production	Well-defined peaks of leaf production coinciding with period(s) of maximum potential productivity	Evergreens with various patterns of leaf production	Short period of leaf production in period of high potential productivity
Phenology of flowering	Flowers produced after (or, more rarely, before) periods of maximum potential productivity	No general relationship between time of flowering and season	Flowers produced at the end of temporarily favorable period
Proportion of annual production devoted to seeds	Small	Small	Large

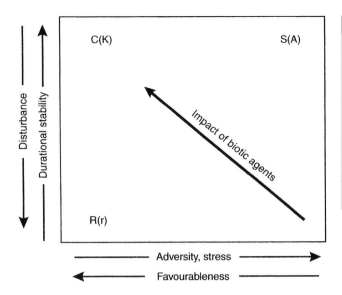

Figure 6.45 Two major forces that influence vegetation structure and the evolution of life-history traits are disturbance and stress (or adversity). The letters outside the parentheses follow Grime (1974, 1977): R, ruderals; C, competitors; S, stress tolerators. The letters inside the parentheses follow Southwood (1977, 1988): r, r-selection; K, K-selection; A, adversity selection (from Keddy 1989).

history types, with the exception that he used the word adversity rather than stress (Figure 6.45). Grime has suggested that different plant communities can also be presented in a triangular phase space that summarizes the relative contribution of these three evolutionary strategies. As a first approximation, the position of each species in this phase space can be determined by two measurements: the position along the C–R axis can be determined by height and capability for lateral spread, and the position along the C–S axis determined by maximum relative growth rate (Figure 6.46).

These suggestions were offered by Grime as an attempt to synthesize the volume of work such as you have encountered in Chapters 2–6. The initial response by many plant ecologists was surprisingly negative. Some of the objections appeared to be based upon misunderstanding of the value of simplification for synthesis. Others appear to have been frustrated that somebody else had thought of something so elegant, and there was even a hint of annoyance that such discoveries should have been made at a red brick university like Sheffield rather than at a more prestigious institution. When I wrote this section in 1999, the very lab that Grime assembled to pursue this research had been dismantled. Some thoughtful criticisms were raised (Taylor et al. 1990), particularly the suggestion that triangular ordinations obscure relationships that might be orthogonal (Loehle 1988b), and you will note that orthogonal axes are used in Figure 6.45. It would seem that this framework is likely to receive wide acceptance, and its application to communities, as opposed to evolutionary types, is one that is likely to grow in the future.

Another way to appreciate this synthesis is to see it as just another example of the great challenge posed by sorting plants into functional types, as seen in Chapter 2. From this perspective, at the most coarse scale, plant types and communities can be sorted into only

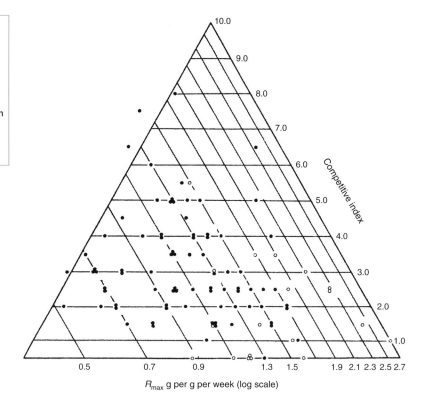

Figure 6.46 Triangular ordination of CSR (from Grime 1979). Plant species are arrayed along two axes. The first is a competitive index (based upon height and capacity for lateral spread) and the second is maximum relative growth rate (based upon screening of seedlings for R_{max}) (from Grime 1974).

three types. The Raunkiaer system (Section 2.3.1), by contrast, yields nine to 13. In some circumstances more groups may be useful or other traits may require greater emphasis, and there are other functional classifications now available for many of the world's vegetation types and groups of species. Examples include herbaceous understory plants in forests (Givnish 1987), wetland plants (van der Valk 1981, Boutin and Keddy 1993), and benthic marine algae (Steneck and Dethier 1994).

The CSR model, then, is not the sole functional classification needed in ecology. The particular classification scheme required will vary with the scale of the problem and the number of species that are encountered (Keddy 1990a). Figure 6.47 shows, for example, one classification scheme for sorting algae into functional groups. It recognizes more groups than the CSR model but many fewer than the number of species. Indeed, it seems likely that properties of plant communities such as stability and predictability are higher when measured at the functional group level rather than the species level: the functional groups may be present in relatively constant amounts, even as the species comprising the functional groups come and go. This tantalizing prospect leads to topics such as assembly rules and guild proportionality – topics of great importance to plant community ecology but beyond the bounds of a book such as this. Students wishing to pursue such topics are referred to the papers assembled in Weiher and Keddy (1999).

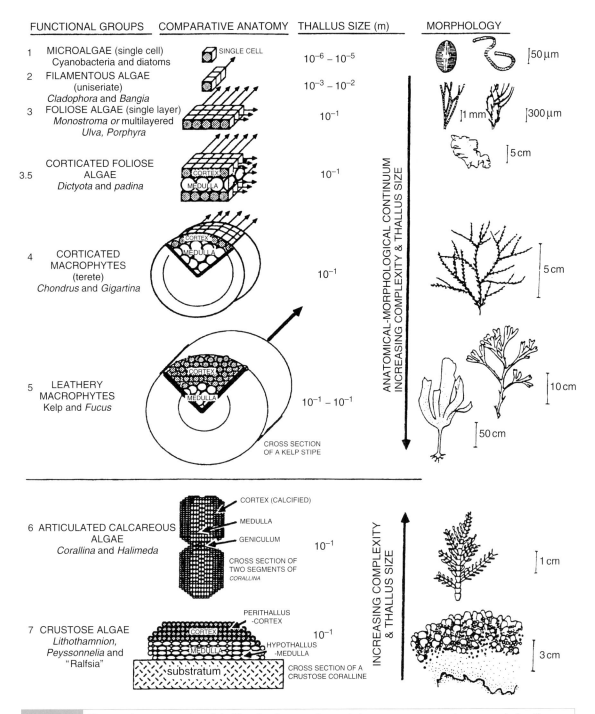

Figure 6.47 Diagramatic representation of algal functional groups. Anatomical components are not drawn to scale, but illustrate tissue differentiation such as between the cortex and medullary regions of the thallus of a macroalga (from Steneck and Dethier 1994).

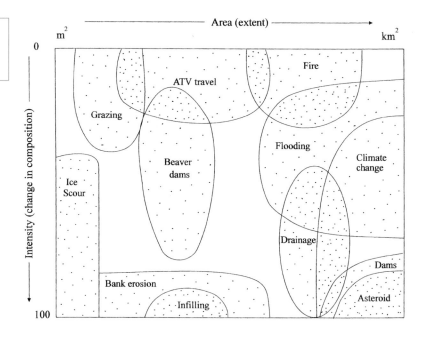

Figure 6.48 The relationship between intensity and area for an array of disturbances in wetlands (from Keddy 2000).

6.9 | Conclusion

It is not my intention to catalog and describe every disturbance that can occur in plant communities. What this chapter has done thus far is establish a basic terminology and list some concrete examples. Let us close by examining the relative scale of different types of disturbance. To develop rigorous ecological theories, there must be some way to compare very different processes. Such comparisons, among sites and processes, are a theme throughout this book. Figure 6.48 compares a wide array of disturbances according to two of the foregoing measurable properties: intensity and area. At the upper left are disturbances that are generally of low intensity and in small patches, such as herbivory. Ice scour is a disturbance that still may occur in small patches but with much higher intensity. Atmospheric deposition of pollutants may produce only small changes in composition, but these may cover very large areas. Finally, there are the effects of huge hydroelectric dams and asteroids that have high intensity and affect large areas. Most of the shaded regions are just best guesses, and serious attempts to better-define regions within this diagram are needed.

Further reading

Connell, J. H. 1978. Diversity in tropical rain forests and coral reefs. *Science* **199**: 1302–1310.

Grime, J. P., G. Mason, A. V. Curtis, J. Rodman, S. R. Band, M. A. G. Mowforth, A. M. Neal, and S. Shaw. 1981. A comparative study of germination characteristics in a local flora. *Journal of Ecology* **69**: 1017–1059.

Sousa, W. P. 1984. The role of disturbance in natural communities. *Annual Review of Ecology and Systematics* **15**: 353–391.

Pickett, S. T. A and P. S. White. 1985. *The Ecology of Natural Disturbance and Patch Dynamics*. Orlando: Academic Press.

Salo, J., R. Kalliola, I. Hakkinen, Y. Makinen, P. Niemela, M. Puhakka and P. D. Coley. 1986. River dynamics and the diversity of Amazon lowland forest. *Nature* **322**: 254–258.

Leck, M. A., V. T. Parker, and R. L. Simpson (eds.) 1989. *Ecology of Soil Seed Banks*. San Diego: Academic Press.

Botkin, D. B. 1990. *Discordant Harmonies: A New Ecology for the Twenty-first Century*. New York: Oxford University Press.

Kuhry, P. 1994. The role of fire in the development of *Sphagnum*-dominated peatlands in western boreal Canada. *Journal of Ecology* **82**: 899–910.

Whelan, R. J. 1995. *The Ecology of Fire*. Cambridge: Cambridge University Press.

Walter, A. 1998. T. Rex *and the Crater of Doom*. New York: Vintage Books, Random House.

Chapter 7

Herbivory

Herbivory as a disturbance. Field studies of herbivory. African mammals. Insects in rain forest canopies. Tortoises on islands. Sheep and slugs in moorlands. Morphological defences. Squirrels and cones. Chemical defenses. Nitrogen and food quality. Coevolution of fruits and herbivores. Exclosure experiments. Herbivorous insects in forests. Land crabs in tropical forest. Mammals in grasslands. Rhinoceroses in floodplain forest. Deer in forests. Small mammals in marshes. Bottom-up or top-down? Modeling the effects of herbivory.

7.1 | Introduction

Growth and reproduction add biomass to plant communities. Disturbances remove biomass. Thus the amount of vegetation in an area will be controlled by the balance between the former (primary production) and the latter. Disturbances can be either abiotic (fire, flooding, landslides) or biotic (herbivory, burrowing, trampling). Herbivory is of particular interest as a disturbance because it is biotic and often selective, and the relationships between plants and herbivores are continually evolving.

It is important that one be aware that the study of herbivory, or plant-herbivore interactions, is made difficult by the many possible ways, both direct and indirect, by which herbivores can influence plants. Further, the relationship is not merely one-way because plants simultaneously influence herbivores. The study of plant–herbivore interactions has led to topics as wide ranging as animal nutrition, the evolution of teeth and guts, kinds of plant defenses, the physiological responses of plants to losing leaves or seeds, and the impacts of herbivores upon soils. Figure 7.1 outlines some of the possible interactions between plants and herbivores. It also shows that micro-organisms become involved as a prominent third party, through their direct effects upon plant growth and indirect effects upon nutrient recycling. This figure does not include the predators and parasites that may simultaneously influence herbivores and thereby indirectly control plant–herbivore interactions. Even so, the boxes and arrows can multiply rapidly. As an exercise, you might try to add new boxes and arrows to Figure 7.1 or even try to sketch out an alternative scheme. (Such sketches may seem elementary, but they outline how science is done: first we ask what kinds

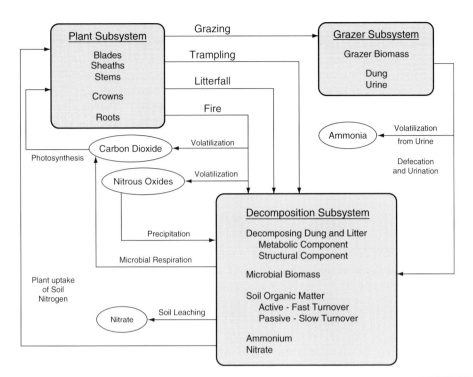

Figure 7.1 Nutrient cycling pathways in grasslands supporting abundant large mammals. Live plant compartments are shown in upper left, grazing mammal compartments in upper right, and soil compartments in lower right. Different pathways of nutrient flow from the plant subsystem to the decomposer subsystem vary in importance among landscape regions depending upon the balances among grazing, fire, litterfall, and trampling. Fast cycles are created where the principal pathway is through grazing, slow cycles where the principal pathway is through litterfall, and pulsed cycles where trampling or fire predominates. These pathways are interdependent and spatially variable, thus creating landscape mosaics of nutrient cycling types (from McNaughton et al. 1988).

of entities there are and what linkages might occur among them. This leads to the challenge of measuring the abundance of the entities (boxes) and the relative importance of the linkages (arrows).)

Rather than elaborate on each box and arrow in Figure 7.1, I will focus this chapter on the central question regarding herbivory: does it have measurable impacts upon the properties of plant communities? This question is a very logical starting point, for if herbivory has no effect on plant communities, or only a minimal effect, then plant ecologists should turn their attention to other factors that do have an impact on plant communities, such as soil resources or mycorrhizae. If, however, the effects of herbivory on plant communities are important then the challenge is to measure the effects, determine how they vary with space and time, and discern what underlying mechanisms might be at work. Note that the question being asked here is not the obvious one of whether herbivores damage *individual* plants. From the perspective of the individual plant, the answer is clear: "The effects of grazing on plants growing in their natural habitats are overwhelmingly detrimental to individual fitness" (Marquis 1991). Whether herbivores have much influence on entire plant communities is rather less obvious.

The logical starting point for answering our query regarding herbivory lies in basic natural history, particularly the observations that field biologists have made on the diets of herbivores. As long as there have been people to watch animals, humans have probably been curious about what animals eat. Of equal interest is what animals tend not to eat or, from the perspective of botanists, what kinds of defenses plants have to deter herbivory. Having laid the foundation for understanding the impacts of herbivory on plant communities with observations on herbivore diets, it is then logical to examine some field experiments that have tried to manipulate the effects of herbivory on plant communities. Next, a look at comparative studies that have sought to draw general conclusions about herbivory by sifting through the results of large numbers of published experiments is useful. Finally, it may be helpful to explore some general models, which help to clarify thinking about the dynamics of plants and herbivores in space and time.

7.2 | Field observations on wildlife diets

What do wild animals eat? Wildlife biologists have investigated this question in two principal ways: they have observed feeding by wild animals, and they have studied feces to reconstruct diets (Holechek et al. 1982). Consider a few examples.

7.2.1 Herbivores in African grasslands

Large herds of grazing mammals once lived in the arid grasslands of North and South America, Eurasia, Africa, and Australia. These ecosystems, dominated by herbaceous plants and grazed by herds of large mammals, probably covered one-third to one-half of the world's surface area until as recently as the last century. The Poaceae (grasses) and mammals with hypsodont dentition both appeared in the Eocene and apparently went, simultaneously, through adaptive radiation from the Miocene to the Pleistocene (McNaughton 1985). The resulting evolutionary diversity of herbivores is illustrated by one mammalian family, the Bovidae (in the order Artiodactyla, containing the buffalo and antelope), which has as many species (78) as the most diverse rodent family, the Muridae (Sinclair 1983). In most areas, large native herbivores have increasingly been replaced by farmland or herds of domestic cattle (McNaughton 1985, Archibold 1995), as illustrated by the fate of the bison in North America (Figure 7.2).

The only remaining large area of ecosystems with native herbivores is found in eastern and southern Africa and much of this is in reserves that were created in the 1900s (e.g., Sinclair 1983, McNaughton 1985, Naiman et al. 1988). In such areas one can recognize three main habitats: forest, savanna, and wetland (Table 7.1), and the distance of a particular habitat from water is often a rather good predictor of herbivore biomass (Figure 7.3). The diets of the African herbivores differ among both species and seasons (Table 7.2). The animals may also be selective about which plant parts they consume; most have a strong preference for green leaves rather than dead leaves and zebras apparently prefer the seeds of awnless grasses such as *Panicum coloratum*. According to Sinclair (1983), shortages of water have placed constant selective pressure upon grazing mammals, and there have been two main evolutionary

Table 7.1. *Seasonal habitat changes for the large herbivores of Rukwa Valley, Tanzania (after Vesey-FitzGerald 1960).*

Animal species				Time of year								
	Jan	Feb	Mar	Apr	May	June	July	Aug	Sept	Oct	Nov	Dec
Elephant	Acacia and escarpment woodlands						floodplain				woodlands	
Buffalo	woodlands, lakeshore and delta grasslands						floodplain				woodlands	
Hippo	fringe river and delta grasslands				wander widely along drainage						river fringe	
Puku					delta and lakeshore grassland all year							
Topi	perimeter grassland, woodland			lakeshore and delta grasslands				Vossia pasture		Acacia		
Zebra	Acacia woodland		perimeter grassland	Acacia parkland			floodplain grassland			Acacia woodland		
Bohor reedbuck				floodplain grassland								
Eland	dry perimeter plains woodland				delta grasslands and Vossia pasture						Acacia	
Giraffe and Impala					Acacia grassland							
Warthog				Acacia grassland and forest edge								
Waterbuck, Duiker, Baushbuck and Steinbuck				woodlands								

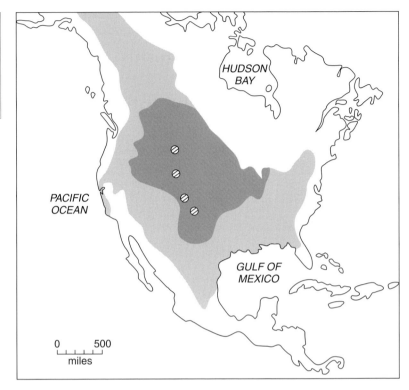

Figure 7.2 The near-extinction of the herds of bison in the late 1800s was the result of exploitation by market hunters with access to high-powered rifles and railways (from Keddy 2001 after Nabokov 1993).

Greatest possible outer extent of the bison range

Probable bison range at mid-nineteenth century

Pockets of bison remaining at the close of the nineteenth century

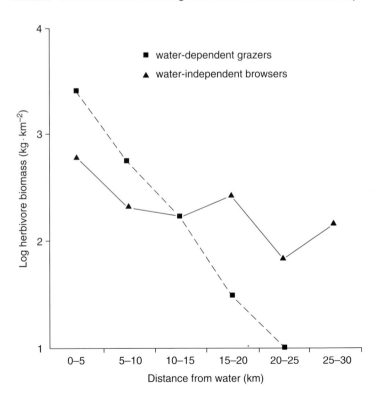

Figure 7.3 Biomass of herbivores at different distances from water during the dry season, Amboseli, Kenya. Water-independent browsers (▲) are less restricted than water-dependent grazers (■) (from Sinclair 1983).

Table 7.2. *The three most important plant species in the wet- and dry-season diets of the four major herbivore species in the Serengeti grasslands. Data are percentages of total consumption. WB, wildebeest; Z, zebra; TG, Thompson's gazelle; B, buffalo (from McNaughton 1985).*

Plant species	Animal species			
	WB	Z	TG	B
	Wet season			
Sporobolus ioclados + S. kentrophyllus	60.8	–	24.8	–
Andropogon greenwayi	11.8	41.7	–	–
Digitaria macroblephara	11.8	11.4	14.3	–
Kyllinga nervosa	–	–	12.4	–
Chloris pycnothrix	–	11.4	–	–
Themedia triandra	–	–	–	44.8
Eragrostis exasperata	–	–	–	17.0
Hyparrhenia filipendula	–	–	–	11.7
	Dry season			
Themeda triandra	63.4	20.6	35.0	35.4
Sporobolus fimbriatus	6.3	–	14.8	–
S. pyramidalis	6.1	–	–	–
Hyparrhenia filipendula	–	20.7	–	26.8
Digitaria macroblephara	–	13.3	–	–
Pennisetum mezianum	–	–	14.9	–
Loudetia kagerensis	–	–	–	12.8

responses. First, there has been a shift from grazing on grasses to browsing on shrubs, browsers being less dependent upon water (Figure 7.3). Second, reproduction has been timed to coincide with the rainy season, when plant growth rates are the highest. Species that have undergone such adaptations include the elephant, white rhinoceros, zebra, hippopotamus, warthog, buffalo, giraffe, and kudu.

Herds of large grazing animals are attractive to humans and popular in game parks and zoos, probably because our minds evolved in savannas and because our ancestors found such animals to be an important source of protein. All the same, insects are potentially far more significant herbivores. Whether measured by their total biomass, by the number of species, or by the rate at which they can reproduce, insects far outclass large mammals. Turn therefore to a study of insect herbivory in tropical forests.

7.2.2 Herbivorous insects in tropical forest canopies

To measure rates of herbivory in the canopy of tropical rain forests, Lowman (1992) selected representative sites in the three major rain forests of New South Wales, Australia. Five tree species, largely evergreen, were selected, and leaf growth was measured monthly for 5 years. Most leaves were produced in a summer flush, and, once expanded, leaves lasted from an average of some 7 months (*Dendrocnide excelsa*) to more than 5 years (e.g., *Doryphora sassafras*). Average leaf losses to herbivores ranged from 4.5 to 42 percent (Table 7.3). In all five species of trees, the major herbivores were predominantly members of the Coleoptera (beetles) in the Curculionidae. The impacts of such high levels of herbivory are unknown, although, interestingly, there was no evidence of mortality of any section of the canopy.

7.2.3 Giant tortoises on islands

While it might be said that insect herbivory is ubiquitous and that it is therefore essential to study, the localized herbivory of giant land tortoises is an equally useful study for a different reason. Although the dinosaurs are extinct, the areas inhabited by giant land tortoises give a glimpse of terrestrial grazing systems dominated by ectotherms. Such grazing systems are now restricted to the Aldabra atoll in the Indian Ocean and the Galapagos off the coast of Ecuador. Tortoises can have extremely high population densities; there are, for example, >25 per hectare on one part of the Aldabra atoll. On Aldabra, there are some 150 000 tortoises (Gibson and Hamilton 1983); in the Galapagos there are fewer, perhaps some 10 000 in total spread across a dozen populations (MacFarland et al. 1974, Pritchard 1996), because of heavy predation from sailors in the 1700s and 1800s. Despite differences in tortoise population density, there are many similarities in the nature of herbivory in the two locations. At both, seasonal drought has a major impact upon the kinds of plants eaten by the tortoises and the habitats in which the tortoises feed. The favored habitat at both places is "tortoise turf," a type of short-cropped vegetation maintained by heavy grazing (Figure 12.9). In the dry season, turf production declines, and tortoises are forced to feed on other plants, particularly shrubs. In the Galapagos, cacti, as well as shrubs, are eaten during dry periods (Hamann 1993).

The usual way to discern whether a herbivore is selective is to compare the availability of food with the actual diet. If the herbivore eats food in direct proportion to its abundance in the habitat, there is no evidence for selectivity. Table 7.4 shows these calculations for Aldabra tortoises; the D/E (diet/environment ratio) is very high for herbs, long grass, and tortoise turf, which shows that the tortoises feed selectively upon these components of the vegetation. Sedges, the grass *Sporobolus virginicus*, and shrub litter are avoided (but note that the sedges and shrub litter together make up more than half the available food). White (1993) is of the opinion that these animals are strongly limited by nitrogen availability; consistent with his view is the observation that tortoises will also feed on carrion (including tortoise) when the opportunity presents itself (Gibson and Hamilton 1983). Moreover, when sedges are eaten, flowers and seeds are consumed, and plant reproductive structures usually have higher levels of both nitrogen and phosphorus.

Table 7.3. *Mean (±SE) leaf longevity and herbivory (the percentage of leaf area eaten) of different cohorts of leaves of five species of rain forest canopy trees in New South Wales, Australia (from Lowman 1992).*

Rain forest type and location	Leaf lifespan (months)	Number of leaves measured	Herbivory (percent)
Dendrocnide excelsa			
Subtropical			
Dorrigo	6.7 ± 0.40	146	32.5 ± 2.6
Mt Keira	7.2 ± 0.70	95	15.5 ± 1.4
Average annual canopy loss (percent)		242	42.0
Toona australis			
Subtropical			
Dorrigo	9.5 ± 0.22	99	6.3 ± 0.3
Mt Keira	7.4 ± 0.14	275	3.3 ± 0.2
Average annual canopy loss (percent)		374	4.5
Nothofagus moorei			
Cool temperate			
New England	22.9 ± 0.21	1967	31
Ceratopetalum apetalum			
Warm-temperate			
Royal	43.0 ± 3.2	395	21.3
Sun only	24.9 ± 1.1	245	26.9 ± 2.0
Shade only	60.1 ± 2.7	150	35.3 ± 2.5
Dorrigo	58.0 ± 4.3	190	24.0
Sun only	26.9 ± 1.8	110	9.4 ± 1.1
Shade only	88.6 ± 4.4	80	35.3 ± 2.7
Average annual canopy loss (percent)		585	22.0
Doryphora sassafras			
Subtropical			
Dorrigo	41.3 ± 1.7	694	15.0
Sun only	22.5 ± 1.1	390	13.4 ± 2.0
Shade only	60.0 ± 1.4	304	16.3 ± 2.2
Warm-temperate			
Royal	50.0 ± 1.9	151	22.7
Sun only	24.0 ± 1.1	81	17.6 ± 2.2
Shade only	76.5 ± 1.3[a]	70	27.8 ± 2.6
Cool-temperate			
New England	53.8 ± 1.7	170	13.6 ± 2.0
Average annual canopy loss (percent)		1015	16.6

Note:
[a]Slightly higher than indicated, because six leaves of the sample size of 1015 leaves were still on the tree after 12 years.

Table 7.4. | *The overall abundance of different foods in the diets and environment of Aldabra atoll tortoises (from Gibson and Hamilton 1983).*

Food	Percent in environment[a]	D/E[b] total
Tortoise turf	15.3	3.99
Mosaic rock	3.75	0.803
Shrub litter	38.5	0.532
Sedges	29.0	0.267
Herbs	0.06	18.3
Long grass	0.36	8.28
Sporobolus virginicus	1.76	0.789

Notes:
[a]Percentage of vegetation (excluding rock).
[b]Percentage in diet/percentage in environment.

7.2.4 Herbivory in anthropogenic landscapes

In contrast to the diverse megafauna of the African savannas, the deforested uplands of the British Isles (and many parts of nearby Europe) have only two major herbivores, slugs and sheep. Because of the distribution of human population, European readers have more likely seen sheep and slugs in fields than they have seen giraffes in savanna, insects in tropical canopies, or tortoises on islands. In Great Britain alone there are more than a million hectares of moorland (Miller and Watson 1983), a landscape (known for its large areas of heather, *Calluna vulgaris*) that was formed during Roman and Medieval times when Britain's original forests were cleared and the land then grazed. The density of the main vertebrate herbivores in the highlands of Scotland in the 1960s was estimated as 50 sheep, 65 red grouse, 10 red deer, and 16 mountain hare per square kilometer. The slug populations are less obvious to the untrained, but species such as *Agriolimax reticulatus* and *Arion intermedius* consume approximately one gram of plant biomass per square meter per month (Lutman 1978) and can reach densities exceeding $10\,m^{-2}$. Despite the abundance of herbivores in moorland, less than 10 percent of the primary production of *C. vulgaris* is actually consumed by herbivores (Miller and Watson 1983).

Red grouse are well studied because of their hunting value. They feed primarily upon *C. vulgaris* shoots but eat only a negligible proportion of the primary production in their territories (Miller and Watson 1978); they therefore have rather little effect, themselves, upon moorland vegetation. The principal effects of grouse on *C. vulgaris* are likely to arise from the human practice of burning moorland to improve the upland areas for hunting grouse. Burning changes plant species composition, stimulating the growth of *Calluna* in particular, and may slow the development of bogs (Rawes and Heal 1978). Further, burning leads to the volatilization of nitrogen, and potassium is leached from the remaining ash.

7.3 | Plant defenses

7.3.1 Evolutionary context

Many plants possess traits, such as spines, thorns, and prickles, which appear to present relatively unambiguous evidence of the need for protection from herbivores (e.g., Crawley 1983, Marquis 1991, Pennings et al. 1998, Raven et al. 2005). Pressure from herbivorous animals can even be inferred from the fossil record. From the late Carboniferous until the late Triassic, all of the big herbivorous dinosaurs were short-necked, low browsers; by the late Jurassic, these were replaced by prosauropod dinosaurs with long necks and anatomy that suggests that the forelegs could be raised off the ground (Figure 7.4). This change in morphology coincides with the time when seed ferns became nearly extinct and conifers began to radiate (Bakker 1978, Coe et al. 1987, Wing and Tiffney 1987). By the Cretaceous, there appears to have been a shift back to big, low browsing species such as ornithischian dinosaurs. During the Cretaceous, dinosaurs also displayed a wide variety of beaks and teeth, which suggests that there was complex partitioning of the plant resources. Bakker (1978) remarks that "the rapid diversification of big Cretaceous low browsers changed the selective pressure on the plant communities. Intense low browsing would have increased mortality among seedlings, thinned out the forest structure, and would have favoured shrubs which could maintain a dynamic steady-state with the herbivores, rapidly regenerating the cropped foliage and colonising areas laid bare by close cropping."

7.3.2 Structures that protect seeds: strobili and squirrels

While all plant tissues are potentially available to herbivores, seeds may be at particular risk because of their value as a food source, which results from their high protein and lipid content. The earliest known seed plants were seed ferns (Pteridospermophyta), first found in the late Devonian, widespread in the Palaeozoic, but now extinct.

Figure 7.4 Late Jurassic (lower) and late Cretaceous (upper) large herbivores compared. Figure represents fully adult individuals shown to scale. In the upper figures each ornithischian is shown browsing close to the ground and also with the maximum vertical reach permitted by the limbs and vertebral articulations. Morrison Fauna (lower): (a) *Haplocanthosaurus*, (b) *Brachiosaurus*, (c) *Camarasaurus*, (d) *Barosaurus*, (e) *Diplodocus*, (f) *Apatosaurus*, (g) *Stegosaurus*, (h) *Camptosaurus* (the largest Morrison low-browser). Kirtland-Fruitland-Ajo Alama Fauna (upper): (a) *Alamosaurus*, (b) *Parasaurolophus*, (c) *Pentaceratops*, (d) ankylosaur. The vertical scale is meters (from Bakker 1978).

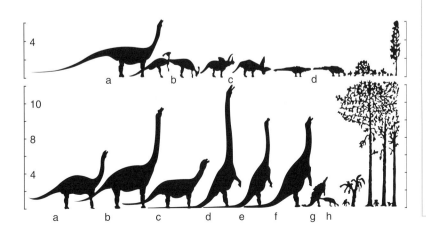

Seeds are a highly desirable food source, therefore one selective pressure that strongly influenced the evolutionary trends observable among seed-bearing plants was the need to protect seeds from predators. Although gymnosperms are technically defined by having the ovule (female gametophyte) produced "naked" on a megasporophyll, structures to protect these naked ovules have appeared in most of the gymnosperms. This seed-protecting structure is usually termed a strobilus and is formed from a series of megasporophylls (Figure 7.5). Strobili may have originated from shoots with widely

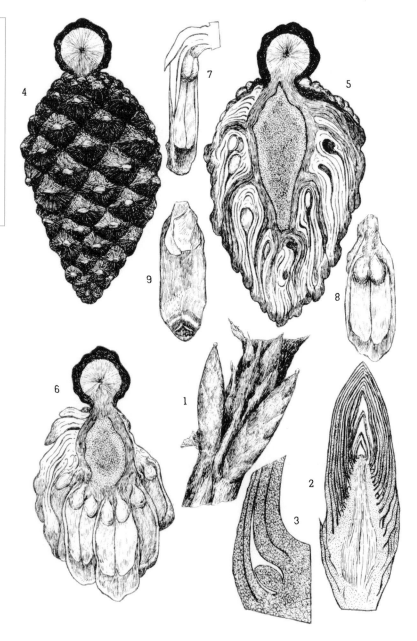

Figure 7.5 Ovuliferous cones of a pine; Monterey pine (*Pinus radiata*): (1) young cones (after pollination), (2–3) longitudinal section, (3) showing an ovule (above a scale) and a bract, (4) mature cone, external view, (5) longitudinal section, (6) dissected cone showing the two winged seeds on each ovuliferous scale, (7–9) views of the scale with seeds on one side and the bract on the other, the cone now much larger than the bract (from Benson 1959).

separated branches and megasporophylls, but as the length of the axis between the branches shortened, and the branches thickened, the typical cone resulted. One can only speculate as to what herbivores may have driven selection for the development of the strobilus, but the persistence of gymnosperms to the present may be regarded as evidence of their success.

Smith (1970) observes, "That some terrestrial animals would have been specialising as seed eaters from an early date is made more plausible by the very high nutritive value of seeds." From the perspective of a herbivore, each strobilus represents a valuable source of energy, albeit one that is well protected. In *Abies amabilis* (Pacific silver fir), for example, a single cone contains up to nearly 400 seeds, which together have a total energy value of 68 000 calories. Smith has observed that squirrels first harvest the cones of *A. amabilis*, which have the highest energy content of conifers, and then harvest from trees whose seeds have progressively lower energy content. In *Pinus ponderosa* (Ponderosa pine), a cone can have up to 150 seeds and therefore contain up to 25 000 calories (Smith 1970). The high caloric value represents a high lipid content, although seeds of one pine species (*Pinus jeffreyi*) also have 20 percent protein. Smith suggests that squirrels and conifers may have coevolved. In the Jurassic, multituberculates, a group of rodent-like mammals, appear in the fossil record at about the time that conifers with multi-appendaged dwarf shoots, as opposed to strobili, start to disappear. Many of the modern genera and species in the Pinaceae start to appear at approximately the same time as placental rodents replace multituberculates.

Another interesting example of coevolution between conifers and squirrels pertains to the specialized cones of some pine species. Certain pines have serotinous cones in which the scales of the strobilus remain sealed by resin until seared by fire; the mature cones then open and the seeds fall onto the burned area. This obvious adaptation to fire means, however, that cones and seeds are retained on the tree and provide a more or less steady supply of seeds for squirrels. Such an adaptation magnifies the selection pressures from herbivores (Table 7.5). Similarly, serotinous cones have exerted selective pressure on squirrels as is demonstrated by the fact that squirrels differ in the design of their jaws and the development of associated musculature (Figure 7.6); squirrels with stronger jaws occur in regions where conifers have serotinous cones. Even within a species differences are observable; red squirrels collected from forests with *Pinus contorta* (lodgepole pine) have significantly heavier jaw musculature than those in forests without this species.

While the strobili of the conifers appear to be a morphological defense against seed herbivory by animals (particularly squirrels), strobili may, however, have other functions. The scales may protect seeds from fire in the same way that bark protects the cambium. The scales and shape of the strobilus may protect the seeds from insects or fungi. Perhaps the entire structure has been retained in spite of the fact that the Cretaceous herbivores it once deterred are now extinct.

Table 7.5. *The selective pressures influencing the characteristics of cones associated with the serotinous habit in lodgepole pine (Pinus contorta) (from Smith 1970).*

Characteristic of the serotinous cone	Factors selecting for the character	Factors selecting against the character
1. Hard bracts, scale bases, and scale apophyses	Squirrels selectively feed on softer cones	The energy cost of building thicker cell walls in the sclerenchymatous tissue
2. Sessile cones	Squirrels occasionally fail to detach sessile cones	–
3. Asymmetrical cones	Squirrels occasionally fail to detach cones with a broad base next to the branch	The energy cost of the enlarged scales
4. Whorled cones	Squirrels occasionally fail to detach cones closely adjacent to each other	Possibly more efficient energy transport to evenly spaced cones
5. Thick vascular trace to the cone	Squirrels occasionally fail to pull off cones with thick vascular traces	Increased energy in vascular tissue
6. Few seeds per cone	Squirrels select cones with more seeds	The energy cost of sterile tissue per seed; lower reproductive output
7. Constant-sized cone crop	Maximizes seeds available for reforestation after frequent fires	Concentrated squirrel feeding pressure on cones produced in small crops

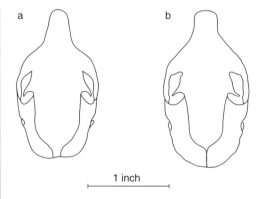
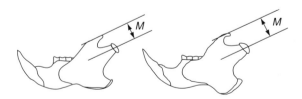

Figure 7.6 Comparison of the skull anatomy of the (a) Douglas squirrel and (b) red squirrel; the latter feeds on serotinous cones of *Pinus contorta*. M is the distance of the moment arm of force applied by the temporal muscles, showing that in red squirrels greater force can be applied by the teeth. The red squirrel skull also has a sagittal crest for attachment of well-developed temporal muscles (from Smith 1970).

a   b

1 inch

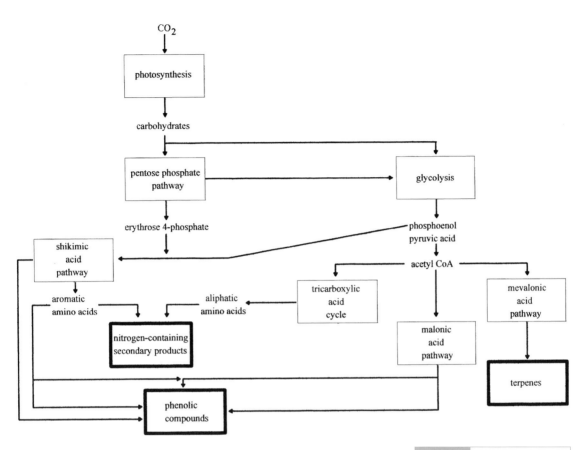

Figure 7.7 Pathways for the production of the three main classes of secondary metabolites (bold boxes) that act as deterrents to herbivory (from Taiz and Zeiger 1991).

7.3.3 Secondary metabolites that protect foliage

The chemical traits of a plant are less obvious than morphological traits but may be equally important in deterring herbivory (Louda et al. 1990, Marquis 1991). While some plant compounds have obvious roles to play in photosynthesis, growth, and reproduction, others do not. These latter "secondary metabolites" were once thought to be just waste products. It has now become clear that many of these compounds play active and important roles in defending plants against herbivores. There are three main groups of anti-herbivore compounds, terpenes, phenolics, and nitrogen-containing secondary products (Figure 7.7), and these are summarized in compendia such as that by Rosenthal and Berenbaum (1991). Over evolutionary time, there appears to have been a gradual transition in the kinds of secondary metabolites involved in plant defense: steroids, sesquiterpenes, and polyacetylene are known only from recently evolved and still rapidly speciating groups such as the Lamiales and Asterales (Figure 7.8).

Consider two examples of chemical anti-herbivore defenses, one from tropical rain forests and the other from temperate-zone wetlands. To study the characteristics of tropical trees that are related to herbivory, Coley (1983) monitored 8600 leaves on

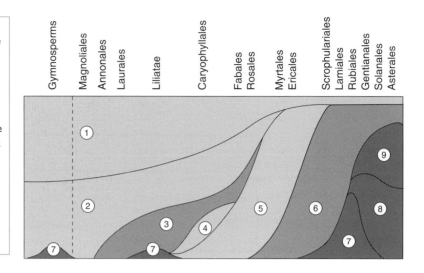

Figure 7.8 Occurrence of secondary metabolites in primitive and derived taxa. In the course of evolution, products of the shikimate pathway (pale shading) became increasingly replaced by those of the alkaloid-synthesis pathway (medium shading) and the mevalonate-acetate pathway (dark shading). (1) lignin; (2) condensed tannins; (3) isoquinoline alkaloids; (4) betalains; (5) gallotannins; (6) indole alkaloids and iridoids; (7) steroids; (8) sesquiterpenes; (9) polyacetylene (from Larcher 2003).

41 tree species to estimate rates of herbivore damage. Rates of herbivory were then related to various leaf properties such as tannin content and presence of hairs. Pioneer tree species had rates of herbivory similar those of persistent tree species of mature forests. Young leaves were grazed far more than old leaves, probably because the young leaves were half as tough, less fibrous, and more nutritious than old leaves. For mature leaves, most of the among-species differences in herbivory could be accounted for by leaf characteristics (Table 7.6).

In contrast with such data from terrestrial plants, there is a striking lack of information on anti-herbivore defense compounds in wetland plants in standard references such as Rosenthal and Berenbaum (1991). There are passing references to glucosinolates (Louda and Mole 1991), coumarins (Berenbaum 1991), flavonoids (McClure 1970), alkaloids (Ostrofsky and Zettler 1986), and possibly iridoid glycosides (Bowers 1991) used by wetland plants to protect themselves from herbivores. Gopal and Goel (1993) list other examples including fatty acids, mustard oils, and steroids, but in general the role of secondary metabolites is still poorly documented. Such compounds may provide defense against herbivores but equally may have other functions perhaps in anti-microbial or allelopathic interactions.

The lack of information on secondary plant metabolites in wetlands led McCanny et al. (1990) to conduct an experiment to determine whether some of these metabolites deter herbivory. They extracted compounds from a series of wetland plants and mixed them into the diet of an herbivorous insect. In some cases, the growth of larvae was cut in half, which provided evidence for the presence of anti-herbivore defense compounds. To see whether plants from different habitats might have different investments in anti-herbivore defenses, a food quality index (as measured by the performance of

Table 7.6. *Correlation coefficients between rates of herbivory and defenses of young and mature leaves in tropical forests. Values are based on 22 pioneer and 24 persistent species using the log-transformed grazing rate (from Coley 1983).*

	Young leaves			Mature leaves		
	Pioneer	Persistent	Both	Pioneer	Persistent	Both
Chemical						
Total phenols (percent dry mass)	0.014	0.030	0.040	−0.145	0.109	−0.099
Tannins – Vanil (percent dry mass)	0.278	0.182	0.190	−0.130	0.023	−0.112
Tannins – Leuco (percent dry mass)	0.220	0.207	0.209	−0.087	0.220	−0.128
Fiber – NDF (percent dry mass)	0.229	0.180	0.254	−0.119	0.056	−0.278[a]
Fiber – ADF (percent dry mass)	0.302	0.095	0.181	−0.318	−0.056	−0.424[a]
Lignin (percent dry mass)	0.213	0.148	0.133	−0.219	0.101	−0.223
Cellulose (percent dry mass)	0.340	0.036	0.195	−0.348	−0.147	−0.473[b]
Physical						
Toughness (N)	0.011	−0.473[a]	−0.045	−0.360	−0.363	−0.515[b]
Hairs – upper (no./mm^2)	0.001	−0.219	−0.146	−0.040	0.000[c]	0.291[b]
Hairs – lower (no./mm^2)	0.062	−0.306	−0.114	0.591[b]	0.089	0.635[b]
Nutritional						
Water (percent)	0.156	−0.082	0.081	−0.027	0.448[a]	0.507[b]
Nitrogen (percent dry mass)	0.028	−0.237	0.004	0.010	0.278	0.287[a]
Tannin: protein ratios						
Total phenols: protein	0.031	0.124	0.093	−0.125	0.037	−0.183
Tannin – Vanil: protein	0.289	0.111	0.167	−0.161	0.049	−0.161
Tannin – Leuco: protein	0.292	0.133	0.191	−0.182	0.145	−0.184

Notes:
[a] $P < 0.05$, one-tailed.
[b] $P < 0.01$, one-tailed.
[c] None of these species is pubescent on the upper surface.

the insect herbivore) was then plotted against the fertility of the habitat typical of each plant species. There was no relationship between the food quality index and soil fertility, plant biomass (Figure 7.9 top), or plant relative growth rates (Figure 7.9 bottom).

7.3.4 Two cautions when interpreting anti-herbivore traits

That plants have various defenses against herbivores might at first be taken as unambiguous evidence that herbivores have a major effect upon plant communities, but there are at least two critical assumptions in such arguments. First, it is necessary to assume that the function of the alleged anti-herbivore trait has been correctly and unambiguously interpreted. For example, do the thorns of vines that scramble along shorelines (e.g., *Smilax* spp.) act to deter herbivores or are they a morphological device for climbing on other plants? Similarly, do secondary metabolites always protect plants from herbivores, or is their main function primarily anti-microbial? The problem of interpretation always complicates comparative evidence.

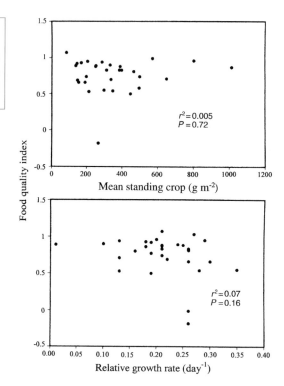

Figure 7.9 The food quality of 30 species of wetland plants is correlated with neither the biomass of the habitat (top) nor the relative growth rate of the species (bottom) (after McCanny et al. 1990).

The second problem with comparative data is that they combine two time scales: evolutionary and ecological. The presence of an anti-herbivore structure indicates that herbivores shaped the evolution of a taxon, but it in no way demonstrates the active occurrence of herbivory in present-day communities. This caveat is by no means trivial or pedantic. In relatively recent times, only about 10 000 years BP, both North America and Australia lost an entire megafauna (Figure 7.10). It has been argued that many plants possess adaptations to dispersal by large mammals that are now extinct (Janzen and Martin 1982); it therefore seems equally plausible that many other plants, such as conifers, could have adaptations to protect themselves from dinosaur herbivores that no longer exist.

7.3.5 Food quality and nitrogen content

Despite having various means of defense against herbivory, plants are a source of food, and nitrogen content is thought to be one of the most important factors determining the food value of plants (Lodge 1991, White 1993). The nitrogen content of aquatic plants, for example, is frequently well below 5 percent (Table 7.7); Gopal (1990) and Lodge (1991) show that emergent, floating, and submersed macrophytes, as well as algae, all have similar nitrogen content, usually of 2–3 percent (with extremes from 1 to at least 5 percent). These are very low values for supporting herbivorous animals. The struggle to extract essential resources such as nitrogen from plant tissues has been the major driving force in the evolution of digestive systems in

Table 7.7. *Atomic composition of different species of wetland plants (after Boyd 1978 and Junk 1983).*

Constituent (percent)	Temperate species		Tropical species	
	N	Mean	N	Mean
Ash	40	14.03	75	14.23
C	28	41.06	–	–
N	27	2.26	75	1.99
P	35	0.25	75	0.19
S	25	0.41	–	–
Ca	35	1.34	75	0.88
Mg	35	0.29	75	0.29
K	35	2.61	75	3.10
Na	35	0.51	75	0.36

Figure 7.10 Some examples of the megafauna that became extinct at the time humans arrived in North America and Australia. North America: (1) *Platygonus*, *Castoroides*; (2) *Bison latifrons*, *Nototherium*. Australia: (3) *Diprotodon optatum*, *Zygomaturus trilobus*, *Euowenia grata*, *Thylacoleo carnifex*; (4) *Procoptodon goliah*, *Sthenurus maddocki*, *Sthenurus atlas*, *Protemnodon brehus*, *Macropus ferragus*; (5) *Progura gallinacea*, *Genyornis newtoni*, *Megalania prisca*, *Wonambi naracoortensis*, *Zaglossus ramsayi*. Human included for scale (after Martin and Klein 1984).

terrestrial animals (Langer 1974, Janis 1976). The presence of a rumen, the maintenance of a rich symbiotic fauna, and increases in gut length are characteristics shared by most grazing animals (Smith and Douglas 1987).

White (1993) describes attempts to control *Salvinia molesta*, an aquatic fern from Brazil that has become a serious weed in many tropical regions. Initial attempts to import and establish insects from Brazil to control *Salvinia* in Australia and Papua New Guinea had variable success; when concentrations of nitrogen in the fern were 1 percent or less dry weight, the imported pyralid moth could not establish: "However, increasing the level of nitrogen in the fern to only 1.3% dry weight by simply adding urea fertiliser to the water can cause an explosive increase in the abundance of the moth and severe damage to the plants" (p. 77). The species of weevil introduced from Brazil to Australia to combat *Salvinia* was also limited by nitrogen availability. In contrast, when Lodge (1991) studied grazing preferences of the crayfish *Orconectes rusticus* among 14 submersed macrophytes, he found that it had a clear preference for certain species of plants; Lodge was, however, unable to detect statistically significant differences in nitrogen content among the plants. Marine crabs (*Armases cinereum*) are also selective feeders in salt marshes; they prefer to feed on *Batis maritima* and *Iva frutescens*, the two species with the softest tissues (Pennings et al. 1998). Plant toughness may well be as important as nitrogen content. On the other hand, whole plant comparisons may conceal real differences in nitrogen content if herbivores are consuming only selected tissues. Sinclair (1983) and White (1993) have described many examples of herbivory where the new growth that occurs after damage is preferentially consumed, and White is of the opinion that this growth has the highest nutrient concentrations. Careful design of feeding trials and consideration of multiple hypotheses (nitrogen content, toughness, secondary metabolites) would appear to be essential in studies of food preference.

7.3.6 Coevolution: a brief preview

Plants apparently face an evolutionary dilemma. On one hand, there has been strong selection to deter herbivory and thereby reduce damage to tissues and reproductive organs, but on the other hand, there appears to have been strong selection to attract animals to distribute pollen and seeds. Indeed, the entire origin of the flowering plants appears to be a product of coevolution with two groups of animals. Herbivorous beetles may well have been the first insects to pollinate flowers, and much of the evolutionary diversification of flowers was likely driven by the increasingly efficient use of insects to disperse pollen. Herbivorous mammals apparently played an important role in dispersing seeds, the consequence of which was the evolutionary diversification of large fleshy fruits.

Flowers and fruits, then, the two key features of the angiosperms, both appear to be examples of coevolution between plants and animals, but even as animals disperse pollen and fruit, they must simultaneously be deterred from consuming ovules and seeds. Many of the fleshy fruits that are very attractive to mammals illustrate this dichotomy by being edible yet simultaneously containing seeds with hard and indigestible coatings. A mammal eats the fruit and either discards the seeds or passes them unharmed through its gut. In either case, the seeds are dispersed. The diversification of fruits to attract herbivores is most dramatic in the world's tropical forests (Figure 7.11). Note the contrast: in the gymnosperms the investment in strobili was usually for the defense of seeds, whereas in angiosperms investment in fruits combines both protection and dispersal.

Figure 7.11 (a)–(e) Fruits and their seeds from Santa Rosa National Park that were probably dispersed by Pleistocene megafauna. The seeds to the right of each fruit represent a normal quantity of seeds found in each fruit. (a) *Hymenaea courbaril* (Fabaceae), (b) *Acrocomia vinifera* (Palmae), (c) *Guazuma ulmifolia* (Sterculiaceae), (d) *Enterolobium cyclocarpum* (Fabaceae), (e) *Apeiba tibourbou* (Tiliaceae) (from Janzen and Martin 1982).

Selection for hard-coated seeds within fruits creates an added problem for plants: to germinate, the young sporophyte must be able to absorb water through this tough coat and then split the coat open. It may even be that selection for thick-coated seeds has sometimes led to an obligate requirement for being passed through a gut. In such cases the seed coat is so thick that germination cannot proceed until the seed coat has been damaged by digestion. What started out as a protective measure may slowly evolve into dependency. This enquiry is continued in Section 8.4.2.

7.4 | Field experiments

Having begun with observations on diet and morphology, it is time to examine field experiments to answer further questions. The principle for studying hebivory is simple (Bender et al. 1984): exclude herbivores from some areas and compare the vegetation in these areas to the vegetation in other control plots. Clements (1935) explains: "The usual type of closure is the exclosure, a fenced area of suitable size which provides protection against the coactions of one or more groups or species of animal. The enclosure is similar in design, but is used to restrict animals to a definite area to permit the direct study of their influence." One could also add other treatments that remove only selected herbivores or even add certain species of herbivores. Figure 7.12 shows an early study of vegetation using a rabbit-proof fence in English grassland (Farrow 1917). Such

Figure 7.12 Rabbit-proof fence across the south side of Cavenham heath – western end (a). Note the difference in the vegetation on the two sides. On the protected side there are many inflorescences, while on the uprotected side there are no inflorescences, the vegetation is nibbled closely down and much bare sand is exposed. (b) Southern rabbit-proof fence on Cavenham heath – eastern end (looking in the opposite direction to photo in (a)). Note greater difference in the luxuriance of the vegetation on the two sides. Note the presence of *Carex arenaria* on the protected side of the fence and its absence on the rabbit attack side (from Farrow 1917).

experiments are easily forgotten: while Crawley's 1983 monograph on herbivory devotes an entire chapter to plant populations, it hardly mentions the importance of properly designed exclosure experiments to the study of herbivory!

7.4.1 Herbivorous insects in deciduous forest canopies

Large numbers of leaf-chewing lepidopterans feed on deciduous forest trees. To quantify these effects, Marquis and Whelan (1994) selected 90 *Quercus alba* (white oak) trees in a mixed oak forest in Missouri. The trees were arranged in triplets, one served as a control, the second had native insects removed (sprayed weekly

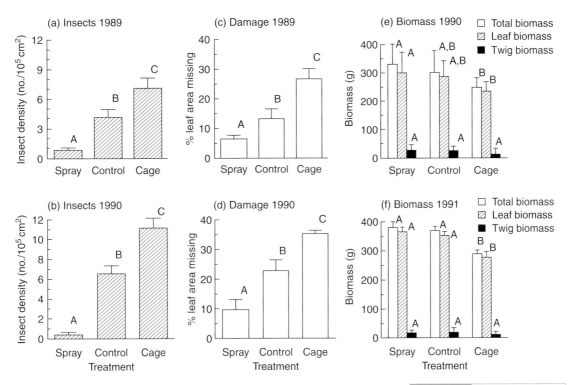

Figure 7.13 Insect density, leaf damage, and biomass production for 90 white oak trees divided into three treatments. In the spray treatment insects were controlled by spraying and hand picking. The controls were left without manipulation. Insectivorous birds were excluded from caged trees. The top row is 1989, the bottom 1990. Letters denote treatments different at the $p < 0.05$ level; histograms include estimates of standard error (from Marquis and Whelan 1994).

with synthetic pyrethroid combined with hand removal), and the third was caged (fine mesh with 3.8-cm holes provided access to insects but not to insect-eating birds). An inventory of the damage to these trees was taken each autumn for 2 years. Figure 7.13 shows that control plants lost roughly 15–25 percent of their leaf surface area depending upon the year. Spraying and hand picking reduced the number of insect herbivores by a factor of 10. The impact of the herbivorous insects is therefore clear, and while the long-term consequences of losing 15–25 percent of leaf area are speculative, one would expect significant reductions in survival, growth, or reproduction.

Remarkably, when insectivorous birds were also excluded, the number of insect herbivores almost doubled and losses of leaf area rose to 25–35 percent. This study therefore provides strong experimental evidence that forest-dwelling birds can enhance the production of forest trees. The birds in this area were typical deciduous forest species and included 17 common spring migrants and 31 spring and summer residents. If migratory bird populations continue to decline, Marquis and Whelan (1994) suggest that concomitant reductions in tree growth are likely. The ability of birds to control tree growth is also an excellent example of "top-down" control (Section 7.6.1).

7.4.2 Land crabs in tropical forest

The absence of mammalian grazers on islands has produced special situations where giant tortoises are the dominant land herbivore

(Galapagos Islands, Aldabra Island, Sections 7.2.3, 12.3.2). Land crabs can also be common herbivores on islands, as well as in coastal areas of the mainland, and crabs can reach densities of $1 \, m^{-2}$ (Kellman and Delfosse 1993). Green et al. (1997) tested for the effects of land crabs (*Gecarcoidea natalis*) in rain forest on Christmas Island in the Indian Ocean. Ten pairs of $5 \times 5 \, m$ plots were used, with one plot in each pair being surrounded by a semi-permeable fence. The fences allowed small invertebrates, as well as lizards and skinks in and out of the enclosed areas but crabs were excluded. Seven fences were constructed under closed forest and three in light gaps. The emergence of seedlings of tropical trees was more than 20 times greater in exclusion plots (plots in exclosures), and the number of species of tree seedlings per plot was also higher (10–12 species in exclosures versus 1 in controls).

Seedlings of trees such as *Maclura cochinchinensis*, *Planchonella nitida*, and *Schefflera elliptica* were common in the exclosures, but none survived for longer than 2 months in control plots. Red crabs can crush propagules of many species with their claws. When propagules were placed in trays on the forest floor, 80 percent or more were removed within 2 weeks. Some of the propagules removed were probably consumed but at least one-quarter were dispersed, and propagules of species such as *Barringtonia racemosa*, *Pandanus christmatensis*, and *Terminalia catappa* were all found inside the entrances of crab burrows. All of the exposed seeds of *Inocarpus fagifer* and *Tristiropsis acutangula* were handled by crabs, but the crabs were unable to penetrate the tough fibrous endocarps; the crabs did, however, eat the pulp of the fruits and drag the seeds to burrow entrances. It may be that crab herbivory has benefits for tropical trees (dispersal) as well as costs (loss of offspring). Crabs and squirrels may, unexpectedly, have a similar function in dispersing trees.

Land crabs, then, may have a substantial impact upon the forests of oceanic islands. The tree canopy on Christmas Island includes many species that are vulnerable to crabs as seedlings. This suggests that occasional periods of low crab density may be necessary for the regeneration of these trees. Over-exploitation of land crabs has so reduced many populations that it may now be difficult to determine what impact they once had upon forest composition. The possibility that harvesting land crabs might entirely change forest composition is yet another reminder that the consequences of human activities upon the environment can be difficult to foresee.

7.4.3 Herbivores in grassland: the Cape Province, the Pampas, and the Serengeti

Elephants are important herbivores in African grasslands, although in many cases, herbivores such as goats have also been introduced. Moolman and Cowling (1994) have provided a valuable comparison of the effects of a native (elephants) and exotic (goats) herbivores, relative to controls. Further, their work, shown in Figure 7.14, was

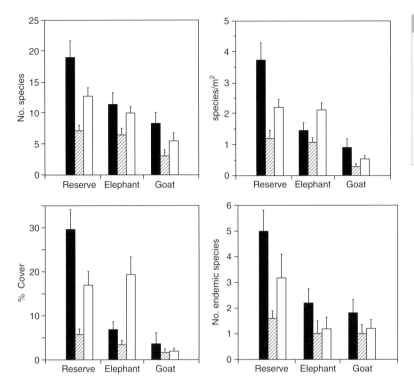

Figure 7.14 Characteristics of three vegetation types found in Addo Elephant National Park in South Africa, and either protected as a botanical reserve or subjected to elephant or goat grazing. The three types are: black bar, open; hatched bar, *Portulacaria* shrubs; white bar, *Euclea* shrubs (from Moolman and Cowling 1994).

carried out in the Cape Province of South Africa where there is a rich succulent flora that includes many hundreds of endemic species, many of which are in the Liliaceae, Asclepiadaceae, Crassulaceae, Euphorbiaceae, and Mesembryanthemaceae. The figure shows that goats have strongly deleterious effects relative to elephants. The diversity in some families, such as the Mesembryanthemaceae, was little affected by herbivory, probably owing to the low palatability of the plants, although total vegetative cover was reduced, and many species were restricted only to the control sites. The Crassulaceae, in contrast, were strongly affected by goats but little affected by elephants. Moolman and Cowling also provide a list of species that indicates the deleterious effects of herbivory.

In another study of herbivory, the subhumid grasslands of central Argentina were subjected to four different grazing regimes. Twenty plant traits were examined (Table 7.8). As grazing increased, there was a shift in morphology from tussock grasses to prostrate stoloniferous plants (Figure 7.15). Thus for a specified grazing regime, plant traits can be used to predict the presence or absence of species.

Facelli et al. (1989) suggest that, unlike African grasslands, the Pampas in South America may have developed under low intensities of natural herbivores. In Argentina the Pampas covers some three-quarters of a million square kilometers. The main wetland area is in the Salado Basin, a flat area of approximately $60\,000\,\mathrm{km^2}$ with mild winters and warm summers. Cattle and horses were introduced to

Table 7.8. *Characteristics of plant species recorded under four grazing regimes in Pampa de San Luis, Argentina (after Díaz et al. 1992).*

Characters
1. Persistence (annual/perennial)
2. Spiny structures
3. Pubescence
4. Average above-ground height
5. Width/length ratio

General plant form

6. Tussock
7. Rosette
8. Prostrate
9. Position of dormant buds
10. Presence of below-ground reserve organs
11. Average leaf length
12. Average leaf width/length ratio
13. Leaf angle
14. Leaf dissection
15. Leaf texture (sclerophyllous leaves)

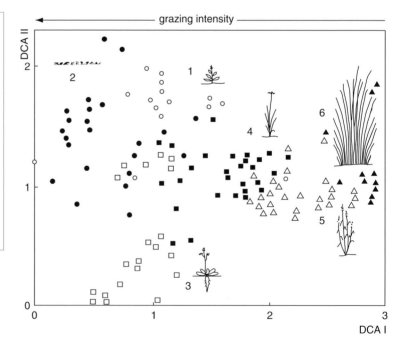

Figure 7.15 DCA ordination of the characters (Table 7.8) × species matrix for grazed grasslands in Argentina. Groups of species (morphological modes) were defined by TWINSPAN: ○, annuals (1); ●, prostrate stoloniferous plants (2); □, rosette plants with below-ground reserve organs (3); ■, graminoids of small-medium height (4); △, graminoids with medium-tall height (5); ▲, tussock grasses (6). Different morphs of a single species are included. DCA axes display standard deviation units (from Díaz et al. 1992).

the area by Spanish settlers in the 1500s, and in the mid 1800s fences were built so that grazing was further intensified in certain areas. As agriculture replaced ranching, natural grasslands were ploughed, except for areas subjected to regular inundation, the flooding Pampa.

Similar trends in grassland use have occurred in the Pantanal and the North American prairies.

In the Pampas, comparison of 1-ha plots that had been grazed steadily (at a stocking rate of roughly one head per 2 ha) and that had cattle excluded for 9 years showed that grazing had major effects on species composition. The ungrazed site had cover that was 95 percent monocots, composed particularly of large tussock grasses; *Paspalum dilatatum* and *Stipa bavioensis* dominated. The tall grasses formed a dense canopy and probably shaded out shorter species. In contrast, the grazed community was comprised of almost 60 percent dicots, many of which were exotic species; *Mentha pullegium* was by far the most common species. Species composition was more variable in the ungrazed site, and this suggests that, in the absence of grazing, the monocots might reach different competitive equilibria according to subtle environmental differences. In the grazed areas, in contrast, the effects of cattle appeared to be so severe as to override environmental heterogeneity.

Returning to Africa, one of the most comprehensive experimental studies of grazing (Belsky 1992) was carried out in Serengeti National Park, Tanzania, a park with $13\,000\,\text{km}^2$ of rolling grasslands, savanna, and open woodlands. To set the scene, rainfall in the park increases from 500 mm in the southeast to 1000 mm in the northwest and produces a vegetation gradient of short-grass (3–5 cm high, *Digitaria* and *Sporobolus*) in the south, through mid-grass (50–100 cm, *Themeda*, *Sporobolus*, *Pennisetum*), up to tall-grass (100–150 cm, *Diheteropogon*, *Elyonurus*, *Hyparrhenia*) in the north. Belsky's experimental design was elaborate and requires attention. At each site, two experimental blocks were selected, and one was enclosed by a chain link fence in order to exclude grazing mammals. Within each block, there were seven treatments: control, two disturbance treatments (deep disturbance, shallow disturbance), fire, and three removal experiments (removal of dominant species, removal of subdominant species, and removal of dominant and subdominant species). Although fire is a kind of disturbance, in this study the term disturbance was applied only to physical churning of the soil. At the end of each growing season, above-ground cover was measured for each species. The analysis then explored comparisons among the treatments (Table 7.9).

Consider just the responses of short-grass vegetation (Table 7.9). First, grazed plots were compared to ungrazed plots. The dominant grasses such as *Sporobolus fimbriatus* increased in the exclosure, whereas small species such as *Cyperus rotundus* declined. Next, disturbed plots were compared in grazed and ungrazed treatments. Some species increased regardless of grazing treatment (e.g., *Melhania ovata*). In other cases, species responded positively to disturbance only in ungrazed plots (e.g., *Harpachni schimperi*), and others increased only in grazed plots (e.g., *Medicago laciniata*). Still others decreased with disturbance (*Sporobolus ioclados*), some declining only in grazed plots (*Kyllinga nervosa*), or ungrazed plots

Table 7.9. *The effects of experimental manipulation on the cover of common grassland species for 5 years following the manipulations in a short-grass community in the Serengeti (+ indicates increased cover and − indicates decreased cover (p < 0.05) due to the treatment). When significant interactions occurred, u indicates that significant changes occurred only in the ungrazed block and g indicates that significant changes occurred only in the grazed block (from Belsky 1992).*

Species	Initial cover of site (percent)	species characteristics	Effects of protection from grazing in year:				Contrast 1: effects of disturbance[a] in year:				Contrast 2: effects of removal of dominant spp. in year:			Contrast 3: effects of early dry-season burn in year:	
			1	2	3	5	1	2	3	5	1	2	5	2	3
Harpachni schimperi	0.2	p,s	+	+	+	+		+u	+u	+u		+u	+u		−
Melhania ovata	0.2	p,t	+	+	+	+	+	+	+	+					
Digitaria macroblephara	3.2	p,t	+	+	+	+	+	−	−		+u	+u	+u		
Sporobolus fimbriatus	11.3	p,t	+	+	+	+	−u	−	−	−u					−u
Sporobolus ioclados	10.9	p,t	+	+			−	−	−	−					
Euphorbia inaequilatera	16.7	a,s	+	−	−	−	+	+g	+g	+g	−u	+g	+g		
Medicago laciniata	0.4	a,s	+												
Chloris pycnothrix	4.7	a,s		−	−	−	+	+g	+g	+g					
Cyperus rotundus	4.2	p,s		−	−	−	+	+u	+u	+u			−g		
Eragrostis papposa	0.3	a,s		−	−	−	+u		+	+			+g		
Indigofera microcharoides	0.4	a,s						+u	+u						
Kyllinga nervosa	0.2	p,s					−	−g	−g	−g	+		+g		
Justicia exigua	0.2	p,s	−	−											
Cynodon dactylon	3.2	p,t													
Digitaria scalarum	21.7	p,t		[ ]	[ ]	[ ]	−	−	−	−g	−				−u
Microchloa kunthii	1.2	p,s		[ ]	[ ]	[ ]	−	−	−	−g		−			
Sporobolus kentrophyllus	7.9	p,t		[ ]	[ ]	[ ]		−g	−g						
Species affected (%)			50	79	64	71	71	82	71	59	24	29	41	0	18

Notes:

a, annual; p, perennial; s, short species (ungrazed height <15 cm); t, tall species (ungrazed height >15 cm); [ ], effects of the grazing treatment could not be determined due to initially unequal cover values in the grazed and ungrazed blocks;
[a] physical churning of soil.

(*S. fimbriatus*). In those plots with dominant species removed, several species increased in the ungrazed plots (*H. schimperi*, *Digitaria macroblephara*). As the final pair of columns in Table 7.9 shows, fire had relatively few effects, although three species showed declines, two of these in ungrazed plots. The table includes a great deal of information and covers only the results for the short-grass community. Detailed results for the other communities can be found in Belsky (1992).

In summarizing the results for the study as a whole, it may be helpful to consider simplification by using factors such as plant traits. Protection from grazing increased the dominance of some species and decreased species diversity as tall species with methods of vegetative propagation shaded out shorter species and out-competed species that reproduce only sexually. Belsky reported that tall species such as *D. scalarum*, *S. fimbriatus*, and *Pennisetum mezianum* tended to replace short species. Even here there were exceptions; the short grass, *H. schimperi*, increased in the exclosure at the short-grass site (Table 7.9) apparently because it was shade tolerant. *Themeda triandra*, in spite of being a tall perennial, declined in exclosures in the mid-grass site, apparently because it is short-lived and has seeds that cannot germinate in shade. In disturbance treatments, in general, annual species and short species tended to increase. Fire had limited effects, its greatest being the stimulation of *T. triandra* regeneration from seed in mid-grass sites. Most other changes caused by fire were negative, presumably as a result of heat damage to shoots and buds. Finally, nearly 50 percent of the species at each site responded significantly to removals, a result that suggests that competition was controlling species' abundances. The many species that decreased when neighbors were removed suggests that commensalism also occurred or that a third species increased after the removal and suppressed other neighbors. Surprisingly, the number of species increasing after removal of neighbors was nearly the same in grazed and ungrazed plots, and this seems to indicate that interspecific competition occurred even in heavily grazed grasslands.

To summarize further, all three grasslands responded more or less similarly to the treatments, and the effects of grazing and disturbance were greater than those of competition and fire. The relative importance of these factors is difficult to assess, however, because the treatments represented different intensities of perturbation; comparing the intensity of perturbations is a difficult problem in all such experiments. The results of this experiment also offer an example of the complexity of possible outcomes in multifactoral, multiyear, and multisite studies – although these are the very studies that are needed in ecology. Extracting meaningful general patterns from such studies will be an ongoing challenge for ecologists. It might be tempting to avoid such complexity by studying only one species, but there would be no way to judge whether the species was typical or aberrant in its responses. The results in Table 7.9 also

Box 7.1 | Experimental design

Why regeneration of beech woods in England and Scotland is so poor was determined by fencing small areas. From some areas, rabbits were excluded; from others, both rabbits and birds; and from still others, field mice as well. By placing beechnuts in each enclosure both on the surface and within the forest litter, it was found that rabbits ordinarily ate very few seeds, birds secured only those on the surface, but mice destroyed almost the entire supply, except a few overlooked in the duff. This simple experiment established the fact that, in a large measure mice are responsible for the failure of the rejuvenation of beech forests.

An exact knowledge of the amount of damage done to the range by rodents and especially of the rate and degree of recovery of the various types of vegetation after rodents have been eradicated has been obtained in a similar manner. Exclosures were made against rodents and cattle, against cattle alone, and against cattle where rodents had been killed. Clipped quadrats from these as well as from enclosures inhabited by jack rabbits and others inhabited by kangaroo rats showed the heavy toll of vegetation taken by these pests, a matter of grave importance, especially in times of drought.

(from Weaver and Clements 1929, pp. 38–39)

Some considerations in designing herbivore exclosure experiments:

1. A well-defined question. Combine your own experience at the site with a careful study of the literature for previous problems with design. Some early examples to consult include (Farrow 1917), Tansley and Adamson (1925), and Baker (1937). Milchunas and Laurenroth (1993) have compiled a dataset for 236 sites where effects of herbivory have been examined.

2. Proper randomization of treatments and controls, including stratification if necessary.

3. Appropriate design. Consider nesting each set of treatments (T_1 to T_n, and controls) to avoid confounding with habitat differences. Consult a standard text on experimental design. Consult a statistician.

4. Verification. Take vegetation measurements before sites are en/exclosed to test for differences before treatments are initiated. Consider using these data as co-variants in analysis. These data may also be used to determine the amount of replication necessary.

5. Type of fencing. Degree of permeability to grazers determined by: (a) height, (b) depth of burial, and (c) mesh size. Possibility of several kinds of fencing to select different kinds of herbivores (yielding treatments T_1 to T_n).

6. Confounding effects. Design en/exclosures to minimize undesirable effects of the exclosure including shading, snow capture, protection from wind, etc. Make extra measurements to test for these effects.

7. Sampling. Avoid areas near fences to minimize problems caused by run-off, shading, toxics from metals, or other confounding fence effects. Avoid pseudo-replication (Hurlbert 1984). Maximize generality (Keddy 1989). Collect vouchers of all species and ensure that they are confirmed by an authority and stored appropriately.

8. Expansion. If resources permit, expand treatments to include resource manipulations (e.g., water, fertilizer) or manipulate other appropriate factors (e.g., fire, insects).

9. Duration. Maintain treatments as long as possible since most ecological studies are very short term. Consider what will be the criteria for ending the experiment. Is there an agency that could take over maintenance and monitoring in the long term?

10. Publish the results. Data buried in unpublished files are of little use to others. Where will the raw data tables be stored for future use by other scientists?

suggest that 5 years was not long enough to find treatment effects, which emphasizes the need for more long-term studies. There was one further problem illustrated by this work. Attentive readers may have noted that there was one large exclosure at each site, a simplification called pseudoreplication (Hurlbert 1984) and one that does not allow for the proper testing of grazing effects. To correctly assess the effects of grazing, it would be necessary to replicate the exclosures and control plots, at each of the three sites, and vastly increase the amount of work necessary.

7.4.4   Effects of rhinoceroses in tropical floodplain forest

Asian lowland forests contain several large herbivores including the Asiatic elephant, greater one-horned rhinoceros, and Javan rhinoceros. Tree diversity is relatively low, but large browser biomass approaches some of the highest values reported from Africa (Dinerstein 1992). More than 300 greater one-horned rhinoceroses (*Rhinoceros unicornis*) occur in Royal Chitwan National Park in Nepal. Two woody species, *Litsea monopetala* (Lauraceae) and *Mallotus philippinensis* (Euphorbiaceae), together comprise one-third of the woody stems, and only six species comprise >95 percent of the stems in the park. Throughout the understorey, *Litsea* showed signs of moderate to heavy browsing and trampling by rhinoceroses. Exclosure experiments showed that *Litsea* growth was enhanced when it was free from browsing for 3 years. Rhinoceroses also distribute the seeds of floodplain trees such as *Trewia nudifloa*, which Dinerstein (1991) considers to be the most common riparian forest tree in Chitwan. Dung piles in floodplain grasslands appear to be important colonization sites for this species. Thirty-seven other plant species have been recorded from rhinoceros latrines, while the flora of the area includes a total of 77 fleshy-fruited species that are dispersed by vertebrates (Dinerstein 1991). Dinerstein (1992) also notes that at the time of his studies, the rhinoceros population was recovering from heavy poaching, so that more natural population levels would be expected to have a greater impact than those he measured.

7.4.5   Large mammals in deciduous forest

White-tailed deer (*Odocoileus virginianus*) are common herbivores in deciduous forests and have the potential to control both herbaceous plants and regeneration by woody plants. Deer tend to have high population densities, largely as a consequence of human activities

Table 7.10. *Damage to trees by deer browsing in 53 woodland tracts in England (from Kay 1993).*

Tree species	Roe sites (39) Mean % shoots damaged	Roe sites (39) Shoots sampled	Fallow sites (10) Mean % shoots damaged	Fallow sites (10) Shoots sampled
Hornbeam	95.7	7	–	–
Willow	60.7	14	–	–
Sweet chestnut	46.3	49	76.2	29
Lime	–	–	55.5	61
Birch	80.5	49	31.8	88
Sycamore	–	–	45.0	18
Hazel	41.3	492	41.4	36
Maple	40.3	38	46.7	6
Ash	23.2	95	71.3	4
Alder	1.2	38	–	–

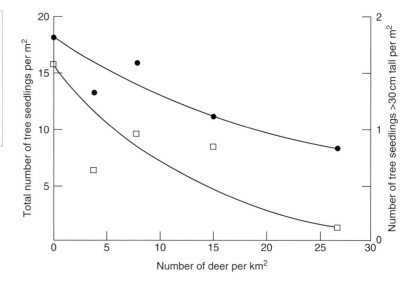

Figure 7.16 Abundance of tree seedlings in experimental enclosures in northern Pennsylvania where white-tailed deer were maintained at different densities for 5 years. ●, All seedlings (left-hand scale); □, seedlings more than 30 cm tall (right-hand scale) (from Newman 1993).

that improve food supplies (agriculture and logging), as well as deliberate management (e.g., winter-feeding) to increase populations for hunters. Deer are also very selective in their feeding habits (Table 7.10). In one study (Tilghman 1989), vegetation was sampled in enclosures where deer were maintained at five experimental densities (0, 10, 20, 40, and 80 deer per 259 ha). Browsing by deer greatly reduced the density and height of tree seedlings (Figure 7.16). Only two tree species, *Prunus serotina* (black cherry) and *Acer pennsylvanicum* (striped maple), were common at high densities of deer. Ferns such as *Dennstaedtia punctilobula* and *Thelypteris noveboracensis* were also

Box 7.2 | Demographic study of the effects of deer browsing

The decline of woodland plants with grazing is illustrated by American ginseng (*Panax quinquefolium*, Figure B7.2a). This plant is becoming increasingly rare from the combination of commercial collecting and overgrazing by deer. McGraw and Furedi (2005) report that 45 percent of the plants they observed had been damaged by grazing. In many cases, all foliage and frequently all flowers and fruits were removed. Plants collected in the past are much larger than those seen now (McGraw 2001), which is consistent with surviving plants being drained of stored energy reserve. Ecologists have constructed demographic models that include rates of seed production and new plant establishment, as well as rates of adult survival for this species (Charron and Gagnon 1991, Nantel et al. 1996). Overall, populations grow and decline slowly, with the largest plants being most important for population growth rate because of their larger seed production. Population viability estimates can be made by projecting population size into the future with a stochastic model, asking how large a population has to be to ensure a 95 percent probability of survival for 100 years (McGraw and Furedi 2005). Applying this model to their data on existing population sizes in central Appalachia, current rates of deer browsing are forecast to eliminate 29 out of 36 known populations within the century with a 99 percent probability. Even the largest population, 406 plants, has a 43 percent probability of becoming extinct before 100 years. Figure B7.2b shows population viability as a function of population size for five different levels of deer browsing.

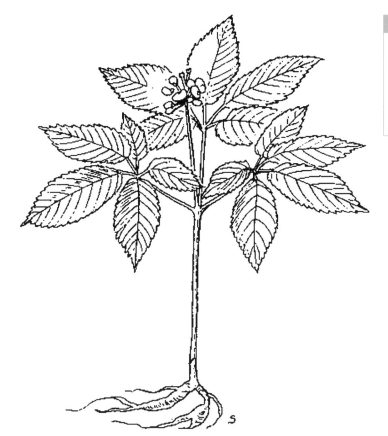

Figure B7.2(a) American ginseng (*Panax quinquefolium*), listed in Appendix II of the Convention on International Trade in Endangered Species of Wild Fauna and Flora, is a member of the Araliaceae (illustration by Marion Seiler, from Radford et al. 1968).

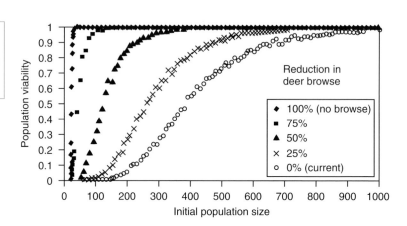

Figure B7.2(b) Population viability of American ginseng as a function of initial population size at five levels of simulated browse (from McGraw and Furedi 2005).

more common at high deer densities. The impacts on other herbaceous species could not be quantified. Overall, there is growing concern that large populations of deer threaten the survival of forests or the rare plant species that some parks are intended to protect (Alverson et al. 1988, Russell et al. 2001). By increasing deer densities, humans change the species composition of forests in unexpected ways. Such changes in the forest may have further unintended effects, such as declines in songbird species (de Calesta 1994, McShea and Rappole 2000).

7.4.6 Effects of an introduced species: nutria

Myocaster coypus is a large (up to 10 kg) South American rodent that was introduced to both North America and Europe. This animal is generally called coypu in Europe (Moss 1983, 1984) and nutria in the United States (Shaffer et al. 1992, Taylor and Grace 1995). Moss describes how animals introduced to fur farms in England about 1929 escaped and multiplied to an estimated 200 000 animals by the 1960s. He observes that coypus "are extremely destructive grazers, uprooting reed and other swamp [marsh] plants to eat the rhizomes," and attributes the loss of fringing reed marshes to grazing by *M. coypus* (Moss 1984). *Myocaster coypus* were introduced to Louisiana in the 1930s for fur farming, escaped during a hurricane, and reached high population levels in Louisiana deltaic marshes (Atwood 1950).

In a study of the effects of *M. coypus*, Shaffer et al. (1992) built four 50 × 40 m exclosures to test whether herbivory was changing the vegetation in deltaic marshes. Their data in Table 7.11 appear to show that, relative to controls, the exclosure plots had much higher cover and more plant species. Plants that were preferred food of *M. coypus* (e.g., *Sagittaria platyphylla, S. latifolia*) dominated the exclosures, while species presumably less preferred (*Justicia ovata, Leersia oryzoides*) dominated the control sites. Although *S. latifolia* was one of the most flood-tolerant species in the study, it was

Table 7.11. *The effects of grazing by* Myocaster coypus *on deltaic wetlands as illustrated by four 40 × 50 m exclosures and paired control areas. Numbers are cover value sums for 30 plots (from Shaffer et al. 1992).*

Species	I Exclosure	I Control	II Exclosure	II Control	III Exclosure	III Control	IV Exclosure	IV Control
Amaranthus tamariscina	–	–	–	–	16	–	–	–
Alternanthera philoxeroides	12	–	–	–	14	–	6	–
Justicia ovata	27	19	31	11	62	40	24	35
Leersia oryzoides	2	–	3	–	51	7	87	27
Paspalum distichum	–	–	–	–	3	3	5	–
Polygonum punctatum	14	1	2	–	52	1	33	12
Sagittaria latifolia	95	1	128	–	82	59	73	22
Sagittaria platyphylla	18	1	11	–	18	4	52	5
Scirpus americanus	–	–	–	–	4	1	9	–
Scirpus validus	1	–	–	–	5	–	6	2
Spartina alterniflora	–	–	–	–	1	–	6	–
Typha domingensis	9	–	–	–	–	–	–	–
Total cover	178	22	175	11	308	115	301	103
Total species	8	4	5	1	11	7	10	6

restricted to higher elevations, which Shaffer et al. attribute to herbivory by *M. coypus* at lower elevations. More recent work in Louisiana by Taylor and Grace (1995) using smaller exclosures showed that the biomass of dominant plant species such as *Panicum virgatum*, *Spartina patens*, and *Spartina alterniflora* increased if *M. coypus* was excluded, but they were unable to detect changes in the number of species.

The secondary effects of herbivory may be more dramatic. Shaffer et al. (1992) suggest that to the direct effects of herbivory, one must add the indirect effects of increased environmental sensitivity in plants that have been damaged. Not only do shoots transport oxygen to rhizomes, below-ground organs allow for regeneration after burial by fresh sediment. Herbivores that feed only on shoots will indirectly damage rhizomes by reducing photosynthetic activity of shoots, but those, like *M. coypus*, that feed on both above- and below-ground parts may be particularly destructive. The presence of *M. coypus* is thought to be a major factor reducing vegetation in the Atchafalaya Delta in Louisiana, not only because the animals consume plants but because remaining plants, which may be damaged, are easily killed by flooding and sedimentation (Shaffer et al. 1992). Since organic matter from plants contributes to the accumulation of marsh soil, nutria may even be reducing the area of wetlands.

7.5 | Empirical relationships

Experiments provide a method for testing whether herbivory causes changes in vegetation and for then exploring the linkages of causation. It is not, however, easy to combine the results of many such experiments to uncover general principles, although there are formal procedures termed meta-analysis for analyzing groups of published studies. In a remarkable piece of work similar to meta-analysis, Milchunas and Laurenroth (1993) used multiple regression analysis to synthesize a data set of 236 sites where grazed and ungrazed tracts of vegetation were compared; more than 30 journals were examined in their entirety, some 500 articles were surveyed, and 97 were used in the analysis. To appreciate the analysis, some terminology is necessary. The two most important dependent variables were: (1) measured changes in species composition and (2) above-ground net primary production (NPP). The effects of the exclosure or, conversely, the effects of herbivory were measured using changes in species composition (Table 7.12). The measure used to assess changes in species composition – 1 minus Whittaker's (1952) index of association – potentially ranged from 0 (no differences between grazed and ungrazed sites) to 1 (completely different ungrazed and grazed sites). NPP was estimated as maximum standing crop. The independent variables included: (1) grazing intensity, (2) years of protection from grazing, (3) evolutionary history of grazing as assessed by a panel of experts, (4) mean annual precipitation, (5) temperature, and (6) latitude. The intensity of herbivory was measured as the percentage of NPP consumed by the grazers; it ranged from a mean of 44 percent in grasslands to 60 percent in forests. The sites covered a range of precipitation from 220 to 1911 mm year^{-1} and latitudes from 0 to 57 °.

Table 7.12 shows that three out of nine potential variables explained 44 percent of the variance in composition for all vegetation types combined. Consumption (0.17) contributed about as much to the cumulative R^2 as did NPP (0.15 + 0.03) while evolutionary history of grazing contributed only 0.09. Species dissimilarity (differences in species composition between grazed and ungrazed areas) for all communities, grasslands plus shrublands, and grassland alone, increased with both NPP and the evolutionary history of grazing (Figure 7.17): that is, the sites with the greatest history of herbivory actually showed a greater response to grazing. This at first seems counterintuitive, for one might suspect that sites with a history of herbivory would be most resistant to grazing. Perhaps it is explained as sites with a history of herbivory having many species able to exploit the changes caused by herbivores. For all communities, species dissimilarity was most sensitive to altering NPP, followed by evolutionary history of grazing, then consumption (Table 7.12,

Table 7.12. *Regression models for plant species dissimilarity of ungrazed versus grazed plant communities and the sensitivity of species dissimilarity to changing an independent variable from a low to a high value while holding other independent variables constant. All communities means grassland, shrubland, forest, mountain (alpine meadow) and desert. Consumption % reflects the strength of herbivory. Dissimilarity values were computed as one minus Whittaker's (1952) index of association (after Milchunas and Lauenroth 1993).*

Habitat	Independent variables	Cumulative R^2	Slope	Final model		
				Sensitivity	Significance	df
All communities	NPP	0.15	1.659×10^{-3}	+0.30	0.000	114
	Consumption (percent)	0.32	4.272×10^{-3}	+0.13	0.000	
	Evolutionary history	0.41	6.569×10^{-2}	+0.20	0.000	
	$(NPP)^2$	0.44	-1.804×10^{-6}		0.033	
	Regression constant		-0.214		0.003	
Grasslands-plus-shrublands, precip. $\leq$ 1000 mm/year	Evolutionary history	0.19	6.447×10^{-2}	+0.20	0.000	96
	NPP	0.32	2.139×10^{-3}	+0.37	0.000	
	Consumption %	0.50	4.903×10^{-2}	+0.15	0.000	
	$(NPP)^2$	0.55	-2.406×10^{-6}		0.002	
	Regression constant		-0.320		0.000	
Grasslands, precip. $\leq$ 1000 mm/year	NPP	0.25	2.849×10^{-3}	+0.47	0.000	68
	$(NPP)^2$	0.40	-3.260×10^{-6}		0.000	
	Consumption (percent)	0.49	3.944×10^{-3}	+0.12	0.000	
	Evolutionary history	0.54	6.690×10^{-2}	+0.20	0.011	
	Regression constant		-0.413		0.001	
Shrublands, precip. $\leq$ 1000 mm/year	Precipitation	0.62	1.071×10^{-3}	+0.53	0.000	59
	Evolutionary history	0.67	7.314×10^{-2}	+0.21	0.002	
	Years of exclosure	0.69	2.404×10^{-3}	+0.10	0.091	
	Regression constant		-0.224		0.001	

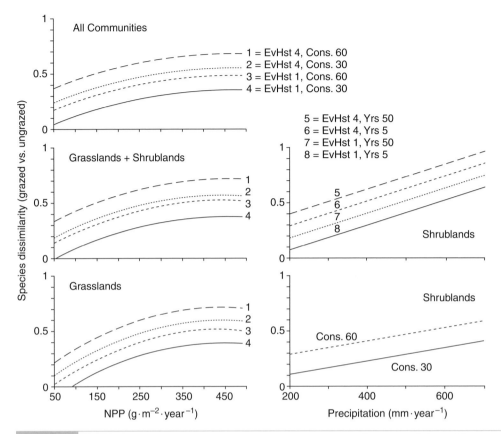

Figure 7.17 Sensitivity analyses of species dissimilarity of grazed versus ungrazed sites around the world computed as 1 minus Whittaker's [1952] index of association based on regression models for all community types combined, grasslands-plus-shrublands, grasslands, or shrublands. A dissimilarity value of 0 indicates no difference between grazed and ungrazed communities, and a value of 1 indicates completely distinct communities. EvHst, evolutionary history of grazing, ranked 1–4 for lower to higher values of past grazing; Cons., consumption – recent grazing intensity (in percentage of above-ground net primary productivity [NPP]); Yrs, years of protection from grazing (from Milchunas and Laurenroth 1993).

column 5). Remarkably then, differences in species composition between grazed and ungrazed areas are more sensitive to physical environmental change (temperature and rainfall largely control NPP) than to altering the intensity of grazing.

A similar dataset was compiled by Cyr and Pace (1993) for a wide variety of habitats with, however, greater emphasis upon wetland and aquatic habitats. The producers were phytoplankton, reef periphyton, submerged macrophytes, emergent macrophytes, and terrestrial plants. Figure 7.18 shows the importance of herbivory when these producers are divided into three groups: aquatic algae, aquatic macrophytes, and terrestrial plants. A striking result depicted in this figure is that aquatic macrophytes are much more like terrestrial plants than aquatic algae. This echoes earlier discussions in Chapter 3 about fertility, when the question was whether wetland plants were limited by phosphorus (as with algae) or by nitrogen (as with many terrestrial plants). For aquatic macrophytes

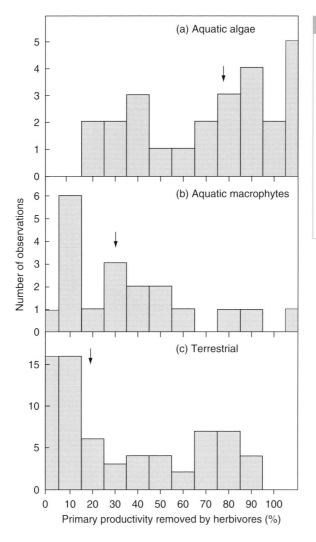

Figure 7.18 Frequency distributions of the proportion of annual net primary productivity removed by herbivores for (a) aquatic algae (phytoplankton $n = 17$ and reef periphyton $n = 8$); (b) aquatic macrophytes (submerged $n = 5$ and emergent $n = 14$ vascular plants); and terrestrial plants ($n = 67$). Arrows indicate median values (aquatic algae 79 percent, aquatic macrophytes 30 percent, terrestrial plants 18 percent) (from Cyr and Pace 1993).

the median proportion of productivity removed by herbivores is 30 percent (compared to 79 percent for algae and 18 percent for terrestrial plants). The relationship between the rate of removal of biomass by herbivores and primary productivity (Figure 7.19 top) is linear with a slope not different from one and suggests that herbivores remove the same proportion of primary productivity across a wide range of fertility levels. The top of Figure 7.19 also shows that consumption rates are apparently an order of magnitude lower for macrophytes than algae.

In the rest of their analyses, Cyr and Pace regrettably combine algae and macrophytes into one "aquatic" category for comparisons with terrestrial plants. Nonetheless, certain general conclusions about herbivores can be extracted. In Figure 7.19 (bottom) the biomass of herbivores is plotted against net primary productivity for both habitats. The two triangles at the upper left are submerged macrophyte beds where herbivore biomass was strikingly high.

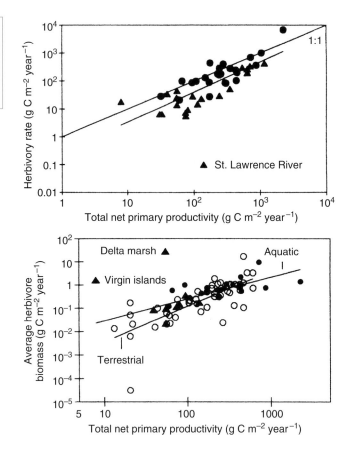

Figure 7.19 Rate of grazing (top) and herbivore biomass (bottom) both increase with net primary productivity. ●, Aquatic algae; ▲, aquatic macropytes; ○, terrestrial plants (from Cyr and Pace 1993).

(The circle at the lower left is a terrestrial tundra site.) Excluding the two outlying triangles, herbivore biomass increases significantly with productivity, and also, excluding the outlying circle, there is no significant difference between the lines for aquatic and terrestrial habitats. Therefore, for a given level of net primary productivity, herbivores reach similar average biomass in aquatic and terrestrial ecosystems.

7.6 | Some theoretical context

7.6.1 Top-down or bottom-up?

The terms "top-down" and "bottom-up" refer to whether the composition of ecological communities is controlled from the top of food webs down, by predators, or whether the control is exercised from the bottom up, with consumers being controlled by plants or resources (e.g., Hunter and Price 1992, Power 1992, Sinclair et al. 2000, Sinclair and Krebs 2001).

At the very least, it is certain that there is some bottom-up control, for the very simple reason that, without plants, the consumers disappear (Hunter and Price 1992). It is therefore quite reasonable to begin with the assumption that vegetation controls wildlife, both through the creation of habitat and production of food. The second issue, whether the consumers also influence or control the producers, turns out to be much less clear. One can naively observe that many areas are green and that since the plants are not being eradicated by herbivores, something else must be controlling herbivore abundance (Hairston et al. 1960), but, as White (1993) argues, a good deal of this green matter has such low nitrogen content that it hardly qualifies as food, and the growing literature on secondary metabolites (Rosenthal and Berenbaum 1991) suggests that much visually apparent green food is well protected from herbivores. Both of these constraints upon herbivory are well documented. Therefore, the issue of whether herbivores control the abundance of plants and the composition of vegetation is open for evaluation. A further complication in the idea of top-down control is the possible effect of predators that feed upon herbivores, the logic being that carnivores could have a positive effect upon plants by having a negative effect upon herbivores, a so-called trophic cascade (e.g., Sinclair et al. 2000, Terborgh et al. 2001). One compelling example of such effects comes from a set of islands created by a hydroelectric impoundment in Venezuela (Terborgh et al. 2001). Islands lacking predators have much larger numbers of herbivores such as iguanas and leaf cutting ants, and as a consequence seedlings and saplings of canopy trees are severely reduced. Thus, there is evidence that top predators would normally protect the trees by controlling herbivores. Another example involves crabs, snails, and marsh plants (Silliman and Bertness 2002). When blue crabs were excluded from small areas of marsh using cages, their prey, the herbivorous periwinkle, destroyed the plants upon which they fed. In this trophic cascade, the authors suggest that commercial trapping of blue crabs could unleash overgrazing by periwinkles, thereby damaging marsh vegetation.

So how widespread is top-down control? Do large carnivores including wolves, lions and alligators often control the composition of plant communities, and does their loss from large areas lead to enormous change in plant communities? The simple answer is probably that we suspect so, but do not yet know. In the short term, we should probably avoid trying to ask simplistic questions about whether control is top-down or bottom-up. Too often, apparently neat dichotomies mislead us (Dayton 1979, Mayr 1982, Keddy 1989). Both processes may operate simultaneously, neither may operate except for rare occasions, or other factors such as habitat productivity (Oksanen 1990), habitat heterogeneity (Hunter and Price 1992), or omnivory (Power 1992) may override their impacts.

Instead of a simple dichotomy, Oksanen et al. (1981) propose that there are at least three different possible kinds of grazing systems along a gradient of increasing primary productivity. The key factor, then, is primary productivity, including the supply of soil resources to the plants. According to their model, herbivore pressure should be most severe in relatively unproductive environments. As primary productivity increases, the impact of herbivory should decline because the growing abundance of herbivores also allows predators to survive and regulate herbivore populations. In very productive systems, herbivory again becomes important owing to the presence of a second tier of predators feeding upon the first tier of predators, thereby once again releasing the herbivores from regulation. Oksanen et al. present a model, building upon work by Fretwell (1977), that shows how such transitions in herbivore–plant relationships might occur, and they also present some data that are qualitatively consistent with these kinds of changes. Sinclair et al. (2000) discuss further how one might test among the many possibilities, and raise may interesting prospects for collaboration between plant ecologists and animal ecologists.

There are further possible effects of animals upon plants. The animals may increase the rates of nitrogen cycling, fertilize plants with their waste products, and even alter competition for nitrogen between plants and soil microbes (recall Figure 7.1). Hence, generalizations about interactions between herbivores and plants, while highly desirable, require further experimental testing. In the meantime, simplistic dichotomies should probably be viewed with caution. Winston Churchill commented in his memoirs of the Second World War that Americans had a tendency to look for grand theories rather than pragmatic solutions to problems. You might therefore find it helpful to focus first on a narrow problem, the *possible* effects of herbivores upon vegetation. The following models are tools for thinking further about the effects of herbivores on the composition of vegetation.

7.6.2 Effects of selective herbivory on plant diversity

Herbivory provides an important tool for managing landscapes in general, and particularly for manipulating plant diversity (Chapters 11, 12). You may therefore be challenged one day to decide whether to increase or decrease the herbivory occurring in a landscape. There is a long list of examples to learn from – including deer in forests (Box 7.2, Latham et al. 2005), cattle in rangeland (Canfield 1948, Milton et al. 1994, McClaran 2003), goats in arid lands (Section 7.4.3, Section 12.2.2) and nutria in wetlands (Section 7.4.6). Although exotic herbivores like goats and cattle often have major negative consequences for the natural vegetation, in other cases, the consequences are less obvious. Predicting the effects of herbivores upon plant diversity is often complicated by the selectivity of herbivores. If herbivores feed mostly upon common plant species, rarer plant species may increase; conversely, if herbivores feed mostly upon rare species, the common species may become even more common. A simple verbal model follows, although a mathematical version is available (Yodzis 1986).

Imagine the following circumstances: a plant community with a mixture of species, some with high competitive ability and some with low competitive ability. The abundance of each species, in the absence of herbivory, tends naturally toward eventual exclusion by the species that is the competitive dominant. Over time, then, species richness will decline. Now introduce a herbivore. What will happen? The effects of this herbivore on the diversity of the plant community are impossible to predict without information about the feeding habits of the herbivore. Consider the two extremes. At one extreme, the herbivore feeds upon the weaker competitors and avoids the dominant. In this case, the herbivore will reduce the diversity of the community. At the other extreme, imagine that the herbivore feeds solely upon the competitive dominant (although cannot entirely eliminate it) and avoids the weaker competitors. In this case, the herbivore will increase the biological diversity of the community. Third, imagine that the herbivore feeds on species in direct proportion to their occurrence in nature; in this case, the effects of herbivory will be small and largely determined by the species' relative degrees of resistance to the damage of herbivory. Yodzis (1986) explores these situations mathematically. Such investigations illustrate that the effects of introducing exotic herbivores or reintroducing extirpated herbivores may be difficult to predict.

Mowing by humans is, in one sense, just a form of herbivory carried out by a relatively unselective herbivore. Mowing usually increases plant diversity (Baker 1937, Grime 1973a, Ellenberg 1988b). This increase in diversity appears to occur because mowing is actually somewhat selective: mowing tends to preferentially remove larger species with dense canopies and thereby allow smaller species, such as rosette forms, to persist. Although mowing has its disadvantages, particularly when we are trying to re-establish natural processes in plant communities, it may be one of the few ways to manage for increased diversity under eutrophic conditions.

7.6.3 A simple model of herbivory

The effects of herbivory upon vegetation, and the response of herbivores to vegetation, can both be explored with simple mathematical models. One of the simplest models adapts the logistic equation, which is widely used by ecologists to describe the growth of populations (Wilson and Bossert 1971). The logistic model assumes that when there are few organisms and abundant resources, growth is (almost) exponential, but when population size increases and resources become scarce, the population growth slows and reaches a level known as the carrying capacity, K. This equation can be equally applied to plant populations (Noy-Meir 1975, Starfield and Bleloch 1991) as

$$\frac{dP}{dt} = \frac{gP(K-P)}{K}$$

where P is the amount of plant material (e.g., biomass/unit area), g is the growth rate, and K is the maximum amount of plant material that a unit area can support. Another way of thinking about this equation, which is more like familiar animal population models, is to consider

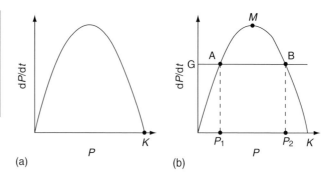

P to be the number of plant cells and K the carrying capacity of plant cells for a particular area of landscape.

To explore the behavior of vegetation without herbivores, one can plot growth rate (dP/dt) against biomass (P), which produces an inverted parabola (Figure 7.20, left). The growth rate of the population of plant cells therefore at first increases as more and more cells are available for photosynthesis, and then it slowly declines as the resources available to each cell become restricted. The botanical logic behind this seems to make sense. When plant biomass is low, each new cell will improve the photosynthetic capacity of the vegetation, but as biomass increases, more and more cells will be needed to provide structural support for photosynthetic cells, and others will be shaded, thus reducing net photosynthetic yield. When the mean photosynthetic yield of all cells just balances their mean respiratory demands, growth will come to a halt; the level K on the horizontal axis of the graph will have been reached. Halfway between 0 and K the growth rate is at a maximum. This is the familiar pattern of logistic growth; the novelty lies solely in applying it to plant biomass. The level of biomass, K, will depend upon environmental factors such as flood duration, growing season, and soil fertility. In the absence of herbivores, all vegetation will tend toward point K.

Now add in a constant grazing pressure from a herbivore. Assuming that the herbivores removed a fixed amount of biomass per unit time, designated G, the equation becomes

$$\frac{dP}{dt} = \frac{gP(K-P) - G}{K}.$$

Since the grazing rate is set to be independent of biomass, one can plot G as a horizontal line across the parabolic model of plant growth (Figure 7.20, right). There is no need to solve the differential equation to learn a good deal about the behavior of such a grazing system; this can be deduced simply from the structure of the equations and the resulting graph (Starfield and Bleloch 1991). Returning to the growth of vegetation, it is apparent that the growth rate is positive only between points A and B, where the growth parabola lies above the grazing rate and biomass therefore accumulates. On either side of this range, the grazing rate exceeds the growth rate. At points A and B, growth just matches grazing.

The next step is to examine stability by considering the consequences of minor perturbations. Consider point B, where the corresponding amount of plant biomass is indicated as P_2. If growing conditions improve slightly, pushing the amount of biomass to the right, the growth rate will fall below the grazing rate, and the vegetation will decline back to level P_2. If, on the other hand, drought or flooding were to reduce biomass slightly below P_2, then simultaneously the difference between the grazing rate and the growth rate increases, so that biomass accumulates, pushing the system back toward point P_2. Since the system returns to point B when it is lightly perturbed, this is called a stable equilibrium point.

Point A, in contrast, is unstable, because the same procedure shows that if the system is perturbed, it slides even further away from point A. If it is perturbed to the left of P_1 say by a drought, then growth rates fall further and further below the grazing rate until the plants disappear; the system slides to the bottom left and collapses. Conversely, if there is a surge of growth above P_1, then the vegetation temporarily escapes from grazing and continues to move to the right because, as biomass increases, the difference between grazing rate and growth rate increases as well. Eventually the entire system slides over to point P_2. Over a broad range of biomass levels, this model of a simple grazing system will return to P_2, the only stable point, after perturbation.

Further herbivore–plant community dynamics can be deduced from the structure of the equation. If the grazing rate was increased above the maximum growth rate (M) – equivalent to sliding the horizontal line above the parabola – the herbivore would graze faster than the vegetation grew. Such a situation would be unstable. Other mathematical models could be used to describe herbivore–plant interactions by, for example, allowing for growth rates to fluctuate in response to rainfall or flooding, or by using a different model for plant growth (Starfield and Bleloch 1991). Scientists have addressed issues such as the interactions between plants competing for light (Givnish 1982) and plant responses to added grazing pressure (Oksanen 1990). If grazing pressure is not constant, but varies with plant biomass, then a variety of outcomes is possible, depending upon the functional responses of the grazer (Yodzis 1989).

7.6.4 Extensions of herbivory models

By making slightly different assumptions, very different models of herbivore–plant dynamics can be generated (Oksanen et al. 1981, Starfield and Bleloch 1986, Yodzis 1989). To illustrate the process of expanding the models, consider the example presented in Yodzis (1989). Again, the plants are assumed to have logistic growth, giving the parabolic curve in Figure 7.21, but instead of the herbivore being represented by a single horizontal line as in Figure 7.20, it is given a more complex harvesting response. This is a type III response (*sensu* Holling 1959) in which the herbivore feeding rate responds in a nonlinear way to the resource levels. Figure 7.21 also adds in three

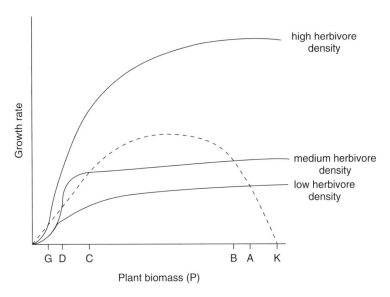

The qualitative structure of a grazing model can depend upon herbivore density. The dashed curve is the logistic growth curve of the vegetation with no herbivore present, and the solid lines are three possible harvesting curves for three herbivore densities (after Yodzis 1989).

different densities of herbivore; for simplicity assume that this density is something that is fixed (perhaps controlled by a farmer) rather than a population with dynamics of its own, which could be a function of P, dP/dt, and dH/dt. For each herbivore density, the growth rate of the plants is given by subtracting the solid curve (grazing rate) from the dashed curve (growth rate). Three outcomes are possible (Figure 7.22). At low herbivore density, shown in the top figure, the system has a single equilibrium point that is stable at $P=A$. Here the biomass removed by the herbivore balances the growth rate of the plants and there are still many plants present. At an intermediate herbivore density, shown in the middle figure, there are three points where the curve intersects the biomass axis (growth rate and grazing rate intersections, Figure 7.21). Points $P=B$ and $P=D$ are stable, while $P=C$ is unstable. In this case, the herbivore and plants can reach an equilibrium at either high (B) or low (D) plant biomass. If the density of herbivores is high enough, the results shown in the bottom figure are obtained, where there is one equilibrium point, G, corresponding to very low plant cover.

May (1977) observes that one can show the equilibrium values and herbivore densities in one diagram (Figure 7.23). The three regions on the horizontal axis correspond to the three situations illustrated in Figure 7.22: low, medium, and high herbivore density. The threshold values that mark the transitions among these three situations are marked as either T_1 or T_2. Yodzis (1989) explains the model as it applies to densities of sheep (please note that I have changed the labeling of the axes in the figure so that they correspond to Yodzis's referenced text, which follows):

If, to start, there are no sheep in the field, the vegetation will eventually reach the value K of biomass density. Suppose we then stock the field with sheep, at a low or intermediate density (that is: with $H < T_2$). If we

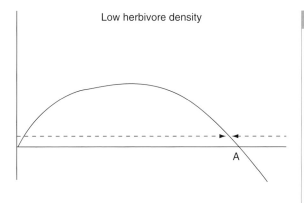

Low herbivore density

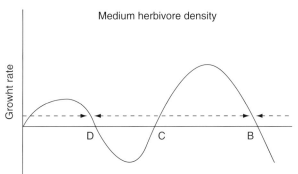

Medium herbivore density

Growht rate

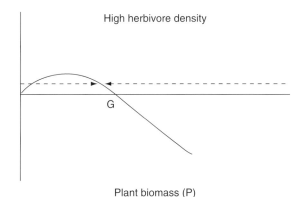

High herbivore density

Plant biomass (P)

Figure 7.22 The growth rate of the vegetation plotted against plant biomass for each of the scenarios in Figure 7.21. At low herbivore density (top), there is one equilibrium point, A. At high herbivore density (bottom), there is another much lower equilibrium point, G. At medium herbivore density, however, there are three equilibrium points, D, C, and B, and of these D and B are both locally stable equilibria. Depending upon circumstances, it is possible to have stable equilibria at either high plant biomass (B) or low plant biomass (D) (after Yodzis 1989).

keep the flock constant for a while, the system will eventually settle into an equilibrium with the vegetation biomass somewhere on the upper solid curve, since we are starting out from a value of P (namely, K) that lies above this curve. And we can increase the density of sheep with no drastic effects, so long as we stay below $H = T_2$: each slight increase in H will just result in a slight decrease in equilibrium vegetation biomass.

However, if we push the sheep density above T_2, even if by only one sheep, a catastrophe will occur.

Beyond T_2, there is in the previous sketch no longer any "upper" stable equilibrium, and the vegetation biomass must plummet to the "lower" stable equilibrium curve! We no longer have a very healthy

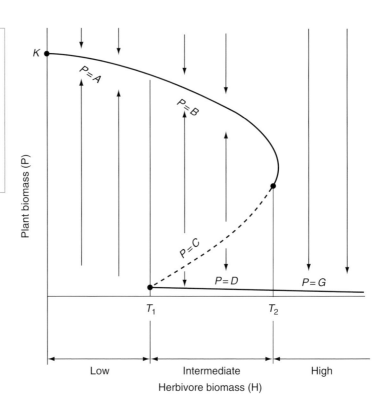

Figure 7.23 The equilibrium values of plant biomass (*P*) plotted against herbivore density (*H*). The arrows show the direction of change in the plant biomass at non-equilibrium, and the different values of *P* correspond to the equilibria shown in Figure 7.22. T_1 and T_2 are threshold values for shifts among the three models (after Yodzis 1989).

pasture: our new "high *H*" flock can subsist, but only rather precariously; the pasture, and our flock of sheep, may suffer severely from some relatively small misfortune such as sparsity of rain.

Worse still, we cannot easily get back to the "upper" stable equilibrium curve. If we remove a few sheep from the pasture to get back into the "intermediate *H*" region, the system will remain on the "lower" stable equilibrium curve, because the vegetation density is below the breakpoint value $P = C$. The only way to get back to the "upper" stable equilibrium curve is by removing enough sheep to get below the threshold $H = T_1$, into the region of "low *H*."

Perhaps you are thinking: isn't it still worth the risk inherent in a high *H* flock, because you do after all, in case there are no little disasters such as a sparsity of rain, have a big flock of sheep. The problem with this is, you've got a big flock of very scrawny sheep, for the level of vegetation biomass density associated with a high *H* flock is very low relative to the saturation density R_0 of the sheep. Therefore, the sheep have only enough food to barely survive: when the vegetation biomass crashes down to the "lower" stable equilibrium curve in the previous sketch, the sheep biomass will crash along with it ….

Notice one more thing about this system. In reality it will be subject to all kinds of unpredictable influences (weather, disease, other grazers, etc.) which will make it fluctuate around any equilibrium. Even if we are below the threshold T_2, if we are too close to T_2 these random fluctuations may bring the vegetation biomass *P* below the breakpoint value *C*, resulting in a "crash" just as if we had overstocked. If you take another look at the previous graph, you will see that the domain of attraction of the upper stable equilibrium $P = B$ is smaller the closer H is to T_2, making the system more susceptible to the kind of crash just described. To be on the safe side, we should not stock too close to T_2.

This kind of possibility makes Hardin's (1968) "tragedy of the commons" all the more poignant.

(pp. 19–20)

Yodzis then describes how a similar model can be formulated to describe the population dynamics of spruce budworm (*Choristoneura fumiferana*). In the earlier chapter on disturbance, fire was discussed as the major disturbance in coniferous forests. In eastern North America, however, there are also periodic outbreaks of spruce budworm which destroy the canopy of coniferous forests every 40 years or so (Holling 1978b). Unlike with fire, understorey trees of the forest remain largely intact and immediately begin to regenerate the coniferous canopy. This produces a resource management dilemma for humans: the pulp and paper industry would like to harvest $\frac{1}{40}$th of the forest every 40 years to maintain steady production of pulp from its mills. The spruce budworm, however, has for thousands of years settled on a system where it harvests, instead, all of the trees once every 40 years. The natural response of foresters is to spray the forest with insecticides to keep the trees alive until they can be harvested. What then seems to happen is that the spruce budworm populations, instead of collapsing after destroying the trees (the normal cycle), remain at permanently high levels, which forces managers to continually spray forests. The results are that pesticide residues threaten both wildlife and humans; indeed, spraying for spruce budworm in the Acadian forests of New Brunswick was one of the classic examples of the abuse of pesticides used by Rachel Carson in *Silent Spring* (1962). Some of the more recent battles between citizens and the forest industry have been summarized in *Budworm Battles* (May 1982).

Given this background, turn to the model in Figure 7.24. This is a representation of herbivore–plant relationships that should now be familiar. In this case, the abundance of plants is represented by leaf area of the trees because this is the food factor to which budworm apparently responds. In the example of sheep herbivory, the density of herbivores is assumed to be under human control; in the case of spruce budworm it is not, and this makes the mathematics much more complicated. May (1977), however, has pointed out that the growth of budworms is much faster than the growth of trees, so for each value of P one might assume that the budworm population will be near equilibrium. Therefore, one can use intuition to get at the slow dynamics of leaf area in relation to budworm density (Figure 7.24).

If one begins at a normal, low budworm density (endemic levels), the budworm is kept under control by predators and the trees are able to grow. The system then moves slowly to the right along the solid curve as leaf area increases. Eventually threshold T_1 is reached,

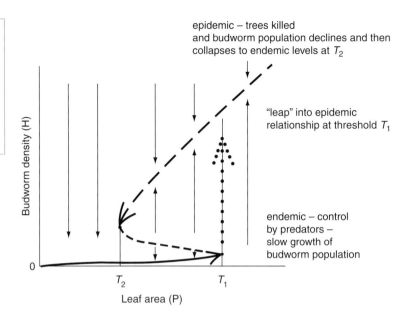

Figure 7.24 A simple model of spruce budworm (*H*, density) and balsam fir (*P*, average leaf area per unit area of forest). This yields a situation similar to that in Figure 7.23, where low endemic levels of budworm suddenly leap into epidemics at T_1 (after Yodzis 1989).

so that the budworm population is no longer in equilibrium; it will erupt to the dashed curve (epidemic levels). The trees, however, cannot withstand the grazing rate of the upper curve, and the system slides slowly back down and to the left. When the threshold T_2 is reached, there is a final crash back down to the lower line, and the process begins anew. This cycle will repeat itself and produce the natural cycles of canopy destruction and forest regeneration that have occurred for millennia. You may wish to read Yodzis's explanation (1989, pp. 104–108) of how the model can be modified to illustrate how spraying with insecticides creates a new stable equilibrium with a fatal flaw – an equilibrium that can be maintained only by continuous spraying. Worse, the model indicates that any cessation of spraying rapidly turns into a worst-case scenario where the forest is rapidly defoliated. (You may also wish to read Ludwig et al.'s (1978) more elaborate model of spruce budworm dynamics.) While the reality is that any model has its limitations, it is now believed that much of eastern Canada has been brought to exactly the situation described, with enormous economic, conservation, and health implications. Those who think that plant ecology is a quiet discipline without important human implications need only attend public hearings on the spraying of spruce budworm to discover how contentious plant ecology really is.

7.7 | Conclusion

This chapter, like so much of biology, is rooted in the careful observation of nature. Observations of herbivory raised questions about how natural selection affects plants, which, in turn, led to a brief discussion of coevolution and mutualism between plants and animals, a topic that will be examined in greater detail in the next chapter. Observations of herbivory generated the need for field experiments, particularly those that used exclosures. Exclosure experiments began with the use of simple fences, such as those shown in Figure 7.12, and advanced through the 1900s to complex multifactorial experiments such as reported in Table 7.9. Once sufficient numbers of experiments were published, it became possible to search for repeating patterns, first in a qualitative manner but then using meta-analyses such as those generated by multiple regression analysis (Table 7.12). Models then helped to further interpret the field observations and experiments.

Return to the question that was raised at the beginning of this chapter: to what extent do herbivores control properties of plant communities (e.g., composition and functions)? The evidence would seem to suggest that herbivores can occasionally have a major effect upon plant communities but that they are often far less important than flooding, drought, or competition in determining composition and function. In many cases, vegetation seems to be controlled from the bottom up: that is, the composition and structure of the vegetation determine the abundance and distribution of herbivores rather than vice versa. There are also clear exceptions, as in the case of deer.

Figure 7.25 Comparison of forage consumption by herbivores and decomposers (including fire) in a variety of African savannas, (a) moist Lamto savanna, Ivory Coast, (b) dry Serengeti savannas, Tanzania, (c) dry Nylsvley savanna, South Africa, (d) semiarid/arid savannas in Marsabit District, northern Kenya (from Deshmukh 1986).

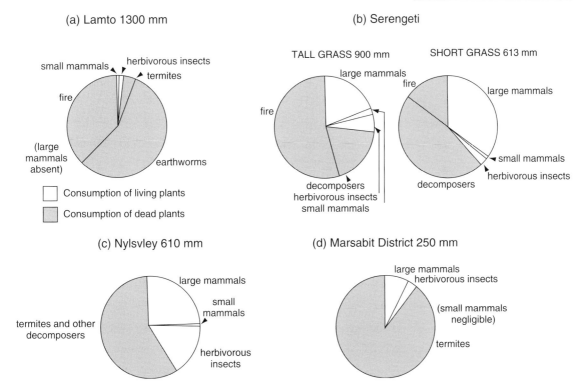

(a) Lamto 1300 mm

small mammals — herbivorous insects — termites
fire
(large mammals absent) — earthworms

☐ Consumption of living plants
▨ Consumption of dead plants

(b) Serengeti

TALL GRASS 900 mm
large mammals — fire
fire
decomposers — herbivorous insects — small mammals

SHORT GRASS 613 mm
large mammals
small mammals — herbivorous insects
decomposers

(c) Nylsvley 610 mm

large mammals
small mammals
termites and other decomposers
herbivorous insects

(d) Marsabit District 250 mm

large mammals — herbivorous insects
(small mammals negligible)
termites

It is important to be aware that herbivory is remarkably inefficient at removing biomass from plant communities. Study after study
over the past 50 years has demonstrated the same startling result: the
vast majority of plant biomass goes straight into the decomposer
food web where it is processed by small invertebrates and micro-
organisms (Figure 7.1). This generalization ranges from arid tropical
grasslands (Deshmukh 1986) to temperate salt marshes (Adam 1990)
to tundra (Oksanen et al. 1997) – although aquatic algae are an
apparent exception (Cyr and Pace 1993). Further, fire often removes
more biomass than decomposers, particularly in tall-grass areas such
as the Serengeti where more than half the biomass is burned
(Figure 7.25). Therefore, while the study of large herbivores and
their impacts on vegetation may seem appealing, one should remember that such studies often deal with animals that process less than
10 percent of the biomass of vegetation.

Plant ecologists are thus faced with three important tasks regarding the study of herbivory. The first is to document the effects of
herbivores on particular ecosystems so that the systems can be wisely
managed, the second is to determine what generalizations about
herbivores might be possible, and the third is to discover the noteworthy exceptions. There is much to be done.

Further reading

Thirgood, J. V. 1981. *Man and the Mediterranean Forest: A History of Resource
Depletion*. London: Academic Press.

Oksanen, L., S. D. Fretwell, J. Arruda, and P. Niemelä. 1981. Exploitation
ecosystems in gradients of primary productivity. *The American Naturalist*
118: 240–261.

Coley, P. D. 1983. Herbivory and defensive characteristics of tree species in a
lowland tropical forest. *Ecological Monographs* **53**: 209–233.

McNaughton, S. J. 1985. Ecology of a grazing ecosystem: the Serengeti.
Ecological Monographs **55**: 259–294.

Louda, S. M., K. H. Keller, and R. D. Holt. 1990. Herbivore influence on
plant performance and competitive interactions. pp. 413–444. In J. B.
Grace and D. Tilman (eds.) *Perspectives on Plant Competiton*. San Diego:
Academic Press.

Rosenthal, G. A. and M. R. Berenbaum. (eds.) 1991. *Herbivores: Their Interactions
with Secondary Plant Metabolites*. San Diego: Academic Press.

Marquis, R. 1991. Evolution of resistance in plants to herbivores. *Evolutionary
Trends in Plants* **5**: 23–29.

Belsky, A. J. 1992. Effects of grazing, competition, disturbance and fire on
species composition and diversity in grassland communities. *Journal of
Vegetation Science* **3**: 187–200.

Milchunas, D. G. and W. K. Laurenroth. 1993. Quantitative effects of grazing
on vegetation and soils over a global range of environments. *Ecological
Monographs* **63**: 327–366.

Cyr, H. and M. L. Pace. 1993. Magnitude and patterns of herbivory in aquatic
and terrestrial ecosystems. *Nature* **361**: 148–150.

Fleischner, T. L. 1994. Ecological costs of livestock grazing in western North America. *Conservation Biology* **8**: 629–644.

Sinclair, A. R. E., C. J. Krebs, J. M. Fryxell, R. Turkington, S. Boutin, R. Boonstra, P. Seccombe-Hett, P. Lundberg, and L. Oksanen. 2000. Testing hypotheses of trophic level interactions: a boreal forest ecosystem. *Oikos* **89**: 313–328.

McClaran, M. P. 2003. A century of vegetation change on the Santa Rita Experimental Range. pp. 16–33. In: USDA Forest Service Proceedings RMRS-P-30. US Department of Agriculture. Ogden: USDA.

Chapter 8

Positive interactions: mutualism, commensalism, and symbiosis

Mutualism, commensalism, symbiosis. Plant–plant co-operation (facilitation, protection, oxygen, shading). Plant–fungus co-operation (mycorrhizae, lichens). Plant–animal co-operation: pollination by birds, seed dispersal by animals (tapir, ants, rodents), the fates of seeds, dodos. The costs of sexual reproduction. The value of sexuality. Animals defending plants. Symbiosis in animal guts: a consequence of cellulose. Models of mutualism. Conceptual obstacles in the study of mutualism.

8.1 | Introduction

8.1.1 Definitions

Mutualism is an interaction between two species or individuals that is beneficial to both. It is, in other words, a $+/+$ interaction, in contrast with competition, which is the reverse, a $-/-$ interaction (Chapter 5). Mutualism is sometimes confused with symbiosis, but the term **symbiosis** denotes merely that two species are living together in close association. Close association is insufficient evidence for the occurrence of mutualism.

Some of the problems and issues that arise in the study of mutualism are related to those that arose in the study of competition (Chapter 5), since the same problems can arise whether one is trying to assess positive or negative interactions among individuals. Further, just as competition can be asymmetric, where one individual experiences more negative effects than the other, so too can mutualism be asymmetric. Since it is, in fact, rather unlikely that both individuals in a mutualistic relationship will receive identical benefits from the association, most mutualistic interactions probably are asymmetric. As the asymmetry becomes more extreme, the relationship tends toward a $+/0$ interaction, in which limiting case one species receives a benefit and the other appears to experience neither a cost nor a benefit from the interaction. This situation is called **commensalism**.

It is often difficult to measure precisely the degree of benefit accruing to each individual in an interaction, so there are many cases where the distinction between asymmetric mutualism and commensalism is unclear. Thus one has to use words such as "mutualism" carefully; the more general term of "positive interactions" may be preferable where the details, costs, and benefits are still unknown. It will become apparent that very few studies have actually measured the benefits of mutualistic interactions, so such limitations will have to be borne in mind in most of the rest of this chapter.

8.1.2 History

One of the earliest uses of the term mutualism was in Pierre van Benden's 1875 book *Les Commensaux et les Parasites* (Boucher et al. 1982). Van Benden recognized many now classic examples of mutualism, including pollination and root-nodulation on legumes. Less than 20 years later the subject of mutualism was reviewed in *The American Naturalist* by Pound (1893). Mutualism also received prominence in *Principles of Animal Ecology*, co-written in 1949 by Warder Allee, a Quaker and pacifist, who in 1951 added a second book, *Cooperation Among Animals with Human Implications* (Allee et al. 1949, Allee 1951). More than 30 years later, Boucher (1985a) compiled an overview that included 15 papers, ranging from the natural history of mutualism (Janzen 1985) to cost-benefit models (Keeler 1985). It remains an important source for those planning to contribute new work to this field.

In spite of more than a century of activity, mutualism has been repeatedly given less attention than interactions such as competition and predation (Table 8.1). There is probably a positive feedback loop

Table 8.1. *The impressions given to students regarding the importance of the three major ecological interactions in the biosphere, as assessed by the number of pages on the topic referred to in the index of some textbooks on ecology (from Keddy 1989).*

Textbook	Mutualism	Competition	Predation
Colinvaux (1986)	1	33	70
Collier et al. (1973)	0 (1)[a]	45	30
Huchinson (1978)	0 (9)	59	6
Krebs (1978)	3	50	32
Lederer (1984)	5	21	4
McNaughton and Wolf (1979)	20	77	71
Odum (1983)	15	17	15
Pianka (1983)	3	74	41
Ricklefs (1979)	3	38	30
Ricklefs (1983)	2	11	14
Smith (1986)	2[b] (1)	19	24
Whittaker (1975)	5 (9)	18	22

Notes:
[a] The number in parentheses is symbiosis, which some authors equate with mutualism.
[b] Mutualism not in index, but present in text.

at work here. Students read less about mutualism, so fewer elect to study it, so fewer examples are published, and so there is less to read about it … and so on. Rather than accept this imbalance, let us pay particular attention to the topic. Consider that it may be most profitable to focus your attention on an area that is little known, rather than looking for problems that are currently popular.

One simple way to break mutualism down into categories is to consider the species involved. There are, for example, plant–plant, plant–fungus, plant–animal, and plant–microbe interactions. The latter three classes are particularly well documented; there are fewer clear examples of plant–plant mutualism, although there are many good examples of plant–plant commensalism.

8.2 | Positive interactions between plants and plants

Plants growing near one another are likely to be drawing from the same pool of resources, and this negative interaction is likely to overwhelm any benefits they might provide to one another. For this reason, plant ecologists have been relatively sceptical about the likelihood of mutual interactions among plants. On the other hand, during early stages of succession, when physical factors are severe, there is evidence at least of commensalism (Clements 1916, Connell and Slatyer 1977, Bertness and Hacker 1994). In this situation, the term "facilitation" is sometimes used instead of "commensalism", emphasizing that one species facilitates invasion by another.

What about the experimental evidence: does it suggest mutualism or commensalism among plants? The first body of evidence is likely to come from environments where there are strong physical constraints upon plant growth, such as deserts, where neighbors may help ameliorate the physical conditions. Here the phenomenon of "nurse plants" is now well established. The second body of evidence, oddly enough, comes from experimental studies of competition, where negative competition provides evidence of positive interaction among neighbors. Examine these in turn.

8.2.1 Nurse plants

In arid environments, shade from neighboring plants may promote the establishment of seedlings. The massive columnar saguaro cactus (*Carnegiea gigantea*), conspicuous in the Sonoran Desert of Arizona, California and Mexico (Figure 8.1), requires shade at the seedling stage. A study of 3299 transplanted saguaro seedlings that were approximately 12 mm high (Turner et al. 1966) reported that all 1200 unshaded plants died within 1 year, whereas 35 percent of the shaded plants survived that period. In addition, seedlings in darker soils had higher mortality rates than those in lighter-colored soils, probably because of the higher temperature reached by dark-colored soil.

Figure 8.1 Saguaro cactus grove in the Sonoran Desert (Saguaro National Monument) where cacti reach 15 m tall. Note the hole drilled in the central plant by a woodpecker or flicker (George A. Grant, courtesy of the U.S. National Parks Service).

The critical time for seedlings was the hot dry period just before the beginning of summer rain. Shrubs such as palo verde (*Cercidium microphyllum*) and creosote bush (*Larrea tridentata*) are therefore termed nurse plants because they protect saguaro seedlings until they are old enough to survive on their own in full sunlight. Turner et al. thought that young saguaros probably become independent from their nurse plant at 5–10 years of age when the saguaro would be 10–15 cm tall. In environments lacking shrubs, they suggest that seedlings may survive by growing on the shaded sides of rocks.

Saguaro regeneration is also reduced by seed predators. Steenbergh and Lowe (1969) observed that a large proportion of the seed crop is consumed in June by birds while the fruit is still on the plant. Doves, thrashers, cactus wrens, woodpeckers, and flickers were all conspicuous consumers. By July, ripe fruits had fallen to the ground where birds, mammals, and insects consumed them. In the early summer, coyote droppings consisted almost entirely of saguaro seeds. Ants also collected seeds. (Regrettably, to what extent these agents disperse seeds rather than destroy them was not discussed.) After germination, seedlings are killed by weevils, cutworms, and moth larvae. Beyond these effects of predators and herbivores, drought (80 percent), frost (12 percent) and erosion (8 percent) were the main causes of seedling death.

Franco and Nobel (1989) extended the work on nurse plants and saguaro in several ways. First, they showed that a second species of cactus, *Ferocactus acanthodes* (barrel cactus), is associated with the perennial bunch grass, *Hilaria rigida*. The *F. acanthodes* seedlings could tolerate higher temperatures, however, and thus 30 percent of the seedlings were able to survive without nurse plants. Second,

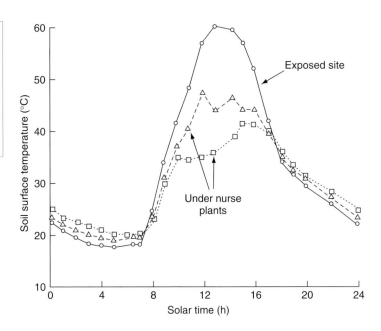

Figure 8.2 Effect of nurse plants on soil temperature shown by the daily course of soil surface temperatures at an exposed location (○) and at the centers of representative *Ambrosia deltoidea* (△) and representative *Cercicium microphyllum* (□) plants on a clear day (after Franco and Nobel 1989).

Franco and Nobel provided added detail on the effects of nurse plants upon the physical environment. On a clear day in the autumn, soil temperatures exceeded 60 °C compared with 47.4 °C or 41.4 °C under nurse plants (Figure 8.2). Daily variation in temperature was also lower under nurse plants. Total soil nitrogen levels were higher under nurse plants. Nurse plants may also reduce the growth rates of seedlings through competition. Based upon effects of temperature, light, and water upon net CO_2 uptake, Franco and Nobel estimated that the depletion of light and water by the nurse plant reduced the growth of *F. acanthodes* seedlings by one-third. These effects, however, may be offset by the greater availability of soil nitrogen.

The beneficial effects of nurse plants have been established elsewhere. *Opuntia* cacti in the Mojave Desert are associated with nurse plant species such as *H. rigida* as well as with other opuntias (Cody 1993). Kellman and Kading (1992) have shown that young pine trees establish better beneath oak trees during sand dune succession in Ontario. In Belize, Kellman (1985) transplanted seedlings of *Xylopia frutescens*, a small tree of thickets, and *Calophyllum brasiliense*, a large rain forest species, to different sites and monitored growth for 3 years. "In both species survivorship and growth of seedlings was superior beneath tree covers and it was unlikely that any open-grown plant would survive to reproduce" (p. 373). Thus, even when savanna habitats are protected from fire, establishment of forest tree seedlings apparently requires the existence of other woody savanna plants to act as nurse trees. Those trees able to use nurse plants are likely to establish the first generation of forest after fire suppression. In the evergreen scrub of central Chile known as matorral, herbaceous plants are clumped beneath shrubs. Jaksic and Fuentes (1980) experimentally removed the shrub canopy from some plots and in others prevented grazing with enclosures. In this habitat, introduced rabbits grazed seedlings outside the shrub canopy.

In conclusion, neighboring plants may produce beneficial effects, particularly in habitats where temperature or grazing is an important environmental constraint (Kellman and Kading 1992). There are likely to be strong trade-offs; any benefits from shade or protection from herbivores have to exceed the costs of increased competition for light and water. Thus it may be expected that nurse plants will be most common where environmental stress is high. The beneficial effect of neighbors may also be a common feature of primary succession. Connell and Slatyer (1977) have emphasized, following Clements (1916), that "facilitation" may be one of the important ecological interactions during primary succession.

However compelling such work seems to be, there is a possible limitation upon these sorts of studies. Returning to the example of the saguaro cactus, one must not forget that this is a very long-lived species and most studies of nurse plants last for only one or a few years. Age distribution analysis of saguaro plants in the Sonoran Desert (Turner 1990) showed that during the period 1790–1960 there were three surges of establishment. Not surprisingly, perhaps, these were periods of abnormal wetness. The most recent surge of establishment, detected in 1974, can be traced back to two unusually intense rainfalls, associated with Tropical Storm Norma (1970) and Hurricane Joanne (1972), rains which in some cases produced temporary lakes and berms of organic debris on receding shorelines. Similarly, the declines observed in saguaro populations during the 1950s were likely related to a quarter century of drought, during which *Larrea* and *Cercidium* cover as well as saguaro establishment declined. It would therefore be possible to argue that the size of saguaro populations is largely a result of long-term and large-scale climatic factors – death during long droughts and brief episodes of establishment during moist periods. In this scenario, nurse plants may be a secondary phenomenon in which ecologists observe seedlings establishing next to neighbors during their brief periods of research, but where a vast majority of the recruitment actually occurs as rarely as once or twice a century.

8.2.2 Stress gradients and competition

Recall from Chapter 5 that a standard design of competition experiments is to grow plants with and without neighbors in order to measure the depression in performance caused by neighbors (recall Chapter 4). The greater the depression caused by neighbors, the higher the intensity of competition. The same experiment can, however, find the unexpected: removing neighbors may produce negative rather than positive results. In the first experiment measuring competition intensity along a gradient, Wilson and Keddy (1986a) studied an exposure gradient on a lakeshore running from open wave-washed sand beaches to sheltered bays where silt and clay accumulated. They found a significant increase in competition intensity from beaches to bays. However, the experiment showed a second unexpected result: the most extreme sites on the wave-washed beaches had negative competition intensity, suggesting that the surrounding vegetation actually protected the transplanted individuals from waves or sunlight.

When this design of experiment was repeated using 60 quadrats equally divided between an open sunny beach and a densely vegetated bay, there was again a significant increase in the intensity of competition from beach to bay (Figure 5.26). Similarly, there were many points showing negative competition intensity. This figure was constructed using two test species simultaneously: the native sedge *Carex crinita* and the invasive gap-colonizer *Lythrum salicaria*. The sedge was more sensitive to the gradient, and if one examines its response to neighbors along the gradient (Figure 8.3(a)) it is obvious that many points lie below zero, and the majority of these are in the low biomass sites (that is, the sites with low fertility and high disturbance from waves). Points with a competition intensity value of −0.5 indicate that *C. crinita* grew 50 percent better with neighbors than without. Since this experiment was also designed to measure above- and below-ground effects, Figure 8.3 also shows that the beneficial effects of neighbors can be found both above (Figure 8.3 (b)) and below (Figure 8.3(c)) ground. These results clearly show that positive interactions can be detected, and that their occurrence and intensity increase with increased physical constraints upon plant growth.

There is one other habitat with prominent physical control – salt marshes. Bertness and Hacker (1994) therefore used the elevation gradient in a salt marsh to test for changes in positive effects with physical stress. The intensity of stress increases with falling elevation, since wave damage, hypoxia, and salinity all increase with tidal flooding. The typical zonation on such shorelines consists of *Iva frutescens* at high elevations and *Juncus gerardi* at low elevations, with a mixed zone in between (Figure 8.4(a)). In each zone, the *Iva* and *Juncus* were planted with and without neighbors. At the high elevation, the growth of both *Iva* and *Juncus* was depressed by neighbors, showing the presence of competition; at the two lower elevations, by contrast, both species benefited from the presence of neighbors. Apparently, at lower elevations, the canopy provided by neighbors reduces evaporation and therefore reduces salinity.

8.2.3 More cases of co-operation

Bertness and Yeh (1994) studied recruitment in the marsh elder (*Iva frutescens*), and found it was influenced by both negative and positive interactions with adult plants. Perennial vegetation usually prevented seedlings from establishing. Adult *Iva* plants first accumulated plant debris that killed the other perennial species, and then protected *Iva* seedlings from radiation and hypersaline soil

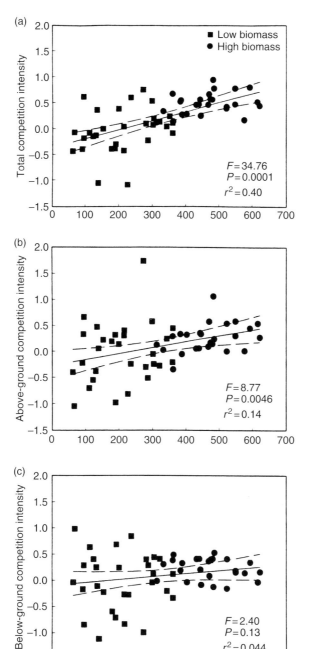

Figure 8.3 The relationship between standing crop and (a) total competition intensity, (b) above-ground competition intensity and (c) below-ground competition intensity using *Carex crinita*. Broken lines give 95 percent confidence bands (from Twolan-Strutt and Keddy 1996).

conditions. Recruitment, they conclude, is dictated by a balance between co-operative and competitive interactions.

The oxygen transported by aerenchyma into hypoxic sediments may also contribute to positive interactions. Callaway and King (1996) showed that under cool conditions (11–12 °C) *Typha latifolia* transported oxygen into sediments, raising oxygen levels from

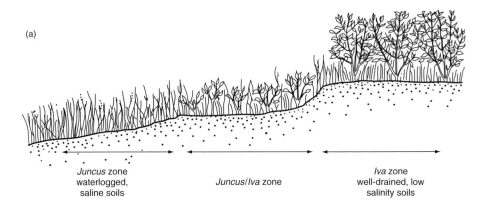

(a)

Juncus zone
waterlogged,
saline soils

Juncus/Iva zone

Iva zone
well-drained, low
salinity soils

Figure 8.4 (a) A schematic diagram of the terrestrial border of a typical New England salt marsh illustrating the major vegetation zones and physical conditions considered in this study. (b) Results of an experiment in which adult *Iva frutescens* and *Juncus gerardi* were transplanted across the terrestrial border of the marsh with and without neighbours. (1) Soil surface salinity (pooled monthly, June–August; $n = 30$/case, +SE) taken adjacent to each transplant; (2) total *Iva* leaf counts 4 months after transplantation; and (3) dried above-ground *Juncus* biomass 4 months after transplantation. For each location and treatment, the data are means of 10 transplants (+SE) (from Bertness and Hacker 1994).

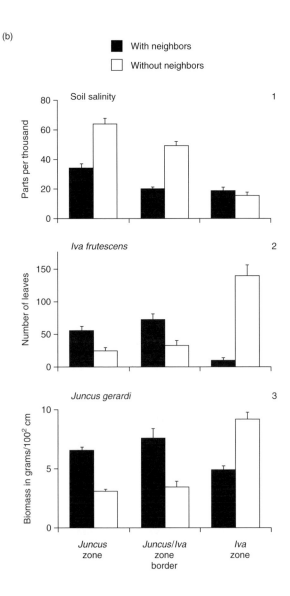

(b)

■ With neighbors
□ Without neighbors

$1\,\mathrm{mg\cdot l^{-1}}$ to near $4\,\mathrm{mg\cdot l^{-1}}$. Enhanced survival of *Salix exigua* and enhanced growth of *Myosotis laxa* were attributed to these increased oxygen concentrations. At higher temperatures, however, the dissolved oxygen levels fell to control amounts, suggesting a shift from facilitation to competition as temperature increased.

In related work, Pedersen et al. (1995) report that the evergreen rosette plant *Lobelia dortmanna*, already known to absorb CO_2 from the rooting zone (Chapter 3), also releases oxygen into the sediment during photosynthesis. This is slightly different from the above case, the oxygen release by *Lobelia* being a by-product of photosynthesis rather than atmospheric oxygen transported by aerenchyma. Such a release of oxygen from roots could lead to aerobic degradation of organic matter, conditions suitable for mycorrhizae, and an aerobic fauna associated with the roots, all of which could be beneficial to other plants. Apparently *Lobelia* roots indeed have arbuscular mycorrhizae and are devoid of root hairs; the mycorrhizae may assist with phosphorus uptake, since the solubility of phosphorus declines under aerobic conditions. Thus, according to Pedersen et al., the release of oxygen into the sediment may produce the benefits of aerobic decomposition and enable the occurrence of mycorrhizae, but the mycorrhizae may be necessary precisely because of the low solubility of phosphorus and loss of nitrogen by denitrification, both caused by the increased oxygen concentrations.

8.2.4 Summary

All the examples above show that plants can have positive effects upon other plants, and that the importance of these positive effects is greatest in extreme environments: deserts, wave-washed beaches, and salt marshes. None of these examples, however, provides conclusive evidence of mutualism; rather, one species benefits from the presence of an already established species ameliorating the environment. This is most likely asymmetric mutualism, perhaps so extreme as to be commensalism. If the plants being "nursed" actually damage their hosts when they eventually become adults and compete with them, it might even be better to term these interactions as parasitism. Short-term measurements of benefits are insufficient to resolve the long-term consequences for the species involved.

These observations make sense if one returns to the original premise (Chapter 5) that similar-sized neighbors likely deplete resources from a common pool. In such circumstances, it is difficult to imagine a positive interaction that could override the obvious negative consequences of competition. If, however, the individuals differed sufficiently from one another, say in size, it might be possible for the smaller to grow upon or beneath the larger, possibly using small patches of resources that are unavailable to (or relatively unimportant to) the larger. This ties in nicely with what is known of competition, that coexistence is most likely to occur at one of two extremes: completely equal or highly unequal competitive abilities (Figure 8.5).

Figure 8.5 Does similarity produce competitive exclusion or coexistence? The answer in part depends upon just how similar two species are. If the species are very similar (left) there is coexistence because the species are so similar that competitive abilities are equivalent and symmetric. Decreasing similarity leads to dominance and competitive exclusion (middle). If the species are sufficiently different, then there is coexistence through resource partitioning or amensalism (right). The bottom figures represent the situations pictorally by sketching possible interactions between barnacles of different sizes on a rock surface; the solid arrows indicate the effect of each competitor upon the other (from Keddy 1989).

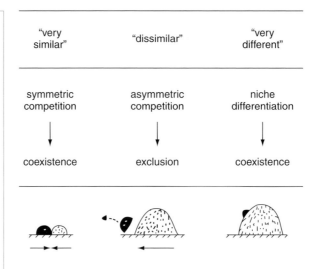

"very similar"	"dissimilar"	"very different"
symmetric competition	asymmetric competition	niche differentiation
↓	↓	↓
coexistence	exclusion	coexistence

Once one looks for examples of commensalism, many more examples can be found, particularly among the much larger number of plants which grow as epiphytes or which depend upon the shade of forest canopies for their survival; in both cases, the interaction is probably strongly asymmetric or commensal. Consistent with Figure 8.5, both epiphytes and understorey plants are much smaller than the canopy trees with which they are associated.

8.3 | Positive interactions between fungi and plants

8.3.1 Ectomycorrhizae and endomycorrhizae

In soils where nutrients are available in low concentrations, fungi provide a vital means of enhancing rates of nutrient uptake. In general, it seems that fungi provide trees with phosphorus (and possibly nitrogen), and in return receive carbohydrates from the trees (Read et al. 1976, Francis and Read 1984, Smith and Douglas 1987, Marschner 1995) (Section 3.4.3). Once thought to be relatively uncommon, it is now clear that mycorrhizae are found in most groups of plants and most habitats. Exceptions include families such as the Chenopodiaceae and Proteaceae.

There are two main groups of mycorrhizae: endomycorrhizae and ectomycorrhizae (Woodward and Kelly 1997, Raven et al. 2005). The former are far more common, occurring in about 80 percent of all vascular plants. Endomycorrhizal fungi are zygomycetes, belonging to the Glomales which contains fewer than 200 mycorrhizal species in the world. Endomycorrhizae appear to be particularly important in the tropics. Ectomycorrhizae, in contrast, are more taxonomically diverse, and most characteristic of temperate zone trees, particularly members of the Fagaceae and Pinaceae, but also including *Eucalyptus* and *Nothofagus*. The Ericaceae and Orchidaceae (recall Figure 3.18) appear to be exceptions to the above generalizations, having rather more specialized relationships with fungi.

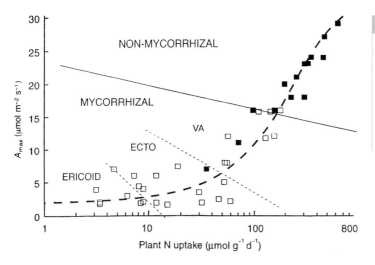

Figure 8.6 The relationship between the uptake rate of nitrogen, the maximum rate of photosynthesis, and mycorrhizal association (VA, vesicular-arbuscular mychorrhizae; ECTO, ectomycorrhizae; ERICOID, ericoid endomycorrhizae) (from Woodward and Kelly 1997).

While the benefits of mycorrhizal associations are often empha-sized, there are also costs. Most mutualisms have both. In the case of mycorrhizae, the benefits are now more or less obvious: the ability to extract nutrients that would otherwise be unavailable, or at least to increase rates of extraction of these nutrients. Further, by using a network comprised of fungal hyphae to extract nutrients, a tree need not allocate as much tissue to roots; hence, stubby roots are often associated with mycorrhizae. As to costs, there is the obvious one – the carbohydrates extracted from the tree to support the fungus. These costs would appear to be substantial, an inference to be drawn from those situations where nitrogen uptake and plant growth are high, and plants do not have mycorrhizae (Figure 8.6). Or, to express it in another way, the highest rates of growth are found in non-mycorrhizal plants in fertile soils. As soil resources decrease, the benefits of mycorrhizae tend to outweigh their costs. To re-emphasize this, the presence of ectomycorrhizae, for example, does not allow plants to grow faster than non-mycorrhizal plants, but it does allow them to grow in habitats that lie outside the tolerance limits of non-mycorrhizal plants. Shrubs in the Ericaceae occupy extremely infertile soils and peat bogs where, in spite of ericoid mycorrhizae, they have extremely low rates of nutrient uptake and inherently low rates of photosynthesis. The relative costs of mycor-rhizal fungi appear to increase from arbuscular mycorrhizae (VA Figure 8.6) through ectomycorrhizae to ericoid mycorrhizae, since each in turn is associated with more extreme conditions of infertility.

Phosphorus has a limited mobility in soils (recall Table 3.5), and it is thought that the rate of movement of phosphorus to plants is limited by rates of diffusion in the soil solution rather than by the ability of roots to absorb phosphorus at low concentrations. Although most soil phosphorus is found in soil organic matter, the approxi-mately 1 percent in solution is the available pool for which most plants must forage (Bolan 1991). This inorganic form consists of

Box 8.1 | The discovery of mycorrhizae by Bernard Frank

It is now understood that most terrestrial plants are unable to survive without the assistance rendered by their associated root fungi, but regrettably, their discoverer did not live to see the wide acceptance of his work. First we must sketch the terrain: Albert Bernard Frank was born in Dresden Germany in 1839. This was a time of turmoil in Germany; in earlier wars, Napoleon had seized territory east of the Rhine and established the Rhine Confederation. It was only in 1813 that allied German troops had driven French troops out of Leipzig, ending French domination of central Europe. Beginning in 1848, revolution came, in part driven by crop failures from Ireland to Russia. It was this year that Karl Marx and Friedrich Engels published the Communist Manifesto, ending eloquently "The proletarians have nothing to lose but their chains. They have a world to win. Workers of the world, unite." Bitter street fights broke out in Berlin, and there was outright insurrection in Paris. By 1862, King William had given the autocratic Otto von Bismarck a free hand to defeat the liberals in the legislature. In spite of these difficult times, Frank obtained his Ph.D in Leipzig in 1865, roughly half a century after French troops had been defeated there, and went on to study a series of botanical problems, including heliotropism, and diseases of beets and grains, although he is now best known for his work on mycorrhizae. Beginning in 1883, he published a series of papers that laid the foundation for the study of fungal associations with plant roots. The following account comes largely from a review by Hatch (1937) published in the obscure *Black Rock Forest Bulletin*.

Having first documented their occurrence in 1883, thereby generating a "storm of criticism" (Hatch 1937, p. 29), Frank followed up in 1887 by distinguishing in "Ueber neue Mycorhizerformen" a new type of mycorrhizal infection, endomycorrhizae. The intracellular infection associated with endo[tropic] mycorrhizae is found in many deciduous forest trees and shrubs including *Fraxinus, Acer, Ulmus, Cornus, Pyrus, Viburnum, Platanus, Juglans, Taxus*. The vociferous opposition to his discoveries gradually subsided, presumably as "most of those participants found, on more careful examination, that fungus roots were abundant" (p. 34). By 1900, the year of his death, another German botanist, Ernest Stahl, published "a thorough study of root condition in the entire plant kingdom" (p. 35), concluding that mycorrhizae were particularly important in infertile soils. Yet long after Frank's death, debate continued, with botanists such as W. B. McDougall repeatedly asserting (ca. 1914–1928) that mycorrhizae, although produced in many plants, were "infrequent, abnormal and pathological structures" (p. 34). Such assertions were sometimes based upon little more than the lack of fleshy fungi associated with trees, the careless assumption being that mushrooms yielded reliable evidence on the existence of mycorrhizae. These sorts of intemperate criticisms delayed the onset of more thorough studies of mycorrhizae until the latter half of the twentieth century, and temporarily robbed Frank of credit for his pioneering work.

varying proportions of phosphates of iron, aluminium and calcium, usually adsorbed onto the surfaces of soil particles. Mycorrhizae have been shown to increase the uptake of phosphorus by plants, particularly from poorly soluble phosphorus sources such as iron and aluminium phosphate. Three mechanisms have been suggested for the increased rates of uptake: exploration of a larger soil volume, faster movement of phosphorus into mycorrhizal hyphae and solubilization of soil phosphorus (Bolan 1991). The latter term refers to the suggestion that mycorrhizae may modify the root environment by exuding hydrogen ions, chelating agents or phosphatase; there is little experimental evidence for such modification.

8.3.2 Ectomycorrhizae and forests

Changes in forest composition along gradients are obvious, and have been well-studied (Chapter 10); changes in their associated fungi are little known or appreciated. Perhaps this is because fungi tend to be buried within the soil or within the tissue of hosts, their presence only being obvious when reproductive structures are present. Yet, mycorrhizal fungi may be the key to forest production. Assuming that one makes the effort to identify both trees and fruiting fungi, the observed positive associations between fruiting bodies and tree species do not prove mutualism is occurring. Such observations only generate the hypothesis that such an interaction is operative. Fungi in forests may be saprophytes, parasites, or mycorrhizal, so the nature of any association between a tree and a fungus is not self-evident. Indeed, it is even possible the pattern of fungi and trees may be independently controlled by physical factors such as soil moisture or depth of humus. The principle is the same as found in the analysis of pattern in vascular plants. One can hypothesize that certain plants are positively associated, one can then do the sampling and the statistical test (e.g., association analysis) to determine if the pattern is statistically significant, but one still cannot say for certain why the positive association occurs without more work.

Some studies have sought to tease apart some of these relationships by explicitly beginning with mycorrhizae. At 11 permanent sample stations, Nantel and Neuman (1992) sampled forest vegetation, the characteristics of the physical environment, and the production of Basidiomycete fungi that were probably ectomycorrhizal. The dry mass of the fungi was used to measure species composition. Some 240 species of ectomycorrhizal Basidiomycetes were recovered, and about half of these could be identified (illustrating the problem of fungal taxonomy and identification that bedevil such research). Unidentified species belonged mostly in the genera *Cortinarius* and *Russula*, as well as the Entolomaceae. Ordination (Section 10.5) was then used to explore the relationships between fungi, trees, and the physical environment. By looking for patterns between fungi and soils while correcting for changes in the tree communities, Nantel and Neuman found some evidence that the Basidiomycetes themselves were controlled by soil factors such as thickness of soil horizons, percent organic matter, nutrient richness of the mineral soil, soil moisture, and pH. Overall, however, they conclude that the patterns they found in the fungi were generally explainable from their biotic interactions with the trees (Table 8.2). The coniferous tree genera had fungal associates different from angiosperms and from one another. For example, the genus *Hygrophorus* was found mainly in *Fagus-Acer* forest, whereas *Leccinum scabrum* was associated only with *Abies*. Other genera such as *Russula* were widely spread across vegetation types, although individual species appeared to differentiate among tree species; *R. fragilis* was found with *Abies balsamea*, whereas *R. roseipes* was with *Picea mariana*.

The limitations in the study above illustrate many of the difficulties in working with symbiotic relationships among plants and fungi under natural conditions:

1. Only half of the fungi could be identified.
2. The fungi were identified only by the presence of their reproductive structures; species that did not sexually reproduce would not be detected.
3. Abundance of fungi was estimated by dry weight of fruiting bodies (mushrooms); there may be little relationship between the physiological activity or biomass of the hyphal networks and the number of mushrooms produced.
4. The production of fungi fruiting bodies varies greatly from one year to the next, and this study examined only two growing seasons.
5. Not all sites were sampled the same year, so that among-year variation could be confounded with between-site variation.
6. There were only 11 stands, and the number of plants and environmental factors greatly outnumbered the sampling stations, which creates difficulties with multivariate techniques.
7. While ordination is a useful tool for describing patterns in vegetation (Section 10.5), it is doubtfully able to distinguish among multiple pathways of causation, in spite of the fact that it is often used in this way.

This list is not intended to criticize this study, but rather to illustrate the difficulties that deter the study of fungus–plant relationships. Of course, so long as scientists choose the easy problems, the tough problems will continue to be ignored, so there are fine opportunities available for those willing to learn about native plants and native fungi. While the knowledge of relationships between mycorrhizal fungi and selected commercial tree species is growing, much less is known about distributions in nature and the complexity of interactions there. This is all the more remarkable when one considers that forest production may be closely related to the ability of fungi to absorb nutrients for trees.

8.3:3 Mycorrhizae in wetlands

In contrast with forests, mycorrhizae may be much less important in wetlands. The main reason seems to be that the lack of oxygen in flooded conditions inhibits the growth of most fungi. A review of the

Table 8.2. *Fungal and tree species associations defined statistically by complete linkage clustering using the chi-square similarity coefficient and importance values of species. To define these associations, the minimum similarity for clusters was arbitrarily fixed at 0.9700. The associations are not necessarily mutualistic (from Nantel and Neumann 1992).*

Cluster	Basidiomycete species	Tree species
1	*Amanita brunnescens*	*Pinus strobus* (tree)
	Suillus granulatus	*Pinus strobus* (sapling)
		Populus grandidentata (sapling)
2	*Amanita porphyria*	*Picea mariana* (tree)
	Russula paludosa	
	Leccinum insigne	
	Russula roseipes	
3	*Amanita citrina*	*Acer rubrum* (sapling)
	Boletus piperatus	*Populus grandidentata* (tree)
	Russula raoultii	*Populus tremuloides* (tree)
4	*Amanita virosa*	*Betula papyrifera* (sapling)
	Cortinarius evernius	*Betula papyrifera* (seedling)
	Russula peckii	
	Clavulina cristata	
	Hebeloma testaceum	
5	*Amanita flavoconia*	*Abies balsamea* (seedling)
	Leccinum scabrum	*Abies balsamea* (sapling)
	Russula fragilis	*Abies balsamea* (tree)
	Russula puellaris	
6	*Amanita fulva*	*Betula papyrifera* (tree)
	Hebeloma sp.	*Populus tremuloides* (tree)
	Russula silvicola	
7	*Hygrophorus laetus*	*Acer rubrum* (seedling)
	Hygrophorums unguinosus	*Populus grandidentata* (tree)
	Nolanea strictior	
	Rozites caperata	
	Boletinus pictus	*Picea glauca* (tree)
	Cortinarius bolaris	*Betula alleghaniensis* (seedling)
	Hygrophorus nitidus	
	Xerocomus subtomentosus	
	Lactarius sordidus	
	Cortinarius flexipes	*Picea glauca* (seedling)
	Cortinarius vibratilis	*Thuja occidentalis* (seedling)
	Hygrophorus miniatus	*Thuja occidentalis* (seedling)
	Leptonia formosa	*Thuja occidentalis* (tree)
	Laccaria laccata	*Picea glauca* (tree)
	Lactarius thyinos	*Betula alleghaniensis* (seedling)
10	*Amanita muscaria*	*Acer saccharum* (seedling)
	Hygrophorus marginatus	*Acer saccharum* (sapling)
	Hygrophorus pallidus	*Acer saccharum* (tree)
	Hygrophorus ceraceus	*Fagus grandifolia* (seedling)

Table 8.2.	(cont.)	
Cluster	Basidiomycete species	Tree species
11	Hygrophorus parvulus Hygrophorus pratensis Paxillus involutus Lactarius lignyotus Leccinum holopus Tylopilus felleus	Pinus strobus (seedling) Picea glauca (tree) Betula alleghaniensis (seedling) Betula alleghaniensis (sapling) Betula papyrifera (tree)
12	Cantharellus cibarius Hebeloma mesophaeum Lactarius glyciosmus Russula claroflava Inocybe umbrina Cortinarius armillatus	Populus grandidentata (seedling) Fagus grandifolia (seedling)
13	Clavulinopsis fusiformis Hygrophorus cantharellus Nolanea lutea Nolanea quadrata Lactarius thejogalus Ramariopsis kunzei Russula cyanoxantha	Betula alleghaniensis (sapling) Acer pennsylvanicum (seedling) Acer rubrum (tree) Betula papyrifera (tree)

distribution of arbuscular mycorrhizae in 843 species in the British flora (Peat and Fitter 1993) yielded two important results for this chapter. First, mycorrhizae are relatively uncommon in wetlands (Figure 8.7), fewer than 50 percent of the plants having mycorrhizae, excepting wet forests where slightly more than 50 percent of the flora is infected. In contrast, in coniferous forest more than 90 percent of the species are infected. Assuming that mycorrhizae are important in augmenting nutrient uptake from infertile soils, it would then seem that this option is not available to many wetland plants. Hence, one may speculate that soil nutrient supplies are even more important in wetlands than in terrestrial habitats. (Might the constraints on mycorrhizae, say, account for the frequency of carnivorous plants in wet as opposed to dry soils?) But Peat and Fitter also found little evidence to support the assumed relationships between mycorrhizae and soil fertility. Percent infection was in the 80 percent range across all soil fertility levels, and, if anything, the abundance of mycorrhizae increased with soil fertility. When the Cyperaceae (an important family in wetlands which often occupies infertile habitats but seems largely non-mycorrhizal) were removed from the analysis, there was no significant relationship between occurrence of mycorrhizae and soil fertility.

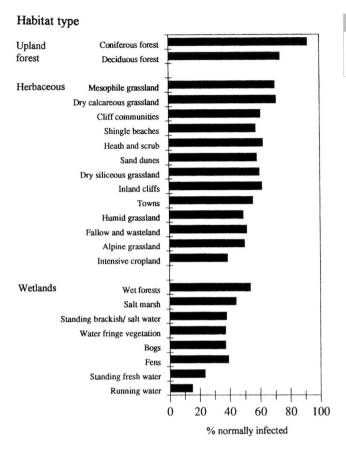

Figure 8.7 The relative abundance of mycorrhizal infection in different habitats (from data in Peat and Fitter 1993).

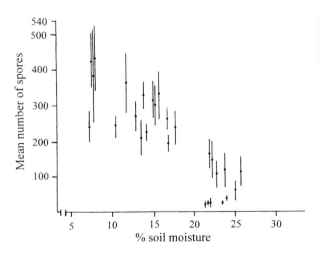

Figure 8.8 Spore counts of arbuscular mycorrhizae plotted against soil moisture in prairie vegetation. One outlier has been removed (after Anderson et al. 1983).

One cannot, of course, generalize from the British flora to the world flora, but this is one of the largest datasets systematically explored. In actual assays in the field, Anderson et al. (1983, 1984) found that the density of spores of mycorrhizal fungi declined with increased soil moisture (Figure 8.8). Rickerl et al. (1994) found that mycorrhizal infection declined with flooding (27 percent infection in dry areas versus less than 1 percent in wet areas), with *Carex atherodes* and *Juncus tenuis* being entirely uninfected. *Scirpus fluviatilis* was non-mycorrhizal in wet sites, but slightly colonized (9 percent infection) in dry areas. In dry areas, but not wet ones, there was also evidence that infection was correlated with the amount of phosphorus in plant tissues. In freshwater marshes, Bauer et al. (2003) found mycorrhizal colonization levels of 3–90 percent, but no trend in infection with hydrologic zone. The level of mycorrhizal colonization of wetland plants may be related to oxygen release by their roots (e.g., *Lobelia dortmanna*, Section 8.2.3).

In summary, it appears that the anoxic conditions in wetlands not only directly stress wetland plants but also inhibit the occurrence of mycorrhizae. Another explanation for low infection rates could be that mycorrhizae exist not, as is commonly assumed, to increase access to soil nutrients, but to increase access to water; in the case of wetland plants, access to soil moisture is obviously not a problem requiring an evolutionary solution. The questions as to why mycorrhizae are least common in wetland plants, and how mycorrhizal and non-mycorrhizal species of plants coexist, still require study.

8.3.4 Costs and benefits of mycorrhizal associations

The measurement of the costs and benefits of mycorrhizal associations requires measurements of transport between partners (Keeler 1985). Smith and Douglas (1987) provide a particularly readable account of interactions between mycorrhizae and their hosts. With respect to the cost of mycorrhizae, little is known, since it is their benefits that have received most interest from scientists. Radioactive-labeled sucrose has been shown to move from plant tissues to fungi in laboratory experiments, but field measurements are considerably more difficult to make. Nonetheless, a few conclusions have been reached. In spruce (*Picea*) forests, carbohydrate consumption by ecto-mycorrhizae is equivalent to some 10 percent of net production. In beech (*Fagus*) forests, ectomycorrhizae account for roughly one-quarter of respiration by beech root systems. These costs are balanced by enhanced rates of growth.

The benefits of mycorrhizae can be assayed using isotopes of nitrogen and phosphorus to document both nutrient uptake by fungi and the consequent movement of nutrients into plant tissues (Smith and Douglas 1987). When $^{32}PO_4$ is added to soil it can appear in tree tissues within 2 days. Two or more plants can be connected by intervening hyphae, and both carbohydrates and mineral nutrients can move from one host to another. The rates of transfer can exceed $20 \, \text{cm} \, \text{h}^{-1}$ for ^{14}C-labeled carbohydrates, particularly if the receiving plant is shaded (Figure 8.9).

To illustrate the importance of careful measurement before designating two partners as mutualistic, consider the Indian Pipe (*Monotropa*) that is generally described as a saprophyte. However,

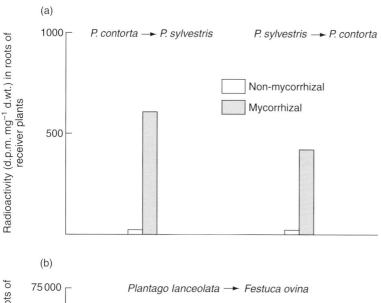

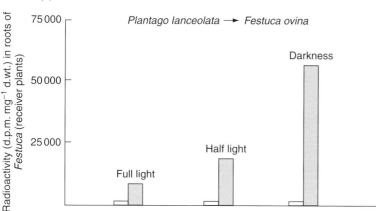

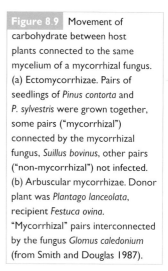

Figure 8.9 Movement of carbohydrate between host plants connected to the same mycelium of a mycorrhizal fungus. (a) Ectomycorrhizae. Pairs of seedlings of *Pinus contorta* and *P. sylvestris* were grown together, some pairs ("mycorrhizal") connected by the mycorrhizal fungus, *Suillus bovinus*, other pairs ("non-mycorrhizal") not infected. (b) Arbuscular mycorrhizae. Donor plant was *Plantago lanceolata*, recipient *Festuca ovina*. "Mycorrhizal" pairs interconnected by the fungus *Glomus caledonium* (from Smith and Douglas 1987).

when ^{14}C-labeled glucose and $^{32}PO_4$ were supplied to neighboring *Pinus* and *Picea* trees, these isotopes were recovered within 5 days from *Monotropa* plants growing 1–2 m away (Björkman 1960). The list of parasitic plants is still growing, and it seems likely that mycorrhizal networks permit a broad range of interactions from competition to commensalism to mutualism to parasitism.

8.3.5 Lichens

One-fifth of all fungi, that is some 13 500 species representing 525 genera, enter into lichen associations (Hawksworth 1988). In the majority of cases the fungus forms the bulk of the tissues, and the phycobiont (cyanobacterium or alga) is restricted to a layer within them (Figure 8.10). The term phycobiont is used since both the cyanobacteria and algae (Chlorophyta, Phaeophyta and Xanthophyta) have been reported from lichen associations (Table 8.3). Normally the species of fungi are exclusively found in lichen associations and

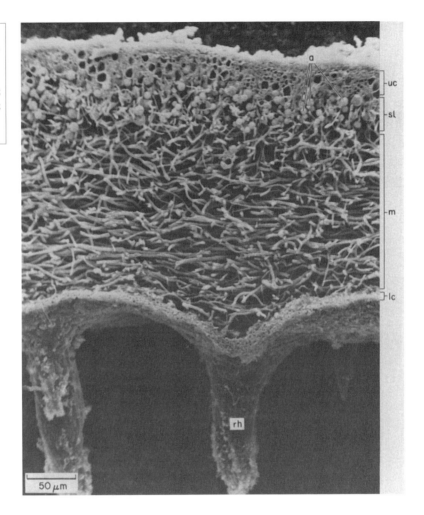

Figure 8.10 Scanning electron micrograph of a transverse section through *Parmelia borreri*, a foliose lichen with *Trebouxia* symbionts. uc, upper cortex; sl, symbiont layer; a, alga; m, medulla; lc, lower cortex; rh, rhizome (from Smith and Douglas 1987).

do not have other independent lives. In contrast, the algae represent free-living species, and at most only 39 genera are involved. In some cases three or four phycobiont species may be involved. In *Solarina*, a cyanobacterium and a green alga form separate layers in the thallus, while in *Placopsis gelida* the cyanobacteria are confined to distinctive structures called cephalodia with the green alga scattered through the main thallus.

The mycobiont receives carbohydrates produced by the phyco-biont. In addition, in the case of cyanobacteria, ammonia fixed from atmospheric nitrogen passes to the mycobiont. The advantages, if any, which accrue to the phycobiont are less clear. It is the phycobionts, after all, which are penetrated by haustoria, and the possibility that lichens are an advanced state of parasitism should not be discounted. That is to say, returning to definitions, not every case of symbiosis should be assumed to be a mutualism or even a product of coevolution. Yet the coevolution of fungi and algae is clearly demonstrated by features such as the production of structures

Table 8.3. *Photobiont genera of bacteria and algae reported as serving as inhabitants in lichen associations. Nomenclature according to source (from Hawksworth 1988).*

	Order	Genera
Cyanobacteria	Chamaesiphonales (incl. Pleurocapsales)	*Hyella*
	Chroococcales	*Aphanocapsa, Chroococcus, Chroococcidiopsis, Gloeocapsa*
	Hormogonales (incl. Stigonematales)	*Anabaena, Calothrix, Dichothrix, Fischerella, Hyphomorpha, Nostoc, Scytonema, Stigonema*
Chlorophyta	Chaetophorales	*Coccobotrys, Desmococcus* (syn. *Protococcus*), *Dilabifilium, Leptosira, Pseudopleurococcus*
	Chloroccocales	*Asterochloris, Chlorella, Chlorococcum, Coccomyxa, Dictyochloropsis, Elliptochloris, Myrmecia, Pseudochlorella* (incl. *Chlorellopsis* sensu Zeitler), *Trebouxia* (incl. *Pseudotrebouxia*), *Trochiscia*
	Chlorosarcinales	*Chlorosarcina, Friedmannia*
	Tetrasporales	*Gloeocystis*
	Trentepohliales	*Cephaleuros, Phycopeltis, Physolinum, Trentepohlia*
	Ulotrichales	*Stichococcus*
Phaeophyta	Ectocarpales	*Petroderma*
Xanthophyta	Mischococcales	*Botrydiopsis*
	Trichonematales	*Heterococcus*

(soredia) which disperse both the mycobiont and the phycobiont simultaneously. Clearly the evolutionary ecology and physiological basis of this symbiosis leaves many questions still unanswered. The question of physiological integration is next examined.

The photosynthetic rate per unit of chlorophyll in the alga is comparable to that of non-lichenized species (the rate per unit area is, of course, much smaller because the phycobiont comprises only 5–10 percent of the volume of the thallus). When lichens are wetted at night by dew, but dry during the day, there can actually be loss of weight as respiratory CO_2 losses at night can exceed those replaced by photosynthesis during the day (Lechowicz 1981). Tracer experiments using ^{14}C show in a range of lichens that a substantial proportion of the photosynthate is released to the host but estimates of quantities have been difficult to obtain; moreover, successful measurements under laboratory conditions do not necessarily provide results applicable to the field. The first lichen species in which movement was demonstrated experimentally was *Peltigera polydactyla*, which has a cyanobacterium (*Nostoc*) as the phycobiont. Using discs of tissue exposed to a radioactive tracer, Smith (1980) found appreciable amounts of radioactive carbon in the fungal tissue within two hours. In this case glucose moves from the cyanobacterium to the fungus. It appears that transfer is usually in the form of a single compound, but the compound differs among the genera of phycobionts (Smith and Douglas 1987). In contrast "[i]t has long been claimed that the fungal host provides its symbionts with mineral nutrients, but there is no experimental evidence either for the movement of nutrients or for the requirement by the symbionts for host-derived compounds. The growth of symbionts is so slow that their needs could probably be satisfied by the normal mineral content of rainwater" (Smith and Douglas 1987, p. 139). In short, this is definitely a case of symbiosis, but without better data on benefits and costs, it seems that this symbiosis is better labeled parasitism than mutualism.

8.4 | Positive interactions between plants and animals

8.4.1 Animals and flowers

Mutual benefits of pollination

Flowers provide two principal sources of food for animals: pollen and nectar. Pollen in particular is a valuable food, containing protein, fats, and carbohydrates. The protein content, from 25 to 33 percent (Percival 1965), is noteworthy in light of White's (1993) thesis that the growth and reproduction of many animals is limited by protein in general and nitrogen in particular. It is generally thought that the earliest example of animal pollination involved beetles consuming pollen attached to strobili with some showy bracts, and incidentally transferring it from one plant to another in their feeding. An interaction that therefore may have started as simple predation also had secondary benefits for the plant; as a consequence, those strobili with bracts that were more attractive to beetles proliferated. In angiosperms we call these bracts "petals." Many of the plants in the Magnoliales have a type of flower reminiscent of a strobilus adapted to beetle pollination. Over time, it is thought, other kinds of insects also began to visit flowers, thereby selecting for other kinds of floral morphologies. Simultaneously, there was selection for flowers containing food other than pollen, and nectar-bearing flowers proliferated.

Nectar is produced by glands, most of which occur within flowers, but some of which, extra-floral nectaries, are borne on adjoining leaves or petioles. Almost any part of a flower can be adapted to produce nectar, including the sepals, petals, stamens, and pistils. Unlike pollen, nectar contains chiefly sugar, particularly sucrose, fructose, and glucose. Sugar content of nectars can range from greater than 70 percent (e.g., Aesculus hippocastanum) to less than 20 percent (Prunus spp.) (Percival 1965). The bulk of large-flowered species with copious nectar occur in the tropics. The large flowers of the banana (Musa spp.), for example, fill nearly to the brim with nectar. Other copious producers include Heliconia spp. and the striking bird of paradise flower (Strelitzia reginae, Figure 8.11). In Protea spp., the flowers are small, but nectar from them is poured into a cup formed from adjoining bracts.

Table 8.4. | *Main classes of anthophilous insects that feed on the products of flowers. Nomenclature according to source (from Percival 1965).*

Hymenoptera	Vespidae	*Vespa*	Social wasps
		Colpa	
		Eumenes	Solitary wasps
	Bombidae	*Bombus* (bumble-bees)	
		Apis (honey-bees)	Social bees
	Colletidae	*Colletes*	
	Andrenidae	*Andrena* (willow and golden-rod bees)	
		Onagrandrena (*Oenothera* bees)	
		Halictus (water lily bee)	
		Halictoides (pickerel-weed bee)	
	Panurgidae	*Panurgus*	Solitary bees
	Megachilidae	*Megachile* (leaf-cutter bees)	
		Osmia	
	Xylocopidae	*Xylocopus* (carpenter bees)	
	Anthophoridae	*Anthophora*	
Diptera	Chironomidae	*Chironomus* (non-biting midges)	
	Mycetophilidae	(fungus gnats)	
	Ceratopogonidae	(biting midges)	
	Tabanidae	*Panagonia* (horseflies)	
	Nemestrinidae	*Megistorhynchus*	
	Bombylidae	*Bombylius* (bee flies)	
	Syrphidae	*Syrphus* (hover flies)	
		Eristalis (drone flies)	
Lepidoptera	Nymphalidae	*Vanessa* (tortoiseshells, peacocks)	
		Pyrameis (painted lady)	
		Heliconius (erato butterflies)	
		Danaus (milkweed butterfly)	
	Sphingidae	*Herse* (*Convolvulus* hawkmoth)	
		Deilephila (striped hawkmoth)	
		Macroglossa (humming-bird hawkmoth)	
	Nocturidae	*Barathra* (cabbage moth)	
		Triphoena (yellow underwing)	
		Pluisa (silvery)	

Three principal groups of animals derive nourishment from flowers: insects, birds, and bats (Percival 1965, Barth 1985, Feinsinger 1993, Endress 1996, Lloyd and Barrett 1996, Raven et al. 2005). Table 8.4 illustrates the breadth of insect types that feed upon products of flowers. Since the coevolution of bees and plants is well appreciated, a less well known example – bird pollination (ornithophily) – will be examined. A majority of bird-pollinated flowers occurs in tropical regions, where four bird families feed on nectar (Table 8.5). Unlike insects, birds take nectar, rather than pollen, as their primary food and most bird flowers therefore produce copious amounts of nectar but otherwise come in a variety of shapes and sizes (Figure 8.11). Large volumes of nectar need a container, so the flowers

Table 8.5. *Major and minor groups of flower-feeding birds (from data in Percival 1965).*

	Locale	Common name	Family
Major			
	Americas	Hummingbirds	Trochilidae
	Africa	Sun-birds	Nectariniidae
	South Africa	Sugarbirds	Promeropidae
	South Pacific	Honey-eaters	Meliphagidae
Minor			
	Hawaiian Islands	Honey-creepers	Drepanididae
	Australia	Brush-tongued lories Lorikeets	Loriidae
	Africa/Australia	White-eyes Silver-eyes	Zosteropidae
	Americas	Tanagers	Thraupidae

often are shaped like funnels or tubes to collect the nectar that is secreted. The flowers may also be stiff and erect, and the petals and sepals reduced in size. Others, in the genera *Salvia* and *Lobelia* for example, are zygomorphic, that is tube-shaped and bilaterally symmetric. Still others such as the genus *Protea* are reduced and completely enclosed in bracts. Vivid colors appear to attract birds by sight, pure red being particularly conspicuous, with vivid blue or green also common.

Hummingbirds are perhaps the best-known example of nectivorous birds; their ability to hover allows them to extract nectar without landing upon the flowers on which they feed. They are most abundant in the tropics of South America, where approximately half of the known species (130 out of 319) occur. As in the Nectariniidae (Figure 8.12), the bill is long and thin so that it is easily inserted into a tubular corolla. The birds in the Loriidae, in contrast, betray their relationship with parrots. Their bill is still compressed to enter flowers, the tongue is large and long and extensile so that it can be thrust deep into flowers, and its tip has papillae that act like a brush.

Now, all these data are very interesting, but of course a mutualism has to have measurable benefit to both parties. The benefit to birds appears clear: a food source. This evidence comes from an array of observations. The sugar content of the nectar can be measured. At least four different families of birds have evolved to use this source of food (Table 8.5), and their bills and tongues are shaped to efficiently extract it (Figure 8.12). Nectivorous birds prefer those flowers with highest nectar content, as evidenced by the vigorous competition for nectar; dominant birds will set up territories and defend them against other visitors (Feinsinger 1976). The benefit to birds, then, seems clear, but what of their plant partner?

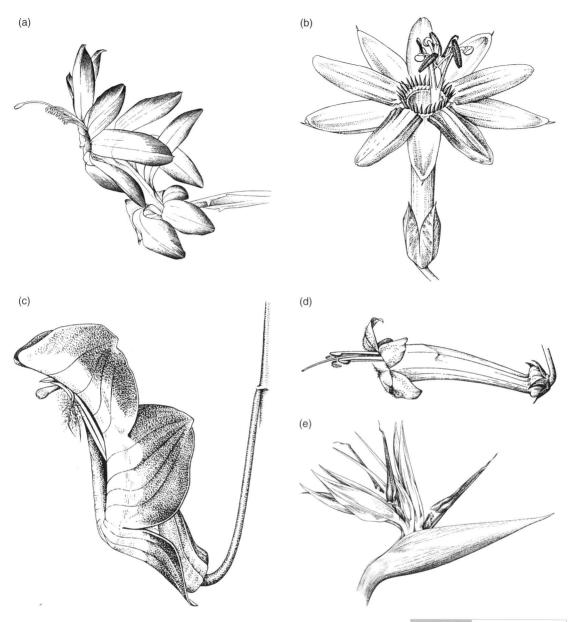

(a)

(b)

(c)

(d)

(e)

Figure 8.11 Bird-pollinated flowers: (a) *Schlumbergera truncata* (Cactaceae), (b) *Passiflora* sp. (subgenus *Tasconia*), (c) *Thunbergia mysorensis*, (d) *Phygelius capensis*, and (e) *Strelitzia reginae* (from Endress 1996).

In a general way, it seems entirely reasonable to assume that plants with flowers visited by birds have higher rates of seed production than if the birds were not present and that these higher rates of seed production outweigh the costs of producing flowers. This, however, is only an assumption (albeit a reasonable one). Some of these benefits have not yet been shown quantitatively, perhaps because it has been assumed that they are obvious. Much of the published work on pollination seems intent on illustrating the complexity and beauty of the assumed mutualism without quantitatively considering both costs and benefits, which raise questions about just how tight pollinator–flower adaptations really are (Vogel 1996).

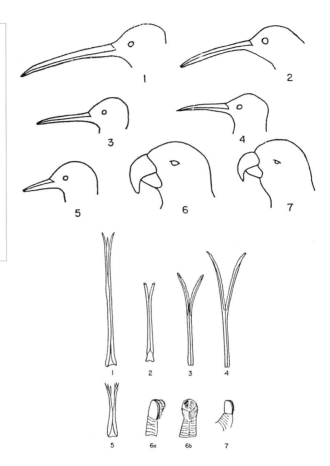

Figure 8.12 Bills (top) and tongues (bottom) of flower-visiting birds. (1) Scarlet-tufted Malachite Sunbird, *Nectarinia johnstoni*, (2) West African Olive Sunbird, *Cyanomitra obscura guineensis*, both Nectariniidae, (3) and (4) two unidentified hummingbirds, both Trochilidae, (5) Oriental White-eye, *Zosterops palpebrosa*, Zosteropidae, (6) Black capped Lory, *Domicella domicella*, (7) Red-collared Lorikeet, *Trichoglossus rubritorques*, both Loriidae. Species nomenclature according to source (from Percival 1965).

Pollination ecology founded by Sprengel and Darwin

Again some history is necessary. The process of pollination was only unravelled in the late 1700s (Table 8.6), and Sprengel's 1793 work was largely overlooked until Darwin re-visited the topic a century later (Percival 1965, Lloyd and Barrett 1996). Sprengels's work was unavailable in English until a chapter was translated by Haase as "Discovery of the Secret of Nature in the Structure and Fertilization of Flowers" (Lloyd and Barrett 1996). It begins

> When I carefully examined the flower of the wood cranesbill (*Geranium sylvaticum*) in the summer of 1787, I discovered that the lower part of its corolla was furnished with fine, soft hairs on the inside and on both margins. Convinced that the wise creator of nature had not created even a single tiny hair without definite purpose, I wondered what purpose these hairs might serve. And it soon came to my mind that if one assumes that the five nectar droplets which are secreted by the same number of glands are intended as food for certain insects, one would at the same time not think it unlikely that provision has been made for this nectar not to be spoiled by rain and that these hairs had been fitted to achieve this purpose.

While Linnaeus had, of course, recognized that plants were sexual organisms (much to the disgust of many of his contemporaries), his chief objective was to use such characteristics to classify plants. Vogel (1996) explains (p. 46) that most biologists believed that the *farina*

Table 8.6. *An historical overview of early treatises on the pollination ecology of angiosperms (from Percival 1965).*

Author	Date	Treatise
C. C. Sprengel	1793	The Secret of Nature in the Form and Fertilization of Flowers Discovered
C. Darwin	1862	The Various Contrivances by Which Orchids are Fertilized by Insects
H. Miller	1873	The Fertilization of Flowers (English translation 1883)
M. Kerner	1894–1895	The Natural History of Plants (2 vols)
P. Knuth	1898	Handbook of Flower Pollination
S. Vogel	1954	Einführung in die Blütenekologie
H. Kugler	1955	Blütenbiologische Typen als Element der Sippengliederung
M. S. Percival	1965	Floral Biology

fecundus (pollen) was carried to the stigma either spontaneously or by small vibrations, in which case insect visits to plants were by mere chance and were irrelevant to fertilization. The color and shape of flowers was thought to have no value other than to "manifest the solemnity of marriage." Indeed, since visiting insects did remove pollen, it was thought more likely that they were detrimental to flowers. Sprengel was therefore "ignored, rejected or ridiculed" when he published his book (Vogel, p. 46). He left the school which employed him the same year the book appeared, and spent the following years as a private scholar, supported by a small pension and housed in an attic in Berlin. His only further treatise on floral ecology was on bee-keeping. His grave is unknown, and there are no portraits of him (Vogel 1996).

Given that Sprengel's work lay unappreciated until Darwin's work on pollination and evolution, much work remains to be done. There are therefore still many unknowns in the evolution of this complex mutualism. The topic is now flourishing; Dafni (1992) lists more than 40 books and 100 key reviews on pollination ecology that appeared between 1971 and 1991. The challenge for today's students is to acquaint themselves with the volume of work available on this topic. Let us look at a few entertaining examples.

Fly pollination: parasitism or mutualism?

One of the most remarkable groups of plants is the Rafflesiaceae, a parasitic and tropical family with 8 genera and some 50 species. The genus *Rafflesia* has 14–15 species in eastern Asia and Malesia (Endress 1996). It is of particular interest because the flowers are among the largest in the angiosperms (Figure 8.13) and because, like increasing numbers of tropical plants, it is threatened with extinction. *Rafflesia* spp. are closely associated with insects, calliphorid flies. These flies are attracted by the odor of carrion. *Rafflesia* spp. mimic this odor; in addition, the blotched, wrinkled perianth

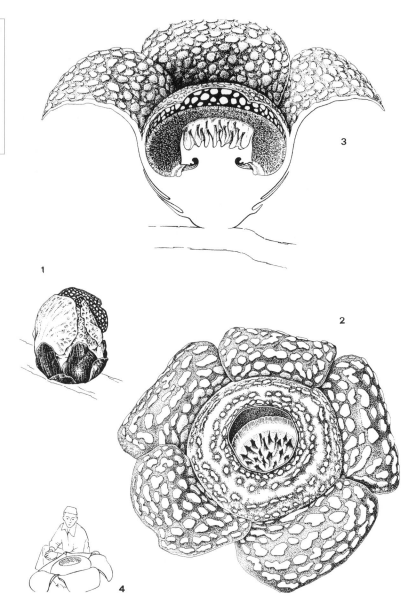

Figure 8.13 *Rafflesia* flowers that mimic carrion. (1) *R. keithii*; floral bud, surrounded by bracts. (2) *R. arnoldii*; open flower. (3) *R. arnoldii*; open flower in schematic longitudinal section, ovary not drawn. (4) *R. arnoldii*, showing enormous size of flower (from Endress 1996).

may simulate diseased animal tissue, and the flower is borne on the ground, simulating a carcass.

The apparently closely related Aristolochiaceae (ca. 400 species) includes the genus *Aristolochia* (ca. 300 species) with tubular flowers up to 1 m long (Endress 1996). Some *Aristolochia* flowers have carrion odors and translucent windows to attract and guide flies through the flower, and in some cases, stiff directional hairs prevent the fly from escaping. The fly remains trapped for unknown lengths of time, presumably accumulating pollen until the hairs wither and allow the fly to escape. Again it is unclear what the costs are to the insect in terms of missed feeding or mating opportunities, so that it is not yet possible to sort these species among categories of mutualism or parasitism.

Another group of carrion flowers occurs in the Asclepiadaceae where one finds "the most elaborate, complicated flowers of all the dicots" (Endress 1996, p. 302). The flowers are so complex and unusual that it may be difficult to imagine how they evolved, but careful study of a related family, the Apocynaceae, reveals many of the preliminary steps leading to the extremes seen in the Asclepiadaceae. Genera such as *Ceropegia* and *Stapelia* are particularly adapted to fly pollination. *Stapelia*, for example, produces purplish, wrinkled, hairy flowers that smell of carrion and are borne low on the plant touching the ground. They resemble small dead rodents. (One that I grew as a houseplant had to be put on a balcony outside when it flowered because my apartment would otherwise smell of rotting flesh. Flies would then lay their eggs on the flowers which would soon be riddled with maggots.)

In some carrion-simulating flowers then, flies are even deceived into oviposition. In such cases, it is unlikely that the flower replaces the nutrition that would be provided by a corpse, in which case, the flower is deceptive and acting as a parasite upon the pollinator population. If, however, the pollinators find food in the flower (the male flowers of *Rafflesia* provide flies with both pollen mush and a slimy exudate from the gynostemium), and if they are not stimulated to oviposit, then the interaction between flies and flowers may be neutral or even beneficial. The exact determination would depend upon the costs to the insect in relation to benefits.

8.4.2 Animals and seed dispersal

The interaction of seed dispersers and plants is so rich in relevant detail and so idiosyncratic from one system to the next that it may appear so chaotic as to be uninteresting to study.

(Janzen 1983, p. 262)

The function of a ripe vertebrate-eaten fruit is to get the seeds into the right animals and keep them out of the wrong animals.

(Janzen 1983, p. 232)

These two quotations from Janzen, widely known for his work on plant–animal mutualism, summarize the essential elements of the study of mutualism between plants and the animals that disperse their seeds. Most mutualisms between plants and herbivores probably originated as simple situations of herbivory or predation, followed by selection upon the plants to lower damage to the seeds as they pass through the mouths and guts of animals. Disentangling the details is not an easy process: "Whenever the function of a trait is not clear, be very suspicious that either the field observations are incomplete or that some of the members of the habitat are not present" (p. 257).

The mere fact that one observes a species feeding upon a fruit and dispersing the seeds does not prove that the species are mutualists or that they coevolved; they may have had an independent geographic origin, with the interaction now observed illustrating only that a predator has found a suitable prey, and a plant has fortuitously encountered a suitable dispersal agent. There is still some disagreement over what essential elements constitute evidence of coevolution (Futuyma and Slatkin 1993), although generally coevolution implies a long history of association between species leading to a set of mutually beneficial traits. The measurement of mutual benefit is certainly insufficient to demonstrate co-evolution; the issue of coevolution involves much more knowledge of past distribution, fossil records, and a good deal of inference. Tightly coevolved plant-dispersal interactions may be particularly rare in the vertebrates, since it is unlikely that any single species of plant could maintain a year round crop of fruits of sufficient quantity and quality to maintain a herbivore species. Exceptions might be fruit bats or rodents, which may feed on a nearly pure diet from one tree species, and insects which, because of the relative differences in size, often do specialize upon a single species of plant as their food source. This suggests two general principles: (1) the larger the herbivore, the less likely it is to have closely coevolved mutualisms with plants; (2) the more diverse a plant community, the lower the food supply of any species, and therefore the less likely coevolution may be. It is important to stress again that mutualism can occur without coevolution.

From the perspective of a plant, the production of fruits involves some challenging physiological modification. Indeed, the presence of fruits and complex biochemistry are regarded as two defining traits of the angiosperms (Raven et al. 2005). Early in development, the carpel must both provide a pathway for the pollen tube to reach the ovule(s) and protect the ovules and ripening seeds from herbivores. Fruit ripening requires that a layer of tissue that has been photosynthetic and well-defended against animals must rapidly transform itself to become non-photosynthetic and not only edible, but attractive. The shift from green fruits to colored fruits is one which we, as primates, quite naturally associate with the idea that a fruit is ripe, that is, edible. It may even be that our color vision is a trait that coevolved with the production of colored fruits for seed dispersal. Controlling the time of ripening, and the degree of visibility, provides some degree of control by plants over which seeds will be eaten, when and by whom.

Measuring the advantages of dispersal proves to be a thorny problem (e.g., Williams 1975, Willson 1984). Some of the possible advantages might include: (1) reduced competition with the parent plant, (2) invasion of new habitats, (3) reduced mortality from predators attracted to the parent, (4) reduced competition from siblings, and (5) reduced incidence of pathogens from the parent plant and siblings. There are also costs of dispersal; in particular, for offspring there are risks of being killed during the process of dispersal and risks of being carried from good habitat into unsuitable habitat. The parent plant, in addition, bears the costs of producing fruits, seed coats, and the surplus offspring necessary for animal dispersal. Thus while one may assume, from the large investments trees make in fruits, that dispersal has been strongly selected for, the actual measurement of the benefits of dispersal has been more difficult. Partly this has been the result of the problem alluded to earlier: that failures of dispersal are much easier to document than successes, particularly when success may be infrequent and distant from the parent (Savile 1956). Data on the benefits of dispersal are, however, accumulating. The challenge has been to measure the "seed shadow" around the parent plant, and the probabilities of survival at different distances from the parent plant. Three examples will be examined: wind dispersal of the annual *Cakile edentula* on sand dunes, tapir dispersal of the tropical palm *Maximiliana maripa*, and bat dispersal of the tropical legume *Andira inermis*.

Cakile edentula

To measure the costs and benefits of dispersal, it is necessary to measure both the distance of each offspring from its parent and the survival and reproductive success of those offspring. Janzen (1971), for example, has suggested that the wide separation between tropical trees of the same species arises out of a combination of (1) declining number of dispersed seeds and (2) increased rates of survival of those seeds, with distance from the parent tree. A principal benefit of dispersal is movement away from the pathogens and herbivores that have established populations associated with the parent tree. Making the measurements to test such a proposal is no easy task. Short-lived annual plants at least remove the difficulty of determining the reproductive output of long-lived trees. Consider the case of the plants in the genus *Cakile* that grow on sand beaches and shingle bars along seacoasts (Rodman 1974).

On a typical sand dune system *C. edentula* plants are distributed from the open sand beach to areas covered by dense grass many meters from the sea. A majority of the seeds is produced by a tiny fraction of the total population found on the open beach; here large plants surrounded by decaying seaweed can produce hundreds of seeds, whereas the plants inland produced as few as one or two seeds. Both survival and reproductive output decline with distance from the sea (Figure 8.14). Near the sea there are high costs to dispersal because every year onshore winds combined with storm waves move a majority of seeds inland into areas with high mortality and low survival rates. Under these conditions it would appear that dispersal is in fact counterproductive. Surely the evolutionary advantage would be associated with remaining in the open beach habitat. The only possible balance is the occasional long distance dispersal that establishes new populations on beaches (*Cakile* was, by way of illustration, the first genus of vascular plants to appear on the new volcanic island of Surtsey (Rodman 1974)), but one would be hard-pressed to compare the benefits of such chance events to the annual costs of dispersal to unsuitable habitats. Is dispersal, then,

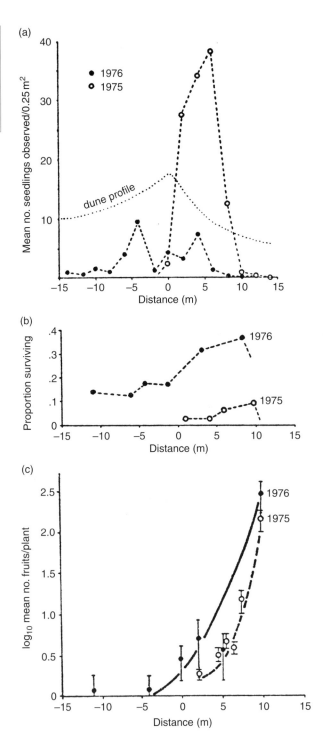

Figure 8.14 Seedling density (a), survival (b), and reproductive output (c) for the annual plant *Cakile edentula* along a sand dune gradient stretching from vegetated dunes (left) to open sand beach (right) (from Keddy 1980).

counterproductive? And in how many other populations of plants are seeds dispersed from good habitats to poor habitats?

Conveniently, the fruits of *Cakile* are two-parted. The distal part, which has a thick buoyant seed coat, breaks off the parent plant, while a smaller proximal section of the fruit remains attached. Each part normally contains a single seed. Thus one might conclude that there has been strong selection to invest half the offspring in the same habitat in which the parents grew. In the case of open sand beaches, the system may not work as intended because large waves tear up the adult plants and disperse the fragments along with the distal seeds. Even here, however, the proximal fruit segments with attached fragments of parent plants may tend to resist landward movement in the wind.

On shingle bars, the reproductive system of the plant has different consequences (Keddy 1980). To appreciate the situation on shingle bars, one must note three critical features of the habitat that differ from dunes. First, because of the gaps between stones, distal seeds roll in the wind only a short distance before falling into a crack. Second, waves tend not to tear up shingle, so that the dead stalks of plants remain in situ, with the proximal seed still attached. As a consequence of these two features, each spring one finds circular seed shadows around the still-rooted remains of dead plants from the previous year. The third feature of this habitat is large patches of wrack (largely dead leaves of *Zostera marina*); some plants therefore, grow in open gravel and others in patches fertilized by wrack.

Where one is able to measure the dispersal from parent plants by counting the number of seedlings germinating at different distances from the center of seedling clusters (Figure 8.15), few are found further than 15 cm. There is a suggestion in both habitats that survival is highest in those plants dispersed more than 25 cm from their parent, but the trend to increased survival is significant only in wrack. The principal cause of mortality in seedlings is a fungal damping-off disease that attacks seedlings at the soil line, and the damp environment provided by wrack not only doubles mortality rates (from 0.2 to 0.5) but also produces significantly higher mortality nearer the parent. Thus in the case of *C. edentula*, it is evident that there is a measurable survival benefit to dispersal away from parents (at least in wrack) because it leads to reduced rates of mortality from fungi. If this were not enough however, in both habitats there are dramatic increases in reproductive output with distance from parent plant: the median reproductive output per plant is much less than 10 near the parent, compared to 50 at long distances. Even a few centimeters of added dispersal can lead to a doubling of reproductive output.

I have gone into this example in some detail because it is one of the few that has measured dispersal distances, survival, and reproductive output of seeds around parent individuals. Further, the differences between sand beaches and shingle beaches illustrate the contrasting selective pressures that may be acting on one species of plant; the benefits of having the released distal fruit section are apparent on shingle beaches. The advantages to a retained fruit section are apparent on sand beaches. And the evidence for successful long-distance dispersal exists, even if these sorts of added benefits are difficult to calculate.

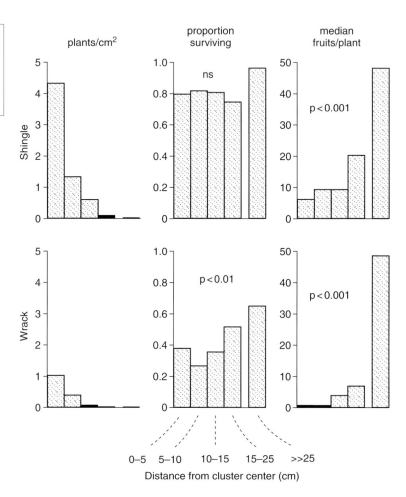

Figure 8.15 Density, survivorship, and reproductive output for *Cakile edentula* plotted against distance from the center of seedling clusters in two habitats (from Keddy 1982).

Tapirs

Palms such as *Maximiliana maripa* produce large-seeded fruits with plentiful, nutritious pulp attractive to mammals such as tapirs. Fragoso (1997) found that tapirs swallowed entire fruits and defecated intact seeds as far as 2 km away from the nearest palm clumps. In contrast, rodents, peccaries, and deer ate the fruits and merely spat out the seeds, most of them falling beneath the crown of the parent plant. Bruchid beetles are important seed predators in the neotropics; their larvae killed 77 percent of the seeds near parent trees, but less than 1 percent of 6140 seeds dispersed by tapirs. Both of these examples provide clear evidence of vastly higher survival at greater distances from parents. Further, the *C. edentula* example also documents greater reproductive output at larger distances. Such examples demonstrate that investments in seed dispersal do indeed lead to higher survival and/or reproductive output of offspring.

Bats and fruits

Bats too may feed on large and relatively visible fruits. Consider the case of *Artibeus jamaicensis* and *A. lituratus*, both of which feed upon fruits of *Andira inermis*, a medium-sized evergreen tree of the coastal lowlands of central America (Janzen et al. 1976). The bats rest in roosts, fly to an *Andira* tree to feed, and then carry back single ripe fruits. These are single-seeded oblong spheres 3–5 cm in length, borne on long stems that project outside the tree canopy. About half of a fruit is eaten, leaving the seed and some pulps to be discarded. Analyses of the fruit suggest that a bat obtains 2.25 kJ from eating half of the pulp. Oxygen consumption rates for the bats yield a resting metabolic rate in the order of 1.5 ml O_2 g^{-1} h^{-1}, compared to >20 ml O_2 g^{-1} h^{-1} while in flight. Therefore, a 45-g *A. jamaicensis* could make a 1266-m round trip and a 60-g *A. lituratus* could make a 951-m round trip at zero profit (Janzen et al. 1976). To simplify it, a bat can forage on a tree 0.5 km away and recover its costs from a single half-eaten *Andira* fruit. Since all but two of the feeding roosts were within 50 m of an *Andira* tree, it is apparent that the costs of foraging are minimal. The benefits to the tree, however, appear to be substantial. Between 54 and 94 percent of the seeds falling under parent trees were attacked and killed by weevils, whereas under bat roosts this was reduced to only 33 percent. Seeds that were dropped in open pastures, while comprising less than 1 percent of the seed crop, had only 10 percent mortality from weevils.

Myrmecochory

Animals eat plant tissues, and some plants exploit this tendency as a means of seed dispersal. In this sense, there is an evolutionary razor being ridden: herbivores must be attracted to disperse the seeds, but at the same time, the foliage of the plant and the seeds themselves must be protected from the herbivore. Unlike the gymnosperms, where strobili exist only to protect seeds from predators, the angiosperms have a structure called the carpel which becomes swollen in order to attract herbivores. Large fleshy fruits in the tropics provide an obvious incentive for seed dispersal, but on first inspection, many other plants lack any conspicuous traits to attract herbivores. One such group, known as myrmecochores, exploit ants to disperse their seeds.

Myrmecochores generally produce not a large fruit, but a small ant-attracting food body called an eliasome (Figure 8.16). Ants carry the seeds back to the nest where the eliasome is removed. The seed coat may be gnawed, but the seed is generally abandoned in the nest. This appears to have at least three advantages to the plant: (1) propagules are dispersed, (2) propagules may be hidden from seed predators, and (3) ant nests may provide particularly suitable germination sites, perhaps being richer in nitrogen and phosphorus than the surrounding forest soils. To determine whether a plant is ant-dispersed one could either examine the seed for the presence of an eliasome, or use feeding trials to observe ant responses to propagules. Beattie and Culver (1981) used both approaches to assay a range of plants typical of temperate deciduous forests. In some species (e.g., *Sanguinaria canadensis*), the presence of white or cream-colored

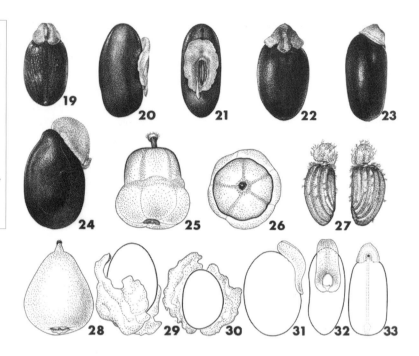

Figure 8.16 Myrmecochorous diaspores: 19–24 and 29–33, seeds showing ant-attracting appendage (eliasome); 25, 26, drupe with distinct eliasome; 27, mericarps with terminal eliasome; 28, drupe; 19, *Monotaxis linifolia*; 20, 21, *Kennedia rubicunda*; 22, 23, *Beyeria viscose*; 24, *Acacia linifolia*; 25, 26, *Leucopogon virgatus*; 27, *Xanthosia pilosa*; 28, *Monotoca scoparia*; 29, 30, *Hibbertia calycina*; 31, 32, *Daviesia mimosoides*; 33, *Bertya rosmarinifolia* (from Berg 1975).

tissue attached to the seed appeared obvious, but it may be difficult for humans to judge the food value of a seed from an ant's perspective. Beattie and Culver therefore put propagules on the ground close to a reproducing adult plant, and watched for an hour, recording the percentage of propagules that were carried at least 10 cm. Altogether they found that 21 out of 91 species were myrmechorous in their study sites; these included woodland genera such as *Asarum*, *Carex*, *Jeffersonia*, *Sanguinaria*, *Trillium*, *Uvularia*, and *Viola*. Further there was a suggestion that the activity of ants was positively correlated with the number of myrmecochorous species at a site. The spatial distribution of individual species may even be produced by the activity of different ant species. Since myrmecochory is not a conspicuous feature of plants, they conclude that many more species might be found to be myrmecochorous. Berg (1975), for example, reported that there are some 1500 myrmecochorous species in the dry heath and sclerophyll vegetation of Australia. Perhaps ant dispersal is particularly appropriate in arid or infertile conditions where resources for construction of fruits are limited and where ant mounds provide fertile microsites for germination in an otherwise restrictive landscape.

Certainly, the use of seeds by ants is well-established in deserts, where three groups of consumers forage for seeds: ants, rodents, and birds (Brown et al. 1986). The ants include both specialized genera of seed-eaters (e.g., *Pogonomyrmex* spp. and *Veromessor* spp.) as well as omnivores (e.g., *Novomessor* spp. and *Solenopsis* spp.). Price and Reichman (1987) have sifted desert soils to determine the distribution of seeds; in general, they are patchily distributed. Yet rodents must locate these seeds and sieve them from the soil with their forepaws or shake them to the surface by vibrating the soil. For small seeds, the time and energy costs may outweigh the gains (Price 1983), so that small seeds may be both less valuable to predators and more easily buried out of sight. If either ants or rodents are removed from experimental plots, the density of seeds in the soil increases (Brown et al. 1986), although their results were far more dramatic in the Sonoran Desert than in the Chihauhuan Desert. The benefits, if any, for the plants are less clear. Whether this is a simple case of outright predation, or whether there is some degree of mutualism remains unclear, and the nature of the interaction may be expected to vary among the three major groups of seed predators as well as the particular species and habitat.

Rodents and mast

Harper notes that, "it may be that it is the act of seed caching that determines which seed among millions is the one that produces the descendent tree" (1977, p. 466). This creates immediate problems for the study of regeneration because it is not the properties of the vast number of seeds that can be measured that results in regeneration – it is the one-in-a-million exceptional case that must be observed. The observation and measurement of exceptional events is highly unlikely – that is why they are exceptional! A principle, reminiscent of the Heisenberg uncertainty principle, limits observations on regeneration: it is the events that can be seen and recorded which, precisely because they are frequent enough to be seen, are unimportant.

The vast majority of woody plants in northern forests are ectomycorrhizal: "The northern representatives, mostly Pinaceae, Fagaceae, Betulaceae, Salicacae, and Juglandaceae, not only pay a high price in carbon to mycorrhizal fungi for allowing them to grow in more uncompromising environments but, being gregarious, must also maintain costly defences against potential herbivores" (Pirozynski and Malloch 1988, p. 235). Many of the animals in these forests are food-storing rodents and birds. The trees produce seasonal supplies of fatty, edible seeds borne in dry unpalatable fruits (nuts and nut-like fruits in angiosperms and strobili in conifers) (Table 8.7). During **mast years** seed production is synchronized, and enormous numbers of seeds are produced. This pattern is observed in temperate conifers (Smith 1970, Janzen 1971), temperate deciduous trees (Smith and Follmer 1972, Jensen 1985), tropical dipterocarps (Janzen 1974, Ashton 1988, Ashton et al. 1988), and bamboos (Janzen 1976). The present-day cue that controls mast years is still poorly understood. The origin is more obvious: once a chance environmental event (such as an exceptionally wet or dry year) produced a degree of synchrony, it would be fine-tuned by predators eliminating the seeds of those individuals that reproduced out of phase.

What should be made of the above facts? Do they show that predation is important, or do they argue for something more – coevolution of trees and animals? The simplest explanation is that mast years and hard-coated seeds are just two means by which these trees endeavor to protect their offspring. But scientists including

Table 8.7. *Characteristics of five species of nuts including feeding rates by gray squirrels (after Smith and Follmer 1972).*

Species	Lipid content (percent)	Mean dry weight (g ± SE)	Calories per nut	Proportion of nut's total energy in the kernel (percent)	Rate of ingest-ing energy from whole nuts (cal/s)	Rate of ingesting metabolizable energy from whole nuts (cal/s)
White oak					27[a]	20[a]
Kernel	4.6	0.40 ± 0.03	1 700	27		
Shell		0.41 ± 0.02	1 900			
Cap		0.64 ± 0.02	2 600			
Bur oak					50	41
Kernel	9.8	4.66 ± 0.19	20 200	45		
Shell		2.04 ± 0.67	7 700			
Cap		4.34 ± 0.17	17 000			
Shumard oak					42	36
Kernel	20.3	2.28 ± 0.07	11 900	66		
Shell		0.87 ± 0.02	3 900			
Cap		0.54 ± 0.03	2 200			
Black walnut					14[a]	13[a]
Kernel	23.1	2.04 ± 0.12	12 700	13		
Shell		12.20 ± 0.25	51 800			
Husk		8.62 ± 0.18	35 300			
Shagbark hickory					19[a]	18[a]
kernel	29.3	1.01 ± 0.06	6 700	21		
shell		2.04 ± 0.05	8 600			
husk		3.89 ± 0.12	16 100			

Note: [a] Overestimate because the squirrels frequently did not consume the entire kernel.

Pirozynski, Malloch, and Janzen believe that coevolution has occurred: "Like nectar and pollen that are offered as a reward for pollination, the edible seed as the currency of 'payment in offspring' seed-dispersal strategy (Janzen 1985) cannot be viewed as accidental but rather signals coevolved mutualism" (Pirozynski and Malloch 1988, p. 238). Further, the great volumes of mast produced by oaks and dipterocarps were probably once dispersed by pigs. In this context, say Pirozynski and Malloch, we may be mistaken to call conifers wind-dispersed when many of their seeds also are edible and simply fall to the ground, much like acorns and nuts. The ancient *Nothofagus* (Section 9.2.1) may be an interesting exception, being "... a fagalian archetype antedating coevolution with seed-dispersing vertebrates" (Pirozynski and Malloch 1988, p. 241), its tiny, apparently wind-dispersed seeds apparently unable to move more than 40 m beyond parent stands (Baylis 1980). Studies of dispersal today must also be undertaken with caution, the pigs that once dispersed dipterocarps may have been eliminated only recently by humans (Janzen 1974).

Zoologists appear to have reached rather similar conclusions, but it is interesting to see the relative emphasis that they put upon the various components of the coevolutionary scheme. Mycorrhizae, for example, are not invoked. Rather, there is a tendency to view the situation first from the point of view of the predator and then consider the responses of the trees:

Squirrels are strictly seed predators on those trees in the deciduous hardwood forests whose seeds are dispersed by the wind, e.g., maple (*Acer*), elm (*Ulmus*), and ash (*Fraxinus*). However, for the species in the families Fagaceae and Juglandaceae, squirrels are both seed predators and dispersing agents for the large, nutlike seeds. The life history of squirrels is too short in comparison to the generation time of trees and squirrels' movements are too great . . . for the individual squirrel to gain any advantage in leaving successful offspring by planting a new generation of food trees for the offspring. The squirrels' behaviour . . . is adaptive to the individual squirrel in spreading nut concentrations to prevent usage by deer. Burying the scattered nuts gets them out of sight of jays and other visual foragers. This process of scatter-hoarding nuts may also reduce the probability that other squirrels will find them, if, as appears to be the case, squirrels have a good sense of location and use it to retrieve the nuts they bury. It would have to be this advantage of reducing theft by other squirrels that would induce individual squirrels to bury walnuts and the thicker shelled hickory nuts because it is highly unlikely that deer and birds can break them open . . . .

Given that dispersing and burying nuts are not altruistic acts of squirrels to benefit trees, how can the interaction between tree seed and squirrel evolve to further the trees' efficiency of seed dispersal? The tree whose seeds are too appealing will have them eaten first and leave no offspring, while the tree whose nuts are too difficult to eat will not have their seeds dispersed. If two species of trees frequently exist together in mixed stands, they will be in the same situation in which both extremes of desirability will lead to failure in seed dispersal. Therefore, it is particularly interesting that oaks and hickories, which are frequently found together in climax forests . . . each have a season of the year in which they are the more desirable food and are more likely to be available for squirrel use if they have been scatter hoarded. It is possible to imagine a balance in selection on the thickness of shells of hickory nuts where too thin a shell makes the average tree too desirable and most seeds are eaten and too thick a shell where the average tree has no seed dispersal because squirrels are using neighboring acorns. This balance coupled with the alternate-year seed production of oaks in the subgenera of red and white oaks would allow squirrels to be effective dispersing agents for three sympatric species of trees. However, the exact nature of the balance in selective pressure on the thickness of acorn and hickory nut shells is further complicated by the numerous insects which also eat the nut kernels and then bore their way out through the shell . . . . But whatever the evolutionary influence of insects, for the various species of mast to coexist, they must reach an evolutionary balance in desirability for squirrels if all species of mast are to be effectively dispersed.

(Smith and Follmer 1972, p. 90)

Quantitative studies of the fates of seeds

Many of these discussions of animals and seed dispersal would benefit from good data on the actual causes of mortality of seeds. Botanists
have, in fact, rather carefully studied the fate of mast, partly because
of the economic and cultural value of woodlands in the European
landscape. Seed production was studied in the Prussian forests in the
late 1800s (Grubb 1977), and the British ecologist A. S. Watt is well-
known for his careful quantitative studies on the seeds of both oak
and beech (Watt 1919, 1923). Watt's important new procedure was to
increase control by placing out counted numbers of seeds in different
habitats, and then censusing them on repeat visits. This enabled him
to determine how long acorns survived in each situation, the value
of leaf litter or burial in preventing destruction, and the different
kinds of damage in different habitats (Cavers 1983). This work was
extended in two studies which are briefly examined here. In the first
case, Jarvis (1964) continued to study the regeneration of oak trees,
but on the Pennine hills of England. He had observed that oak seemed
unable to regenerate when the ground was covered by the grass
Deschampsia flexuosa. Jarvis confirmed Watt's finding that acorns
could survive only under a cover of leaves, and no leaves would
accumulate in the grazed turf of *D. flexuosa*. His sample sizes were
also much larger than those of Watt. The effects of surface litter are
apparent in Table 8.8. Gardner (1977) carried out similar studies upon
the reproduction of ash trees using nets to catch seeds and estimate
seed production. Figure 8.17 shows the results for 3 years. Although
the number of seeds produced varied by several orders of magnitude,

Table 8.8. | *The survival of acorns in and around oak woods in
the English Pennines during the winter and spring for 2 years
(1958–1960). Small rodents were the main predators (from Cavers
1983 after Jarvis 1964).*

Situation	Total no. acorns distributed	Sound acorns remaining after 2 weeks	
		No.	Percent
On surface of litter of:			
Deschampsia flexuosa (grass)	3350	0	0
Pteridium aquilinum (bracken)	1225	0	0
Holcus mollis (grass)	325	0	0
Calluna vulgaris (heather)	50	0	0
Oak leaves	475	4	0.8
Beneath surface litter of:			
D. flexuosa and leaves	165	42	25.5
P. aquilinum and leaves	120	11	9.2
Oak leaves	665	127	19.1

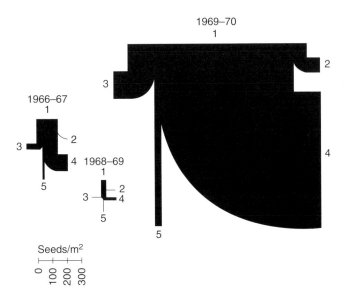

Seeds/m²

a large proportion was consumed by small mammals each year. But also, in each of these years, some seeds escaped predation and survived to germinate. In the fourth year of his study, all the seeds were either damaged by moth larvae (75 percent) or eaten by small mammals (25 percent). One year, however, is a short period of time for trees that can live several centuries, and for a tree population to remain stable, it is only necessary that one seed out of millions survives to adult size.

Coevolution of *Sideroxylon* and the dodo: a cautionary tale

The situation with rodents and mast is dissatisfying because it does not provide the most compelling example of mutualism, obligate dependence between a single animal species and a single plant species. Ecologists were therefore intrigued when such an example was announced. Temple (1977) reported that a Mauritian tree called the tambalacoque (*Sideroxylon grandiflorum* in the Sapotaceae) produced a fleshy fruit with a single large seed. This fruit is a drupe, with a large stone (a single seed encased in a hard endocarp) covered in a 5-mm-thick layer of tenacious fleshy pulp. The endocarp is about 4 cm wide and 5 cm long, with a shell ranging from 0.5 to 1.5 cm thick. Temple asserted that this tree had not reproduced for some 300 years, since the time when dodos became extinct. When, however, the seeds of the tree were force-fed to turkeys, some of them germinated. These three seeds, Temple asserted, were the first *S. grandiflorum* seeds to germinate in more than 300 years, and such observations "provide empirical support for the hypothesis that the fruits of [*S. grandiflorum*] had become highly specialized through coevolution with the dodo. After the dodo became extinct, no other animal on Mauritius was capable of ingesting the large pits. As a result, [*S. grandiflorum*] has apparently been unable to reproduce for 300 years and nearly became extinct." (I have changed the name in the quotation and text as the name of the tree has changed since Temple's paper appeared.) Thus, as the logical consequence of the coevolutionary race between seed predators and their prey (a kind of evolutionary escalation), the seed coats become steadily thicker to protect the seed from digestion, and soon the seeds become dependent upon digestion by their predator in order to escape from the thickened seed coat. This story is more dramatic than that of squirrels and mast, or ants and seeds, and has become a popular feature of introductory ecology textbooks. (Was it in yours?)

A re-evaluation of the dodo and tambalacoque story (Witmer and Cheke 1991) has since cast doubt on many of its appealing aspects. The problems include the following:

1. While *S. grandiflorum* had reproduced infrequently, there was evidence for young trees in published surveys.
2. A 1941 paper had described how the endocarp ruptures along a circular line, producing a cap which splits off, a feature shared with several other Mauritian tree fruits. Many other trees have thick seed coats, among these the large nuts in the genera *Juglans* and *Carya*, and in these the hard endocarp splits along a zone of weakness to allow germination.
3. There is rather little evidence that the seeds require abrasion to germinate, although the removal of pulp from the fruits, which the turkeys would also have likely done, certainly does seem to reduce mortality of seeds or seedlings from fungi.
4. Dodos were probably generalist feeders, given that they could be kept alive on long sea journeys.
5. There are other (now extinct) species that might have been capable of dispersing the tree, including large billed parrots (*Lophopsittacus mauritianus*) and two species of endemic giant tortoises (*Geochelone* spp.).

Thus the most charitable interpretation of the revised evidence appears to be the same kind of diffuse mutualism postulated for rodents and mast.

Witmer and Cheke also argue that if dodos were primarily granivorous as the evidence suggests: "they presumably destroyed most of the tambalacoque seeds they consumed." In light of the previous studies in this chapter, this is not a refutation of Temple's argument, since the production of surplus offspring may be an entirely acceptable cost of dispersal (recall 'payment in offspring', under rodents and mast). Even if the dodos had destroyed most of the seeds they ate, those that escaped might have been more than enough to maintain populations of the tree. The argument for close coevolution, for the evolution of intricate and obligate mutualisms, even among these comparatively isolated island species, does not seem to hold up under closer scrutiny. However: "attractive ideas, once entrenched, are difficult to change even in the face of contradictory evidence" (Witmer and Cheke 1991, p. 133), and it will be interesting to see how long this story lasts in textbooks.

In closing, there is good evidence for mutualism in the dispersal of fruits by animals, but obligate examples are rare and possibly non-existent. Most examples appear to be of the diffuse kind described for squirrels and mast. The contrast between the relatively precise mutualisms described for pollinators and flowers, and the relatively coarse mutualisms of dispersers and fruit, remains a noteworthy and possibly significant evolutionary enigma.

8.4.3 The costs of sexual reproduction

Many of the mutualisms found in the angiosperms are conspicuously associated with sexual reproduction. Both the flower and the fruit fall into this category. In order to understand the appearance of these structures, their mutualistic interactions with animals, and their possible coevolutionary origins, it may help to back up. Why is there sexual reproduction anyway? The easy answer to this, and one too often heard and accepted, is that sex is necessary for evolution to occur. While it is indeed true that a long-term consequence of sex is evolution, this does not convincingly explain its value in the short term. All structures have costs and benefits. Where substantial costs are observed, close scrutiny is necessary to determine what benefits might exist. Any structure for which the costs greatly outweigh the benefits seems unlikely to persist for long.

Some of the costs of sexual reproduction are obvious: these include the energetic cost of producing flowers and nectar, the resources expended in producing fruit, and the ancillary damage caused by herbivores attracted by the fruit. In addition to these, there are opportunity costs. Each meristem that produces flowers and fruit is a meristem that could have produced more foliage to enhance photosynthesis and adult survival. In the extreme case of asexuality, one could imagine trees that produce only two kinds of meristems: some continue to grow and produce leaves; others fall to the forest floor and grow into new genetically identical individuals. While some plants do indeed produce vegetative bulblets that are essentially dispersed meristems (e.g., *Cystopteris bulbifera*, *Lysimachia terrestris*) this is a relatively uncommon strategy, and is always accompanied by a sexual reproductive mechanism as well.

In addition to the resource costs and the opportunity costs, there is a further significant hidden cost in sexual reproduction that is called the "cost of meiosis" (Williams 1975). Consider two individuals: let one be parthenogenetic and produce dispersed meristems identical to itself; let the other produce haploid eggs that require fertilization. The relative success of these two individuals will illustrate the relative success of asexual and sexual reproduction. Each offspring of the asexual organism will contain complete copies of the parental genotype, whereas each offspring of the sexual organism will contain only one-half of the parental genotype. Therefore, merely by undergoing meiosis to produce eggs, the sexual organism cuts in half its contribution to offspring. Any gene that cuts reproductive fitness in half would appear to have very high costs indeed,

Table 8.9. *Expected differences between sexually and asexually produced offspring (from Williams 1975).*

Asexual (mitotically standardized) offspring	Sexual (meiotically diversified) offspring
Large initial size	Small
Produced continuously	Seasonally limited
Develop close to parent	Widely dispersed
Develop immediately	Dormant
Develop directly to adult stage	Develop through a series of diverse embryos and larvae
Environment and optimum genotype predictable from those of parent	Environment and optimum genotype unpredictable
Low mortality rate	High mortality rate
Natural selection mild	Natural selection intense

and, from this perspective, the persistence of sexual reproduction becomes a problem. Why do parthenogenetic individuals not predominate in most populations, and why do plants, in particular, not allocate all reproductive output to asexual offspring? So far, "nothing remotely approaching an advantage that could balance the cost of meiosis has been suggested" (Williams 1975, p. 11). That statement is still true today.

It is unconvincing to try to argue that some long-term benefit arising out of the continuing potential for evolution is sufficient to balance the immediate loss of 50 percent of a genome each generation. Surely some short-term benefit of meiosis to individuals can be found. One proposal supposes that meiosis and sexual recombination are of immediate value in any case where offspring are likely to face a different environment from that of the adult. This explanation seems reasonable, for wherever one looks in the plant, animal, or fungal kingdoms, one finds that the asexual propagules usually develop immediately and near the parent, whereas sexual propagules are usually dormant and widely dispersed (Table 8.9). The further away the offspring disperses into space or time, the lower the probability that it will encounter the same environment as its parent, and therefore the greater the value of meiosis and recombination. In Chapter 4 (Section 4.2.5) we encountered Williams's three models for life history evolution that address the trade-offs between sexual and asexual reproduction – the aphid-rotifer, strawberry-coral and elm-oyster models. These models had a number of similar components, particularly an environment that was spatially and temporally variable (see also Maynard Smith 1978). This seems to be a realistic assumption to make, particularly for sessile organisms like plants. Perhaps the amount of environmental heterogeneity is so great, that, in plants at least, the maintenance of sexual reproduction can be justified solely as a consequence of environmental uncertainty. In this situation, the benefits of sexual variation, and the benefits of dispersal, are apparent in the short run. Whether they can be shown to actually outweigh the cost of meiosis remains to be seen. Here we will continue with other studies of costs and benefits of sexuality in light of the cost of meiosis.

8.4.4 Experimental tests of the value of sexuality

Are there measurable advantages to out-crossing?
There is every reason to believe that flowers and insects coevolved. Those plants that attracted pollinators tended to leave more genetically variable (out-crossed) young, and those insects that visited plants tended to find food that increased their own survival and reproduction. It is the benefit to plants that interests us here. What is the selective pressure that has produced plants pollinated by animals? The enormous complexity of plant sexual systems (Barrett 2002), including di- and tri-morphic flowers, seems driven by the necessity to ensure out-crossing. Darwin himself was strongly interested in the presumed benefits of out-crossing, a passion possibly driven, according to one biography (Desmond and Moore 1991), by his suspicion that his troubled children were a consequence of marriage to his cousin. In practice, a century later, there is still a paucity of actual measurements of the assumed benefits of out-crossing (Antonovics 1984, Schaal 1984), and remarkably, when such measurements are made, the benefits of out-crossing are subtle. Consider two examples.

The legume *Lupinus texensis* is a winter annual endemic to the calcareous soils of central Texas where it forms large, showy populations of thousands of plants each with up to 30 inflorescences of 7–60 flowers. Schaal (1984) created two groups of plants: selfed and out-crossed. He then measured aspects of their subsequent germination, growth, and reproduction. There were no significant differences in seed set, seed viability, seed weight, or germination. There were small, but statistically significant differences in the number of leaves at 4, 6, and 8 weeks, and slightly higher life spans in the progeny of out-crossed plants (selfed 140 ± 77 days; out-crossed 165 ± 63 days). Reproductive output was only 88 flowers in selfed plants as opposed to 109 in out-crossed plants, but no significance test was reported. Schall concluded, however, that a "strong inbreeding depression clearly exists." Inbreeding depression, or its reverse, out-crossing vigour, is suggested but not tested or conclusively shown by the data above. Even if the ratio of 88/109 were significant, it in no way balances the cost of meiosis.

The widespread grass, *Anthoxanthum odoratum*, has been extensively studied by British ecologists. It is possible to obtain genetically uniform progeny by cloning tillers, and one can then ask whether these progeny fare better or worse when moved to adjacent habitat patches. Plants from seeds can be grown to the same size, providing an equivalent source of sexually produced tillers. Antonovics (1984) grew some 2500 tillers in such an experiment, reporting that

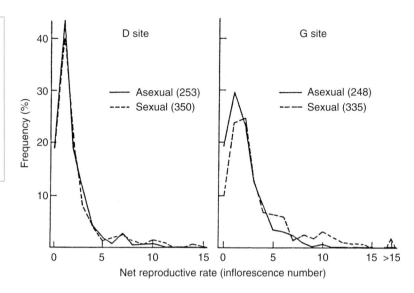

Figure 8.18 Frequency distribution of net reproductive rate in the grass *Anthoxanthum odoratum* for sexually produced half-sibs (genetically variable) and asexual clone (non-variable) progeny arrays, planted at two sites within a field and grown over 2 years. Sample sizes are in parentheses (from Antonovics 1984).

genetically variable material significantly out-yielded the genetically uniform. The ratio of relative fitness was 1:0.97 at one site, and 1:0.80 at another; by the second year the ratios had grown to 1:0.63 and 1:0.42. These figures suggest a much higher benefit of sexuality in *Anthoxanthum* than *Lupinus*, although the frequency distributions of reproductive output seem less compelling (Figure 8.18).

Remarkably, while both authors emphasize the value of genetic variation, neither rise to Williams's challenge by asking the obvious question: are the higher reproductive values of sexually produced offspring high enough to balance the cost of meiosis? Such studies at least provide potential methods for further investigation into why angiosperms have life cycles emphasizing out-crossing and dispersal. A review of some dozen studies that have explicitly tested for the benefits of genetically diverse offspring also found little support for the proposition (Cheplick 1992). That pool of studies, however, had only seven species to draw upon, all of which were herbaceous plants from temperate zones that are found in disturbed areas (e.g., *Abutilon theophrasti*, *Anthoxanthum odoratum*, *Plantago lanceolata*); any conclusions would therefore lack generality. There may even be benefits to interacting with siblings (Nakamura 1980), and, indeed, there is some evidence that, if anything, the negative effects of intraspecific competition decrease with increasing genetic relatedness (Cheplick 1992).

Are pollinators efficient?

In pollination by animals, the animals transfer the gametes (or more precisely, gametophytes) between plants. The inefficiency of pollen transfer may further increase costs of sexual reproduction. Consider the example of the orchid *Epidendrum ciliare*, an epiphytic species that is widespread in the neotropics (Figure 8.19). Orchids are of particular interest in the assessment of costs and benefits of pollination because their complex flower structures and pollination

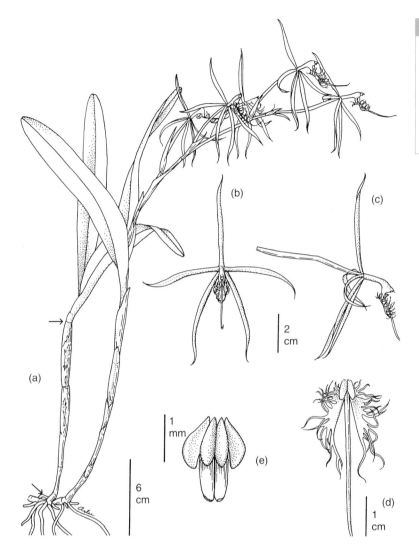

(a)

(b)

(c)

(d)

(e)

2 cm

1 mm

6 cm

1 cm

Figure 8.19 *Epidendrum ciliare*, a neotropical orchid. (a) Plant habit. The arrows indicate the points of measurement for stem (pseudobulb) length. (b) Flower, front view. (c) Flower, side view. (d) Free portion of the labellum. (e) Pollinarium. (from Ackerman and Montalvo 1990.)

systems illustrate the intense evolutionary pressures for out-crossing rather than self-fertilization.

Let us digress for some background on orchids. They are one of the largest plant families in the world, there being some 775 genera comprising 19 500 species (Judd et al. 2002). (Most other families are an order of magnitude smaller (Groombridge 1992).) Orchid pollination has been intensively studied for more than a century; indeed one of Darwin's monographs was entitled *On the Various Contrivances by Which British and Foreign Orchids Are Fertilised by Insects* (1862), and he followed it in 1876 by *The Effects of Cross and Self Fertilisation in the Vegetable Kingdom*, which addressed the role of cross fertilization in producing vigorous offspring.

While orchids can occupy a wide array of regions and habitat types, from northern peat bogs to the branches of trees in tropical forests, typically they are animal-pollinated tropical herbs that flourish in moist forests. The pollen grains are typically stuck together in large masses called pollinia that usually attach to the pollinator as a single package; thus, pollination is an all-or-nothing event that yields offspring fathered by a single donor plant (Nilsson 1992). The seeds are dust-like and wind dispersed (Figure 4.6). Comparative studies suggest that the primitive type of orchid was a sympodial plant with fleshy roots, elongate stems, spiral, plicate leaves, and a terminal inflorescence with erect anthers and soft, sticky pollen (Dressler 1983). Other traits of the primitive orchid appear to be net-veined leaves, climbing habit, three-locular ovaries, crustose seed coats, and fleshy fruits. The subfamily Epidendroideae has the greatest diversity, containing over 15 tribes including the Triphoreae, Malaxideae, saprophytic Gastrodieae, Arethuseae, and Calypsoeae. Some genera are exceedingly large, including *Pleurothallis* (1120 species), *Bulbophyllum* (1000), *Dendrobium* (900), *Epidendrum* (800), and *Habenaria* (600) (Judd et al. 2002).

The morphology of orchid flowers is often closely connected with that of the pollinating species. The length of the nectar-containing spurs and the position of pollinia may be such that a single species of insect is required for pollination. Some 8000–10 000 species of orchids act by deceit; they may mimic the mates or food supplies of insects. *Ophrys* orchids, for example, bloom when male competition is at a peak owing to a shortage of virgin females. The flower lip resembles the body and crossed wings of a female insect. Floral fragrances even contain compounds identical to female pheromones. The diversification of the orchid family may be related to several traits. Single male parentage, dust-like seeds, and pollinator specificity all appear to be particularly well represented in this family, although not unknown in other groups. Yet, in spite of more than a century of effort, many basic questions remain unanswered. Even the relative importance of pollinators and resources in determining seed set is still in doubt. Nilsson (1992) asks, "Orchids need pollinators, but are pollinators dependent upon orchids?" He concludes that there is no evidence that the pollinators are dependent upon orchids for nectar; they may still be mutualists with the orchids, but are not obligately so.

Returning now to one natural population of *Epidendrum ciliare* in Puerto Rico, the rate of fruit maturation was only from 5 to 15 percent. To test whether this was caused by lack of pollinators, Ackerman and Montalvo (1990) hand-pollinated flowers and found that this tripled fruit production. Thus, lack of pollination apparently constrained reproduction in these natural populations, but even when it was augmented, other factors caused fully half the flowers to fail to produce fruits. Further, the total mass of seeds declined as fruit set increased, suggesting that in any case resources for fruits and seeds were limited, and that increasing the number of flowers that were pollinated only reduced the resources available for each fruit. There were also long-term costs to higher rates of pollination and fruit set: the number of inflorescences, flowers, and flowers per inflorescence declined relative to controls. It seems that these orchids have sufficient resources to accommodate only the natural pollination rate of 15 percent, and increases in pollination frequency only damage the plant by draining it of resources. Ackerman and Montalvo conclude: "At this stage we need models that predict just how much natural fruit production results in maximisation of reproduction over the lifetime of individuals . . . trade-offs may exist between allocation for increased pollinator attractiveness and future reproduction."

Life without sex

As arguments arising from the cost of meiosis might suggest, sexual recombination has indeed been lost from some plant groups (Section 4.2.5). Genera with apomixis include *Taraxacum*, *Crepis*, *Hieracium*, and *Antennaria*, all of which are in the Asteraceae. Apomixis may happen in a number of ways. A diploid embryo may arise directly from diploid tissue of the parent. A diploid gameto-phyte may be produced ameiotically, giving rise to a diploid egg cell. In some groups, such as *Poa* and *Potentilla*, there *is* pseudogamy – the plants are apomictic, but produce functional pollen, and still require pollination and partial fertilization before they set seed. (The off-spring are produced from the maternal genes, with the pollen serving only to fertilize the endosperm (Maynard Smith 1978).) The great majority of flowering plants have hermaphroditic flowers, and apomic-tic varieties seem always to have originated from such species. Many apomicts also show clear evidence of hybrid origin. Often these groups form swarms of genetically distinct but closely related "species."

The costs of sexuality were measured using *Antennaria parviflora*, a complex in which one can find both sexual and asexual forms. This small herbaceous "species" is distributed across much of western North America. Sexual populations contain both male and female plants, and are nearly absent at altitudes above 3100 m. Bierzychudek (1980) found that apomictic females produce significantly more via-ble seeds per capitulum than sexual females. The sexual females not only produce fewer ovaries per captiulum, but less than half of them are fertilized. Hence, seed production by sexual females is lower than that of apomicts (this is in addition to the cost of meiosis already incurred). By growing sexuals and apomicts in six different experimen-tal conditions, it was possible to compare the range of habitats tolerated by each group. If the habitat variation hypothesis is correct, one would expect that sexually produced offspring would be more variable and therefore able to tolerate a wider range of conditions. Bierzychudek (1980) reports that, in all cases, the apomicts showed equal or superior performance. When four field environments were compared, there was no significant difference detectable between the two groups. A further advantage to the apomicts lies in their ability to found a new colony from a single seed, and, as might be expected, they have a larger geo-graphic range. In short, Bierzychudek was unable to find evidence for the alleged benefits of sexual reproduction within *Antennaria*.

The benefits of out-breeding have also been extensively studied in animals, usually again under the topic of "inbreeding depression."

That is, it is again the costs of inbreeding rather than the benefits of out-breeding upon which attention has been focused. Inbreeding depression has been found in baboons, lions, hawks, sparrows, mice, and snails (Pusey and Wolf 1996). It is questionable again, however, whether the documented costs of inbreeding are anywhere high enough to balance the cost of meiosis (a topic also neglected in Pusey and Wolf's review).

How many seeds will a plant produce? And why?

A large number of factors could be postulated to control seed production, including diversion of resources to asexual reproduction, the number of ovules per ovary, physiological ovule abortion, rate of visitation by pollinators, the size of seeds, or the availability of resources to produce viable seeds and fruits. It would be an easy (and all too common) option for an author to try to impress students with all the remarkable possibilities, leaving an impression of the virtuosity of his knowledge, the inadequacy of the reader, and the perplexing complexity of nature. Instead, let us avoid all three of these options. Let us consider just how one might determine which factors are most important, rather than discussing all the factors that might be important. The task of any scientist, after all, is to find simplicity where it is appropriate, leaving complexity only for those realms where no generalizations are yet known.

What simple measurable characteristics of plants might predict seed output? Shipley and Dion (1992) collected data on 285 herbaceous plants representing 57 temperate zone species, and made measurements of characteristics including the number of seeds produced, the mean weight of seeds, and the mean above-ground weight of shoots. Figure 8.20 shows that the number of seeds was negatively related to the weight of a seed, as would be expected if resources were limiting seed production, and evolutionary options were constrained to the continuum between few large seeds or many small seeds. As well, the number of seeds was positively correlated with shoot size (Box 3.3), again suggesting a resource-based explanation, as larger plants have proportionately larger volumes of resources to allocate to offspring.

The allometric relationship for seed number per ramet (N_s), vegetative ramet weight (W_v in grams), and individual seed weight per ramet (W_a in grams) was:

$$N_s = 1.4 \, W_v^{0.93} W_a^{-0.78}.$$

This equation predicts that an increase in weight of above-ground tissues in a ramet leads to an almost proportional increase in seed production, since the allometric slope of W_v (0.93) is not significantly different from 1. In contrast, the increase in average seed weight leads to a less than proportionate decrease in seed number, since the allometric slope of W_a (-0.78) is significantly less than 1. These two factors alone accounted for 81 percent of the variance in seed

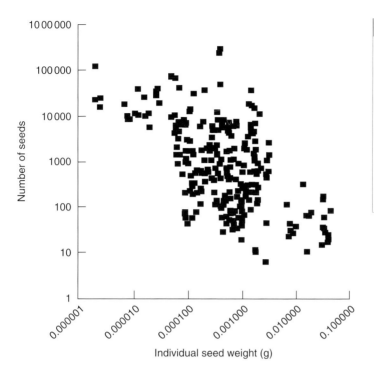

Figure 8.20 The number of seeds produced by a plant is negatively correlated with individual seed weight ($r = 0.60$). In this example, seed number is expressed per ramet (shoot); these data represent 285 ramets from 57 herbaceous species from a variety of habitats including wetlands, old fields, and woodlands in the vicinity of Montreal, Canada. Note the logarithmic scale (from Shipley and Dion 1992).

number among ramets. In other words, conclude Shipley and Dion, all of the other aspects of plant reproductive systems from phylogenetic history to pollination mechanisms can together explain only a further 19 percent of the variation in seed production among plant species.

Of course, Shipley and Dion examined only herbaceous temperate zone plants, leaving two obvious and important groups (woody plants, tropical plants) to be examined in the future. Meanwhile, the general lesson for students seems to be that if one sets out to prove that the world is complicated, one can certainly do so, but if one sets out to find simple quantitative relationships, they too may be present.

8.4.5 Animals defending plants

The genus *Acacia* has about 1000 species distributed throughout the drier portions of the tropics and subtropics. A small subset of this genus confined to the New World (e.g., *Acacia cornigera, A. sphaerocephala, A. hindsii, A. collinsii, A. melanoceras*) is known as swollen-thorn acacias (Figure 8.21). This subset shares a number of distinctive traits: (1) enlarged stipular thorns, (2) enlarged foliar nectaries, (3) modified leaflet tips called Beltian bodies, and (4) nearly year-round leaf production even in areas with a distinct dry season (Janzen 1966). These acacias are known as myrmecophytes because of their obligate mutualism with colonies of ants living within their thorns. In the case of

Figure 8.21 (a) *Acacia collinsii* in a heavily grazed pasture in southwestern Nicaragua. Note bare basal circle cleared of vegetation by the ant, *Pseudomyrmex nigrocincta*. (b) *A. cornigera* type A (1) and type B (2) thorns; same tree, Veracruz, Mexico. (c) *A. hindsii* type Z (1) and type B (2) thorns; same tree, Nayarit, Mexico. (d) Leaf of *A. hindsii*, same tree as (c). (e), (f) raised petiolar nectary of *A. cornigera*; greenhouse seedling, seed from Guanacaste, Costa Rica. (g) Beltian bodies on tips of pinnules of *A. cornigera*, same seedling as (f) (from Janzen 1966).

Acacias, the obligate ants are in the genus *Pseudomyrmex*, a genus of approximately 150 species restricted to the New World. This account of ant–acacia interactions comes largely from the review by Janzen (1966).

When a queen ant colonizes a tree, she either cuts her own entrance hole to a thorn or uses one cut by a previous worker or queen. Having laid her eggs in the thorn, she forages for nectar from the petiolar nectaries (Figure 8.21e) and for solid food from the Beltian bodies (Figure 8.21g). Over time, a colony may grow as large as 30 000 individuals, at which point it may also occupy neighboring trees within 3–10 m. The costs for the acacia are considerable. A 2-m acacia produces about 1 ml of nectar per day, the entire sugar source of the associated ant colony. (In the absence of ants, these nectaries are visited by a large number of kinds of Hymenoptera, beetles, cockroaches, and flies.) The Beltian bodies are constricted leaflets containing large thin-walled cells apparently full of proteins and lipids; the ants harvest them, cut them up, and feed them to larvae. (Beltian bodies are named for Thomas Belt, who first described their function in *The Naturalist in Nicaragua* in 1874.) The canopy of a 2-m-tall acacia can bear a kilogram of swollen thorns, and a 4-m plant, 3 kg (Janzen 1966). This weight of thorns requires tough and resilient wood. Unlike other acacias, the stumps sprout rapidly after fire, even during the dry season; this is apparently necessary if the ant colony is not to starve waiting for new shoots to appear.

The benefits of this relationship must be relatively great to balance the costs. The principal benefit appears to be the protection of the acacia from predation and competition. The ants are aggressive and will bite and sting any herbivore that attempts to feed upon the plant; observers describe ants rushing to the ends of twigs and throwing themselves into the air to land on visitors. Table 8.10 compares the incidence of herbivorous insects on acacias with and without ant colonies. The ants also kill the shoots of vines or other neighboring plants that touch the acacia. There are therefore bare areas around ant-occupied acacias, whereas other species are swamped by vines and over-topped by surrounding trees. Experiments have confirmed these inferences; when ant colonies were killed, the acacias were rapidly defoliated by herbivores and overgrown by vines (Janzen 1967). Finally, there may be some secondary benefits to the mutualism. The shoots of swollen-thorn acacias appear to lack the protective fibrous tissues of other acacias and grow more quickly than other acacias. They also may need to allocate less energy to the production of anti-herbivore defense compounds.

Table 8.10. *Incidence of phytophagous insects on shoots of* Acacia cornigera *with and without* Pseudomyrmex ferruginea, *an ant, in Temascal, Mexico, during the first part of the rainy season (daylight* n = 1241; 1109; *night-time,* n = 847; 793, *after Janzen 1966).*

Time/occurrence	With ants	Without ants
Daylight		
Shoots with insects (percent)	2.7	38.5
Mean no. insects/100 shoots	3.9	88.1
Night-time		
Shoots with insects (percent)	12.9	58.8
Mean no. insects/100 shoots	22.6	270.1

8.4.6 Microbes in animal guts

The degradation of cellulose by micro-organisms

The next interaction does not involve plants directly as a partner, yet it is one that is irrevocably driven by plants all the same. It has already been noted (Section 3.4.6) that plants have used cellulose as the primary structural molecule. This polymer has strong chemical bonds and uses minimal amounts of soil resources. Cellulose is therefore difficult to digest, and when it is digested, provides low levels of nutrition (Duchesne and Larson 1989, White 1993). For example, grass in temperate regions contains 10–35 percent cellulose, 10–25 percent hemicellulose, 2–12 percent lignin, and 25 percent soluble sugars per unit dry weight. The diet of animals such as ruminants and termites is therefore dominated by carbohydrates. In both these major groups of herbivores, symbiotic micro-organisms are essential to sever the chemical bonds in the cellulose. Here, drawing extensively upon the book on symbioses by Smith and Douglas (1987), are some examples; most of the details are of vertebrates, but most of the same principles apply to invertebrates. There are two main classes of herbivores: those in which the main site of microbial activity is the foregut, and those in which it is the hindgut. In foregut symbioses, the surplus microbial biomass can be digested in the lower regions of the gut, whereas in hindgut symbioses the surplus microbes are discharged with the faeces and lost to the host.

In the large herbivores, the ungulates or hoofed mammals, the two main groups are the perissodactyls and the artiodactyls (Figure 8.22). Both use fermentation to digest cellulose. The only surviving perissodactyls are horses, rhinos, and tapirs, but during the Eocene they were the dominant group of medium- to large-sized herbivores (Langer 1974, Janis 1976). In perissodactyls fermentation occurs in the hindgut (a sac at the junction of the large and small intestines called the caecum) whereas in artiodactyls, fermentation occurs in the foregut (in advance of the stomach in a chamber called the rumen).

Foregut fermentation, including ruminants

Foregut symbioses have evolved independently in four orders of mammals, including at least three times within the order Artiodactyla (Table 8.11). In all cases, part of the foregut has become enlarged and modified to form a multi-chambered organ with an anaerobic environment and dense populations of bacteria (or in some cases, protozoa). These chambers contain high concentrations of volatile fatty acids, which are the main product of fermentation of the plant material. The substantial investment required to digest cellulose is illustrated by the weight of these foreguts – between 10 and 30 percent of body weight.

Within the rumen, pH is regulated by copious amounts of saliva rich in compounds with high buffering capacity. The host grinds the food into small particles to maximize the surface area of food particles for bacterial attack. In camels and ruminants, the food may be

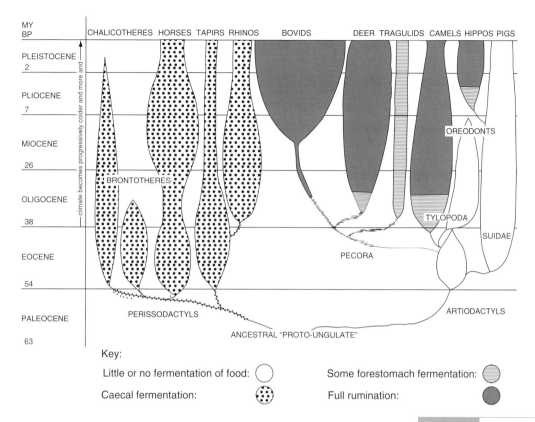

Key:

Little or no fermentation of food: ◯

Some forestomach fermentation: ◐

Caecal fermentation: ⦿

Full rumination: ●

Figure 8.22 Summary of ungulate evolution and gut type during the Tertiary (from Janis 1976).

returned to the mouth after a period of fermentation and ground more finely yet. This is termed, colloquially, chewing the cud. This practice may have evolved to allow herbivores to rapidly consume foliage when feeding conditions were good, and then process it further under less-exposed conditions. In this case, a rumen also acts like the cheek pouches of small mammals, allowing larger amounts of biomass to be transported for later consumption.

Ruminants (Figure 8.23 top) have been intensively studied owing to their importance in agriculture. The rumen fluid is maintained at constant pH and temperature to degrade and ferment the ingested food. Most of the fatty acids produced pass directly through the rumen wall into the host. The gases in the rumen, largely CO_2 and methane, maintain an anaerobic environment. (Surplus gas is removed by belching; hence the connection between the huge populations of ruminants maintained to feed humans, and the increasing concentration of atmospheric methane. Some estimates suggest that 10 percent of the energy intake of the host is lost in methanogenesis.) Rhythmic contractions of the muscular rumen wall mix the contents. Periodically portions of the contents are passed to the omasum (Figure 8.23) where water, bicarbonate from the saliva, and the remaining fatty acids are absorbed by sheets of tissue; the rate of passage is about one-third of the rumen contents each day. Finally, the abomasum completes digestion; the remainder of the

Table 8.11 *Characteristics of symbiosis in the foreguts of herbivorous mammals (from Smith and Douglas 1987).*

Host	No. chambers[a]	Weight (percent total body weight)	pH	Concentration of VFAs[b] (mM)	Symbionts Bacteria	Symbionts Protozoa
Order Marsupialia						
Family Macropodidae (kangaroos)	3	15	4.6–8.0	100–140	+	+
Order Primatia						
Subfamily Colobinae (colobus monkeys)	3	10–20	5.5–7.0	90–220	+	–
Order Edentata						
Family Bradypodidae (sloths)	2	20–30	5.2–6.7	40–95	+	–
Order Artiodactyla						
Family Hippopotamidae	3	?	5.0–5.7[c]	110–120	+	+
Family Camelidae	2	10–17	6.4–7.0	80–120	+	+
Suborder Ruminantia (e.g. deer, cattle)	3	10–15	6.0–7.0	90–140	+	+

Notes:
[a] Excluding the true stomach.
[b] VFA, volatile fatty acid.
[c] Values from carcasses, probably underestimates pH in living animals.

alimentary tract is not substantially different from that of other animals.

The rumen symbionts also contribute to the nitrogen economy of the host (Figure 8.24). Nitrogenous compounds are degraded to ammonia, some of which is absorbed by the host and used in the synthesis of amino acids. Further nitrogen is removed when the symbionts themselves are digested in the abomasum. Ruminants produce urea as the main nitrogenous waste product. Some of this is excreted in the urine, but some is transported directly back to the rumen or indirectly via the salivary glands. Many of the rumen micro-organisms can degrade urea back to ammonia, which is then reused by the host. When animals feed on nitrogen-poor diets (probably the rule in non-agricultural animals), up to 50 percent of the urea is recycled in this way. Rumen micro-organisms therefore simultaneously contribute to energy reserves and the nitrogen recycling of the host organism.

The micro-organisms themselves appear to number some 200 species of bacteria and some 50 species of protozoa. Each milliliter of rumen fluid supports 10^9–10^{10} bacteria and 10^4–10^5 protozoa! Some of the genera of bacteria include *Bacteroides*, *Ruminococcus*, *Selenomonas*, and *Methanobacterium*. The protozoa are dominated

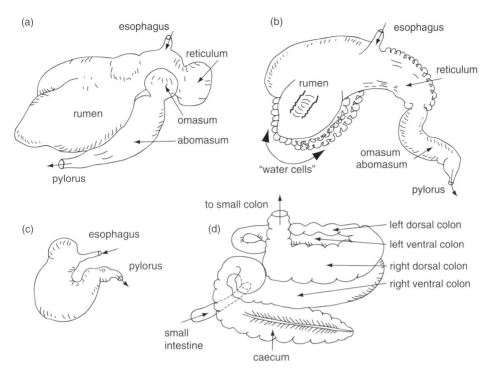

Figure 8.23 The digestive apparatus in ruminant perissodactyls (top) and artiodactyls (bottom). Food enters via the esophagus and leaves through the pylorus in both the (a) cow rumen and stomach and (b) camel rumen and stomach. Part (c) shows the horse stomach and (d) the cecum and colon (from Janis 1976).

by two groups of ciliates in the orders Entodiniomorphida and Trichostomatida. These protozoans are obligate anaerobes and can survive only under rumen conditions. They feed on carbohydrates and may be responsible for 30–60 percent of the fermentation in the rumen. Experiments in which protozoans have been eliminated from the rumen, either by rearing uninfected young animals or by treatment with chemicals that kill the protozoa, find that the growth of the animals is unaffected. This suggests that these are not essential components of the rumen community, although experiments under agricultural conditions may again produce different results from those in wild animals. On the other hand, commensals may well be present in the rumen.

Hindgut fermentation

Hindgut fermentation in mammals is somewhat less dramatic, but driven by most of the same constraints (Janis 1976). Although it is sometimes asserted that the more ancient perissodactyls have a more primitive form of digestion, Janis has another interpretation: "The so-called 'inefficiency' of the perissodactyls, resulting from the evolution of a cecal site of fermentation, arises because the strategy of selecting fibrous herbage was developed early in their evolution. The ruminant artiodactyls did not adopt this sort of diet until they were of a sufficiently large body size for a rumen fermentation site to be physiologically possible" (p. 722).

Those wanting an introduction to hindgut fermentation and to symbionts in the insects can begin by consulting Smith and Douglas

(1987). The introduction to ruminants above should be enough to emphasize the important role plants can play in driving positive relationships among other groups of organisms and to illustrate the many challenges posed in assuming plant diets. Note the dramatic relationship between gut capacity and diet (Table 8.12). Further, recall that the complexities of gut structure and the need for microbial symbioses can be traced back to that early event in the Earth's history wherein cellulose became the major constituent of cell walls

Table 8.12. *The relationship between gut capacity and diet in mammals (from Smith and Douglas 1987).*

		Average absolute capacity of gut region (l)		
Animal	Total gut length: body length	Foregut (stomach)	Midgut (small intestine)	Hindgut (cecum, colon, rectum)
Ox (ruminant)	20:1	253	66	38
Horse (non-ruminant herbivore)	12:1	18	64	130
Pig (omnivore)	6:1	8	9	10
Dog (carnivore)	4:1	4	4	1

Figure 8.24 The nitrogen pathways within ruminants. Note in particular the pathway that returns metabolic wastes back into the rumen (from Smith and Douglas 1987).

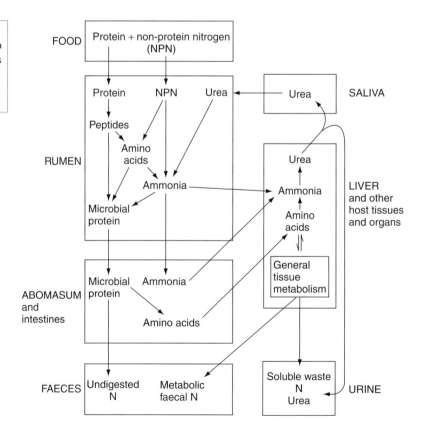

in plants. Although the world may indeed seem very green, the consumption and digestion of plant tissue is by no means easy.

8.5 | Mathematical models of mutualism

8.5.1 Population dynamics models

Mathematical models for mutualism go back to work in the 1930s (Boucher 1985b, Wolin 1985) when Gause and Witt (1935) applied the Lotka–Volterra competition equations to mutualism. As with competition, many different mathematical formulations are possible; in this section only two will be examined. The first is based upon the Lotka-Volterra models familiar from introductory ecology ($dN_1/dt = r_1 N_1 \ [(K_1 - a_{11}N_1 - a_{12}N_2)/K_1]$ and $dN_2/dt = r_2 N_2 \ [(K_2 - a_{22}N_2 - a_{21}N_1)/K_2]$). One may take these original Lotka–Volterra equations and, instead of assuming that neighbors cause negative effects, the coefficients are positive to indicate that interspecific neighbors have reciprocated beneficial effects upon each other. One can then explore the effects of the negative effects of intraspecific competition and the beneficial effects of interspecific mutualism (Figure 8.25). It is necessary to have as a mathematical artifact a negative carrying capacity because a positive density of the mutualistic partner is required for population increase (that is, $dN_1/dt = 0$ must have a positive intercept

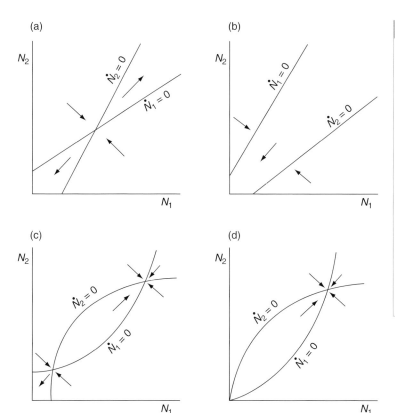

Figure 8.25 Isoclines for two-species models of obligate mutualism. Using a modified Lotka–Volterra competition equation, (a) shows a situation where the isoclines intersect at an unstable saddle point (extinction occurs below critical densities and population explosion occurs above them) and (b) shows a situation where there is no equilibrium point and both species become extinct. Using a second, more complex model, (c) shows the case where there is an unstable equilibrium point and a stable equilibrium point (species coexist provided densities are sufficiently large) and (d) shows the case where there is always coexistence (from Wolin 1985).

on the N_2 axis). Such a model yields two outcomes. The linear isoclines will intersect at a single equilibrium point that is an unstable saddle point when $a_{12}a_{21}/a_{11}a_{22} > 1$ (Figure 8.25(a)). Extinction occurs below critical densities and population explosion occurs above them. This illustrates the rather unsatisfactory nature of many mutualism models, since each population increases the other's density, leading to a steady (and unrealistic) increase in population sizes (May 1973). If, on the other hand, $a_{12}a_{21}/a_{11}a_{22} \leq 1$, both populations simply become extinct (Figure 8.25 (b)). This too is rather unsatisfactory from the point of view of model building.

If, however, one uses a different model and assumes that the per-capita benefit of mutualism decreases with increasing density, mutualism cannot override all density-dependent effects. As population densities increase, the benefits of mutualism are slowly outweighed by the costs of competition. In such a case, the isoclines are curvilinear and there is an asymptote at some density of partners where costs balance benefits. Population explosion is prevented if one or both species acts in this manner. Figure 8.25(c) illustrates a scenario with one unstable and one stable equilibrium point; Figure 8.25(d) is a scenario with only a single stable equilibrium point.

Wolin (1985) and Boucher (1985b) introduce some other kinds of models of mutualism. Facultative (as opposed to obligate) mutualism models tend to predict species persistence, particularly as one species can survive in the absence of the other. As with models of competition, models of mutualism help one to think about the nature of species interactions but may be far removed from biological reality.

8.5.2 Cost-benefit models

While research on mutualism might begin by documenting the rich degree of interaction among living organisms, studies must eventually become more quantitative. Population dynamics models (Section 7.6.3, 7.6.4) are useful to help one understand how various scenarios might proceed though time, but ultimately cost-benefit models are needed to study evolution. In fact, it is only when both costs and benefits are measured that one can be certain that there is true mutualism involved in an interaction.

The chief problems in developing such cost-benefit models include: (1) measuring costs and benefits, (2) putting all costs and benefits into a common currency, and (3) developing an appropriate quantitative framework in which to insert the measured costs and benefits. Models now exist for pollination, myrmecochory, mycorrhizal fungi, ants with fungus gardens, and mixed feeding flocks (Keeler 1985). To apply cost-benefit models one needs to envisage a population of individuals in which there are three classes of individuals: successful mutualists that assist another organism and receive assistance in return, unsuccessful mutualists that provide assistance but receive no reward, and non-mutualists that make no investments in mutualism and receive no return. For a population to be mutualistic, the fitness of the successful mutualists must be greater than that of either the non-mutualists or the unsuccessful mutualists. Further, the total fitness of all mutualists, successful or not, must exceed those who do not try. If it does not, that trait or behavior will be lost from the population.

Consider, says Keeler (1985), the case of animal pollination (zoophily) as opposed to self-pollination. Let w_z be the fitness of zoophilous individuals and w_s be the fitness of self-pollinators. Further, let:

$$w_z = pw_f + qw_u,$$

where w_f is the fitness of zoophilous individuals that are pollinated (fertilized) and w_u is the fitness of those that are unpollinated; p and q are their respective frequencies ($p + q = 1$).

To measure any w, one must define it as benefit minus cost. Ideally these would be measured in terms of contribution to the next generation, such as seeds produced or number of surviving offspring. Calories might be a useful choice of measurement, although grams of nitrogen or phosphorus might be more critical in some situations. To obtain the benefit one might combine the two measurements, using N, the proportion of seeds set, and v, the relative fitness of these seeds, to yield Nv. The cost I_z would be the investment in floral displays and rewards for pollinators. The variables N and p are clearly related, but Keeler separates them to emphasize the difference between plants receiving no pollen and plants with unfilled seeds in the fruits. Both N and v apply to both successfully (f) and unsuccessfully (u) pollinated zoophils, so that the equation above becomes:

$$w_z = p(N_f v_f - I_z) + q(N_u v_u - I_z).$$

If the species is an obligate outcrosser, $N_u v_u = 0$, in which case;

$$w_z = pN_f v_f - I_z,$$

and, for simplicity, replacing f with z.

$$w_z = pN_z v_z - I_z.$$

Similarly, for self-pollinating individuals:

$$w_s = N_s v_s - I_s,$$

in which case, for mutualism to occur, $w_z > w_s$ (note that this is incorrectly given in Keeler 1985) or:

$$pN_z v_z - I_z > N_s v_s - I_s.$$

It is likely that I_z will be greater than I_s, that is to say, zoophilous species generally make a greater investment in floral displays than self-pollinating species. Other things being equal, then, they should produce fewer seeds. If there is to be mutualism, v_z must exceed v_s, that is, the fitness of outcrossed seeds must be greater than that of inbred seeds.

This quantitative excursion should serve to illustrate the problems in testing for the presence of mutualism, evaluating different components of pollination ecology, and then measuring the intensity of mutualistic interdependence. Interestingly this model leads to nearly identical conclusions from qualitative assessments of the costs of meiosis: somehow there must be substantial benefits to out-crossing. Further, these benefits are necessary for plant–pollinator mutalisms to arise.

8.6 | Mutualism and apparent competition

Much of the work above concerns interactions among small numbers of individuals or species. The difficulty in interpreting all such experiments is compounded by (the nearly inevitable) connections to many other species through webs of competition and predation. A parable may clarify this point:

> Darwin's observations of bumblebees and red clover led him to extrapolate that since field mice, who prey on bumblebee nests, were relatively scarce near villages, they could account for the prevalence of red clover there. The mice are presumably scarce there because of predation by domestic cats. A German scientist then continued to extrapolate that since cats were responsible for the prevalence of red clover, and since red clover was a staple food of cattle and since British sailors thrived on bully beef, one could conclude that Britain's dominant world position as a naval power was ultimately determined by the presence of cats. Thomas Huxley, tongue planted firmly in cheek, went on to note that old maids were the main protectors of cats, thus showing that the British empire owed its existence to the spinsters of England.
>
> (Vandermeer et al. 1985, p. 326)

Thus, while it is one thing to measure the change in abundance of a species, either positive or negative, it is often devilishly difficult to understand the cause of the change.

The careful design of experiments can help minimize such indirect effects, but the problem remains inherent in most experiments. When one species is removed from a community, a multitude of other effects will accompany its removal. In medicine, such unexpected consequences of a treatment are called "side-effects"; in ecology, we can be less sanguine in sorting treatment effects into "intended effects" and "side-effects". Side-effects might occur when a species increases after the removal of a neighbor, not because of lack of competition with the neighbor, but because that neighbor attracted a species of grazing insect that attacks the test species. The many possible interactions that could create the appearance of competition (side-effects in medical parlance) have been called "apparent competition" (Connell 1990, Holt and Lawton 1993). Holt and Lawton are of the opinion that apparent interaction may be particularly likely in insect assemblages because parasitoids can limit their hosts to levels at which resource competition is unimportant. The same problems arise in teasing mutualisms out from complex interactions among species; in this case, it is equally possible that some cases of mutualism are "apparent mutualism" caused by indirect effects of competition or predation.

Another example of indirect effects can be found among ants tending homopteran parasites on plants (Vandermeer et al. 1985). If only three players (ants, homopterans, plants) are considered alone, the ant has a negative effect upon the plant, since it protects the homopteran that feeds upon the plant. But if one then considers more species of herbivores, it seems that the ants are at the same time excluding other insect herbivores, with the consequence that the plant still benefits from the interaction: "In other words, the incorrect conclusion that the ant must have a negative effect upon the plant derives from having conceived of a four dimensional system (ant–homopteran–plant–herbivores) as a three-dimensional one" (p. 332). But the situation may be more complex still; in the case of ants on black locust trees (*Robinia*), the protection from other herbivores that the tree receives may be balanced by the protection the ant provides the homopteran with its own suite of enemies! What then, is the "real" effect of the ants upon the tree? It is dependent on the relative strength of each pathway. It is near certain that the ecological consequences of shared natural enemies include a wide array of unexpected indirect impacts (Holt and Lawton 1994). Detecting and measuring mutualism amidst complex species interactions remains a challenge.

8.7 | Conclusion

Have we reached an impasse? Having convinced ourselves that mutualism is important in nature, we seem equally to have found that there are innumerable obstacles to ever detecting its presence and strength in specific situations. It is not pleasant to face an impasse, but it is far better to see it for what it is than to carry on pretending that problems do not exist. Until an obstacle is identified, and labeled, solutions cannot be sought. While such problems are left for bright young students to resolve, a few thoughts on progress in the study of mutualisms follow. First, it is important to understand the attitudinal obstacles that have arisen.

1. The search for nature nuggets
Many people are attracted to the study of biology because they like nature. This is by no means an obstacle in itself since an intimate knowledge of nature is an excellent foundation for any aspiring ecologist. But too many people fail to grow beyond the simple study of natural history, collecting facts and observations as if all were of equal value. Collecting data about nature is *not* an end in itself, it is merely a single part of the scientific process. Of the literature on mutualism, it may be noted that far too much is little more than a collection of nature stories without a theoretical context and without a hypothesis-driven impetus.

2. The confusion between mutualism and divine order

Those who escape the pull of nature study alone may fall prey to a second conceptual obstacle. One can become insensitive to the importance of co-operative interactions for fear of falling into the naive spirituality that often comes with their occurrence. A majority of human beings, it is safe to say, still believe in some sort of "divine balance of nature." It rains *so that* plants can grow. Plants produce flowers *in order to* make the world pretty, or *in order to* feed bees. Birds sing *in order to* make the world pleasant, or because they are happy. In this view, there is divine order and inherent purpose for everything. The study of mutualism could easily be treated as evidence of a divine order; indeed creationists regularly use the examples of complex mutualism to allegedly "prove" that evolution cannot occur. The belief in divine order was certainly a prominent theme in Victorian England, and there is little doubt that Darwin's long delay in publishing his ideas on evolution was a consequence of his realization that natural selection replaced divine order with a simple materialistic explanation for the diversity of life.

A scientist studying competition or predation follows the revolutionary Darwinian view of nature as a struggle for resources. This comfortably continues the historical trend in biology of replacing naive views of divine order by scientific materialism. Mutualism has the inherent risk of falling back into a simplistic view of divine order of nature. Perhaps defining mutualism as "mutual exploitation" would make the evolutionary basis of co-operative interactions clearer.

3. The failure to measure

The third obstacle is the tendency of scientists to be satisfied after merely showing that an apparent mutualism occurs. Stopping at this point is a sort of intellectual *coitus interruptus*. A similar problem occurs in the study of competition; authors seem to think that once they have found evidence of competition, their work is done. I spent the better part of a book (Keddy 1989) documenting this problem and suggesting ways to get off this dead end path. The same analysis can be applied to mutualism. Fundamentally, demonstrating that an apparent mutualism occurs is not an end in itself – it is just a beginning. The important next step is to *measure* the benefits accruing to each partner (just as in a competitive interaction where one measures the costs to each competitor) (Keeler 1985, Smith and Douglas 1987). The benefits might be measured in calories, grams of nitrogen, number of offspring produced, or decreased rates of mortality. Ideally, these benefits should be compared to control individuals lacking their partner (in the same way, one measures competition intensity with reference to individuals without neighbors). Figure 8.26 illustrates the procedures and comparisons necessary. Without *measurement*, and without *controls*, it is impossible to quantify the strength of mutualism or accurately distinguish between asymmetric mutualism and outright commensalism (Figure 8.27).

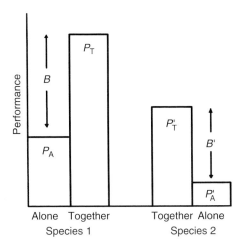

Figure 8.26 Comparisons and calculations for measuring the effects of a possible mutualism (P_A = performance alone, P_T = performance together).

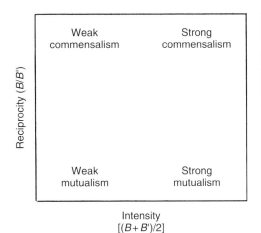

Figure 8.27 A possible way to compare mutualisms based upon intensity and reciprocity calculated using the results from Figure 8.26. How many published studies could be plotted in this diagram?

With measurement, a series of important questions can be answered:

1. What benefits accrue to each partner?
2. If many mutualistic interactions are measured, where does the mean fall along the continuum between mutualism and mere commensalism?
3. Do different habitats have different proportions of mutualistic interactions or different intensities of them?
4. How is mutualism balanced to ensure that neither participant exploits the other?
5. Do some species engage in mutualism with multiple partners, and if so, what then are the answers to questions 1–4?

In short, nature is assembled from pair-wise interactions: competition, predation, mutualism, and commensalism. Mutualism is implicated in many interactions between plants and fungi and between plants and animals. There is much work to be done in taking the study of mutualism from the realm of natural history to rigorous science.

Further reading

Janzen, D. H. and P. S. Martin. 1982. Neotropical anachronisms: the fruits the gomphotheres ate. *Science* **215**: 19-27.

Janzen, D. H. 1983. Dispersal of seeds by vertebrate guts. pp. 232-262. In D. J. Futuyma and M. Slatkin (eds.) *Coevolution*. Sunderland: Sinauer.

Boucher, D. H., S. James, and K. H. Keeler. 1982. The ecology of mutualism. *Annual Review of Ecology and Systematics* **13**: 315-347.

Smith, D. C. and A. E. Douglas. 1987. *The Biology of Symbiosis*. London: Edward Arnold.

Williamson, G. B. 1990. Allelopathy, Koch's postulates and the neck riddle. pp. 143-162. In J. B. Grace and D. Tilman (eds.) *Perspectives on Plant Competition*. San Diego: Academic Press.

Simon, L., J. Bousquet, R. C. Lévesque, and M. Lalonde. 1993. Origin and diversification of endomycorrhizal fungi and coincidence with vascular land plants. *Nature* **363**: 67-69.

Bertness, M. D. and S. D. Hacker. 1994. Physical stress and positive associations among marsh plants. *The American Naturalist* **144**: 363-372.

Endress, P. K. 1996. *Diversity and Evolutionary Biology of Tropical Flowers*. Paperback edition 1994 (with corrections). Cambridge: Cambridge University Press.

Chapter 9

Time

Scales of investigation. Methods. The origin of angiosperms. Pangea. Gondwana. Laurasia. Glossopteris. Araucaria. Nothofagus. Ginkgo. Proteaceae. Quaternary events. Glaciation. Loess. Pluvial lakes. Drought. Sea level decrease. Migration. Hominids. Flooding. Succession. Definitions. Deglaciated valleys. Peat bogs. Sand dunes. Forests. Predictive models. Historical views on succession.

9.1 | Introduction

We assume that our universe has three spatial dimensions and one temporal dimension. While these assumptions appear invalid at very small (subatomic) or very large (galactic) scales, they are an adequate means for describing the macroscopic world that we share with other living organisms (Ferris 1988). Although the measurement of space has been readily done, the quantification of time has posed more of a problem. Accurate measurement of time was a constant challenge to early navigators until John Harrison invented his chronometer. When Captain Cook returned from his second voyage in July 1775, he reported that Harrison's timepiece "exceeded the expectations of its most zealous advocate and by being now and then corrected by lunar observations has been our faithful guide through all vicissitudes of climates" (Sobel 1995, p. 150). Its reliability permitted Cook to accurately estimate his longitude for making maps of the South Sea Islands. Cook insisted on taking it with him again on his third and fatal expedition.

While accurate clocks were essential for initiating the period of global exploration in the 1800s (e.g., Box 2.1), the time problem for ecologists has usually been of a different kind: our species lives for a mere "three score and ten" ($<10^2$ years), while many ecological processes occur on a time scale exceeding 10^6 years. How is one to study processes that take longer than a lifetime?

1. *Ignore them.* One can shift one's attention to population biology or physiology in order to study processes that occur over much shorter periods of time.
2. *Find zoned communities.* Zoned communities on shorelines and mountainsides present an obvious sequence of changes in vegetation. If one assumes that the spatial sequence represents a

temporal sequence, then measuring properties of different zones will allow description of their sequential change in time. If one assigns times to locations in these sequences, say by means of historic lava flows or radiocarbon dates of organic matter, one can be more precise.

3. *Use historical documents.* Historical records of vegetation can be assembled and used to reconstruct changes over time. This technique is valuable for changes over a century or so, but earlier than this, historical records are increasingly fragmentary, the names given species may be unreliable, and the observations may be qualitative rather than quantitative. This procedure is particularly valuable in Europe where written historical accounts go back a thousand years or more. This will be explored in more depth in Chapter 12.

4. *Study fossil assemblages.* For example, peat bogs and lake sediments preserve pollen, plant and insect fragments, charcoal, and diatoms from earlier times. Cores taken from these habitats summarize past changes in vegetation. If annual layers of sediment can be counted, these changes can be given an exact chronology; if not, radiocarbon dates can provide estimates of elapsed time since burial. The study of pollen in sediments (palynology) has been a vital tool for the study of events on scales from 10^2 to 19^4 years. For longer time scales, fossils in dated rocks allow paleobotanists to reconstruct the evolution of plants and their changing distributions over many millions of years. Cores, pollen studies, and fossils are discussed in depth in books such as Flint 1971, Delcourt and Delcourt 1991, Stewart and Rothwell 1993, and Levin 1994.

Figure 9.1 Environmental disturbance regimes, biotic responses, and vegetation patterns viewed in the context of four space-time domains (from Delcourt and Delcourt 1988).

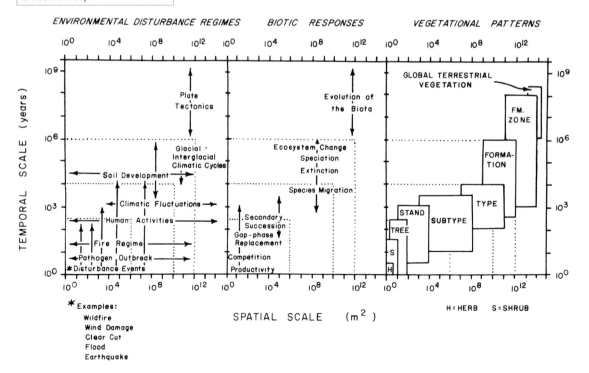

In summary, the processes that ecologists observe will depend upon the scale of time investigated (Figure 9.1). At extremely long scales ($>10^6$ years) entire new orders of plants may evolve, and the location of entire continents may shift. In contrast, at short time scales (10^2–10^3 years), modern species and ecological interactions such as competition and grazing are likely to be important. This chapter examines three major events that occurred at three very different time scales and are of great significance to plant ecology: (1) the origin of flowering plants and continental drift, (2) the effects of the ice age on plant distributions, and (3) ecological succession.

9.2 | $>10^6$ years: the origin of the angiosperms and continental drift

The origin of the angiosperms, or the flowering plants, is a mystery, but one being resolved through careful examination of various clues. Clues to the origin of the angiosperms can be found in diverse disciplines, and understanding the significance of these clues requires an ecologist to have a good knowledge of the fossil record, geology, plant anatomy, and the systematics of tropical plants.

Whether dominance is defined in terms of biomass, number of families, or number of species, the angiosperms are now the dominant group of plants on Earth. During the Cretaceous Period (65–140 million years BP), their fossils show up in both increasing number and frequency (Figure 9.2). Where and how did the flowering plants originate? This inquiry is best begun with a review of the conditions on Earth just prior to the emergence of the angiosperms (Axelrod 1970, Stewart and Rothwell 1993).

At this time the single continent of the late Precambrian had split in two forming Gondwana in the south and Laurasia in the north. The dominant plants of the time were the gymnosperms – species that produce seeds but do not protect them within carpels, as the angiosperms do. True flowers and double fertilization are also absent. The diversity of gymnosperms at this time should be appreciated; consider some examples. One order, now extinct, the Glossopteridales (Stewart and Rothwell 1993), was first discovered in 1828 when certain tongue-shaped leaves were named *Glossopteris*. At first different fragments of these plants were given different names, but as the number and quality of fossils found improved, it became clear that this order consisted of woody plants with ovules. High quality specimens even allowed paleobotanists to take sections of ovules and stems. These fossils are distributed across India, Australia, South Africa, South America, and Antarctica (with one possible exception in Mexico), which suggests that the Glossopteridales were restricted to Gondwana. Permineralized trunks, 40 cm in diameter, have been

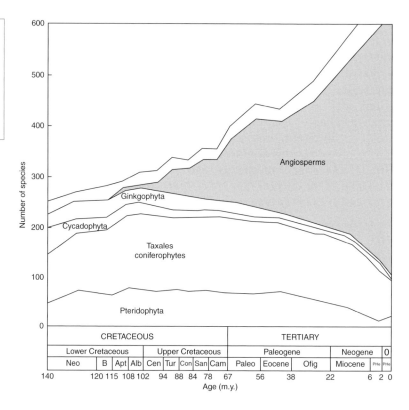

Figure 9.2 Changes in diversity, at the species level, of major plant groups represented in the late Mesozoic and Cenozoic eras. The data used in the graphs are predominantly from the Northern Hemisphere (from Niklas et al. 1985).

found in late Permian rocks. The group is now extinct, as are the Cordaitales and Voltziales.

In contrast to the Gondwana distribution of Glossopteridales, the Ginkgoales were circumpolar (Stewart and Rothwell 1993). Fossils of the Ginkgoales are known from Alaska, Greenland, Scandinavia, Siberia, and Mongolia as well as from the Southern Hemisphere. One species in this group has survived to the present, *Ginkgo biloba*, known from the deciduous forests of Asia. In contrast to all the gymnosperm orders discussed above, the Coniferales is still widely distributed, with 51 genera and some 500 species. They are widespread in the fossil record back as far as the early Devonian.

The gymnosperms (both extinct and living forms) provide the context for the evolution of angiosperms. The study of the ovulate structures of gymnosperms has uncovered an entire sequence of reproductive structures ranging from leaves with attached ovules to ovules with leaves nearly fused around them (Figure 9.3), the latter giving the appearance of a carpel. Some Jurassic rocks contain undoubted angiosperm fossils (palm wood; *Propalmophyllum* in France, *Sassendorfites* in Germany, *Phyllites* in England, *Palmoxylon* in Utah), and the very early Cretaceous rocks in France and California contain angiosperm fruits (Axelrod 1970). Many of the characters of modern groups can be seen in fossils in rocks of the middle Cretaceous (ca. 100 million years BP), including *Archaeanthus* which apparently represents the Magnoliales (Figure 9.4); others like *Caloda* were

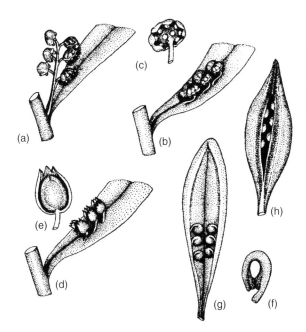

Figure 9.3 Stages in the evolution of the carpel from glossopterid ancestors. (a) Modified "gonophyll" with pinnate ovulate "sporangiophore" in the axil of a leaf. (b) Adnation of "sporangiophore" with adaxial surface of leaf leaving two rows of *Ligettonia*-like capitula (c). (d), (e) Reduction in number of ovules per capitulum from several to one as in *Denkania*. (f) Fusion of cupule-like capitulum with integument of ovule to form bitegmic ovule. (f), (g) Inversion of ovules to produce anatropous ovules. (h) Reflexing of leaf margins to enclose two rows of ovules in a carpel (from Stewart and Rothwell 1993).

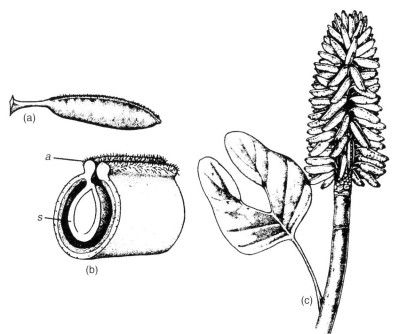

Figure 9.4 *Archaeanthus linnenbergeri*, a mid-Cretaceous representative of the Magnoliales. (a) Reconstruction of single follicle. (b) Section through follicle; adaxial ridge (*a*), seed (*s*). (c) Reconstruction of leafy twig bearing many helically arranged conduplicate carpels (follicles) (from Dilcher and Crane 1985).

evidently wind-pollinated (Figure 9.5) but are not clearly related to an existing group:

It is important to keep in mind that the characteristics by which we recognize angiosperms did not evolve simultaneously from a gymnosperm ancestor at the end of the Jurassic or Lower Cretaceous. Instead, many groups of gymnosperms evolved one or more characteristics that we associate with angiosperms prior to the Lower Cretaceous. Some of

Figure 9.5 *Caloda delevoryana*, a mid-Cretaceous wind-pollinated plant. (a) Reconstruction in early fruiting stage prior to fruit abscission. (b) Reconstruction of secondary axis showing a cluster of carpels (from Dilcher and Kovach 1986).

(a)

(b)

these groups became extinct, while others evolved new characteristics of particular selective advantage (the carpel and double fertilization, for example) in combination with already established characteristics such as reticulate venation or tectate pollen.

(Stewart and Rothwell 1993, p. 452)

The absence of earlier angiosperm fossils suggests that angiosperms were not growing in lowland areas during pre-Cretaceous times; fossil Jurassic and Triassic floras are well known, yet contain few angiosperms. It is therefore presumed that angiosperms evolved in uplands, where fossilization was infrequent, and that their sudden appearance in the Cretaceous marks their invasion of lowland sites where fossilization was more common (Axelrod 1970). Some of the earliest fossil groups were the Magnoliales (containing the modern magnolias, Figure 2.3), the Hamamelidales, and the Juglandales (with catkins evidently allowing for wind pollination) (Stewart and Rothwell 1993). A rich bed of early Tertiary age in southern England includes fossils of monocots, some of which can be assigned to modern genera such as *Potamogeton*, *Scirpus*, *Mariscus*, and *Typha* (Collinson and Hooker 1987) and many additional fossil floras containing angiosperms have been found (Friis et al. 2006).

It seems reasonable to assume that the conditions required by the early angiosperms were warm and frost free. Presently, more than half of the 300-odd families known occur primarily in tropical to subtropical regions. Further, some of the most primitive families in existence today are found in environments that are warm and frost free:

> To judge from modern evolutionary studies, open areas in a region of regular drought would provide an ideal setting for early angiosperm evolution. These sites would be the more exposed, better drained slopes, dry intermontane valleys, and rock slopes, areas where a dry season would provide a powerful stimulus for rapid, continuing evolution.
>
> (Axelrod 1970, p. 282)

To better understand the current distribution of the angiosperms, we must turn to the conditions of the world during and just before the Cretaceous. During the Triassic and Jurassic, Gondwana separated from Laurasia as the Tethys Sea opened (ca. 250 million years BP, Figure 9.6). This event appears still to exert control over the present distribution of many plant species, since the flora of the Southern Hemisphere, which is largely derived from Gondwana, is much more diverse than of those areas derived from Laurasia. The present plant diversity of the Southern Hemisphere suggests that the climatic conditions of Gondwana were more favorable to plant growth than those of Laurasia:

> ... an analysis of the climatic requirements of ancient taxa that are still living (e.g., cycads, araucarians, tree ferns, podocarps, redwood) demonstrates that they have survived chiefly in areas of very high equability .... This is also true of the more 'primitive' angiosperm alliances – magnolioids, annonids, hamamelids – as well as the surviving primitive members of the major angiosperm orders.
>
> (Axelrod 1970, p. 290)

Regrettably, most botanists live in the parts of the world derived from Laurasia and less is known about the more diverse flora of the Southern Hemisphere. The travels of the early plant geographers, however, took them to those parts of the world derived from Gondwana, and their travels may be conceived of as journeys back in time, as they would have encountered representatives of the ancient taxa. Many of the surviving ancient plants are found today in regions of the world that derived from Gondwana: South America, Africa, Australia, New Zealand, and India. Consider three important plant groups that follow this pattern.

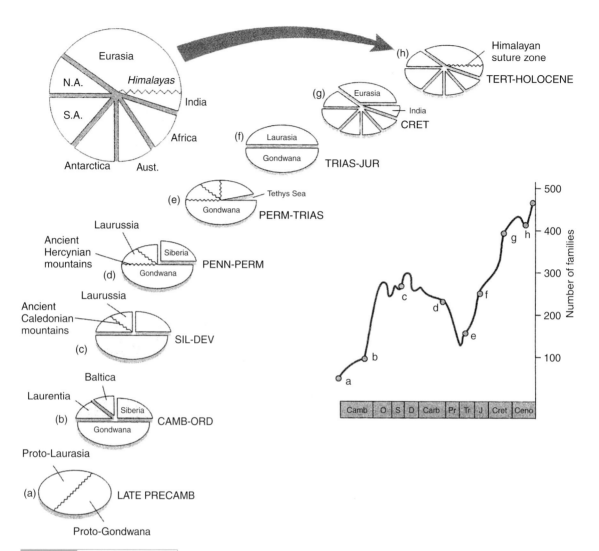

Figure 9.6 Continental fragmentation and the diversity of life show a clear relationship from Cambrian to recent time (after Levin 1994).

9.2.1 Temperate evergreen forests

The southern beech (*Nothofagus*) today is found exclusively in the Southern Hemisphere, in areas such as Tasmania, the temperate montane forests of New Guinea and New Caledonia, and the Fuegian area, although the fossil distribution of *Nothofagus* extends to Antarctica (Humphries 1981) (Figure 9.7). *Nothofagus* tends to form nearly pure stands on the east coast of the Andes, for example, although in other cases it grows mixed with gymnosperms such as *Araucaria*, *Podocarpus*, and *Dacrydium* (Archibold 1995).

The gymnosperms in the Podocarpaceae and Araucariaceae also have a similar distribution (Scagel et al. 1965, Farjon 1998). Podocarps lack strobili, instead ovules are borne singly on the tips of stalks. In some species, such as *Podocarpus spicatus*, the ovules are arranged in two rows along an axis, in the axil of a bract, thus simulating a strobilus. Investigations of fossil pollen indicate that the Podocarpaceae was widespread in Asia, Europe, and North America as well as the Southern

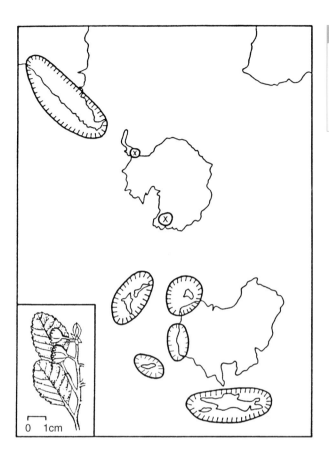

Figure 9.7 The modern distribution of the genus *Nothofagus* (southern beech). *Nothofagus* pollen, of Oligocene age, has been found at the two sites in Antarctica marked with crosses (after Pielou 1979).

Hemisphere where 18 genera now occur (Table 9.1). Fossil wood from the Araucariaceae is known from the Triassic, and foliage compressions are known from the Jurassic to the present. Pollen of *Araucaria* has been reported from Tertiary rocks in Europe (Scagel et al. 1965).

9.2.2 Deserts

The desert floras of the Southern Hemisphere contain two groups of species. One group has presumably been derived from adjacent mesic floras, but the other appears to be an ancient desert flora from Gondwana, a flora of early Cretaceous or greater age. Examples include *Colletia, Forchammeria, Larrea, Adansonia, Fagonia, Koeberlinia,* and *Simmondsia*:

> Relatively free and isolated from competition by northern shrubs, and surviving under a more equable climate, some bizarre ancient taxa have persisted in larger numbers in austral lands, not only in the semidesert to desert areas, but also in the dry tropical forest, savanna, and thorn scrub vegetation adjacent to them. But in North America and the Eurasian region, they were subjected to more extreme climates and were unable to compete with the new xerophytes that originated there and have largely supplanted them.
>
> (Axelrod 1970, p. 311)

Table 9.1. *Distribution of the genera of Podocarpaceae that have five or more species (based on Farjon 1998; Quinn and Price 2003).*

Genus	No. species	Distribution
Podocarpus	105	Japan, Taiwan, s China, Nepal, Indonesia, Australia, Tasmania, New Zealand, Fiji, Philippines, Central and South America, Caribbean islands,; e and s Africa, Madagascar
Dacrydium	16	s China, Thailand, Indonesia, New Guinea, New Zealand, Fiji, Philippines
Dacrycarpus	9	s China, Burma, Philippines, Malaysia, Indonesia, New Guinea, Fiji, New Zealand
Prumnopitys	9	Australia, New Caledonia, New Zealand, Chile to Venezuela and Costa Rica
Afrocarpus	6	e and s Africa, Madagascar
Nageia	6	Japan, s China, e India, Malaysia, Indonesia, New Guinea, New Britain
Falcatifolium	5	Philippines, Malaysia, Indonesia, New Guinea, New Caledonia
Phyllocladus	5	e India, Philippines, Malaysia, Indonesia, Papua New Guinea, Australia, Tasmania, New Zealand
Retrophyllum	5	Malaysia, Indonesia, New Caledonia, Brazil, Venezuela, Colombia

Evidence of this extirpation can be found from the fossil record. Genera found in the late Cretaceous and Paleocene fossil floras of the United States (*Araucaria*, *Astronium*, *Lomatia*, and *Schinus*) still occur in South America.

9.2.3 Tropical floras

Many tropical plant groups are spread across South America, Africa, and Asia – 54 forest plant families are pantropical (Figure 9.8). At one time it was postulated that these species somehow spread across the ocean by means of birds or ancient land bridges; in light of continental drift theories, however, we now understand that these groups were once widespread on Gondwana. The distribution of the subgroups, such as the eight families shared by South America and India/Australia (Figure 9.8), can be explained by allowing for extinction of these groups in Africa. As Gondwana split into smaller fragments, which drifted across climatic zones, it is reasonable to imagine that extinctions occurred and account for the variation in the taxa that survive in these regions:

> ... as the Australian plate moved into lower middle latitudes following Eocene time, it entered the permanent high-pressure belt of low precipitation at the south margin of the tropics. As a result, the

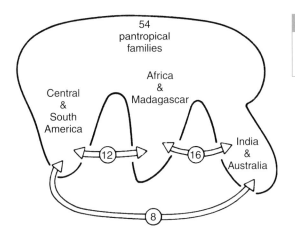

Figure 9.8 Schematic representation of the ranges of families of tropical forest plants (from Pielou 1979).

temperate rainforest, composed of southern beech [*Nothofagus*], araucarias, podocarps, proteads, and other evergreen dicots that had covered much of the continent, was progressively restricted to moist equable southeast Australia – Tasmania. During this movement, many taxa underwent severe restrictions in range, and others must have become extinct. Some that were in the region survive as relicts on offshore lands such as New Caledonia, Fiji, and New Zealand.

(Axelrod and Raven 1972, p. 229)

As continents drift across the latitudes, two other consequences, aside from outright extinction, are possible: evolutionary diversification within the continent or collision with other regions, which contain their own flora. In the case of evolutionary diversification, the species already present diversify to occupy the available habitats. The family Proteaceae, for example, has expanded to about 80 genera and 1770 species (Judd et al. 2002) and the Restionaceae to some 53 genera and 485 species in the Southern Hemisphere (Figure 9.9). Axelrod and Raven (1972) say:

Rafting lands to new climatic belts has provided new opportunities for evolution. As Australia moved into a zone of warmer drier climate, plant genera such as *Acacia*, *Eucalyptus*, *Casuarina*, *Melaleuca*, *Hakea*, and *Eremophila* ... proliferated into scores of new species adapted to progressively drier, more continental climates.

(p. 230)

When regions collide, as a result of continental drift, floras mix and species not previously exposed to competition may be driven to extinction. To illustrate this process, consider an animal example: the well-known case of New World vertebrates. Vertebrates are a useful example because their bones fossilize well, and they have received a good deal of paleontological study. Before the land link between North and South America formed in the Pliocene, North and South America had no families of terrestrial

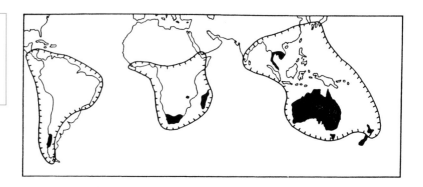

Figure 9.9 The ranges of the angiosperm families Restionaceae (black) and Proteaceae (outlined). *Banksia serrata*, an Australian member of the Proteaceae (from Pielou 1979) is shown below.

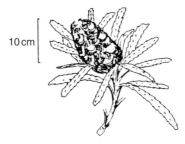

10 cm

mammals in common. After the link formed, 15 families spread northward and 7 southward, and over time many of the southern families disappeared:

> Many families that were endemic to South America in the early Pliocene are now extinct and their places have been taken by invaders from North America such as various ungulates, rodents, carnivores and rabbits. The faunal richness of the Americas as a whole has been drastically reduced.
>
> (Pielou 1979, p. 58)

As discussed above, Axelrod is of the opinion that the desert floras in the Southern Hemisphere have been spared this sort of competition from northern species. In the case of Australia, mixing did not lead to extinction but to greater diversity:

> Eventually as the Australian plate moved northward and particularly after New Guinea emerged in tropical latitudes, many plants and animals from Asia entered the region for the first time.
>
> (Axelrod and Raven 1972, p. 229)

For some reason, collision with Asia did not deplete the flora of Australia to the same degree as it depleted the flora of India.

There are many problems for paleobotanists to solve regarding the origin and diversification of the angiosperms, but based upon current understanding, both the present distribution of ancient plant genera (e.g., *Araucaria*, *Podocarpus*, *Nothofagus*) and the present diversity in other genera (e.g., *Acacia*, *Eucalyptus*, *Banksia*) can best be accounted for by events that happened millions of years ago.

Box 9.1 | Mr. Hofmeister and the vanishing gametophyte

The evolution of plant life cycles

Sadly, plant life cycles are too often taught, if at all, through memorizing the stages and tissue types in the life cycle of a flowering plant. This is hardly an inspiration to further study in botany. Although the preface states that I assume you know some basic botany, increasingly, given the emphasis on teaching physiology and genetics, it seems that one can no longer presuppose familiarity with the alternation of generations. Yet, the alteration of generations is arguably the most important theory synthesizing life history and evolution in the plant kingdom.

To understand the theory, and its implications for evolution and ecology, we need to begin, not with the flowering plants, but rather with the life cycle of primitive plants such as *Rhynia* (Figure 1.11), *Lepidodendron* (Figure 1.13), or modern seedless plants such as ferns. In these plants, we can still see clearly two entirely different life history phases, the sporophyte (which is diploid) and the gametophyte (which is haploid). The sporophyte has cells that undergo meiosis, producing large numbers of haploid cells (spores). Each spore develops into a gametophyte that produces sperm and/or egg cells. The fusion of egg and sperm then produces a diploid sporophyte. The sporophyte and gametophyte generations therefore alternate. Most vascular plant fossils (e.g., Figures 1.11 and 1.13) represent the sporophyte stage, but gametophytes, while rarer, have also been found (Figure B9.1a).

This alternation of generations would seem to be rather inefficient and improbable. Why should a plant have two life history phases at all? Why should plants that live on land have sperm that must swim through water to reach eggs? The answer illustrates a profound and frequently misunderstood point in evolution: natural selection does not create a perfect solution to environmental hazards. Natural selection can only modify an existing situation by weeding out the worst alternatives. The alternation of generations appears to have been directly inherited from the algae, where it is widespread and appears in many different guises. All early land plants, both extinct forms and those which can be thought of as living fossils, have a conspicuous alteration of generations (Kenrick and Crane 1997, Taylor et al. 2005.) In such plants, the ferns being the best known example, both life history stages are free-living and independent of one another. In theory, one could go into a forest and seek either gametophytes or sporophytes of these species. In practice, the sporophytes are much larger and more obvious, and so they tend to receive most of the attention from botanists. Gametophytes are rarely seen.

Swimming sperm could severely limit reproduction, particularly in drier circumstances. Large areas of land might then have remained largely uninhabited by plants. The history of plant evolution can be viewed as a clash between the stress imposed by drought, and the inherited raw material of an algal life cycle better-suited to water. Seeds and pollen arise as a consequence.

The origin of seeds and pollen

Some living and many fossil plants are heterosporous – that is, the sporophyte produces two types of spores, large ones (megaspores that become female gametophytes) and small ones (microspores that become male gametophytes). *Selaginella* is the common example studied in botany courses. Should some ancestral plants have delayed dispersal of the megaspores, perhaps by something as simple as an imperfectly-rupturing sporangium, the female gametophytes could have matured while still attached to the sporophyte. This minor aberration could have had multiple short term advantages including (1) protection of the gameto-phyte from predators, (2) continued provision of water and nutrients by the sporophyte, and (3) a general reduction in the time required for a complete life cycle. A female gametophyte retained upon the sporophyte is the precursor to the ovule and seed.

Microspores which would otherwise have dispersed to the ground, developed into male gametophytes, and released sperm, could equally have been dispersed by wind to adjacent shoots possessing female gametophytes. Male gametophyte dispersal through the air would have been the precursor to pollen. Most of the vascular plants, including the conifers and the flowering plants, now have seeds and pollen.

The vanishing gametophyte

The gametophyte stage is still prominent in the life cycle of most primitive plants. It remains the dominant life history phase in mosses. Early fossils of gametophytes are even larger than those of present plants, with antheridia (sperm producing organs) and archegonia (egg producing organs) borne on stalked gametangiophores (Figure B9.1a). The evolutionary history of plants illustrates continued pressure to reduce the size and complexity of this reproductive stage.

The stages in the reduction of gametophytes are represented by varying living plant groups (Figure B9.1b). In the seedless vascular plants, represented by ferns and their allies, gametophytes are still free living. In general we can reconstruct the following sequence of events: female gametophytes were at first retained within the sporangia of the sporophyte, then reduced to ovules protected within cones, and finally, in the case of flowering plants, reduced to a mere handful of cells in what is cryptically named the "embryo sac." In a less dramatic trend, male gametophytes, became reduced in size until, in the case of flowering plants, they become a mere vegetative nucleus within a pollen grain. One can view this trend in two ways, both of which have value. If we focus upon the extreme modification and reduction in the gametophytes achieved by natural selection, we see a strong and consistent evolu-tionary trend through the entire plant kingdom. If we focus instead on the continued occurrence of alternation of generations, we see a conserved and unifying algal life cycle in spite of the enormous evolutionary diversification that has occurred in vascular plants.

A unifying theory

Remarkably, this essential unifying theory of plant evolution was largely unraveled by a single botanist, Wilhelm Hofmeister (1824–1877). Hofmeister (Figure B9.1c) was largely self-taught, having left school at the age of 15 to work as an apprentice in a book and music shop in Leipzig. Yet he became "one of the most notable scientists in the history of plant biology" (Kaplan and Cooke 1996). Note that while he did this vital research on plants, Mr. Hofmeister was not a tenured professor – he supported himself, and carried out most of his research on his own time, largely from 4 to 6 in the morning before going to the store (Goebel 1905). He was only 27 when he

Figure B9.1(a) Reconstruction of a gametophyte preserved as a 400 million year old fossil. The eggs and sperm were produced on top of the stalked structures (termed gametangiophores) in archegonia and antheridia, which can be seen microscopically in slides made from the fossils (Taylor et al. 2005). Note the apparent similarity to modern liverworts like *Marchantia* that are often studied in botany courses (from Kenrick and Crane 1997).

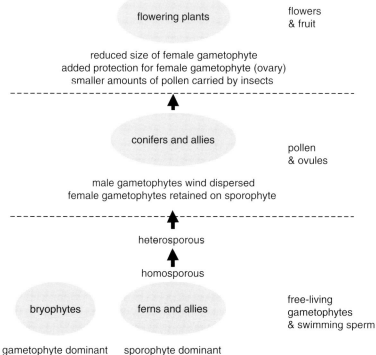

Figure B9.1(b) Major trends in the evolution of the alternation of generations, beginning at the bottom with the free-living gametophytes and swimming sperm typical of early land plants. (Although the diagram shows that the early land plants were homosporous, the spores apparently developed into male and female gametophytes (Taylor et al. 2005).)

Figure B9.1(c) Wilhelm Hofmeister (1824–1877) uncovered the alternation of generations in plants and published a monograph on the topic in 1851 (from Goebel 1905).

Figure B9.1(c) Wilhelm Hofmeister (1824–1877) uncovered the alternation of generations in plants and published a monograph on the topic in 1851 (from Goebel 1905).

published his ground-breaking monograph that documented the alternation of generations in plants. This appeared in 1851, eight years before Darwin published *The Origin of Species*. Not until 1863 (at the age of 39) was Hofmeister employed as a professor.

9.3 | $>10^4$ years: the Pleistocene glaciations

The Pleistocene is the second to last epoch in the Earth's history; it was a period of climatic instability that began about 2 million years ago during which extensive ice sheets and other glaciers formed repeatedly (e.g., Delcourt and Delcourt 1991, Levin 1994). For this reason, its popular name is the "Ice Age." The Pleistocene and the Holocene (the last 10 000 years) together comprise the Quaternary Period. Although there have been many ice advances and retreats in the Earth's history, much of its surface has been shaped by the last great period of glacial advance and retreat – a period which ended only about 10 000 years ago. No student of plant ecology can afford to be ignorant of the effects that the last ice advance had upon the landscape. The effects are often very local and their results may vary from heavily scoured landscapes lacking soil, to great terminal moraines, to

wind-deposited soils, to large lakes. Thus the influences in any particular area should be examined in more detail than a text like this can
provide. It is, however, essential that you learn about Quaternary Period
events that shaped your particular region of the world; this will require
you to seek out relevant monographs and papers. The comments here
will serve only to place these specific details in a larger context.

Now a comment on names. The defining event of the Pleistocene
has been the repeated advance of large sheets of ice. In general, the
advances and retreats consisted of four major advances interspersed
with three major warm periods. The names of the advances differed
depending upon where the field-work had been done. In North
America they were named, from youngest to oldest, Wisconsinan,
Illinoian, Kansan, and Nebraskan; in Great Britain, Devensian,
Wolstonian, Anglian, and then a further series of at least four other
advances. In Europe they were Weichselian, Saalian, Elsterian, and
then a different set of at least three advances. It has proven difficult
to put these together in one large picture, particularly as the numbers
of advances and retreats have expanded with our knowledge of
glacial geology. In fact, marine isotope records suggest that a much
more complicated series of advances and retreats occurred
(Section 1.10), although ice core records indeed show four glacial
periods (Figure 1.17(b)).

9.3.1   Erosion and deposition by glacial ice

During the last glacial advance and retreat, substantial portions of
the Earth were covered by ice as little as 25 000 years ago, and many
temperate areas were uncovered only within the last 10 000 years. As
the ice retreated, it left behind the present-day topography. Soil was
scoured away and pushed south of the ice margin. (American farmers
now grow corn using the soil that was once on my Canadian land.)
The landscape was ground flatter in the north and then covered with
a variety of glacial deposits from moraines and eskers to clay and
sand plains (Figure 9.10). You should obtain a physiographic map of
your own home landscape in order to develop an appreciation of the
local impacts of events near the end of the Pleistocene Epoch. As one
example of the influence of glacial history, consider the quite remarkable changes in the shape and drainage of the Great Lakes during this
period (Figure 9.11). The distribution of many vegetation types in this
area can still be best explained by past events. For example, the
distribution of the nationally rare plant, *Rhexia virginica*, is still associated with areas once covered by glacial Lake Algonquin. The southern-
most location of the arctic species *Saxifraga aizoon* is in a canyon that
formed when once the Great Lakes drained through Algonquin Park.
The extensive pine forests of the upper Ottawa Valley occur on an old
delta where a glacial river drained into the Champlain Sea.

9.3.2   Loess

Wind moved large volumes of soil exposed during glacial events.
Deposits of wind-blown soil, called loess, cover large areas of

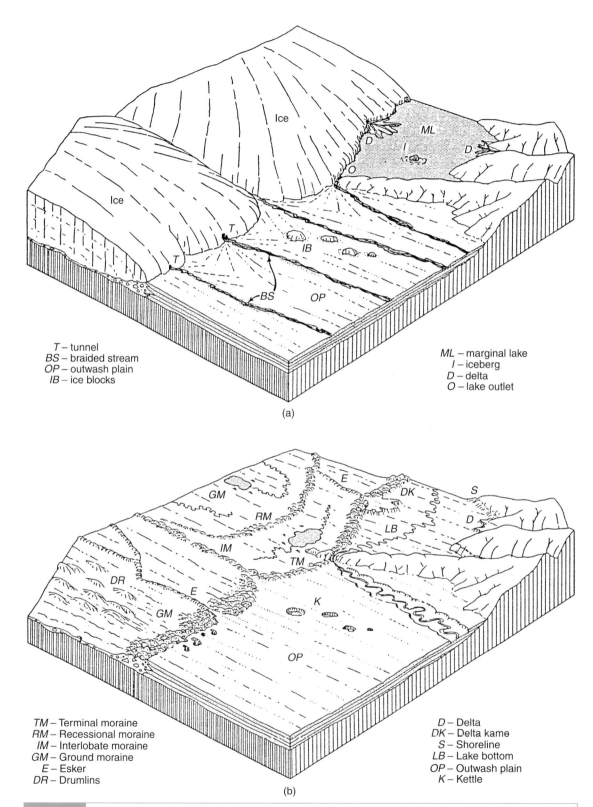

T – tunnel
BS – braided stream
OP – outwash plain
IB – ice blocks

ML – marginal lake
I – iceberg
D – delta
O – lake outlet

(a)

TM – Terminal moraine
RM – Recessional moraine
IM – Interlobate moraine
GM – Ground moraine
E – Esker
DR – Drumlins

D – Delta
DK – Delta kame
S – Shoreline
LB – Lake bottom
OP – Outwash plain
K – Kettle

(b)

Figure 9.10 Landforms produced near the margin of an ice sheet. (a) Ice margin in almost stagnant condition. (b) Ice entirely gone, revealing subglacial forms (from Strahler 1971).

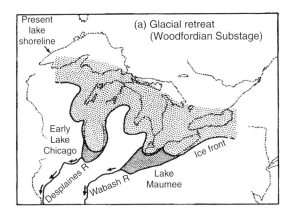

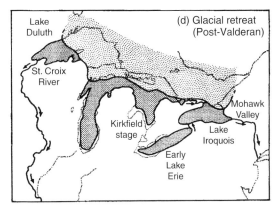

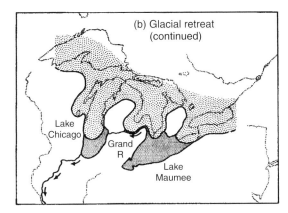

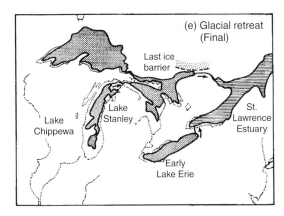

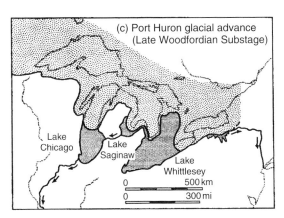

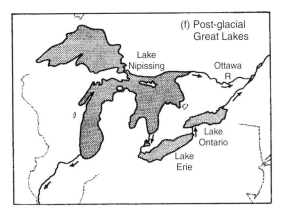

Figure 9.11 Sequence of stages in the development of the Great Lakes (from Strahler 1971).

the Northern Hemisphere: the central and northwestern United States, Alaska, the east European plain (Figure 9.12), and southern Europe. It is thought that loess was derived from the floodplains of braided rivers draining away from the glaciers as well as from glacial debris. The deep deposits of loess in China appear to have been swept in from the Gobi Desert; in places they are 100 meters thick.

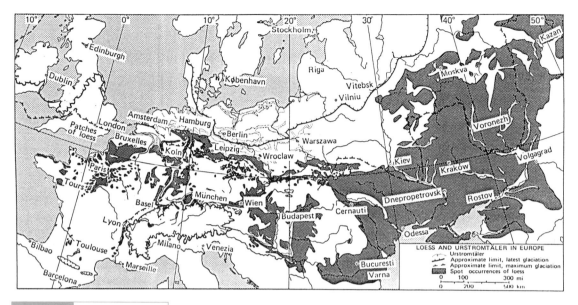

Figure 9.12 Loess and loess-like deposits in Europe (from Flint 1971).

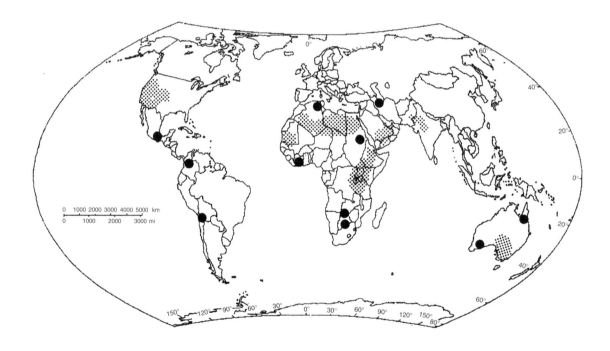

Figure 9.13 Over the last 30 000 years pluvial lakes have formed in and then disappeared from the shaded regions of the Earth. Dots show isolated lakes (after Street and Grove 1979).

9.3.3 Pluvial lakes

Changes in water balance south of ice sheets caused the accumulation of water in previously arid areas (Flint 1971). Large lakes formed in areas such as the southwestern United States, central Australia, and Africa (Figure 9.13). Many of these lakes are now entirely dry or greatly reduced in size.

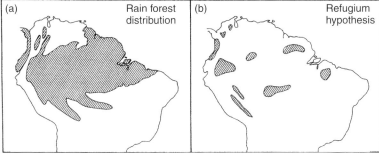

Figure 9.14 (a) Rain forest currently covers the Amazon basin in northern South America. Current evidence indicates that this region remained forested during the last glacial period. (b) The falsified hypothesis. It has been suggested that the rain forest may have shrunk to small refugia during ice advances, but current data provide no evidence to support this hypothesis (Colinvaux et al. 1996, 2000, 2001) (after Pielou 1979).

9.3.4 Drought and tropical forests

Just as some areas became wetter during glacial advances (Figure 9.13), other areas may have become drier. Tropical forests currently cover the Amazon basin (Figure 9.14(a)). How, if at all, did these forests change during colder, glacial periods? Perhaps changes in these rain forests were minimal, since this area is near the equator and far from advancing ice sheets. Alternatively, perhaps drier periods allowed savanna to invade substantial areas of the Amazon, and perhaps the rain forests contracted to isolated refugia (Figure 9.14(b)). The hypothesis of isolated refugia (e.g., Haffer 1969) has seemed attractive to many, since each ice advance would have fragmented the forests, allowing periods of isolation and speciation. If this had happened, the cycle of glacial periods (Figure 1.17(b)) might have acted as diversity pump, conveniently explaining both the high diversity of the Amazonian forests, the higher numbers of species in certain regions, and the distributions of some species. (This model may also appeal to another audience for another reason, since it implies that rain forests may be relatively insensitive to disturbance, and that large areas may be lost with few consequences for diversity.) Of course, one might equally argue that it was the very absence of recurring disturbance that allowed so many species to evolve and survive in the Amazon, and that some regions have species (if they do) as a consequence of other factors like more kinds of habitats (Chapter 11).

Contrasting hypotheses are a part of science, and knowledge increases only when data are collected to test among them. Given the enormous area of Amazonia, and the many concerns about the loss of primary (frontier) rain forests (Chapter 12), these contrasting hypotheses need to be tested, and the incorrect one(s) discarded.

Here is a challenge: how does one test whether savanna invaded the Amazon during drier periods tens of thousands of years ago? There are at least three sources of biological data available. The first is the Amazon delta. If the rain forests periodically receded, this should be mirrored in changes in the characteristics of sediments in the delta. Samples of Amazon River detritus taken from coastal sediment indicate that the Amazon basin remained continually forested, at least up to 70 000 years ago (Kastner and Goñi 2003).

A second source of evidence could come from sediment cores taken from lakes. Periods of savanna should be marked by layers having pollen grains from grasses and other savanna plants. Finding good pollen records is much more difficult in the Amazon than at higher latitudes (Colinvaux et al. 2001). The Amazon basin has few old lakes with long sediment records, and further, many rain forest trees produce little pollen that could drift into lakes, since the pollen is dispersed by animals. These problems have been slowly overcome, and a number of cores taken for study (including a 40 000 year pollen record from Lake Pata on a 500–600 m tall inselberg, a rock outcrop that emerges above the rain forest (Colinvaux et al. 1996). This core, and others like it, show no evidence of periods of savanna expanding into the rain forest (Colinvaux et al. 2000, 2001). A third source of evidence comes from fossil plants. Fossil plant assemblages that predate the Quaternary glaciations show that high plant diversity occurred long before such hypothetical refugia might have formed (Wilf et al. 2003). Hence, this evidence indicates that the map of refugia in Figure 9.14(b) is wrong, and that the Amazonian rain forests were relatively unaffected by changing climate during the ice ages. Moreover, the hypothesis is not needed to explain tree diversity, since this diversity predated the Quaternary. In the words of Colinvaux et al. (2001): "All geological data from Amazonian landforms imply continuous humid weathering throughout late Tertiary and Quaternary times . . .. All available Amazonian pollen data, without exception and including new data, imply biome stability . . .. The 'aridity with refuges paradigm' now impedes Amazonian research and should be discarded."

Although the evidence is now clear that savannas did not recently intrude into Amazonia, savannas are widespread elsewhere in South and Central America, and in the world, and their distribution is very sensitive to drought and fire. In drier climates, or drier locations, savanna can replace forests. Recurring fire is a natural part of this process (Figure 9.15), and the type of savanna that forms will depend up fire frequency (Myers et al. 2006). In tropical landscapes with high fire frequencies, most species of trees survive only in narrow strips of forest along water courses (termed riparian forest or gallery forest). During wetter periods with lower fire frequency, the forest may expand into upland areas, while during drier periods with higher fire frequency, the forest may shrink to the margins of rivers. In order to investigate the potential importance of riparian forests as refugia for forest plants, Meave and Kelmman (1994) explored an area of Belize that was mostly savanna, and enumerated the tropical tree species they encountered in riparian forests. A total of 292 species was found in a cumulative sample of only 1.6 ha. Some tracts of riparian forest had as many tree species as continuous forests elsewhere in Central America. Moreover, small changes in flood frequency and soil fertility can produce different types of riparian forest (Veneklaas et al. 2005), which may further increase the number of species of trees that can survive in landscapes that are largely

Figure 9.15 In drier climates, and in drier locations, tropical broadleaf forests can be replaced by open savanna. Recurring fire is a natural part of this process. In fire-dominated landscapes, narrow strips of forest along watercourses may be the only remnants of broadleaf forest in the landscape. (Caribbean pinelands of the Rio Platano Biosphere Reserve in Honduras, courtesy Ronald Myers).

savanna. Hence, all the evidence suggests that the refugium hypothesis mapped in Figure 9.14(b) is incorrect.

In summary, we know that drought and fire can shift the relative distribution of forest and savanna in a landscape. The hypothesis that drought reduced Amazonian rain forests to small refugia during the last ice age (Figure 9.14(b)) is not supported by current evidence. However, there is good evidence that in drier climates elsewhere, where drought and fire do allow savanna to expand, water courses are an important refuge for trees to escape recurring fire.

9.3.5 Sea level decrease

The enormous amounts of water locked into glacial ice lowered sea levels by as much as 100 m. This would have opened up new areas of habitat along previously submerged coastal plains, as well as created land bridges between some continents. The continental margins of eastern North America, for example, appear to have had a rich wetland flora appropriately called the Atlantic Coastal Plain flora; peat

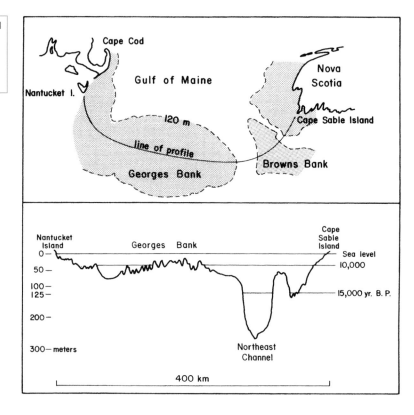

Figure 9.16 Changes to sea level in relation to a profile from Nantucket Island, Massachusetts, to Cape Sable Island, Nova Scotia (from Keddy and Wisheu 1989).

balls recovered from offshore illustrate how well developed the peatlands in these areas were. When the sea level rose, most of this habitat was submerged, which left widely spaced fragments of this distinctive wetland habitat along the eastern coast of North America. The distribution of *Sabatia kennedyana* in the Carolinas, Cape Cod, and southwestern Nova Scotia suggests that at one time these areas were connected by land, but when the sea level rose the areas of *S. kennedyana*'s distribution were no longer contiguous (Figure 9.16).

Similarly, Beringia would have been exposed enough to allow an exchange in fauna and flora between Eurasia and northern North America. During the peak of the ice age, this connection between the two continents was covered by xeric tundra, which provided food for large grazing mammals and allowed them to survive as they migrated across the land bridge. Snow sheep, musk-oxen, moose, lynx, and black bear arrived from Siberia (Hopkins 1967, Pielou 1979). Another species that is thought to have migrated eastward across this land bridge was a hominid known as *Homo sapiens*.

9.3.6 Migration

Changes in sea levels, pluvial lake levels, and ice cover would have forced major changes in the distributions of plant and animal species. Picture the world's vegetation types at the maximum of the last ice advance; Figure 9.17 shows that the vegetation of eastern North

(a) Present

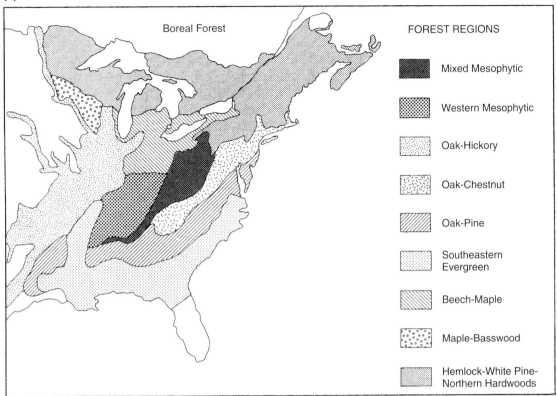

(b) Past

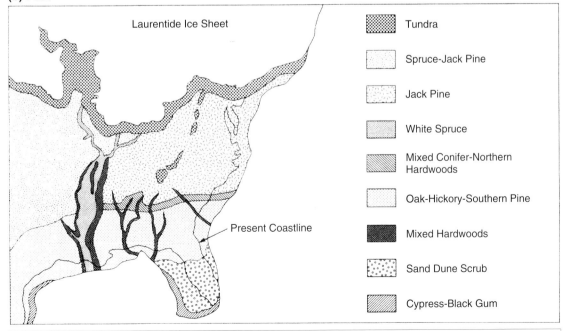

Figure 9.17 (a) Major associations within the deciduous forests of eastern North America, and (b) reconstruction of the vegetation of eastern North America during the Wisconsin glacial maximum about 18 000 years BP (from Archibold 1995).

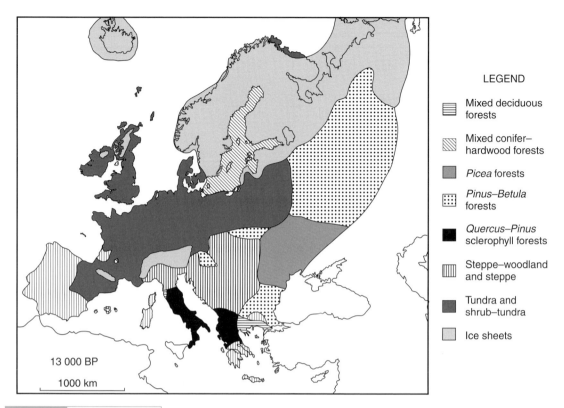

LEGEND

≡ Mixed deciduous forests

╲ Mixed conifer–hardwood forests

■ *Picea* forests

⋮ *Pinus–Betula* forests

■ *Quercus–Pinus* sclerophyll forests

▥ Steppe–woodland and steppe

■ Tundra and shrub–tundra

□ Ice sheets

13 000 BP

1000 km

Figure 9.18 Simplified paleo-vegetation map of Europe for 13 000 BP based upon palynological data (from Huntley 1990).

America was vastly different from that today. In Europe, temperate zone trees such as *Carya*, *Liquidambar*, *Robinia*, and *Tsuga* became extinct around this time, perhaps because the Alps prevented southward migration as the ice advanced (Daubenmire 1978). Figure 9.18 shows the vegetation of Europe at 13 000 BP. Note the restriction of deciduous forests to two small regions, one on the west coast of Italy and the other north of the Adriatic Sea.

While species distributions today are obviously different from distributions in the past, knowledge of how plant species responded to the various dramatic changes that occurred is still incomplete. This has led to debates about whether the world's vegetation zones are, in fact, in equilibrium with today's climate or whether they represent delays in migration following the retreat of the ice. Palynological research carried out over the last half of the twentieth century tends to confirm that there was rapid recolonization northward as the ice retreated (Figure 9.19). The need for accurate reconstructions of past events has now been given an added impetus by fears that we are altering Earth's climate (Section 1.10). Establishing a connection between climate and vegetation in the past provides a vital tool for forecasting changes in vegetation.

9.3.7 Hominids

Modern humans (*Homo sapiens*) appear during the last Pleistocene interglacial, about 100 000 years ago. At this time Neanderthals

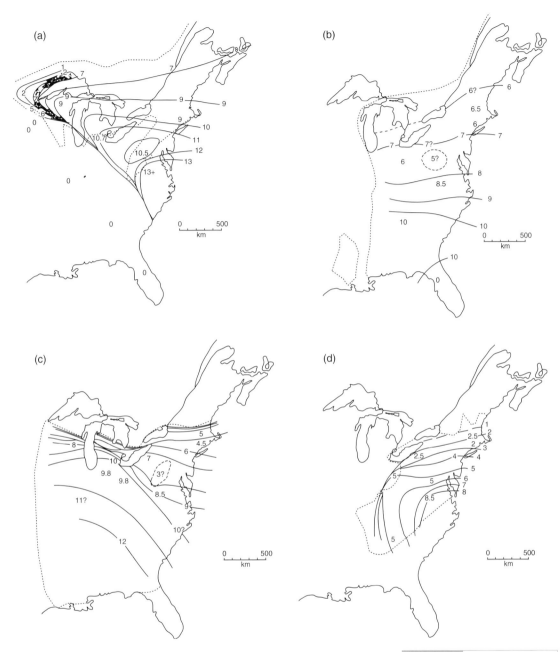

Figure 9.19 The northward migration of trees as the continental glaciers receded. (a) white pine, (b) chestnut, (c) hickory, (d) beech. Note that each species apparently re-invaded from slightly different refugia, some of which may have been on the now-flooded continental shelf. Solid lines mark the advancing frontiers at 1000-year intervals and dotted lines surround the modern ranges of the species (from Davis 1976).

(H. neanderthalensis) were in Europe and parts of Asia. It is thought that H. sapiens arrived in North America only some 10 000 years ago by crossing the Bering land bridge, although archaeologists are still struggling to date the exact time of arrival (Pringle 1996). As H. sapiens spread across North America, there was a massive die off of large mammals, and paleo-ecologists still argue about whether climate change or over-hunting was responsible for this wave of extinction. The fact that similar waves of extinction are associated with the arrival of humans in other areas including Australia and Easter Island (Section 12.3.2) suggests that even our

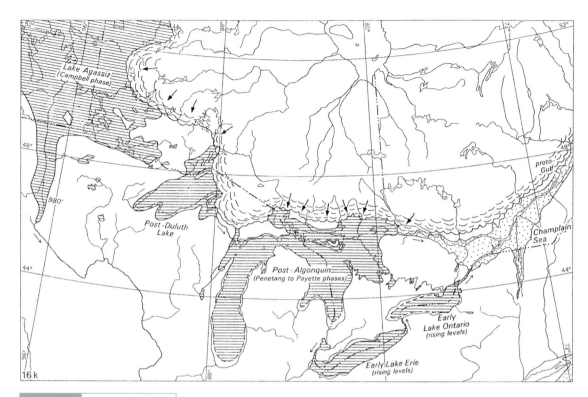

Figure 9.20 As the continental ice sheet retreated, the Great Lakes began to take their modern form. The Atlantic Ocean flooded southern Quebec, eastern Ontario, and northern New England, forming the shallow Champlain Sea. During one short period about 11 200 BP, the receding ice allowed melt water to flow from glacial Lake Algonquin directly along the margins of the ice sheet and into the Champlain Sea. Relict plants such as *Saxifraga aizoon* still dot the ancient route of this glacial outlet (from Douglas 1972).

ancestors were busily destroying the new lands they encountered. In the period since the last major glaciation, our species has spread around the world and multiplied until its numbers (in mid-2006) exceed six and a half billion.

9.3.8 Flooding

At the time the glaciers finally began to retreat, the weight of glacial ice had depressed northern areas so much that sea water flooded far inland. The Champlain Sea formed in eastern North America (Figure 9.20), the Hudson Bay lowlands were inundated (Glooschenko 1980, Abraham and Keddy 2005), and much of northern Russia and Scandinavia were submerged. As these regions still continue to rebound from the weight of the ice, they emerge from beneath the sea with lines of raised beaches (Stevenson et al. 1986, Bégin et al. 1989). Similarly, in South America the entire Amazon valley appears to have been drowned about 15 000 BP. During this period, a large freshwater lake 1500 km long and up to 100 km wide may have extended inland from the mouth of the Amazon (Irion et al. 1995, Müller et al. 1995). Sediments deposited in this lake would have produced deltas in the middle Amazon.

In summary, the effects of ice advances and retreats, and the associated changes in climate and sea level, caused major changes in the biota of the Earth. Such major changes provide the physiographic and ecological template upon which more recent processes are laid.

9.4 | $>10^2$ years: plant succession

9.4.1 Succession

Succession refers to the sequence of changes in vegetation that occurs after a site is disturbed – a sequence of events that normally leads to the re-establishment of the vegetation that was initially removed. If the disturbance is minor, and the soil and propagules remain, the recovery of the vegetation is usually rapid; this is termed **secondary succession**. Examples of secondary succession include the steps by which forests invade clearings that have been created by storms or logging; the soil is generally intact, and propagules either remain in the soil or are available from adjacent stands of forest. If the disturbance is more severe, and the soil and propagules are also destroyed, a much longer series of events called **primary succession** begins. In this case, the soil itself must be re-established and propagules may have to invade from distant sources. Examples of primary succession include the sequence of changes in which sand dunes become forest, shallow water becomes peat bog, and severely burned sites or sites with deep volcanic debris become forest. Frequently it is possible to distinguish a number of distinctive stages through which recovering communities pass; these are termed **seres**. When the process of change ends, because the vegetation is in balance with the climate, or because the species in the final sere are capable of maintaining themselves and restricting further invasion (these are really just two different ways of saying the same thing), the **climax** is reached.

Elton (1927), an early father of animal ecology, was discouraged by even the thought of studying succession:

> The writer has found that it is almost impossible to make even a superficial study of succession in any large and complicated community, owing to the appalling amount of mere collecting which is required, and the trouble of getting the collected material identified. When one has to include seasonal changes throughout the year as well, the work becomes first of all disheartening, then terrific, and finally impossible.
>
> (p. 28)

Impossible or disheartening, plant ecologists must face the fact that vegetation changes occur. Chapter 6 provided some examples of succession and surveyed the many kinds of disturbance that occur in natural vegetation. Succession is one of the key concepts in ecology, yet one that has at times been overused. As a consequence, it has occasionally become fashionable to move to the opposite extreme and deny that succession occurs. The truth in this case lies somewhere in between these extremes, although my own inclination is certainly to emphasize the many ways in which the concept of succession is of value. Before considering the debates that have occurred regarding succession, it is useful to examine some real

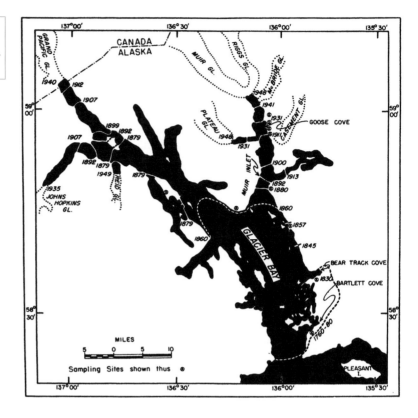

examples of succession, with particular emphasis upon primary succession, since many of the examples in Chapter 6 provided an introduction to secondary succession.

9.4.2 Examples of succession

Succession after the retreat of glaciers: deglaciated valleys

The Glacier Bay region in Alaska provides a 200-year-long perspective on succession. It is possible to determine, for an array of sites, how long each has been uncovered by glacial ice (Figure 9.21), revealing a chronoseqence of ecological communities (recall Section 3.8.2). The dates are based upon evidence such as the number of rings in trees growing on moraines, corroborated by written records and photographic surveys. The vegetation in the study area changes with site age. The youngest sites have mosses in the genus *Rhacomitrium* along with vascular plants such as *Equisetum variegatum*, *Dryas drummondii*, and *Salix arctica*. The oldest sites are forested by *Picea sitchensis* along with *Tsuga heterophylla* and *T. mertensiana*. This shift from bryophytes to dense forest is typical of pioneer succession in other deglaciating sites. An overview of work done at this site is provided by Crocker and Major (1955) and Kershaw and Looney (1985).

Crocker and Major joined an expedition to the site in 1952 to study changes in soils along this successional gradient. A number of important trends were apparent. Over the first 100 years, the pH

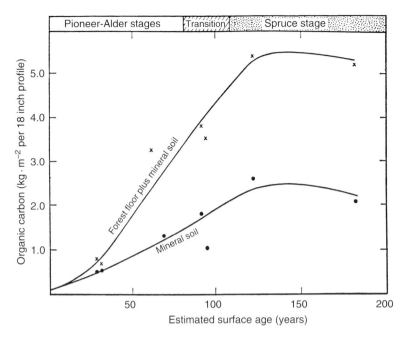

Figure 9.22 Organic carbon accumulation in mineral soil and on the forest floor under *Alnus crispa* (from Crocker and Major 1955).

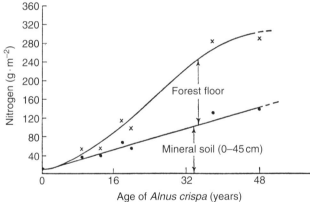

Figure 9.23 Accumulation of nitrogen in the mineral soil and on the forest floor under *Alnus crispa* (from Crocker and Major 1955).

of the upper 5 cm of soil declines from above 8.0 to 5.0. The rate of decline is most rapid during the first 50 years and changes only slightly after 100. Over the same time period, the amount of organic carbon rises steadily (Figure 9.22). Total nitrogen rises rapidly over the first hundred years but declines once *Picea* (spruce) becomes established (Figure 9.23). The rapid increase in soil nitrogen appears to be produced by *Alnus crispa*, a shrub known to fix nitrogen.

In 1984 Bormann and Sidle (1990) revisited this area and sampled the biomass and nitrogen content of the vegetation at four sites which corresponded to a seral sequence that progresses from *Alnus*-dominated sites (ca. 60 years old) to *Picea* forest (ca. 210 years old). Biomass appears to reach a peak of 300 tonnes·ha^{-1} after a century and a half (Figure 9.24) and total nitrogen shows similar patterns but reaches an asymptote half a century sooner. Since the volume of

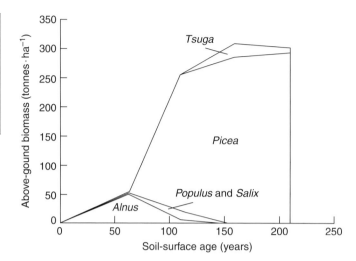

Figure 9.24 Distribution of the above-ground biomass by species in chronosequence at Glacier Bay, Alaska. Note that estimates are based on single large quadrats and that no estimates of between-stand variation are available (from Bormann and Sidle 1990).

wood declined slightly over the 100- to 200-year period, increased respiration by non-photosynthetic tissues seems unlikely to have set the upper limit in biomass. Rather, say Bormann and Sidle, the asymptote and the lower productivity of older stands is perhaps instead caused by limited nutrients (you may wish to review Section 3.8.2 for more on this topic).

Succession in peat bogs

The accumulation of partially decayed plant debris in peat bogs, particularly *Sphagnum* mosses, can produce deep accumulations of peat in wet habitats. Over time, as the peat deepens, plants lose contact with underlying mineral soil. This general process of peat bog succession has been understood and described for more than a century (Gorham 1953, 1957, Gore 1983, Keddy 2000). Eventually, peat accumulates to such a depth that the vegetation is little affected by the underlying topography and instead becomes largely controlled by climate (Foster and Glaser 1986). Figure 9.25 shows how the landscape becomes blanketed with peat. The final stage is an ombrotrophic bog – one in which the peat is deep enough that rainfall provides the only source of nutrients. How long does the process take? Compared to most geological processes it is rapid, since many areas now covered with peat were covered with ice as little as 10 000 years ago.

The intensive study of cores taken from peat bogs, and radiocarbon dating, allow us to reconstruct the process of bog formation. There are three hypotheses that might explain how large peatlands form.

1. There could be initiation of peat accumulation across a broad area, with steady accumulation of peat but no lateral expansion, in which case the area of the bog would remain unchanged but the depth would increase steadily through time.

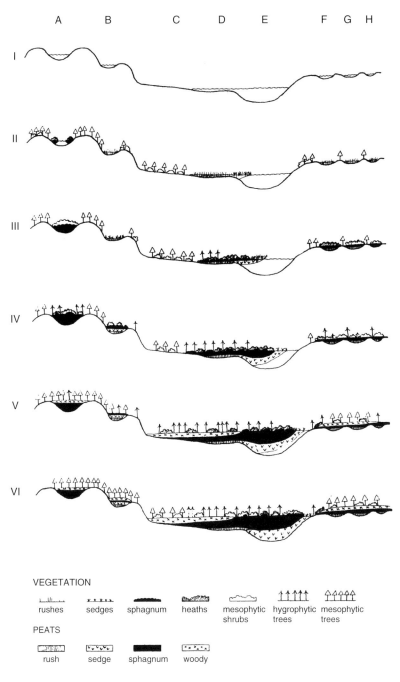

Figure 9.25 The development over time of peatlands in landscapes on the Precambrian shield, showing both the events in closed drainage (A, B, F, G, H) and situations where there is more seepage or water movement (C, D, E) (from Danereau and Segadas-Vianna 1952).

VEGETATION

| rushes | sedges | sphagnum | heaths | mesophytic shrubs | hygrophytic trees | mesophytic trees |

PEATS

| rush | sedge | sphagnum | woody |

2. Peat could begin to accumulate at a number of individual sites followed by expansion and fusion of the separate peat islands into one large bog.

3. Peat might also begin to accumulate at one site and gradually increase both in depth and area.

Consider the Hammarmossen Bog in the Bergslagen region of central Sweden; this bog developed on a broad, flat outwash plain

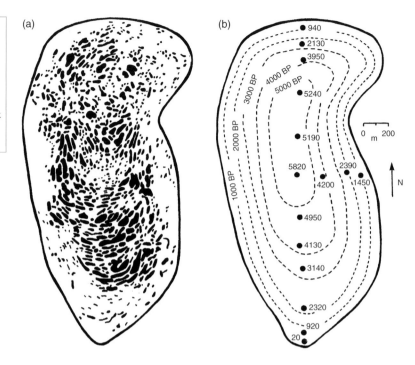

Figure 9.26 A top view of the Hammarmossen bog in Sweden, showing the distribution and size of open water pools (a) and basal radiocarbon dates with interpolated isochrones for bog expansion (b). The peat is 4 m thick at the center of the bog (from Foster and Wright 1990).

left by melting ice. To discriminate among the three models for bog formation, Foster and Wright (1990) took peat cores from a series of locations in this bog and obtained radiocarbon dates from the bottom of each core near the mineral soil. Figure 9.26(a) shows the general outline of this bog, with the open-water pools covering its surface; the adjoining sketch gives contours of bog age as determined by radiocarbon dating. The bog began forming some 6000 years BP, with growth initiated near the center under what is now the deepest peat. It seems clear that, in this case, the bog has not only grown upward by peat accumulation (the peat depth near the middle is some 4 m, giving a rate of accumulation of 0.67 mm per year), but it has also expanded laterally at a rate of some 200 m per thousand years.

The careful dating of pools also allowed Foster and Wright to study the process by which pools form on the surface of raised bogs. They conclude that "pool development is the result of biological process under hydrological control." Pools apparently begin as small hollows on relatively steep slopes covered by shallow peat. As the peat accumulates, these hollows turn into pools. Presumably the rate of peat accumulation in the hollows is less than that of the adjoining ridges, so that over time the peat rises around the depression. At the same time, the water table rises. The plants near the center of the depression are gradually killed and replaced by open water. Adjoining pools may coalesce to produce larger pools.

During periods of drought, the peat as well as the surface vegetation may burn. At a minimum, burning can create ash-filled depressions to serve as regeneration sites for bog species, or, if the peat burns deeper, a temporary pool. In some cases, the peat can burn right down to the underlying mineral soil, in which case the process of peat accumulation and bog formation would start over (Wein 1983, Kuhry 1994, White 1994). The studies outlined above reinforce our understanding of succession and help clarify the mechanisms involved. Peat bogs may be one of the ecosystem types coming closest to the strict Clementsian view of ecosystems as super organisms (Section 10.5.1).

Succession on sand dunes

A preponderance of the studies of succession have been carried out on soil sequences in post-glacial landscapes of the Northern Hemisphere. How far can one extrapolate from such studies? Walker et al. (1981) observed that: "The effects of prolonged soil weathering are absent in such areas and field evidence is biased toward the recognition of progressive stages to a climax since insufficient time has elapsed for retrogressive stages to be important." What, in other words, would happen if longer periods of time were allowed to elapse?

To answer this question, we will examine the study of a large sand dune system on the subtropical coast of Queensland in extreme eastern Australia. Six of the dunes that form this system depict a successional sequence that extends through the late Quaternary Period. Regrettably, absolute radiocarbon dates were not available, but dune ages in the range of 30 000 years are suggested. Some of the woody genera present at the site will be familiar from Section 9.2.3: *Banksia*, *Eucalyptus*, and *Acacia*. Along this sequence of dunes, biomass at first increases where trees such as *Banksia serrata*, *Eucalyptus intermedia*, and *Angophora woodsiana* occur, but then it falls again as these trees are replaced by shrubs and sedges. Similarly, canopy cover is high on the intermediate dunes but rapidly declines on the oldest dunes. On the oldest dunes, phosphorus and calcium have been leached from the surface to a depth of many meters (Figure 9.27).

Atmospheric deposition of nutrients is apparently unable to balance the rates of leaching, and the authors suggest that other activities such as burning, logging, and grazing may increase the rates of nutrient loss. It therefore appears that along this dune sequence there is at first a succession to forest cover, but as rain continues to leach nutrients from the soil, there is regression to an infertile open shrubland. Thus, conclude Walker et al. (1981), the younger dunes show a **progressive** sequence, and the older dunes a **retrogressive** sequence. The term retrogressive is slightly misleading, however, because the vegetation on the oldest dunes is not the same as the vegetation on the younger dunes (Figure 9.28). Biomass and soil nutrients may show retrogression, but the species composition continues unidirectional change to sedges (*Caustis recurvata*, *Coleocarya gracilis*) and shrubs (*Acacia ulicifolia*, *Aotus lanigera*) that occur only on the oldest dunes. The degree to which this model applies to other tropical systems and other infertile soils remains to be seen.

Similar patterns may occur elsewhere where sandy soils and high rainfall coincide. Near the Gulf Coast of Veracruz, Mexico, there is an

Figure 9.27 Nutrients in six dune systems (1 youngest to 6 oldest) at various depths. (a) Total soil phosphorus (ppm), (b) total soil calcium (ppm) (from Walker et al. 1981).

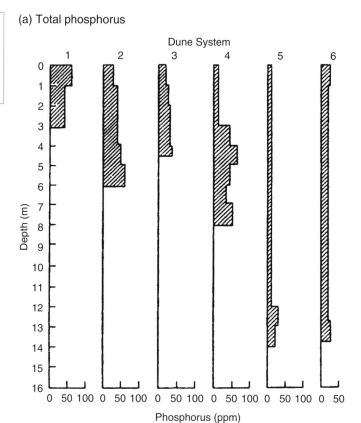

(a) Total phosphorus

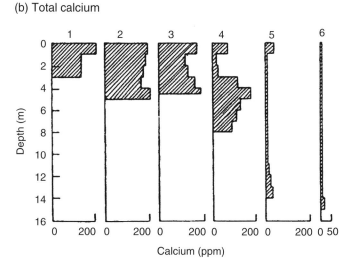

(b) Total calcium

Figure 9.27 Nutrients in six dune systems (1 youngest to 6 oldest) at various depths. (a) Total soil phosphorus (ppm), (b) total soil calcium (ppm) (from Walker et al. 1981).

extensive system of Pleistocene age dunes covered by low semi-deciduous forest; rainfall exceeds 1300 mm, most of which falls between June and September. Measurements, by Kellman and Roulet (1990), show high infiltration rates and leaching of soil nutrients: "The successional pattern that emerges from these data is of an early phase of succession in which biomass increases, and

(a)

(b)

Figure 9.28 Photographs contrasting the high and low stature and biomass of forests developed on dunes of (a) recent (ca. 10 000–20 000 years) versus (b) ancient (ca. 200 000–400 000 years) origin on the dune system at Cooloola, Queensland. The individual shown in the photograph is about 1.65 m tall (from Peet 1992).

increased quantities of nutrients are cycled, but during which absolute loss of nutrients increases even more rapidly. This is followed by a much longer phase in which soil mineralogical changes are induced by weathering, and result in a less leaky system" (pp. 673–674). These later successional forests cycle large quantities of nutrients and have a much lower output of nutrients. At this stage of succession, fine roots are concentrated in the upper 20 cm of the soil, presumably to enhance the recapture of nutrients from litter.

Succession and fire in coniferous forests

Forests composed of conifers are common at high latitudes and high altitudes, as well as upon infertile soils of sand plains and dunes. The vast boreal forests of the Northern Hemisphere support the largest continuous stands of conifer forest, some 15.8 million km^2

compared with about 3.3 million km^2 in mountainous areas (Archibold 1995). Because of their high resin content and evergreen foliage, conifers burn easily. When fire occurs, the underlying soil of the forested area may also burn, since it is often comprised of peat formed from understorey mosses and tree needles. The dominant kind of fire is a high intensity crown fire that can easily cover 10 000 ha and sometimes more than 400 000 ha (Heinselman 1981). The frequency of fire changes with both vegetation and climate; cycles of 100–150 years are typical of lichen woodlands in the extreme north, while those in eastern North America are longer (150–300 years). In drier areas of the west, surface fires of low intensity may burn every 25 years or so, whereas on floodplains *Picea alba* stands may avoid fire for 300 years. In spite of the frequency of fire, gymnosperms in general do not sprout from burned stumps; co-existing angiosperms (hardwoods) such as *Quercus*, *Acer*, *Fraxinus*, *Alnus*, *Corylus*, and *Vaccinium*, however, do resprout after fire.

Heinselman distinguishes two types of fires: those that burn the organic layer, and those that do not. When the soil organic matter is not deeply burned, tree seedlings often have difficulty in establishing. Shrubs, herbs, and grasses adapted for post-fire regeneration resprout in the first year, while species such as *Aralia* and *Rubus* germinate from buried seeds. If the organic layer is also consumed, few buried propagules will remain, and most rhizomes and root systems that could sprout are also killed. Bryophytes such as *Marchantia*, *Funaria*, and *Ceratodon* are abundant on moist sites. Dense regeneration of conifers usually occurs. A mosaic of different fire intensities will then produce an array of different forest types. As biomass accumulates through succession, and twigs, needles, and peat accumulate under the trees, the risk of fire steadily increases. The proportion of old forests with a dense understorey of moss and peat will therefore depend on the fire frequency, which will in turn depend largely upon the climate.

Succession and fire have been extensively studied in the Boundary Waters Canoe Area, Minnesota. The latter has 215 000 ha of natural coniferous forests typical of the Precambrian shield country of central North America. Deglaciation occurred some 16 000 years BP and left behind coarse-textured soils formed on gravel, sand, and bare rock outcrops. The Boundary Waters Canoe Area was once populated by the Sioux and then by the Chippewa. By the late 1800s European settlements had begun to form. The forest types in the area include lowland conifers and spruce bogs, with pine, spruce or birch mixed with lichen outcrops in the uplands. In an extensive study of these particular forests, Heinselman (1973) examined tree rings, fire scars, and historical records to reconstruct the fire history of the area. He found that virtually all forest stands dated from one or more fires that had occurred since 1595 AD, and 83 percent of the area burned resulted from just nine fire periods: 1894, 1875, 1863–4, 1824, 1801, 1755–9, 1727, 1692, and 1681 (Table 9.2). The mean length of time between major fires was

Table 9.2. *Virgin forest areas (never logged, cleared or roaded) of the Boundary Waters Canoe Area, Minnesota, by stand origin year, as of March 1973 (land areas only) (from Heinselman 1973).*

Stand origin year	Area in 1973 (acres)	Percent of total	Cumulative percent of total
1971	2 032	0.5	0.5
1967	128	–	0.5
1936	7 968	1.9	2.4
1925	400	0.1	2.5
1918	576	0.1	2.6
1917	1 856	0.4	3.0
1914	32	–	3.0
1910	34 000	8.2	11.2
1904	1 952	0.5	11.7
1903	2 368	0.6	12.3
1900	512	0.1	12.4
1894	96 944	23.2	35.6
1890	32	–	35.6
1889	256	0.1	35.7
1887–8	176	0.1	35.8
1885–7	384	0.1	35.9
1882	288	0.1	36.0
1881	9 968	2.4	38.4
1875	90 614	21.8	60.2
1871	5 856	1.4	61.6
1863–4	83 600	20.1	81.7
1854	8 112	2.0	83.7
1846	2 656	0.6	84.3
1827	912	0.2	84.5
1824	1 616	0.4	84.9
1822	6 128	1.5	86.4
1815	5 200	1.3	87.7
1803	176	0.1	87.8
1801	17 072	4.1	91.9
1796	5 840	1.4	93.3
1784	432	0.1	93.4
1766	48	–	93.4
1755–9	12 240	2.9	96.3
1747	768	0.2	96.5
1739	160	–	96.5
1727	3 408	0.8	97.3
1712	240	0.1	97.4
1692	1 472	0.4	97.8
1681	8 560	2.0	99.8
1648	64	–	99.8
1610	720	0.2	100.0
1595	16	–	100.0
Total	415 782	100.0	100.0

26 years, and historical data seem to indicate that these were particularly dry periods. Figure 9.29 shows some of the earliest recorded burns.

The landscape of this area is a mosaic of forest types recovering from different intensities of fire. Peatland succession may be occurring in the lowlands, unless the process is interrupted by fire burning the organic soils. The uplands, however, are patches of different-aged stands produced by fire. At the time of Heinselman's study there had been a policy of fire control in place for some 60 years, but even so, the canopy trees were still the first generation of trees to repopulate burned areas. Herbaceous species such as *Aralia hispida* and *Corydalis sempervirens* also reappear abundantly after fire. Succession in such areas is constantly interrupted by fire, and the term recovery or regeneration may be better applied to such short periods of vegetation change (Heinselman 1981). Yet, over even the short term of a few decades, there are still increases in stand biomass, soil organic matter, and woody debris, so typical trends associated with succession occur over even these relatively short time periods. In the absence of fire, more shade-tolerant forests of *Thuja occidentalis* and *Tsuga canadensis* might be expected to grow and replace the fire-dependent species.

This replacement by shade-tolerant species can be evaluated to some extent by examining forests on islands where fires are infrequent (although edge effects and wind damage are likely much greater). One island in Heinselman's study had *Pinus resinosa* trees that were 378 years old. Another had *Pinus strobus* approaching 370 years old. These older stands go through a stage of senescence in which arboreal lichens and terrestrial mosses proliferate. As mosses, branches, and dead wood accumulate, the area's susceptibility to fire increases steadily (Heinselman 1981). *Pinus strobus* in particular may be so long-lived that it is rarely replaced before a new fire destroys the stand. Distinctive tree species distributions may result from fire; *Thuja occidentalis* "has almost literally been driven to the lakeshores by fire" (p. 358). The species is so uncommon on uplands that one might assume that it needs abundant water to grow, but on ridges and islands where fires have been infrequent, it can occur. Many lakeshores are lined with old *Thuja* that, upon close examination, are found to be fire-scarred on the side away from the lake.

Closer to the east coast of North America, where there are deeper soils, more rainfall, and milder winters, a variant of the Boreal Forest known as the Acadian Forest occurs. The mixture of species here varies with local soils and climate. When Wein and Moore (1977) did an analysis of historical fires, they found much lower fire rotation periods – 1000 and 5000 years for the mean and median, respectively. The diversity of forest types in New Brunswick enabled Wein and Moore to sort fire data by forest type (Table 9.3), and the data showed that conifer forests had the highest burn rates and deciduous forest the lowest.

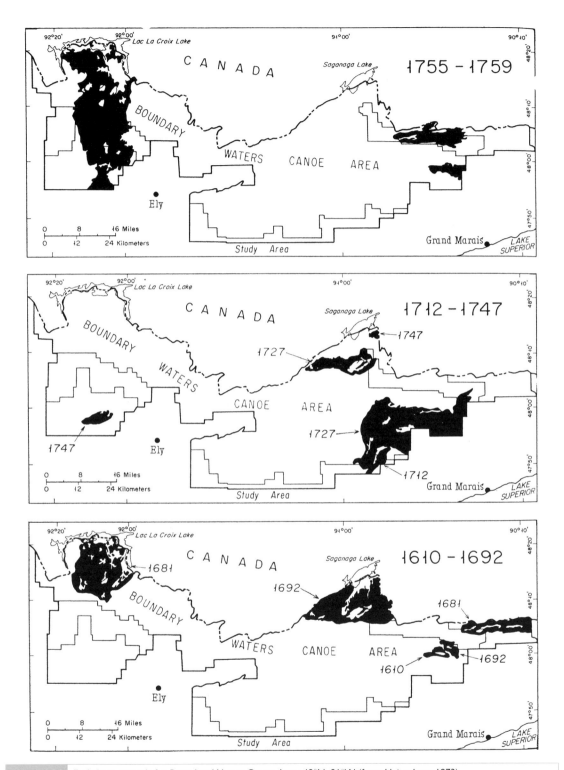

Figure 9.29 Early burn records for Boundary Waters Canoe Area; 48°N, 91°W (from Heinselman 1973).

Table 9.3. *Properties of fire in the Acadian Forest of maritime Canada illustrated by the major vegetation types in eight areas of New Brunswick (from Wein and Moore 1977).*

Vegetation type and approximate area ($\times 10^3$ ha)		Mean annual burn		Annual fire size (ha)		Mean annual no. fires
		ha	percent	mean	median	
Red spruce-hemlock-pine	2591	5418	0.21	681	69	7
Sugar maple-yellow birch-fir	1655	2569	0.16	1152	61	2
Spruce-fir coast	197	253	0.13	295	52	1
Sugar maple-hemlock-pine	1005	731	0.07	149	49	3
Sugar maple-hemlock-pine	1202	480	0.04	204	51	2
Fir-pine-birch	522	68	0.01	230	122	<1
Fir-pine-birch	99	2	<0.005	71	71	<1
Sugar maple-ash	305	8	<0.005	30	27	<1

Succession, fire and vital traits in Tasmanian rain forests

Fire-dominated ecosystems are common around the world. Now, to the opposite side of the globe – the wet sclerophyll and rain forests of Tasmania. The dominant trees of these rain forests are *Nothofagus cunninghamii* and *Atherosperma moschatum*. The normal sequence of succession progresses from sedges and shrubs through a wet sclerophyll forest dominated by *Eucalyptus* and *Acacia* species to a mixed forest with *Eucalyptus* towering over a rain forest understorey. If no fire occurs, the *Eucalyptus* cannot regenerate, and so they are ultimately lost from the community.

To analyze and simplify this situation, Noble and Slatyer (1980) recognized a set of "vital attributes" – traits critical to the role that a species plays in a vegetation replacement sequence. These vital attributes were as follows: (1) method of arrival or persistence at a site during and after disturbance, (2) ability to establish and grow to maturity, and (3) time taken to reach critical stages. The first group of vital attributes, describing arrival and persistence, were summarized using four "life stages": juvenile (J), mature (M), present only as propagules (P), and locally extinct (E). The second group of traits yielded a much larger set of possibilities; depending upon how long various attributes persisted through the succession, many life history types could be created by the different timing of the four "life stages." Eight of these "are biologically feasible and probably common in nature" (p. 9). Finally, the third group of traits summarized the timing of events during succession, and this required the following three attributes: time to reproductive maturity (*m*), the life span of the species (*l*), and the time taken for propagules to be lost from the community and for the species to become locally extinct (*e*). Sifting through the various combinations of all these vital attributes yields eight common types (Figure 9.30).

The complexity of this procedure (seven pages of text and figures) may cause a reader to doubt that this really qualifies as simplification. Indeed, the results may be more easily described, as in

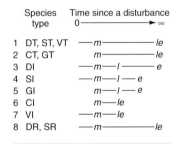

	Species type	Time since a disturbance 0 ────────▶ ∞
1	DT, ST, VT	—*m*————*le*
2	CT, GT	*m*————*le*
3	DI	—*m*—*l*——*e*
4	SI	*m*—*l*—*e*
5	GI	*m*—*l*—*e*
6	CI	*m*——*le*
7	VI	—*m*—*le*
8	DR, SR	—*m*————*le*

Figure 9.30 Life stage characteristics for each of eight species types in relation to disturbance in Tasmanian forests. The critical events are the time to reach reproductive maturity (*m*), the longevity of the species population (*l*), and the longevity of its propagule pool (*e*) (after Noble and Slatyer 1980).

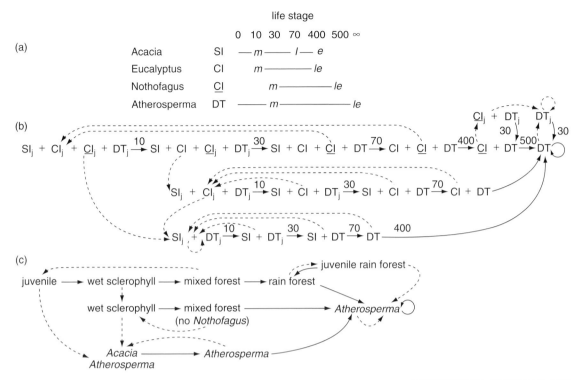

Figure 9.31 The vegetation replacement sequence for Tasmanian wet sclerophyll rain forest: (a) vital attribute data required to derive the replacement sequence shown in (b) – the underlined CI is used only to distinguish *Eucalyptus* and *Nothofagus* in the replacement sequence; (c) summarizes (b). Solid lines show transitions in periods with no disturbance, while broken lines show transitions due to disturbance (from Noble and Slatyer 1980).

Heinselman's work, with a half-dozen species names. At the same time, however, the outcome of eight tree types does summarize a number of distinctive life histories that may occur well beyond the particular Tasmanian forest stands examined. For example, *Acacia dealbata* is an SI species (long-lived propagule **S**tore; **I**ntolerant of shading) that reaches reproductive maturity early, has a short life span of some 70 years, after which it survives only as seeds, and the seeds remain viable for about 400 years. *Eucalyptus* (both *E. regnans* and *E. delegatensis*) are CI species (short-term propagule storage often in the **C**anopy) having similar early reproduction but persisting as adults for some 400 years; the seed source disappears when the adults disappear. *Nothofagus cunninghamii* is also a CI species, but it matures at 30 years and adults persist for 500 years. *Atherosperma moschatum* is a climax species that can regenerate in its own shade. It is a DT species (seeds widely **D**ispersed; **T**olerates wide range of site conditions).

Figure 9.31 shows what happens after a fire occurs in a mixed species stand – region (b) uses the vital types terminology, and region (c) summarizes the forest stands verbally. At the far left, all species are assumed to be present as juveniles (indicated by the subscript letter j). A transition occurs after 10 years when *Acacia* and *Eucalyptus* reach reproductive maturity and can produce seeds. After 30 years the rain forest species also reach maturity. Reproduction of *Acacia* ceases because it has the I attribute, and after about 70 years living plants will have senesced and died; owing to the S attribute, the seed pool, however, persists. The forest will now be a mixed forest with *Eucalyptus* emergent above a rain forest understorey. After 400 years the *Eucalyptus* is lost, and since it has the C vital attribute, a short-lived seed pool, no viable seeds will remain. If the rain forest is undisturbed for a further 100 years, DT replaces itself resulting in pure *Atherosperma* rain forest. The dashed arrows show the effects of fire on each stage in the replacement sequence. The various combinations of fire and recovery can, according to Noble and Slatyer, produce the classical sequences of succession as well as other possibilities.

9.4.3 Predictive models for plant succession

While studies of interactions among plants may provide important insight into the processes that drive successional change, such studies may be of little value for making predictions of the kind that managers need in order to manage vegetated landscapes. Matrix models offer a means to make these kinds of predictions. Imagine a landscape with n different vegetation types. Further imagine that information is available from two time periods, perhaps from aerial photographs or even old maps. It is then possible to assign a probability for each different vegetation type turning into another vegetation type. Each such transition can be represented as an element in this $n \times n$ matrix, with the diagonal giving the probabilities that each vegetation type remains unchanged. It is possible to represent this matrix by a flow chart of changes among vegetation types, perhaps with the higher probabilities represented by thicker arrows. Figure 9.32 presents an example from forests in central Newfoundland, where the boreal forest is apparently unstable; when disturbed by logging or fire, the vegetation becomes barrens covered with *Kalmia latifolia*, an ericaceous shrub. Similar barrens can be found in Nova Scotia and across northern Canada. Such transitions have important consequences for the sustainability of logging and the management of protected areas.

If one is prepared to make the assumption that future changes in an area will be similar to those that occurred in the past (and obviously this assumption requires careful evaluation), then one can assume that the probabilities of the vegetation changes represent a stationary Markov chain, in which case two predictive capacities arise (Waggoner and Stephens 1970). First, multiplying the matrix by itself will predict the vegetation components in the next time period. Second, it is possible to evaluate the steady state, when further transitions will result in a constant proportion of vegetation types in each of the n classes.

In one example, Aaviksoo et al. (1993) classified Estonian wetlands into 17 different vegetation types such as sedge fen, swamp forest, reeds, and bogs. Instead of photographs, peat cores were used to estimate transition probabilities among the 17 classes. Each 25 cm of peat corresponded to approximately 100–300 years. In this case, many possible transitions were documented, and no single

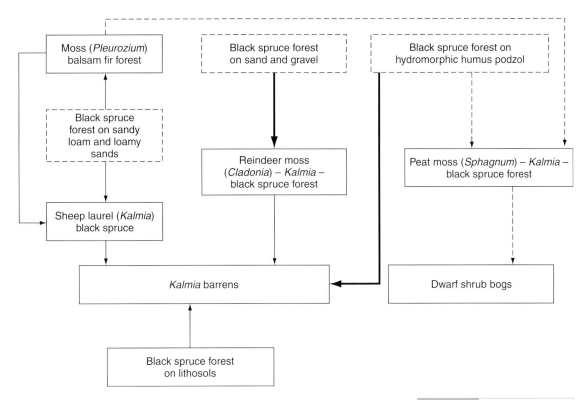

Figure 9.32 Succession illustrated by flow diagrams. Logging of black spruce forest in Newfoundland can create dwarf shrub bogs or *Kalmia latifolia* barrens when spruce fails to regenerate. If the probability of change associated with each arrow can be measured (arrow thickness proportional to probability), matrix models can be used to predict the nature of future landscapes (from Weetman 1983).

successional sequence could be found. When projected forward, however, the model showed that the proportion of willow, reed, and sedge wetlands declined, and raised bog with *Sphagnum fuscum* steadily increased as peat accumulated.

Other workers have tried to combine mechanistic assumptions about the interactions of trees in order to produce predictive models for landscapes (Botkin 1977, 1990; Shugart et al. 1981, Urban and Shugart 1992, Austin et al. 1997). This approach has been particularly successful where forests have few species and where a few ecological characteristics, such as shade tolerance, are useful for predicting species interactions. Such models can also be modified to include the effects of different kinds of disturbance, such as fire or logging, in order to predict the kinds of landscape that would arise. One well-known example is the JABOWA model which, like FORET, simulates the behavior of a forest by simulating the growth of individual trees in 10×10 m plots. Trees grow by gathering resources within the plot (light is assumed to be a key resource), and the model explores competitive interactions among the trees (Botkin 1977). Large areas of landscape are divided into plots 10 m on a side. Trees grow by gathering resources within this patch, and light is assumed to be a key resource.

Owing to the size of this model, there is room here to explore only its basic conceptual structure. For example, a tree growing in the open collects radiant energy in proportion to its leaf area, and its growth will also be proportional to leaf area. The equation for growth can then be modified to incorporate the effects of shading by neighbors, as well as allow for different degrees of tolerance to shade. For regeneration to occur, patches must arise, their frequency being determined by mortality rates of adults. New saplings are added each year, based upon the amount of light available and relative tolerances to shade (and with temperature and soil moisture considered as well). If, for example, light levels are high, shade-intolerant species such as cherry are added. If light is very low, only shade-tolerant species such as beech are added.

While such models seem useful, Rigler (1982) and Peters (1992) have expressed doubt about the validity of large-scale computer models, which have large numbers of coefficients. They have pointed out that as the number of species increases, the number of pairwise interactions increases rapidly to the point where the model becomes unwieldy (see also Wimsatt 1982, McIntosh 1985, Rigler and Peters 1995). In contrast, Starfield and Bleloch (1986) have argued that the real challenge is to simplify nature intelligently, and some workers therefore continue to use large simulation models (e.g., Mitsch and Jørgensen 1990, Ondok 1990, Sklar et al. 1990). Perhaps the apparent utility of the JABOWA model arises out of two fortunate circumstances. First, the number of trees in temperate deciduous forests is relatively small, so a species by species approach is not overwhelming. Second, strong asymmetric competition structures the forest around a single process, competition for light. Similarly, models of succession in wetlands are conveniently driven by accumulation of peat (Gorham 1953, 1957, Foster and Wright 1990). Perhaps some systems, such as temperate forests and peatlands, are inherently easier to simplify.

9.4.4 Synthesis

A book like this has two ways to deal with a controversial topic: it can review the last hundred years of writings on succession, in which case the writer must introduce ideas that did not stand the test of time, and eddies of conflict that generated more heat than light and more confusion than clarity. Sometimes it is best to just let these past misunderstandings fade from memory. But this risks exposing students to repeating these past mistakes. I will tend toward the latter course, while trying to inoculate students against fruitless debate by stressing a few landmarks. Those who wish to dive into the topic more fully can consult reviews such as those in West et al. (1981), McIntosh (1981, 1985), Botkin (1990), and Glenn-Lewin et al. (1992).

To start at the very beginning, there are many situations wherein one may observe the zonation of plant communities: along latitudinal gradients on mountainsides, around lakeshores, along the edges of old fields, and across sequences of sand dunes. Sometimes, but not always, these sequences represent patterns of ecological succession. Consider the example of shorelines in more detail, although one could follow the same arguments using any of the above cases. The sequence of plant communities along shorelines (Figure 9.33) appears to follow a temporal trend. The sequence occurs as wetland

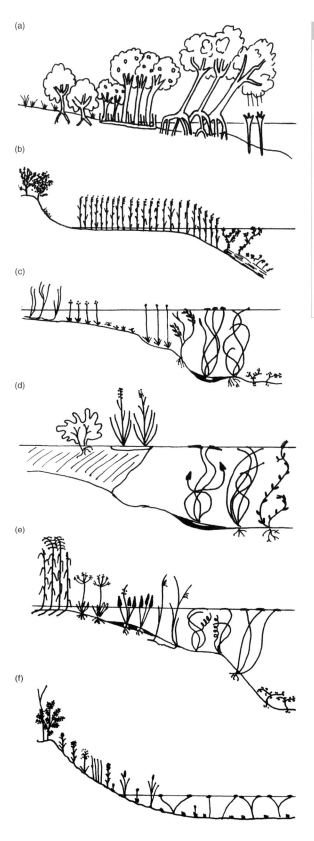

(a)

(b)

(c)

(d)

(e)

(f)

Figure 9.33 The zonation of vegetation on shorelines has been described in many studies. (a) Mangrove swamp of the Caribbean (after Bacon 1978); (b) eastern shore of Lake Kisajno, northeastern Poland, a typical small-lake phyto littoral (after Bernatowicz and Zachwieja 1966); (c) sandy shoreline (after Dansereau 1959); (d) bog (after Dansereau 1959); (e) St. Lawrence River (after Dansereau 1959); (f) Wilson's Lake, Nova Scotia (after Wisheu and Keddy 1989b). Frequently these are interpreted as illustrating successional trends from shallow water to terrestrial vegetation (illustrations by Rochelle Lawson, from Keddy 2000).

areas gradually fill with detritus and turn into land. Vegetation zones can parallel the progress of the temporal sequence: "Zonation, therefore, is taken to be the spatial equivalent of succession in time, even in the absence of direct evidence of change" (Hutchinson 1975, p. 497). This view has been held for both peatlands (e.g., Dansereau and Segadas-Vianna 1952) and small marshes along lakes (e.g., Pearsall 1920, Spence 1982). In each of these circumstances, the organic matter produced by the wetland, combined in some cases with sediment trapped by the vegetation, gradually increases the elevation of the substrate and turns shallow water into marsh and marsh into land.

Gorham (1953) traces this understanding of succession back to at least the early 1800s. J. A. De Luc's book *Geologic Travels*, published in 1810, recognized six discrete stages in the transformation of a lake into a peaty meadowland. Further, De Luc proposed that the rate of succession is greatest on shallow shores; on steep shores the vegetation zones will be narrow and the process of change through time nearly non-existent. Walker (1970) also drew attention to Gough's (1793) account of how lakes are converted to dry land by the accumulation of organic matter, so that "the margin of the pond will be progressively advanced" and the land thereby produced "will, in time, be covered with a bed of vegetable earth" the upper limit of which is set by dry periods because exposure to air will allow decomposition. Such observations were systematized as a successional sequence called a **hydrosere** by Tansley (1939). Walker has thoroughly studied vegetation transitions across a series of 20 sediment cores and found that indeed there is a repeatable sequence of **seres** that occurs (Figure 9.34).

The importance of succession as a general phenomenon in plant communities was repeatedly emphasized and systematized by Clements (e.g., Clements et al. 1929), and the use of the terms such as **sere** and **climax** are essentially his. In his treatise, Clements (1916) recognized a number of mechanisms and processes involved in succession. Succession depends upon the kind of disturbance that initiated it (nudation), the propagules that remained in the soil (residuals), the arrival of migrants at the site (migration), the success of the migrants at establishment and growth (ecesis), and how the migrant plants altered their biotic environment (reaction). As the species grow, interactions become important (competition). These successional processes continue until an equilibrium is reached between the species on the site and their environment. Perhaps the only process missing from Clements's categories is the effects of animals (MacMahon 1981), but by 1935 Clements is using the word coaction to include three different categories: "namely interactions between plants, those between plants and animals, and those that concern animals directly or primarily" (pp. 333–344). Clements (1916) also notes that primary succession takes longer than secondary because "the physical conditions are for a long time too severe for the vast majority of migrants, as well as too severe for the rapid increase of

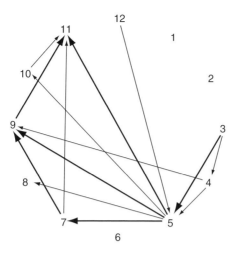

Figure 9.34 Frequencies of transition between 12 vegetation stages (ranging from open water (1) through reed swamp (5) to bog (11) to mixed marsh (12)) in 20 pollen cores from a range of wetlands including small lakes, valley bottoms, and coastal lagoons in the British Isles (top, transition diagram; bottom, tabulated frequencies) (from Walker 1970).

	SUCCEEDING VEGETATION												
	1	2	3	4	5	6	7	8	9	10	11	12	T
1	·	·	·	·	·	·	·	·	·	·	·	·	0
2	·	·	·	1	1	·	·	·	·	·	·	·	2
3	·	·	·	2	5	·	·	·	·	·	·	·	7
4	·	·	1	·	3	·	1	·	2	1	·	·	8
5	·	·	·	·	·	1	4	3	5	2	4	·	19
6	·	·	·	·	·	·	·	1	·	·	·	·	1
7	·	·	·	·	·	·	·	·	4	1	3	·	8
8	·	·	·	·	·	·	1	·	1	1	·	·	3
9	·	·	·	·	1	·	1	·	·	1	5	·	8
10	·	·	·	·	·	·	·	·	·	·	4	·	4
11	·	·	·	·	·	·	·	·	2	1	·	·	3
12	·	·	·	·	2	·	1	·	·	·	·	·	3
T	0	0	1	3	12	1	8	4	14	7	16	0	66

ANTECEDENT VEGETATION

the pioneers" (p. 71). McIntosh (1985) has outlined Clements's views as well as those of colleagues who offered "opposing" interpretations of ecological change, and he observes that: "Clements's ideas, like those of prophets generally, have been widely used and misused by his adherents and detractors; and careful rereading of his major accounts of succession . . . is often required to distinguish his actual ideas from what they are said to be" (McIntosh 1981, p. 10).

Gleason was a well-known opponent, an early reductionist who felt that the emphasis should be upon the individual responses of plants to their environments (Section 10.5.1); more recently, population biologists, who quite naturally see nature as a collection of populations, have tended to embrace the Gleasonian view (Harper 1977). (I use the words *feel* and *embrace* in the sentence above because the debates between Gleason and Clements, and their later adherents, have tended to be remarkable for their emphasis upon feelings rather than hard data (Section 10.6).) In 1917, Gleason laid out 28 numbered statements to summarize his views. Portions of three of them are offered below:

> The development and maintenance of vegetation is therefore merely the resultant of the development and maintenance of the component individuals, and is favored, modified, retarded, or inhibited by all causes which influence the component plants. [1]
>
> The actual mature immigrant population of an area is therefore controlled by two sets of factors: the nature of the surrounding population ... and the environment, selecting the adapted species. [9]
>
> The common cause of succession is an effective change in the environment. [25]

In spite of all that has been written about "Clements versus Gleason" it is hard to imagine that Clements would seriously disagree with any of the above points, and the debate, if there is one, is really about subtle differences in emphasis. Humans can always superimpose their views upon nature; what is required is to know whether succession is a useful concept or not, and if it is useful, what constraints should be placed upon its use. Students of plant ecology are at some risk of having to read great volumes of words about succession and of being misled by many "modern" proponents of succession, who would have one believe that they have something new and clever to say on the matter (when in fact they have not read the original work, a point made independently by both Jackson (1981) and Booth and Larson (1999)). One might therefore be best advised to read Clements (1916), Gleason (1917), and then (with a great deal of scepticism) a modern synthesis (like this one; see also Sections 10.5 and 10.6, Box 10.2).

Returning to this synthesis, succession may be ubiquitous and closely related to zonation in situations such as peatlands, where organic matter accumulates, but even De Luc apparently understood that his 1810 generalization did not apply to all sites, not even to the steeper shores of lakes. With the explosion of ecological studies in the later 1900s, it became clearer that there are many natural disturbances that delay, or even restart, proposed successional sequences. As the effects of fires, floods, storms, and droughts were better documented and understood, many "temporal" sequences could perhaps be better understood as dynamic balances between successional processes and disturbance events (e.g., Pickett and White 1985). Simultaneously, population biologists began placing increasing emphasis on the mechanistic interactions among species, leading Horn (1976, 1981) to suggest that succession was best understood as a "statistical result of a plant-by-plant replacement process." Connell and Slatyer (1977) were stimulated to try to recognize a number of different mechanisms involved in this process.

If nothing else, this emphasis upon mechanisms tended to rehabilitate the concept of succession, although a close reading of early work by Clements illustrates that he too thought rather carefully about the mechanisms by which change might occur. Perhaps many of Clements's critics were responding to a caricature of his views rather than reading them carefully. The importance of disturbance, the complexity of responses to it, and consideration of mechanisms of change have, if nothing else, challenged scientists to rethink many of their ideas about succession, stability, and predictability in nature (Botkin 1990).

Along with a gradual shift in emphasis toward the study of the dynamics of individuals in patches within landscapes, the ubiquity of buried seed reserves became evident and their importance a subject of investigation. It became apparent that buried seeds were more than mere detrital accumulations; seed reserves held the potential for community regeneration, and in many cases disturbance triggered the re-emergence of species from their reserves of buried seed (e.g., Harper 1977, Leck et al. 1989). Charles Darwin himself had commented on the remarkable number of seedlings that emerged from a spoonful of mud, and, increasingly, soils have been found to be vast repositories of buried seeds (e.g., Salisbury 1970, van der Valk and Davis 1976, 1978, Leck et al. 1989). This fact led van der Valk to propose that many zonation patterns were not successional sequences, but rather represented short-term responses of plant communities to local changes in the environment.

A thorough review of experiments on competition and succession (Wilson 1999) offers three general conclusions: (1) facilitation (Chapter 8) is relatively uncommon except in the most stressed sites in early primary succession; (2) competition (Chapter 5) is an important force that occurs soon after disturbance when early successional plants begin to influence one another; (3) the intensity of competition increases through time. Therefore, trends known from natural spatial gradients (Chapters 5, 8) appear similar to those found along temporal gradients. Perhaps this should not seem too surprising since many of the same factors change, including soil organic matter, and biomass. Wilson presents three scenarios in Figure 9.35: primary succession, secondary succession on poor soil, and secondary succession on rich soil. In all three cases, facilitation occurs early in succession when physical stress is most prevalent. In all three cases, competition intensity increases through time and root and shoot competition increase simultaneously. On poor soils, however, root competition eventually becomes predominant, whereas on rich soils, shoot competition becomes predominant.

If one regards deciduous forest as one endpoint of succession, then it would be instructive to evaluate two parts of Wilson's trifurcation by comparing above- and below-ground competition in forest sites with and without rich soil. Fortunately, exactly this study has been done. Putz and Canham (1992) measured above-ground competition in different forests. In their work, above-ground competition was reduced by using a winch to pull neighboring trees back from test plots, and below-ground competition was reduced by digging trenches around plots to isolate a tree from the roots of neighbors. On rich soil, increased light produced the greatest increase in tree growth (consistent with predominance of competition for light), whereas on poor

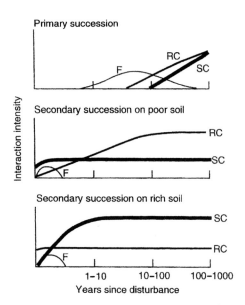

Figure 9.35 Postulated trends in intensity of root and shoot competition (RC, SC) and facilitation (F) during primary and secondary succession (from Wilson 1999).

soil, trenching produced the greatest growth (consistent with the predominance of competition for nutrients or water). This experiment tends to confirm one essential feature of Wilson's synthesis regarding secondary succession.

9.5 | Conclusion

Over time there has been a progression of views on ecological change, the earlier ones emphasized long-term unidirectional succession; the later ones emphasize the short-term responses of organisms to changing environmental conditions. Two specific examples nicely illustrate this shift in emphasis. In 1952, Dansereau and Segadas-Vianna could draw zonation profiles of peat bogs in eastern North America and confidently relate them to succession diagrams ending in climax vegetation of *Picea mariana* or *Acer saccharinum* (these being named the *Picetum marianae* and *Aceretum saccharophori* associations). The many other vegetation types they named were considered to belong to one of three stages of bog succession: pioneer, consolidation, and sub-climax, all of which led, by means of peat accumulation, from open water to woodland. In 1996 Yu et al. described zonation of a single shoreline swamp at Rice Lake (just north of Lake Ontario), with a zonation sequence not unlike that discussed by Dansereau and Segadas-Vianna. Aided by sediment cores, and studies of pollen and plant macrofossils, Yu et al. (1996) found two main stages in the vegetation history. An open marsh stage, with sedge genera such as *Carex* and *Eleocharis*, persisted for some 2700 years with no successional change, a situation they explain by fluctuating water levels. Then, about 8300 years BP, there was a transition to perennials associated with wet meadows (e.g., *Verbena hastata*, *Lycopus americanus*, and *Carex* spp.) and by about 7500 years BP a transition to cedar swamp. This change coincided with a regional period of warm and dry climate. The adjoining lake levels dropped and the swamp went dry about 1000 years later. Then during a cooler and wetter period, lake levels rose and the cedar swamp reappeared. Yu et al. (1996) conclude: "Paleoecological data for the past 11 000 years show that there were no significant successional changes of marsh communities for about 2700 years .... When change did occur, it was ultimately controlled by allogenic [external] factors such as climate and water level changes." Further, when the climate changed: "The herbaceous marsh converted directly to cedar swamp without the shrub-marsh and (or) alder-thicket stages."

These studies illustrate the change in perspective that has occurred over the last 50 years. It would be far too easy, however, to merely suggest that a correct view (dynamics) has replaced a wrong one (succession). Even Dansereau and Segadas-Vianna note that fluctuating water levels can control and even reverse vegetation succession and that factors such as fire could also cause vegetation to regress. Yu et al. (1996) would have to concede that at Rice Lake, trees are now growing in accumulations of 2 m of peat and several more of organic silt, thereby elevating the swamp forest above what would otherwise be open water. Whether one therefore focuses upon succession or short-term dynamics would appear to be somewhat a matter of emphasis and perspective: general patterns as opposed to site histories, large-scale processes as opposed to small-scale dynamics, and classification as opposed to processes.

These developments leave one with two questions about succession. What purpose or advantage is there in describing changes through time under this name when the sequence of events and the species change from site to site? If there is some value, then under which circumstances is this term correctly applied? Succession is a valuable term, particularly in habitats where unidirectional change is largely driven by one factor, because this allows one to make useful generalizations about vegetation patterns. The concept of succession can be usefully applied, for example in peatlands where the accumulation of peat shapes vegetation patterns and in forests where the effect of the accumulation of organic matter after fires is unambiguous. In other cases, such as the shores of large lakes and rivers or in small gaps within mature forests, the value of succession is weak, and, if anything, confuses rather than clarifies the causes of patterns seen in the vegetation.

Further reading

Clements, F. E. 1936. Nature and structure of climax. *Journal of Ecology* **24**: 254–282.

Dansereau, P. and F. Segadas-Vianna. 1952. Ecological study of the peat bogs of eastern North America. *Canadian Journal of Botany* **30**: 490–520.

Walker, D. 1970. Direction and rate in some British post-glacial hydroseres. pp. 117–139. In D. Walker and R. G. West (eds.) *Studies in the Vegetational History of the British Isles*. Cambridge: Cambridge University Press.

Horn, H. 1976. Succession. pp. 187–204. In R. M. May (ed.) *Theoretical Ecology: Principles and Applications*. Philadelphia: W. B. Saunders.

Connell, J. H. and R. O. Slatyer. 1977. Mechanisms of succession in natural communities and their role in community stability and organization. *The American Naturalist* **111**: 1119–1144.

West, D. C., H. H. Shugart, and D. B. Botkin (eds.) 1981. *Forest Succession: Concepts and Application*. New York: Springer-Verlag.

Delcourt, H. R. and P. A. Delcourt. 1991. *Quaternary Ecology: A Paleoecological Perspective*. London: Chapman and Hall.

Pielou, E. C. 1991. *After the Ice Age: The Return of Life to Glaciated North America*. Chicago: University of Chicago Press.

del Moral, R. and L. C. Bliss. 1993. Mechanisms of primary succession: insights resulting from the eruption of Mount St. Helens. *Advances in Ecological Research* **24**: 1–66.

Petit, J. R., J. Jouzel, D. Raynaud et al. 1999. Climate and atmospheric history of the past 420 000 years from the Vostok ice core, Antarctica. *Nature* **399**: 429–436.

Wilson, S. D. 1999. Plant interactions during secondary succession. pp. 629–650. In L. R. Walker (ed.) *Ecosystems of Disturbed Ground*. Amsterdam: Elsevier.

Flannery, T. 2005. *The Weather Makers: How Man is Changing the Climate and What it Means for Life on Earth*. New York: Atlantic Monthly Press.

Chapter 10

Gradients and plant communities: description at local scales

Vegetation description. Profile diagrams. Block diagrams. Forest site types. Vegetation cover types. Vegetation templates. Summary displays. Indirect gradient analysis. Use and abuse of multivariate models. Measurement of similarity. Ordination techniques. Sea cliff vegetation. Riverine wetlands. Functional summaries. Vegetation classification. Phytosociology. Site classification and land management. Direct gradient analysis. The importance of null models and tests. Salt marsh zonation. Freshwater shoreline zonation. Emergent wetland zonation. On the existence of communities: the null model perspective.

10.1 | Introduction

Early explorers encountered plant species and vegetation types that were entirely unknown in Europe. Some of the methods for describing patterns in vegetation at the global scale were introduced in Chapter 2, but the description of vegetation at smaller than global scales continues to be a challenging issue in plant ecology. Accurate description is essential for both scientific research and conservation.

In the most basic way, accurate description is a first step in any scientific inquiry. Even large experiments need description – the selection of each dependent variable requires a decision about which properties are most appropriate to describe the possible responses of manipulated communities. In the case of conservation applications, accurate description provides methods to divide landscapes into ecologically similar units, which can then guide the selection of new protected areas, or suggest those areas most appropriate for urban development. Further, once each vegetation unit in a landscape is delineated, it is then possible to select the most appropriate management activities such as grazing, logging, or reforestation. A perusal of any recent journal of plant ecology is therefore likely to yield at least one paper on techniques of vegetation description. On one hand, many of the techniques (and the debates about them) seem entirely unnecessary. On the other hand, what remains is the fact that patterns are the foundation for studies of mechanism and techniques of prediction. The questions seem to be:

1. Which measurable properties are most useful for describing vegetation?
2. How do these properties change in space and time?

3. Which patterns in these properties generate important questions about mechanisms?
4. Which patterns in these properties usefully synthesize essential aspects of vegetation?

In this chapter we will survey some of the methods used to describe vegetation, explore their value in scientific research and landscape management, and then re-visit their value in basic scientific research.

10.2 | Describing pattern along obvious natural gradients

The description of species and vegetation distributions in relation to natural gradients is an obvious starting point for examining pattern in local plant communities. An observer can often readily see the changes in vegetation with altitude, amount of flooding, soil depth, or salinity. The task then is to choose a method for describing the vegetation and plot the changes in vegetation along this gradient. This approach is often called **direct gradient analysis** (Whittaker 1973a). In contrast, **indirect gradient analysis** uses statistical methods to extract gradients from vegetation data (Section 10.3). There is a long tradition of direct gradient analysis, from Tansley and Chipp (1926) and Weaver and Clements (1929) to Whittaker (1973b) and Orloci (1978). Consider a few examples.

In his classic book on tropical rain forests, Richards (1952) advocates making profile diagrams: "A narrow rectangular strip of forest is marked out with cords, the right angles being obtained with the help of a prismatic compass. In Rain Forest the length of the strip should not usually be less than 200 ft. (61 m); 25 ft. (7.6 m) has proved a satisfactory width. All small undergrowth and trees less than an arbitrarily chosen lower limit of height are cleared away. The positions of the remaining trees are then mapped and their diameters noted . . . ." The result is a **profile diagram** through a tract of forest (Beard 1944, Richards 1952, Beard 1973). Profile data from several sites can be arranged along a gradient such as rainfall, as in Figure 10.1. Rainfall effects can be found at quite local scales in mountainous areas or on islands. This tool, while laborious, has the advantage of producing a visual representation of the vegetation community, including obvious changes in physiognomy. It does not, however, show changes in taxonomy or diversity in any quantitative way. Similarly, the gradient along which the plants are arranged is qualitative.

The gradients along which species are distributed can be made much more explicit. Let us move from Trinidad to Estonia where soil depth, soil moisture, and pH are three critical gradients along which plant species are distributed (Frey 1973). A two-way profile diagram shows the distribution of principal tree species along gradients of moisture and soil type (Figure 10.2). This type of **block diagram** provides an excellent, quick introduction to the landscapes of a

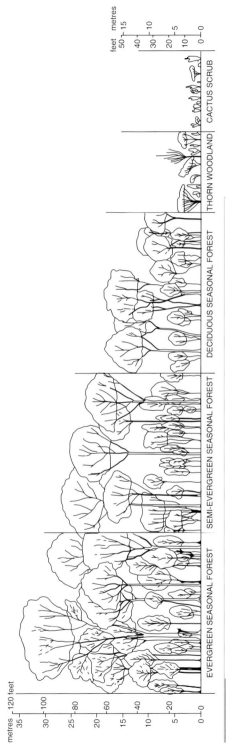

metres ┌120 feet
35 ┤
30 ┤─100
25 ┤─80
20 ┤
15 ┤─60
10 ┤─40
5 ┤─20
0 ┴─0

feet metres
50 ┬15
40 ┤
30 ┤─10
20 ┤─5
10 ┤
0 ┴0

EVERGREEN SEASONAL FOREST | SEMI-EVERGREEN SEASONAL FOREST | DECIDUOUS SEASONAL FOREST | THORN WOODLAND | CACTUS SCRUB

Figure 10.1 A formation-series for communities on Trinidad affected by increasing drought from left to right (Beard 1944).

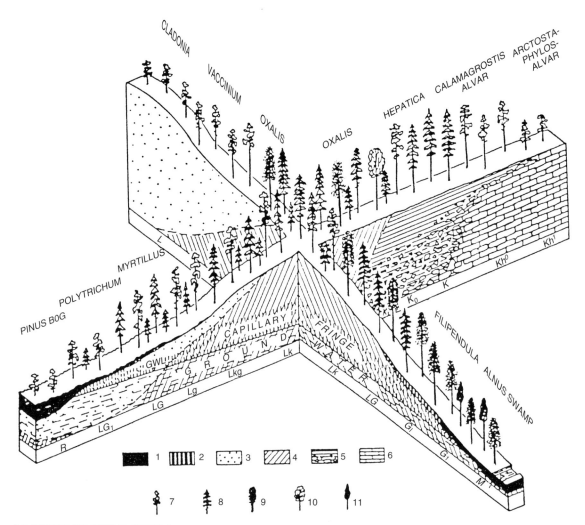

Figure 10.2 The interrelations of Estonian forest site types and their ecological position in the network of complex habitat factors: (1) peat, (2) organic-mineral, (3) sand, (4) non-calcareous moraine, (5) calcareous moraine, (6) limestone, (7) *Pinus sylvestris*, (8) *Picea abies*, (9) *Betula* spp., (10) *Populus tremula*, (11) *Alnus glutinosa* (from Frey 1973).

region. Different segments of the gradient may represent different forest site types that may require different forestry practices.

More quantitative information about the vegetation can be added by replacing the sketches of plants with measured levels of abundance. Depending upon the study, these might include the cover, density, biomass, or canopy cover of a species. These measures are particularly common in the American tradition. Thus Whittaker (1956) described tree distributions along gradients of altitude and exposure in the Great Smoky Mountains by plotting the percent of the stand comprised by each species (Figure 10.3). While some detail about the physiognomy is lost in such diagrams, information on individual species and diversity is captured. Comparable examples can be found in Whittaker (1960) and Peet (1978). Often, the names of one or a few abundant species are used to identify **vegetation cover types** dominated by those species. The different types can

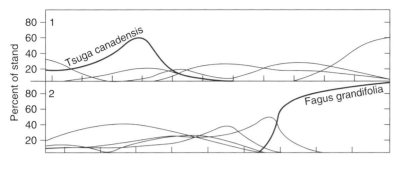

Figure 10.3 Distribution of selected tree species in the Great Smoky Mountains, USA. Relative density (percent of stems 2 cm and over) is shown for each species. (1) Dominance of *Tsuga canadensis* along a moisture gradient at 1070–1380 m elevation. (2) Dominance of *Fagus grandifolia* along an elevation gradient in mesic sites (from Whittaker 1956).

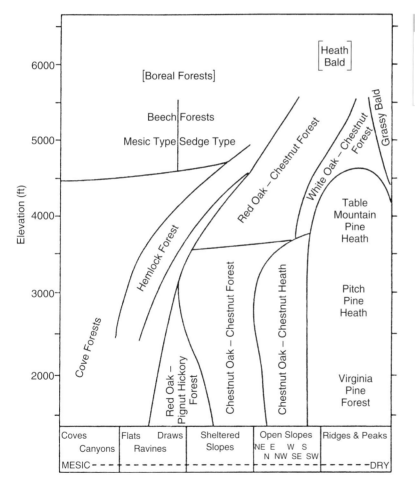

Figure 10.4 Non-boreal vegetation types in the Great Smoky Mountains, USA, displayed with respect to elevation and topographic-moisture gradients (from Whittaker 1956).

then be plotted along one or more measured environmental axes (Figure 10.4). Frequently the delineation of vegetation cover types is made subjectively based upon the familiarity of an ecologist with the vegetation of the region, although quantitative techniques do exist for this purpose (Section 10.4).

Maps of vegetation types along environmental gradients need not be ends in themselves – they can be used as **vegetation templates** upon which other data are plotted. Figure 10.5 shows a vegetation template for the Colorado Front Range of western North America. Look more closely at the axes and the fine dashed lines. If one were to start at low elevation in a ravine (origin of the graph), and begin climbing, one would start in riparian (floodplain) forest and eventually reach mixed mesophytic (deciduous) forest at an altitude of about 2200 m. If one continued climbing to 2500 m one would then enter coniferous forest with *Picea engelmannii* and *Abies lasiocarpa*. Above 3400 m one would encounter alpine vegetation. If one tired of climbing after reaching the mixed mesophytic forest, and began

Figure 10.5 Species richness in relation to elevation and topographic-moisture gradients in the Colorado Front Range. Solid lines are species richness isopleths starting at 13 species per 0.1 ha and increasing by increments of 9 species. Dashed lines denote boundaries of forest types (from Peet 1974).

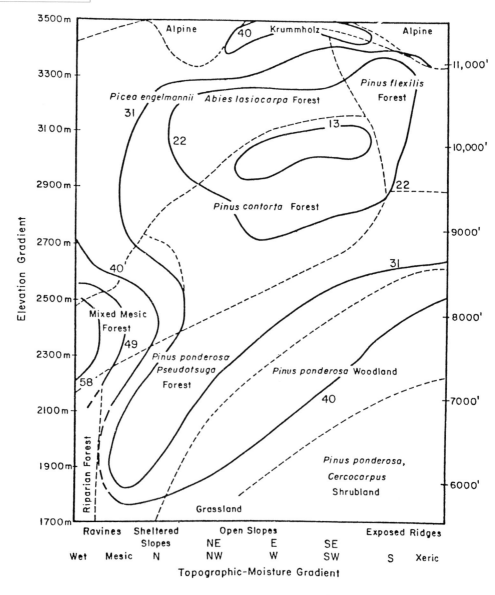

walking along the 2400-m-elevation contour (that is, to the right on the graph), one would reach open slopes and pass into a different coniferous forest comprised of *Pinus ponderosa* and *Pseudotsuga menziesii*. If one continued to walk along this contour out onto an exposed dry ridge top, one would find oneself in *Pinus ponderosa* woodland. Peet tabulated the species richness of the vegetation and plotted this information as isopleths (solid lines) on the same figure. The mixed mesophytic forests have the highest richness (approaching 60 species), whereas the open slopes at 3000 m have the lowest richness (less than 13). Such template would be a valuable tool for describing vegetation in a park guide and for showing the distributions of other organisms, in the same way Peet plotted richness.

Finally, the data on vegetation can be simplified still further with the objective of producing a **summary display** of the environmental factors that control the vegetation types of an entire region. In this case, the vegetation gradients may not be actual gradients studied step by step in the field; rather, the display is a means of abstracting and depicting the kinds of vegetation that would be found if one were able to sort all of the existing vegetation types along a few axes. These sorts of summary displays can be very helpful in condensing large amounts of information about landscapes into one diagram; a good analogy might be the periodic table of the elements. For example, Gopal et al. (1990) bravely tried to represent all the world's types of wetland vegetation in one diagram (Figure 10.6). The two main axes were duration of waterlogging and fertility. Superimposed upon duration of waterlogging was the amplitude of water level changes, and superimposed upon fertility was whether the water came from

Figure 10.6 Wetland type related to water level changes and nutrient supply (after Gopal et al. 1990).

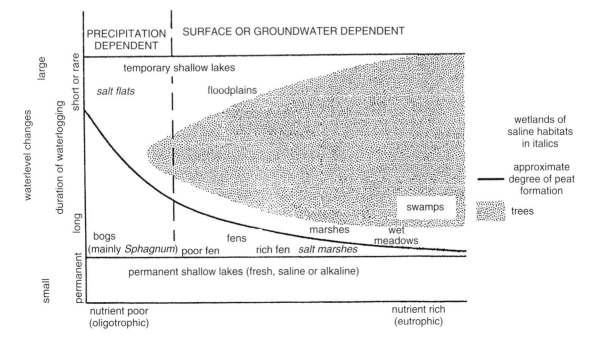

precipitation or groundwater. The major vegetation types (bogs, fens, marshes, swamps, salt flats, and floodplains) were then plotted. Further, the region dominated by trees was shaded in. Unlike a profile diagram, a diagram such as this conveys little information about any particular fen or bog; the strength lies rather in the context into which a particular bog is placed.

The examples above illustrate some of the common ways in which natural gradients have been used to describe vegetation. The major features that distinguish them from one another are the dependent variables (used to represent the vegetation) and the independent variables (used to describe the environmental controls upon vegetation) selected. The appropriate variables very much depend upon the question being posed by the researcher and the needs of his or her audience. A formal test of the community unit hypothesis might require considerable statistical sophistication, whereas a report for the citizens managing a local nature reserve may require self-explanatory pictorial clarity. One might combine several approaches; a profile diagram through a swamp might be combined with a summary diagram of the entire landscape for example. Although many important questions in ecology now require quantitative methods and field experiments, for many other purposes such as conservation and inventory work, clear descriptions are still invaluable. Before continuing with more sophisticated versions of gradient analysis, it would be helpful to make sure that you completely understand each of the figures above. You should be able to place yourself mentally in the vegetation at any point in any of the above figures and then imagine moving along an axis, visualizing the vegetation as you do so.

Through the early history of ecology, the emphasis was very much upon describing such vegetation patterns. However, along the way a subtle change began to occur. From such representations of species along gradients, scientists began drawing inferences about the underlying mechanisms causing the distributions. This is a dangerous (if necessary) step, because causation cannot be deduced from simple observations. (Were this to be so, we could prove to our satisfaction that having breakfast causes the Sun to rise, because one seems always to occur with the other.) Yet these sorts of distribution diagrams were soon being applied to one of the most contentious debates in plant ecology: whether or not vegetation communities exist. We shall return to this topic in the final section of this chapter.

10.3 | Multivariate methods for pattern detection

Sometimes the patterns in plant distributions and vegetation types are less obvious than those we have seen above. When patterns are not obvious, or when you want a quantitative rather than qualitative view of the pattern, there are two multivariate statistical tools that you can apply: ordination and classification. The objective of **ordination** is to create a simplified representation of the pattern of continuous variation in vegetation. The objective of **classification** is to sort different vegetation types into a limited number of groups. In both cases one begins with descriptive data from a large number of sample units. Typically, one has a list of s plant species occurring in a long list of q quadrats (that is, an s × q matrix of observations). This type of data set is very common in plant ecology. The matrix can be very large, with hundreds of species or quadrats, in which case it may not even be possible to guess the patterns that exist without a statistical tool. We will begin with ordination, reserving classification for Section 10.4. In practice, however, both begin with the same type of data matrix, they are often similar in approach, and often both can be found in a single statistical package.

Ordination does not extract something new from the data; rather it is a means of reducing the dimensionality of the data so that previously hidden patterns become evident. In general this means taking the data from an *n*-dimensional cloud of points (where each dimension represents the abundance of one particular species and each point in the cloud represents a quadrat) to two dimensions (or rarely three) which can be neatly laid out on the page of a journal. Although the complex statistics involved provide ordination with a superficial appearance of rigor, a simple analogy may be the process of taking a complex three-dimensional object like a frog or a porcupine, and reducing to a two-dimensional array by driving a large truck over it. In doing so, certain aspects of the shape are emphasized, and certain others are distorted. The objective of the multivariate technique it to squash the data in a way that emphasizes the patterns and minimizes the distortion, but fundamentally there is no way to reduce the dimensionality of the data (or a frog) without introducing some degree of artificiality.

10.3.1 The data matrix

To appreciate the results of an ordination, one must first clearly visualize the dataset itself. In the simplest possible case, the data consist of a rectangular matrix of s species abundances in q quadrats (Figure 10.7); such a dataset might be used in any number of analytical procedures. A more elaborate matrix can be created when extra rows are added for environmental measurements made in each quadrat. Part of the difficulty of combining environmental measurements with species data is that their differences in statistical structure risks further distortions during data analysis. There is also a basic conceptual issue: does the ecologist want the physical factors to influence the patterns that are extracted, or only to add these factors in after the vegetation patterns have already been extracted? In the first case the physical factors are included to create the patterns, in the second they are applied only to interpret possible causes of the patterns. This conceptual dichotomy illustrates again why it is important to determine your objectives clearly before embarking on data collection, much less choosing the technique for ordination of the

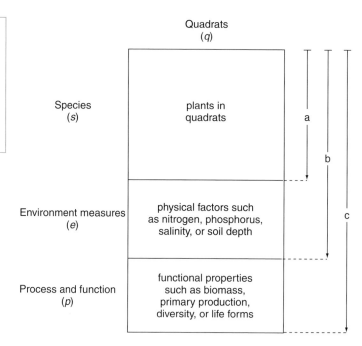

Figure 10.7 The raw data for ordination normally consist of a matrix of measures for s species in q quadrats (region a). Increasingly, environmental measures are analyzed simultaneously with the species data (region b). Data on process and function can also be incorporated (region c).

resulting data. Finally, Figure 10.7 shows that it is also possible to add rows in the matrix for other properties of vegetation such as primary production, biomass, or diversity.

10.3.2 Measuring similarity

Having selected the kind of raw data to be used in the data matrix (Section 10.3.1), the next step in ordination is to calculate the similarity of every possible pair of quadrats. There is a large number of possible measures of similarity, and these have been conveniently tabulated by Legendre and Legendre (1983), who advise that the choice of a particular measure depends largely upon the objectives of the researcher. We will touch lightly on a few examples here, but it is imperative to consult a more authoritative source (e.g., Orloci 1978, Gauch 1982, Legendre and Legendre 1983, Digby and Kempton 1987, Krebs 1989) before making your decision. Here I want you to focus upon why one does ordination (or classification), and how it fits into the larger strategic picture of plant ecology. These are valuable tools, but they should be used to accomplish a purpose in a research program, not just because the technique happens to exist.

There is one fundamental dichotomy in measures of similarity. The appropriateness of a measure depends upon whether the data matrix has only presence or absence data, or whether the data matrix has measures of abundance for each species.

Presence/absence data

With presence or absence data, the usual measure of similarity for a pair of quadrats is based upon the number of species that are found in both quadrats and the number that are absent from both quadrats.

To picture this, imagine that a pair of quadrats has been cast into a 2×2 contingency table (Figure 10.8). If the number of joint occurrences of species, a, and joint absences of species, d, is divided by the total number of species being examined, the result is the simple matching coefficient:

$$\frac{a+d}{a+b+c+d}.$$

In many cases, the joint occurrences of species will be more informative than the joint absences. Similarity may then be expressed simply as the number of joint occurrences of species, a, divided by the number of species in the two quadrats combined. This yields the Jaccard coefficient, which, although it dates back to 1901, is still a common and valuable measure of similarity for ecological purposes:

$$\frac{a}{a+b+c}.$$

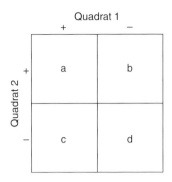

Figure 10.8 Similarity in species composition between two quadrats can be expressed in a 2×2 contingency table where a is the number of species present in both quadrats, d is the number of species absent from both quadrats, b is the number of species present only in quadrat 2, and c is the number of species present only in quadrat 1.

Abundance data

If the species abundances are known for each quadrat, say as counts of individuals or measures of biomass or cover, it is then possible to use another class of measures of similarity. One of the most obvious will be familiar from secondary school analytical geometry courses: the Euclidean distance between the two sample units in n-dimensional space, where each dimension represents one of n species. If the difference in abundance along each of these n axes is measured, the degree to which the two quadrats, i and j, differ in species composition is

$$\Sigma \sqrt{(x_{ik} - x_{jk})^2}/n$$

where $\sqrt{(x_{ik} - x_{jk})^2}$ is the Euclidean distance between quadrats i and j for species k and n is the number of species.

Another common measure of similarity is the correlation coefficient, where the similarity of quadrats is assessed by the degree to which species abundances in the two quadrats are correlated. If both samples have the same species with the same abundances, the similarity is 1. The correlation coefficient, which would be familiar to most of you, is however susceptible to problems caused by joint zeros (species absent from both quadrats), or when a few common species swamp the others. As far back as 1949, Cole noted that simple presence or absence data are often more informative than measures of correlation based upon species abundances.

The point here is not to summarize all the measures of similarity, since they have been fully enumerated elsewhere (e.g., Legendre and Legendre 1983, Digby and Kempton 1987). Rather, the point is to understand the tactical objective: to measure the similarity of each pair of quadrats sampled. Whatever the final decision on the measure of similarity, the result will be a matrix of similarities for each pair of quadrats. This similarity matrix is the intermediate step between the raw data matrix and the ordination. Since there are q quadrats in the data matrix, the similarity matrix will be $q \times q$. Since the measure of similarity is usually symmetrical (the similarity of quadrat 1 compared to quadrat 2 is the same as quadrat 2 compared to 1), only the values on one side of the diagonal need to be reported. The diagonal, which consists of similarities for each quadrat compared to itself, can be omitted.

In summary, we begin with a raw data matrix. A measure of similarity is then used to transform these data into a similarity matrix. The similarity matrix is the input for the next step: ordination or classification. The objective of the ordination or classification is to take the information in the similarity matrix, and present it in a pictorial manner that is easier to comprehend. Since we find it difficult to think in more than three dimensions, the usual objective is to find a means to represent the patterns of similarity in two or three dimensions.

10.3.3   Ordination techniques

The final decision required of the investigator is to select a technique for ordination. This will in part be determined by the kind of raw data available for preparing the similarity matrix. The techniques available for ordination include Bray Curtis ordination, principal component analysis, factor analysis, reciprocal averaging, canonical correspondence analysis, and detrended correspondence analysis, listed roughly in order of their historical use by plant ecologists. The trade-offs among these approaches can be explored in papers such as Gauch and Whittaker (1972), Gauch and Wentworth (1976), and Gauch et al. (1977). One of the biggest problems with many techniques is their tendency to take linear relationships in the data and bend them into curves in the ordination; this happens even when entirely artificial data are used (Gauch and Whittaker 1972). The second axis of the ordination, therefore, frequently reflected not a real environmental gradient but simply the curvature created by the technique itself (rather like the way in which flattening an animal will generally create a protuberance to one side or another). Newer techniques such as reciprocal averaging (RA) and detrended correspondence analysis (DCA) tend to minimize this curvature but then so too does the earliest Bray Curtis ordination (Gauch et al. 1977). Since new techniques are continually being developed, it is important to consult the most recent literature before choosing a technique. At the same time, the most recent techniques are often the least well understood; for all their weaknesses, the Bray Curtis approach and principal components analysis (PCA) are at least relatively simple and their deficiencies well known. By using such basic techniques, one also avoids being seduced by a technique with such complex algorithms that one can no longer understand them entirely.

10.3.4   Ordinations based upon species data

Figure 10.9 shows the results of an ordination of sea cliff vegetation in England using an early technique called principal components

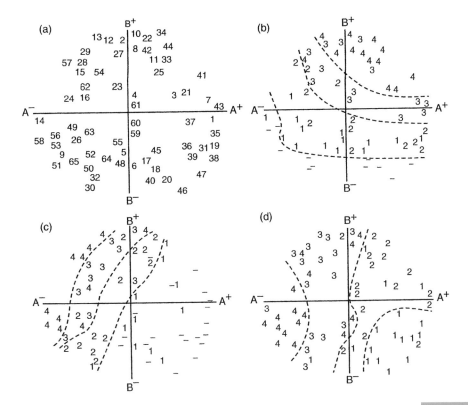

Figure 10.9 An ordination of sea cliff vegetation using principal components analysis. (a) distribution of 65 quadrats along the first two PC axes, (b) abundance of *Festuca rubra*, a dominant grass species, (c) abundance of *Armeria maritima*, (d) salinity of each quadrat measured as conductivity (after Goldsmith 1973a).

analysis (Goldsmith 1973a). While this technique has now been replaced by more elaborate ones, the patterns are still evident. The array shows a distribution of data points, each representing a quadrat, plotted according to the first two principal components (Figure 10.9(a)). Note that in this example, the data matrix consisted only of species abundances in each quadrat; the pattern reflects the changes in composition of the vegetation compressed into two dimensions. To interpret the possible environmental causes of these patterns, one might return to one's knowledge of the natural history of these species. For example, *Armeria maritima* is found in exposed and saline sites, and so its abundance in one portion of the ordination space might suggest that these are the quadrats from exposed and saline cliff faces (Figure 10.9(c)). By plotting the abundance of species for each point, one can see that different points represent dominance by different plant species. Alternatively, if one wanted to explore environmental factors more directly, one could superimpose measurements of environmental factors, such as soil salinity, on each point. Gradients in soil salinity could then be visualized (Figure 10.9(d)), and one might tentatively conclude that soil salinity is an important factor controlling plant distributions on sea cliffs.

Another reason for beginning with Goldsmith's work, apart from the simplicity and clarity of the patterns he found, is the remarkable fact that he did not stop his enquiry after doing the ordination. Based upon these patterns he hypothesized that competition was a major factor controlling species distributions and that salinity controlled the outcome of competition. Then he actually did the experiments (Goldsmith 1978) to test these hypotheses! This is such a rare feature of ordination studies that it deserves recognition. Another example can be found in the work of Larson on lichens and their distribution on cliff faces; the initial ordination work (Larson 1980) led to hypotheses about physiological responses to temperature, moisture, and drought and these hypotheses were tested with an extensive series of growth chamber experiments (e.g., Larson 1982, 1989).

10.3.5 Ordinations combining species and environmental data

In Goldsmith's (1973a) work (Figure 10.9), the ordination was based only upon the plant species, and the physical factors were then explored in a second stage. Alternatively, one might combine physical factor data and species data in one large matrix, or even expand the data further by adding in factors such as plant diversity or productivity. Recall Figure 3.13 that showed the results of a factor analysis of an expanded data matrix for a freshwater marsh in southern Canada. Since little was known about relationships among species, biomass, diversity, and fertility, Auclair et al. (1976a) sought patterns by combining all of these different measures in one dataset. The particular technique, factor analysis, is no longer widely used, but in practical terms, it still illustrates rather well the nature of the results of ordination. In Figure 3.13 at the upper right, it is evident that soil fertility, productivity, and the abundance of *Typha angustifolia* are all closely associated in this wetland. The upper left shows that fire incidence, species density, and the abundance of *Carex lanuginosa* are associated. This figure also incorporates a third dimension by using different types of dots, with the open circles being positive (raised above the surface of the page) and the dark ones being negative (falling below the surface of the page).

One of the strengths of ordination is its ability to incorporate and display many environmental factors and vegetation characteristics that are correlated to varying degrees at different scales. One frequently attends seminars where someone will point out that the factor under study is actually correlated with others, as if this observation were a clever and original criticism of the research. In fact, the world of plant ecology is filled with strongly correlated factors. This is not a problem so much as a simple statement of reality. On a hillside, say, where moisture, soil depth, temperature, and vegetation may all be correlated, it may not even make much sense to ask about the independent effects of each of these factors, for even if one factor could be isolated from all others, the fact remains that the others co-vary in nature.

To emphasize this point, and further illustrate the strength of ordination, consider the practical example of herbaceous vegetation on rock outcrops within forest (Figure 10.10(a)). At the large scale, there is variation caused by geology and climate. At more local scales, aspect, slope and elevation will vary among sites. Superimposed upon this variation are biotic processes such as dispersal, competition, mycorrhizae and grazing, and correlated physical factors such as soil moisture, depth of snow cover, growing season, soil temperature, wind speed, and so on. To study any one of these factors in isolation would be misleading because none of them occurs in isolation. Therefore, the best procedure seems to be to describe the multivariate variation in vegetation and relate it to multivariate variation in the environment. Therefore, Wiser et al. (1996) collected species presence and cover data for 154 100-m^2 samples from 42 Appalachian peaks from 11 locations in the mountains of North Carolina. A total of 294 vascular plant species was recorded. Environmental factors included topographic position, vertical relief, surface fracturing, exposure, rock type (mafic, felsic, intermediate), and outcrop area. In smaller plots, lichen cover, seepage, pH, organic content, and soil nutrients were recorded.

A hierarchical classification using the now standard technique of TWINSPAN (Section 10.4.2) was first used to sort the vegetation samples into nine different community types (Figure 10.10(b)). Only vegetation data were used in the analysis, but note that the dominant vegetation types are associated with different elevations at first, and then with rock type and exposure. The *Aronia arbutifolia – Kalmia latifolia* community, for example, occurs on shallow slopes over felsic bedrock (granite domes) at low to mid elevations. In contrast, the *Selaginella tortipila – Carex umbellata* vegetation occurs below 1600 m on felsic bedrock in the southern part of the study area. When the vegetation samples are ordinated using detrended correspondence analysis (DCA), the nine community types can then be superimposed on two DCA axes (Figure 10.10(c)). The *Selaginella – Carex* community falls lowest on axis 1, for example, and the *Coreopsis – Schizachyrium* community falls lowest on axis 2. Finally, superimposed upon the same ordination axes are the environmental factors. Each factor is labeled and oriented to indicate its relative contribution to the two axes; the longer the line, the greater the effect. Thus, plant communities to the left, low on axis 1, have higher solar radiation and higher pH, whereas those to the right, high on axis 1, have higher elevation and fracturing. The combination of all these analyses, as Figure 10.10 shows, provides a detailed snapshot of the vegetation and environmental factors on high elevation rock outcrops and a solid footing for conservation planning, or future experimental work aimed at unraveling cause and effect.

10.3.6 Functional simplification in ordination

When the results of ordination are presented, species names are often used. The problem with this approach is that there are so many plant species in the world that most of us know only a limited flora. The names on the axes are therefore largely meaningless to many readers. Even if one recognizes the names, they are of limited use in drawing ecological conclusions from the data. Why should this be surprising; after all, names are something put on plants by humans, they are not natural properties of plants or ecosystems. When one tries to interpret ordination axes using species names, one is usually drawing upon some additional knowledge about each species: its size, its tolerance of salinity, or some other trait. The problem is that the reader who is unfamiliar with the species does not know the traits unless they are explained on a case-by-case basis. This suggests that it might be very useful to plot plant traits upon the ordination; these might include competitive ability or relative

Figure 10.10 Multivariate analysis of high altitude rock outcrops in the Appalachian Mountains. (a) The *Selaginella tortipila/Carex umbellata* vegetation type on Hawksbill Mountain. (b) Hierarchical classification of 154 100-m² plots into nine vegetation types using TWINSPAN. (c) DCA ordination of all plots coded by the nine TWINSPAN communities. (d) Environmental correlations superimposed over plot locations in DCA space (from Wiser et al. 1996).

(a)

(b)

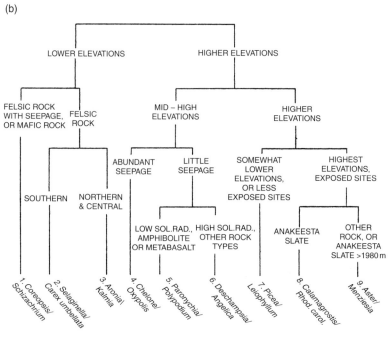

(c)

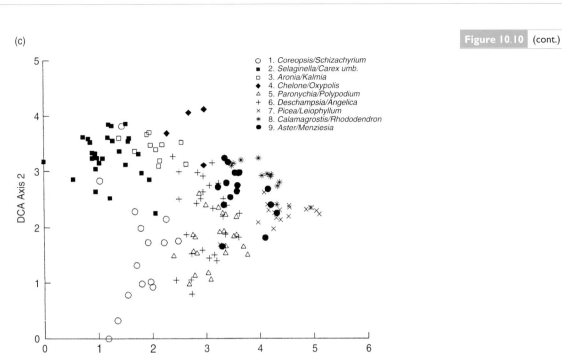

1. *Coreopsis/Schizachyrium*
2. *Selaginella/Carex umb.*
3. *Aronia/Kalmia*
4. *Chelone/Oxypolis*
5. *Paronychia/Polypodium*
6. *Deschampsia/Angelica*
7. *Picea/Leiophyllum*
8. *Calamagrostis/Rhododendron*
9. *Aster/Menziesia*

Figure 10.10 (cont.)

(d)

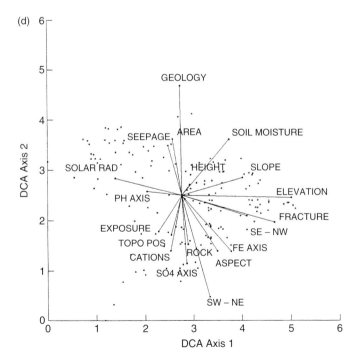

growth rate (as measured in independent experiments). This is rarely done. Even when factors such as fertility and litter mass are included, as in Figure 3.13, there is still a good deal of effort involved in interpreting the results, particularly for the non-specialist. One could,

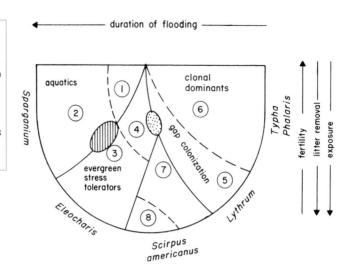

Figure 10.11 Summary of dominant plant species and processes along shorelines of the Ottawa River, Canada derived from an ordination of plant species overlaid by environmental factors. The hatched and stippled regions show the locations of *Scirpus acutus* and *Spartina pectinata*, respectively (from Day et al. 1988).

however, simplify the results by subjectively extracting the key factors and plotting them in simplified form. One would then combine the main species associations with the key factors thought to be producing them. (Of course, such a figure would be placed in the Discussion of the paper, not the Results.) Another study of riparian wetlands used this approach to produce a functional summary of herbaceous vegetation types, where both dominant species (e.g., *Sparganium eurycarpum*) and processes (e.g., gap colonization) were combined (Figure 10.11).

10.4 | Vegetation classification

Classification divides landscapes and vegetation into discrete groups. Vegetation types are often delineated on the basis of species composition, but classification schemes vary depending upon their purpose.

In selecting a classification scheme one needs to consider objectives carefully. As a research tool, classification may have limited value, tending to obscure the interactions that occur among species along gradients. One is reminded of Pielou's (1975) warning about ecologists who are more interested in finding the elusive "homogeneous ecosystem" than in studying the gradients that occur in real systems. Further, classification may suffer from the same problems as ordination – being applied mindlessly too often as a substitute for a properly thought out research question. When it comes to the practical task of managing real landscapes and plant communities, or planning reserve systems, some method of vegetation classification is essential. For example, if one is managing large tracts of mixed deciduous forest, those regions dominated by oak may need to be burned to produce oak regeneration; if one does not have a vegetation map indicating areas of oak forest, one cannot proceed with appropriate management. Similarly, in designing a reserve system to protect the different ecosystems of the world, one cannot know how many reserves are needed without first identifying ecosystem types. A list of major vegetation types provides an objective template for judging when a reserve system is complete. As well, procedures such as gap analysis, to detect ecosystem types not yet included in the reserve system (Section 12.4.1), are entirely dependent upon the adequacy of the classification scheme (Noss and Cooperrider 1994). At present, most vegetation classification schemes are developed by individual land management agencies, according to agency objectives. Gradually, consistent global systems such as maps of ecoregions (Olson et al. 2001, Figure 2.12) are emerging.

No single classification scheme will fill every need; reserve selection may emphasize the natural diversity of vegetation and land forms, whereas management of large mammals may require knowledge of only a few cover types, and management of an endangered species may require mapping of some very specific feature significant only to the particular species. In designing and applying vegetation classification schemes, we should strive to make the best possible use of existing data and to incorporate the latest understanding of vegetation dynamics.

10.4.1 Phytosociology

Phytosociological systems of vegetation classification are particularly well developed in Europe. Here there has been an emphasis upon classifying stands of vegetation rather than studying changes along gradients, and a number of classification schemes have been developed. The most widely used system is that of the Zurich-Montpellier school of phytosociology (Westhoff and van der Maarel 1973, Mueller-Dombois and Ellenberg 1974, Beeftink 1977). This system is based entirely upon the plant species cover in standard sample areas. The vegetation therein is then classified hierarchically, going downward through classes, orders, alliances, to associations. Each level in the hierarchy is identified using parts of the names of the defining species along with a special suffix to indicate the level (Table 10.1). Thus a tract of salt marsh dominated by *Spartina maritima* would be in the Class Spartinetea, Order Spartinetalia, Alliance Spartinion, and Association Spartinetum maritimae. Table 10.2 illustrates the application of this technique to salt marsh communities in The Netherlands.

Once such tables are prepared for different sites, it becomes possible to recognize the geographical distribution of specific vegetation types and the relationship between these vegetation types and the environmental gradients (Figure 10.12). In this classification system, a plant community is termed a "phytocoenose," a quadrat becomes a "relevé," and communities become "syntaxa." The use of this approach may be most suitable in European landscapes that are largely mosaics of vegetation types resulting from past agriculture, grazing, and forestry regimes. It seems less useful in those areas of the world where natural gradients remain. All students of plant ecology should be familiar with this system since it is widely used in the European scientific literature.

Table 10.1. *Levels and units of the formal hierarchy of the Zurich-Montpellier school of sociology from highest (division) to lowest (subvariant), with suffixes and examples of the construction of names based on denominating taxa (from Westhoff and van der Maarel 1973).*

Syntaxon	Suffix	Examples	Denominating taxa
Division	-ea	Querco-Fagea	genus *Fagus*
Class	-etea	Phragmitetea	*Phragmites australis*
		Querco-Fagetea	*Quercus robur*
		silvaticae	*Fagus sylvatica*
Order	-etalia	Littorelletalia	*Littorella uniflora*
		Festuco-Sedetalia	*Festuca* and *Sedum* L. div. spp.
Alliance	-ion	Agropyro-Rumicion crispi	*Agropyron repens*,(syn.; *Elytrigia repens*) and *Rumex crispus*
		Alnion glutinosae	*Alnus glutinosa*
Suballiance	-ion (-esion)	Ulmion carpinifoliae (Ulmesion)	*Ulmus carpinifolia*
Association	-etum	Ericetum tetralicis	*Erica tetralix*
		Elymo-Ammophiletum	*Elymus arenarius, Ammophila arenaria*
Subassociation	-etosum	Arrhenatheretum elatioris brizetosum	*Briza media*
Variant		ibid., *Salvia* variant	*Salvia pratensis*
Subvariant		ibid., *Bromus* subvariant	*Bromus erectus*

10.4.2 Classification and land management

There are many statistical methods for classifying vegetation data. Sneath and Sokal (1973) provide a particularly lucid introduction to the topic, although there are many other sources you could also consult (e.g., Legendre and Legendre 1983, Pielou 1984, Digby and Kempton 1987, Gnanadesikan 1997). All have the objective of organizing a set of quadrats into clusters having similar species composition. Just as with ordination, one begins with the samples by quadrats ($s \times q$) data matrix shown in Figure 10.7, one selects a measure of similarity and then one applies a statistical technique (algorithm) to obtain the clusters. You may have noticed that I slipped a common classification method into the ordination discussion in Section 10.3.6 (Figure 10.10(b)), in order to present the Appalachian Mountains example in its entirety. In that case, the classification tool was TWINSPAN (two-way indicator species analysis), which not only sorts quadrats into clusters, but organizes them hierarchically and identifies indicator species for each cluster. In the Appalachian example, the resulting clusters were then superimposed upon the ordination in Figure 10.10(c). Note in this example that the habitat interpretations (e.g., "lower elevations") in the TWINSPAN diagram (Figure 10.10(b)) were added later to assist with interpreting the data, and are not a part of the TWINSPAN output.

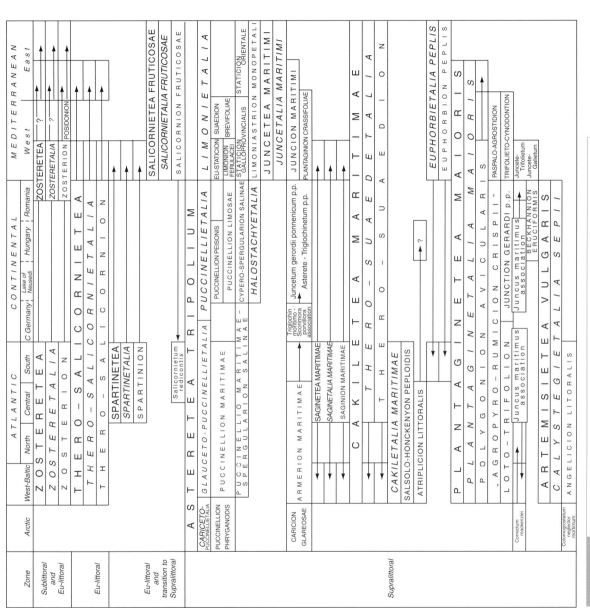

Figure 10.12 Geographical distribution of the European higher salt marsh syntaxa (from Beeftink 1977).

Table 10.2. *Zurich-Montpellier classification of salt marsh communities in the southwestern Netherlands based on Braun-Blanquet species abundance measures (from Westhoff and Van der Maarel 1973).*

Classes	Thero–Salicornietea	Spartinetea		Asteretea tripolii	
Orders	Thero–Salicornietalia	Spartinetalia		Glauco–Puccinellietalia	
Alliances	Thero–Salicornion	Spartinion		Puccinellion maritiimae	
Associations	*Salicornietum strictae*	*Spartinetum maritimae*	*Spartinetum townsendii*	*Puccinellietum maritimae*	*Halimionetum portulacoidis*
Column	1	2	3	4	5
Number of relevés	14	24	30	124	40
Character–taxa of the associations					
Salicornia europaea coll.[1]	100(1– –3)	33(+ –2)	14(+ –2)	78(+ –2)	40(+ –1)
Spartina maritima	14(+)	100(2– –4)	—	6(+)	—
Fucus vesiculosus f. *volubilis*	—	79(+ –5)	7(2– –3)	4(+ –2)	—
Spartina townsendii agg.	86(+ –1)	79(+ –2)	100(3– –5)	50(+ –2)	35(+ –2)
Puccinellia maritima[2]	25(+ –1)	33(+ –1)	30(+ –1)	100(3– –5)	92(+ –2)
Halimione portulacoides	8(+)	—	33(r– –1)	83(+ –2)	100(3– –5)
Artemisia maritima	—	—	—	5(+ –1)	—
Armeria maritima	—	—	—	6(+ –1)	—
Carex extensa	—	—	—	—	—
Puccinellia distans	—	—	—	—	—
Puccinellia fasciculata	—	—	—	—	—
Puccinellia retroflexa	—	—	—	—	—
Scirpus maritimus var. *compactus*[3]	—	—	27(+ –2)	—	—
Faithful taxa of Puccinellion maritimae					
Bostrychia scorpioides	—	17(+ –4)	14(+ –2)	21(+ –4)	37(+ –4)
Character–taxa of Armerion maritimae					
Juncus gerardi	—	—	—	2(+)	—
Festuca rubra f. *litoralis*	—	—	—	14(+ –2)	62(+ –1)
Glaux maritima	—	—	10(r– –1)	50(+ –2)	15(+ –1)
Parapholis strigosa	—	—	—	—	—
Agrostis stolonifera var. *compacta* subvar. *salina*	—	—	—	—	—
Character–taxon of Puccinellio–Spergularion salinae					
Spergularia salina	—	—	—	—	—
Character–taxa of Glauco–Puccinellietalia					
Spergularia media	—	—	7(r– +)	73(+ –2)	42(+ –2)
Limonium vulgare ssp. *vulgare*	8(+)	8(+)	30(r– +)	73(+ –2)	60(+ –2)
Character–taxa of Asteretea tripolii					
Aster tripolium	50(+ –2)	33(+ –2)	77(r– –2)	98(+ –2)	97(+ –2)
Triglochin maritima	8(+)	—	27(r– –2)	86(+ –4)	62(+ –2)
Plantago maritima	—	—	20(r– –1)	65(+ –4)	65(+ –2)
Other taxa					
Suaeda maritima	50(+ –1)	12(+ –2)	37(+ –1)	64(+ –2)	60(+ –2)
Atriplex hastata	—	—	77(+ –2)	25(+ –2)	5(+)
Elytrigia pungens	—	—	7(r– +)	1(+)	22(+)
Lolium perenne	—	—	—	—	—
Plantago coronopus	—	—	—	—	—
Phragmites communis	—	—	—	—	—

Addenda

Column 1: *Zostera noltii* 29(+ –2); Column 7: *Centaurium pulchellum* 17(+ –2), *Carex distans* 5(+), *Sagina maritima* 2(+), *Solanum dulcamara* 2(+); Column 8: *Centaurium pulchellum* 57(r– –2), *Carex distans* 29(r– –2), *Juncus maritimus* 29(r– –1), *Lotus tenuis* 29(2), *Hippophae rhamnoides* 29(r– +), *Trifolium fragiferum* 14(r), *Sonchus arvensis* 14(r), *Trifolium repens* 14(r), *Centaurium littorale* 14(+)[0]; Column 9: *Polygonum aviculare* 41(+ –2), *Elytrigia repens* 22(+ –1), *Potentilla anserina* 8(+ –1), *Plantago major* 24(+ –2), *Leontodon autumnalis* 5(+), *Trifolium repens* 11(+)[0], *Coronopus squamatus* 8(+ –2), *Matricaria inodora* 11(+)[0], *Bromus mollis* 8(+), *Ranunculus sceleratus* 16(+ –1)[0], *Poa annua*

[1] In the alliances Thero–Salicornion and Spartinion represented by *S. stricta* Dum.
[2] Preferential character–taxon of the association; also selective character taxon of the alliance Puccinellion maritimae and exclusive character–taxon of the order Glauco–Puccinellietalia.
[3] Also character–taxon of the alliance Halo–Scirpion.
N.B. The superscript [0] is a convention meaning that the taxon is represented by stunted individuals.

Armerion maritimae			Puccinellio–Spergularion salinae			Halo–Scirpion
Artemisietum maritimae	Juncetum gerardii	Junco–Caricetum extensae	Puccinellietum distantis	Puccinellietum fasciculatae	Puccinellietum retroflexae	Halo–Scirpetum maritimi
6	7	8	9	10	11	12
61	64	7	37	10	12	19
$30(+ -1)^0$	$42(+ -1)^0$	$14(+)^0$	$35(+ -2)^0$	$70(r- -2)^0$	$100(1- -2)^0$	—
—	—	—	—	—	—	—
—	—	—	—	—	—	—
13(+)	20(+ -2)	—	$8(+)^0$	—	17(r)	37(+ -2)
43(+ -2)	31(+ -2)	14(+)	62(+ -1)	90(r- -3)	25(r- -1)	26(1- -3)
98(+ -3)	62(+ -1)	—	5(+)	—	—	—
93(+ -3)	59(+ -1)	—	8(+ -1)	—	—	—
2(+)	90(+ -3)	14(r)	—	—	—	—
—	—	100(1- -4)	—	—	—	—
—	—	—	100(1- -5)	$20(r- -2)^0$	17(r - +)	—
—	—	—	—	100(2- -4)	17(r)	—
—	—	—	—	—	100(1- -4)	—
—	—	—	$32(+ -2)^0$	$10(+)^0$	$8(r)^0$	100(3- -5)
5(+ -2)	—	—	—	—	—	—
—	86(+ -5)	100(2- -4)	14(+ -2)	30(+)	—	5(+)
100(3- -5)	97(+ -5)	86(+ -3)	35(+ -3)	10(r)	—	—
33(+ -1)	98(+ -3)	100(2- -3)	35(+ -3)	30(r- -2)	—	11(+)
5(+ -1)	64(+ -3)	43(+ -2)	19(+ -2)	10(+)	8(+)	—
—	11(+ -1)	100(+ -3)	65(+ -2)	30(+ -2)	—	42(+ -4)
—	—	—	97(+ -3)	80(+ -2)	100(r- -2)	—
72(+ -2)	47(+ -1)	14(+)	19(+ -1)	20(1- -2)	8(+)	—
66(+ -2)	91(+ -3)	57(r- -2)	$3(+)^0$	—	—	—
100(+ -2)	72(+ -2)	71(r- -1)	65(+ -3)	100(r- -3)	100(+ -4)	74(+ -2)
29(+ -1)	77(+ -2)	29(+)	5(+ -1)	50(r- -2)	8(r)	16(+ -1)
72(+ -3)	98(+ -3)	100(+ -2)	11(+)	—	8(+)	—
31(+ -1)	$20(+ -1)^0$	—	$38(r- -1)^0$	$30(r- -1)^0$	$8(1)^0$	—
11(+)	$5(+)^0$	—	$62(+ -2)^0$	$40(r)^0$	—	63(1- -3)
31(+ -2)	28(+ -2)	—	30(+ -2)	—	—	32(+ -2)
—	2(+)	—	30(+ -3)	10(r)	—	—
—	2(+)	29(+)	11(+ -1)	10(1)	$25(+)^0$	—
—	2(+)	$43(r- +)^0$	30(+ -3)	$10(r)^0$	$67(r- -2)^0$	11(+ -2)

11(+ -2), *Cochlearia officinalis* 11(+), *Festuca arundinacea* 8(+), *Cirsium arvense* 5(+ -1), Poa trivialis 3(3), *Hordeum secalinum* 3(1), *Taraxacum* sp. 5(+), *Sonchus arvensis* 3(+), *Poa pratensis* 3(+), *Solanum nigrum* 3(+), *Senecio vulgaris* 3(+), *Anagallis arvensis* 3(+), *Leontodon nudicaulis* 3(+); Column 10: *Centaurium pulchellum* 10(+), *Plantago major* $20(r)^0$, *Matricaria inodora* $10(r)^0$, *Bromus mollis* 10(+), *Sagina maritima* 40(+ -2), *Juncus bufonius* 40(r- -2), *Hordeum marinum* 10(r), *Samolus valerandi* 10(r); Column 11: *Bromus mollis* 8(r); Column 12: *Ranunculus sceleratus* 5(+), *Cochlearia officinalis* 5(+), *Atriplex littoralis* 5(+).

To illustrate the application of classification to land management, we will focus upon the boreal forests near Hudson Bay in Canada, as summarized in a document called *Field Guide to Forest Ecosystem Classification for the Clay Belt, Site Region 3E* developed by a consortium of government agencies concerned with forest management in northern Ontario (Jones et al. 1983b). This report begins: "If management knowledge and experience are to be organised, communicated and used effectively, a practical, clear system for classifying [forest] stands (ecosystems) is needed to ensure that each manager knows what the others are talking or writing about" (p. 1).

The first step in understanding the value of this document in particular and classification in general is to explain the title. What are Site Regions? The province of Ontario has been divided into 13 Site Regions based upon landform and climate (Figure 10.13). Each Site Region is divided, in turn, into Site Districts. Site Region 1E, for example, refers to tundra-like lowlands along the coast of Hudson Bay; Region 7E refers to rich deciduous forest along the north shore of Lake Erie. Site Region 3E, popularly called the clay belt, was formed at the end of the last ice age when Lake Barlow-Ojibway formed at the margin of the retreating ice (Baldwin 1958). The lake lasted about 2000 years and apparently drained some 11 000 years BP, leaving 70 000 square miles between James Bay and the Great Lakes with a thick layer (ca. 70 m deep) of lacustrine clay. The drainage is poor, and extensive peatlands now cover much of the area. In peatlands, *Picea mariana* is the dominant tree; in occasional well-drained areas such as rock outcrops or sandy ridges, *Pinus banksiana* is common.

To construct the guide, a large number of vegetation samples was collected, ordinated using detrended correspondence analysis, and then classified into 23 vegetation types using TWINSPAN. These were simplified to 14 "operational groups" for management purposes: "No classification is of practical use if the management staff cannot allocate any stand to its class quickly in the field using only a few easily recognised diagnostic features. Further, there should be only a sensible number of classes to cover the whole range of forest conditions if the number of management prescriptions is to be reasonable" (Jones et al. 1983a, pp. 1–2). The classification was combined with the ordination to produce an array of the 23 vegetation types in the two-dimensional phase space defined by the ordination axes. Operational groups were overlaid on the results (Figure 10.14). Each operational group has a name, ranging from the driest, OG1, "Very Shallow Soil Over Bedrock" to a peatland, OG14 "Chamaedaphne," referring to the dominant ericaceous shrub in this habitat. The guide provides a short key using indicator species to enable a manager to rapidly assign a site to one of these 14 operational groups.

Figure 10.15 summarizes the vegetation and physical factors in this classification. In the upper left, OG1 is dominated by Pj (jack pine, *Pinus banksiana*) whereas OG14 (lower left) has Sb (black spruce,

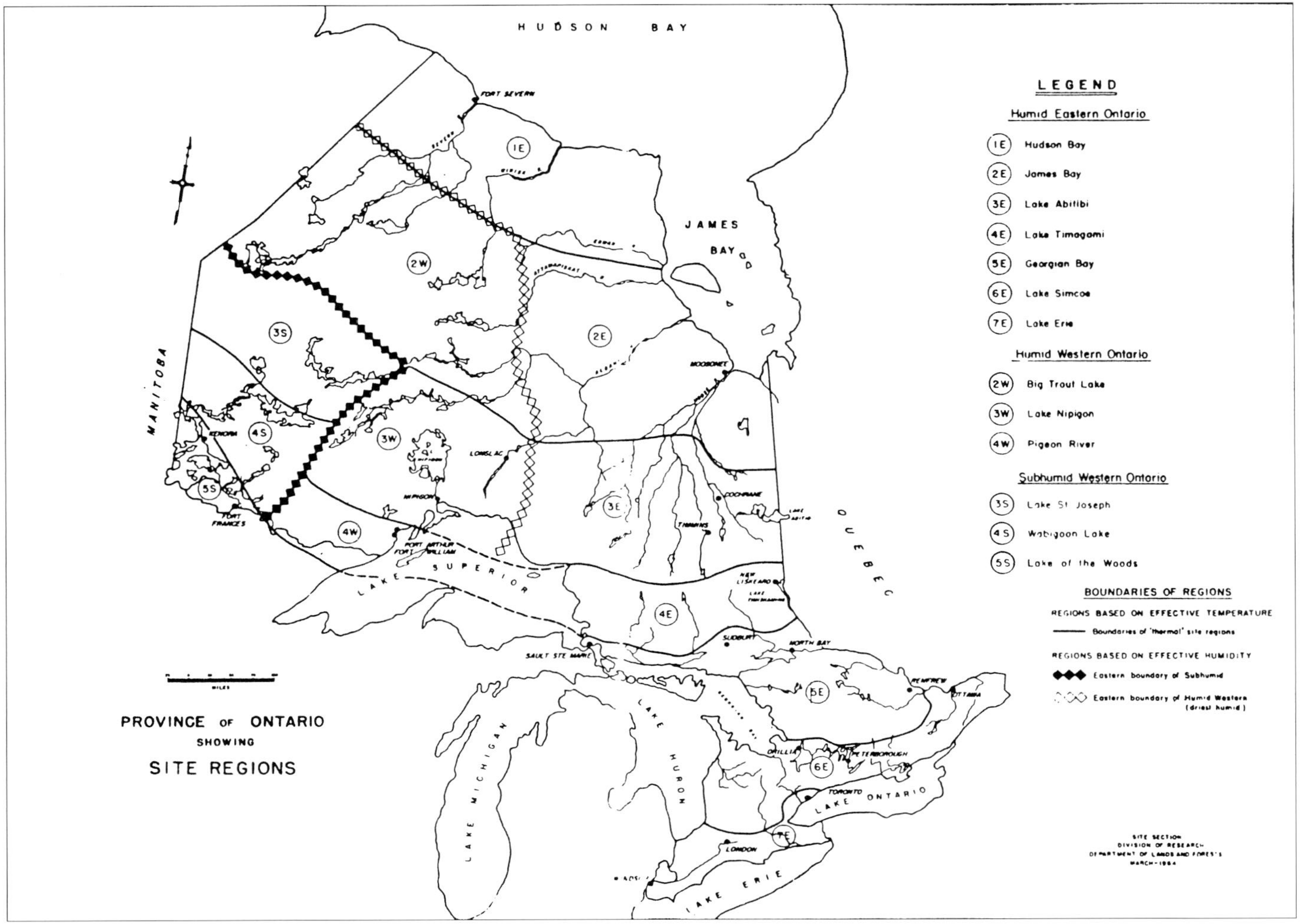

Figure 10.13 Ontario, Canada can be divided into 13 site regions based upon landform and climate (from Hills 1961).

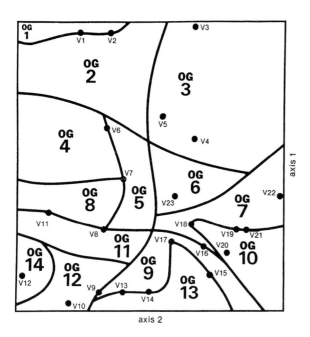

FEATHERMOSS - COARSE SOIL
OG 4
Sb (&/or Pj) - Feathermoss on
Fresh-Moist
Sandy or Coarse Loamy Soil

FEATHERMOSS - FINE SOIL
OG 5
Sb (&/or Pj) - Feathermoss on
Fresh-Moist Fine Loamy-Clayey Soil

LYCOPODIUM
OG 6
Lycopodium - Herb Poor on
Fresh-Moist Loamy Soil

MIXEDWOOD - HERB RICH
OG 7
Hardwood/Mixedwood - Herb Rich on
Fresh-Moist Fine Loamy-Clayey Soil

FEATHERMOSS - SPHAGNUM
OG 8
Sb - Feathermoss - Sphagnum on
Moist Fine Loamy-Clayey Soil with
20-39 cm. Organic Matter

CONIFER - HERB/MOSS RICH
OG 9
Conifer Mixed - Herb Rich on
Moist Fine Loamy-Clayey Soil

HARDWOOD - ALNUS
OG 10
Hardwood - Alnus - Herb Rich on
Moist Fine Loamy-Clayey Soils
with Thick Black Organic-Mineral Forest Humus Form

LEDUM
OG 11
Sb - Ledum on
Wet Moderately Decomposed Organic Soil with
Thick Surface Fibric Horizon

ALNUS - HERB POOR
OG 12
Sb - Alnus - Herb Poor on
Wet Moderately Decomposed Organic Soil with
Thick Surface Fibric Horizon

ALNUS - HERB RICH
OG 13
Sb (&/or Ce/L) - Alnus - Herb Rich on
Wet Well Decomposed Organic Soil with
Thin Surface Fibric Horizon

CHAMAEDAPHNE
OG 14
Sb - Chamaedaphne on
Wet Poorly Decomposed Organic Soil with
Thick Surface Fibric Horizon

operational group names

VERY SHALLOW SOIL OVER BEDROCK
OG 1
Sb &/or Pj - Feathermoss - Lichen on
Very Shallow Soil over Bedrock

VACCINIUM
OG 2
Pj (& Sb) - Vaccinium - Feathermoss - Lichen on
Dry or Fresh Sandy Soil

DIERVILLA
OG 3
Hardwood/Mixedwood - Vaccinium - Diervilla - Herb Poor on
Fresh Sandy or Loamy Soil

Figure 10.14 Ordination and classification divide a region of northern Ontario (site region 3E in Figure 10.13) into 14 operational groups, associated with different vegetation, soil types and water availability (from *Field Guide to Forest Ecosystem Classification for the Clay Belt, Site Region 3E*, published by the Ontario Ministry of Natural Resources, © Queen's Printer for Ontario, 1983. Reproduced with permission.)

Picea mariana); the codes are those in standard use by Ontario government foresters. The understorey vegetation changes from feathermoss (*Dicranum* spp.) in OG1 to *Sphagnum* in OG14. Soil texture is bedrock in OG1, and organic matter (peat) in OG14. Finally, the soil moisture regime ranges from dry-fresh in OG1 to very wet in OG14. In short, the array in Figure 10.14 summarizes the vegetation types found in the clay belt of northern Ontario, from jack pine on rock ridges to ericaceous peat bogs with black spruce in the wet sites. In between one finds other conditions, such as Sw (white spruce, *Picea glauca*) on loam with a rich herbaceous understorey (e.g., OG7).

The guide then provides a short biography of each operational group (Figure 10.16) with a profile of the community and a summary of the vegetation and soils. Note that it is keyed back to the ordination in Figure 10.14 with a shaded region in the small ordination diagram at the upper left. Simply flipping through the 14 pages with

1. tree species

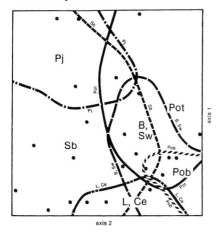

2. understory vegetation

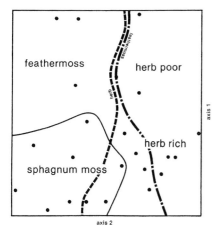

3. soil texture

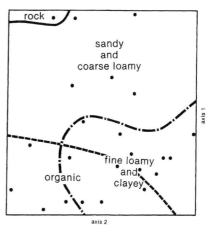

4. soil moisture regime

Figure 10.15 Four factors superimposed upon the ordination and classification presented in Figure 10.14. The codes for tree species include Pj (jack pine, *Pinus banksiana*), Sb (black spruce, *Picea mariana*), Pot (trembling aspen, *Populus tremuloides*), Pob (balsam poplar, *P. balsamifera*), Sw (white spruce, *picea glauca*) and B (birch, *Betula* spp.) (from *Field Guide to Forest Ecosystem Classification for the Clay Belt, Site Region 3E*, published by the Ontario Ministry of Natural Resources, © Queen's Printer for Ontario, 1983. Reproduced with permission.)

the biographies provides a rapid reconnaissance of the communities to be expected in the vast area of site region 3E. Managers can therefore prescribe different land use strategies according to the operating group. Jack pine on rock ridges might, for example, be clear cut and then burned to enhance regeneration, whereas wet peatlands might be left untouched. Intermediate sites, such as OG6, might be clear-cut and then replanted. Similarly, if one has the objective of setting up a park system to represent the vegetation diversity of this region, one would want to ensure that the park system contained large enough examples of these 14 operating groups that they would persist through time. If a gap analysis of the existing system were conducted one might similarly discover that one OG was not represented, and this would guide one in seeking a representative example of this OG to add to the park system.

Figures 10.14 to 10.16 not only illustrate the procedure of classification used in one section of the boreal forest of Ontario, but they

Figure 10.16 A typical one-page biography of an operational group, in this case the example of black spruce and jack pine in shallow soil on rock ridges (OG1). Each operational group requires a different set of management guidelines (from *Field Guide to Forest Ecosystem Classification for the Clay Belt, Site Region 3E,* published by the Ontario Ministry of Natural Resources, © Queen's Printer for Ontario, 1983. Reproduced with permission.)

very shallow soil over bedrock

Sb &/or Pj - Feathermoss - Lichen on Very Shallow Soil over Bedrock

DESCRIPTION

VEGETATION

COMMON FOREST COVER TYPES:
Rock, Pj, Pj-Sb

VEGETATION TYPES:
V1[4] V7[3] V2[1] V11[1] V23[1]

TREE LAYER:
Black Spruce, Jack Pine, occasionally Larch and Cedar.

SHRUB LAYER:
Vaccinium angustifolium, Black Spruce, Balsam Fir, and occasionally Jack Pine and White Birch regeneration.

HERB LAYER:
None - very few.

MOSSES:
Pleurozium schreberi, Dicranum polysetum, Polytrichum juniperinum, Dicranum fuscescens.

LICHENS:
Cladina mitis, C. rangiferina.

GROUND SURFACE:
Varying proportions of exposed rock, feathermoss and coniferous litter. Occasionally local concave pockets contain Sphagnum moss.

SOIL

SOIL TYPES:
S1

FOREST HUMUS FORM:
Fibrimor[6] Humimor[4]

DEPTH OF ORGANIC MATTER:
(3-10 cm)[8] (>10 cm)[2]

TEXTURE:
Will vary depending on nature of rock and types of adjacent deposits.

MOISTURE REGIME/DRAINAGE:
(0-1)[8] (>1)[2]/VR-R; local concave pockets can be wetter/more poorly drained.

CARBONATES:
Usually absent but will depend on nature of adjacent deposits.

also provide a series of steps that could be used in any other vegetation region. The field guide from which these figures are reproduced contains other elements, including keys to ecosystem types based upon plant species, descriptions of the soils, and a section on plant recognition with line drawings so that field workers can quickly assign sites to operational groups. I describe this example in some detail not only to illustrate the role of classification, but to provide some inspiration to young ecologists who may face a similar task in another part of the world.

10.5 | Gradients and communities

10.5.1 | Clements and Gleason

We have now seen how natural gradients provide a useful starting point for describing pattern in plant communities (Section 10.2). We have also examined how gradients can be detected by applying ordination techniques to species × sample matrices (Section 10.3). Gradients also figure prominently in one of the major debates of plant ecology (Whittaker 1962, McIntosh 1967, Colinvaux 1978, Shipley and Keddy 1987), usually framed as a debate between two American ecologists, Frederick Clements (1974–1945) and Henry Gleason (1882–1975). Since both Clements and Gleason wrote extensively, any summary of their work is bound to be an oversimplification, and textbooks are forced by space limitations to present caricatures of their views. Essays that attempt more detail often fall into using quotations from different periods of their careers, which usually generates more confusion and leads away from the original topic of debate (the structure, if any, of plant communities) toward separate topics – how the views of two scholars changed with time, and even how they understood or misunderstood the meaning of words such as "random" (e.g., Nicolson and McIntosh 2002). Before we know it, an important topic – the nature and meaning of pattern in ecological communities (a topic that could inspire new work) – becomes the frustrating attempt to try to interpret 50-year-old quotations from long dead scholars whose views likely changed during their careers.

Yet one cannot ignore this topic. It involves two important historical figures in ecology. It raises the important issue of how structured ecological communities actually are. Moreover, those of you who are already familiar with the topic from introductory texts may expect a more nuanced treatment of the debate. Further, the topic reminds us that, contrary to the impressions left by some books (e.g., Strong et al. 1984, Gotelli and Graves 1996), the issue of structure in communities, and the use of null models to examine it, is a traditional approach, not a radical new topic in ecology (Box 10.1). There is also an important lesson for future work. The debate illustrates the folly into which we fall when we argue about topics without explicitly describing what measurements are needed to distinguish between alternatives. It therefore issues a challenge to us: either frame an argument in a measurable way, or ignore it and move on to something more fruitful. So let us revisit the topic with the advantage of nearly a century of hindsight.

In general, Clements is presented as an ecologist who argued for strongly integrated communities with consistent, recurring species composition (community units) that were somewhat like super organisms:

> The developmental study of vegetation necessarily rests upon the assumption that the unit or climax formation is an organic entity ... As an organism the formation arises, grows, matures, and dies. Its

response to the habitat is shown in processes or functions and in structures which are the record as well as the result of these functions. *(p. 3)*
The climax formation is the adult organism, the fully-developed
community, of which all initial and medial stages are but stages of
development. *(p. 125)* Finally, all of these viewpoints are summed up in
that which regards succession as the growth or development and the
reproduction of a complex organism. *(pp. 3–4)*

Clements (1916)

Gleason is presented as his antagonist who in 1917 published a
counter-treatise "The structure and development of the plant association." In one familiar sentence, Gleason says:

The development and maintenance of vegetation is therefore merely the
resultant of the development and maintenance of the component individuals, and is favoured, modified, retarded or inhibited by all causes
which influence the component plants.

(p. 464)

Who could disagree? I'm not convinced that if Clements were available for interview, that he would argue with this statement. If there is
a difference between the two, it seems to be a matter of degree (see
Box 10.2).

10.5.2   The temporary victory of the Gleasonian view

Many ecology texts give the impression that the matter has been
resolved in favor of Gleason's individualistic approach (see Colinvaux
(1978) for a particularly readable summary). This "individualistic"
approach is based on each individual species having its own distribution
independent of other species with which it may occasionally occur.

Two types of evidence are usually presented to support this view.
The first is the use of ordination (Section 10.3) to describe species
distributions along gradients; ordination often seems to show continuous variation in species associations (individualistic/continuum
approach). The second is the description of species distributions
along natural gradients such as those in Section 10.2. When plotted
and viewed by eye, few distributions (e.g., Figure 10.3) show strong
evidence of discrete communities.

What has been missed in relating this story are two simple counter-
observations:

1. Ordination is a technique designed to array species along gradients
   of vegetation composition. The fact that one uses a gradient-seeking
   technique and then (surprise!) finds gradients is not particularly
   conclusive evidence for continuous variation in species composition. Not surprisingly, if instead one uses techniques of classification, one can recognize apparently discrete communities.
   Ordination and classification each find what they are designed
   to look for – vegetation gradients and vegetation types, respectively.
   Indeed, although Whittaker's data are often used to support the
   individualistic approach, Whittaker himself (1956) divides forest
   vegetation into discrete types.

2. Examining species distributions along gradients by eye is inconclusive. Without criteria of falsification, and without null models, debates can continue indefinitely. Certainly Whittaker's data (Figure 10.3) do not show clearly demarcated plant communities along elevation gradients. But are these species distributions actually random? Perhaps they are even over dispersed from interspecific competition (Weiher and Keddy 1995b). Or perhaps they are clustered but the data are noisy and a statistical test is needed to find pattern within the noise. There are other possibilities too: real communities might be obscured by "blended" or "blurred" boundaries (*sensu* Pielou 1975).

Much effort could have been saved if ecologists had consulted James's (1907) essay on pragmatism:

> The pragmatic method is primarily a method of settling metaphysical disputes that otherwise might be interminable ... whenever a dispute is serious, we ought to be able to show some practical difference that must follow from one side or the other's being right.
>
> (p. 10)

James's essay is still delightful reading. He was a philosopher who wrote to be understood rather than to impress others by his scholastic virtue, and his style still has lessons for young scholars.

10.5.3   Null models and patterns along gradients

Oddly, many of the assessments of communities and patterns seem to have overlooked the enormous body of research that used statistical techniques to appraise the degree to which species are positively and negatively associated with one another, or with particular habitats. (Early examples included Cole (1949) and Greig-Smith (1957).) The null model, that there are no positive or negative associations (that species are randomly distributed with respect to one another), has now been repeatedly falsified.

Patterns of association are, of course, only pieces of evidence for communities, but many authors (e.g., Diamond 1975, Strong et al. 1984, Gotelli and Graves 1996) have minimized this body of studies, and overlooked just how thorough the studies of pattern have been (e.g., Cole 1949, Greig-Smith 1957, Agnew 1961, Kershaw 1973, Dale 1999). A quite separate body of studies also grew up using data from species along gradients (Pielou 1977, Dale 1999). In her short academic career, Chris Pielou produced a stream of papers and books addressing the search for pattern in nature. In her books one finds many methods for testing null hypothesis of community structure. Although she does not appear to have been familiar with James's (1907) ideas about pragmatism, her approach is what he advocated more than half a century earlier. Do communities exist? Well, what can be measured along gradients

Box 10.1 Getting the history right: null models in ecology

How might we determine whether plants are organized into communities, or merely randomly distributed with respect to one another? A review (Harvey et al. 1983) and an entire book (Gotelli and Graves 1996) have dealt with this topic. Unfortunately for historical accuracy, the book asserts that the term "null models" was invented in 1981 by American zoologists meeting in Florida. At best, this fundamentally misrepresents the short-term historical record (Keddy 1998), since other ecologists had already developed null models for plant communities. For example, decades earlier, P. Greig-Smith, and later, E. C. Pielou, presented many null models for the organization of communities, and discussed methods to test them (e.g., Greig-Smith 1952, 1957, Pielou 1975, 1977). However, even these writings on null models were built upon a foundation created by statisticians for whom the concept of a null model (e.g., the binomial, the Poisson, and the normal distribution) stretches back at least to the pioneering work (*Statistical Methods for Research Workers*) of Sir R. A. Fisher (1925) (Figure B10.1).

One of the earliest null model seems, in fact, to be attributable to Raunkiaer, whose global study of plant growth forms we encountered in Chapter 2. He understood the need for a random model against which he could judge observed patterns in growth form. Long before the age of Monte-Carlo computer programs, he describes how he selected 1000 species at random from the world's flora, and constructed a life-form spectrum for this group, which he then used as a reference spectrum against which to compare the life-form spectra of specific climates

Figure B10.1 Portrait in 1929 of Sir R. A. Fisher (1890–1962) whose work formed the basis for many modern techniques of statistical theory and methods (from Fienberg and Hinkly 1980).

(Table 2.4). Since my reference copy of Raunkiaer's original work (an English translation from the Danish edited by Tansley) is a badly tattered photocopy obtained on interlibrary loan (and since his original papers were published in Danish, German or French), I assume that many readers are unlikely to have access to the originals. Moreover, many readers or writers may accept without evidence the impressions provided by Gotelli and Graves. I will therefore quote from Raunkiaer's work at more than usual length.

Raunkiaer (1908) introduced the classification of plants into 10 life-forms, and tabulated these life-forms for an array of different climatic types. He begins his discussion with the observation that Nanophanerophytes are abundant in the Seychelles. Recall that Phanerophytes are trees and shrubs with buds (meristems) borne above the surface of the ground even under extreme conditions (Figure 2.8). Nanophanerophytes are the smallest of the phanerophytes being less than 2 m tall (Table 2.3), thereby including a wide range of shrubs typical of Mediterranean climates, fynbos, semi-deserts and peatlands.

> But what do these numbers mean? Are we to conclude from the fact that the Nanophanerophytes are the best represented life-form that it is the Nanophanerophytes that are particularly characteristic of the humid and hot tropical regions? By no means! The large number of Nanophanerophytes (sic) might perhaps mean that this life-form is very common in the world taken as a whole . . . what we lack is a standard, a 'normal spectrum' with which to compare the spectra of the various regions, and by means of which the value of the individual numbers can be determined. It is most reasonable to suppose that a normal spectrum of this kind might be found in the spectrum of the whole world, that is to say the percentage of each life-form in the flowering plants of the world.
>
> (Raunkiaer 1908, p. 115)

He goes on to describe the difficulty of obtaining a random sample of the world's flora, particularly given that the Compositae (now Asteraceae) alone then had some 13 000 species. In 1908 he had a spectrum for 400 species "even though 400 be too small a number . . . I shall use a spectrum founded on this number as a preliminary normal spectrum" (p. 16). By 1918 he reported that he had completed the monumental task. He first describes the difficulty in obtaining a list of the species in the global pool from which he could make a random selection.

> I came upon the difficulty that there was no comprehensive descriptive list of Phanerogams of the whole earth which represented a conglomeration approximately as uniform and homogeneous as a mass of seeds which one can thoroughly mix by shaking. If there were available a catalogue of all the Phanerogams in which the different species were arranged alphabetically according to their scientific names without reference to the genus it might be assumed that we should have such a mixture; but a catalogue of this sort does not exist.
>
> (Raunkiaer 1918, p. 429)

The need for a list without reference to genus is critical, "since the species of the same genus very often belong, all or in great part, to the same life-form . . .." (p. 429). Raunkiaer has already glimpsed, then, the problem of defining what random sample truly means when some groups of species are closely related to one another. He uses the analogy of trying to mix seeds thoroughly when some of them are stuck together.

Table B10.1. *Raunkaier's normal spectrum of plant life-forms (percent) for the globe based initially on a sample of 400 plant species and, later, a sample of 1000 species (Raunkaier 1918).*

No. species in sample	Plant life-form									
	S	E	MM	M	N	Ch	H	G	HH	Th
400	1	3	6	17	20	9	27	3	1	13
1000	2	3	8	18	15	9	26	4	2	13

He describes the problem of selecting 1000 species from the catalog of vascular plants called the *Index Kewensis*, which, at that time, recognized some 140 000 plant species (although the accepted figure today approaches 300 000, Groombridge 1992). To get around the problem that these species are organized by genus:

> I therefore took groups of species with certain intervals between them and between the species of each group. I chose ten groups, each of one hundred species, the ten groups being so distributed in the *Index Kewensis* that the first began on p. 150, the second on p. 400, the third on p. 650, &c., that is at intervals of 250 pages, and I chose in each of the hundred columns beginning at the above designated starting-points the last cited species .... It is very possible that another method of selection would have been better .... In the year 1908 I determined the life-forms of the first 400 species, and in the same year published the normal spectrum calculated from them .... In the autumn of 1916 I determined the life-forms of the remaining 600 ...'
>
> (Raunkiaer 1918, p. 430)

He compares his normal spectrum based on a sample size of 400 with that of 1000, reproduced here in Table B10.1. Next, he sorts the 1000 species used to define the normal spectrum into four groups (Gymnosperms, Monocotyledons, Choripetalae and Gamopetalae) and calculates the percentage found in each group. Using another compendium, Engler and Prantl's *Natürlichen Pflanzenfamilien* (as well as other sources), he then determines the total number of species known at the time (139 953) and the percentage of these species found in each of the four groups. Finally, he compares the calculated percentages based on his sample of 1000 to the actual percentages determined using the entire flora and finds that "The correspondence between the actual and calculated numbers in the two series of percentages must be considered very good" (p. 433). The Choripetalae showed the greatest difference. "... the difference between the calculated and actual percentage (49.8–46.4) amounts to 3.4, and is thus greater than twice but smaller than three times the mean error [±1.6], quite a satisfactory approximation" (p. 433).

that would support or refute the idea of discrete communities? How does one assign probabilities to the outcomes? Since Pielou's work is so often either overlooked or misunderstood, let us trace the history of the gradient approach to testing for the existence of discrete plant communities.

10.6 │ Empirical studies of pattern along gradients

The observation of plants along gradients usually reveals distinctive "zones" where different species apparently dominate sections of the gradient. This is called zonation. There are three major uses for quantitative studies of zonation.

1. Although there are many pictures of zonation (recall Section 10.2) and a vast literature describing zonation, there is no way to summarize or compare such descriptive studies except with measurable properties.
2. There are many theories of resource and habitat use (e.g., Miller 1967, MacArthur 1972, Pianka 1981, Weiher and Keddy 1995b) that may be evaluated using zoned plant communities.
3. The question about whether discrete communities occur has raged on for decades, and there is no way to slay this dragon and end the debate conclusively except to actually measure the degree to which plant distributions exhibit individualistic or community patterns.

It is this third use that we will explore here. Since statistical analysis of zoned communities is likely less familiar, and has fewer monographs to consult than ordination, I will give rather more detail in this section.

From the perspective of distributions along gradients, the "community unit" concept proposes that when species distributions are plotted along some gradient or gradient-complex whose rate of change is constant, there exist groups of species, i.e., "communities," which occur in sequence along the chosen gradient (Whittaker 1975). Within each grouping most species have similar distributions and the end of one group coincides with the beginning of another. The "individualistic" concept, in contrast, proposes that "centres and boundaries of species distributions are scattered along the environmental gradient" (Whittaker 1975) and no distinct groups of species are predicted to exist. These alternatives are illustrated in the top part of Figure 10.17.

Following Pielou (1975, 1977), explicit hypotheses regarding these two concepts can be formulated using upper and lower boundaries of species along gradients (Figure 10.17, bottom). The **community unit hypothesis** states that:

1. There should be significantly more boundaries (both upper and lower) in some intervals of the gradient than in others, i.e., boundaries are clustered.
2. The number of upper and lower boundaries per interval should increase and decrease together along the gradient.

Figure 10.17 The individualistic and community unit hypotheses (a) recast into a testable form (b) (after Shipley and Keddy 1987).

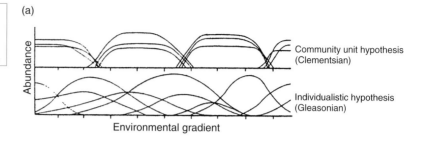

Figure 10.18 Species may be distributed along gradients in a manner that is overdispersed (left) like shingles on a roof, random (middle), or underdispersed (right) like pages of a book. Underdispersed boundaries are usually called clustered boundaries. Statistical tests can distinguish among these possibilities (from Keddy 2001).

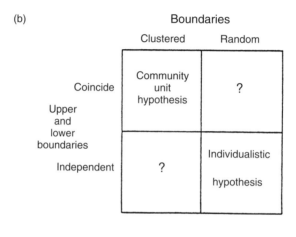

The **individualistic hypothesis** states that:

1. The average number of boundaries (both upper and lower) in each interval of the gradient should be equal except for random variation about the mean.
2. The number of upper boundaries per interval of the gradient should be independent of the number of lower boundaries.

At one extreme (Figure 10.18 left), distributional limits of species may be overdispersed, like the shingles on a roof; at the other extreme (Figure 10.18 right) they are clustered (Pielou 1975, Underwood 1978, Weiher and Keddy 1995b). The middle case is a random distribution.

Now to some examples. The first comes from salt marshes. Pielou and Routledge (1976) collected data on species distributional limits in five sets of salt marshes at different latitudes in eastern North America. They found in many transects that species boundaries were

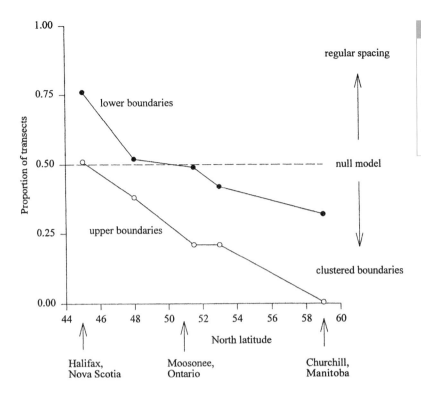

Figure 10.19 The clustering of species boundaries in relation to latitude for salt marshes. The higher the latitude, the lower the proportion of transects with clustered boundaries. Note: the lower the proportion, the greater the degree of boundary clustering (after Pielou and Routledge 1976).

significantly clustered – there were zones of species with similar distributional limits. Salt marsh zonation therefore looks similar to the right side of Figure 10.18. Moreover, the upper limits clustered more than the lower limits, irrespective of latitude (Figure 10.19). The study clearly showed that with proper sampling methods and appropriate null models, it was possible to find measurable patterns in zoned vegetation.

The causes of such patterns cannot be deduced solely from statistical analyses of pattern. Nonetheless, Pielou and Routledge did find evidence that biological interactions were responsible for some of these patterns. Their logic was as follows. If zonation was solely the result of physiological responses to salinity and inundation, then species' upper and lower distributional limits would be independent. If, however, one species set the limits of another through competition, then there would be a tendency for the upper limits of one species to coincide with the lower limits of the other. Using a set of 40 transects near Halifax, Nova Scotia, they found that distributional limits of species tended to coincide ($p < 0.001$). Therefore, they concluded that competition could produce some of the observed patterns in salt marshes. Regrettably, the test was too crude to compare the intensity of competition among latitudes.

The next example comes from a lakeshore – data on zonation from a small, sandy lake near the Great Lakes. Axe Lake has an array of zonation patterns, from those associated with open sand beaches,

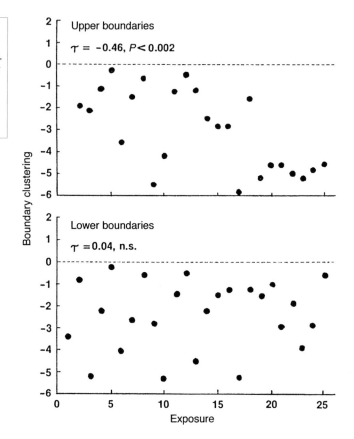

Figure 10.20 The clustering of species boundaries in relation to exposure to waves for a small lake. The more negative the measure of clustering, the more clustered are the boundaries. The dashed line presents the null model (from Keddy 1983).

to those of fertile bays, to floating bogs (Keddy 1981b, 1983). The flora of this lake and its array of vegetation types appear in many ways typical of the northern temperate zone. The following patterns were found:

1. Both the upper and lower boundaries of species were clustered. Just as Pielou and Routledge (1976) showed, there were certain elevations where more species reached their limits than would be expected by chance alone. This is shown in Figure 10.20 where the measures of boundary of clustering for all 25 transects fall below zero.

2. The degree to which species distributions were clustered (the intensity of the zonation on a shoreline) increased with exposure to waves. This occurred because exposure to waves increased the clustering of upper boundaries (Figure 10.20, top); lower boundaries were unaffected (Figure 10.20, bottom).

3. The locations of boundary clusters were pushed up the shoreline as exposure to waves increased. This can be seen in the field distributions of species, where aquatics such as *Lobelia dortmanna* moved up the shoreline (Figure 10.21). It showed up in the joint distribution of species as a landward shift in the distributional limits of all species (Figure 10.22).

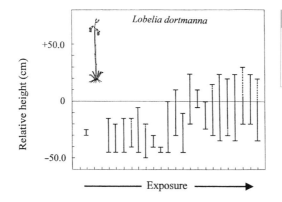

Figure 10.21 The relative height occupied by a shoreline plant as a function of exposure to waves; zero marks the August water line (after Keddy 1983).

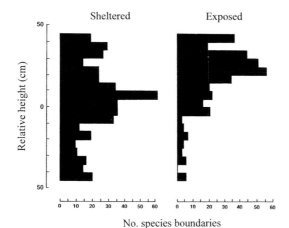

Figure 10.22 The relative height of species distributional limits (upper and lower boundaries combined) for shoreline plants in 10 transects sheltered from waves (left) and 10 transects exposed to waves (right) (from Keddy 1983).

Our third zonation investigation was carried out in a freshwater riparian marsh. It explored all four possibilities for patterns along a gradient that are shown in Figure 10.17 (bottom) and were pointed out by Whittaker (1975). Shipley and Keddy (1987) collected data on species boundaries from 13 transects in the marsh. As with the example from Axe Lake, the distribution of species boundaries was tabulated for 5-cm increments of elevation. Along this gradient the-dominant species changed from *Carex crinita* to *Acorus calamus* to *Typha angustifolia* with increasing water depth. These data were analyzed using analysis of deviance, which is analogous to analysis of variance, but does not assume normality in the error structure of the model. They found that both upper and lower boundaries were clustered (Figure 10.23). This was clearly contrary to the individualistic concept. But they also found that the pattern of clustering was different between upper and lower boundaries – a result inconsistent with the community unit concept. They therefore concluded that rather than a simple dichotomy between two models, there was a need to erect multiple models for species relationships that occur in nature. In

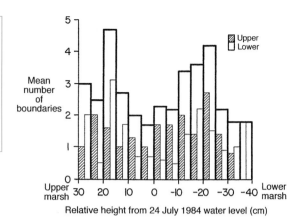

Zonation in a riparian marsh. The mean number of species boundaries in each 5-cm height interval is plotted against relative height. Within each rectangle the mean number of upper boundaries (hatched) and lower boundaries (clear) are shown (from Shipley and Keddy 1987).

other words, more than 50 years of debate about patterns had dragged on (Box 10.2), in part because the patterns were not expressed in clear testable form. This example illustrates the power of zonation pattern analysis as a research tool in ecology.

The study described above had two significant weaknesses. First, it tested a broad general model with data from a single wetland. Second, it used only data on the distributional limits of species. In our final example of zonation studies, Hoagland and Collins (1997) tried to rectify these deficiencies. First, they collected data from 42 wetland sites. Second, they measured three attributes of zonation patterns: (1) boundaries of species distributions, (2) modes of species response curves, and (3) nested structure. The use of three properties not only provides a more powerful way to test among competing models, but it also allows the creation of new kinds of distribution models. Hoagland and Collins examined their results in light of the following four contrasting models of zoned vegetation:

1. The highly deterministic community unit model of Clements (1936) could be interpreted to imply that plant communities are comprised of distinguishable associations of species with little overlap in species distributions among associations. This model can be portrayed as a series of species response curves in which the starting and ending points of species distributions are clustered (Figure 10.24(a)).
2. Other interpretations of this community unit model are possible. Clements (1936) described the occurrence of "predominants," species that were dominant and spanned one or more associations. Figure 10.24(b) shows a model in which boundaries and modes of response curves are clustered yet some species response curves are nested within the curves of other, more dominant, species.
3. The individualistic distribution of species (Gleason 1926) and the continuum concept of vegetation (Whittaker 1967) are represented

---

Box 10.2 | A possible synthesis: Gleason, Clements and a community structure continuum

It is likely that Clements and Gleason now suffer from misrepresentation, their names now providing convenient labels for two possible situations that need names (Figure B10.2). At one extreme (Figure B10.2, left) lie situations where species have almost no interactions with other species, or at least no more than expected by chance; such random aggregations of species probably should not be called a community at all. At the opposite extreme (Figure B10.2, right) lie groups of species with tightly integrated relationships, a situation that would deserve the term community. Neither end of the continuum is likely to be found in nature. The terms Gleasonian and Clementsian really just refer to different locations along this organizational continuum. There may be historical reasons for holding on to the terms Gleasonian and Clementsian as opposing regions of the continuum. You should know that other scholars (Nicolson and McIntosh 2002) believe that my view continually misrepresents Gleason as being too far to the left in Figure B10.2. But perhaps, like many terms in ecology, they erect a "false dichotomy" (*sensu* Keddy 2001) that encourages meaningless argumentation.

The position of a community along the structure continuum might be assessed using two different kinds of data – descriptive or experimental. In the first case, the matrices can represent measures of interspecific association using standard association measures such as χ^2. Alternatively, a thorough set of experiments such as we saw in Chapters 5 and 8 would measure the amount of competition or mutualism between each pair of species. Data on pattern are far more available, and easier to collect than data on species interactions, but in the long run, it is likely to be the latter that will be needed to arrange communities along this continuum.

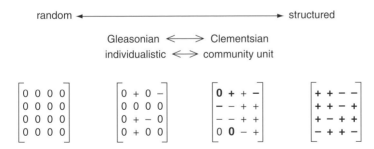

Figure B10.2 The strenghts and types of association between species in a community can be shown in a matrix. Some may lack any interactions (left) and might not even be called a community. Others may have intense positive and negative interactions and be considered a tightly-structured community (right). In this context, Gleasonian and Clementsian views merely represent different regions of this continuum, though neither occupies the extreme.

---

in Figure 10.24(c) as a series of broadly overlapping species response curves with randomly distributed starting and stopping boundaries, and modes, along an environmental gradient.

4. Dominant species may be regularly spaced and encompass several curves of subordinate species; the hierarchical continuum model predicts that modes and boundaries of species response curves are random, but because distributions are hierarchical, it predicts that species distributions are nested (Figure 10.24(d)).

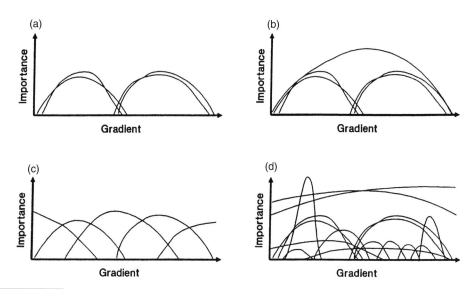

Figure 10.24 Four possible patterns of species growing along gradients. The top two (a, b) represent the community model; whereas the lower two (c, d) represent the continuum model. The right hand pair (b, d) possess the additional feature of being nested (from Hoagland and Collins 1997).

Three test statistics were used to discriminate among these models in the 42 wetland sites. The three test statistics were as follows:

1. Morisita's index (Hurlbert 1990) was used to determine whether or not species boundaries were clustered:

$$I = Q \sum_{i=1}^{Q} \left(\frac{n_i}{N}\right) \left(\frac{n_i-1}{N-1}\right),$$

where Q is the number of quadrats, n_i is the number of starting and stopping boundaries in the ith quadrat, and N is the total number of boundaries.

2. The degree of aggregation (P) of species modes was determined using the sample variance of distance between modes (Poole and Rathcke 1979):

$$P = \frac{1}{k+1} \bullet \sum_{i=0}^{k} \{y_{i+1} - y_i - [1/(k+1)]\}^2$$

where k is the number of species, $y_{i+1} - y_i$ is the distance between modes, and $1/(k+1)$ is the mean of $y_{i+1} - y_i$. If $P = 1$, modes are randomly distributed; if $P < 1$, modes are regularly distributed; and if $P > 1$, modes are aggregated.

3. Nestedness was determined by using the index of Wright and Reeves (1992):

$$N_c = \sum_{i=1}^{K-1} \sum_{m=i+1}^{K} \sum_{j=1}^{S} X_{ij} X_{mj},$$

where S is the total number of species, K is the number of quadrats, and species richness of quadrat $i >$ quadrat m. $X_{ij} = 1$ if species j is present in quadrat i and 0 if it is absent (same for X_{mj}, quadrat m,

Table 10.3. *Summary of six models of distribution along gradients (based on the distribution of boundaries of species response curves, modes of species response curves, and degree of nestedness of species distributions) and the prevalence of these models in a set of 42 transects from wetlands in Minnesota and Oklahoma (after Hoagland and Collins 1997).*

	Boundaries clustered	Modes clustered	Distributions nested	Examples found
Community-unit	yes	yes	no	0
Nested community-unit	yes	yes	yes	3
Alternative model	yes	no	yes	7
Alternative model	no	yes	yes	16
Continuum	no	no	no	0
Nested continuum	no	no	yes	16

species *j*). This index counts the number of times that the presence of a species in a quadrat correctly predicts its presence in quadrats that are more species-rich. The value of N_c was then used to calculate a relative nestedness index:

$$C = \frac{N_c - E\{N_c\}}{\max\{N_c\} - E\{N_c\}}$$

where $E\{N_c\}$ is the expected value and max $\{N_c\}$ is the value of N_c for a perfectly nested matrix. C ranges from 0 (complete independence) to 1 (perfect nestedness). Cochran's Q was used to test for significance of nested species distributions.

All 42 transects were nested (Table 10.3). This is an important generalization. Hoagland and Collins interpret this as evidence for "hierarchical" community structure. Given the many uses of the word hierarchy, it may be more useful to simply use the descriptive result: nested patterns are the rule in zoned vegetation.

Clustering of boundaries occurred in only 10 out of 42 transects; thus the continuum model is more prevalent in the wetlands they studied than indicated by Pielou and Routledge (1976), Keddy (1983), or Shipley and Keddy (1987). Unfortunately the use of Morisita's index, rather than previously used indices, raises the possibility that the prevalence of the continuum model in Hoagland and Collins (1997) data may be an artifact of the test used. Such problems emphasize the need for methodological consistency.

More than half of the transects did not fit any of the four models described above (Table 10.3). Seven had clustered boundaries but unclustered modes, whereas 16 had clustered modes but unclustered boundaries. This work shows the merit of applying a battery of tests to analyze zonation patterns. The differences among the transects and among published studies suggest that ecologists require several different models to describe zonation patterns in nature; Dale (1999) provides the most recent compendium of approaches.

10.7 | Conclusion

Here, in summary, are the main questions that ordination, and to a lesser extent, classification, can answer:

1. Are there any patterns or trends in the data?
2. Which sets of species tend to co-occur?
3. Which environmental factors tend to be associated with these patterns?

The principal objective of this chapter was not to authorize you to carry out different kinds of gradient analyses, but rather to equip you to understand research papers or consulting reports that include them. The secondary objective was to advise those of you who use such tools to do so wisely. You should think about what these techniques can and cannot do, and use them sparingly. Too often, they are used unnecessarily, perhaps just to create a false sense of sophistication. Perhaps a simple sketch like a block diagram (Figure 10.2) will suffice, or perhaps there is another tool like statistical analysis of patterns along gradients (Section 10.6) that would answer your question more clearly. Your research, and your sampling, should always be driven by one or a few clearly stated questions.

You should know what you plan to do with the results of your work before collecting the data. If you want to explore patterns of continuous variation, you will likely want to use ordination. If you want to assign the sample units to discrete groups, you will likely want to use classification. You may even want to use both – but do not do so simply because of the easy availability of computer software. In other cases, neither may help answer your question. There are also multiple types of data that can be collected (presence/absence? biomass? visual cover?), multiple ways of comparing quadrats (matching coefficient? Jaccard? Euclidean distance?), and multiple techniques to consider (principal component analysis? factor analysis? multidimensional scaling? structural equation modeling?). All of these decisions should be made before you collect data. There is a growing number of books that deal solely with the advantages and disadvantages of different approaches (e.g., Whittaker 1967, 1973b, Orloci 1978, Gauch 1982, Legendre and Legendre 1983, Digby and Kempton 1987, Tabachnick and Fidell 2001, Grace 2006) – the manual that comes with a particular sofward package should never be your sole reading in this field.

It may be useful to remember that the mere application of computing power does not guarantee good science. Nor is it a substitute for being able to identify plants and their habitats. Although it predates computers and multivariate statistics, you might keep in mind an observation by Tansley, one of the founders of plant ecology: "Besides stimulating many good biological minds, ecology had a great attraction for weaker students, because it was so easy to describe particular bits of vegetation in a superficial way, tending to bring the subject into disrepute" (Tansley 1987, p. 6).

While multivariate descriptive techniques are sometimes overused, there remain many cases of complex plant communities where patterns that are now described subjectively might be better summarized and communicated with multivariate tools. Every plant ecologist should, therefore, have an understanding of the value of these techniques and what multivariate analysis can and cannot tell us. When circumstances demand ordination, then one should carefully specify the nature of the sampling, choose the most appropriate technique, seek advice from someone already familiar with the technique, fully describe the patterns, and be explicit about the hypotheses that are generated.

Further reading

Gleason, H. A. 1926. The individualistic concept of the plant association. *Bulletin of the Torrey Botanical Club* **53**: 7–26.

Mueller-Dombois, D. and H. Ellenberg. 1974. *Aims and Methods of Vegetation Ecology*. New York: John Wiley and Sons.

Goldsmith, F. B. and C. M. Harrison. 1976. Description and analysis of vegetation. pp. 85–155. In S. B. Chapman (ed.) *Methods in Plant Ecology*. Oxford: Blackwell Scientific.

Gauch, H. G. Jr. 1982. *Multivariate Analysis in Community Ecology*. Cambridge Studies in Ecology. Cambridge: Cambridge University Press.

Legendre, L. and P. Legendre. 1983. *Numerical Ecology*. Amsterdam: Elsevier.

McIntosh, R. P. 1985. *The Background of Ecology Concept and Theory*. Cambridge Studies in Ecology. Cambridge: Cambridge University Press.

Digby, P. G. N. and R. A. Kempton. 1987. *Multivariate Analysis of Ecological Communities*. London: Chapman and Hall.

Shipley, B. and P. A. Keddy. 1987. The individualistic and community-unit concepts as falsifiable hypotheses. *Vegetatio* **69**: 47–55.

Wiser, S. K., R. K. Peet, and P. S. White. 1996. High-elevation rock outcrop vegetation of the southern Appalachian Mountains. *Journal of Vegetation Science* **7**: 703–722.

Chapter 11

Diversity

Three main patterns: area, habitat variation, latitude. Some evolutionary considerations. Some examples of diversity: Mediterranean climates, carnivorous plants, deciduous forests, endemic species. Four models describing diversity at smaller scales: intermediate biomass, competitive hierarchies, intermediate disturbance/gap dynamics, centrifugal organization. Relative abundance patterns. Evenness and diversity. Laboratory experiments. Field experiments. Conservation.

11.1 Introduction

How many kinds of plants are there altogether? And why do some areas of the world have more plant species than others? In some textbooks and reviews, students new to these questions are referred to articles such as Hutchinson (1959) and May (1988) – both of which conspicuously ignore plants! In his essay entitled "Homage to Santa Rosalia" Hutchinson (1959) wrote "[W]hy are there so many kinds of plants? As a zoologist I do not want to ask that question directly, I want to stick with animals but also get the answer." May (1988) makes one single statement (without a reference) on plant diversity and then moves on to animal diversity! Yet, plants constitute over one-quarter of a million species (Groombridge 1992) and over 99 percent of the Earth's biomass (Whittaker 1975), while the number of species of fungi has been estimated at 1.65 million (Hawksworth 1990).

In this chapter we will explore the factors that allow so many different species of plants to occur and to coexist. The approach emphasizes two questions:

1. What environmental factors are correlated with plant diversity at specified scales?
2. What methods have provided evidence about the nature and causes of these patterns?

11.2 Large areas have more plant species

One of the most fundamental observations in ecology is the increasing number of species encountered with increased time spent searching for them, or with increased area of habitat explored. (Time and

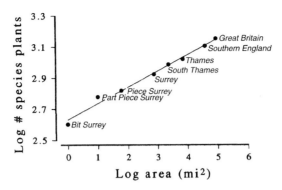

Figure 11.1 A species–area curve for the plants of the Surrey region of Great Britain constructed in 1859 (from Rosenzweig 1995).

area are often related, in that the more time you spend searching, the more ground you are likely to cover.) The relationship between species and area can be quantified as:

$$S = c A^z,$$

where S is the number of species, A is the area and c and z are constants (Rosenzweig 1995). This exponential relationship is conveniently made linear by taking logarithms of both sides

$$\log S = \log c + z \log A,$$

in which case the constant ($\log c$) represents the intercept of the line and the slope is given by z. This relationship was first quantified more than a 100 years earlier using plant species in England (Figure 11.1). The English countryside is a particularly good region in which to study such patterns because so many amateur naturalists there have studied plant distributions, providing a rich and relatively accurate database. Now this linear relationship has been documented for many kinds of plant and animal species and for many natural areas of landscape. These studies have revealed that typical values of z for large, contiguous areas of habitat range from 0.12 to 0.18. For isolated patches such as islands, z tends to be much higher, from 0.25 to 0.35. The mechanisms that produce this pattern likely change with area. At the small scale, say within a square meter, the number of species is likely in part determined by the size of the plants (which will determine the number of individuals that can fit into a quadrat), the amount of competition among species, and the degree to which they partition the habitat. At larger scales, differences among quadrats becomes more important, with areas having many endemics, or areas having more variable environments likely to have higher z values. To explore such issues, Williams (1964) compiled data from no less than 244 sites differing in size and location in one figure, finding, not unexpectedly, that the number of species increased with area, and the relationship was particularly strong at scales above $1 \, \text{km}^2$ (Figure 11.2). More recent work (which, typically, has overlooked Williams's pioneering contribution) suggests that z is low at small scales ($z = 0.1$–0.2 at scales less than $100 \, \text{m}^2$), increases at

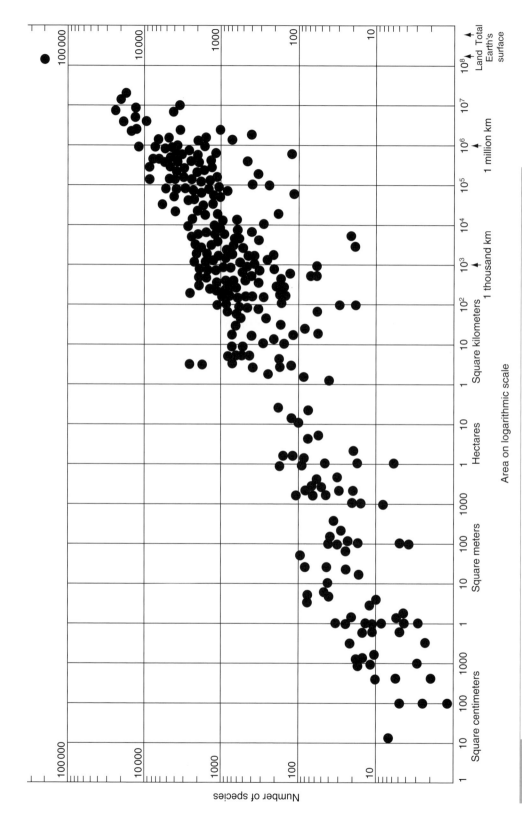

Figure 11.2 The number of species of flowering plants recorded in floras of 244 areas of different sizes throughout the world (after Williams 1964).

intermediate scales ($z = 0.4$–0.5 at scales of 1 ha to 10 km^2), and then falls back to 0.1–0.2 at even larger scales – at least in the east of the English county of Berkshire. The reasons for such changes remain unclear, although some hypotheses are offered in Williams (1964), Rosenzweig (1995), and Crawley and Harral (2001).

One of the great values of the species-area model is its immediate applicability to the conservation of biological diversity. The model says quite explicitly that the greater the area of habitat protected in a reserve system, the greater the number of species that will be included. Moreover, it tells us what this relationship is: for every doubling of area there will be an increase of roughly 20 percent in the number of species. There is some common sense logic to this: some species are naturally rare, have very small geographic ranges, or require very specific kinds of unusual habitat, and so will be encountered only by searching relatively large areas of landscape.

Viewed from the other direction, the species-area model has a depressing reverse logic. As the area of natural landscapes decreases (as forests are logged, prairies are plowed, wetlands are drained, and rangeland is overgrazed), species will disappear with mathematical certainty. Exactly how fast will they disappear? Every time the area of natural habitat is reduced by one-half, the number of species will fall by one-fifth. We will return to rates of extinction in natural habitats in the final chapter, but it is sobering to appreciate just how striking the reduction has already been in many natural ecosystems – the longleaf pine savannas of the southeastern United States have lost more than 95 percent of their original geographical area (Platt 1999). Too many natural vegetation types have already been pushed to the extreme lower left of Figure 11.2. But why do species become extinct in smaller areas? The model does not say. In each case there is a special cause. The last individual might be felled by a logging company, or eaten by a goat, or killed by an exotic insect, or flattened under a new highway, or desiccated when its habitat is drained for development. The number of explanations can be nearly as large as the number of species. But in the broad general sense, the reason for rising rates of extinction is the steady loss in area of natural vegetation in the world. In Chapter 12 we will explore this problem further, and examine some possible courses of action.

11.3 | Areas with more kinds of habitat have more species

In his 1931 treatise, du Rietz observes "The more different habitats there are in a country, the greater will be the number of species; the more uniform the habitats, the smaller will be the number of species. A plain has not as great a chance of attaining wealth in species as a mountain country." (p. 15). That is, the more kinds of habitat there are, the more kinds of plants there tend to be. This is largely because each species of plant has physiological and morphological adaptations that are of benefit in specific sets of environmental conditions, so plants specialize (to varying degrees) on particular habitats – marsh plants are found in marshes, cliff plants are found on cliffs, carnivorous plants are found in infertile soils, and so on. There is an additional reason why habitat and plant diversity tend to be correlated. Some plants have relatively weak abilities to compete with other plants, and so are restricted to those habitats that the stronger competitors cannot occupy. These weaker competitors have been called "fugitive species" (Horn and MacArthur 1972), "interstitial" species (Grubb 1987), or "peripheral" species (Keddy 1990b).

Hence, plants are distributed among different habitats according to their physiological requirements and their relative competitive abilities. Although the species-area pattern provides a good general model, in most cases there is a rather complicated set of factors controlling the occurrence of each species. Unusual microhabitats will often enhance local diversity. A good example comes from my early days as a park naturalist in Algonquin Provincial Park in Ontario. Here, amidst a largely forested landscape with acidic bed rock and soils, there was one isolated location for a small arctic plant called *Saxifraga aizoon* – the north-facing walls of one canyon where calcium-rich water seeped out of the rock. This canyon was once a river produced by melting glaciers at the end of the last ice age. The presence of this plant in Algonquin Park therefore involved multiple factors including dispersal by an ancient river and survival since the last ice age on cold north-facing rock walls that trees could not occupy. No cliffs, no alkaline water seeping from the cliff, no *S. aizoon*. It is this way with many other unusual species, which is what inspires many field botanists in their search for rare plants.

For similar reasons, in any fixed area of landscape, the greater the range in altitude, the more different kinds of vegetation there will be. This is an old idea, and so I illustrate it with an old figure reproduced from Oosting's 1956 textbook, *The Study of Plant Communities*, which shows how vegetation zones change with altitude in the arid mountains of southwestern North America (Figure 11.3). Note the alpine tundra at the highest altitudes. Alpine tundra is found even on mountains near the equator if they are sufficiently high; in East Africa, for example, alpine tundra with giant senecios and lobelias is found above 3700 m, with permanent snow above 4600 m (Richards 1952). Earlier (Figure 10.4) we saw another example of changes in vegetation with altitude in the Great Smoky Mountains, where the highest elevations have heath areas called "balds." While the most obvious factor influencing species distributions is the lower temperature at higher elevations, this is not the only factor. Ridges drain quickly, and tend to be dry, whereas valleys accumulate water and tend to be wet. Soil erodes from the tops of slopes and accumulates in valleys, producing fertility gradients. Slopes that face the south are warm, whereas slopes that face north are cool (hence the diagonal zonation lines in Figure 11.3). Often, too, mountains have exposures

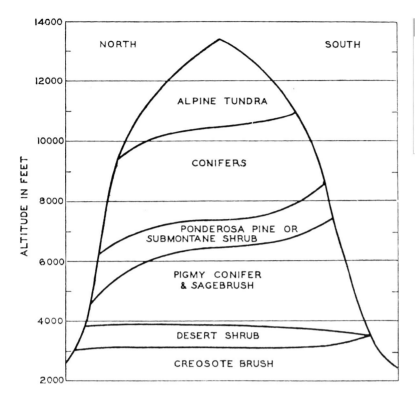

Figure 11.3 Changes in vegetation with altitude on mountainsides in southwestern North America, showing how topographical variation can increase the number of vegetation types (and hence plant species) found in an area (from Oosting 1956, after Woodbury 1947).

of different kinds of rock types that form different soil types (Figure 10.10, also from the Great Smoky Mountains). For all these reasons, the number of kinds of habitats for plants (and hence the number of kinds of plants) increases with topographical variation. This is one reason why mountainous areas such as the Himalayas, the Andes, and the Caucasus tend to be biological hot spots of plant diversity at the global scale (Myers et al. 2000, a topic of focus in Chapter 12).

It might be reasonable to raise an objection now – surely some relatively flat areas, such as the Amazon floodplain, also have a lot of plant species. Does this not contradict the above rule? It might. But we can rescue the idea of habitat variability by arguing that flooding creates many different moisture regimes, and that each moisture regime also has a characteristic set of plant species (Figure 11.4). Perhaps a few centimeters of water in a floodplain is the equivalent of many meters of elevation on a mountainside. Or perhaps the constant disturbance from erosion and deposition creates a mosaic of new habitats, each of which has its characteristic set of species (Figures 6.12, 6.13). Or perhaps the Amazon is not as diverse as it first seems – studies of botanical diversity suggest that the adjoining Andes and the coastal Atlantic Forests have more plant species (Figure 12.13). Or perhaps over such vast areas, even though there are few kinds of different habitats, there has been insufficient time for any one plant species to force another into extinction. While there are many hypotheses, the answer for lowland tropical rain

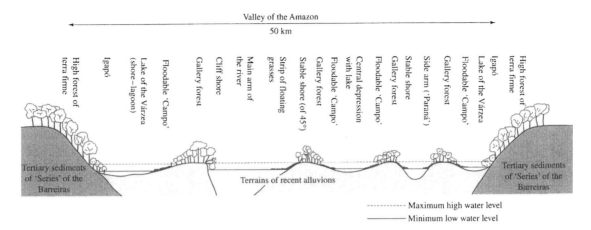

Valley of the Amazon

50 km

High forest of terra firme

Igapó

Lake of the Várzea (shore–lagoon)

Floodable 'Campo'

Gallery forest

Cliff shore

Main arm of the river

Strip of floating grasses

Stable shore (of 45°)

Gallery forest

Floodable 'Campo'

Central depression with lake

Floodable 'Campo'

Gallery forest

Stable shore

Side arm ('Paraná')

Gallery forest

Floodable 'Campo'

Lake of the Várzea

Igapó

High forest of terra firme

Tertiary sediments of 'Series' of the Barreiras

Terrains of recent alluvions

Tertiary sediments of 'Series' of the Barreiras

---------- Maximum high water level

———— Minimum low water level

Figure 11.4 Cross-section through the Amazon valley, illustrating how the physical conditions provide a template that generates different vegetation types (from Keddy 2000, after Sioli 1964).

forest is yet unresolved (Richards 1952, Hubbell and Foster 1986). But even if we do not understand the exact reasons why there are so many kinds of plants in lowland tropical forests, the species-area relationship still works there just as it does everywhere else.

But then the Amazon is not alone – there are other flat areas with large numbers of species. Two of the best known are the heathland plant communities of South Africa (fynbos) and southern Australia (kwongan), where large numbers of similar-looking species co-occur. Rosenzweig (1995) uses the term "species flocks" to designate many apparently redundant species within one functional type.

11.4 | Equatorial areas have more species

Most plant species occur in tropical regions (Table 11.1, Figure 11.5). Three main groups of vascular plants have been tabulated (Groombridge 1992). The Pteridophytes, most of which are native to the moist tropics, include some 12 000 species. The gymnosperms, although locally important in terms of biomass in selected types of conifer forests, total probably 600 species. The angiosperms include some 250 000 species. When Linnaeus first began classifying plants, he started with the northern temperate flora and by 1764 had already listed 1239 genera. Although he had hoped that his classification system would apply to the tropics as well (Mayr 1982), as the great expeditions of global exploration such as those of von Humboldt (Box 2.1) returned with cargoes of pressed specimens, it became clear that the tropics contained an array of species far greater than anyone had anticipated (Edmonds 1997).

There is still no general agreement on the factors responsible for high tropical diversity (Huston 1994, Rosenzweig 1995, Rohde 1997, Gaston 2000, Willig et al. 2003). It seems likely that the two overriding factors for plants are warmth (in particular, absence of freezing conditions) and moisture. One way ecologists have sought to understand causes of diversity is to explore relationships between plant diversity and measured climatic factors. Australia is a

Table 11.1. *Distribution of higher plant species (pteridophytes, gymnosperms, angiosperms) by continent (after Groombridge 1992).*

Area	No. plant species
Latin America (Mexico through South America)	85 000
Tropical and subtropical Africa	40 000–45 000
North Africa	10 000
Tropical Africa	21 000
Southern Africa	21 000
Tropical and subtropical Asia	50 000
India	15 000
Malaysia	30 000
China	30 000
Australia	15 000
North America	17 000
Europe	12 500

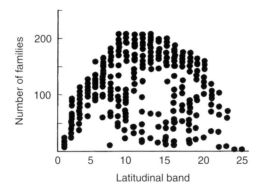

Figure 11.5 The number of families of seed plants plotted for 24 bands of latitude from north (left) to south (right). The equator lies between bands 12 and 13 (from Gaston et al. 1995).

particularly good example, since it contains many different vegetation types, and a rich flora derived from Gondwana. Figure 11.6 illustrates the changes in overstorey species diversity with both latitude (e.g., warm temperate, subtropical, tropical) and moisture availability. Irrespective of latitude, drier environments have fewer overstorey species and all three latitudes converge where the evaporative coefficient falls to 0.03. Moreover, within the subtropical and tropical climate types, the evaporative coefficient is able to account for more than 90 percent of the variation in overstorey species. This coefficient is derived from the equation:

$$MI = E_a/E_o,$$

where MI is the monthly moisture index, E_a is the actual evapotranspiration (cm·month^{-1}) and E_o is the pan evaporation (class A pan; cm·month^{-1}) (Specht and Specht 1993). The greater the MI, the more actual evapotranspiration approaches that measured experimentally:

$$MI = k(P - R - D + S_e),$$

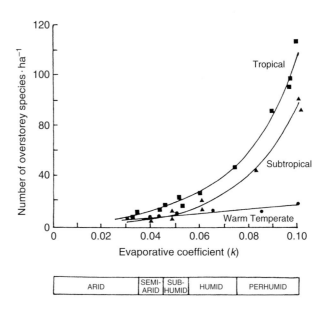

Figure 11.6 The relationship between overstorey (trees and tall shrubs) species richness and moisture availability in tropical, subtropical, and warm temperate plant communities in Australia (from Specht and Specht 1993).

where P is precipitation, R is runoff, D is drainage (all measured in $cm \cdot month^{-1}$), and S_e is extractable soil water (cm at the beginning of the month). Measuring the values of k allows climates to be divided into arid ($k < 0.035$), semi-arid, subhumid, humid and perhumid ($k > 0.075$) (Specht and Specht 1989).

In the tropics and subtropics, the ratio of understorey to overstorey species remains fairly constant with k values above 0.03 (Figure 11.7(a), (b)). In the temperate zone, the proportion of understorey species drops as k increases, although the diversity of cryptogams (non-seed-producing plants including ferns and bryophytes) somewhat compensates (Figure 11.7(c)). The diversity of the understorey is controlled by the structure of the overstorey since it regulates the amount of solar radiation that penetrates the canopy. Thus, the annual production of the overstorey canopy may be an excellent predictor of diversity. Consider the difference in the nature of forest canopies: at one extreme, in tropical monsoon climates, the growing season extends for 10 months and total shoot growth can exceed $11\,000\ kg \cdot ha^{-1}$, whereas at the other extreme, semiarid temperate climates, the growing season may be a few months long and total shoot growth an order of magnitude lower at some $1100\ kg \cdot ha^{-1}$. A complicating factor is the effectiveness of the canopy at intercepting direct sunlight; this actually increases at higher latitudes because the angle of elevation of the Sun's rays declines with increasing latitude, so a given area of canopy can actually intercept direct sunlight over a larger area of understorey. This may help explain the precipitous drop in seed plant diversity in Figure 11.7(c).

In another analysis of Australian forests Austin et al. (1996) used multiple regression models to seek predictors of tree diversity. The order of variables entered in the model was: temperature, plot size,

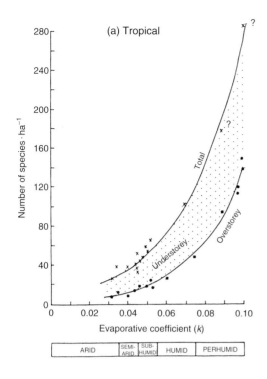

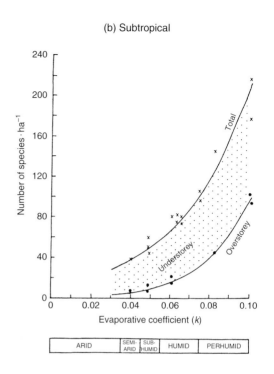

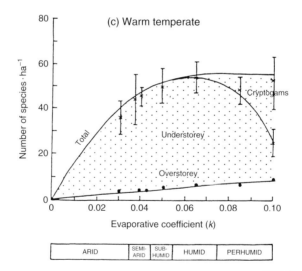

Figure 11.7 Overstorey and understorey species richness versus evaporative coefficient for plant communities in three regions of Australia (from Specht and Specht 1993).

topography, rainfall, radiation, seasonality of rainfall, and a soil nutrient index based upon the phosphorus content of the bedrock. Figure 11.8 shows how the total tree diversity can be represented in a phase space whose outer limits are set by sampled rainfall and temperature combinations. Austin et al. showed that temperature (vertical axis) seems to be more important than rainfall (horizontal axis) in controlling species diversity.

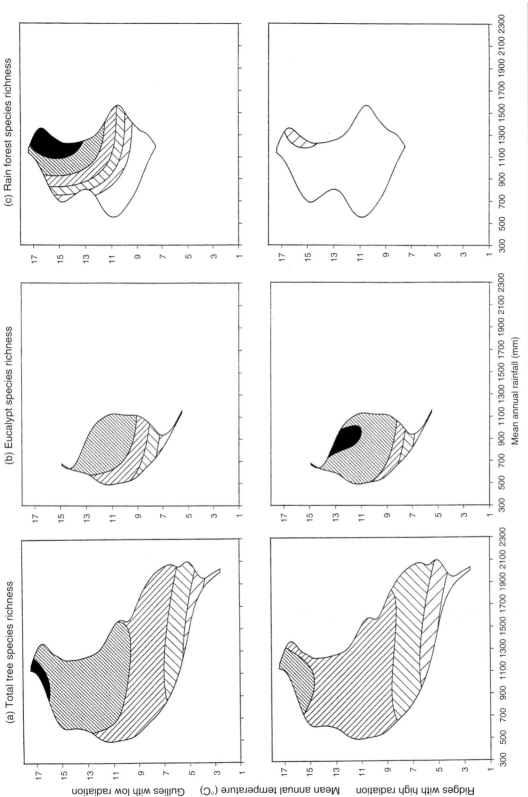

Figure 11.8 Tree species richness in southwestern New South Wales, Australia. (a) total number of tree species per 0.1 ha in the temperature and rainfall space, and in two topographic positions. Both plots are displayed for granites with intermediate nutrient levels. The region outside the envelope represents unsampled rainfall and temperature combinations. (b) Contour plots of eucalypt species richness model on intermediate nutrient level with aseasonal rainfall for gullies and ridges. (c) contour plots of rain forest species richness on intermediate nutrient level, soft sediments for gullies and ridges. Rain forest species occur only in areas with summer rainfall, so only this section of the environmental space is shown. Shading as in (a) (from Austin et al. 1996).

(●) above 8.0; (▨) 4.0–8.0; (▧) 2.0–4.0; (▨) 1.0–2.0; (▨) 0.5–1.0; (▨) below 0.5. (b) Contour plots of eucalypt species richness model on intermediate nutrient level with aseasonal rainfall for gullies and ridges. (■) above 3.0; (▨) 2.0–3.0; (▨) 1.5–2.0; (▨) 1.0–1.5; (▨) 0.5–1.0; (▢) below 0.5. (c) contour plots of rain forest species richness on

(a) Total tree species richness

(b) Eucalypt species richness

(c) Rain forest species richness

Mean annual rainfall (mm)

Mean annual temperature (°C)

Gullies with low radiation

Ridges with high radiation

Eucalypts showed different responses than rain forest species, reaching greatest abundance on ridges. The pattern from southern Africa (Hoffman et al. 1994), where plant richness is negatively correlated with potential evapotranspiration, is apparently the opposite, leading to the suggestion that the complete picture is a unimodal pattern similar, as we shall see below, to that observed at much smaller scales (Section 11.7).

Rather than focussing on immediate effects of climate, we will explore an alternative set of hypotheses to explain high species richness in equatorial areas that emphasizes evolutionary time. Actually, we should probably not call them alternative hypotheses. This would be somewhat circular reasoning: if warm and moist conditions predict woody plant diversity today, it is precisely because such requirements evolved in past environments. The paleobotanist Axelrod (1970) observed that far back in the fossil record woody species were restricted to "equable conditions," by which he apparently meant absence of freezing conditions or severe drought. Latham and Ricklefs (1993a,b) postulate that the current distribution of diversity still betrays the Cretaceous origins of this flora in warm regions, and that there has been insufficient time to produce woody forms adapted to colder climates. It may also be that woody forms of plants are simply unable to cope with the cold conditions (freezing tolerance) at higher latitudes. Expounding on this theory, Latham and Ricklefs (1993a) suggest that:

> [I]f colonization of temperate habitats occurred from the wet tropics or seasonally moist subtropics, we might expect diversity in temperate biomes to be highest in those habitats with warmer and more moist conditions.
>
> (p. 310)

Following a similar logic, Raunkiaer developed his life-form classification for terrestrial plants based upon the position of their meristems during the unfavorable season (see summaries in Shimwell 1971, Kershaw and Looney 1985). He found that, at high latitudes, over-wintering meristems were produced low to the ground where they could be sheltered from freezing conditions by snow, leaf litter, or even soil (Table 2.4). His general conclusions were that phanerophytes (species with exposed meristems) were restricted to warmer areas, whereas geophytes and cryptophytes (Figure 2.8) were better suited to colder areas. The observed diversity gradient in trees could therefore also be explained simply as an obvious transition in life-form to cryptophytes and geophytes at high latitudes.

In summary, we can begin exploring diversity guided by three provisional rules:

1. The larger the area, the greater the number of species.
2. The larger the variation in environmental conditions, the greater the number of species.
3. The closer to the equator, the greater the number of species.

11.5 | Some evolutionary context

11.5.1 Four key events

At the largest scales of space and time, four evolutionary events provide the essential context for examining species diversity. Given the temptation to think only about contemporary patterns, let us re-emphasize these ancient events.

1. Adaptation to the land. Recall from Chapter 1 that about 400 million years ago, early land plants evolved and entered new habitats in which adaptive radiation could occur (Scagel et al. 1969, Stewart and Rothwell 1993, Kenrick and Crane 1997). *Rhynia* and *Asteroxylon* (Figure 1.11) are two well-known examples.

2. Life cycles adapted to drought. About 350 million years ago, the gymnosperms solved the problem of reproducing in dry environments (Section 9.2); seeds are found independently in a number of different orders including three extinct ones (Pteridospermales (seed ferns), Bennettitales, and Cordaitales), as well as the extant orders Gnetales, Ginkgoales, Cycadales, and Coniferales. Only the latter order is a common member of today's terrestrial communities, with the conifers having 8 families, some 50 genera and hundreds of species. Gymnosperms range from the largest of all trees, *Sequoiadendron giganteum* of California, to the bizarre *Welwitschia mirabilis*, which consists of only two spreading leaves and a bowl-like stem supporting strobili, and is found in a small area of the southwestern deserts of Africa.

3. Land mass separation by the Tethys Sea. During the Triassic and Jurassic, Gondwana separated from Laurasia as the Tethys Sea opened (ca. 250 million years BP, Figure 9.6). This event still appears to control the distribution of many plant species, since the flora of the Southern Hemisphere, largely derived from Gondwana, is still much more diverse than that of Laurasia.

4. Angiosperm appearance. Just over 100 million years ago in the early Cretaceous, the angiosperms proliferated. These plants produced flowers, protected the ovules within a bract called the megasporophyll (popularly known as the pistil), and had double fertilization. With the addition of the angiosperms, the total number of plant species doubled by the end of the Tertiary, and all other plant groups declined (Figure 9.2). The angiosperms now dominate all terrestrial plant communities, except at the high latitudes and altitudes where conifers are still abundant (Archibold 1995). A high rate of increase in the angiosperms may have been triggered by the same catastrophic event that caused the extinction of the dinosaurs and ended the Mesozoic about 65 million years ago: a collision with a meteor (Section 6.4.3). This produced an impact equivalent to 100 million megatons of high explosive. Owing to the angle of arrival, North America was particularly affected, with the heat generated from atmospheric friction likely exceeding 1000 times that of the Sun (Flannery 2001).

11.5.2 Some characteristics of angiosperms

One important feature of the angiosperms was a shorter life cycle achieved through the reduction of the gametophyte stage to little more than a few cells borne on the sporophyte (Box 9.1). This drastic reduction in the complexity of the life cycle and a relatively short generation time hastened natural selection and evolution. In addition, some angiosperms initiated a second feature of their life cycle – using insects to efficiently carry pollen from one plant to another (Percival 1965). The gymnosperms are dependent upon wind pollination and have vast numbers of microstrobili to dispense clouds of pollen into the atmosphere; the pollen is passively spread to any nearby receptive megastrobilus. The use of insects is a much more precise distribution mechanism. While it is widely understood that this greatly reduced the amount of pollen produced, a second consequence seems to have been generally overlooked (but see Regal 1977). Clouds of wind-dispersed pollen place a severe restriction upon the number of coexisting species (and possibly also upon rates of speciation), since neighbors can flood each other with pollen grains, reducing the possibilities of reproductive isolation.

Flowers, in contrast, allow for a nearly endless diversification of reproductively isolated species, even if they are within close proximity. Instead of neighbors being flooded with pollen, each can remain reproductively isolated behind barriers set up by flower design and type of insect pollinator (see Ehrlich and Raven 1964, Percival 1965, Crepet and Friis 1987, Futuyma and Slatkin 1993 for further discussions on co-evolution). This was the key step in rapid evolution and survival of angiosperm diversity. It may be noteworthy that existing stands of conifers still consist of only a few species represented by large numbers of individuals of each kind. In contrast, in the tropics, where one finds a vast array of complex flower types and complex methods of cross-pollination, individuals of the same species can be widely separated from one another. This feature of the angiosperms is beautifully expressed in Perry's (1986) book on tropical forest canopies:

> Some tropical trees produce massive amounts of flowers in an opulent display of color and aroma that can be seen for miles around. Since individuals of the same species may be separated by hundreds of yards or even miles, it is thought that these flowers act as "billboards" to help pollinators locate familiar sources of pollen and nectar within the confusing array of hundreds of tree species that make up a jungle community.
>
> (p. 59)

In other words, the evolution of insect pollination allowed for the partitioning of biomass into many more reproductively isolated units, and this simply could not have happened to the same degree in the gymnosperms given their reproductive system.

Secondary metabolites that protect foliage from herbivores may also have made an important contribution to the dominance of angiosperms. The development of new secondary metabolites such as indole alkaloids and iridoids, steroids, sesquiterpenes, and polyacetylene may be of particular significance, since these are found in recently evolved and rapidly evolving plant groups (Figure 7.8).

11.5.3 Physiological constraints on diversity are likely additive

The number of species in an area is sometimes called the **species pool** to emphasize that it provides the pool of raw materials from which ecological communities are assembled (Keddy 1992, Eriksson 1993, Pärtel et al. 1996, Weiher and Keddy 1999, Grace 1999, 2001). Table 11.2 shows some examples. There is currently no general theory of how particular environmental factors determine the size of the species pool for a region (Grace and Pugesek 1997, Grace 2001), although it seems likely that each physiological constraint acts as a barrier (or filter, Keddy 1992) to a certain subset of the flora. Recall the many physiological stresses that restrict the growth of plants that we explored in Chapters 3 and 4. A barrier to greater diversity exists either because of the lack of an evolutionary solution to a particular stress, or, more likely, because any solution produced by evolution has metabolic costs, and the greater such costs, the higher the probability of extinction. A quantitative example is provided by van der Werf et al. (1988), who measured the respiratory costs of ion uptake in a species of sedge, finding that the proportion of ATP demand for ion uptake alone ranged from 10 to 36 percent!

Table 11.2. *Species pool values from a range of regions around the world (from Bond 1997).*

Region	Area $(10^3 km^2)$	No. Species	Species density $([10^3 km^2]^{-1})$
Mediterranean climate regions			
Cape Floristic Region	90	8 578	95.3
Cape Peninsula	0.47	2 256	13.7
California Floristic Province	324	4 452	13.7
SW Australia	320	3 600	11.25
Greece	130	6 000	30.8
Temperate regions			
British Isles	308	1 443	4.7
Eastern North America	3 238	4 425	13.7
Europe (Flora Europea)	10 000	10 500	1.05
Tropical rain forests			
Panama	80	c. 8 300	103.75
Malaysian Peninsula	130	c. 8 000	61.5
Ivory Coast	320	c. 4 700	14.7

We might therefore learn about large-scale climate effects on plants by studying the effects of other strong gradients. Consider salinity as another kind of extreme condition that challenges the tolerance limits of plant species (e.g., Chapman 1940, Sculthorpe 1967, Tomlinson 1986, Adam 1990). Some plants have adapted to these extreme challenges, but there are added metabolic costs just as there are for ion uptake in the example above. In flooded and saline environments these added costs would include the need to cope with anaerobic soil environments. This requires either inefficient energy extraction by fermentation instead of respiration, or specialized structures for transporting oxygen to the roots. Salinity further raises the cost of maintaining osmotic balance; there must be either mechanisms to exclude the uptake of unnecessary sodium and chloride ions, or special organs to excrete them. Even herbaceous plants have had difficulty occupying areas with the combination of flooding and salinity. The difficulty woody plants have had meeting this challenge is illustrated by the very low diversity of mangrove swamps (Tomlinson 1986), even in tropical regions where the nearby freshwater floodplains have some of the most diverse woody plant floras on Earth (Grubb 1987, Gentry 1988).

It may well be that the costs of these stresses are additive. Coping with one stress (flooding, under freshwater, tropical conditions) might be fairly easily solved and metabolically affordable. Two factors, flooding and salinity, might be more difficult to solve, and, if solved, prohibitively expensive. Although in warm areas trees can grow in saline water, the resulting mangrove swamps have relatively low diversity. Further north, where cold is an added constraint, woody plants cannot occupy saline habitats at all. Perhaps there is no evolutionary solution to three stresses – flooding, salinity, and cold – combined. More likely, the energetic costs are simply prohibitive.

Competition may also provide a further limitation on the occurrence of species. The presence of neighbors raises the metabolic constraints on plants by increasing the cost of acquiring light and nutrients (Keddy 1989). Hence, the first species to solve an evolutionary problem (such as flooded saline conditions) may obtain great added advantage by being able to occupy a habitat without neighbors – as the proliferation of mangrove species may illustrate. But once one species occupies the habitat, the metabolic costs increase for all later arrivals, since these species have to tolerate the same physical limitations plus the costs of competition with the first species. The pressures of competition combined with those of the metabolic costs of adaptation may well place an upper limit on diversity in habitats with extreme environments. Figure 11.9 illustrates the sort of patterns that might result: habitats with intermediate levels of biomass (and species interactions) appear to have the largest species pools. At the far left, low nutrient supplies may limit the number of species, whereas on the right, the existence of strong competitors for light may reduce the number of species.

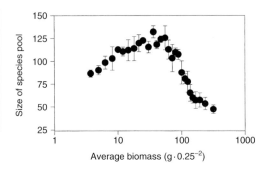

Figure 11.9 The size of species pools plotted against the average biomass of wetland habitats. Each dot represents a mean value calculated from five randomly selected sets of 50 quadrats, with bars showing 95% CIs (from Wisheu and Keddy 1996).

Ultimately, the number of species in any habitat, in any pool, and in any region depends upon rates of speciation and survival of species. Figure 11.10 shows that taxa such as the Apiaceae and Asteraceae are relatively recent and have the most rapid rates of speciation. In contrast, the Theaceae and Nymphaeaceae have existed for a longer period of time and have lower rates of speciation. The Sapindaceae, Annonaceae and Lauraceae have relatively low rates of speciation and short durations. The causes of these differences are largely speculative.

11.6 | Examples of plant species diversity

11.6.1 Mediterranean climate regions

Five areas of the world have a Mediterranean type of climate with warm, dry summers and cool, wet winters (Figure 4.15). In order of decreasing size these are the Mediterranean basin, coastal California, southwestern Australia (kwongan), central Chile, and the cape of South Africa (fynbos). The species pool for each region has been estimated by Cowling et al. (1996) in Table 11.3. Fynbos has one of the largest species pools in the world. Many of the species are sclerophyllous shrubs that appear superficially similar, but Cowling et al. (1996) attribute the high plant diversity to relatively low growth rates and the reshuffling of competitive hierarchies after fires. There are some distinctive features of species pools in these areas. The Southern Hemisphere family Proteaceae is very well represented in both the fynbos and kwongan. These two areas also appear to have converged in a number of other ways: they share high diversity, a high incidence of species with obligate dependence upon fire for re-seeding, serotinous seed storage in the canopy, and seed dispersal by ants (myrmecochory, Section 8.4.2). Other genera have rapidly diversified into this habitat including *Eucalyptus* (>300 species), *Acacia* (>400 species), and *Erica* (> 500 species). Of course fire is an important factor in other environments where species richness is comparatively lower (e.g., boreal forest). The difference in diversity between these areas influenced by fire is latitude, with higher diversity found at lower latitudes. Across all five regions there is a clear relationship between species richness and area (Figure 11.11). The southwestern region of

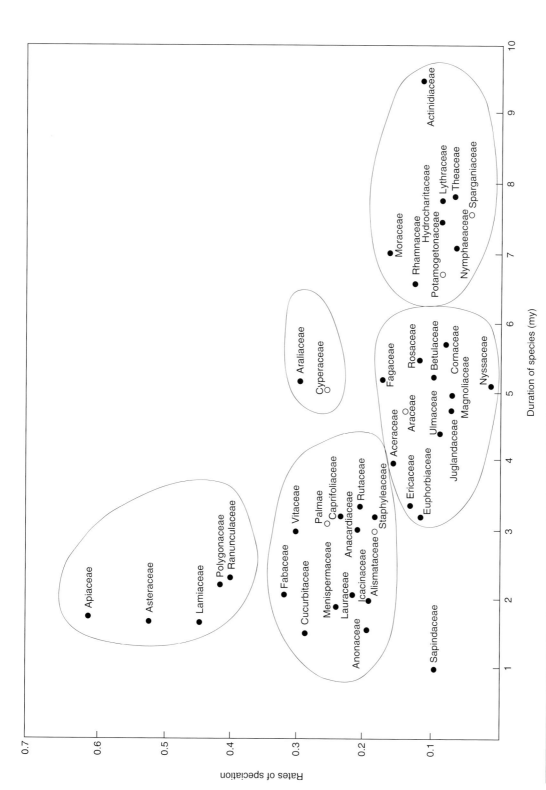

Figure 11.10 Mean species-origination rate versus mean species duration for representative families of angiosperms (● dicotyledonous families, ○ monocotyledonous families). The solid lines are drawn subjectively around groups of families (from Niklas et al. 1985).

Table 11.3. *Plant species diversity of Mediterranean climate regions (from Cowling et al. 1996).*

Region	Area (10^6km^2)	Native flora (no. species)
Coastal California	0.32	4 300
Central Chile	0.14	2 400
Mediterranean Basin	2.30	25 000
Cape	0.09	8 550
SW Australia	0.31	8 000

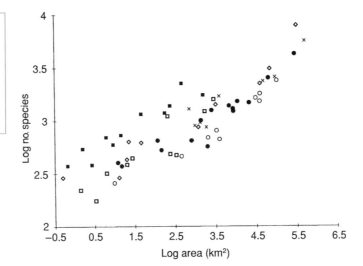

Figure 11.11 Species–area relationships from Mediterranean climate regions. ◇, SW Australia; ■, Cape (SW) (South Africa); □, Cape (SE) (South Africa); ×, Mediterranean Basin; ○, central Chile; ●, coastal California (from Cowling et al. 1996).

the Cape has, on average, 1.7 times the diversity of southwestern Australia, about 2.2 times the diversity of the southeastern Cape, coastal California, and the Mediterranean basin, and 3.3 times the diversity of central Chile.

11.6.2 Carnivorous plants

Extreme environmental conditions provide opportunities for the diversification of species over evolutionary time. In very infertile soils, for example, plants have evolved a wide array of devices for trapping insects in order to compensate for severe shortages of nitrogen and phosphorus. In fact, carnivory evolved in seven different plant families including about 600 species (Table 11.4) (Pietropaolo and Pietropaolo 1986, Givnish 1988), and Givnish estimates that carnivory evolved independently at least six times.

Unless extreme conditions persist through time, the plants that have adaptations to these conditions will be lost from the global pool of species. Carnivorous plants are now threatened by a number of factors that simultaneously reduce the area of infertile and wet habitat. Vast areas of wetland are lost through drainage, infilling, or the construction of dams (Dugan 1993, Dynesius and Nilsson 1994,

Table 11.4. *Summary of diversity in the global pool of carnivorous plants (from Pietropaolo and Pietropaolo 1986).*

Family	Genus	No. species	Geographic distribution	Type of trap
Byblidaceae	*Bybis*	2	Australia	Passive flypaper
Cephalotaceae	*Cephalotus*	1	SW Australia	Passive pitfall
Dioncophyllaceae	*Triphyophyllum*	1	West Africa	Passive flypaper
Droceraceae	*Aldrovanda*	1	Europe, Asia, Africa, Australia	Active
	Dionaea	1	North and South Carolina, USA	Active
	Drosera	120	omnipresent	Passive flypaper
	Drosophyllum	1	Morocco, Portugal, Spain	Passive flypaper
Nepenthaceae	*Nepenthes*	71	area surrounding and including the East Indies	Passive pitfall
Sarraceniaceae	*Darlingtonia*	1	California and Oregon, USA and western Canada	Passive pitfall
	Heliamphora	6	northern South America	Passive pitfall
	Sarracenia	9	North America	Passive pitfall
Lentibulariaceae	*Genlisea*	14	tropical Africa, tropical South America, Madagascar	Passive lobster
	Pinguicula	50	Northern Hemisphere, South America	Passive lobster
	Polypompholyx	2	Australia	Active mousetrap, suction type
	Utricularia	ca. 300	omnipresent	Active mousetrap, suction type

Mitsch and Gosselink 2000). In the remnant areas of wetland, nutrients are accumulating through run-off from agricultural activities, discharge from sewers, and deposition in precipitation (Box 3.2) (Ehrenfeld 1983, Moss 1983, Moore et al. 1989, Keddy 2000). As the area of suitable habitat declines, it is inevitable that the number of species in the habitat will also decline (MacArthur and Wilson 1967, Noss and Cooperrider 1994). Superimposed upon this is the market for these plants among collectors. Perhaps the most threatened carnivorous plant is *Dionaea muscipula*, the venus fly trap (Figure 11.12), which is highly valued by collectors and greenhouse owners because of its active mechanism of trapping insects. The single member of this genus is endemic to the infertile coastal plains of North and South Carolina where it occupies peatlands on sand plains ("Pocosins" Richardson 1981), and is often associated with other more common carnivorous plants such as *Drosera*, *Pinguicula*, and *Utricularia* species (Estill and Cruzan 2001). The combination of habitat loss in the Pocosins and poaching by unscrupulous collectors has threatened the survival of this species in the wild.

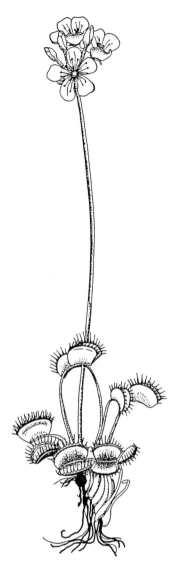

Figure 11.12 Venus fly trap, *Dionaea muscipula*, with inflorescence (from Pietropaolo and Pietropaolo 1986).

11.6.3 Deciduous forests

The southern Appalachians support one of the world's richest deciduous forests, particularly in the region known as "mixed mesophytic forest" (Figure 9.17). There are five species of magnolia, ten species of oak, and seven species of hickory, along with a rich array of other woody plants (Braun 1950, Stupka 1964). The other two principal areas of deciduous forest occur in western Europe and eastern Asia (Archibold 1995). Once these forest areas were contiguous, as illustrated by the fact that the species and genera still have distributions encompassing these three regions, but continental drift and climate change have now isolated them from one another (Braun 1950, Pielou 1979).

The large number of tree species in deciduous forests in North America can be accounted for by a number of factors depending upon the breadth of space and time being considered. History is certainly important (Braun 1950, Latham and Ricklefs 1993a,b). During the ice age, tree species in North America were able to migrate southward along the mountains; in contrast, trees in Europe may have been trapped by the Alps and driven to extinction. Temperate-zone trees such as *Carya*, *Liquidambar*, *Robinia*, and *Tsuga* became extinct in Europe around this time (Daubenmire 1978); as a result, these species, known from past interglacial eras, no longer occur in Europe. The high number of tree species presently found in North American deciduous forests is also probably due to the variation in topography (Figure 10.4) – differences in slope, aspect, altitude, and exposure provide habitat variation.

11.6.4 Diversity, biogeography, and the concept of endemism

A species is **endemic** when it is restricted to a small geographical range. One example is the venus fly trap, mentioned above, which occurs only in a small area of southeastern North America (Estill and Cruzan 2001). Although endemism is a relative term, it is useful since it draws attention to species with relatively small geographic ranges. Areas may have large numbers of endemic species because of either high rates of evolution of new taxa (neoendemics) or high rates of survival of old taxa (paleoendemics). Sites with many endemics often have high diversity and are therefore important target areas for conservation. To study endemism, Cowling and Samways (1995) collected data on endemism in 52 regions from tropical rain forest to polar deserts. As possible causal variables they considered area, latitude, altitudinal range, mean annual rainfall and mean annual temperature. Latitude was the strongest single predictor of the number of endemics, accounting for more than half of the variation. Areas nearer the equator tended to have more endemics (Figure 11.13(a)). Mean annual rainfall was also important, but contributed little to the final multivariate model because log mean annual rainfall is correlated with latitude ($r^2 = 0.58$). The second most important variable in the analysis was therefore area, with larger areas tending to have more endemic species (Figure 11.13(b)). This is not surprising

(a)

(b)

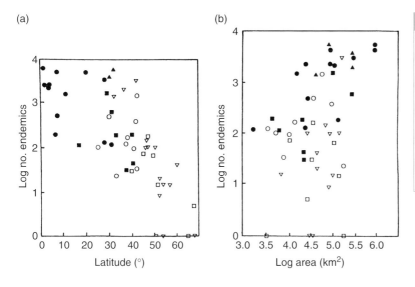

Figure 11.13 Number of endemic species plotted against (a) latitude and (b) area for 52 regions on continental landmasses. ●, tropical and subtropical forest and savanna; ○, temperate forest and woodland; ▲, mediterranean climate shrubland and woodland; ■, warm desert and steppe; □, cold desert and steppe, ▽, boreal forest and tundra (from Cowling and Samways 1995).

given the general relationship between species richness and area (Section 11.2). In addition, larger areas might also provide a wider array of habitats for speciation of neoendemics or refuges for survival of paleoendemics. The best fit model ($r^2 = 0.63$) was:

$$\text{log endemic species} = 1.54 - 0.042 \text{ latitude} + 0.466 \text{ log area}.$$

A regression model such as this one is useful for further investigation. Not only does it show that diversity generally increases in the manner indicated, but also that residuals can be examined to find anomalies. Strong positive deviation from the relationship occurred in seven sites including: four Mediterranean climate regions (southwestern Australia, coastal California, southwestern Cape, central Chile) and two Asian regions (Caucasus, Tien Shan-Alai). The middle-Asian regions are still poorly known, although the Tien Shan-Alai region alone has 3370 endemic plant species (Major 1988). Clearly such areas deserve more attention in conservation planning. Strong negative deviation occurred in seven areas, five of which were polar desert and tundra which had been glaciated during the Pleistocene Epoch. The other two were temperate forests in the Carolinas of southeastern North America and tropical forests in the Ivory Coast of West Africa. Perhaps the explanation for the latter two areas lies in their history: there is no source of tropical forest species adjacent to the Carolinas, and during the Pleistocene rain forest was eliminated from much of West Africa.

11.7 | Models to describe species diversity at smaller scales

We have seen above that area, habitat variation, and latitude can explain much of the large-scale variation in plant diversity. Ecologists

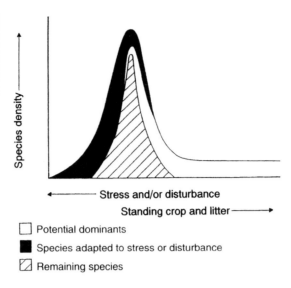

Figure 11.14 A model illustrating the impact of stress and/or disturbance on species richness (density) and species composition (after Grime 1973a,b, 1979).

have also sought models to describe plant diversity at smaller scales, and there is an enormous number of such models (Keddy 2001, 2005b). Some models are entirely theoretical – their task is to explore the consequences of certain assumptions – and while they may be elaborate, they may have little or nothing to do with reality. Pragmatic models, by contrast, are based upon actual patterns in data. We may not yet understand why these patterns occur, but that is the task of future experimenters. Here I introduce four pragmatic models that apparently describe diversity at local scales.

11.7.1 Intermediate biomass

Grime (1973a, 1979) observed that British grasslands with intermediate levels of biomass appeared to have the largest numbers of plant species. He postulated a general unimodal relationship, the "humped-back" model, between plant species richness and above-ground biomass (Figure 11.14). In addition to suggesting the pattern, he suggested two possible mechanisms: stress and disturbance. Species richness is low at low biomass because of high levels of stress or disturbance, and only a few plants can tolerate these extremes. Species richness is low at high biomass because of dominance by a few strong competitors that create closed canopies.

Ecologists have since tested for this pattern elsewhere. A useful model applies to more than one location. Figure 11.15 shows its application to Mediterranean grasslands. In European grasslands (Figure 11.16) phosphorus alone apparently has an enormous influence on diversity, although the maximum richness is strongly skewed to the left.

A useful model also applies to more than one habitat. The intermediate biomass model has been explored in fens (Wheeler and Giller 1982), lakeshores (Wisheu and Keddy 1989a), interior wetlands

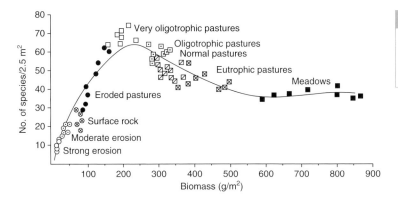

Figure 11.15 The relationship between the number of species and biomass for grasslands in the Mediterranean region of Spain (from Puerto et al. 1990).

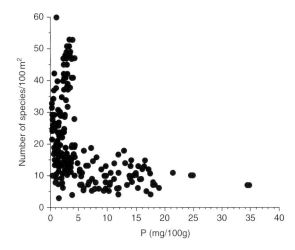

Figure 11.16 Plant species richness in relation to soil phosphorus for a set of European pastures (from Janssens et al. 1998).

(Moore et al. 1989), and coastal wetlands (Gough et al. 1994). For a large sample of interior wetlands, Figure 11.17(a) shows that plant diversity is highest in low biomass sites, although the pattern is strongly skewed to the left, and may be more of an envelope with an upper limit rather than a simple line. If rare species alone are considered (Figure 11.17(b)), the vast majority occur in those sites with very low standing crop (less than 100 g/0.25 m²). For this reason, Moore et al. (1989) argue that infertile sites are of particular significance to the conservation of plant diversity.

This is likely to become a larger issue with time, as nutrient-laden precipitation, run-off and groundwater fertilize these habitats that were once infertile (e.g., Ehrenfeld 1983, Ellenberg 1985a, Newman et al. 1996, Keddy 2000, Matson et al. 2002, Box 3.2). The presumed mechanism is the increase in biomass with fertility, and the resulting rise in competition intensity, which leads to the replacement of smaller and more slow-growing plant species by tall canopy-forming dominants. Eutrophication, then, pushes the plant community from the left to the right of Figures 11.14–11.17. Although there are exceptions to this pattern (e.g., at small scales, Moore and Keddy (1989a), in

Figure 11.17 The relationship between plant species richness and soil fertility (measured as above-ground biomass) for shoreline wetlands based on 401 0.25-m² quadrats from wetlands in Ontario, Quebec, and Nova Scotia, Canada. (a) all species, (b) species considered nationally rare (from Moore et al. 1989).

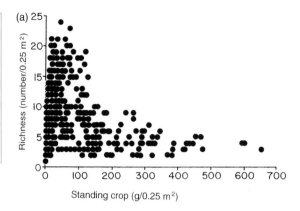

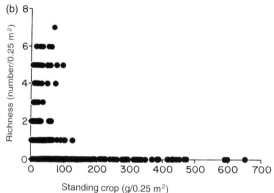

saline marshes, Gough et al. (1994)), overall, the "humped-back" model provides a useful tool for describing vegetation and, perhaps more importantly, for predicting response to management. Grime's management paper (1973b) can be adapted to most herbaceous vegetation types.

11.7.2 Competitive hierarchies

A few species typically dominate any particular habitat. These species also tend to share a few key traits, typically, the ability to preempt light (Keddy and Shipley 1989, Keddy 2001). Most of the remaining species in the community (the majority) must survive amidst a matrix formed by these dominant species. This generalization has emerged from many experiments in which sets of species were grown in all possible pairs to study their relative competitive performance. Consider one example. Wilson and Keddy (1986b) grew seven wetland plants in all possible pairwise combinations (Table 5.2, Section 5.4.1). A review of many such pot experiments documented that this is a recurring pattern – species are apparently organized into hierarchies with dominants and subordinates (Keddy and Shipley 1989, Shipley 1993). Often, the dominants are larger canopy-forming species able to intercept light and shade neighbors (Keddy and Shipley 1989, Keddy 2001). In other experiments, ecologists have removed dominant species from experimental communities, finding that other species respond positively and diversity often increases (e.g., Gurevitch and Unnasch 1989, Brewer 1998, Jutila and Grace 2002).

Given the experimental and statistical evidence that plant communities are organized in strong competitive hierarchies, a new question about diversity arises. Given this strong tendency for dominance by a few strong competitors, how do so many other species manage to survive? This leads rather naturally to intermediate disturbance models.

11.7.3 Intermediate disturbance

In a world with strong competitors, how do so many other plant species manage to survive? One answer seems to be that recurring disturbance creates gaps among these competitors, and many (if not most) other species survive in such gaps. This idea occurred to an entire cohort of ecologists nearly simultaneously in the late 1970s and early 1980s – with a set of papers including Grubb (1977), Connell (1978), Grime (1979), Huston (1979), White (1979), and Pickett (1980), and Sousa (1984). Chapter 6 explored many aspects and examples of disturbance. Disturbance, you will recall, should be defined rather narrowly, as a factor that removes biomass from a community (Grime 1979).

Intermediate disturbance models (Figure 11.18) postulate that diversity is controlled by two contradictory forces: rate of disturbance and rate of recovery from disturbance. Both of these control the rate at which strong competitors exclude weak ones. Think about disturbance from grazing animals. If grazing is very light, a few canopy-forming plants may shade out all neighbors – and diversity will be low. If grazing is very intense, nearly all species will be eaten, leaving only a few very unpalatable species (or even bare soil.) Both extremes have low diversity. But now imagine intermediate amounts of grazing which are sufficient to reduce, but not eliminate, the dominant competitors, and create gaps in which other species can survive. This intermediate level of disturbance will allow more species to coexist, and there will be some specific rate of disturbance that will allow the greatest number of species to coexist. Hence the name – intermediate disturbance. The second axis on the figure is necessary because the rate at which plants grow new biomass will determine how much disturbance will be needed to maximize diversity.

When a disturbance produces relatively small gaps still surrounded by intact vegetation, the term gap-dynamics is often used to describe the disturbance. Many kinds of trees will regenerate only in gaps that are created when one or more mature trees are killed (e.g., Shugart et al. 1981, Denslow 1987, Botkin 1993). Which species colonizes a gap often depends as well upon the size of the gap (Figure 6.41). Even small gaps can enhance recruitment in grasslands (Brewer 1999, Jutila and Grace 2002). Diversity of landscapes can be increased by gaps created by landslides (Guariguata 1990), storms (Seischab and Orwig 1991), volcanic eruptions (del Moral and Wood 1993), and floodplain deposition (Salo et al. 1986).

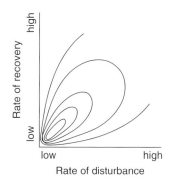

Figure 11.18 The number of plant species in a habitat (and the biomass) is a consequence of a dynamic equilibrium between the rate of disturbance and the rate of recovery from disturbance. The inner ellipsoid has the highest number of plant species (after Huston 1979 in which these axes are designated "frequency of [biomass] reduction" and "rate of [competitive] displacement").

This model has important implications for plant conservation. If the rate of disturbance is altered (say, by changing fire regimes in a landscape), or if the rate of recovery is altered (say, by increasing eutrophication), diversity will change. There is one complication in applying the model to a natural habitat. If we ask the question of whether a disturbance, such as fire or grazing, will increase or decrease diversity, it is obvious from inspection that the answer depends upon where the system is located in two-dimensional space. Grazing can increase diversity if the system is at the upper left of Figure 11.18, or it can decrease diversity if the system is at the lower right. Thus, one often cannot give a simple answer to the question of whether a particular factor will increase or decrease diversity – it depends upon the history and current state of the system. This is called contingency.

The conservation implications of the intermediate disturbance model are illustrated by the next example which introduces a study at one of the largest scales of which I know – fire and plant diversity in boreal forests. (The other large-scale application of this model may be the Amazonian floodplains discussed in Section 6.3.2, Figure 6.13.) Boreal forests are heavily dependent upon fire for regeneration, and landscapes often consist of mosaics of forest dating from fires of different ages (Heinselman 1973, 1981, Rowe and Scotter 1973, Wein and Moore 1977, Archibold 1995). Suffling et al. (1988) set out to test whether an intermediate frequency of forest fires would lead to highest vegetation diversity at the landscape scale in accordance with predictions of intermediate disturbance models. Their study area was a large tract of forest in northwestern Ontario. The forests here are dominated by fire-dependent species such as *Pinus banksiana* and *Picea mariana* in the rock barrens of the west and grade into *Abies balsamea* and *Picea mariana* in the east. Forest fire records showed an increase in fire frequency from east to west, with the exception of a fire-prone area on shore deposits, eskers, and rock barrens along the shoreline of former Lake Agassiz (Figure 11.19). The diversity of forest types (as measured by the Shannon index of diversity) was strongly related to fire history (Figure 11.20). Maximum diversity occurred at intermediate fire frequencies of 0.25 percent of the land burnt each year.

Forest fire control might lead to increased diversity in some fire-prone habitats (at the far right of the figure), but overall it will reduce landscape diversity in areas with intermediate to low disturbance (Suffling et al. 1988). They might have added that, at a larger scale, there is a further diversity issue. If all vegetation types are maintained with the same fire frequency, then similar diversity patterns will be found along the entire transect they studied. Maintaining low, intermediate and high fire frequencies in both the eastern and the western portions of the region will maximize diversity at a still higher scale. Suffling et al. emphasize correctly that fire control will force the entire landscape to the far left side of Figure 11.20, reducing the diversity of vegetation types (and presumably the number of component species). Maximum diversity is attained by having some sites at the maximum

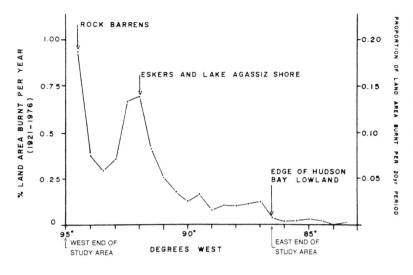

Figure 11.19 Regional variation in forest fire occurrence in the boreal forest of northern Ontario. The climatically induced trend is complicated by relatively dry geomorphological features that increase local forest fire occurrence from 91° to 93° longitude (from Suffling et al. 1988).

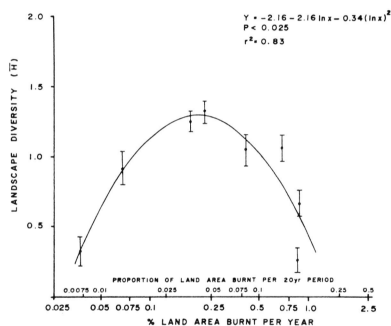

Figure 11.20 The relationship between beta or landscape diversity (*H*) and disturbance by forest fires in eight 250-km² samples (from Suffling et al. 1988).

along with sites representing both extremes. Managing for diversity within a single park, then, is not the same as managing for landscape and vegetation diversity over a park system as a whole.

11.7.4 Centrifugal organization

We know from Section 11.3 that heterogeneous environments support more kinds of plants. One model that can summarize these patterns is called the centrifugal model (Keddy 1990b, Wisheu and Keddy 1992). Consider a landscape that contains multiple biomass gradients, each controlled by a different limiting factor. At one end of each gradient, which we shall call the core habitat, nutrients and

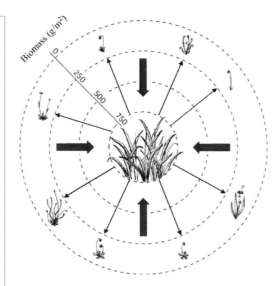

Figure 11.21 In the centrifugal model, biomass gradients (thin arrows) radiate outward from one central high biomass habitat. This "core" habitat is dominated by a few large leafy species that are superior competitors for light. The low biomass end of each axis represents a different kind of extreme habitat with one or more strong environmental constraints, and each is often occupied by stress-tolerant species. Many have rosette growth forms, such as genera including *Armeria, Castilleja, Drosera, Eriocaulon, Hieracium, Isoëtes, Lobelia, Parnassia, Pinguicula, Sabatia,* or *Saxifraga*. Eutrophication increases biomass causing convergence (thick arrows) in species composition upon a few common species.

water are freely available, which allows a closed canopy to develop and here light becomes a limiting resource. Think, for example, of floodplains where the core habitat is dominated by *Phragmites* and *Typha*, or old fields with *Solidago* and *Aster* in the core habitat. At the low biomass end of each gradient, however, quite different factors may limit plant growth – say, drought, flooding, high or low pH, low nitrogen, low phosphorus, or grazing. In order to tolerate such limiting factors, plants require different kinds of adaptations, and thus the low biomass end of each gradient supports a different set of plant species. Consider the different kinds of species found in low biomass habitats such as chalk grassland, sea cliffs, alvars, sandy shorelines, rock outcrops, etc. The resulting pattern can be represented by a set of gradients radiating outward from the core habitat (where light is the main constraint) to peripheral habitats (where a wide array of factors can be limiting) (Figure 11.21). Many unusual genera occur in peripheral habitats, including *Armeria, Asplenium, Castilleja, Coreopsis, Drosera, Eriocaulon, Isoëtes, Lobelia, Lycopodium, Ophioglossum, Parnassia, Pinguicula, Sabatia, Saxifraga* and *Utricularia* (e.g., Fernald 1921, 1922, 1935, Peattie 1922, Soper and Maycock 1963, Goldsmith 1973a,b, Moore et al. 1989, Wisheu and Keddy 1989b).

Several predictions can be made from this model. First, while the intermediate biomass model (Section 11.7.1) focuses upon a corridor of diversity at intermediate levels of biomass, the centrifugal model emphasizes that over multiple gradients, it is the lower biomass habitats that likely support the largest number of plant species. Thus, the larger the number of extreme environments, the higher the total diversity is likely to be. In terms of reserve design and selection, the centrifugal model draws attention to the need to ensure that extreme and/or unusual kinds of environmental conditions are included. It may be the atypical habitats that contribute most to total plant diversity – rock outcrops (Wiser et al. 1996, Shure

1999), alvars (Belcher et al. 1992, Catling and Brownell 1995), wet meadows (Peattie 1922, Hill and Keddy 1992, Sorrie 1994), or cliffs (Soper and Maycock 1963, Goldsmith 1973a).

The centrifugal model also predicts probable responses to eutrophication. As noted earlier (Section 11.7.1), eutrophication is a growing threat to plant diversity, as it allows larger canopy-forming plants to exclude smaller, stress-tolerant plants (Keddy 2000). Eutrophication will force plant communities that are initially different to converge into one light-limited habitat, thereby leading to even larger losses of plant diversity (Figure 11.21, thick arrows) – a growing problem world-wide (e.g., Ehrenfeld 1983, Ellenberg 1985, Newman et al. 1996, Keddy 2000). A specific kind of plant is usually eliminated by eutrophication – creeping or rosette species which depend upon sites with low biomass and high light availability. Examples of such sensitive species can be found in many vegetation types: *Poterium sanguisorba* and *Carex flacca* in chalk grassland (Austin 1968), *Lobelia dortmanna*, *Eriocaulon septangulare*, and *Sabatia kennedyana* in wetlands (Wisheu and Keddy 1989b), *Armeria maritima* on sea cliffs (Goldsmith 1973b), and *Hieracium floribundum* in old fields (Reader and Best 1989).

One of the most intensively studied cases of eutrophication damaging native species comes from the Everglades (Loveless 1959, Davis and Ogden 1994, Newman et al. 1996). These were once a vast rain-fed wetland, with extremely low nutrient levels, producing a unique vegetation type of species adapted to wet, infertile conditions. As the sugar industry began to exploit the northern Everglades, vast amounts of nutrient-rich water poured south, fertilizing these wetlands. The consequence was the invasion of a tall, rapidly growing wetland plant – cattail (*Typha*). Cattails changed not only the plant species, but also the suitability of the wetlands for indigenous wildlife. Plumes of invading cattail now mark where nutrients flow into the Everglades. Although court cases brought by environmental groups have led to some efforts to reduce nutrient input, it remains to be seen whether this process can be halted or reversed (Sklar et al. 2005). Currently, the Florida sugar industry provides a textbook case of eutrophication.

J. S. Beard (1944) described centrifugal patterns in tropical forests. Rain forest, the core community, occurs where conditions are optimal for growth.

> We may begin by envisaging a mesic or optimum habitat where availability of moisture – and thus every condition for plant growth – is as ideally favorable as it can be in the tropics ... the land must be well-drained, the soil deep and permeable, moisture must be available in sufficient quantity throughout the year and the situation sheltered from violent winds. There must be neither inundation nor seasonal drought, evaporation must be moderate and frost unknown. Such conditions naturally favor the tallest, most luxuriant and most complex type of vegetation in the American tropics, the vegetal optimum, rain forest. Rain forest is by no means so common in the tropics as is popularly supposed, for these ideal growth conditions are rare.
>
> (p. 134)

Five vegetation types are produced by different kinds of constraints: the seasonal formation (seasonal lack of rainfall), the dry evergreen formation (constant lack of available moisture), the montane formation (cold and exposed), the swamp formations (flooding), and the marsh or seasonal swamp formations (alternating inundation and desiccation). Each of these five, he notes, is the product of an environmental factor that inhibits the occurrence of rain forest.

> These series are additional to the single optimum formation, rain forest. Each series consists of stages between the optimum and the extremely adverse and thus the head of each series approached closely to the optimum ... the series may be regarded as radiating outwards from the optimum like the spokes of a wheel or, better, three-dimensionally like radii from the centre of a sphere.
>
> (p. 135)

11.8 | Relative abundance – dominance, diversity, and evenness

So far, we have used species richness – the number of species in a quadrat or region – as a measure of diversity. This measure can be a misleading measure of diversity, since often a large proportion of the biomass is locked into the tissues of a few dominant species. The small fraction of biomass not locked up in the dominant species is then partitioned among a much larger number of relatively uncommon species. In a completely even community, each species would have an equal proportion of biomass (it would have an abundance of b/s where b is community biomass and s is the number of species). Such a situation maximizes a property of diversity called **evenness** (Peet 1974, Pielou 1975). The greater the departure from evenness, the greater the biomass concentration within a few species.

The number of species and the evenness of a community are best illustrated with a **ranked abundance list** – the abundance of each species (measured in biomass, number of individuals, cover, or some similar measure) plotted against its order in a sequence from most abundant to least abundant. Figure 11.22 shows an example from vascular plant communities in the Great Smoky Mountains, and Figure 11.23 shows examples from wetlands. These kinds of ranked abundance lists are small-scale examples of a larger scale phenomenon, the canonical or log-normal distribution. The log-normal pattern is found in nearly all large samples: a few species are common (they dominate the sample) while most other species are uncommon (each is represented by only a few individuals). The analysis of the log-normal pattern is beyond the scope of this text, but you should know that there are many studies available to you in other sources such as Preston (1962a,b), Pielou (1975) and May (1981).

Sometimes one wants a single number to measure diversity. This means that one number is used to summarize all the information

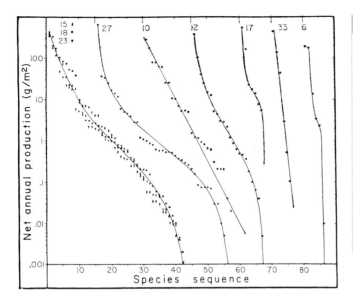

Figure 11.22 Dominance–diversity curves for vascular plant communities in the Great Smoky Mountains. For each curve, points represent species plotted by net annual above-ground production and order in the species sequence from most to least productive. For the sake of clarity, the curves have been arbitrarily spaced out, their origins being separated by 10 or 15 units along the sequence axis. The numbers across the top refer to sample sites and the first curve is based on data for three sites (from Whittaker 1965).

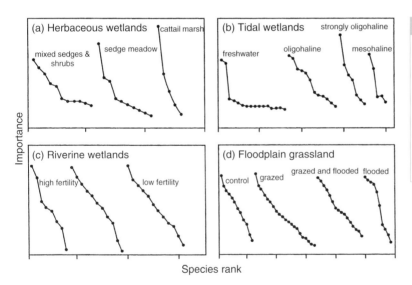

Figure 11.23 Ranked abundance lists (dominance–diversity curves) for four wetland types. (a) herbaceous (after Gosselink and Turner 1978), (b) tidal (after Latham et al. 1994), (c) riparian (after Weiher and Keddy unpublished), (d) floodplain grassland (after Chaneton and Facelli 1991) (from Keddy 2000, courtesy E. Weiher).

in a ranked abundance list, both the number of species overall, and the relative abundance (or evenness) of the species. Two measures are commonly used: Simpson's index (Simpson 1949) and the Shannon–Weaver index (Shannon and Weaver 1949) (Box 11.1). More on the relative merits of these (and other diversity measures) can be found in sources such as Peet (1974) and Pielou (1975).

Returning to ranked abundance lists, the traditional approach to exploring such patterns has been to develop statistical models that produce different relative abundance patterns (Whittaker 1965, May 1981), with the assumption that such models might suggest something about the processes generating these patterns in real data (Pielou 1975, 1977). Four models are commonly used:

Box 11.1 | **Diversity indices**

The formula for Simpson's diversity index is:

$$C = \sum_{i=1}^{s} (p_i)^2$$

The formula for the Shannon-Weaver (Shannon-Wiener) diversity index is:

$$H' = -\sum_{i=1}^{s} (p_i)(\ln p_i)$$

where C and H' are index numbers, s is the total number of species in the sample, and p_i is the proportion of all individuals in the sample that belong to species i.

Broken stick (MacArthur 1957). Assumes the simultaneous random division of resources among species, as if points were randomly assigned along a stick of wood that is then broken into pieces, the length of each piece representing the abundance of a species.

Geometric (Whittaker 1965, 1972). Assumes that each species takes a constant fraction of the available resources, availability being defined as resources not already allocated to the preceding set of dominant species. This assumes a strict hierarchy of competitive dominance.

Log-normal (Preston 1962a,b). The ranked abundance pattern that is associated with Preston's early descriptions of the canonical distribution of commonness and rarity.

Zipf–Mandelbrot (Frontier 1985). The most recent addition to the class of ranked abundance models, which assumes a successional process such that the entry of species into a community is dependent upon changes caused by those species already present.

Each of these models produces slightly different theoretical ranked abundance lists. Figure 11.24 shows an example of each fitted to real ecological data. The most notorious of such models is the broken stick model that my doctoral supervisor, Chris Pielou, frequently criticized. In her opinion, it made the most unlikely assumptions of the entire set of such models, and she attributed its popularity and persistence to the fact that most ecologists could imagine breaking a stick, but few could do the calculations for, say, a geometric model. The relative merits of most of these models were extensively explored in the 1970s (e.g., Pielou 1977, May 1981), but it seems fair to conclude that all such modeling brought little understanding of the origin and persistence of differences in relative abundance. The tantalizing patterns remain.

The most comprehensive study of ranked abundance lists comes from three sets of British grasslands (Wilson et al. 1996). The Monks Wood experiment, established in 1978, allowed natural colonization

Table 11.5. *The percentage of best-fits to four models of species' relative abundance in three grassland data sets (from Wilson et al. 1996).*

Location	Broken stick	Geometric	General log-normal	Zipf–Mandelbrot
Monks Wood	1	29	43	27
Park Grass				
1991	2	28	46	24
1992	2	28	22	48
Compton	0	58	42	0
Total	5	143	153	99

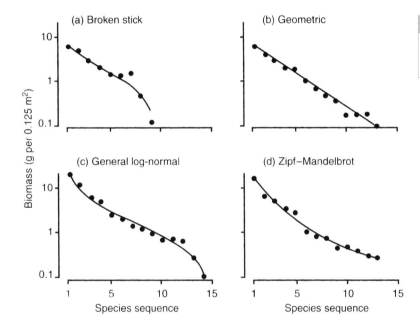

Figure 11.24 Four models of relative abundance fitted to data from British grasslands (from Wilson et al. 1996).

and succession with annual hay mowing in mid-August. The Park Grass experiment, established in 1856, includes different fertilization and mowing regimes (Box 11.2). The Compton experiment, initiated in 1987, explores factors thought to create grasslands with high species richness. Considering these grasslands collectively, the general log-normal model most frequently described the relative abundance of plant species (Table 11.5). A further analysis showed that it fit significantly better in plots fertilized with phosphorus. Changes in weather may also cause fluctuations in the patterns of ranked abundance. The data from the Park Grass experiment are presented for two separate sampling years. In 1991, the general log-normal model was most frequent ($n = 46$), whereas in 1992 the Zipf–Mandelbrot model was most frequent ($n = 48$).

Documenting the relative frequencies of these ranked abundance lists is an important contribution. The next step is to explore changes

Box 11.2 Rothamsted, the Park Grass Experiment

Most ecological experiments run for short periods of time, owing to practical constraints such as the length of a human career, the short nature of most grants, and in many cases, the duration of PhD research. As a consequence, long-term experiments have been rare in ecology, the Rothamsted experiments being a notable exception. Not only do they illustrate the value of long-term work, but they also provided the impetus for Sir R. A. Fisher's statistical studies that revolutionized thinking about variation in nature, and provided the quantitative arsenal that we now take for granted (Box 10.1). So let us examine these three monumental and intertwined stories, Rothamsted itself, the park grass plots, and Ronald Fisher.

According to Johnston (1994), J. B. Lawes, later Sir John, inherited the Rothamsted estate, which included an old manor house and about 100 ha, in 1822, when he was only eight years old. His father had died, leaving family fortunes at a low ebb. After some time at Oxford, Lawes returned home and had a bedroom at the Manor converted into a laboratory; here he worked on a variety of projects including medicinal plants. He finally took out a patent for the manufacture of superphosphate, and in 1843 starting commercial production at a factory in Deptford, London. On 1 June 1843 he appointed J. H. Gilbert (later Sir Henry), a chemist by training, to assist him in field and laboratory experiments on nutrition of crops and animals. Today some of their experiments continue, and are apparently the oldest continual agricultural experiments in the world. Their partnership continued for 57 years, and together they published some 150 scientific papers and 300 popular articles for farmers.

Gilbert had earned a doctorate at Giessen in Germany as a student of Professor Liebig, a leading figure in the history of plant nutrition, still known for "Liebig's Law of the Minimum." The first edition of Professor Liebig's treatise on agriculture was published in 1840, and it rapidly went through several subsequent editions. Gilbert earned his doctorate in 12 months, returning to England to work at University College London and then in industry in Manchester before moving to Rothamsted. The principal field experiments he established there focused upon agricultural species, turnips (1843), winter wheat (1843), beans (1847), crops in rotation (1848), clover (1849), spring barley (1852), oats (1869), and finally, of most interest to community ecologists, the only experiment involving plants in mixture, the park grass studies of permanent pasture (1856).

Here we shall largely pass over the details of the experiments themselves, particularly the ones on agriculture, except for Figure B11.2(a), which shows the dramatic improvement in yields of wheat through time as fertilizer, herbicides and fungicides were incorporated into agricultural practice.

Fisher was hired at Rothamsted in 1919, nearly a century after the founding of the Statistical Society of London by Adolphe Quetelet in 1834 (Barnett 1994). Although Fisher was at first regarded as flighty, it soon became apparent that he had great ability, and the director of the station, Sir John Russell, concluded that he "was in fact a genius who must be retained." Over his period at Rothamsted, Fisher developed and introduced such essential concepts as factorial design, interaction of main effects, analysis of variance, and blocking to account for the heterogeneity of fields. Figure B11.2(b) shows the layout of the

(a)

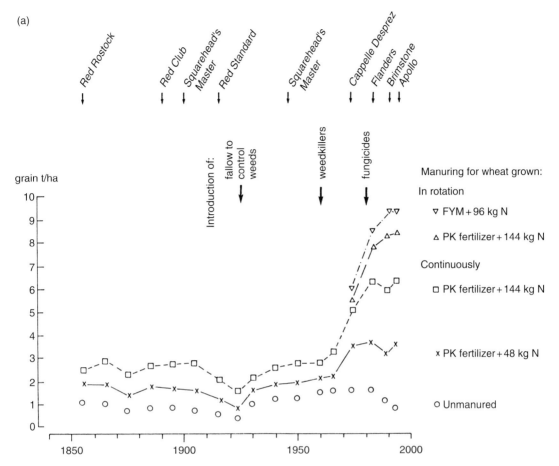

Figure B11.2(a) Yields of winter wheat grown at Broadbalk, Rothamsted, from 1852 to 1990 with fertilizers and with farmyard manure showing the effects of changing cultivars, the introduction of weed control and fungicides, and crop rotation to minimize effects of soil-borne pathogens (courtesy A. E. Johnston, updated from Johnston 1994).

Park Grass experiments. Although the design clearly indicates a desire to study the effects of fertilization, we should now recognize the design as deficient in at least three ways. There is a decided lack of replication to measure variation among plots receiving the same treatment. The design does not appear randomized, similar treatments appearing instead to be adjacent to one another. The design is not factorial for the study of interactions among the treatments. The very fact that most of us can see these inadequacies at once serves only to illustrate how fundamentally Fisher has changed the way we think about the design and analysis of experimental data.

The Park Grass plots themselves continue to be of interest to ecologists (Silvertown et al. 2006); one of the more interesting examples of this work (Silvertown 1980, Silvertown et al. 1994) shows that fertilization consistently led to steady declines in plant diversity (Figure 11.27); in contrast, effects of rainfall were minor. Further, within any plot, there now appears to be some sort of botanical equilibrium at the coarse scale: the relative proportions of three groups (grasses, legumes, and other species) show no trends over recent time. In contrast, however, individual species within each group have continued to fluctuate widely. There thus appeared to be a dynamic equilibrium at one scale, but not the other.

Figure B11.2(b) The layout of Park Grass, Rothamsted, UK. Treatments (every year except as indicated). *Nitrogen* (applied in spring): N1, N2, N3, sulfate of ammonia supplying 48, 96, 144 kg N ha^{-1}; N1*, N2*, nitrate of soda supplying 48, 96 kg N ha^{-1}; (N2), (N2*), last applied 1989. *Minerals* (applied in winter): P 35 kg; K 225 kg; Na 15 kg; Mg 10 kg ha^{-1}; Si silicate of soda at 450 kg ha^{-1} of water-soluble powder; plot 20, rates of fertilization in years when FYM not applied: 30 kg N*, 15 kg P, 45 kg K ha^{-1}. *Organics* (each applied every fourth year since 1905): FYM, 35 tonnes ha^{-1} farmyard manure (bullocks) (1989, 1993); fish meal (about 6.5% N) to supply 63 kg N ha^{-1} (1991, 1995). *Lime*: a,b,c lime applied as needed to maintain pH 7, 6, and 5 respectively; d no lime applied (pH range 3.5 (plot 11/1) to 5.7 (plot 17) (from Barnett 1994).

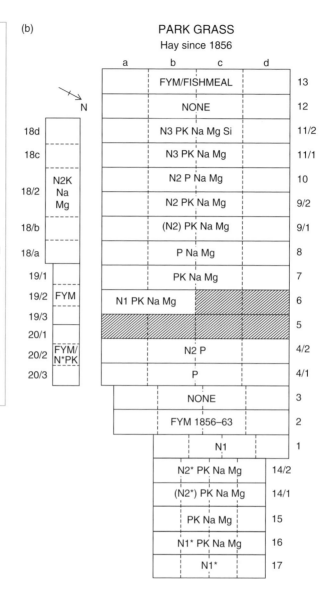

The Park Grass experiments, and others, continue at Rothamsted. Recognizing the value of this work, many other sites for long-term ecological research have been established over the last few decades. The valuable association of long-term experiments with large tracts of native vegetation also illustrates the close connection possible between systems of protected areas and scientific research. There is a sort of symbiosis here, with the natural areas providing sites for research which otherwise would not be possible and the research providing insight into management and protection of the reserve system. The results of long-term experiments should enliven and enrich future texts on plant ecology, and may be one of the most important and least expected long-term contributions by Lawes and Gilbert.

that occur with known factors such as primary production, successional stage, soil fertility, or rainfall. While mechanisms are still
poorly understood, the ubiquity of competition and competitive
hierarchies in vegetation (Chapter 5) suggests that competition
plays a significant role in causing these dominance patterns. The
sensitivity of the shape of the relationship to the addition of phosphorus also suggests a mechanism involving competition. However,
the connection will be clearly established only when independent
measures of relative competitive ability can be used to predict positions in ranked abundance lists or when dominant plants are
removed to test for release of the subordinates.

11.9 | Laboratory experiments on richness and diversity

Small plant communities that are created artificially are called
microcosms. Microcosm experiments are relatively artificial in the
restricted number of species used, and in the few environmental
factors that are manipulated. Unlike field experiments, they sacrifice
realism for precision (Diamond 1986). The advantage of microcosms
for community-level research is the degree of control they allow over
the key environmental factors. Their use has been increasing (Fraser
and Keddy 1997) and a number of studies directly address questions
regarding biodiversity (e.g., Grime et al. 1987, Naeem et al. 1994,
Weiher and Keddy 1995a).

Grime et al. (1987) made artificial grassland communities to
examine the effects of mycorrhizal infection, soil structure, and
grazing on plant species diversity. They found that mycorrhizae can
increase diversity by increasing the biomass of the subordinate plant
species relative to that of the dominant plant species. Perhaps the
transfer of mineral nutrients and sugars through mycorrhizae
reduces the intensity of competition and encourages species coexistence on fertile soils.

Weiher and Keddy (1995a) made artificial wetland communities
to examine the effect of 24 different combinations of habitat factors
on diversity. At the end of two growing seasons, species richness was
significantly affected by fertility in eight different habitat types
(Figure 11.25). After 5 years (Table 11.6), species richness was strongly
affected by fertility level (column 3) and year (column 5) for all treatments. Beyond this, only two of the six treatments (rows 1 and 2)
strongly affected species richness – water depth and fluctuation of
water level.

Vivian-Smith (1997) also made artificial wetland communities to
study the effects of small-scale habitat variation on diversity. There is
a good deal of evidence that heterogeneity can increase richness by
allowing for differential establishment of seedlings (e.g., Harper

Table 11.6. *The results of a 5-year competition experiment using 20 species in 24 habitats (combinations of variables in column 1). F-values are shown for repeated-measures three-way ANOVA of species richness, main effects, and two-way interaction terms (from Weiher and Keddy 1995a).*

Environmental variable	Treatment	Fertility	Treatment × fertility	Year	Treatment × year	Fertility × year
Depth of water	195.60***	47.48***	9.67***	153.66***	46.11***	9.36***
Fluctuation of water level	73.75***	46.76***	5.28*	99.13***	48.44***	5.41**
Presence/absence of litter	0.89	220.40***	8.65**	169.00***	4.98**	6.47**
Texture (sand, gravel, cobbles)	0.50	77.63***	0.35	296.58***	1.88	12.14***
Starting time	5.88**	56.96***	7.87**	268.52***	0.95	6.54**
Presence/absence of Typha	0.05	81.87***	2.55	84.58***	3.52*	4.06*

Notes:
$^{*}p < 0.05.$ $^{**}p < 0.01.$ $^{***}p < 0.001.$

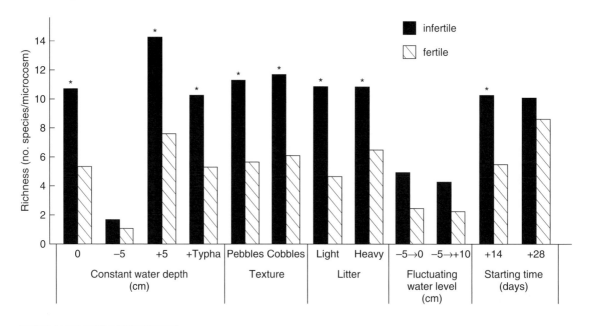

Figure 11.25 Species richness after two growing seasons for 12 artificially created wetland habitats at two levels of fertility. Significant differences in richness between fertility treatments at $p = 0.001$ are indicated by an asterisk (from Moore and Keddy 1989b).

1965, Grubb 1977, Keddy and Constabel 1986). In this experiment, some containers had a flat peat-sand mixture, and some had five artificial peat hummocks raised 2.5 cm above the surrounding substrate. Three seed mixtures were then sown into these two treatments: an artificial seed mixture, a natural seed bank, and a combination of the two. Figure 11.26 shows that heterogeneous treatments had significantly more species, regardless of the seed source used.

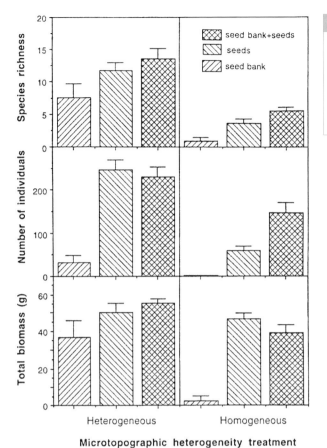

Figure 11.26 Experimental plant community responses (species richness, number of individuals, and total biomass) to substrate heterogeneity and seed source treatments (values shown are means +1 SE) (from Vivian-Smith 1997).

11.10 | Field experiments on richness and diversity

Experimental manipulation of independent variables in the field is more realistic, but burdened with the problem of complexity and how to disentangle the myriad natural factors that influence community pattern. Two of the most common field manipulations are based on the two fundamental forces that structure plant communities: fertility and disturbance (Grime 1979, Huston 1979, Tilman 1982). Increasing numbers of field experiments also manipulate species composition (Tilman et al. 1996), but such methodology is suspect owing to the enormous differences among the types of plants used (e.g., Huston 1997, Grime 2002).

The longest-running manipulative experiment is the Park Grass Experiment at Rothamsted, England (Box 11.2). Begun in 1856, the treatments involve different fertilizer regimes on hay-meadow grassland. The original objective was to study the effects on hay yield, but ecologists have found it valuable for answering broader questions. Silvertown (1980) describes more of the history of the site and shows that over the years, species diversity has progressively

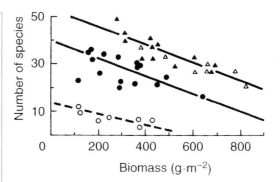

Figure 11.27 Species richness in experimental plots in the Park Grass experiments at Rothamstead, UK. The plots in the top line represent the situation before fertilization; the bottom two lines illustrate the effects of fertilization (open symbols, acidified; closed symbols, not acidified when fertilized). The top line (triangles) precedes the bottom lines by 80 years. In all three cases, across time and treatments, the slopes are nearly identical (from Keddy 2001, after Silvertown 1980).

declined in the nutrient-enriched treatments (with a corresponding increase in biomass). The pH of the soil was found to be another important factor controlling species richness, where soils with lower pH had lower species richness (Figure 11.27). The decline in species richness with nutrient enrichment has been found in many other studies (e.g., Grime 1973a,b, 1979, Huston 1979, Austin and Austin 1980, Tilman 1982), including wetlands (e.g., Willis 1963, Moore et al. 1989, Verhoeven et al. 1996).

In an elegant experiment that combined both fertilization and the experimental removal of the dominant plant species, Gurevitch and Unnasch (1989) were able to illustrate close connections among fertilization, competitive dominance, and reduced diversity. The sandy, nutrient-poor fields that they studied had some 15 herbaceous plant species, but this number declined to 6 with the application of N-P-K fertilizer. These effects could be entirely avoided by removing the one dominant species (Figure 11.28), in which case both fertilized and unfertilized plots had a mean of 18 species. This provides clear evidence that the decline in richness with fertilization is a result of competition from the dominant species. That is, it appears that increasing the resource supply increases monopolization. Presumably this is because the added nutrients allowed the dominant grass, *Dactylis glomerata*, to more effectively shade its neighbors (although Gurevitch was unable to detect a significant increase in *Dactylis* biomass after fertilization). Further, evidence for increased competition at higher resource levels comes from the greater difference between controls and treatments at high as opposed to low fertilities. This experiment, like that of Carson and Pickett (1990), tends to confirm the view that adding resources merely allows an already dominant species to further exclude the others by increasing its competitive effects upon neighbors.

In a revealing extension of the Gurevitch experiment, Carson and Pickett (1990) explored the effects of four different treatments on old fields in New Jersey: (1) added macronutrients, (2) added water, (3) added light (achieved by tying back tall plants to remove their shade from a plot, and (4) added disturbance (achieved by digging with a hand trowel early in the growing season). These fields are normally dominated by goldenrods and asters, with *Solidago canadensis* and *Aster*

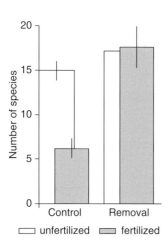

Figure 11.28 The number of plant species in an old field with sandy soil declined after addition of fertilizer (left histograms), but this change did not occur if the dominant species, *Dactylis glomerata*, was also removed (right histograms). Plots were 2 × 0.5 m; responses were measured after two growing seasons; vertical lines show 1 SE for $n = 5$ replicates (after Gurevitch and Unnasch 1989).

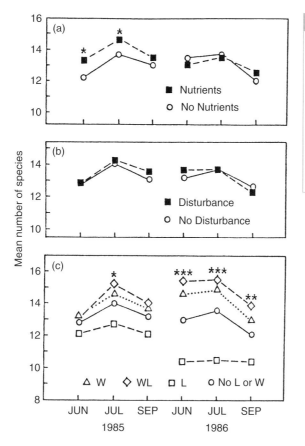

Figure 11.29 The effects of (a) increased nutrients, (b) disturbance and (c) increased water and light on species richness (mean number of species per 1.0×0.5 m plot). For (a) and (b) significant differences between treatments and within a date are indicated by asterisks. For (c), significant interactions for a given date are indicated by asterisks ($^*p < 0.5$, $^{**}p < 0.01$, $^{***}p < 0.001$) (from Carson and Pickett 1990).

pilosus most common, and *S. graminifolia*, *S. juncea*, *S. rugosa*, and *S. nemoralis* also found. The mean number of species was temporarily increased by the addition of nutrients (Figure 11.29(a)), but this effect disappeared in the second year. Disturbance had no effect upon the number of species in either year (Figure 11.29(b)). The principal factors increasing diversity were apparently the removal of the canopy and the addition of water (Figure 11.29(c)).

11.11 | Implications for conservation

Ecological management and conservation is a rapidly growing field. There are new journals dedicated to the topic, as well as clearly stated objectives for the maintenance of biodiversity (e.g., Noss and Cooperrider 1994, Table 11.7), and new global maps of where diversity is concentrated (Myers et al. 2000). There is a very important, and still frequently misunderstood, connection among local species diversity, the species pool, and global biodiversity. Conserving "biodiversity" (e.g., Groombridge 1992, Reid et al. 1993, Noss 1995, Myers et al. 2000) requires one to think about the regional species

Table 11.7. *Four fundamental land management objectives for maintaining native biodiversity of a region (from Noss and Cooperrider 1994).*

Represent, in a system of protected areas, all native ecosystem types and seral stages across their natural range of variation.

Maintain viable populations of all native species in natural patterns of abundance and distribution.

Maintain ecological and evolutionary processes, such as disturbance regimes, hydrological processes, nutrient cycles, and biotic interactions.

Manage landscapes and communities to be responsive to short-term and long-term environmental change and to maintain the evolutionary potential of the biota.

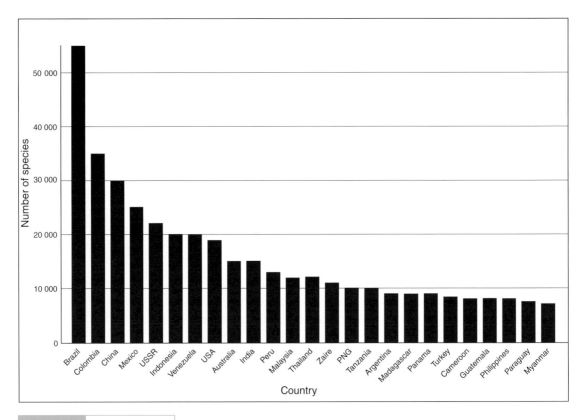

Figure 11.30 The 25 most plant-rich countries (from Groombridge 1992).

pool for an area. It also requires setting clear priorities. Money, time, and resources will always be limited, so it is imperative to concentrate upon those regions of the world that have the highest biological diversity.

While political boundaries are highly artificial, they do provide the administrative units within which conservation programs must be designed and implemented. Figure 11.30 shows that Brazil is therefore a global priority, being the only country with more than 50 000 plant species within its borders. Columbia, China, and Mexico are next on the list, each having more than 25 000 plant species. In contrast, Figure 11.31 shows that most ecological research occurs

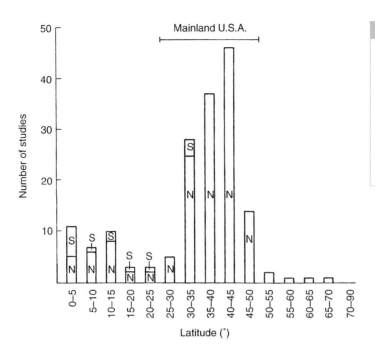

Figure 11.31 The latitudinal distribution of ecological research based upon 167 papers from *Ecology* randomly selected from the period 1976–1985. Given that both diversity and surface area per degree of latitude decline with increasing latitude, the appropriate null models would have a maximum at the left and decline to the right (from Keddy 1989).

within the northern temperate zone. This divergence between priority and effort will need to be addressed by future generations of ecologists. At the largest scale, the challenge is to maintain the species pool of the entire planet or at least of a region. Most managers, however, must focus on maintaining or increasing diversity at only one location. *It is entirely possible that attempts to increase local diversity can actually reduce diversity at a larger scale*, that is, reduce the regional species pool. We will explore two examples.

The New Jersey Pine Barrens support many rare plants, in part because the habitats are so infertile. This infertility means that carnivorous plants are particularly well represented in the flora. Ehrenfeld (1983) found that experimentally nutrient-enriched sites supported nearly three times the number of species (73) as pristine sites (26). Enrichment increased local biodiversity by allowing the invasion of common, exotic species that were adapted to higher nutrient levels and already part of the regional species pool. It also resulted in the loss of native, uncommon carnivorous plants that occupy only infertile habitats, and thus reduced the regional species pool overall. The flora of infertile sites is 88 percent native species, 12 percent of which are carnivorous. The more development that occurs, the more fertility increases, and the more native species (particularly carnivorous plants) are replaced by invasive species.

Overgrazing of rangelands by domestic livestock and the subsequent loss of native plant diversity is a universal problem in semi-arid areas and has been a problem for several thousand years (Thirgood 1981, Hughes 1982). It has been a particularly contentious issue in southwestern North America, where ranchers pay a nominal fee to graze their cattle on publicly owned grasslands, and where over-grazing is implicated in conversion of grassland to shrubland, loss of the native biota, as well as increased erosion (e.g., Archer 1989, Fleischner 1994, Noss and Cooperrider 1994, McClaran 2003). The most obvious step seems to be to simply reduce grazing pressure – at least so long as critical thresholds have not been exceeded, a topic to which we shall return in the next chapter (Section 12.6.4). Other interventions may do more harm than good for biological diversity. Consider the Vail rangeland in eastern Oregon (Heady and Bartolome 1977, Heady 1988). In this case, efforts at "rehabilitation" primarily consisted of ploughing and seeding a monoculture of non-native grass (*Agropyron pectiniforme*). Although marginal benefits to wildlife were reported (Heady 1988), little evidence exists to support such claims (Noss and Cooperrider 1994). For native plants, such programs can be quite destructive. For example, it has led to the invasion of non-native noxious weeds such as medusahead (*Taeniatherum asperum*) (Noss and Cooperrider 1994).

The general rule is that *if attempts at increasing local diversity are achieved by increasing populations of globally common species, local management is probably counterproductive*. Management for maintaining "biodiversity" makes sense only if one takes a global perspective as the context for evaluating local actions.

11.12 | Conclusion

We will spend the entire next chapter dealing with the conservation of plant diversity. But if we are to engage in successful conservation, we must have some understanding of the fundamental evolutionary and ecological forces that determine plant diversity at global, regional, and local scales. Table 11.8 provides one such summary. We also need to appreciate how little is currently known of the details and mechanisms that cause and maintain diversity. Two very different methods of investigation, description and experimentation, are needed. While global patterns in diversity are increasingly understood (Gaston 2000, Myers et al. 2000, Willig et al. 2003), there has been only limited success in predicting species richness from environmental factors. We have seen here that at the large scale, area, habitat variation, and distance from the equator are important factors. At the smaller scale, factors such as competitive exclusion and intermediate disturbance become increasingly important. Overall, we are remarkably ignorant of factors controlling diversity. Willig et al. (2003) suggest that there are 30 hypotheses for possible causes of the latitudinal diversity gradient alone! We therefore need to approach management for conservation with a certain modesty, or we risk making things worse rather than better.

In the short term, a top priority must be the establishment of nature reserve systems that efficiently represent the largest possible

---

Table 11.8. *A summary of the major factors that control diversity in plant communities at different temporal and spatial scales.*

Large temporal and spatial scales (global species pool)
1. The isolation of continents allows increased plant diversity by permitting the evolution of new species and persistence of different floras on different continents
2. The angiosperm life cycle allows for greatly increased rates of speciation
3. The angiosperm method of pollination allows more species to coexist within a landscape
4. More than one major physical constraint on plant growth (e.g., salinity and flooding) reduces the species pool

Medium temporal and spatial scales (regional species pool)
1. Gradients allow for the coexistence of more species within a landscape, and the longer the gradients and more kinds of gradients, the more species occur
2. For any one gradient, the number of species is highest at intermediate levels of productivity
3. Within any segment of a gradient, disturbance and gap dynamics allow more species to coexist
4. There is little evidence that habitat specialization on narrower sections of gradients allows more species to coexist

Small temporal and spatial scales (local species pool)
1. A few species often dominate a site at the expense of most others
2. Increased amounts of productivity associated with factors such as higher soil fertility or longer growing season tend to increase the degree of dominance by these few species
3. Species density reaches a maximum at intermediate levels of fertility and disturbance
4. Patches with extreme infertility or disturbance tend to support distinctive species, thereby increasing the size of the local species pool

---

pool of native species (Scott et al. 1987, Myers 1988, Pressey et al. 1993, Noss and Cooperrider 1994). This will buy time while we refine management methods to ensure the persistence of biodiversity through time. Given that roughly one-third of the world's flora is at risk of extinction (Pitman and Jørgensen 2002) there remains a great deal of work for plant ecologists to accomplish.

Further reading

Williams, C. B. 1964. *Patterns in the Balance of Nature*. London: Academic Press.

Whittaker, R. H. 1965. Dominance and diversity in land plant communities. *Science* **147**: 250–260.

Pielou, E. C. 1975. *Ecological Diversity*. New York: John Wiley and Sons.

Huston, M. A. 1979. A general hypothesis of species diversity. *The American Naturalist* **113**: 81–101.

Specht, A. and R. Specht. 1993. Species richness and canopy productivity of Australian plant communities. *Biodiversity and Conservation* **2**: 152–167.

Rosenzweig, M. L. 1995. *Species Diversity in Space and Time*. Cambridge: Cambridge University Press.

Cowling, R. M. and M. J. Samways. 1995. Predicting global patterns of endemic plant species richness. *Biodiversity Letters* **2**: 127–131.

Zobel, M. 1997. The relative role of species pools in determining plant species richness: an alternative explanation of species coexistence? *Trends in Ecology and Evolution* **12**: 266–269.

Willig, M. R., D. M. Kaufman, and R. D. Stevens. 2003. Latitudinal gradients of biodiversity: pattern, process, scale and synthesis. *Annual Review of Ecology, Evolution and Systematics* **34**: 273–309.

Keddy, P. A. 2005. Putting the plants back into plant ecology: six pragmatic models for understanding, conserving and restoring plant diversity. *Annals of Botany* **96**: 177–189.

Chapter 12

Conservation and management

Some historical context. Ancient Assyria and Rome. Deforestation of the Mediterranean region. More vegetation types at risk. Louisiana wetlands. Oceanic islands: Easter Island and the Galapagos. Boreal forests. Protection of representative vegetation types. Principles for the design of reserve systems. Hot spots. Primary forests. Large wetlands. The Guyana highlands. Value of wilderness. Fragmentation: fens and deciduous forests. Functions and management. Two perspectives on conservation. Change through geological time. Ecological footprints. Thresholds. Restoration. Indicators. Monitoring. The thin red line. Where does one go from here?

12.1 | Introduction

It is time to put the picture together. We began the book by exploring how plants have evolved and how plant communities have formed in response to fundamental factors such as resources, stress, disturbance, and herbivory. We have also encountered selected examples of how humans interfere with these ecological processes that create and maintain plant communities, such as overgrazing arid grasslands (Section 4.3.2), introducing exotic species that feed on wetland plants (Section 7.4.6), logging boreal forests (Section 9.4.3), or fertilizing infertile plant communities (Section 11.6.2). There are nearly 300 000 plant species in the world, but as human populations increase, and as we disrupt the natural forces that create plant communities, the destruction of plants and vegetation will accelerate. This is not an exaggeration. In some parts of the world, more than 90 percent of the natural primary vegetation has already been cleared. The list includes: southern central China, Sri Lanka, Burma, Madagascar, West Africa and southeastern Brazil (the Atlantic Forest) (Myers et al. 2000). Not only will individual species of plants vanish, but as entire vegetation types and ecosystems disappear, there will be the loss or distortion of important processes in the biosphere, such as carbon and nitrogen cycling. All plant ecologists will therefore need to consider their personal responsibilities and the role of their discipline in these broader concerns of humanity. In taking such a perspective, it is important to understand that environmental problems are not something newly created by either twenty-first century technology or a single group of human beings.

A few basic, almost common sense, principles provide the foundation for applied plant ecology or, as it is sometimes called, conservation biology. It is, perhaps, most effective to illustrate these basic principles by providing examples of vegetation types exposed to different kinds of pressures and risks. This chapter considers examples including desertification in Mediterranean landscapes, loss of wetlands in Louisiana, effects of introduced goats on the Galapagos Islands, and effects of logging on boreal forests. It then proceeds to a discussion of priorities for action. First, there is the urgent need for comprehensive reserve systems. Second, it will explore processes of degradation in landscapes, how these exhibit critical thresholds, and how they include losses in ecological function. Finally, we will consider the challenges posed by restoring landscapes so they can support plants and vegetation, as well, of course, as animals and people. There is reason for optimism, and vast areas of the Earth will require enlightened activity to restore ecological functions and natural vegetation.

12.2 | Some historical context

12.2.1 Ancient Assyria

Let us begin with one of the earliest written human epics, Gilgamesh. This epic is also of interest because it predates the Christian Bible, yet describes an ancient flood. Recent archaeological work has provided some interesting context for this early flood story of both Jewish and Christian traditions. Sandars (1972) recounts how in 1839 a young Englishman, Austen Henry Layard, spent some years excavating archaeological sites in Mesopotamia. One of the most significant discoveries was thousands of broken tablets from the palace of Nineveh. Nineveh was an Assyrian city that fell in 612 BC to a combined army of Medes and Babylonians. The destruction was so complete that the city never rose again. Included in the ruins was the entire library of Assurbanipal "King of the World, King of Assyria." Over 25 000 broken tablets from this library were taken to the British Museum, and eventual decipherment revealed an epic immeasurably older than Homer's *Iliad*, the fragments of which are now known as *The Epic of Gilgamesh*. One section of this epic narrates how there was a flood: "The rider of the storm sent down the rain ... a black cloud came from the horizon; it thundered within where Adad, lord of the storm, was riding ... For six days and nights the winds blew, torrent and tempest and flood overwhelmed the world ..." (pp. 110–111). This epic also has a boat full of survivors who come to rest on a mountain and who release a dove to search for land.

In an early part of the epic, Gilgamesh and his companion, Enkidu, travel to a mysterious cedar forest (which Sandars places in northern Syria or southwest Persia): "They gazed at the mountain of cedars, the dwelling-place of the gods ... The hugeness of the cedar rose in front of the mountain, its shade was beautiful, full of comfort ..." (p. 77). They encounter a monstrous guardian of the forest, Humbaba, whom they kill with their swords: "They attacked the cedars, the seven splendours of Humbaba were extinguished" (p. 83). *The Epic of Gilgamesh* therefore records an early episode of deforestation followed by destructive flooding.

12.2.2 Deforestation in Ancient Rome and the Mediterranean

Moving into the realm of recorded history, the Roman civilization originated with the Etruscans, who "reclaimed Tuscany from forest and swamp" and built drainage tunnels to take the overflow from lakes (Durant 1944). The early history of Rome is little known, in part because the Gauls burned the city in 390 BC, presumably destroying most historical records. Although Rome was built on seven hills, it was not a healthy location: "rains, floods and springs fed malarial marshes in the surrounding plain and even in the lower levels of the city" (p. 12), but Etruscan engineers built walls and sewers for Rome, and "turned it from a swamp into a protected and civilized capital." One of the main sewers, the *Cloaca Maxima*, was large enough that wagons loaded with hay could pass beneath its arches; the city's refuse and rain water passed through openings in the streets into these drains and then into the Tiber "whose pollution was a lasting problem in Roman life" (p. 81). Meanwhile, deforestation occurred apace to provide building materials and fuel.

The famed Cedars of Lebanon, for example, now live only as literary references; the trees themselves vanished into the shipbuilding yards of the Egyptians, Phoenicians, Jews, Romans, and Ottomans. Grazing by goats prevented regeneration of these forests and converted the Mediterranean countries into an increasingly barren landscape (Thirgood 1981, Hughes 1982). Twenty-five centuries ago, Plato was well aware of the consequences of these activities; he bemoans how "there has been a constant movement of soil away from the high ground and what remains is like the skeleton of a body emaciated by disease. All the rich soil has melted away, leaving a country of skin and bone" (Plato, *Criterias III*, in Thirgood 1981, p. 36).

It is not a coincidence that the Tiber "was perpetually silting its mouth and blocking Rome's port at Ostia; two hundred vessels foundered there in one gale … About 200 BC vessels began to put in at Puteoli, 150 miles south of Rome, and ship their goods overland to the capital" (p. 78). Some 100 years later Julius Caesar had great plans "to free Rome from malaria by draining Lake Fucinus and the Pontine marshes, and reclaiming these acres for tillage. He proposed to raise dikes to control the Tiber's floods; by diverting the course of that stream he hoped to improve the harbour at Ostia, periodically ruined by the river's silt" (p. 193). These plans were cut short when he was assassinated by a group of conspirators in 44 BC who saw in these and other ambitions the dangerous beginnings of a potential despot.

The effects of several thousand years of human settlement on Mediterranean forests are summarized in Figure 12.1. It illustrates how relatively small human populations can degrade entire landscapes. Over several thousand years, humans have changed the

Phoenicia (ca. 3000 BC)

Some 5000 years ago, it is believed Semites from the east occupied the narrow coastal plain and established a series of settlements that developed into the Phoenician cities of Tyre, Sidon and Beirut. From the third millennium B.C., these were centers of trade and culture. According to early sources, Lebanon was "an oasis of green with running creeks" and "a vast forest whose branches hide the sky". The population grew and the Phoenicians were forced to migrate and colonize, to engage in manufacture and maritime trade; and to exploit the sloping land. These activities together formed the basis of their trading civilization. Phoenician achievements as cultivators in first breaking away from the hydraulic agriculture of the flatlands and establishing a permanent agriculture on slopes, are no less significant than their capacity as traders, while their maritime power and a good portion of their trade was founded on their exploitation of the forest. In classical times, Mount Lebanon appears an economic hinterland, its forests providing wood for export. Lebanese cedar became the first great commercial timber. The forests of the Lebanon range not only made Phoenicia a dominant seapower and trading nation, but, from an early date, supplied the civilizations of Egypt and Mesopotamia with choice timber for temples and palaces, and with essential oils and resins. Indeed, the fame and the rise and fall of the Phoenician civilization can be closely related to the availability of timber. As early as the Third Dynasty, 5000 years ago, timber is known to have been rafted from Lebanon to Egypt. (Thirgood 1981, p. 95–96)

Greece (ca. 500 BC)

Contemporary Attica may accurately be described as a mere relic of the original country. There has been a constant movement of soil away from the high ground and what remains is like the skeleton of a body emasculated by disease. All the rich soil has melted away, leaving a country of skin and bone. Originally the mountains of Attica were heavily forested. Fine trees produced timber suitable for roofing the largest buildings; the roofs hewn from this timber are still in existence. The country produced boundless feed for cattle, there are some mountains which had trees not so very long ago, that now have nothing but bee pastures. The annual rainfall was not lost as it is now through being allowed to run over the denuded surface to the sea, it was absorbed by the ground and stored ... the drainage from the high ground was collected in this way and discharged into the hollows as springs and rivers with abundant flow and a wide territorial distribution. Shrines remain at the sources of dried up water sources as witness to this. (Plato, *Criterias III*, in Thirgood 1981, p. 36)

Lebanon (ca. 1960)

... In the Lebanon mountains ... the scene had to be witnessed to be believed for there one can see the most incredible scenes of wanton destruction of the last remnants of these beautiful trees. Not only are the last trees sought out and hacked down for timber and fuel, but one sees mature trees being lopped and actually felled in order to provide goat fodder. So heavy is goat grazing ... that the flocks have already consumed nearly all forms of vegetation within their reach. The shepherds, unperturbed, have therefore resorted to felling the last remnants of high forest in order to satisfy the empty bellies of their ravenous flocks. It is an astonishing sight to see a fine cedar or silver fir tree felled for this purpose and then to see hundreds of hungry goats literally pounce upon it the moment it falls to earth and devour every vestige of foliage from the branches. It does not take many minutes for such a flock to strip a tree of its foliage. The felled tree has then served the shepherd's purpose and is left to rot where it fell, he then turns his attention to the next tree and so on. (FAO 1961 in Thirgood 1981, p. 73)

Spain (ca. 1500)

The final destruction of the forests of Spain was initiated in medieval times. While the original extent of the forests of central Spain is uncertain ... the entire country was predominantly wooded. The Phoenicians, Greeks, Carthaginians and Romans all built ships on the Iberian coast. With the development of Catalanian and Castilian sea power, these encroachments on the forest cover of the coastal mountains became more extensive and by the fifteenth century, ship wood had to be imported from the Hanseatic League from as far away as Scandinavia. Around 1600, there was also considerable trade in barrel wood and boards between Hamburg and Spain. During the sixteenth century, naval dominance by Spanish shipbuilders attained its highest mark. At this time, Spain is said to have possessed almost 2000 seaworthy ships. Ships of more than 1000 tons were built and, with an average life of 15–20 years and 150 000 cubic feet of wood used in the building of a 1400 ton ship, the drain during the wooden ship era is evident. (Thirgood 1981, p. 49)

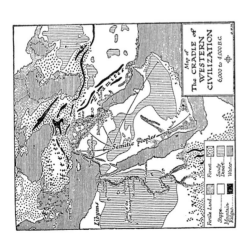

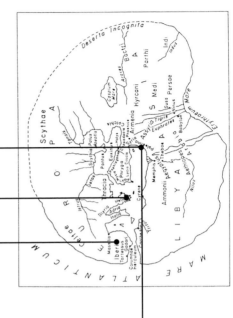

The world of the ancients according to Herodotus (fifth century BC) (from Thirgood 1981)

Figure 12.1 Cumulative effects of grazing upon Mediterranean forests, beginning at upper right (from Thirgood 1981, Wells 1956).

Mediterranean basin from a land of forests and streams to a land that is denuded and eroded. The great sea fleets of history – the sea-going ships of the Phoenician, Egyptian, Persian, Greek, Carthaginian, Roman, Muslim, Spanish, and Napoleonic eras – were constructed from the trees that once covered the Mediterranean hillsides. Each ship took a toll. The forests might have been able to withstand the pressures of cutting, except that grazing by livestock, particularly goats, killed any tree seedlings that regenerated. The present number of goats alone in this region likely exceeds 100 million. Until these great herds of grazing animals are removed, forests will be unable to re-establish (Thirgood 1981).

12.3 | Vegetation types at risk

As human populations continue to grow, and as people demand ever higher standards of living, the pressures on the Earth's natural plant communities are accelerating. About one-half of all the primary production of the Earth's natural communities is already diverted away from natural systems and into humans (Vitousek et al. 1986). Half of the available fresh water is also appropriated for humans (Postel et al. 1996). Many species have become extinct, some hover near extinction, and others are in serious decline (Ehrlich and Ehrlich 1981, E. O. Wilson 1993, Pitman and Jørgensen 2002). Indeed, it has been said that we are about to enter a period of biological catastrophe of a scale last seen at the end of the Cretaceous (Section 6.4.3) – a new period of extinction driven by humans. Many vegetation types now exist as only small fragments of their original distribution. Each natural vegetation type has its own story. I will present a few here that are typical. We shall then look at how we design natural area systems to protect natural vegetation diversity, and how we restore vegetation that is already damaged or degraded.

12.3.1 The destruction of Louisiana's alluvial forests

One might try to explain away the degradation of Mediterranean forests by arguing that human beings a thousand years ago could not be expected to understand the consequences of their behavior for the environment of their homelands. Let us therefore look at relatively recent human activity in the New World, and let me use coastal Louisiana as the case study. One could take any part of the world and find related patterns and events, but Louisiana, where I completed this book, is my choice here. You might challenge yourself to write a similar account of your own home region.

Louisiana is located on the Gulf of Mexico on the Gulf coastal plain, a region created by sedimentation in shallow coastal waters. The sediments that form contemporary Louisiana eroded from uplands far to the northwest (Rocky Mountains) and northeast (Appalachian Mountains), being carried here primarily by the Mississippi River (Figure 12.2). The central feature of southern Louisiana is the

Figure 12.2 The Mississippi River drains all of central North America between the Rocky Mountains and the Appalachians. (a) The sediment it carries has, over millions of years, built much of the central United States and the north shore of the Gulf of Mexico. Vast swamps of baldcypress and tupelo occupied the floodplain near the mouth of the Mississippi River. (b) This giant baldcypress was cut by the Lyon Lumber Company in the Maurepas Swamp around 1900 (source: Al Dranguet, Department of History and Political Science, Southeastern Louisiana University, Hammond).

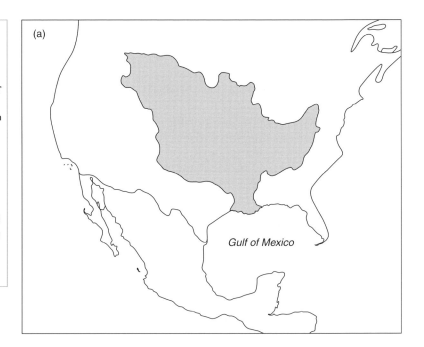

(a)

Gulf of Mexico

(b)

19 400 km^2 deltaic plain of the Mississippi River, an area that supports 41 percent of the coastal wetlands in the coterminous United States (Shaffer et al. 2005). The development of the landscape in southern Louisiana is described in Bernard and Leblanc (1965), Boyd and Penland (1988), Coleman et al. (1998), Boesch et al. (1994), and Gosselink et al. (1998). Today the Mississippi River may be thought of as scenic, but the region left a forbidding impression on some early visitors. In 1837 one traveler from Europe wrote:

> It is not like most rivers, beautiful to the sight ... not one that the eye loves to dwell upon as it sweeps along .... It is a furious, rapid, desolating torrent,

loaded with alluvial soil . . .. [I]t sweeps down whole forests in its course,
which disappear in tumultuous confusion, whirled away by the stream
now loaded with the masses of soil which nourished their roots, often
blocking up and changing the channel of the river, which, as if in anger at
its being opposed, inundates and devastates the whole country round . . .

(Barry 1997, p. 96)

The youngest parts of Louisiana have been newly built out into
the Gulf of Mexico over just the past 5000 years. As the Mississippi
River enters the sea, the sediments (an annual load of some
6.2×10^{11} kg, Coleman et al. 1998) settle and accumulate below
the surface of the water. Coarse sediments accumulate closest to
where the river enters the sea, whereas fine particles are carried
further. An engineer named Eads once lowered himself to the
bottom of this river in a self-made diving bell and later described
his experience:

The sand was drifting like a dense snowstorm at the bottom . . .. At sixty-
five feet below the surface I found the bed of the river, for at least three
feet in depth, a moving mass and so unstable that, in endeavoring to find
a footing on it beneath my bell, my feet penetrated through it until I
could feel, although standing erect, the sand rushing past my hands,
driven by a current apparently as rapid as that on the surface.

(Barry 1997, p. 26)

During flood periods, the river flows up and over older deposits,
laying down new layers of sediment and forming natural levees. Thus
the deltaic sediments build up above the level of the ocean, producing
dry land (Figure 12.3(a)–(c)). As areas of the delta build up from accumulated sediment, water is naturally diverted to lower areas. The
higher areas then begin to subside as the sediments settle, allowing
the sea to creep inland (Figure 12.3(d), (e)); eventually the delta may
subside until only a small chain of islands or even just a shoal remains
(Boyd and Penland 1988). The natural vegetation of much of southern
Louisiana would be fresh or saltwater marshes, mixed with swamps
of baldcypress and tupelo.

During periods of falling sea level, such as occurred during the ice
ages, land formation would accelerate. During periods of rising sea
levels, such as we are in now, deposition by the river may fail to keep
pace with sea level rise, and saline water may move inland, converting the freshwater swamps and marshes back into brackish marsh,
salt marsh, or open water (Figure 12.3(d), (e)). Since the 1930s,
Louisiana has lost some 3950 km^2 (1525 mi.^{2}) of coastal wetlands,
and there is an ongoing debate as to how much this rate of loss is
natural and how much it has been accelerated by human intervention in the natural deltaic cycles.

If it were possible to view the last 10 000 years from a satellite with
a time-lapse camera, the Mississippi River would be seen to snake
back and forth from east to west across the northern Gulf of Mexico,
switching deltas every 1000 to 2000 years. At least five major deltas
can be distinguished (Figure 12.4), each with an average thickness of

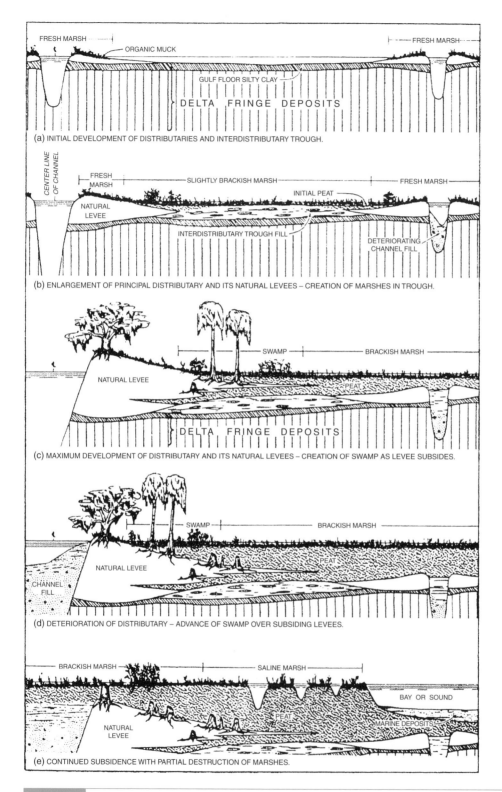

Figure 12.3 The different kinds of wetland communities found in the Mississippi River delta depend upon the rate of sediment deposition (top three panels) and the rate of sea level rise (bottom two panels) (after Bernard and LeBlanc 1965).

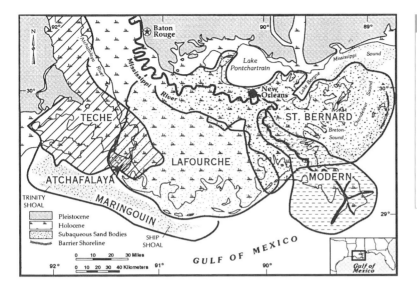

Figure 12.4 The location of the delta of the Mississippi River has shifted every few thousand years. New Orleans is built upon the now abandoned St. Bernard Delta, while active deposition today continues in the Modern Delta and the Atchafalaya Delta (from Boesch et al. 1994). Without a dam maintained by the U.S. Army Corps of Engineers, the Mississippi would likely drain entirely into the Atchafalaya region.

35 m (Coleman et al. 1998), and corresponding to a period of active sedimentation by the Mississippi River.

The oldest sediments are now those furthest to the west. About 5000 years ago the Mississippi swung back to the east, laying down the St. Bernard Delta and trapping fresh water to produce both Lake Maurepas and Lake Pontchartrain. Left alone, the Mississippi would now swing back westward and drain directly down the Atchafalaya basin at the bottom left of Figure 12.4. The new delta at the mouth of the Atchafalaya is being built at a rate of 120 to 200 ha per year (Coleman et al. 1998). If not for a barrier built by the Army Corps of Engineers, it is likely that the Mississippi River would cease flowing through New Orleans.

Since it was produced by flowing water, southern Louisiana is very flat. As the Mississippi River approaches the ocean, it flows down a negligible slope. For the last 725 km, the bed of the river is actually below sea level – 4.6 m below sea level at Vicksburg and over 52 m below sea level at New Orleans! In the words of Barry (1997) "for 450 miles or more, the water on the bottom of the river has no reason to flow at all" (p. 39).

Yearly flooding by the Mississippi River is the major factor controlling vegetation patterns. Even a difference of a few centimeters in elevation can make an enormous difference in the duration of flooding, and hence in the plant communities (recall Section 4.6.3). Many native trees are relatively intolerant of flooding; the notable exceptions, baldcypress (*Taxodium distichum*) and tupelo (*Nyssa* spp.), form enormous swamps, particularly where rivers reach the coast. Where trees cannot grow, herbaceous species such as cord grass (*Spartina* spp.), reeds (*Scirpus* spp.), and arrowhead (*Sagittaria* spp.), produce extensive areas of marsh.

Humans and the Louisiana environment

Europeans have wrought massive changes to the landscape of all of Louisiana, and the coastal regions are no exception. So extreme have the effects been that it is sometimes difficult to accurately reconstruct the original plant and animal communities. The great prairies are all but gone, reduced from hundreds of thousands to mere tens of hectares (millions to hundreds of acres). Over a few centuries Louisiana changed from a thinly populated region where natural processes predominated, to one with high population density where the landscape is largely controlled for human use.

Most histories of Louisiana place emphasis upon humans rather than landscape, but careful reading of published histories (e.g., Taylor 1984) allows one to extract some ecological themes. There were indigenous Americans in what is now Louisiana when Europeans began colonizing the Gulf Coast region. The Caddo, Atakapa, Tunica, Natchez and Chitimacha were the five dominant indigenous cultures of Louisiana. Typical villages had fewer than 500 people. The men hunted, and the women farmed corn, beans, squash, and sweet potatoes. The history of European settlement begins with New Orleans, which has had a convoluted history involving ownership by France, Spain, England, and the young United States, not to mention a period of administration by John Law's Company of the West in the early 1700s and brief participation in the doomed confederacy in the 1860s. From the perspective of human impacts upon the vegetation, there have been three over-riding factors: human population size, agriculture, and logging.

New Orleans was founded in 1717 when Louisiana was a French colony. New colonists were badly needed, but the city was so unpopular that when French convicts were offered release from prison if they would go to Louisiana, "Most preferred prison in France to freedom in America" (Taylor 1984, p. 9). A century and a half later, in the 1860s, New Orleans was considered to be the most unhealthy city in the nation. There were no sewers, except for ditches adjacent to streets. Frequent epidemics occurred (Taylor 1984). The streets were lower than the Mississippi River, and could be submerged by spring floods, hurricanes or heavy rain. Hurricanes regularly caused flooding that inundated the lower areas of the city. The first recorded hurricane hit in 1719, two years after the city was founded.

Sugar cane and cotton
Some of the wealth that built Louisiana came from burgeoning sugar plantations. Cane cultivation required eradication of the indigenous bottomland forests, drainage, construction of levees, and harvesting of fuel wood from any remaining forest remnants. While sugar was cultivated in the extreme south, cotton was more suited to the rest of Louisiana. Cotton cultivation produced another series of changes in the land. Again, the native forests were replaced by fields and protected by artificial levees to reduce flooding. Since labor was relatively expensive, and land was cheap,

> ... the cotton planter attempted to produce as much cotton as possible per worker rather than per acre. This practice led to rapid exhaustion of

the soil except along rivers and bayous, here frequent flooding deposited soil that maintained fertility; but at the time, that did not matter. More land could always be cleared and brought under the plow. Indeed, many cotton planters in Louisiana, or their fathers, had already exhausted lands farther east.

(Taylor 1984, pp. 65–66)

Cypress swamps

Baldcypress is the most flood-tolerant tree on the delta and has been commercially exploited for several centuries (Conner and Buford 1998). Its wood is resistant to rot, strong, and yet easy to work. In Louisiana, the timber trade began around 1700. Because cypress swamps were flooded for much of the year, harvesting was at first a seasonal occupation. By 1725, loggers learned to girdle the trees during the late summer and winter to kill them, after which the wood dried enough to float during high water in the spring. Loggers would work from boats or rafts to fell the tree, trim the branches, cut the trunks to log lengths, and build them into rafts. These rafts could then be floated to mills for processing. The May Brothers Company in Garden City, Louisiana once constructed a levee 2 m in height around a swamp to flood it in order to float out the logs. Ditches were also dug through swamps to carry floating logs. Early logging, then, not only removed the forest, but the spread of levees and drainage ditches began to change water levels that were essential for the re-growth of cypress trees.

Large-scale commercial logging of cypress accelerated after the Civil War when the Timber Act of 1876 declared that swampland was unsuitable for cultivation. Large tracts sold for 60 cents to $1.20 per hectare (25–50 cents per acre). Shortly thereafter, pull boats were introduced (Figure 12.5). Using cables and winches, they could pull in trees from as far away as 1500 m (almost a mile). Canals could be dug at 3000-m intervals, and entire forests systematically removed.

Figure 12.5 Pull boats allowed large-scale logging in cypress swamps (from Williams 1989).

Logs were winched toward the canals along runs spaced some 45 m part. Each run gradually was gouged into a mud- and water-filled ditch 1.8–2.4 m deep. In some places, logs were pulled into canals from one point, in which case pull boat runs radiated outwards like spokes in a wheel (Figure 12.6). Both parallel and radiating ditches are still visible to visitors flying into New Orleans today.

Dredges were often used to create secondary canals for pull boats. These canals were from 3 to 12 m wide, and from 2.4 to 3 m deep, resulting in the partial drainage of many swamps. In other areas, railway lines were laid. Between 1880 and 1910, a mere 20 years, the length of railroad in Louisiana increased from 1050 to more than 8850 km! Logging reached a peak in the early 1900s, with a billion board feet being cut in 1913. One early logger said:

> We just use the old method of going in and cutting down the swamp and tearing it up and bringing the cypress out. When a man's in here with all the heavy equipment, he might as well cut everything he can make a board foot out of; we're not ever coming back in here again.
>
> (Conner and Buford 1998, p. 280)

The entire Mississippi floodplain has had a similar history of deforestation (Llewellyn et al. 1996, Shaffer et al. 2005). Frequently, the baldcypress forests simply failed to regenerate. All along Lake Pontchartrain, for example, one can see areas of marsh with stumps, debris and the occasional stunted cypress trees as evidence of the carnage that took place between 1870 and 1920. Further, the pull boat ditches enhanced runoff from the wetlands, likely contributing to permanent changes in the water table. When the water table falls, the soil begins to decompose, so it is thought that drainage ditches actually caused gradual lowering of the land. Debris from baldcypress forest might have built up the level of the land, keeping ahead of rising sea level, but with the trees gone, the process stopped. The balance between land and sea was altered, and the former forests changed into open marsh and then open water. As if this were not enough, in areas near the coast where sea levels are rising, the old ditches serve as conduits to carry surges of salt water back into the marsh. The salt water kills young baldcypress trees. Pull boat logging, therefore, not only removed the forest, but permanently changed the physical nature of the landscape.

Artificial levees have also caused serious damage to wetlands. New Orleans was founded on a natural levee of the Mississippi River created by river floodwaters, and, by 1726, artificial levees from 1.2 to 1.8 m in height provided additional protection for the city. Levees were gradually extended upstream and downstream from New Orleans, and then to the opposite bank. As the levees grew in length and height, the water was confined to narrower areas, and so, naturally, the water began to rise higher. By 1812 there were more than 240 km of levee on each side of the river. Following severe floods, the federal government proclaimed the Swamp Land Acts of 1849 and 1850 which gave the swamps and

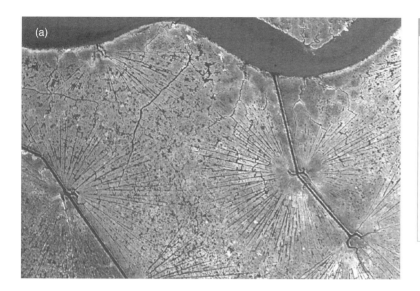

(a)

Figure 12.6 An aerial view of the wetlands south of Pass Manchac in Louisiana (a) shows the scars left by pull boat logging (Figure 12.5) that occurred about 100 years ago. The typical logging operation is sketched in (b). Larger channels were dredged to allow the pull boats to enter the swamps and smaller channels were gouged into the mud as the cypress tress were dragged toward the pull boat. These channels have permanently altered the hydrology of the floodplain (from Williams 1989)

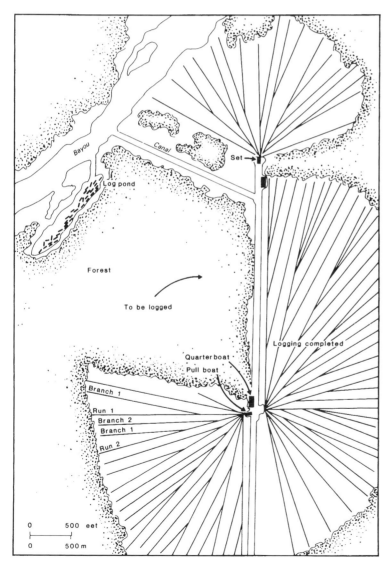

Bayou

Canal

Set

Log pond

Forest

To be logged

Logging completed

Quarterboat
Pull boat

Branch 1
Run 1
Branch 2
Branch 1
Run 2

| 0 | 500 | eet |
| 0 | 500 | m |

land overflowed to the state. The sale of these lands to private owners was to provide money for constructing improved levees (Davis 2000). In 1858 the length of levees exceeded 1600 km (Barry 1997). In some cases these levees rose to a height of 11.5 m. Today 3545 km of levee have been built to corral the Mississippi waters – 2586 km along the Mississippi itself and 959 km along the banks of the Red and Arkansas rivers and in the Atchafalaya basin (U.S. Army Corps of Engineers 2004).

Increasing resources are now being allocated to restoring the baldcypress forests of Louisiana. It is a race against time, since rising sea level and subsiding land are allowing the sea to creep further inland each year. Once marshes are saline, they cannot be replanted to forest. It is sobering to think that even if baldcypress trees can be replanted, it will be a thousand years until Louisiana recovers its forest. Logging companies profited by cutting growth that began a thousand years ago, from trees that were already 500 years old when Columbus discovered the New World, trees that were already large before there were telescopes or printing presses, much less electricity and telephones. Ancient trees are a form of ecological capital that cannot easily be replaced. This much time must elapse again; at four generations per century, it will be some 40 generations from now, around 3000 AD, before these marshlands might again support the ancient cypress trees that were common here until the early part of the last century.

In summary, some of the major effects of humans on alluvial forest have included: (1) clearing for cotton and cane plantations, (2) logging of baldcypress, (3) construction of logging ditches and shipping canals that altered fresh water flows and enhanced salt water intrusion, and (4) construction of artificial levees that reduced the natural spread of fresh water and silt. These, by themselves, have produced major changes in the vegetation of southern Louisiana. Superimposed upon these have been further stresses, but there is insufficient space to describe them: the spread of non-native organisms (e.g., nutria, tallow trees), the discharge of nitrogenous fertilizer in regions higher in the Mississippi watershed, suppression of natural fire regimes, over-harvesting of food species (e.g., bison and passenger pigeons (now extinct in Louisiana), alligators, drum, menhaden and crabs), urban sprawl around Baton Rouge and New Orleans, and the discharge of toxic wastes from chemical industries along the lower Mississippi River.

In late summer 2005 two hurricanes, Katrina and Rita, hit the Louisiana coast within the same month. More than 1000 people were killed and some 25 000 ha of marsh was converted to open water, while estimates of property loss exceed 50 billion dollars and projected economic damages may exceed 100 billion dollars. My house, too, was damaged by these events. As this book goes to press, debates about the future of coastal Louisiana continue. Some wish to rebuild coastal communities as before but with stronger levees, while others recommend comprehensive restoration of coastal wetlands, and others suggest admitting defeat and withdrawing from coastal areas entirely. The debate is bound to be intensified by new data

Table 12.1. *Plant communities of Louisiana judged at risk of disappearing from the landscape of the southeastern United States (after White et al. 1998).*

Status	Plant community
>98 percent loss (critically endangered)	Wet and mesic coastal prairies
85–98 percent loss (endangered)	Longleaf pine
	Mississippi terrace prairie, calcareous prairie, Fleming glades
	Live oak, live oak-hackberry
	Prairie terrace-loess oak forest
	Mature forest, all types
	Short-leaf pine-oak-hickory
	Mixed hardwood-loblolly pine
	Xeric sandhill
	Stream terrace-sandy woodland-savannah
70–84 percent loss (threatened)	Saline prairie
	Upland longleaf pine
	Live oak-pine-magnolia
	Spruce pine-hardwood flatwoods
	Xeric sandhill woodlands
	Flatwood ponds
	Slash pine-pondypress-hardwood
	Wet hardwood-loblolly pine
60–70 percent loss	Southern mesophytic forest
	Calcareous forest
50–60 percent loss	Hardwood slope forest
	Freshwater marsh, interior saline marsh, interior salt flat
	Scrub-scrub swamp
	Baldcypress-tupelo swamp
	Bayhead swamp
	Small stream forest
	Bottomland hardwoods
	Cedar woodlands

(e.g., Miller et al. 2005, Dowdeswell 2006), which suggest that sea level will rise higher and faster than previously anticipated. You may wish to consult recent sources for the latest on the story of coastal Louisiana, and treat this issue as a case study of how humans will (or will not) cope with changing climate and sea level.

Louisiana is a small area, but an illustration of the extensive environmental damage caused by humans across southeastern North America (Williams 1989, Silver 1990, Turner 1994, Stein et al. 2000). Table 12.1 shows the status of the distinctive types of ecosystems on the southeastern coastal plain of North America. This table does not list individual species that are at risk, but rather entire plant communities, involving perhaps dozens or even hundreds of individual species. Several categories of risk are recognized (White et al. 1998): critically endangered (more than 98 percent lost), endangered (85–98 percent lost), and threatened (70–84 percent lost). There are 14 critically endangered communities, 25 that are listed as endangered and 11 that are considered threatened. Of these, an astonishing 18 – about one-third – occur in Louisiana. Examples include wet coastal prairies (critically endangered), all types of mature forest (endangered), dry sandhill communities (endangered), longleaf pine forests (endangered), live oak-pine-magnolia (threatened) and flatwood ponds (threatened).

12.3.2 Islands: Easter Island and the Galapagos

The long-term results of population growth in a limited world may be deduced by studying the fate of human societies where isolation created a strict boundary to expansion. According to Diamond (1994), more than a dozen isolated civilizations on islands have collapsed so completely that no survivors remained! Easter Island: "the most remote habitable scrap of land in the world" (p. 365) is famous for its hundreds of giant stone statues of heads, statues that were carved and dragged many miles overland by a Stone Age people (Figure 12.7).

Figure 12.7 Easter Island monoliths in front of the Rano Raraku quarry (from Englert 1970).

Easter Island, created by three volcanic eruptions, is just 170 km^2 and lies isolated by thousands of kilometres of ocean from any other land. When the Polynesians first arrived in the fifth century BC, the island was covered with palm forest. According to Diamond (2004) and Wright (2004), population density grew to 60 people per square kilometre, and soon the forests were cleared. The large statues for which the island is known could no longer be transported and erected without logs to use as rollers and levers. For a generation or so after the last tree was felled, old lumber could still be used, but soon there was insufficient wood to build ocean going canoes (cutting off the food supply) or to provide roof beams (cutting off the supply of housing). By the time Europeans arrived (the Dutch explorer, Jacob Roggeveen, arrived on Easter day in 1722), there had been destitution, multiple clan wars, and many of the survivors lived in caves. The remaining sources of protein were humans and closely-guarded chickens.

The decisive moment came when the last tree was cut. How is it that this island society was unable to appreciate the need for conservation? In the words of Wright (2004):

> We might think that in such a limited place, where from the height of Terevaka, islanders could survey their whole world at a glance, steps would have been taken to halt the cutting, to protect the saplings, to replant . . . . The people who felled the last tree could *see* that it was the last, could know with complete certainty that there would never be another. And they felled it anyway.
>
> (p. 60)

Although Easter Island seemed to offer a clear cut story with an important lesson, you should know that there are sceptics who question both the details of the story and the lesson (Young 2006). Critics suggest that European diseases and slave raiding may have been responsible for the population decline. Even the name, Easter Island, is questioned – the current residents call the island Rapa Nui. Future archaeological studies might help clarify details of the history and resolve some of this controversy – unless the evidence is eradicated by bulldozers. In the latest phase of Easter Island history, residents are planning a casino, golf course, hotels and resorts. Perhaps its role as a modern morality tale continues.

Let us now consider another isolated archipelago off the west coast of South America, the one that the young Charles Darwin visited in 1835 and where he was stimulated to think about natural selection – the Galapagos Islands. These islands are of conservation interest because they already have a degree of protection in Galapagos National Park (created in 1968), and they have a rich endemic flora and fauna.

The history of the Galapagos was surveyed by Rose (1924); Lack (1947) summarizes this history as being "mainly a tale of disaster, tempered by squalid crime." The human population was under 10 000 in 1989. The island of Pinta has been the focus of recent vegetation studies, and therefore offers some interesting examples of island

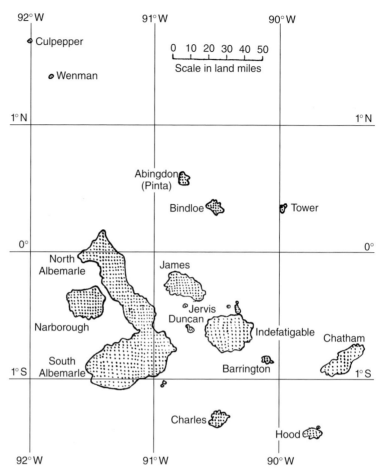

Figure 12.8 The island of Pinta in the Galapagos Islands (from Lack 1947).

conservation (Hamann 1979, 1993, Whelan and Hamann 1989). Pinta makes up only 0.75 percent of the total land surface of the archipelago; it is somewhat isolated even from the rest of the Galapagos islands, being one of the northern islands and one rarely visited by scientists and tourists. This island is 59 km^2 and has an altitudinal range of 650 m (Figure 12.8). Because of the variation in elevation, the diversity of plants and animals is higher than that of the other Galapagos islands. No less than 180 taxa of higher plants are known, of which 59 are endemic to the Galapagos; two taxa *Scalesia baurii* ssp. *hopkinsii* (the Pinta sunflower-tree) and *Alternanthera filifolia* spp. *pintensis* are endemic to Pinta. There are no native land mammals and only three native reptiles – the giant tortoise, marine iguana, and lava lizard.

Many areas on the island are open forest known as dry season deciduous steppe forest in which *Bursera graveolens* and *Opuntia galapageia* form an open-canopied tree layer with a scattered shrub understorey. Grazing by tortoises can create a distinctive type of vegetation, in which forested areas are interspersed with open, meadow-like areas (Figure 12.9). The meadows contain herbaceous species that continually grow new tissue the tortoises consume; in the absence of grazing,

Figure 12.9 A tortoise meadow created by grazing, surrounded by woody species which would otherwise dominate the landscape (from Hamann 1993).

tree-like forms predominate, often with foliage higher than tortoises can reach. On less fertile islands where droughts are particularly severe, tortoises have an elevated front on their carapace which allows them to reach higher to consume the lower foliage of woody plants and cacti (Figure 12.10). These sorts of obvious differences in tortoises are one kind of evidence of the nature of natural selection (even if, as is so often the case, the birds get most of the attention).

As with other isolated islands, buccaneers and whalers took a heavy toll on the animal life. During the 1600s to 1800s, it is estimated that more than 100 000 tortoises were taken off the islands, often to be carried away alive, and tied to the deck as a source of fresh meat on the long voyage across the Pacific. Two of the original 15 subspecies were hunted to extinction. In addition, the Pinta Island tortoise appears to be represented by a single remaining individual, Lonesome George, who today lives at the Charles Darwin Research Station on Santa Cruz Island. American whalers took 4545 tortoises from Pinta during the period 1831–1868 alone; the last known female was taken in 1901, and the last three males were collected by the California Academy of Sciences in 1906. Lonesome George was discovered in 1971 and caught in 1972; no further tortoises have been seen on Pinta, but a single, dried tortoise scat found in 1981 brings hope that Lonesome George may not be the last (Pritchard 1996).

In the 1950s goats were introduced to Pinta, where they multiplied extremely rapidly and soon had a very negative impact on the vegetation. It is thought that a local fisherman introduced one male and two female goats, but by the early 1970s, it is estimated that some 10 000 goats were present. Closed forest and scrub were opened, soil erosion started, and natural regeneration of several plant species was prevented. The Galapagos National Park Service began a goat eradication campaign, and the last goats were killed in 1990. Permanent quadrats are being used to monitor the recovery of plants.

Figure 12.10 The shape of the front of the carapace allows some Galapagos tortoise subspecies to reach higher than others in search of food during drought (from Pritchard 1996).

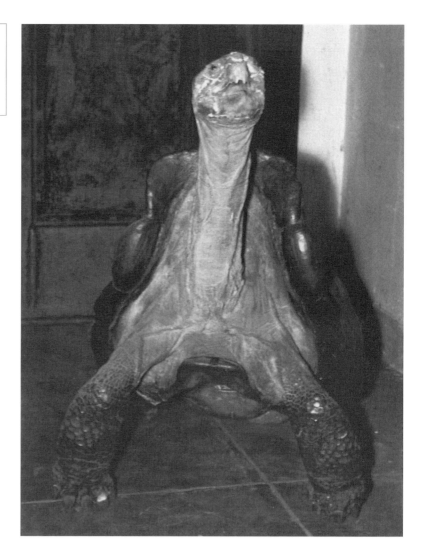

While the short-term recovery of vegetation is to be expected, and is indeed occurring, the longer-term prospects are problematic. The destructive overgrazing by goats has ended, but now the island lacks a large herbivore, and the meadows once created by tortoises can be expected to gradually fill in with woody plants (Figure 12.11). "So absence of grazers will perhaps in the long term lead to both the disappearance of herb-grass meadows as a vegetation type on Pinta, and to the disappearance from Pinta of an endemic species, which is only known from this island and Marchena" (Hamann 1993). What of those species that may require tortoises for processing and dispersing their seeds? In the absence of further discoveries of tortoises from this island, conservation managers are faced with a dilemma. Should nothing be done? Should another subspecies of tortoise be introduced to replace the native population? Can Lonesome George be mated with the most genetically similar species and his offspring used to repopulate the island?

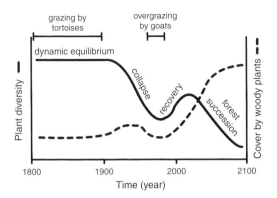

12.3.3 Boreal forests

A recent study of frontier forest, defined according to seven criteria by Bryant et al. (1997), showed that fully half of the world's frontier forests lie within two countries: Russia and Canada (nearly 7 million km^2 of frontier forest). Within Canada, the entire southern margin of the boreal forest is considered to be under medium or high threat, and the same is true of Eurasia. In Canada, there are 10 national parks within the boreal forest that together comprise 83 000 km^2, but these parks represent only 15 of the 48 recognized types of boreal forest. As great areas of remaining boreal forest are clear-cut, largely by the pulp and paper industry, there is increasing debate about whether clear-cutting is an appropriate management tool. As the vast majority of the boreal forest lies outside existing and proposed parks, what management is appropriate here? Some argue that clear-cutting simulates fire; others insist that it does not. Heinselman's (1981) observations on the importance of different intensities of fire would seem relevant, since clear-cutting will generally remove the trees but not the buried seeds or roots of hardwood trees. Thus in order to obtain good conifer regeneration, it is often necessary to use herbicides to kill the regenerating herbaceous plants and hardwoods.

One important study on the effects of logging was recently completed in an area of Canada known as the clay belt (Section 10.4.2) because it is covered with thick flat deposits of clay. The clay belt is dominated by extensive stands of *Picea mariana*. The intermixed deciduous species produce large volumes of seed and can re-sprout from stumps or roots. Despite the efficiency with which deciduous species multiply and disperse, they are, however, subordinate to the conifers, presumably because the evergreen conifers are more tolerant of the extremes of boreal climate.

Data from 131 clear-cut stands were compared with 250 stands that had regenerated naturally after fire (Carleton and MacLellan 1994). Multivariate analysis of these data showed that after accounting for site effects such as soil type and moisture availability, the kind of disturbance was very important in controlling the regenerating forest.

In particular, it was possible to distinguish among three different kinds of disturbance: wildfire, horse logging, and mechanized logging. In general, *Abies balsamea* dominated woodlands produced after fire. This same species was common at sites that were logged using horses, presumably because seedlings in the understorey were not damaged and could rapidly replace the removed trees. Areas that had recently been logged with heavy equipment, however, tended to regenerate with deciduous species rather than conifers; the intense disturbance had somehow tipped the balance against conifer regeneration, so that the trees once suppressed by conifers were instead becoming dominant. Carleton and MacLellan conclude: "Comparison between postfire and postlogged woody vegetation data provides evidence of a massive conversion from needle-leaved, conifer-dominated ecosystems to broad-leaved, deciduous forest and shrub ecosystems as a result of logging activity." A long-term study of regeneration in monitored strip-cuts shows many of the same patterns; particularly the risk of conversion from conifers to hardwoods (Jeglum 1983).

In conclusion, boreal forests normally consist of a mosaic of conifers of different sizes and ages regenerating from past fires with cycles of around one to two centuries (see also Section 11.7.4). The reintroduction of fire to national parks, and perhaps to non-park areas, will remain a future challenge for plant ecologists. Parks Canada is committed to "have fires burn whenever feasible and reintroduce fire where man has altered the natural balance through fire's exclusion" (Lopoukhine 1983). Fire will first be restored within two pilot national parks, Kluane and Nahanni, perhaps conveniently two of the most northern and isolated parks in the system.

12.4 | Protection of representative vegetation types

12.4.1 Designing reserve systems

As the twenty-first century begins, the first challenge for plant ecologists is to ensure that significant areas of landscape are protected from further degradation of structure and function. Once these areas are protected, the next generation of managers will have to grapple with their wise management. One challenge in setting up networks of protected areas is to make future management as easy as possible. The design of reserves, and of reserve systems, is a topic that deserves an entire book (e.g., Shrader-Frechette and McCoy 1993, Noss and Cooperrider 1994); a brief introduction has been provided by Noss (1995). There are six basic steps to follow when designing and maintaining a representative reserve system (Figure 12.12):

1. *Classification* of landscape based on physical features (topography, surficial geology, soils) and vegetation types (including serial stages) to enumerate the habitat types that are present and should be represented in the system of protected areas.

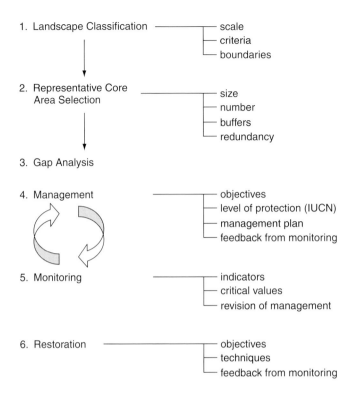

1. Landscape Classification
   - scale
   - criteria
   - boundaries

2. Representative Core Area Selection
   - size
   - number
   - buffers
   - redundancy

3. Gap Analysis

4. Management
   - objectives
   - level of protection (IUCN)
   - management plan
   - feedback from monitoring

5. Monitoring
   - indicators
   - critical values
   - revision of management

6. Restoration
   - objectives
   - techniques
   - feedback from monitoring

Figure 12.12 Six steps toward a functioning reserve system.

2. *Identification* of core protected areas that represent the habitats identified in 1. Topics to be considered at this stage include area, number, redundancy, and buffer zones.

3. *Gap analysis*, that is, reinspection of step 2 to determine if any habitat types are misssing.

4. *Management* of each site/core area to retain values that led to the area's initial selection. This will be a growing challenge to young plant ecologists.

5. *Monitoring* the results of management to ensure management achieves the desired outcome. This requires selecting indicators, determining critical limits for them, and, most importantly, ensuring that management practices change if management objectives are not being met.

6. *Restoration* may be required if the best example of an ecosystem type is already damaged, or if it has been lost entirely and an attempt at re-creation is made.

Beginning with the core protected area, the **size** of each protected area of landscape should be large enough to retain the diversity of vegetation types and full array of species present. The well-documented relationship between species richness and area (Section 11.2) shows that, in general, the bigger the site the more species that are likely to be protected. Big areas have two particular merits. Big areas are important to maintain large mobile predators that need large territories (Weber and Rabinowitz 1996). As well, the bigger the site, the greater the possibility that natural processes can continue to generate or maintain habitat diversity. A boreal forest reserve, for example, has to be large enough to allow wild fires to produce a mosaic of forest stands of different ages (Section 12.3.3). An alluvial wetland reserve ought to be large enough to allow flooding and bank erosion to continue unabated (Section 6.6.3). If these processes are missing, it may be impossible to retain the biological characteristics of the reserve, and it certainly will compound the difficulties and costs of management. Many other factors can be used to select core protected areas including naturalness, significance, rare species, ecological functions, and value for research (Table 12.2). Each protected area needs to be surrounded by a **buffer zone**; in this zone, land-use practices may have to be regulated to higher standards than elsewhere in order to ensure that nutrients, pollution, or exotic species are not carried into the protected site from immediately adjoining areas. Biosphere reserves (an international conservation designation given by the United Nations Educational, Scientific and Cultural Organization, UNESCO) provide an example of such an arrangement, with protected core areas, such as a national park, surrounded by larger landscapes in which human use considers the viability of the core area.

Table 12.2. | *Some important factors for selecting and prioritizing natural areas for conservation. These are listed in approximate order of importance.*

Factor	Comments
Area	All important ecological values and functions increase with area
Naturalness	Minimal alteration to natural patterns and processes
Representation	Serves as an example of one or more important ecosystem types
Significance	Relative global importance: existing area of this habitat, rates of loss, percent of habitat type protected, better examples protected elsewhere?
Rare species	Globally and regionally significant species present
Diversity	Supports many native species
Productivity	Good production of commercial species (but high production may reduce rare species and diversity)
Hydrological functions	Flood reduction, groundwater recharge
Social functions	Education, tourism, recreation
Carrier functions	Contribution to global life support system: oxygen production, nitrogen fixation, carbon storage
Food functions	Harvesting of species for human consumption
Special functions	Spawning or nesting area, migratory stop over
Potential	Potential for restoration to recover lost values and functions
Prospects	Probability of long-term survival: future threats, buffer zones, possibilities for expansion, patrons, supporting organizations
Corridors	Existing connections to other protected areas or site itself is a corridor
Science function	Published work on site, existing use by scientists, existing research station, potential for future research

At a broader scale, protected areas should **represent** habitat types that are of significance at the local, regional, or global scale. This is why we spent some time exploring the classification of vegetation types in Chapters 2 and 10. A particular reserve may represent a common vegetation type and serve as a protected example of a common landscape feature, or it may represent a rare vegetation type. Protection of both typical and rare features are complementary objectives for setting up reserve systems. A candidate core area also needs to be considered in the context of habitat types already protected: are there similar examples already protected? Are there more important vegetation types that are not yet protected? This process is often termed "gap analysis," and algorithms now exist to evaluate reserve scenarios in order to maximize the ecological value of a reserve system (Scott et al. 1987, Pressey et al. 1993, Rodrigues et al. 2004). The objective is to define the smallest number of sites needed to achieve certain goals, such as providing one, two, or three protected areas for each species or each community type.

12.4.2 Hot spots of biological diversity

With six billion people multiplying and encroaching upon the natural areas of Earth, reducing them to ever smaller remnants, it is important to know which areas of the Earth are the highest priority for conservation efforts. We cannot save everything. One promising approach has been the identification of "hot spots," relatively small regions of the Earth that have very high biological diversity. The first publication on hot spots, prepared by Myers (1988), was based entirely upon plant species richness and identified 18 global hot spots. More recent work has expanded the list to 25 (Figure 12.13). The criterion for hot spot designation is that the area must have at least 0.5 percent of all plant species worldwide as endemics. Table 12.3 supplements the map in Figure 12.13, listing the 25 hot spots, the number of plant species they contain in total, and the number of endemics. This tells us something about their relative conservation **value**. Table 12.3 also shows the relative degree of **risk**, indicated by the percent of primary vegetation that remains in each hot spot. Some of the areas most at risk according to this criterion are the Philippines (97 percent lost) and Indo-Burma (95 percent lost). The hot spots with the lowest risk seem to be central Chile, New Caledonia, and the Succulent Karoo of South Africa – but even these have already lost more than 70 percent of their natural vegetation cover! Myers et al. (2000) estimate that the 25 hot spots in total contain more than 133 000 plant species and 9645 vertebrates species – species that are confined to a total of only 2.1 million square kilometers or 1.4 percent of the Earth's land surface.

The richest hotspot for plants is the Tropical Andes of South America (Young et al. 2002, Conservation International 2006) – with approximately 45 000 plant species (Table 12.3). This region extends from elevations as low as 0.5 km to peaks exceeding 6 km, and spans a latitudinal range from Argentina to Venezuela. Recall that von Humboldt visited this area early in his career (Box 2.1) and set a

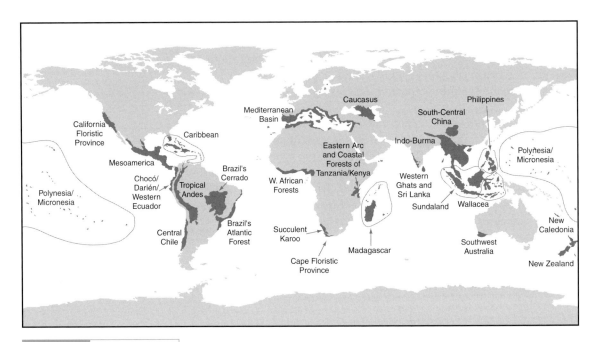

Figure 12.13 Twenty-five hotspots with high plant diversity (from Myers et al. 2000). See Table 12.3.

world altitude record while climbing Mount Chimborazo. The hotspot includes tropical forests, montane cloud forests, thorn scrub, high elevation grasslands, and alpine communities (páramo). Overall, it contains roughly a sixth of all plant species in the world. Such high plant diversity in the Andes is consistent with earlier chapters, where we encountered the importance of gradients in general, and altitude in particular, in generating plant diversity (Figure 10.4, Figure 11.3).

The final column in Table 12.3 shows the number of square kilometers of hot spot area that were protected when that table was compiled in 2000. The word "protected" must be used with caution since some protected areas may exist only on paper, and are still at risk from factors including deforestation, settlement, and even changing climate. Even so, the good news is that an area slightly in excess of $800\,000\,\text{km}^2$ has some form of protected status, and this makes up 38 percent of the land area in hotspots. A gap analysis of the global protected areas system in 2004 found that many species remain unprotected, particularly those restricted to the mountains of South and Central America, and to islands in the Arabian Sea and South Pacific Ocean (Rodrigues et al. 2004). While 11.5 percent of the Earth's surface has been protected within reserves at the time of writing this book, the process of acquisition and protection will have to be accelerated and focussed in the coming decades.

12.4.3 Primary forests

Another approach to setting priorities is to identify areas of primary forest – forest that has not yet been subjected to commercial logging. Not all areas of primary forest have high biological diversity. The boreal forest of the north, for example, has relatively low plant

Table 12.3. *More information on the 25 hotspots of plant diversity mapped in Figure 12.13, ordered by the number of plant species found (Myers et al. 2000).*

	Original extent of vegetation (km²)	Plant species	Endemic plants (% of global plants, 300 000)	Percent of original extent remaining	Percent of area protected
New Zealand	270 500	2 300	0.60	22.0	87.7
New Caledonia	18 600	3 332	0.90	28.0	10.1
Eastern Arc and coastal forests of Tanzania/ Kenya	30 000	4 000	0.50	6.7	100.0
Western Ghats/ Sri Lanka	182 500	4 780	0.70	6.8	100.0
Succulent Karoo	112 000	4 849	0.60	26.8	7.8
SW Australia	309 850	5 469	1.40	10.8	100.0
Caucasus	500 000	6 300	0.50	10.0	28.1
Polynesia/Micronesia	46 000	6 557	1.10	21.8	49.0
Philippines	300 800	7 620	1.90	3.0	43.3
Cape Floristic Province	74 000	8 200	1.90	24.3	78.1
Western African forests	1 265 000	9 000	0.80	10.0	16.1
Chocó/Darién/Western Ecuador	260 600	9 000	0.80	24.2	26.1
Brazil's Cerrado	1 783 200	10 000	1.50	20.0	6.2
Central Chile	300 000	10 000	0.50	30.0	10.2
California Floristic Province	324 000	10 000	0.70	24.7	39.3
Wallacea	347 000	10 000	0.50	15.0	39.2
South-Central China	800 000	12 000	1.20	8.0	25.9
Caribbean	263 500	12 000	2.30	11.3	100.0
Madagascar	594 150	12 000	3.20	9.9	19.6
Indo-Burma	2 060 000	13 500	2.30	4.9	100.0
Brazil's Atlantic Forest	1 227 600	20 000	2.70	7.5	35.9
Mesoamerica	1 155 000	24 000	1.70	20.0	59.9
Mediterranean Basin	2 362 000	25 000	4.30	4.7	38.3
Sundaland	1 600 000	25 000	5.00	7.8	72.0
Tropical Andes	1 258 000	45 000	6.70	25.0	25.3
Totals	17 434 300	N/A	44.0	12.2	37.7

diversity, but may have other important features such as wilderness values and carbon storage functions. On the other hand, any primary forests in areas such as Madagascar, Brazil or the Philippines are also likely to be of great value for biological diversity.

A study on the loss of world forests (Bryant et al. 1997) concludes that while the greatest areas at risk are in the boreal regions, the greatest threats to biodiversity occur in Brazil and Colombia. Brazil has by far the largest remaining area of frontier forest, more than 2 million km², with some 36 000 plant species therein (Table 12.4).

Table 12.4. *Ten countries with the highest plant diversity in their frontier forests (from Bryant et al. 1997).*

Global rank	Country	Frontier forest (1000 km^2)	Estimated no. plant species within frontier forests (thousands)[a]	Approximate percentage of the country's plant species found within frontier forests
1	Brazil	2284	36	65
2	Colombia	348	34	70
3	Indonesia	530	18	65
4	Venezuela	391	15	75
5	Peru	540	13	75
6	Ecuador	80	12	65
7	Bolivia	255	10	60
8	Mexico	87	9	35
9	Malaysia	47	8	50
10	Papua New Guinea	172	7	70

Note:
[a] Frontier forest plant species richness was estimated by multiplying the country's higher totals per unit area (standardized for size, using a species-area curve) by the country's total frontier forest area.

Note that while the area of forest at risk in Colombia is much smaller, it contains nearly as many plant species. The map in Figure 12.14 shows that vast areas of this region are at medium or high levels of threat, with further areas not assessed owing to a lack of data.

12.4.4 Large wetlands

Wetlands perform a variety of ecological services including primary production, carbon sequestration, flood control, the removal of nutrients from water, food production, and maintenance of biological diversity (Sather and Smith 1984, de Groot 1992, Keddy 2000, Mitsch and Gosselink 2000). Often these services are directly related to the area of the wetland. For example, there is a direct relationship between the area of wetlands and fish production, in both Africa (Welcomme 1976, 1979) and the Gulf of Mexico (Turner 1977). Given that other functions too are likely to be related to area, it may be helpful to identify the largest wetlands in the world. Figure 12.15 and Table 12.5 show that the two largest wetlands in the world are the West Siberian Lowland and the Amazon River basin. The former is a vast peatland, which may have great significance as a reservoir of stored carbon. The latter has the largest flow of fresh water in the world, and supports some of the world's highest diversity of trees and fish.

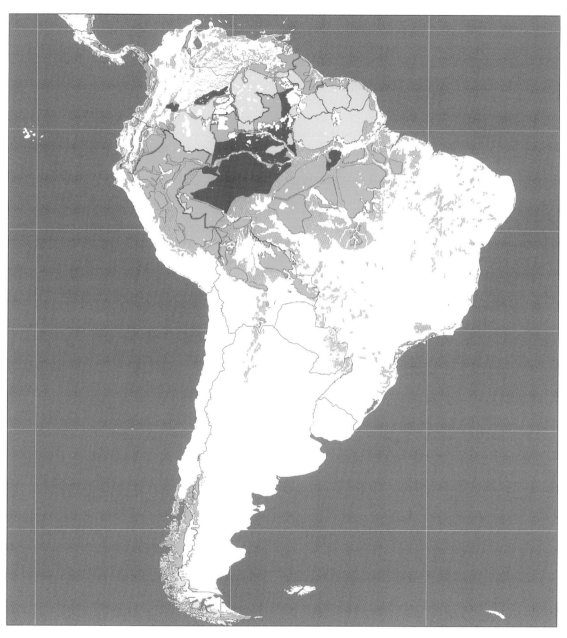

FRONTIER FORESTS UNDER
LOW OR NO THREAT:
large, intact natural forest ecosystems
that are relatively undisturbed and
large enough to maintain all of their
biodiversity.

FRONTIER FORESTS UNDER
MEDIUM OR HIGH THREAT:
ongoing or planned human activities
(e.g. logging, agricultural clearing,
mining) will, if continued, significantly degrade these frontiers.

NON-FRONTIER FORESTS:
secondary forest, plantations, degraded
forest, and patches of primary forest
not meeting this study's criteria as
frontier.

FRONTIER FORESTS
UNASSESSED FOR THREAT:
insufficient information prevented
evaluating the threat level of these
frontiers.

Figure 12.14 Threatened frontier forests of South America (from Bryant et al. 1997). For a global context, see Table 12.4.

Table 12.5. *The world's largest wetlands, with areas rounded to the nearest 1000 km² (from Fraser and Keddy 2005).*

Rank	Continent	Wetland	Description	Area (km²)
1	Eurasia	West Siberian Lowland	Bogs, mires, fens	2 745 000
2	South America	Amazon River basin	Floodplain forest and savanna, marshes, mangrove	1 738 000
3	North America	Hudson Bay Lowland	Bogs, fens, swamps, marshes	374 000
4	Africa	Congo River basin	Swamps, riverine forest, wet prairie	189 000
5	North America	Mackenzie River basin	Bogs, fens, swamps, marshes	166 000
6	South America	Pantanal	Savannas, grasslands, riverine forest	138 000
7	North America	Mississippi River basin	Bottomland hardwood forest, swamps, marshes	108 000
8	Africa	Lake Chad basin	Grass and shrub savanna, marshes	106 000
9	Africa	River Nile basin	Swamps, marshes	92 000
10	North America	Prairie potholes	Marshes, meadows	63 000
11	South America	Magellanic moorland	Bogs	44 000

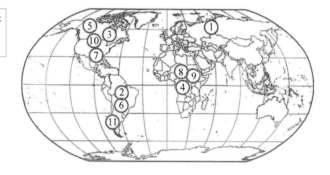

Figure 12.15 The world's largest wetlands (from Keddy and Fraser 2005). See Table 12.5.

1 West Siberian Lowland
2 Amazon River basin
3 Hudson Bay Lowland
4 Congo River basin
5 Mackenzie River basin
6 Pantanal

7 Mississippi River basin
8 Lake Chad basin
9 River Nile basin
10 Prairie potholes
11 Magellanic moorland

12.4.5 New discoveries of species in the Guyana highlands

Some poorly known areas of the world are still yielding new discoveries. One example is the sandstone tepui of the Guyana highlands in northern South America. Tepui are table mountains from 1000 to 1600 m above sea level formed from fragments of an old plateau capped by Precambrian sandstone and now isolated within a larger area of lowland forest. The soil is thick, sandy, and acidic, with

(a)

(b)

Figure 12.16 General view of the vegetation on tepui, or inselbergs, showing patches of herbaceous and shrub vegetation, dominated by (a) *Stylosanthetum guianensis* and (b) *Pepinietum geyskesii* (from Sarthou and Villiers 1998).

scattered areas of peat. The plateaux are waterlogged during the rainy season (April–October) and dry in the winter. Lowland forests, montane forests, scrublands, savannas, sub-tepui grasslands, and highland vegetation can all be found in relatively small geographical areas.

In Brazil, at least 12 different vegetation types can be found on tepuis, ranging from open vegetation rooted in rock crevices to bogs (Prance and Johnson 1991). The list of species from bogs includes genera such as *Drosera*, *Saxofridericia*, *Xyris*, and *Utricularia*. Four plant families dominate the flora: Rubiaceae, Melastomataceae, Orchidaceae, and Cyperaceae. In nearby French Guyana, Sarthou and Villiers (1998) identified six vegetation types, dominated by Cyperaceae, Poaceae, Lentibulariaceae, and Bromeliaceae; they use the German name "inselberg" to describe these isolated rock outcrops (Figure 12.16). New species of amphibians, reptiles and mammals continue to be described from these habitats (e.g. Ochoa et al. 1993, Myers and Donnelly 1997).

12.4.6 Economic growth, human welfare, and wilderness

A major obstacle to protection is the view that protecting ecosystems means withdrawing them from human use and thereby reducing human economic welfare. The functions performed by wetlands illustrate that this simplistic protect-versus-use dichotomy does not exist; shrimp and fish production are, for example, dependent upon salt marshes and floodplains (Welcomme 1976, Turner 1977). Functions (such as food production, carbon storage, and watershed protection) may provide economic arguments for preservation. Even if the obvious production functions are ignored, however, there is a further merit to protected areas: contrary to expectation, it appears that they actually stimulate economic activity (Rasker and Hackman 1996). Owing to the importance of this assertion, it is necessary to spend some time on this example.

Rasker and Hackman begin by examining the difficulty encountered when protecting natural areas for large carnivores. There is a belief that a choice is required between environment and economy: "A belief that, however appealing, carnivore conservation is a luxury we cannot afford because the opportunity cost in terms of jobs and resources forgone is too high." This is a commonly heard argument around the world; what may be surprising is the paucity of data for or against it. Rasker and Hackman set out to test this proposition by comparing economic indicators for two regions in northwestern Montana. Four counties with large protected areas (Flathead, Lewis and Clark, Teton, Powell) are compared to three resource-extractive counties (Lincoln, Sanders, Mineral). The wilderness counties total about 3.4 million ha (839 000 protected), whereas the resource-extractive counties total nearly 2 million ha (33 000 protected). These particular resource-extractive counties were chosen because the conflicts between jobs and environment are intense and because timber harvesting and hard rock mining have traditionally played an important part in their economies. Although these are only counties, they are the size of nations in many other parts of the globe. If, indeed, "locking up" land in reserves causes economic hardship, then the counties with protected areas should show reduced economic performance relative to the counties with few protected lands. Figure 12.17 shows the striking results. Based on a range of economic indicators, which included personal income growth (a) and unemployment rate (b), counties with large protected areas performed well. The results for these counties were above the USA and Montana averages and also above the means for the resource-extractive counties: "From 1969 to 1992 wilderness counties added new jobs and income in every non-agricultural sector of the economy. The resource-extractive counties lost more than 1,300 jobs in the construction, transportation, and public utilities sectors." The resource-extractive counties also suffered from higher unemployment rates. Rasker and Hackman conclude:

> The bulk of growth in the Greater Yellowstone was in industries that do not rely on natural resources extracted from the ecosystem.

(a)

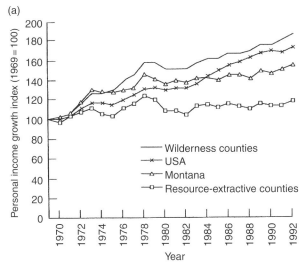

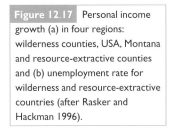

Figure 12.17 Personal income growth (a) in four regions: wilderness counties, USA, Montana and resource-extractive counties and (b) unemployment rate for wilderness and resource-extractive countries (after Rasker and Hackman 1996).

(b)

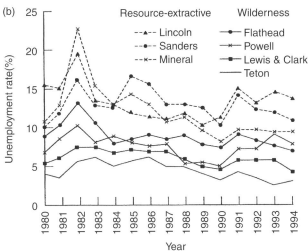

From 1969 to 1992 more than 99% of all the new jobs and personal income (and 88% of existing jobs) came from industries other than mining, logging, and ranching or farming . . .. Research on the economy of the Greater Yellowstone has uncovered a new paradigm for economic development in the West: protection of the wild and scenic character of the landscape and the quality of life in local communities serves as a magnet to retain local people and their businesses. These qualities are a vital part of the economic well-being of local residents . . ..

12.5 | Fragmentation of natural landscapes

The importance of large reserves, and interconnected reserve systems, is reinforced by the array of problems that arise when managers try to protect isolated fragments of habitat. These problems are particularly severe wherever there has been a long history of human modification of the landscape (Box 12.1). Consider two examples: fen fragmentation in England and forest fragmentation in North America.

12.5.1 Fens in agricultural landscapes

The fens of Huntingdonshire in western England occur adjacent to The Wash along the coast with the North Sea. The following account comes entirely from Sheail and Wells (1983) and sources therein. These wetlands extend inland some 60 km from the ocean. The coastal areas are tidal marsh; in the more upland areas, the depth and character of the peat reflect differences in local drainage; in between, along the River Nene, there are more alkaline conditions and a series of lakes created by the meandering river. The largest lake is Whittlesea Mere, which, in 1697, was said to be three miles broad and six miles long; most of this is less than 2 m deep. The number and area of lakes may have declined since the medieval period onwards, and, in 1826, Whittlesea Mere dried up completely during one summer. The Domesday survey of 1086 outlined the various rights or privileges on the lakes, and later documents also drew attention to value for fish production and hunting for waterfowl. Settlement along the fen edge was both in the fenland and the arable upland and pasture, and in the 1600s records from the manorial court at Upwood reveal attempts to regulate land use, including rights of grazing in the fen and of excavating turf for fuel. Farmers were forbidden from digging over "10 000 cesses of turf from the fen in one year."

By the 1700s the number and variety of species in the area had begun to fall. Waterfowl were perhaps over-hunted, distinctive butterflies may have been over-collected, but habitat destruction was probably the most important factor contributing to the decrease. In 1844 an Act of Parliament combined the drainage of the Huntingdonshire fen with the improvement of watercourses further downstream. It was not until 1850 that the last of the meres, Whittlesea Mere, could be drained. Both windmills and steam scoop wheels were used for further draining fens, and in 1851 this area was the first site in England where a centrifugal pump from the Netherlands was used. In the 1890s an observer recorded: "all is gone – reeds, sedges, the glittering water, the butterflies, the gypsies, the bitterns, the wild fowl, and in its place . . . a dreary flat of black arable land, with hardly a jack snipe to give it a charm and characteristic attraction."

The first attempt at preservation was made in 1910, with the purchase of 137 ha of the Woodwalton Fen. At the same time, the water table was falling, in part from peat cutting. In some cases, the peat cutting provided disturbed sites for unusual plants to colonize, but extensive cutting removed seed sources and also changed the nature of the peat. Woody plants began to invade the fen; some trees had established on the nature reserve as early as the 1860s, and by

Box 12.1 | Conservation of tropical forest in the Caribbean: ca. 1650–1950

Forest fragmentation is not a new problem. In his classic book on the vegetation of the Antilles, Beard (1949) gives an overview of the forces destroying forest, and the administrative actions taken by the British. These islands each support between 120 and 193 tree species, with 13–47 of these being endemic. The four main vegetation types are rain forests, montane forests, seasonal forests, and dry evergreen forests, but one can find everything from cacti on rocky slopes to mangrove swamps: "The large number of types present is perhaps surprising in view of the small size of the islands, and is due principally to the very wide climatic variations within each of the mountainous islands" (p. 51).

The activities of Europeans began when Columbus made his second voyage to America and landed at Dominica in 1493:

> The earliest settlers were yeoman farmers, small-holders, who cultivated indigo, cotton, and tobacco. About 1650, sugar-cane was introduced and, with negro slaves to work it, proved enormously profitable. During the succeeding century great numbers of slaves were brought over from Africa and every piece of land suitable for growing sugar was taken up. Coffee and cacao were grown in some of the localities that were too wet for sugar. Large properties became the rule and many of the landowners were fabulously wealthy. After the Napoleonic Wars the sugar industry began to get into difficulties and a period of decline set in.
>
> (p. 29)

> The clearing of land probably reached its maximum at the time of the Napoleonic Wars. After that erosion and the depression in sugar began to cause areas of poor or degraded land to be abandoned and revert to bush. . . . After the abolition of slavery a new onslaught occurred on the interior forests of the larger and more mountainous islands. The labouring classes, now free to go where they would, preferred an independent existence and the practice of subsistence agriculture on their own account, to working for wages on the estates of their late masters. . . . The peasant prefers shifting cultivation in the mountains to permanent cultivation of lower lands. . . . However, destruction of the forests upon the rainy interior mountain slopes could not but have serious effects upon stream-flow and water-control and after some years public opinion began to be aware of this fact. In consequence, an officer of the Indian Forest Service, Mr. E. M. D. Hooper, visited all the islands in 1886 and presented a series of reports in which he recommended the reservation of forests.
>
> (p. 31)

> . . . in 1903, St. Kitts had passed a Forest Ordinance, the first in the Caribbean. A Forestry Board was set up which in effect was a committee of the planters who owned lands running up into the mountains. Under the ordinance, no land under forest at the time at which it came into force (i.e. 1903) or which became reforested at any subsequent time, might be cleared or cut over except with the permission of the Forestry Board. It appears that a good deal of felling and shifting cultivation was going on high in the mountains at the time. The effect of this ordinance, which has been consistently well enforced, has been to create a large central block of forest which is now mostly well-advanced second growth. As mountain cultivations were exhausted and abandoned they reverted to bush and the Board gave no permits for new clearings. The Board also refused to permit the felling of any trees, except for the personal use of estate owners, and this is still their policy. The central forest is in effect a Forest Reserve, though it has no legal status as such.
>
> (p. 32)

1931 most of the reserve was covered by "dense impenetrable thickets of sallow bushes." This was largely the result of the falling water table. Drainage ditches were partially blocked to maintain water levels during times of drought, and in 1935 a portable pump was used to raise water from neighboring drains into the reserve during dry weather. It would, of course, be possible to cut out the invading woody plants, but what would be the point if the fen was dried out? Drainage ditches beyond the reserve were deepened further after the Second World War, and in 1972 a clay-cored bank was constructed on the northern and western perimeter of the reserve so as to reduce the amount of water percolating out of the reserve and into the ditches. A photograph in Sheail and Wells shows a small rectangular plot of land, largely wooded, forlornly surrounded by drainage ditches and agricultural land. The Holme Fen National Nature Reserve, 256 ha set aside in 1952, is 3 km away. It has some species associated with undrained fenland such as *Calluna vulgaris*, *Erica tetralix*, and *Cladium mariscus*, but it too is being invaded by scrub and trees as the water table falls.

12.5.2 Deciduous forests in agricultural landscapes

Similar problems arise in forested landscapes (e.g., Lovejoy et al. 1986, Wilcove et al. 1986). Clearing forests for agriculture not only reduces the total area of forest, but it also divides the remaining forested area into increasingly smaller islands (Figure 12.18). There are a number of important consequences of fragmentation: the disappearance of animals and plants that require continuous habitat, the increase in organisms that exploit edge habitat (including invasive species from adjoining farmland), and selection for those species able to rapidly disperse to, and successfully colonize, new habitat islands (e.g., Burgess and Sharpe 1981, Harris 1984, Freemark and Merriam 1986, Terborgh 1989, Terborgh et al. 2001). As a consequence, the flora and fauna of the remnant islands of forest increasingly diverge from that of the original landscape (Section 12.5.3).

A first conservation challenge in such circumstances is to identify and protect the largest remaining fragments, since these are likely to be significant reservoirs of native species, particularly if their shapes tend to minimize the proportion of edge habitat. The next step is to try to re-connect the islands by forested corridors.

In the case of temperate deciduous forests in North America (Pearce 1993, Figure 12.18), there is a further serious problem – introduced insects and diseases that attack trees (Mueller-Dombois 1987, Little 1995). This process may be accelerated by air pollution which weakens the trees, making them more susceptible to herbivores and diseases. Too often, these are viewed on a case-by-case basis, the loss of chestnuts (*Castanea dentata*) in one decade, elms (*Ulmus americana*) in another, and butternut (*Juglans cinerea*) in yet another. The cumulative effect is the loss of a significant number of species with many unknown secondary effects. Over time the forest vegetation is degraded, but short-lived humans may miss this larger picture.

(a)

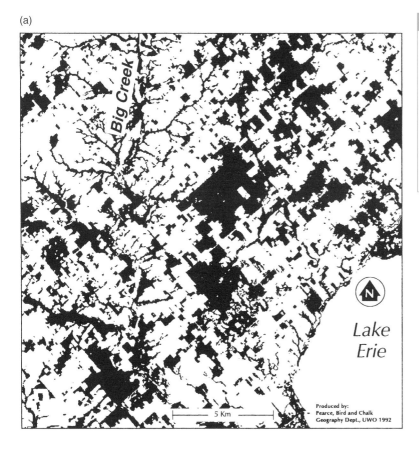

Lake Erie

Produced by:
Pearce, Bird and Chalk
Geography Dept., UWO 1992

5 Km

Figure 12.18 Forest cover (a) and patch sizes (b) in heavily farmed southern Ontario, northwest of Lake Erie (from *Size and Integrity Standards for Natural Heritage Areas in Ontario: Proceedings of a Seminar*, published by the Parks and Natural Heritage Policy Branch of the Ontario Ministry of Natural Resources, © Queen's Printer for Ontario, 1993. Reproduced with permission.)

(b)

Size class	No. of patches	Percent	Area (ha)	Percent
<3 ha	8912	80.6	6575	9.6
3–24 ha	1795	16.2	14 424	21.1
25–49 ha	172	1.6	6035	8.8
50–99 ha	86	0.8	5898	8.6
100–499 ha	80	0.7	16 029	23.7
500–1000 ha	12	0.1	7610	11.1
>1000 ha	6	0.1	11 530	16.9
Total	11 064	100.0	68 282	100.0

Significant areas of European forest have also been damaged. In 1999 more than 100 000 trees across Europe were assessed, and almost a quarter of them were considered moderately or severely damaged (Fischer et al. 2000). This process of *waldsterben* is now attributed to the mixture of air pollutants that are stressing these forests. Table 12.6 shows a similar disturbing trend in the forests of eastern North America. Even large reserves such as the Great Smoky Mountains may now be threatened by air pollution and exotic insects.

Table 12.6.	*Over the last century a series of epidemics has struck the deciduous forest trees of eastern North America (from examples in Little 1995 and U.S.D.A. 2004). The increasing frequency of outbreaks may be partly due to the stress caused by heavy metals, acid rain, ozone, and ultraviolet light – all factors implicated in the extensive forest die-backs already documented in Europe (waldsterben). Will North American forests be next?*	

Decade	Tree species	Agent

1870	Oak and aspen
	  Quercus spp.
	  Populus spp.
		Gypsy moth, *Lymantria dispar*

1910–1930	American chestnut *Castanea dentata*	fungus, *Cryphonestria parasitica*
	Elm, *Ulmus* spp.	Dutch elm disease, *Ceratocystis ulmi*
1950	Hemlock, *Tsuga* spp.	Hemlock wooly aphid, *Adeiges tsugae* on trees with N deposition on foliage
	American beech *Fagus grandifolia*	scale insect, *Cryptococcus fagi* fungus, *Nectria coccinea*
1970s	Flowering dogwood *Cornus florida*	fungus, *Discula* spp.
	Sugar maple *Acer saccharum*	acid rain
	Ash *Fraxinus* spp.	Ash yellow mycoplasma
1980s	Red spruce *Picea rubens*	acid rain, ozone, and balsam wooly aphid
	Fraser fir *Abies fraseri*	same as above
	Butternut *Juglans cinerea*	Butternut canker fungus
1990s	Ash, *Fraxinus* spp.	Emerald ash borer, *Agrilus planipennis*

12.5.3 How much is enough?

In Chapter 11, we saw how larger areas of land support more kinds of plants, and how this was governed by the species–area equation, and modified by factors such as topography. Many conservation problems could have been avoided if large reserves of natural vegetation, with boundaries based on ecological criteria and wide buffers, had been established in the first place. The extra costs needed to expand the size of a protected area may be more than balanced if they help to avoid the high, long-term costs of intensive management required to maintain small islands of habitat. As we saw in the chapter on grazing (Section 7.6.1), small areas that cannot support large carnivores may experience increased herbivore densities, with significant damage to the remaining plants, a process Terborgh et al. (2001) called "ecological meltdown." It is not yet possible to predict all the management problems that will be faced in 10, 20, or a 100 years. Yet it is inescapable that small reserves with unrealistic boundaries will leave many species at risk and a legacy of increased management costs to future managers and taxpayers.

Fens (Section 12.5.1) and deciduous forests (Section 12.5.2) situated in agricultural landscapes are just two of many possible examples of isolated reserves in changing landscapes. Such examples serve to re-emphasize many of Noss's (1995) guidelines, including the need for large reserves, with buffer strips, functioning as part of an interconnected system. Sinclair et al. (1995) point out the risks posed by change within reserves themselves and provide examples to show that, while protection reduces the rate of decline in habitats, habitats nonetheless continue to decline after protection, albeit at a slower rate. Sinclair et al. therefore stress that managers must place added emphasis upon **habitat renewal** within reserve systems. In a landscape undisturbed by human activity, natural habitat loss tends to be balanced by disturbance and succession, which renew different habitat types, but many of these dynamic processes are inoperative or partially operative in currently protected landscapes. Since natural habitats are still in decline at the global scale (Figure 12.19), the challenge for conservationists and managers is to ensure that natural habitats continue to be renewed within the reserve systems. Habitat renewal requires sufficiently large reserves to accommodate natural dynamics. Alternatively, reserve maintenance will involve increasingly expensive intervention by managers to attempt to simulate these processes. It might be possible to apply adequate fire or grazing regimes, and possibly meet flooding requirements, but certainly not to carry out processes necessary to maintain meander systems or deltas.

The commonly stated goal of natural area conservation programs – protecting 12 percent of a landscape in reserves (World Commission on Environment and Development 1987) – is not based upon scientific criteria (Sinclair et al. 1995). It was based on an ad hoc calculation that was derived by assuming that, since 4 percent of the Earth's landscape was protected, three times this amount would be a reasonable goal. As Noss (1995) comments: "There is a danger that such an ad hoc number will become a standard before we have any evidence that it is sufficient to protect biodiversity." He therefore suggests that, after the first steps have been taken in establishing a reserve network (mapping out a preliminary network with core reserves, buffer zones, and continuity), one should identify the species, still extant in the region, that has the largest area requirement and then estimate how much area is needed to provide for both short-term and long-term viable populations of that species. A second step would be to identify the extirpated native species with the largest area

Figure 12.19 Examples of habitat loss. (a) Extent and loss of forested area shown as a proportion of total land area for each region. □, São Paulo State, Brazil, total area 229 450 km²; ●, Madagascar, total area 587 000 km²; ○, Thailand, total area 513 520 km²; ■, Costa Rica, total area 50 990 km²; ▲, Vancouver Island, British Columbia, Canada, total area 32 000 km². (b) Proportional loss of wetland habitat on the Canadian prairies based on total wetland area in 1950: □, Manitoba 1903 km²; ○, Alberta, 4064 km² (from Sinclair et al. 1995).

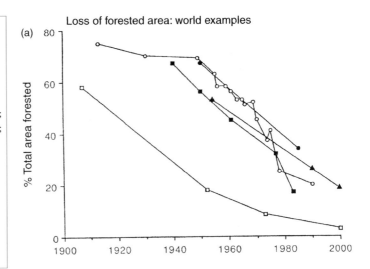

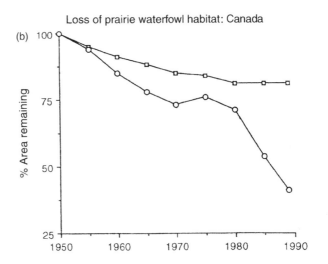

requirement, which could reasonably be reintroduced, and again estimate the area required for short-term and long-term population survival. If the reserve system is not sufficient to maintain long-term viable populations of these species, plans must be made to enlarge the network or enhance connectivity within the system or to adjoining regions.

12.6 | Function, management, and thresholds

12.6.1 Two perspectives

There are two rather different perspectives on the management and conservation of ecosystems. On one hand, ecological communities could be viewed primarily in terms of their **function**: living machines that provide services to humans. As long as these services are performed, the management goal is achieved. From this perspective, for example, all the different types of wetlands from northern peatlands to tropical mangrove swamps can be grouped into just three main categories based on water control as a function – donors, receptors, or conveyors of water (Figure 12.20). The fact that there are bogs, fens, marshes, and swamps, with different plant and animal species, different rates of disturbance and different fertility levels, may be unimportant from a functional perspective. On the other hand, these same communities could be viewed primarily in terms of their **structure**: that is, as natural communities of living organisms. One would then strive to conserve the patterns, processes, and species diversity within the individual communities. As long as the communities retain their normal complement of species, processes, and patterns one may assume that conservation is adequate.

Although these perspectives tend to divide plant ecologists, and their studies (and their clients!) into two rather different groups, they are not as independent, or as isolated, as they sometimes seem. While the wetland type may be unimportant for classification according to

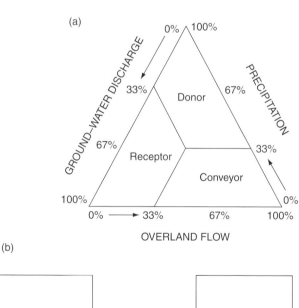

(a)

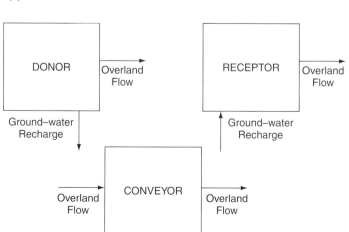

(b)

Figure 12.20 Three sources of water to wetlands corresponding to (a) the functional classes of wetlands and (b) the hydrological functions of each class (after Brinson 1993a ,b).

the function of water regulation, the particular vegetation types in conveyor wetlands, for example, will matter very much to humans concerned with fish that feed in alluvial forests, orchids that grow in wet prairies, and ducks that breed in sedge marshes. Similarly, if the primary concern is methane production and its contribution to global warming, one's main goal may be to determine how much is produced by each wetland type, and how different environmental factors regulate methane production within each. If each species of plant releases an equal amount of methane to the atmosphere, one need not be concerned with which species occur. On the other hand, if one discovers that some species are much more efficient than others at producing methane, it may be necessary to shift species composition to reduce methane generation. Vegetation types, of course, have multiple functions: a single wetland or forest will have a role in controlling hydrology, yielding wildlife, retaining sediment, producing methane, fixing nitrogen, and supplying human recreation. The functional and structural perspectives have to be combined in order to understand the multiple consequences of different management actions. Since vegetation performs multiple functions, one of the most thorny problems of management is ensuring that management for one function or goal does not cause loss of other equally important functions. It is all too easy to focus upon a single problem, a single function, or a single species and ignore everything else.

The functional and structural perspectives clearly overlap when one considers the function of ecosystems in maintaining biodiversity. First, there is a close connection between the global function of maintaining biodiversity, and the patterns and processes that occur within individual communities. Second, a function is carried out by the species that are present to perform that function. Table 12.7 shows the principal functions carried out by the Earth's ecosystems.

The functions carried out by any specific ecosystem are, by definition, the sum of the processes carried out by individual species. The more kinds of species, the greater the number of functions likely to be performed. We have seen examples throughout this book of such functions. Plants in general remove carbon dioxide from the atmosphere. Cyanobacteria and flowering plants in the Fabaceae fix atmospheric nitrogen. Plants with mycorrhizae move nitrogen and phosphorus from soil into biomass. Roots stabilize soil and reduce erosion. Plant tissues store nitrogen and phosphorus that otherwise would flow into watercourses. Seeds and fruits support multiple species of wildlife, with a nearly infinite number of details – some plants produce seeds that have eliasomes that will feed ants, other plants produce nuts that will support small mammals. Acacias have hollow thorns that support ant colonies. Nurse plants provide shade that allows cacti to regenerate. Early successional species change soil properties and the light regime, allowing invasion by a different suite of species. Any management that changes the composition or structure of vegetation will change functions as well.

Table 12.7.	*Principal functions carried out by the Earth's ecosystems (after de Groot 1992).*

Regulation functions

1. Protection against harmful cosmic influences
2. Regulation of the local and global energy balance
3. Regulation of the chemical composition of the atmosphere
4. Regulation of the chemical composition of the oceans
5. Regulation of the local and global climate (incl. the hydrological cycle)
6. Regulation of run-off and flood prevention (watershed protection)
7. Water catchment and groundwater recharge
8. Prevention of soil erosion and sediment control
9. Formation of topsoil and maintenance of soil fertility
10. Fixation of solar energy and biomass production
11. Storage and recycling of organic matter
12. Storage and recycling of nutrients
13. Storage and recycling of human waste
14. Regulation of biological control mechanisms
15. Maintenance of migration and nursery habitats
16. Maintenance of biological (and genetic) diversity

Carrier functions – providing space and suitable substrate for:

1. Human habitation and (indigenous) settlements
2. Cultivation (crop growing, animal husbandry, aquaculture)
3. Energy conversion
4. Recreation and tourism
5. Nature protection

Production functions

1. Oxygen
2. Water (for drinking, irrigation, industry, etc.)
3. Genetic resources
4. Medicinal resources
5. Raw materials for clothing and household fabrics
6. Raw materials for building, construction and industrial use
7. Biochemicals (other than fuel and medicines)
8. Fuel and energy
9. Fodder and fertilizer
10. Ornamental resources

Information functions

1. Aesthetic information
2. Spiritual and religious information
3. Historic information (heritage value)
4. Cultural and artistic inspiration
5. Scientific and educational information

Ehrlich and Ehrlich (1981) describe the loss of species from communities as analogous to the loss of rivets from the wings of an aeroplane. A certain number of rivets can be lost without the wings falling off because there is some redundancy of function, but eventually, if too many are lost, function is impaired and you crash! As a first approximation, one may assume that most functions in vegetation communities are carried out by more than one species; this is why species fall naturally into functional groups. If one species is lost, another may perform its function, but if too many are lost, that function is no longer performed. The degree of redundancy, and hence the safety margin, is still an unknown.

A word of warning to you before reading further about ecosystem functions. The well-demonstrated importance of ecosystem functions, from fish production to carbon storage, is currently being sidetracked by a stream of minor but well-publicized papers that entirely ignore the obvious large-scale examples given above (from Welcomme 1979 to de Groot 1992), substituting artificial mixtures of small numbers of species (e.g., Tilman et al. 1996, Naeem 2002). In my opinion, this is an example of scientists knowing rather little about plants and caring rather little about conservation, pretending to have an interest in both (e.g., Tilman and Pacala 1993, Loreau 2000, Kinzig et al. 2002), while ignoring all the important issues of biodiversity conservation (Keddy 2005b). Not only does this distract researchers from more pressing issues in science and conservation, but it consumes money needed for more important work, and perhaps worst of all confuses a new generation of students as it finds its way into textbooks (Keddy 2004, 2005b). Many plant ecologists have serious concerns about both the experimental designs and the rather cavalier analysis of the data (e.g., Givnish 1994, Huston 1997, Wardle et al. 2000, Grime 2002, Keddy 2005b), but there is no obvious end in sight – and of course, the more criticisms that are published, the more people are attracted to the controversy. If function and diversity interest you, I suggest you start by reading de Groot (1992) and then move on to Pimm (2001).

12.6.2 Plant communities are dynamic

While the safety margin is unknown, we can say with certainty that the greater the loss of species and functions, the more human survival is put at risk. The persistence of ecosystems and communities, then, is a necessary foundation for the persistence of human civilization (Holling 1978a, Christensen et al. 1996, Pimm 2001). Persistence, however, is a dangerous word if it creates the impression that the future is static or that dynamic changes in ecosystems have to be suppressed. In fact, we have seen many kinds of dynamic changes in plant communities, from fire to river meanders to grazing, and these are an essential part of maintaining and restoring biological diversity and ecological function.

Before considering land management further, let us digress to a broad overview of the degree to which change is natural in plant communities. Humans can damage ecosystems by suppressing natural dynamics, just as much as they can by altering the landscape through the damming of rivers, cutting of forests, diking of salt marshes, ploughing of prairies, and draining of peatlands. Since the biota and the ecosystems of the Earth have naturally changed steadily through time, management decisions should be based on a broader appreciation of vegetation dynamics – hence the lengthy chapter on disturbance. Forested wetlands, for example, have existed for millions of years, but they have changed as the fauna and flora of Earth evolved. Coal swamps dominated by *Lepidodendron* trees (Figure 12.21) no longer exist, and even they were subject to alternating wet and dry periods. Similarly, over merely the last 30 000 years, the world has seen the formation of great pluvial lakes in the southwestern United States, Africa, and Australia (recall Figure 9.13). In Africa, these lakes reached their maximum extent around 9000 BP; in the southwestern United States, between 12 000 and 24 000 BP; and in Australia earlier still, perhaps 26 000–30 000 BP. Imagine the extensive areas of wetlands and the clouds of migratory waterfowl that once must have occupied those areas of the Earth that are now arid flats or remnant saline lakes. Our own millennium appears to be one of the most arid in the late Quaternary (Figure 12.22).

We often fear change, extinguishing forest fires, stabilizing lake water levels, and building dams to stop spring flooding. As plant ecologists we need to overcome these fears and learn to work with change. This does not mean that one must accept that all changes wrought by humans are desirable or even acceptable, but working with naturally dynamic systems is the real and practical situation with which one must contend. Of course, one of the complex problems of conservation and management is to decide which changes are acceptable and which are not. Allowing fire to destroy areas of forest or allowing meander systems to erode a floodplain are often acceptable; allowing introduced species to spread is unacceptable. Allowing tortoises to crop vegetation in the Galapagos would be desirable; introducing goats to accomplish the same objective would not. One option allows a natural process to continue, the other causes a rapid change that is not intrinsic to particular vegetation types. Although plant communities will always change with time, the *processes* that they undergo and the *functions* that they perform must be maintained. The immediate challenges facing plant ecologists therefore fall into two areas: (1) protecting representative ecosystems and (2) maintaining their ecological functions. In the longer term, we may turn our attention to the restoration of damaged systems.

12.6.3 Ecological footprints for human cities

The changes in function and structure that we have caused around the world, in the Mediterranean, in Louisiana, and on Easter Island and the Galapagos, were carried out to increase the flow of resources to one species – humans. Human populations have grown by taking

Figure 12.21 Wetlands have changed through time, as illustrated by the origin and disappearance of coal swamps and their associated flora and fauna (courtesy the Field Museum, #GE085637c, carboniferous forest).

Figure 12.22 Lake level status for 1000-year time periods for the past 30 000 years in three parts of the world (after Street and Grove 1979).

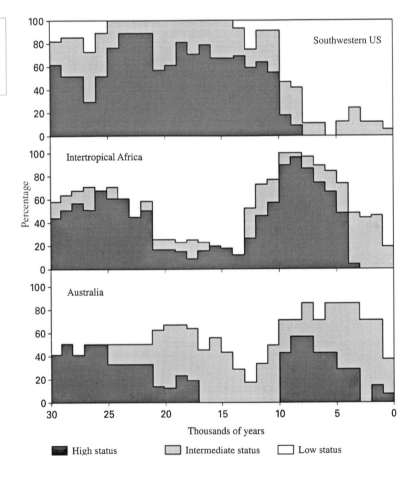

food and energy from other species – species that then declined or disappeared. As human populations continued to increase, the local landscape was no longer able to support the human populations there, requiring imports from other times and places. How can humans import across time? They deplete resources that have accumulated over many centuries, such as baldcypress and sequoia trees that are more than a thousand years old, or they go back millions of years for fuel, such as coal and oil. Imports from other places are achieved by transportation of resources such as oil, timber, and food from other geographic regions.

The importation of resources from other times and places continues throughout the world, particularly in urban centers. It may well be that humans have already exceeded the Earth's steady-state carrying capacity. Humans may now be maintaining population size (and subsidizing continued growth) not by consuming the annual production of ecosystems, but by drawing down accumulated resource capital such as stocks of long-lived fish and old forests. Like a family living not on a steady income, but on their cash reserves, such a process will end abruptly when the reserves are exhausted. To measure the effects of urban populations drawing upon resources outside their own region, Rees and Wackernagel (1994) introduced the concept of an "ecological footprint" for a city or country. To determine the size of this footprint, it is necessary to consider the various resources that a city consumes on a per-capita basis, multiplied by its population size. The energy needs of the typical citizen of a developed county, if met from current photosynthesis rather than fossil fuels, would require some 3.5 ha for production of ethanol. Food production would require a further 1.1 ha of agricultural land, and the paper consumed would require 0.5 ha of prime forest in continuous production. Summing these three needs alone shows that a typical urban area in North America such as Vancouver, Canada (population about 2 million) requires the resources from 22 times as much land as it actually occupies. Consumption in the Netherlands is lower on a per-capita basis, yet even so the country now consumes far more resources than are generated within its own political boundaries, $110\,000\,\mathrm{km}^2$ for food and forestry products and $360\,000\,\mathrm{km}^2$ for energy (Figure 12.23). Modern developed countries are therefore not only based upon past land degradation (contrast top and bottom of Figure 12.24) but currently accelerate this process over much larger areas of the Earth.

12.6.4 Thresholds

Arid grasslands illustrate the sensitivity of stressed ecosystems to degradation by human activities. Overgrazing of these grasslands may convert them to shrublands (Archer 1989, Sayre 2003). It can threaten the survival of indigenous plants and animals (Noss and Cooperrider 1994, Milchunas et al. 1998). Overgrazing can also threaten food production for indigenous human populations (Milton et al. 1994). In extreme cases of overgrazing, the vegetation cover is stripped from

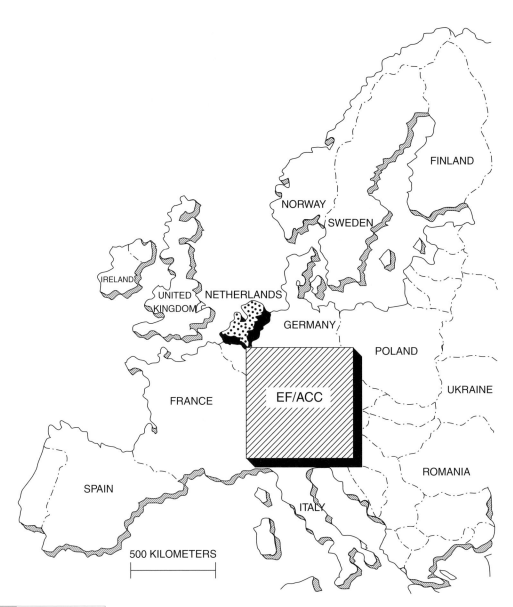

Figure 12.23 Not only has the environment of the Netherlands already been degraded by human activity (Figure 12.24), but its current population consumes resources from an area (square) 14 times the size of the country (Rees and Wackernagel 1994).

the land and erosion is greatly accelerated. The remaining soil may also become salinized. These and other negative effects of overgrazing may not occur as smooth transitions, but rather as a series of steps (Figure 12.25). The edge of each step represents a **threshold**, a situation where a rather small amount of added grazing can make an enormous difference in ecological function. You may recall the models for grazing in Section 7.6.4, Figure 7.23, where similar sudden transitions could occur. Figure 12.25 shows four stages in degradation. The stages are separated by thresholds.

In the early stages of degradation, removing the grazing will allow recovery to occur. As the negative consequences of overgrazing accumulate, however, a transition threshold is crossed. At this point,

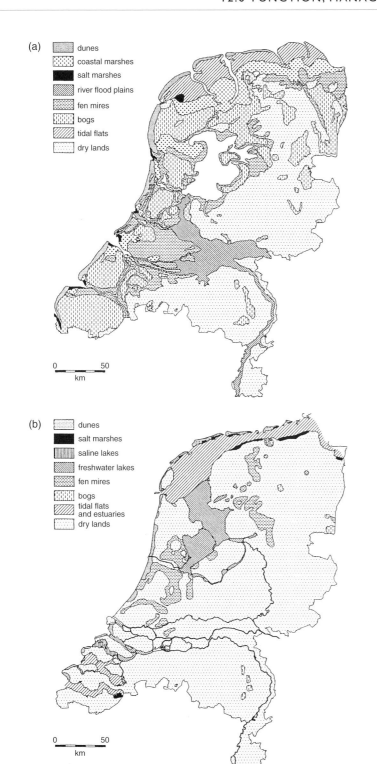

(a)
- dunes
- coastal marshes
- salt marshes
- river flood plains
- fen mires
- bogs
- tidal flats
- dry lands

0 ___ 50
km

(b)
- dunes
- salt marshes
- saline lakes
- freshwater lakes
- fen mires
- bogs
- tidal flats and estuaries
- dry lands

0 ___ 50
km

Figure 12.24 Wetlands in the Netherlands. (a) 100 AD and (b) present distribution (from Wolff 1993).

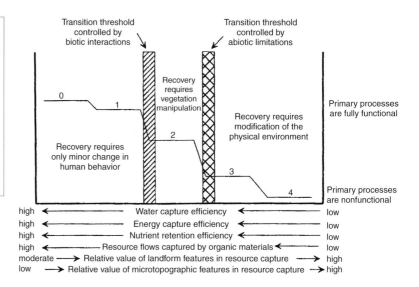

Figure 12.25 Two thresholds can be recognized in the degradation (from stages 0 to 4) of arid grassland subjected to overgrazing. After the first threshold is passed, the vegetation must be manipulated to re-establish the original plant community. After the second threshold is passed, the physical environment must also be modified for any recovery to occur (after Whisenant 1999).

cessation of overgrazing may be insufficient to allow recovery. The system may remain in a degraded state unless expensive management is applied. This management might include reseeding, burning, herbicide treatment or selective cutting of weedy plants. All of these may have other unwanted consequences. With further overgrazing, a second transition threshold is crossed. Even more costly intervention may be necessary. In extreme cases, it may be necessary to use heavy equipment to cut trenches to trap water and to artificially replant vegetation in such trenches. Needless to say, this kind of management is a costly and undesirable substitute for ecologically sustainable grazing. Grazing intensity is, of course, only one of many factors acting on grasslands: others include precipitation, the history (if any) of grazing before humans introduced cattle, and the type of grassland (Milchunas et al. 1998).

Although Figure 12.25 uses the example of rangeland, you should understand that all communities and ecosystems will degrade if humans interfere sufficiently with primary production or reproduction. Degradation refers to a series of typical events that includes loss of larger species, replacement of slow-growing species by fast-growing ones, and lower rates of nutrient retention (Rapport et al. 1985, Freedman 1995). You should think about how Figure 12.25 might be modified to represent the ecosystems around your own home. Thresholds greatly complicate ecosystem management because it is often difficult to explain to land users how a small amount of added damage can lead to a great shift in ecological function – until that shift has actually occurred. At this point, it is not an easy matter to reverse the process. Overall, the past centuries have seen a steady shift in the Earth's vegetation types from the left side to the right of Figure 12.25. Think, for example, of the Mediterranean forest mentioned in Section 12.2.2. Who at the time would have believed that one could pass thresholds that would reduce this to semi-desert?

Overall, it is reasonable to conclude that increasing areas of the Earth's surface are shifting to the right side of the figure. Many plant ecologists will likely be employed trying to reverse this degradation. The problem you will face is the challenge of pushing the landscape and its vegetation in the opposite direction – from the degraded right side of the figure to the more pristine left side. This process has a name – or actually multiple names – but the best known is "ecological restoration." Let us turn now to the problems and opportunities associated with restoring damaged habitats.

12.7 | Restoration

Each plant community is the consequence of many environmental factors acting simultaneously. It follows, then, that we can manipulate vegetation by changing one or more of those factors. One can, for example, change flooding regimes, reduce the amount of nitrogen in floodwaters, remove cattle that are overgrazing, reintroduce natural grazers, or allow fire. Each such modification of an environmental factor is an act of management. Any management program should be undertaken only with a specific objective in mind and with an understanding of the known quantitative linkages that allow one to forecast the results of the manipulation. Put more simply, you should ask: what is the problem I am trying to solve, and what is the objective of my management? Only when your objectives are clearly articulated, can you determine whether or not your management has been successful.

The idea of setting measurable targets for management deserves more emphasis (Noss 1995). Noss begins with Leopold's 1949 essay on land ethics:

> A thing is right when it tends to preserve the integrity, stability, and beauty of the biotic community. It is wrong when it tends otherwise.

Leopold did not explain what he meant by integrity, and although the word is increasingly used by managers, it is still poorly defined (e.g., Woodley et al. 1993, Noss 1995, Higgs 1997). Noss is of the opinion that the difficulty of defining integrity does not reduce its value; other terms such as justice, freedom, love, and democracy are also vague and slippery, yet this has not kept scientists, philosophers, and policy makers from thinking about them and from being guided by their intent (Rolston 1994). Rather than enter the realm of discussion here, I will adopt the view that integrity has three essential components: (1) maintaining biological diversity, (2) ensuring ecosystem persistence through time, and (3) maintaining performance of ecological functions. These components are all measurable and therefore operational, even if the term integrity is not. All are also inter-related – if diversity declines, functions will naturally be impaired. Similarly, the continued performance of functions is probably essential for persistence. All these aspects of integrity are equally considered as the basis for "ecosystem management"

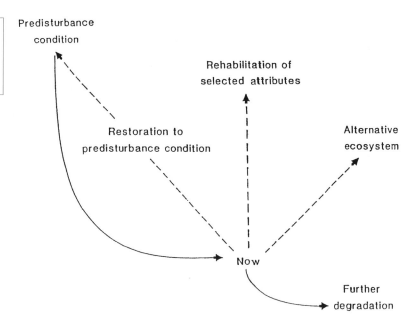

Figure 12.26 Some of the options available to managers responsible for degraded ecosystems (from Cairns 1989 after Magnuson et al. 1980).

(e.g., Christensen et al. 1996, Grumbine 1997). The proliferation of terms synonymous with wise management should not distract us – the task is fundamentally to set wise goals and ensure that the best possible science is brought to bear on the achievement of those goals.

Managers will rarely inherit a landscape with entirely intact and pristine ecosystems; in most cases there will already have been considerable loss in the area of native vegetation, reductions in function, and declines in biological diversity. Two of the principal challenges facing managers are: (1) deciding to what degree it is possible to reverse these undesirable changes, and (2) implementing the programs to reverse them. There are a variety of technical terms for the specific options open to managers (Figure 12.26) depending upon the objectives of management for a particular site. The objective of **restoration** is the re-creation of vegetation types that have either been degraded or entirely lost from the landscape (e.g., Lewis 1982, Jordan et al. 1987, Galatowitsch and van der Valk 1994). You should be aware that this idea arises under many other names, including, "ecosystem management" (e.g., Christensen et al. 1996, Grumbine 1997), the "maintenance of ecological integrity" (e.g., Woodley et al. 1993, Noss 1995), "rehabilitation" (Cairns 1988), and "reconstruction" (Allen 1988, Saunders et al. 1993). Whatever label one uses, the principles are similar: all involve the use of indigenous species and natural environmental factors to re-establish communities that will persist without continued human interference.

Restoration is often treated as a new discipline, but it has a long history. Clements (1935) discusses, in a paper that is still well worth reading, the degree to which research in ecology influenced landscape management. In this work, he draws in part upon his studies of carrying capacity in grazing lands in the American southwest (Sayre

2003). In these naturally arid grasslands, both shrubs and cacti occur naturally, but a combination of drought and overgrazing damaged the grasslands so severely that there was a die-off of livestock in the 1880s. As a consequence, livestock were excluded from much of a 21 000 ha experimental grassland, the Santa Rita Experimental Range, between 1903 and 1915 (McClaran 2003). Botanists then monitored the recovery of the vegetation and, after grazing was restored in 1915, carried out "hundreds of experiments and manipulations" (p. 17) to explore the interactions of livestock grazing, rodents, and vegetation. Further back, Phipps (1883) wrote a treatise on forest restoration, and Larson (1996) describes a 107-year-old restoration experiment established by William Brown, an arboriculturalist from Scotland who was hired as a professor of agriculture at the University of Guelph in 1874. The site of Brown's restoration experiment, a former gravel pit, was planted with 14 species of trees, of which 10 are still present. Larson (1996) observes that this "represents an example … of an ecosystem that was planned and built based on the best information and principles available at the time."

Students should appreciate, therefore, that restoration, ecosystem management, and, for that matter, conservation have deep historical roots. Yet while these topics are now global concerns, perspectives vary. The principal differences come about because of contrasting cultural and biological reference points. In regions settled for many centuries, management goals focus on the maintenance of familiar historical landscapes created by humans (e.g., European species rich pastures typical of the eighteenth and nineteenth centuries). In more recently settled regions, such as North America or Australia where humans have had less impact, the goal of restoring ecosystems to pre-European settlement conditions (e.g., large tracts of forest, prairie, or desert with viable populations of native animals) can be practical. The same dichotomy can arise locally: within cities, small tracts of semi-natural greenspace cannot be expected to support wolves or condors, but large wild spaces may be practical only a few hours away. There is a natural balance between these two views. In densely populated areas of more recently settled areas, there may have to be increasing use of intensive management in order to maintain small examples of desired ecosystem types. Equally, in areas that have been settled for hundreds of years, it may still be possible to plan for natural composition rather than cultural familiarity. In the long run, there is the inspiring prospect of rewilding – minimizing human impacts on large areas of landscape to allow natural processes such as fire, flooding and climate to re-establish wilderness containing naturally regulating animal populations (Soulé and Noss 1998, Foreman 2004). Building a global network of wild landscapes is an inspiring goal for the next generation of ecologists.

The task at hand is clear. There is a need for: (1) increased protection for natural habitats around the world, (2) habitat restoration, and (3) the use of science as a basis for conducting habitat management programs.

12.8 | Indicators

It is one thing to set noble goals, such as maintaining the life-supporting functions of ecosystems, or restoring the integrity of forests. It is quite another to agree upon how progress towards these goals can be measured. Yet, without establishing desired, attainable, and measurable management outcomes (objectives) and without repeated measurement of how plant communities are changing through time (monitoring), we cannot determine whether ecosystems are being well-managed; neither can we make decisions about how to alter management to make it better. Holling (1978a) therefore introduced the concept of **adaptive ecosystem management** to describe an ongoing iterative process: start with management decisions based upon the objectives and the best scientific information available, monitor the results and compare them to the desired management outcome, adjust management practices accordingly, monitor the results of management and compare, adjust practices accordingly, and so on. This allows for management practices to evolve as human knowledge grows, enabling us to get closer and closer to the management goal as time passes.

There are two key issues in monitoring: (1) what **indicators** should be measured to help us make management decisions, and (2) what are the **critical values** of each indicator that characterize healthy as opposed to degraded ecosystems? Engineers, for example, have decided upon the indicators that are required by car drivers to monitor car performance – gauges for speed, engine temperature, and fuel supply are nearly universal. Most such gauges also have regions marked in red to indicate that an undesirable level has been reached. Similarly, doctors have a standard set of indicators to measure and monitor human health such as temperature and blood pressure. It would be best if there were a short list of indicators or gauges for ecosystems or the biosphere that all scientists agreed upon, but no consensus has yet been reached (e.g., Rapport et al. 1985, Rapport 1989, Keddy 1991, Adamus 1992, McKenzie et al. 1992, Keddy et al. 1993).

Two obvious indicators of ecosystem condition that might apply to all ecosystems are primary production and decomposition. The selection of other indicators might depend upon the particular ecosystem one is monitoring. The most obvious indicators are **physical factors**, particularly in bodies of water. In lakes, it is traditional to measure the concentration of phosphorus, which indicates the potential for algal growth (Vallentyne 1974, International Joint Commission 1980). In streams, water temperature and dissolved oxygen are measured because they are indicators of fish habitat quality (Steedman 1988). But the link between physical factors and biological processes is often not straightforward. Hence the search for measurable **biological properties** of living systems. This has generated a good deal of debate about which properties will provide the most useful information about the health of ecosystems (e.g., Rapport et al. 1985, Rapport 1989, Keddy 1991, Adamus 1992, McKenzie et al. 1992, Keddy et al. 1993). There is, however, an emerging consensus that at least one group of indicators should address large organisms, particularly **large carnivores**, a group that is especially at risk of extinction (Rapport et al. 1985, Soulé and Noss 1998). Another group should consider **keystone species**, which create habitat that allows an entire suite of other species to occupy a landscape – examples that we have seen here include animals such as beavers and alligators (Section 6.3.3). Large carnivores and keystone species may at first seem out of place in a plant ecology text. But, we saw in Chapter 7 how large carnivores may regulate herbivores, thereby controlling the composition of vegetation (a trophic cascade) – indeed, the loss of wildflowers from deciduous forests in North America may be connected to the loss of wolves and cougars that once controlled deer. Similarly, we saw in Chapter 6 how, from the perspective of plants, alligators and beavers (not to mention prairie dogs and bison) create patches of habitat for selected species of plants. One might also make the case to zoologists that many species of trees are keystone species in landscapes. Certainly, wildlife managers now recognize the enormous number of animal species that are dependent upon old dead trees, called "snags" (Tubbs et al. 1987, McComb and Muller 1983).

Consider the challenge of devising indicators for conservation of deciduous forest. Table 12.8 shows some potential indicators and their critical values, extracted from published studies of old growth stands of deciduous forest in eastern North America. One might argue that there are overlooked elements – perhaps it is necessary to directly monitor other characteristics such as the activity of mycorrhizae that maintain tree growth, or the abundance of amphibians that form the base of many food webs. Another option is to monitor surrogates for these functions. For example, instead of monitoring mycorrhizal fungi or amphibians directly, one might measure the amount of dead wood on the forest floor (coarse woody debris, Table 12.8), since this provides a source of food for fungi and habitat for amphibians. In other cases, one might select certain species to monitor, so-called **indicator species**, with the assumption that the presence of such species indicates that the rest of the ecosystem is functioning normally. From the perspective of plants, these might include plant species known to be sensitive to environmental change, or animals that pollinate them or disperse seeds. As with animals, slow-growing plant species that take many years to mature are likely to be more at risk than fast-growing species that reproduce rapidly.

At present, it is physical factors and indicator species that are most often monitored. But indicators that provide information about life-supporting functions of entire ecosystems are certain to become more important.

Table 12.8. *A preliminary list of indicators for evaluating temperate deciduous forest and suggested critical values for them (after Keddy and Drummond 1996).*

Property	Measurement	Relative condition of forest		
		Good	Intermediate	Low
Stand indicators				
1. Tree size	Basal area (m^2)/ha	>29	20–29	<20
2. Canopy composition	Proportion of shade-tolerant tree species (American beech, sugar maple, basswood, hemlock)	>70%	30–70%	<30%
3. Coarse woody debris	Megagrams/ha, presence of large decaying logs ($\geq$8 logs/ha)	>20, both firm and crumbling	10–20, either firm or crumbling	<10, no large logs present
4. Herbaceous layer	Number of ephemeral plant species	$\geq$6	2–5	<2
5. Corticulous bryophytes	Number of bryophyte species	$\geq$7	2–6	<2
6. Wildlife trees	Number of snags/10 ha ($\geq$50.8 cm dbh)	$\geq$4	1–3	<1
7. Fungi	No information available			
Landscape indicators				
8. Avian community	Number of forest interior species	>5	2–4	<2
9. Large carnivores	Number of species present	$\geq$6	3–5	<3
10. Forest area	Hectares	>10^5	10^2–10^5	<10^2

12.9 | Conclusion

We are at a point in human history when the threat to our civilization and our planet from our own species is rapidly increasing. Even if we doubt the likelihood of the most gloomy scenarios, such as nuclear war, nuclear winter, and mass starvation, we cannot doubt the accumulating, insidious effects of deforestation, pollution, desertification, soil erosion, drainage of wetlands, and rising rates of extinction (Leopold 1949, Meadows et al. 1974, E. O. Wilson 1993, Pimm 2001). Perhaps the world will end as T. S. Eliot put it, "not with a bang, but with a whimper." In either case, ecologists are like the legendary thin red line of British soldiers; we stand between our civilization and the ecosystems upon which it depends. These ecosystems are mute, we alone provide them with voices, and we have the potential to shape positive future action.

In the words of Dave Foreman (2004):

Students need to understand whose shoulders they stand on, how much work has already been done, where twenty-first century ideas of conservation come from, and how important their future work is for the diversity of life. They must know that, despite the terrifying extinction crisis in which we find ourselves, there is hope. They can make things better.

(p. 7)

Action has several components. With respect to our own activities, there is the responsibility to work on significant problems rather than allowing our minds to flit about and be occupied by each curiosity of nature that catches our attention. One can avoid conducting research on indiscriminately selected minor problems. Equally, one can avoid being seduced by trivial but well-publicized issues, such as the diversity and ecosystem function debate mentioned above. Time is short. There are few good plant ecologists. You have the responsibility to act in defense of the world's ecosystems. To remain silent in the face of folly is irresponsible (Box 12.2).

At the beginning of this book, I introduced the discipline of plant ecology, and began with the origin of plants themselves and their consequent impacts upon the biosphere. Far from those first thoughts, this text ends. You may already be preparing to put this book back on its shelf. Before doing so, we must ask where one goes from here. I hope that I have managed to convey to you the importance of plants in the biosphere, the remarkable diversity that exists in the plant kingdom, and some of the excitement (and frustrations!) of research in plant ecology. I also hope that you feel like you have met some of the remarkable personalities that have shaped our view of plant ecology. Even people such as Fritz Haber, who now may seem repugnant, are a part of our history – they too have affected the world. Please take the time to read some of the original work that I have mentioned, and get to know these people better.

It would be entirely normal at this point to feel utterly overwhelmed by the volume of data and the amount of work that has already been done. Sometimes this can be discouraging rather than inspiring! Keep in mind that it took me more than 25 years of working in plant ecology to collate what I have tried to share with you here. I have tried to prepare a bit of a shortcut, by writing for you the book that I wish I had had when I was just starting my university studies and working in Algonquin Provincial Park. All the same, you have to be patient. If you learn just a little more each week, if you read even one original paper each week, it will all add up.

You may also be considering a research project of your own and wondering how to begin. This is one of the reasons to become an apprentice to older scientists – they have been through this already. If you want to pursue a research career, look around and see who is willing to spend time sharing their knowledge with you, and who is doing the sort of research that excites you. In any case, Figure 12.27 reminds one that fundamentally the path forward is straightforward. There is a set of independent variables (Figure 12.27, left). These produce a series of measurable properties at each level of

Box 12.2 | The Sinking of the *Rainbow Warrior*

Who will rid me of this turbulent priest?

(W. Shakespeare, Henry II)

On September 15, 1971 a small group of Canadians sailed into the Pacific Ocean on an old 24-meter fishing boat called the *Phyllis Cormack* to challenge the most powerful nation on earth, the United States of America, which was carrying out nuclear tests in the Aleutian Islands. On 30 September the crew was arrested by the U.S. Coast Guard as they neared Amchitaka. The nuclear bomb was detonated on 7 November 1971; they had not stopped the test, but they had launched Greenpeace, which was destined become one of the world's most powerful and active environmental groups.

The French government became the target of a Greenpeace campaign, in 1972 when the Canadian expatriate David McTaggart sailed the *Vega* to the Moruroa Atoll in the South Pacific. One of the French ships, a 4000-tonne minesweeper called *La Paimpolaise* rammed his ship. The following year he returned; this time a group of French commandos boarded the *Vega* and McTaggart and his companion were beaten so severely that McTaggart was partially blinded in one eye. The French seized cameras, and imprisoned the crew, but unbeknownst to them, Ann-Marie Home smuggled out a 35-mm film canister in her vagina (Gidley and Shears 1986). The protest and the beating were reported around the world. In 1974 the French announced an end to atmospheric nuclear testing. The use of brutal force against environmental activists had, however, only begun.

The French continued nuclear testing in the Pacific Ocean in spite of growing world opposition. In 1985 Greenpeace again set out for the Moruroa, this time at the helm of the *Rainbow Warrior*, a ship that had already been active in disrupting the Icelandic and Spanish whaling fleets in the late 1970s. However while the ship was anchored in Auckland harbor, divers from the French secret service planted two bombs on the ship, one adjacent to the engine room, and the other in the propeller assembly. Shortly before midnight of 10 July the first blast went off; most of the crew scrambled to safety, but a second blast killed the ship's photographer, Fernado Pereira.

The French refused to apologize, and went ahead with their tests, detonating two neutron bombs within the space of 2 days. The commandos who carried out the attack almost certainly escaped; two arrested French agents (Captain Dominique Prieur and Major Alain Mafart) pleaded guilty to murder in a New Zealand court and were each sentenced to 10 years in prison.

Since then, the list of murdered and imprisoned environmental activists has steadily grown, although few have received the international attention that surrounded the sinking of the *Rainbow Warrior*. Far too many died in third world countries in defense of tropical forests, where lack of a free press has contributed to death in obscurity. Others still languish in prison. I tell this story here for several reasons. No young scientist should be naïve enough to believe that scientific study, publication and rational arguments alone will be sufficient to save the biosphere from continued damage. People willing to put their lives on the line will always be necessary, and in spite of the fact that they may lack PhDs, their importance should not be underestimated.

Figure B12.2 A sad end for the *Rainbow Warrior* and sailor Pereira in Auckland Harbour (from Morgan and Whitaker 1986).

Fernando Pereira was only 25 when he died. You could consider what else you might do to carry on with the tasks he and other murdered activists have been unable to complete before their deaths. To share the responsibility, each of us could join and financially support at least one global conservation group. The World Wildlife Fund and The Nature Conservancy have a particular focus on protecting natural habitats. There are, of course, many other worthy global, national, and local groups. Find one year your home, and support them as well.

Further reading

The Sunday Times Insight Team. 1986. *Rainbow Warrior: The French Attempt to Sink Greenpeace*. London: Century Hutchinson Ltd.

Dyson, J. 1986. *Sink the Rainbow! An Enquiry into the "Greenpeace Affair"*. Toronto: Harcourt Brace Jovanovich Canada Ltd.

Gidley, I. and R. Shears. 1986. *The Rainbow Warrior Affair*. Toronto: Irwin Publishing.

Hunter, R. H. 1979. *Warriors of the Rainbow: A Chronicle of the Greenpeace Movement*. New York: Holt, Rinehart and Winston.

Figure 12.27 Plant ecology is the study of (1) how independent variables (left) determine vegetation properties (center) and (2) the consequences of the foregoing linkages for other components of the landscape and biosphere (right).

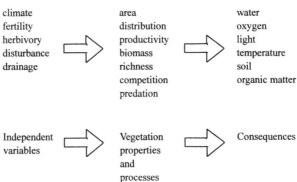

Figure 12.27 Plant ecology is the study of (1) how independent variables (left) determine vegetation properties (center) and (2) the consequences of the foregoing linkages for other components of the landscape and biosphere (right).

organization in plant communities (Figure 12.27, middle). In turn, plant communities provide functions and services (Figure 12.27, right). Our task as scientists is to uncover these relationships and convey them clearly and effectively to others.

Further reading

Carson, R. 1962. *Silent Spring*. Boston: Houghton Mifflin.

Ehrlich, A. and P. Ehrlich. 1981. *Extinction: The Causes and Consequences of the Disappearance of Species*. New York: Random House.

Cairns, J. 1989. Restoring damaged ecosystems: is predisturbance condition a viable option? *The Environmental Professional* **11**: 152–159.

de Groot, R. S. 1992. *Functions of Nature*. The Netherlands: Wolters-Noordhoff.

Groombridge, B. 1992. *Global Biodiversity: Status of the Earth's Living Resources*. London: Chapman and Hall.

Pressey, R. L., C. J. Humphries, C. R. Margules, R. I. Vane-Wright, and P. H. Williams. 1993. Beyond opportunism: key principles for systematic reserve selection. *Trends in Ecology and Evolution* **8**: 124–128.

Noss, R. F. and A. Y. Cooperrider. 1994. *Saving Nature's Legacy*. Washington, DC: Island Press.

Bryant, D., D. Nielsen, and L. Tangley. 1997. *The Last Frontier Forests: Ecosystems and Economies on the Edge*. Washington, DC: World Resources Institute.

Constanza, R., R. d'Arge, R. de Groot, S. Farber, M. Grasso, B. Hannon, K. Limburg, S. Naeem, R. O'Neill, J. Paruelo, R. Raskin, P. Sutton, and M. van den Belt. 1997. The value of the world's ecosystem services and natural capital. *Nature* **387**: 253–260.

Myers, N., R. A. Mittermeier, C. G. Mittermeier, G. A. B. da Fonseca and J. Kent. 2000. Biodiversity hotspots for conservation priorities. *Nature* **403**: 853–858.

Fraser, L. H. and P. A. Keddy (eds.) 2005. *The World's Largest Wetlands: Ecology and Conservation*. Cambridge, UK: Cambridge University Press.

Questions for review

25 review questions, final exam questions, or assignments

1. Pick one book from the further reading lists and write a 3–5 page report on how that book advances the field of plant ecology.
2. If early vascular plants had free-living gametophytes, why was it the gametophyte stage rather than the sporophyte stage that became reduced with time? There are multiple hypotheses to offer, not just one. How might you test them?
3. Does the Southern Hemisphere have more kinds of plants than the Northern Hemisphere? If so, what does this mean for global conservation?
4. Write a short environmental history for your region of the world. You may use the section in Chapter 12 on Louisiana as a model if you wish.
5. Where is the nearest natural area that has carnivorous plants or orchids? Write a short description of the habitat and offer some hypotheses that might explain the occurrence of these plants there.
6. Which ecoregion do you live in, and what kind of natural disturbance was prevalent in your ecoregion 1000 years ago?
7. You buy a set of fifty small islands in the Mediterranean to experimentally explore re-creation of the native forests of that region. Describe the treatments that you might use, with emphasis upon experimentally investigating the possible impacts of natural herbivores and predators.
8. Nitrogen is a scarce resource. Members of the Fabaceae can fix atmospheric nitrogen using symbiotic bacteria living in root nodules. Why do all plants not have such root nodules?
9. "There is no real difference between lichens and vascular plants, except that vascular plants are larger." Marshall the evidence for and against this generalization.
10. If nutrients limit plant growth, then adding nutrients should increase the diversity of plants in a habitat. Use the concept of competition to explain why this assertion is false.
11. Can plants cause lower sea levels? Explain the linkages that make this possible. If you are inspired to go further, look for quantitative evidence as to whether it is probable. Consult Lackner, K. S. 2003. A guide to CO_2 sequestration *Science* 300: 1677–1678 for more information.
12. How did glaciation over the past 100 000 years affect your region of the world? Make the list as long as possible.

13. Why do some plants, such as orchids, have very small seeds? Why do some plants, such as oaks and walnuts, have rather large seeds? What are the trade-offs between the two? Read some recent studies on this issue.

14. List some common ways that plants defend themselves from herbivores. Which seem to be prevalent in your part of the world? Can you identify several local plants that are particularly palatable or particularly unpalatable?

15. Read more about parasitic plants. Under what circumstances is it thought that parasitism becomes advantageous? Name some examples of parasitic plants in your local flora.

16. Where is the nearest location to you that has fossil plants? What age are the fossils? Describe the general type of plant community represented by these fossils.

17. Explain how the study of pollen grains in lake sediment allows plant ecologists to reconstruct the history of plant communities, including the frequency of fire.

18. Is it true that northern peatlands likely have more gametophytic tissue that any other habitat on earth?

19. You inherit 10 million dollars with the instructions that you must use the money to buy one of the most important vegetation types remaining in the world to donate to The Nature Conservancy. How might you go about making the decision rationally? What criteria would you consider?

20. You are hired by a rich patron to restore a 10 000 acre property to its "natural state." Describe how you would decide what state that would be. Then list some of the techniques you could use to carry out that restoration.

21. You manage an enormous tract of forest. Local residents want you to kill the large predators in the forest. Describe the possible consequences of such actions upon the plants, using examples from this book or from other sources.

22. What are the advantages and disadvantages of evergreen leaves? Give some examples of habitats where evergreen leaves are particularly common.

23. Find three examples of the following in scientific journals (do not use examples mentioned in the book): stress, disturbance, herbivory, competition, mutualism.

24. This book mentions a number of historical figures in plant ecology. Who was overlooked and should be added to a future edition? Write a box for that person (and send it to me).

25. What topic do you wish had been discussed in this book that was not? Write a short piece that you think should have been included in a section of the book (send this to me too).

References

Aaviksoo, K., M. Ilomets, and M. Zobel. 1993. Dynamics of mire communities: a Markovian approach (Estonia). pp. 23–43. In B. C. Patten (ed.) *Wetlands and Shallow Continental Water Bodies*, Vol. 2. The Hague: SPB Academic Publishing.

Abraham, K. F. and C. J. Keddy. 2005. The Hudson Bay lowland. pp. 118–148. In L. H. Fraser and P. A. Keddy (eds.) *The World's Largest Wetlands: Ecology and Conservation*. Cambridge: Cambridge University Press.

Abrahamson, W. G. and M. Gadgil. 1973. Growth form and reproductive effort in goldenrods (*Solidago*, *Compositae*). *The American Naturalist* **107**: 651–661.

Ackerman, J. D. and A. M. Montalvo. 1990. Short- and long-term limitations to fruit production in a tropical orchid. *Ecology* **71**: 263–272.

Adam, P. 1990. *Saltmarsh Ecology*. Cambridge: Cambridge University Press.

Adamus, P. R. 1992. Choices in monitoring wetlands. pp. 571–592. In D. H. McKenzie, D. E. Hyatt, and V. J. McDonald (eds.) *Ecological Indicators*. London: Elsevier Applied Science.

Aerts, R. 1996. Nutrient resorption from senescing leaves of perennials: are there general patterns. *Journal of Ecology* **84**: 597–608.

Agnew, A. D. Q. 1961. The ecology of *Juncus effusus* L. in North Wales. *Journal of Ecology* **49**: 83–102.

Allee, W. C. 1951. *Cooperation Among Animals with Human Implications*. New York: Schuman. (Revised edition of *Social Life of Animals*. 1938. New York: Norton.)

Allee, W. C., A. E. Emerson, O. Park, T. Park, and K. P. Schmidt. 1949. *Principles of Animal Ecology*. Philadelphia: Saunders.

Allen, E. B. 1988. *The Reconstruction of Disturbed Arid Ecosystems*. Boulder: Westview Press.

Allen, E. B. and M. F. Allen. 1990. The mediation of competition by mycorrhizae in successional and patchy environments. pp. 367–389. In J. B. Grace and D. Tilman (eds.) *Perspectives on Plant Competition*. San Diego: Academic Press.

Allison, S. K. 1995. Recovery from small-scale anthropogenic disturbances by northern California salt marsh plant assemblages. *Ecological Applications* **5**: 693–702.

Alvarez, W. 1998. *T. rex and the Crater of Doom*. New York: Vintage Books.

Alverson, W. S., D. M. Waller, and S. J. Solheim. 1988. Forests to deer: edge effects in northern Wisconsin. *Conservation Biology* **2**: 348–358.

Anderson, R. C., A. E. Liberta, L. A. Dickman, and A. J. Katz. 1983. Spatial variation in vesicular-arbuscular mycorrhizal spore density. *Bulletin of the Torrey Botanical Club* **110**: 519–525.

Anderson, R. C., A. E. Liberta, and L. A. Dickman. 1984. Interaction of vascular plants and vesicular-arbuscular mycorrhizal fungi across a soil moisture-nutrient gradient. *Oecologia* **64**: 111–117.

Anderson, R. C., J. S. Fralish, and J. M. Baskin. 1999. *Savannas, Barrens, and Rock Outcrop Plant Communities of North America*. Cambridge: Cambridge University Press.

Antonovics, J. 1984. Genetic variation within populations. pp. 229–241. In R. Dirzo and J. Sarukhán (eds.) *Perspectives on Plant Population Ecology*. Sunderland: Sinauer.

Archer, S. 1989. Have southern Texas savannas been converted to woodlands in recent history? *The American Naturalist* **134**: 545–561.

Archibold, O. W. 1995. *Ecology of World Vegetation*. London: Chapman and Hall.

Arthur, W. 1982. The evolutionary consequences of interspecific competition. *Advances in Ecological Research* **12**: 127–187.

Arthur, W. 1987. *The Niche in Competition and Evolution*. Chichester: Wiley.

Ashton, P. S. 1988. Dipterocarp biology as a window to the understanding of tropical forest structure. *Annual Review of Ecology and Systematics* **19**: 347–370.

Ashton, P. S., T. J. Givnish, and S. Appanah. 1988. Staggered flowering in the Dipterocarpaceae: new insights into floral induction and the evolution of mast fruiting in the seasonal tropics. *The American Naturalist* **132**: 44–66.

Atwood, E. L. 1950. Life history studies of the nutria, or coypu, in coastal Louisiana. *Journal of Wildlife Management* **14**: 249–265.

Auclair, A. N. D., A. Bouchard, and J. Pajaczkowski. 1976a. Plant standing crop and productivity relations in a *Scirpus-Equisetum* wetland. *Ecology* **57**: 941–952.

Auclair, A. N. D., A. Bouchard, and J. Pajaczkowski. 1976b. Productivity relations in a *Carex*-dominated ecosystem. *Oecologia* **26**: 9–31.

Austin, M. P. 1968. An ordination study of a chalk grassland community. *Journal of Ecology* **56**: 739–757.

Austin, M. P. 1982. Use of a relative physiological performance value in the prediction of performance in multispecies mixtures from monoculture performance. *Journal of Ecology* **70**: 559–570.

Austin, M. P. and B. O. Austin. 1980. Behaviour of experimental plant communities along a nutrient gradient. *Journal of Ecology* **68**: 891–918.

Austin, M. P., J. G. Pausas, and A. O. Nicholls. 1996. Patterns of tree species richness in relation to environment in southeastern New South Wales, Australia. *Australian Journal of Ecology* **21**: 154–164.

Austin, M. P., J. G. Pausas, and I. R. Noble. 1997. Modelling environmental and temporal niches of eucalypts. pp. 129–150. In J. E. Williams and J. C. Z. Woinarski (eds.) *Eucalypt Ecology: Individuals to Ecosystems*. Cambridge: Cambridge University Press.

Axelrod, D. I. 1970. Mesozoic paleogeography and early angiosperm history. *The Botanical Review* **36**: 277–319.

Axelrod, D. I. and P. H. Raven. 1972. Evolutionary biogeography viewed from plate tectonic theory. pp. 218–236. In J. A. Behnke (ed.) *Challenging Biological Problems: Directions Toward Their Solution*. Oxford: Oxford University Press.

Bacon, P. R. 1978. *Flora and Fauna of the Caribbean*. Trinidad: Key Caribbean Publications.

Bailes, K. E. 1990. *Science and Russian Culture in an Age of Revolutions. V. I. Vernadsky and his Scientific School, 1863–1945*. Bloomington, IN: Indiana University Press.

Baker, H. 1937. Alluvial meadows: a comparative study of grazed and mown meadows. *Journal of Ecology* **25**: 408–420.

Baker-Brosh, K. and R. K. Peet. 1997. The ecological significance of lobed and toothed leaves in temperate forest trees. *Ecology* **78**: 1250–1255.

Bakker, R. T. 1978. Dinosaur feeding behaviour and the origin of flowering plants. *Nature* **274**: 661–663.

Bakker, S. A., C. Jasperse, and J. T. A. Verhoeven. 1997. Accumulation rates of organic matter associated with different successional stages from open water to carr forest in former turbaries. *Plant Ecology* **129**: 113–120.

Baldwin, W. K. W. 1958. *Plants of the Clay Belt of Northern Ontario and Quebec*. National Museum of Canada, Bulletin No. 156.

Ball, P. J. and T. D. Nudds. 1989. Mallard habitat selection: an experiment and implications for management. pp. 659–671. In R. R. Sharitz and J. W. Gibbons (eds.) *Freshwater Wetlands and Wildlife*. U.S. Department of Energy. Proceedings of a symposium held at Charleston, South Carolina, March 24–27, 1986.

Barko, J. W. and R. M. Smart. 1978. The growth and biomass distribution of two emergent freshwater plants, *Cyperus esculentus* and *Scirpus validus*, on different sediments. *Aquatic Botany* **5**: 109–117.

Barko, J. W. and R. M. Smart. 1979. The nutritional ecology of *Cyperus esculentus*, an emergent aquatic plant, grown on different sediments. *Aquatic Botany* **6**: 13–28.

Barnett, V. 1994. Statistics and the long-term experiments: past achievements and future challenges. pp. 165–183. In R. A. Leigh and A. E. Johnston (eds.) *Long-term Experiments in Agricultural and Ecological Sciences*. Proceedings of a conference to celebrate the 150th anniversary of Rothamsted Experimental Station, held at Rothamsted, July 14–17, 1993. Wallingford: CAB International.

Barrett, S. C. H. 2002. The evolution of plant sexual diversity. *Nature Reviews Genetics* **3**: 274–284.

Barry, J. M. 1997. *Rising Tide. The Great Mississippi Flood of 1927 and How it Changed America*. New York: Simon and Schuster.

Barth, F. G. 1985. *Insects and Flowers: The Biology of a Partnership*. Princeton: Princeton University Press. Translated from 1982 German edition by M. A. Biederman-Thorson.

Barthlott, W., S. Porembski, E. Fischer, and B. Gemmel. 1998. First protozoa-trapping plant found. *Nature* **392**: 447.

Baskin, J. M. and C. C. Baskin. 1985. A floristic study of a cedar glade in Blue Licks Battlefield State Park, Kentucky. *Castanea* **50**: 19–25.

Bauer, C. R., C. H. Kellogg, S. D. Bridgham, and G. A. Lamberti. 2003. Mycorrhizal colonization across hydrological gradients in restored and reference freshwater wetlands. *Wetlands* **23**: 961–968.

Baylis, G. T. S. 1980. Mycorrhizas and the spread of beech. *New Zealand Journal of Ecology* **3**: 151–153.

Beard, J. S. 1944. Climax vegetation in tropical America. *Ecology* **25**: 127–158.

Beard, J. S. 1949. *The Natural Vegetation of the Windward and Leeward Islands*. Oxford: Clarendon Press.

Beard, J. S. 1973. The physiognomic approach. pp. 355–386. In R. H. Whittaker (ed.) *Ordination and Classification of Communities*. Part V. The Hague: W. Junk.

Beattie, A. J. and D. C. Culver. 1981. The guild of myrmecochores in the herbaceous flora of West Virginia forests. *Ecology* **62**: 107–115.

Beeftink, W. G. 1977. The coastal salt marshes of western and northern Europe: an ecological and phytosociological approach. pp. 109–155. In V. J. Chapman (ed.) *Ecosystems of the World 1: Wet Coastal Ecosystems*. Amsterdam: Elsevier Scientific Publishing Company.

Bégin, Y., S. Arseneault, and J. Lavoie. 1989. Dynamique d'une bordure forestière par suite de la hausse récente du niveau marin, rive sud-ouest du Golfe du Saint-Laurent, Nouveau-Brunswick. *Geographie Physique et Quaternaire* **43**: 355–366.

Begon, M. and M. Mortimer. 1981. *Population Ecology: A Unified Study of Animals and Plants*. Oxford: Blackwell.

Belcher, J., P. A. Keddy, and P. M. C. Catling. 1992. Alvar vegetation in Canada: a multivariate description at two scales. *Canadian Journal of Botany* **70**: 1279–1291.

Belcher, J. W., P. A. Keddy, and L. Twolan-Strutt. 1995. Root and shoot competition intensity along a soil depth gradient. *Journal of Ecology* **83**: 673–682.

Bell, A. D. 1984. Dynamic morphology: a contribution to plant population ecology. pp. 48–65. In R. Dirzo and J. Sarukhán (eds.) *Perspectives on Plant Population Ecology*. Sunderland: Sinauer.

Bell, R. A. 1993. Cryptoendolithic algae of hot semiarid lands and deserts. *Journal of Phycology* **29**: 133–139.

Belsky, A. J. 1992. Effects of grazing, competition, disturbance and fire on species composition and diversity in grassland communities. *Journal of Vegetation Science* **3**: 187–200.

Bender, E. A., T. J. Case, and M. E. Gilpin. 1984. Perturbation experiments in community ecology: theory and practice. *Ecology* **65**: 1–13.

Benecke, P. and R. Mayer. 1971. Aspects of soil water behavior as related to beech and spruce stands: some results of water balance investigations. pp. 153–168. In H. Ellenburg (ed.) *Integrated Experimental Ecology: Methods and Results of Ecosystem Research in the German Solling Project*, Vol. 2. Ecological Studies: Analysis and Synthesis. New York: Springer.

Benson, L. 1950. *The Cacti of Arizona*, 2nd edn. Tucson: University of Arizona Press.

Benson, L. 1959. *Plant Classification*. Lexington: D.C. Heath and Company.

Benzing, D. H. 1990. *Vascular Epiphytes: General Biology and Related Biota*. Cambridge: Cambridge University Press.

Berbee, M. L. and J. W. Taylor. 1993. Dating the evolutionary radiations of the true fungi. *Canadian Journal of Botany* **71**: 1114–1127.

Berenbaum, M. R. 1991. Coumarins. pp. 221–249. In G. A. Rosenthal and M. R. Berenbaum (eds.) *Herbivores: Their Interactions with Secondary Plant Metabolites*. San Diego: Academic Press.

Berg, R. Y. 1975. Myrmecochorous plants in Australia and their dispersal by ants. *Australian Journal of Botany* **23**: 475–508.

Bernard, H. A. and R. J. Leblanc. 1965. Résumé of the quaternary geology of the northwestern Gulf of Mexico province. pp. 137–185. In H. E. Wright and D. G. Frey (eds.) *The Quaternary of the United States*. Princeton: Princeton University Press.

Bernatowicz, S. and J. Zachwieja. 1966. Types of littoral found in the lakes of the Masurian and Suwalki Lakelands. *Komitet Ekolgiezny-Polska Akademia Nauk* **XIV**: 519–545.

Bertness, M. D. and S. D. Hacker. 1994. Physical stress and positive associations among marsh plants. *The American Naturalist* **144**: 363–372.

Bertness, M. D. and S. M. Yeh. 1994. Cooperative and competitive interactions in the recruitment of marsh elders. *Ecology* **75**: 2416–2429.

Bessey, C. E. 1915. The phylogenetic taxonomy of flowering plants. *Annals of the Missouri Botanical Garden* **2**: 109–164.

Bierzychudek, P. 1980. The demographic consequences of sexuality and apomixis in *Antennaria*. pp 293–307. In S. Kawano (ed.) *Biological Approaches and Evolutionary Trends in Plants*. London: Academic Press.

Billings, W. D. and H. A. Mooney. 1968. The ecology of arctic and alpine plants. *Biological Reviews* **43**: 481–529.

Binford, M. W., M. Brenner, T. J. Whitmore, A. Higuera-Gundy, E. S. Deevey, and B. Leyden. 1987. Ecosystems, paleoecology and human disturbance in subtropical and tropical America. *Quaternary Science Reviews* **6**: 115–128.

Björkman, E. 1960. *Monotropa hypopitys* L. an epiparasite on tree roots. *Physiologia Plantarum* **13**: 308–327.

Black, D. (ed.) 1979. *Carl Linnaeus: Travels.* Nature Classics. New York: Charles Scribner's Sons.

Bliss, L. C. and W. G. Gold. 1994. The patterning of plant communities and edaphic factors along a high arctic coastline: implications for succession. *Canadian Journal of Botany* **72**: 1095–1107.

Blizard, D. 1993. *The Normandy Landings D-Day: The Invasion of Europe 6 June 1944.* London: Reed International Books.

Boesch, D. F., M. N. Josselyn, A. J. Mehta, J. T. Morris, W. K. Nuttle, C. A. Simenstad, and D. P. J. Swift. 1994. Scientific assessment of coastal wetland loss, restoration and management in Louisiana. *Journal of Coastal Research*, Special Issue No. 20.

Bohlen, P. J., S. Scheu, C. M. Hale, M. A. McLean, S. Migge, P. M. Groffman, and D. Parkinson. 2004. Invasive earthworms as agents of change in north temperate forests. *Frontiers in Ecology and the Environment* **8**: 427–435.

Bolan, N. S. 1991. A critical review on the role of mychorrhizal fungi in the uptake of phosphorus by plants. *Plant and Soil* **134**: 189–207.

Bond, W. J. 1997. Functional types for predicting changes in biodiversity: a case study in Cape fynbos. pp. 174–194. In T. M. Smith, H. H. Shugart, and F. I. Woodward (eds.) *Plant Functional Types.* Cambridge: Cambridge University Press.

Boot, R. G. A. 1989. The significance of size and morphology of root systems for nutrient acquisition and competition. pp. 299–311. In H. Lambert *et al.* (eds.) *Causes and Consequences of Variation in Growth Rate and Productivity of Higher Plants.* The Hague: SPB Academic Publishing.

Booth, B. and D. W. Larson. 1999. Impact of history, language, and choice of system on the study of assembly rules. pp. 206–229. In E. Weiher and P. Keddy (eds.) *Ecological Assembly Rules: Perspectives, Advances, Retreats.* Cambridge: Cambridge University Press.

Borhidi, A. 1992. The serpentine flora and vegetation of Cuba. pp. 83–95. In A. J. M. Baker, J. Proctor, and R. D. Reeves (eds.) *The Vegetation of Ultramafic (Serpentine) Soils.* Andover: Intercept.

Bormann, B. T. and R. C. Sidle. 1990. Changes in productivity and distribution of nutrients in a chronosequence at Glacier Bay National Park, Alaska. *Journal of Ecology* **78**: 561–578.

Bormann, F. H. and G. E. Likens. 1981. *Pattern and Process in a Forested Ecosystem.* Second corrected printing. New York: Springer-Verlag.

Boston, H. L. 1986. A discussion of the adaptation for carbon acquisition in relation to the growth strategy of aquatic isoetids. *Aquatic Botany* **26**: 259–270.

Boston, H. L. and M. S. Adams. 1986. The contribution of crassulacean acid metabolism to the annual productivity of two aquatic vascular plants. *Oecologia* **68**: 615–622.

Botkin, D. B. 1977. Life and death in a forest: the computer as an aid to understanding. pp. 213–33. In A. S. Hall and J. W. Day (eds.) *Ecosystem Modelling in Theory and Practice.* New York: John Wiley and Sons.

Botkin, D. B. 1990. *Discordant Harmonies: A New Ecology for the Twenty-first Century.* New York: Oxford University Press.

Botkin, D. B. 1993. *Forest Dynamics.* Oxford: Oxford University Press.

Boucher, D. H. 1985a. *The Biology of Mutualism: Ecology and Evolution.* New York: Oxford University Press.

Boucher, D. H. 1985b. The idea of mutualism, past and future. pp. 1–28. In D. H. Boucher. *The Biology of Mutualism: Ecology and Evolution.* New York: Oxford University Press.

Boucher, D. H., S. James, and K. H. Keeler. 1982. The ecology of mutualism. *Annual Review of Ecology and Systematics* **13**: 315–347.

Boutin, C. and P. A. Keddy. 1993. A functional classification of wetland plants. *Journal of Vegetation Science* **4**: 591–600.

Bowers, M. D. 1991. Iridoid glycosides. pp. 297–325. In G. A. Rosenthal and M. R. Berenbaum (eds.) *Herbivores: Their Interactions with Secondary Plant Metabolites*. San Diego: Academic Press.

Boyd, C. E. 1978. Chemical composition of wetland plants. pp. 155–168. In R. E. Good, D. F. Whigham, and R. L. Simpson (eds.) *Freshwater Wetlands: Ecological Processes and Management Potential*. New York: Academic Press.

Boyd, R. and S. Penland. 1988. A geomorphologic model for Mississippi River delta evolution. *Transactions Gulf Coast Association of Geological Societies* **38**: 443–452.

Brackenridge, J. B. and R. M. Rosenberg. 1970. *The Principles of Physics and Chemistry*. New York: McGraw-Hill.

Braun, E. L. 1950. *The Deciduous Forest of Eastern North America*. New York: Hafner.

Brewer, J. S. 1998. Effects of competition and litter on a carnivorous plant, *Drosera cappilaris* (Droseraceae). *American Journal of Botany* **85 N 11**: 1592–1596.

Brewer, J. S. 1999. Effects of fire, competition and soil disturbances on regeneration of a carnivorous plant (*Drosera capillaris*). *The American Midland Naturalist* **141**: 28–42.

Bridges, E. M., N. H. Batjes, and F. O. Nachtergaele (eds.) 1998. *World Reference Base for Soil Resources: Atlas*. Leuven, Belgium: ACCO.

Brinson, M. M. 1993a. Changes in the functioning of wetlands along environmental gradients. *Wetlands* **13**: 65–74.

Brinson, M. M. 1993b. *A Hydrogeomorphic Classification for Wetlands*. Technical Report WRP-DE-4. U.S. Army Corps of Engineers, Washington, D.C.

Brooks, R. R., R. D. Reeves, and A. J. M. Baker. 1992. The serpentine vegetation of Goiás State, Brazil. pp. 67–81. In A. J. M. Baker, J. Proctor, and R. D. Reeves (eds.) *The Vegetation of Ultramafic (Serpentine) Soils*. Andover: Intercept.

Brown, J. F. 1997. Effects of experimental burial on survival, growth, and resource allocation of three species of dune plants. *Journal of Ecology* **85**: 151–158.

Brown, J. H., D. W. Davidson, J. C. Munger, and R. S. Inouye. 1986. Experimental community ecology: the desert granivore system. pp. 41–61. In J. Diamond and T. J. Case (eds.) *Community Ecology*. New York: Harper and Row.

Browne, J. 1995. *Charles Darwin: Voyaging*. Princeton: Princeton University Press.

Bryant, D., D. Nielsen, and L. Tangley. 1997. *The Last Frontier Forests: Ecosystems and Economies on the Edge*. Washington: World Resources Institute.

Burch, W. Jr. 1999. *Daydreams and Nightmares – A Sociological Essay on the American Environment*. Madison: Social Ecology Press.

Burdon, J. J. 1982. The effect of fungal pathogens on plant communities. pp. 99–112. In E. I. Newman (ed.) *The Plant Community as a Working Mechanism*. Oxford: Blackwell.

Burger, J. C. and S. V. Louda. 1995. Interaction of diffuse competition and insect herbivory in limiting brittle prickly pear cactus, *Opuntia fragilis* (Cactaceae). *American Journal of Botany* **82**: 1558–1566.

Burgess, R. L. and D. M. Sharpe (eds.) 1981. *Forest Island Dynamics in Man-dominated Landscapes*. New York: Springer-Verlag.

Buss, L. W. 1988. *The Evolution of Individuality*. Princeton: Princeton University Press.

Cairns, J. (ed.) 1980. *The Recovery Process in Damaged Ecosystems*. Ann Arbor: Ann Arbor Science.

Cairns, J. (ed.) 1988. *Rehabilitating Damaged Ecosystems*. Vol. 1 and 2. Boca Raton: CRC Press.

Cairns, J. 1989. Restoring damaged ecosystems: is predisturbance condition a viable option? *The Environmental Professional* **11**: 152–159.

Cairns-Smith, A. G. 1985. *Seven Clues to the Origin of Life: A Scientific Detective Story*. Canto edition 1990. Cambridge: Cambridge University Press.

Callaway, R. M. and L. King. 1996. Temperature-driven variation in substrate oxygenation and the balance of competition and facilitation. *Ecology* **77**: 1189–1195.

Campbell, B. D., J. P. Grime, and J. M. L. Mackey. 1991. A trade-off between scale and precision in resource foraging. *Oecologia* **87**: 532–538.

Campbell, B. D., J. P. Grime, and J. M. L. Mackey. 1992. Shoot thrust and its role in plant competition. *Journal of Ecology* **80**: 633–641.

Canfield, R. H. 1948. Perennial grass composition as an indicator of condition of southwestern mixed grass ranges. *Ecology* **29**: 190–204.

Caputa, J. 1948. Untersuchungen über die Entwicklung einiger Gräser und Kleearten in Reinsaat und Mischung. *Landwirtschaftliches Jahrbuch der Schweiz* **62**: 848–975.

Carleton, T. J. and P. MacLellan. 1994. Woody vegetation responses to fire versus clear-cutting logging: a comparative survey in the central Canadian boreal forest. *Ecoscience* **1**: 141–152.

Carpenter, S. R., S. W. Chisholm, C. J. Krebs, D. W. Schindler, and R. F. Wright. 1995. Ecosystem experiments. *Science* **269**: 324–327.

Carroll, G. 1988. Fungal endophytes in stems and leaves: from latent pathogen to mutualistic symboint. *Ecology* **69**: 2–9.

Carson, R. 1962. *Silent Spring*. Boston: Houghton Mifflin.

Carson, W. P. and S. T. A. Pickett. 1990. Role of resources and disturbance in the organization of an old-field plant community. *Ecology* **71**: 226–238.

Catling, P. M. and V. R. Brownell. 1995. A review of the alvars of the Great Lakes region: distribution, floristic composition, biogeography and protection. *The Canadian Field-Naturalist* **109**: 143–171.

Catling, P. M. and V. R. Brownell. 1998. Importance of fire in alvar ecosystems – evidence from the Burnt Lands, Eastern Ontario. *The Canadian Field-Naturalist* **112**: 661–667.

Catling, P. M., J. E. Cruise, K. L. McIntosh, and S. M. McKay. 1975. Alvar vegetation in southern Ontario. *Ontario Field Biologist* **29**: 1–25.

Cavers, P. B. 1983. Seed demography. *Canadian Journal of Botany* **61**: 3578–3590.

Chaneton, E. J. and J. M. Facelli. 1991. Disturbance effects on plant community diversity: spatial scales and dominance hierarchies. *Vegetatio* **93**: 143–156.

Chapin, III, F. S. 1980. The mineral nutrition of wild plants. *Annual Review of Ecology and Systematics* **11**: 233–260.

Chapin, III, F. S., P. M. Vitousek, and K. Van Cleve. 1986. The nature of nutrient limitation in plant communities. *The American Naturalist* **127**: 48–58.

Chapman, V. J. 1940. The functions of the pneumatophores of *Avicennia nitida* Jacq. *Proceedings of the Linnean Society of London* **152**: 228–233.

Charron, D. and D. Gagnon. 1991. The demography of northern populations of *Panax quinquefolium* (American ginseng). *Journal of Ecology* **79**: 431–445.

Cheplick, G. P. 1992. Sibling competition in plants. *Journal of Ecology* **80**: 567–575.

Christensen, N. L., R. B. Burchell, A. Liggett, and E. L. Simms. 1981. The structure and development of pocosin vegetation. pp. 43–61. In C. J. Richardson (ed.) *Pocosin Wetlands: An Integrated Analysis of Coastal Plain Freshwater Bogs in North Carolina*. Stroudsburg, Pennsylvania: Hutchinson Ross Publishing Company.

Christensen, N. L., A. M. Bartuska, J. H. Brown, S. Carpenter, C. D'Antonio, R. Francis, J. F. Franklin, J. A. MacMahon, R. F. Noss, D. J. Parsons, C. H. Peterson, M. G. Turner, and R. G. Woodmansee. 1996. The report of the Ecological Society of America Committee on the Scientific Basis for Ecosystem Management. *Ecological Applications* **6**: 665–691.

Clarke, D. and N. J. Hannon. 1969. The mangrove swamp and salt marsh communities of the Sydney district. II. The holocoenotic complex with particular reference to physiography. *Journal of Ecology* **57**: 213–234.

Clay, K. 1990. The impact of parasitic and mutualistic fungi on competitive interactions among plants. pp. 391–412. In J. B. Grace and D. Tilman (eds.) *Perspectives on Plant Competition*. San Diego: Academic Press.

Clements, F. E. 1916. *Plant Succession: An Analysis of the Development of Vegetation*. Pub. 242. Washington, DC: Carnegie Institute.

Clements, F. E. 1933. Competition in plant societies. In *News Service Bulletin*. Washington: Carnegie Institution of Washington, April 2, 1933.

Clements, F. E. 1935. Experimental ecology in the public service. *Ecology* **16**: 324–363.

Clements, F. E. 1936. Nature and structure of climax. *Journal of Ecology* **24**: 254–282.

Clements, F. E., J. E. Weaver, and H. C. Hanson. 1929. *Plant Competition*. Washington, D.C.: Carnegie Institution of Washington.

Cloud, P. 1976. Beginnings of biospheric evolution and their biogeochemical consequences. *Paleobiology* **2**: 351–387.

Cloudsley-Thompson, J. L. 1996. *Biotic Interactions in Arid Lands*. Berlin: Springer-Verlag.

Clymo, R. S. and J. G. Duckett. 1986. Regeneration of *Sphagnum*. *New Phytologist* **102**: 589–614.

Clymo, R. S. and P. M. Hayward. 1982. The ecology of *Sphagnum*. pp. 229–289. In A. J. E. Smith (ed.) *Bryophyte Ecology*. London: Chapman and Hall.

Cody, M. L. 1993. Do cholla cacti (*Opuntia* spp., Subgenus Cylindropuntia) use or need nurse plants in the Mojave Desert? *Journal of Arid Environments* **24**: 1–16.

Coe, M. J., D. L. Dilcher, J. O. Farlow, D. M. Jarzen, and D. A. Russel. 1987. Dinosaurs and land plants. pp. 225–258. In E. Friis, W. G. Chaloner, and P. R. Crane (eds.) *The Origins of Angiosperms and Their Biological Consequences*. Cambridge: Cambridge University Press.

Cole, L. C. 1949. The measurement of interspecific association. *Ecology* **30**: 411–424.

Coleman, J. M., H. H. Roberts, and G. W. Stone. 1998. Mississippi River Delta: an overview. *Journal of Coastal Research* **14**: 698–716.

Coleman, R. G. and C. Jove. 1992. Geological origin of serpentines. pp. 1–17. In A. J. M. Baker, J. Proctor, and R. D. Reeves (eds.) *The Vegetation of Ultramafic (Serpentine) Soils*. Andover: Intercept.

Coley, P. D. 1983. Herbivory and defensive characteristics of tree species in a lowland tropical forest. *Ecological Monographs* **53**: 209–233.

Colinvaux, P. 1978. *Why Big Fierce Animals are Rare: An Ecologist's Perspective*. Princeton: Princeton University Press.

Colinvaux, P. 1986. *Ecology*. Toronto: Wiley and Sons.

Colinvaux, P. 1993. *Ecology 2.* New York: Wiley and Sons.

Colinvaux, P. A., P. E. De Oliveira, J. E. Moreno, M. C. Miller, and M. B. Bush. 1996. A long pollen record from lowland Amazonia: forest and cooling in glacial times. *Science* **274**: 85–88.

Colinvaux, P. A., P. E. De Oliveira, and M. B. Bush. 2000. Amazonian and Neotropical plant communities on glacial time-scales: the failure of the aridity and refuge hypotheses. *Quaternary Science Reviews* **19**: 141–169.

Colinvaux, P. A., G. Irion, M. E. Räsänen, M. B. Bush, and J. A. S. Nunes de Mello 2001. A paradigm to be discarded: geological and paleoecological data falsify the Haffer & Prance refuge hypothesis of Amazonian speciation. *Amazoniana* **16**: 609–646.

Collinson, M. E. and J. J. Hooker. 1987. Vegetational and mammalian faunal changes in the Early Tertiary of southern England. pp. 259–304. In E. Friis, W. G. Chaloner, and P. R. Crane (eds.) *The Origins of Angiosperms and Their Biological Consequences.* Cambridge: Cambridge University Press.

Colwell, R. K. and E. R. Fuentes. 1975. Experimental studies of the niche. *Annual Review of Ecology and Systematics* **6**: 281–309.

Connell, J. H. 1978. Diversity in tropical rain forests and coral reefs. *Science* **199**: 1302–1310.

Connell, J. H. 1990. Apparent versus "real" competition in plants. pp. 9–26. In J. B. Grace and D. Tilman (eds.) *Perspectives on Plant Competition.* San Diego: Academic Press.

Connell, J. H. and R. O. Slatyer. 1977. Mechanisms of succession in natural communities and their role in community stability and organization. *The American Naturalist* **111**: 1119–1144.

Conner, W. H. and M. A. Buford. 1998. Southern deepwater swamps. pp. 261–287. In M. G. Messina and W. H. Conner (eds.) *Southern Forested Wetlands. Ecology and Management.* Boca Raton: Lewis Publishers.

Connolly, J. 1986. On difficulties with replacement-series methodology in mixture experiments. *Journal of Applied Ecology* **23**: 125–137.

Conservation International. 2006. *Biodiversity Hotspots. Tropical Andes.* (www.biodiversityhotspots.org/xp/Hotspots/andes/) accessed 24 July 2006.

Corfield, T. F. 1973. Elephant mortality in Tsavo National Park, Kenya. *East African Wildlife Journal* **11**: 339–368.

Cowling, R. M. 1990. Diversity components in a species-rich area of the Cape Floristic Region. *Journal of Vegetation Science* **1**: 699–710.

Cowling, R. M. and M. J. Samways. 1995. Predicting global patterns of endemic plant species richness. *Biodiversity Letters* **2**: 127–131.

Cowling, R. M., P. W. Rundel, B. B. Lamont, M. K. Arroyo, and M. Arianoutsou. 1996. Plant diversity in mediterranean-climate regions. *Trends in Ecology and Evolution* **11**: 362–366.

Craighead, F. C., Sr. 1968. The role of the alligator in shaping plant communities and maintaining wildlife in the southern Everglades. *The Florida Naturalist* **41**: 2–7, 69–74.

Crandell, D. R. and H. H. Waldron. 1969. Volcanic hazards in the Cascade Range. pp. 5–18. In R. Olson and M. Wallace (eds.) *Geologic Hazards and Public Problems.* Conference Proceedings. U.S. Government Printing Office.

Crawford, R. M. M. 1982. Physiological response to flooding. pp. 453–477. In O. L. Lange, P. S. Nobel, C. B. Osmond, and H. Ziegler (eds.) *Physiological Plant Ecology II.* Encyclopedia of Plant Physiology. Berlin: Springer-Verlag.

Crawley, M. J. 1983. *Herbivory: The Dynamics of Animal/Plant Interactions.* Oxford: Blackwell.

Crawley, M. J. and J. E. Harral. 2001. Scale dependence in plant biodiversity. *Science* **291**: 864–868.

Crepet, W. L. and E. M. Friis. 1987. The evolution of insect pollination in angiosperms. pp. 181–201. In E. Friis, W. G. Chaloner, and P. R. Crane (eds.) *The Origins of Angiosperms and Their Biological Consequences*. Cambridge: Cambridge University Press.

Crocker, R. L. and J. Major. 1955. Soil development in relation to vegetation and surface age at Glacier Bay, Alaska. *Journal of Ecology* **43**: 427–448.

Cronquist, A. 1991. Asterales. pp. 721–726. In *Angiosperms: The Flowering Plants*. pp. 596–765, Vol. 13. *The New Encyclopaedia Britannica*, 15th edn. Chicago: The University of Chicago.

Cronquist, A. 1993. A commentary on the general system of classification of flowering plants. pp. 272–293. In Flora of North America Editorial Committee. *Flora of North America*, Vol. 1. *Introduction*. New York: Oxford University Press.

Cyr, H. and M. L. Pace. 1993. Magnitude and patterns of herbivory in aquatic and terrestrial ecosystems. *Nature* **361**: 148–150.

Dacey, J. W. H. 1980. Internal winds in water lilies: an adaptation for life in anaerobic sediments. *Science* **210**: 1017–1019.

Dacey, J. W. H. 1981. Pressurized ventilation in the yellow water lily. *Ecology* **62**: 1137–1147.

Dafni, A. 1992. *Pollination Ecology: A Practical Approach*. Oxford: Oxford University Press.

Dale, M. 1999. *Spatial Pattern Analysis in Plant Ecology*. Cambridge: Cambridge University Press.

Dansereau, P. 1959. Vascular aquatic plant communities of southern Quebec. A preliminary analysis. *Transactions of the Northeast Wildlife Conference* **10**: 27–54.

Dansereau, P. and F. Segadas-Vianna. 1952. Ecological study of the peat bogs of eastern North America. *Canadian Journal of Botany* **30**: 490–520.

Darwin, C. 1871. The descent of Man and selection in relation to sex. In M. J. Adler (ed.) *Great Books of the Western World*, 2nd edn, Vol. 49. Chicago: Encyclopaedia Britannica.

Darwin, C. 1888. *Insectivorous Plants*. 2nd edn. London: John Murray. Revised by F. Darwin.

Darwin, C. R. 1881. *The Formation of Vegetable Mould Through the Action of Worms, with Observations on Their Habits*. London: Murray.

Darwin, F. (ed.) 1950. *Charles Darwin's Autobiography: With his Notes and Letters Depicting the Growth of the Origin of Species*. New York: Henry Schuman.

Daubenmire, R. 1978. *Plant Geography: With Special Reference to North America. Physiological Ecology*. New York: Academic Press.

Davis, D. W. 2000. Historical perspective on crevasses, levees, and the Mississippi River. In C. E. Colten (ed.) *Transforming New Orleans and its Environs, Centuries of Change*. Pittsburgh: University of Pittsburgh Press.

Davies, B. R. and K. F. Walker. 1986. *The Ecology of River Systems*. Dordrecht: W. Junk Publishers.

Davis, M. B. 1976. Pleistocene biogeography of temperate deciduous forests. pp. 13–26. In R. C. West and W. G. Haag (eds.) *Geoscience and Man*, Vol. 13. *Ecology of the Pleistocene, a Symposium*. Baton Rouge: School of Geoscience, Louisiana State University.

Davis, S. and J. Ogden (eds.) 1994. *Everglades: The Ecosystem and its Restoration*. Del Ray Beach: St. Lucie Press.

Dawkins, R. 1976. *The Selfish Gene*. Oxford: Oxford University Press.

Day, R. T., P. A. Keddy, J. McNeill, and T. Carleton. 1988. Fertility and disturbance gradients: a summary model for riverine marsh vegetation. *Ecology* **69**: 1044–1054.

Day, W. 1984. *Genesis on Planet Earth*, 2nd edn. New Haven: Yale University Press.

Dayton, P. K. 1979. Ecology: a science and a religion. pp. 3–18. In R. J. Livingston (ed.) *Ecological Processes in Coastal and Marine Systems*. New York: Plenum Press.

de Calesta, D. S. 1994. Effect of white-tailed deer on songbirds within managed forests in Pennsylvania. *Journal of Wildlife Management* **58**: 711–718.

Deckers, J. A., F. O. Nachtergaele, and O. C. Spaargaren (eds.) 1998. *World Reference Base for Soil Resources: Introduction*. Leuven, Belgium: ACCO.

de Duve, C. 1991. *Blueprint for a Cell: The Nature and Origin of Life*. Burlington: Neil Patterson.

de Groot, R. S. 1992. *Functions of Nature*. Groningen: Wolters-Noordhoff.

Delcourt, H. R. and P. A. Delcourt. 1988. Quaternary landscape ecology: relevant scales in space and time. *Landscape Ecology* **2**: 23–44.

Delcourt, H. R. and P. A. Delcourt. 1991. *Quaternary Ecology: A Paleoecological Perspective*. London: Chapman and Hall.

del Moral, R. 1983. Competition as a control mechanism in subalpine meadows. *American Journal of Botany* **70**: 232–245.

del Moral, R. and L. C. Bliss. 1993. Mechanisms of primary succession: insights resulting from the eruption of Mount St. Helens. *Advances in Ecological Research* **24**: 1–66.

del Moral, R. and S. Y. Grishin. 1999. Volcanic disturbances and ecosystem recovery. pp. 137–160. In L. R. Walker (ed.) *Ecosystems of Disturbed Ground*. Ecosystems of the World Series. Amsterdam: Elsevier Science.

del Moral, R. and D. M. Wood. 1993. Early primary succession on the volcano Mount St. Helens. *Journal of Vegetation Science* **4**: 223–234.

del Moral, R., J. H. Titus, and A. M. Cook. 1995. Early primary succession on Mount St. Helens, Washington, USA. *Journal of Vegetation Science* **6**: 107–120.

Denslow, J. L. 1987. Tropical rain forest gaps and tree species diversity. *Annual Review of Ecology and Systematics* **18**: 431–451.

Deshmukh, I. 1986. *Ecology and Tropical Biology*. Palo Alto: Blackwell Scientific.

Desmond, A. and J. Moore. 1991. *Darwin*. New York: Warner Books.

de Wit, C. T. 1960. On competition. *Verslagen van Landbouwkundige Onderzoekingen* **66**: 1–82.

Diamond, J. M. 1975. Assembly of species communities. pp. 342–444. In M. L. Cody and J. M. Diamond (eds.) *Ecology and Evolution of Communities*. Cambridge: Belknap Press of Harvard University Press.

Diamond, J. M. 1986. Overview: laboratory experiments, field experiments, and natural experiments. pp. 3–22. In J. M. Diamond and T. J. Case (eds.) *Community Ecology*. New York: Harper and Row.

Diamond, J. 1994. Ecological collapses of past civilisations. *Proceedings of the American Philosophical Society* **138**: 363–370.

Diamond, J. 2004. Twilight at Easter. *New York Review of Books* LI (5) (March 25). pp. 6–10.

Díaz, S., A. Acosta, and M. Cabido. 1992. Morphological analysis of herbaceous communities under different grazing regimes. *Journal of Vegetation Science* **3**: 689–696.

Dickerson, R. E. 1969. *Molecular Thermodynamics*. New York: W. A Benjamin Inc.

Digby, P. G. N. and R. A. Kempton. 1987. *Multivariate Analysis of Ecological Communities*. London: Chapman and Hall.

Dilcher, D. L. and P. R. Crane. 1985. *Archaeanthus*: an early angiosperm from the Cenomanian of the western interior of North America. *Annals of the Missouri Botanical Garden* **71**: 351–383.

Dilcher, D. L. and W. L. Kovach. 1986. Early angiosperm reproduction: *Caloda delevoryana* gen. et sp. nov., a new fructification from the Dakota Formation (Cenomanian) of Kansas. *American Journal of Botany* **73**: 1230–1237.

Dinerstein, E. 1991. Seed dispersal by greater one-horned rhinoceros (*Rhinoceros unicornis*) and the flora of *Rhinoceros* latrines. *Mammalia* **55**: 355–362.

Dinerstein, E. 1992. Effects of *Rhinoceros unicornis* on riverine forest structure in lowland Nepal. *Ecology* **73**: 701–704.

Dirzo, R., C. C. Horvitz, H. Quevedo, and M. A. López. 1992. The effects of gap size and age on the understorey herb community of a tropical Mexican rain forest. *Journal of Ecology* **80**: 809–822.

Dodson, C. H. 1991. Orchidales, pp. 738–746. In *Angiosperms: The Flowering Plants*. pp. 596–765, Vol. 13. *The New Encyclopaedia Britannica*, 15th edn. Chicago: The University of Chicago.

Douglas, R. J. W. 1972. *Geology and Economic Minerals of Canada*. Ottawa: Geological Survey of Canada.

Dowdeswell, J. A. 2006. The Greenland Ice Sheet and global sea-level rise. *Science* **311**: 963–964.

Dressler, R. L. 1983. Classification of the Orchidaceae and their probable origin. *Telopea* **2**: 413–424.

Drew, M. C. 1975. Comparison of the effects of a localized supply of phosphate, nitrate, ammonium and potassium on the growth of the seminal root system, and the shoot, in barley. *New Phytologist* **75**: 479–490.

Duchesne, L. C. and D. W. Larson. 1989. Cellulose and the evolution of plant life. *Bioscience* **39**: 238–241.

Dugan, P. (ed.) 1993. *Wetlands in Danger*. New York: Oxford University Press.

Duncan, R. P. 1993. Flood disturbance and the coexistence of species in a lowland podocarp forest, south Westland, New Zealand. *Journal of Ecology* **81**: 403–416.

Durant, W. 1944. *Caesar and Christ*. New York: Simon and Schuster.

du Rietz, G. E. 1931. *Life-forms of Terrestrial Flowering Plants*. Acta Phytogeographica Suecia. III. Uppsala: Almqvist and Wiksells.

Dynesius, M. and C. Nilsson. 1994. Fragmentation and flow regulation of river systems in the northern third of the world. *Science* **266**: 753–762.

Earth Impact Database. 2006. (http://www.unb.ca/passc/ImpactDatabase) accessed 12 Sept. 2006.

Edmonds, J. (ed.) 1997. *Oxford Atlas of Exploration*. New York: Oxford University Press.

Ehrenfeld, J. G. 1983. The effects of changes in land-use on swamps of the New Jersey Pine Barrens. *Biological Conservation* **25**: 353–375.

Ehrlich, A. and P. Ehrlich. 1981. *Extinction: The Causes and Consequences of the Disappearance of Species*. New York: Random House.

Ehrlich, P. and P. H. Raven 1964. Butterflies and plants: a study in coevolution. *Evolution* **18**: 586–608.

Eissenstat, D. M. and E. I. Newman. 1990. Seedling establishment near large plants: effects of vesicular-arbuscular mycorrhizae on the intensity of plant competition. *Functional Ecology* **4**: 95–99.

Ellenberg, H. 1985. Veränderungen der Flora Mitteleuropas unter dem Einfluß von Düngung und Immissionen. *Schweizerische Zeitschrift für Forstwesen* **136**: 19–39.

Ellenberg, H. 1988a. Floristic changes due to nitrogen deposition in central Europe. In J. Nilsson and P. Grennfelt (eds.) *Critical Loads for Sulphur and Nitrogen*. Report from a workshop held at Skokloster, Sweden, March 19-24, 1988.

Ellenberg, H. 1988b. *Vegetation Ecology of Central Europe*. 4th edn. Cambridge: Cambridge University Press. Translated by G. K. Strutt.

Ellison, A. M. and E. J. Farnsworth. 1996. Spatial and temporal variability in growth of *Rhizophora mangle* saplings on coral cays: links with variation in insolation, herbivory, and local sedimentation rate. *Journal of Ecology* **84**: 717-731.

Elton, C. 1927. *Animal Ecology*. London: Sidgwick and Jackson Ltd.

Encyclopaedia Britannica. 1991a. Vol. 16. p. 500. Chicago: Encyclopaedia Britannica Inc.

Encyclopaedia Britannica. 1991b. Vol. 12. p. 41. Chicago: Encyclopaedia Britannica Inc.

Encyclopaedia Britannica. 1991c. Vol. 16. p. 481. Chicago: Encyclopaedia Britannica Inc.

Endress, P. K. 1996. *Diversity and Evolutionary Biology of Tropical Flowers*. Paperback edition (with corrections). Cambridge: Cambridge University Press.

Englert, S. 1970. *Islands at the Center of the World: New Light on Easter Island*. New York: Charles Scribner. Translated by W. Mulloy.

Environment Canada. 1976. Marine Environmental Data Service, Ocean and Aquatic Sciences. *Monthly and Yearly Mean Water Levels,* Vol. 1. *Inland*. Ottawa: Department of Environment.

Eriksson, O. 1993. The species-pool hypothesis and plant community diversity. *Oikos* **68**: 371-374.

Ernst, W. 1978. Discrepancy between ecological and physiological optima of plant species: a re-interpretation. *Oecologia Plantarum* **13**: 175-188.

Estill, J. C. and M. B. Cruzan. 2001. Phytogeography and rare plant species endemic to the southeastern United States. *Castanea* **66**: 3-23.

Facelli, J. M., R. J. C. Leon, and V. A. Deregibus. 1989. Community structure in grazed and ungrazed grassland sites in the flooding Pampa, Argentina. *The American Midland Naturalist* **121**: 125-133.

Farjon, A. 1998. World Checklist and Bibliography of Conifers. Royal Botanical Gardens at Kew, Richmond, UK.

Farrow, E. P. 1917. On the ecology of the vegetation of Breckland. III. General effects of rabbits on the vegetation. *Journal of Ecology* **5**: 1-18.

Faulkner, S. P. and C. J. Richardson. 1989. Physical and chemical characteristics of freshwater wetland soils. pp. 41-72. In D. A. Hammer (ed.) *Constructed Wetlands for Wastewater Treatment. Municipal, Industrial, and Agricultural*. Chelsea: Lewis Publishers.

Fedorov, A. V., P. S. Dekens, M. McCarthy, A. C. Ravelo, P. B. deMenocal, M. Barreiro, R. C. Pacanowski, and S. G. Philander. 2006. The Pliocene paradox (mechanisms for a permanent El Niño). *Science* **312**: 1485-1489.

Feinsinger, P. 1976. Organisation of a tropical guild of nectivorous birds. *Ecological Monographs* **46**: 257-291.

Feinsinger, P. 1993. Coevolution and pollination. pp. 282-310. In D. J. Futuyma and M. Slatkin (eds.) *Coevolution*. Sunderland: Sinauer.

Fernald, M. L. 1921. The Gray Herbarium expedition to Nova Scotia 1920. *Rhodora* **23**: 89-111, 130-171, 184-195, 233-245, 257-278, 284-300.

Fernald, M. L. 1922. Notes on the flora of western Nova Scotia 1921. *Rhodora* **24**: 157-164, 165-180, 201-208.

Fernald, M. L. 1935. Critical plants of the upper Great Lakes region of Ontario and Michigan. *Rhodora* **37**: 197-222, 238-262, 272-301, 324-341.

Fernández-Armesto, F. 1989. *The Spanish Armada: The Experience of War in 1588*. Oxford: Oxford University Press.

Ferris, T. 1988. *Coming of Age in the Milky Way*. Anchor Books edition 1989. New York: Doubleday.

Fienberg, S. E. and D. V. Hinkley (eds.). 1980. *R. A. Fisher: An Appreciation*. New York: Springer-Verlag.

Firbank, L. G. and A. R. Watkinson. 1985. On the analysis of competition within two-species mixtures of plants. *Journal of Applied Ecology* **22**: 503–517.

Fischer, R., W. De Vries, W. Seidling, P. Kennedy, and M. Lorenz. 2000. *Forest Condition in Europe*. 2000 Executive Report. United Nations Economic Commission for Europe/European Commission, Geneva and Brussels.

Fisher, R. A. 1925. *Statistical Methods for Research Workers*. London: Oliver and Boyd.

Fitter, A. H. and R. K. M. Hay. 1983. *Environmental Physiology of Plants*. London: Academic Press.

Flannery, T. 2001. *The Eternal Frontier: An Ecological History of North America and its Peoples*. Melbourne: Text Publishing.

Flannery, T. 2005. *The Weather Makers: How Man is Changing the Climate and What it Means for Life on Earth*. New York: Atlantic Monthly Press.

Fleischner, T. L. 1994. Ecological costs of livestock grazing in western North America. *Conservation Biology* **8**: 629–644.

Flint, R. F. 1971. *Glacial and Quaternary Geology*. New York: John Wiley and Sons.

Fonteyn, P. J. and B. E. Mahall. 1978. Competition among desert perennials. *Nature* **275**: 544–545.

Fonteyn, P. J. and B. E. Mahall. 1981. An experimental analysis of structure in a desert plant community. *Journal of Ecology* **69**: 883–896.

Forde, B. and H. Zhang. 1998. Response: nitrate and root branching. *Trends in Plant Science* **3**: 204–205.

Foreman, D. 2004. *Rewilding North America: A Vision for Conservation in the 21st Century*. Washington, D.C.: Island Press.

Forman, R. T. T. 1964. Growth under controlled conditions to explain the hierarchical distributions of a moss, *Tetraphis pellucida*. *Ecological Monographs* **34**: 1–25.

Forman, R. T. T., D. Sperling, J. Bissonette, A. P. Clevenger, C. D. Cutshall, V. H. Dale, L. Fahrig, R. France, C. R. Goldman, K. Heanue, J. A. Jones, F. J. Swanson, T. Turrentine, and T. C. Winter. 2002. *Road Ecology: Science and Solutions*. Washington: Island Press.

Foster, A. S. and E. M. Gifford, Jr. 1974. *Comparative Morphology of Vascular Plants*. 2nd edn. San Francisco: W. H. Freeman and Company.

Foster, D. R. and P. H. Glaser. 1986. The raised bogs of south-eastern Labrador, Canada: classification, distribution, vegetation and recent dynamics. *Journal of Ecology* **74**: 47–71.

Foster, D. R. and H. E. Wright, Jr. 1990. Role of ecosystem development and climate change in bog formation in central Sweden. *Ecology* **71**: 450–463.

Fowler, N. 1981. Competition and coexistence in a North Carolina grassland. II. The effects of the experimental removal of species. *Journal of Ecology* **69**: 843–845.

Fox, J. F. 1977. Alternation and coexistence of tree species. *The American Naturalist* **111**: 69–89.

Fragoso, J. M. V. 1997. Tapir-generated seed shadows: scale-dependent patchiness in the Amazon rain forest. *Journal of Ecology* **85**: 519–529.

Francis, R. and D. J. Read. 1984. Direct transfer of carbon between plants connected by vesicular-arbuscular mycorrhizal mycelium. *Nature* **307**: 53–56.

Franco, A. C. and P. S. Nobel. 1989. Effect of nurse plants on the microhabit and growth of cacti. *Journal of Ecology* **77**: 870–886.

Fraser, L. H. and P. Keddy 1997. The role of experimental microcosms in ecological research. *Trends in Ecology and Evolution* **12**: 478–481.

Fraser, L. H. and P. A. Keddy (eds.). 2005. *The World's Largest Wetlands: Ecology and Conservation.* Cambridge: Cambridge University Press.

Freedman, B. 1995. *Environmental Ecology.* 2nd edn. San Diego: Academic Press.

Freedman, B., W. Zobens, T. C. Hutchinson, and W. I. Gizyn. 1990. Intense, natural pollution affects arctic tundra vegetation at the Smoking Hills, Canada. *Ecology* **71**: 492–503.

Freemark, K. E. and H. G. Merriam. 1986. The importance of area and habitat heterogeneity to bird assemblages in temperate forest fragments. *Biological Conservation* **36**: 115–141.

French, B. M. 1998. *Traces of Catastrophe: A Handbook of Shock-Metamorphic Effects in Terrestrial Meteoric Impact Structures.* LPI Contribution No. 954. Houston: Lunar and Planetary Institute.

Fretwell, S. D. 1977. The regulation of plant communities by food chains exploiting them. *Perspectives in Biology and Medicine* **20**: 169–185.

Frey, R. W. and P. B. Basan. 1978. Coastal salt marshes. pp. 101–169. In R. A. Davis (ed.) *Coastal Sedimentary Environments.* New York: Springer-Verlag.

Frey, T. E. 1973. The Finnish school and forest site types. pp. 403–433. In Whittaker, R. H. (ed.) *Ordination and Classification of Communities.* Part V. The Hague: W. Junk.

Friedmann, E. I. 1982. Endolithic microorganisms in the antarctic cold desert. *Science* **215**: 1045–1053.

Friis, E. M., K. R. Pedersen, and P. R. Crane. 2006. Cretaceous angiosperm flowers: Innovation and evolution in plant reproduction. *Palaeogeography, Palaeoclimatology, Palaeoecology* **23**: 251–293.

Frontier, S. 1985. Diversity and structure in aquatic ecosystems. *Oceanography and Marine Biology Annual Review* **23**: 253–312.

Futuyma, D. J. and M. Slatkin. 1993. The study of coevolution. pp. 459–464. In D. J. Futuyma and M. Slatkin (eds.) *Coevolution.* Sunderland: Sinauer.

Galatowitsch, S. M. and A. G. van der Valk. 1994. *Restoring Prairie Wetlands: An Ecological Approach.* Ames: Iowa State University Press.

Gardner, G. 1977. The reproductive capacity of *Fraxinus excelsior* on the Derbyshire limestone. *Journal of Ecology* **65**: 107–118.

Gaston, K. J. 2000. Global patterns in biodiversity. *Nature* **405**: 220–227.

Gaston, K. J., P. H. Williams, P. Eggleton, and C. J. Humphries. 1995. Large scale patterns of biodiversity: spatial variation in family richness. *Proceedings of the Royal Society of London Series B-Biological Sciences* **260**: 149–154.

Gauch, H. G. Jr. 1982. *Multivariate Analysis in Community Ecology.* Cambridge Studies in Ecology. Cambridge: Cambridge University Press.

Gauch, H. G. Jr. and T. R. Wentworth. 1976. Canonical correlation analysis as an ordination technique. *Vegetatio* **33**: 17–22.

Gauch, H. G. Jr. and R. H. Whittaker. 1972. Comparison of ordination techniques. *Ecology* **53**: 868–875.

Gauch, H. G. Jr., R. H. Whittaker, and T. R. Wentworth. 1977. A comparative study of reciprocal averaging and other techniques. *Journal of Ecology* **65**: 157–174.

Gaudet, C. L. 1993. Competition in shoreline plant communities: a comparative approach. PhD thesis. Ottawa: University of Ottawa.

Gaudet, C. L. and P. A. Keddy. 1988. A comparative approach to predicting competitive ability from plant traits. *Nature* **334**: 242–243.

Gause, G. F. and A. A. Witt. 1935. Behavior of mixed populations and the problem of natural selection. *The American Naturalist* **69**: 596–609.

Geis, J. W. 1985. Environmental influences on the distribution and composition of wetlands in the Great Lakes basin. pp. 15–31. In H. H. Prince and F. M. D'Itri (eds.) *Coastal Wetlands*. Chelsea: Lewis Publishers.

Gentry, A. H. 1988. Changes in plant community diversity and floristic composition on environmental and geographical gradients. *Annals of the Missouri Botanical Garden* **75**: 1–34.

Gibson, A. C. and P. S. Nobel. 1986. *The Cactus Primer*. Cambridge: Harvard University Press.

Gibson, C. W. D. and J. Hamilton. 1983. Feeding ecology and seasonal movements of giant tortoises on Aldabra atoll. *Oecologia* **56**: 84–92.

Gidley, I. and R. Shears. 1986. *The Rainbow Warrior Affair*. Toronto: Irwin Publishing.

Given, D. R. and J. Soper. 1981. *The Arctic-Alpine Element of the Vascular Flora at Lake Superior*. Publications in Botany No. 10. Ottawa: National Museums of Canada.

Givnish, T. J. 1982. On the adaptive significance of leaf height in forest herbs. *The American Naturalist* **120**: 353–381.

Givnish, T. J. 1984. Leaf and canopy adaptations in tropical forests. pp. 51–84. In E. Medina, H. A. Mooney, and C. Vásquez-Yánes (eds.) *Physiological Ecology of Plants of the Wet Tropics*. The Hague: Dr. Junk.

Givnish, T. J. 1987. Comparative studies of leaf form: assessing the relative roles of selective pressures and phylogenetic constraints. *New Phytologist* **106** (Suppl.): 131–160.

Givnish, T. J. 1988. Ecology and evolution of carnivorous plants. pp. 243–290. In W. B. Abrahamson (ed.) *Plant-Animal Interactions*. New York: McGraw-Hill.

Givnish, T. J. 1994. Does diversity beget stability? *Nature* **371**: 113–114.

Glaser, P. H. 1992. Raised bogs in eastern North America – regional controls for species richness and floristic assemblages. *Journal of Ecology* **80**: 535–554.

Glaser, P. H., J. A. Janssens, and D. I. Siegel. 1990. The response of vegetation to chemical and hydrological gradients in the Lost River peatland, northern Minnesota. *Journal of Ecology* **78**: 1021–1048.

Gleason, H. A. 1917. The structure and development of the plant association. *Bulletin of the Torrey Botanical Club* **44**: 463–481.

Gleason, H. A. 1926. The individualistic concept of the plant association. *Bulletin of theTorrey Botanical Club* **53**: 7–26.

Glenn-Lewin, D. C., R. K. Peet, and T. T. Veblen (eds.) 1992. *Plant Succession: Theory and Prediction*. Population and Community Biology. No. 11. London: Chapman and Hall.

Glooschenko, W. A. 1980. Coastal salt marshes in Canada. pp. 39–47. In C. D. A. Rubec and F. C. Pollet (eds.) *Proceedings of the Workshop on Canadian Wetlands*. Saskatoon, Saskatchewan. Environment Canada, Lands Directorate, Ecological Land Class. Series No. 12.

Gnanadesikan, R. 1997. *Methods for Statistical Data Analysis of Multivariate Observations*. 2nd edn. New York: Wiley.

Goebel, K. 1905. Wilhelm Hofmeister. *The Plant World* **8**: 291–298.

Goldberg, D. E. 1982a. The distribution of evergreen and deciduous trees relative to soil type: an example from the Sierra Madre, Mexico, and a general model. *Ecology* **63**: 942–951.

Goldberg, D. E. 1982b. Comparison of factors determining growth rates of deciduous vs. broad-leaf evergreen trees. *The American Midland Naturalist* **108**: 133–143.

Goldberg, D. E. 1990. Components of resource competition in plant communities. pp. 27–49. In J. B. Grace and D. Tilman (eds.) *Perspectives on Plant Competition*. San Diego: Academic Press.

Goldberg, D. E. and K. Landa. 1991. Competitive effect and response: hierarchies and correlated traits in the early stages of competition. *Journal of Ecology* **79**: 1013–1030.

Goldberg, D. E. and P. A. Werner. 1983. Equivalence of competitors in plant communities: a null hypothesis and a field experimental approach. *American Journal of Botany* **70**: 1098–1104.

Goldsmith, F. B. 1973a. The vegetation of exposed sea cliffs at South Stack, Anglesey: I. The multivariate approach. *Journal of Ecology* **61**: 787–818.

Goldsmith, F. B. 1973b. The vegetation of exposed sea cliffs at South Stack, Anglesey: II. Experimental studies. *Journal of Ecology* **61**: 819–829.

Goldsmith, F. B. 1978. Interaction (competition) studies as a step towards the synthesis of sea-cliff vegetation. *Journal of Ecology* **66**: 921–931.

Goldsmith, F. B. and C. M. Harrison. 1976. Description and analysis of vegetation. pp. 85–155. In S. B. Chapman (ed.) *Methods in Plant Ecology*. Oxford: Blackwell Scientific.

Gopal, B. 1990. Nutrient dynamics of aquatic plant communities. pp. 177–197. In B. Gopal (ed.) *Ecology and Management of Aquatic Vegetation in the Indian Subcontinent*. Dordrecht: Kluwer Academic Publishers.

Gopal, B. and U. Goel. 1993. Competition allelopathy in aquatic plant communities. *The Botanical Review* **59**: 155–210.

Gopal, B., J. Kvet, H. Loffler, V. Masing, and B. C. Patten. 1990. Definition and classification. pp. 9–15. In B. C. Patten (ed.) *Wetlands and Shallow Continental Water Bodies*, Vol. 1. *Natural and Human Relationships*. The Hague: SPB Academic Publishing.

Gore, A. J. P. 1983. Introduction. In A. J. P. Gore (ed.) *Ecosystems of the World 4A. Mires: Swamp, Bog, Fen and Moor*. Amsterdam: Elsevier Scientific Publishing Company.

Gore, A. 2006. *An Inconvenient Truth. The Planetary Emergency of Global Warming and What We Can Do About It*. New York: Melcher Media/Rodale.

Goremykin, V. V., K. I. Hirsch-Ernst, S. Wölfl, and F. H. Hellwig. 2003. Analysis of the *Amborella trichopoda* chloroplast genome sequence suggests that *Amborella* is not a basal angiosperm. *Molecular Biology and Evolution* **20**: 1499–1505.

Gorham, E. 1953. Some early ideas concerning the nature, origin and development of peat lands. *Journal of Ecology* **41**: 257–274.

Gorham, E. 1957. The development of peat lands. *The Quarterly Review of Biology* **32**: 145–166.

Gorham, E. 1979. Shoot height, weight and standing crop in relation to density of nonspecific plant stands. *Nature* **279**: 148–150.

Gorham, E. 1990. Biotic impoverishment in northern peatlands. pp. 65–98. In G. M. Woodwell (ed.) *The Earth in Transition*. Cambridge: Cambridge University Press.

Gorham, E. 1991. Northern peatlands role in the carbon cycle and probable responses to climatic warming. *Ecological Applications* **1**: 182–195.

Gosselink, J. G. and R. E. Turner. 1978. The role of hydrology in freshwater wetland ecosystems. pp. 63–78. In R. E. Good, D. F. Whigham, and R. L. Simpson (eds.) *Freshwater Wetlands: Ecological Processes and Management Potential*. New York: Academic Press.

Gosselink, J. G., J. M. Coleman, and R. E. Stewart, Jr. 1998. Coastal Louisiana. pp. 385–436. In M. J. Mac, P. A. Opler, C. E. Puckett Haecker, and P. D. Doran (eds.) 1998. *Status and Trends of the Nation's Biological Resources*, 2 Vols. Reston: U.S. Department of the Interior, U.S. Geological Survey.

Gotelli, N. J. and G. R. Graves. 1996. *Null Models in Ecology*. Washington, D.C.: Smithsonian Institution Press.

Gough, J. 1793. Reasons for supposing that lakes have been more numerous than they are at present; with an attempt to assign the causes whereby they have been defaced. *Memoirs of the Literary and Philosophical Society of Manchester* **4**: 1–19. In D. Walker. 1970. Direction and rate in some British post-glacial hydoseres. pp. 117–139. In Walker, D. and R. G. West (eds.) *Studies in the Vegetational History of the British Isles*. Cambridge: Cambridge University Press.

Gough, L., J. B. Grace, and K. L. Taylor. 1994. The relationship between species richness and community biomass: the importance of environmental variables. *Oikos* **70**: 271–279.

Gould, S. J. 1977. *Ever Since Darwin: Reflections in Natural History*. New York: W. W. Norton and Company.

Grace, J. B. 1993. The effects of habitat productivity on competition intensity. *Trends in Ecology and Evolution* **8**: 229–230.

Grace, J. B. 1999. The factors controlling species density in herbaceous plant communities: an assessment. *Perspectives in Plant Ecology, Evolution and Systematics* **2**: 1–28.

Grace, J. B. 2001. The roles of community biomass and species pools in the regulation of plant diversity. *Oikos* **92**: 193–207.

Grace, J. B. 2006. *Structural Equation Modeling and Natural Systems*. Cambridge: Cambridge University Press.

Grace, J. B. and B. H. Pugesek. 1997. A structural equation model of plant species richness and its application to a coastal wetland. *The American Naturalist* **149**: 436–460.

Grace, J. B. and D. Tilman (eds.) 1990. *Perspectives on Plant Competition*. San Diego: Academic Press.

Grant, M. C. 1993. The trembling giant. *Discover* **4**(10): 82–89.

Green, P. T., D. J. O'Dowd, and P. S. Lake. 1997. Control of seedling recruitment by land crabs in rain forest on a remote oceanic island. *Ecology* **78**: 2472–2486.

Greenslade, P. J. M. 1983. Adversity selection and the habitat templet. *Nature* **242**: 344–347.

Greig-Smith, P. 1952. Use of random and contiguous quadrats in the study of the structure of plant communities. *Annals of Botany* **16**: 293–316.

Greig-Smith, P. 1957. *Quantitative Plant Ecology*. London: Butterworths.

Grime, J. P. 1973a. Control of species density in herbaceous vegetation. *Journal of Environmental Management* **1**: 151–167.

Grime, J. P. 1973b. Competitive exclusion in herbaceous vegetation. *Nature* **242**: 344–347.

Grime, J. P. 1974. Vegetation classification by reference to strategies. *Nature* **250**: 26–31.

Grime, J. P. 1977. Evidence for the existence of three primary strategies in plants and its relevance to ecological and evolutionary theory. *The American Naturalist* **111**: 1169–1194.

Grime, J. P. 1979. *Plant Strategies and Vegetation Processes*. Chichester: John Wiley.

Grime, J. P. 1994. The role of plasticity in exploiting environmental heterogeneity. pp. 1–19. In M. M. Caldwell and R. W. Percy (eds.) *Exploitation of Environmental Heterogeneity by Plants: Ecophysical Processes Above- and Belowground*. San Diego: Academic Press.

Grime, J. P. 1997. The humped-back model: a response to Oksanen. *Journal of Ecology* **85**: 97–98.

Grime, J. P. 2002. Declining plant diversity: empty niches or functional shifts? *Journal of Vegetation Science* **13**: 457–460.

Grime, J. P. and R. Hunt. 1975. Relative growth-rate: its range and adaptive significance in a local flora. *Journal of Ecology* **63**: 393–422.

Grime, J. P. and D. W. Jeffrey. 1965. Seedling establishment in vertical gradients of sunlight. *Journal of Ecology* **53**: 621–642.

Grime, J. P., G. Mason, A. V. Curtis, J. Rodman, S. R. Band, M. A. G. Mowforth, A. M. Neal, and S. Shaw. 1981. A comparative study of germination characteristics in a local flora. *Journal of Ecology* **69**: 1017–1059.

Grime, J. P., J. M. L. Mackey, S. H. Hillier, and D. J. Read. 1987. Floristic diversity in a model system using experimental microcosms. *Nature* **328**: 420–422.

Grishin, S. Y., R. del Moral, P. V. Krestov, and V. P. Verkholat. 1996. Succession following the catastrophic eruption of Ksudach volcano (Kamchatka, 1907). *Vegetatio* **127**: 129–153.

Groombridge, B. (ed.). 1992. *Global Biodiversity: Status of the Earth's Living Resources*. London: Chapman and Hall.

Grover, A. M. and G. A. Baldassarre. 1995. Bird species richness within beaver ponds in south-central New York. *Wetlands* **15**: 108–118.

Grubb, P. J. 1977. The maintenance of species-richness in plant communities: the importance of the regeneration niche. *Biological Reviews* **52**: 107–145.

Grubb, P. J. 1987. Global trends in species-richness in terrestrial vegetation: a view from the Northern Hemisphere. pp. 99–118. In J. H. R. Gee and P. S. Giller (eds.) *Organization of Communities Past and Present*. Oxford: Blackwell Scientific Publications.

Grumbine, R. E. 1997. Reflections on "What is ecosystem management?" *Conservation Biology* **11**: 41–47.

Guariguata, M. R. 1990. Landslide disturbance and forest regeneration in the Upper Luquillo mountains of Puerto Rico. *Journal of Ecology* **78**: 814–832.

Guerlac, H. 1975. *Antoine-Laurent Lavoisier, Chemist and Revolutionary*. New York: Charles Scribner's Sons.

Gurevitch, J. and R. S. Unnasch. 1989. Experimental removal of a dominant species at two levels of soil fertility. *Canadian Journal of Botany* **67**: 3470–3477.

Haber, L. F. 1986. *The Poisonous Cloud. Chemical Warfare in the First World War*. Oxford: Clarendon Press.

Haffer, J. 1969. Speciation in Amazonian forest birds. *Science* **165**: 131–137.

Hairston, N. G., F. E. Smith, and L. B. Slobodkin. 1960. Community structure, population control, and competition. *The American Naturalist* **XCIV**: 421–425.

Hamann, O. 1979. Regeneration of vegetation on Santa Fe and Pinta Islands, Galápagos, after the eradication of goats. *Biological Conservation* **15**: 215–236.

Hamann, O. 1993. On vegetation recovery, goats and giant tortoises on Pinta Island, Galápagos, Ecuador. *Biodiversity and Conservation* **2**: 138–151.

Harper, J. L. 1965. The nature and consequence of interference amongst plants. *Genetics Today* **2**: 465–482.

Harper, J. L. 1967. A Darwinian approach to plant ecology. *Journal of Ecology* **55**: 247–270.

Harper, J. L. 1977. *Population Biology of Plants*. London: Academic Press.

Harper, J. L. 1982. After description. pp. 11–25. In E. I. Newman (ed.) *The Plant Community as a Working Mechanism*. Oxford: Blackwell.

Harper, J. L. and J. Ogden. 1970. The reproductive strategy of higher plants. I. The concept of strategy with special reference to *Senecio vulgaris* L. *Journal of Ecology* **58**: 681–698.

Harper, J. L. and J. White. 1974. The demography of plants. *Annual Review of Ecology and Systematics* **5**: 419–463.

Harper, J. L., B. R. Rosen, and J. White. 1986. *The Growth and Form of Modular Organisms*. London: The Royal Society.

Harris, L. D. 1984. *The Fragmented Forest: Island Biogeography Theory and the Preservation of Biotic Diversity*. Chicago: University of Chicago Press.

Hartman, J. M. 1988. Recolonization of small disturbance patches in a New England salt marsh. *American Journal of Botany* **75**: 1625–1631.

Harvey, P. H., R. K. Colwell, J. W. Silvertown, and R. M. May. 1983. Null models in ecology. *Annual Review of Ecology and Systematics* **14**: 189–211.

Hatch, A. B. 1937. The physical basis of mycotrophy in *Pinus*. *The Black Rock Forest Bulletin*, No. 6. 17 pp.

Hawksworth, D. L. 1988. Coevolution of fungi with algae and cyanobacteria in lichen symbioses. pp. 125–148. In K. A. Pirozynski and D. L. Hawksworth (eds.) *Coevolution of Fungi with Plants and Animals*. London: Academic Press.

Hawksworth, D. L. 1990. The fungal dimension of biodiversity: magnitude, significance, and conservation. *Mycological Research* **95**: 641–655.

Hayati, A. A. and M. C. F. Proctor. 1991. Limiting nutrients in acid-mire vegetation: peat and plant analyses and experiments on plant responses to added nutrients. *Journal of Ecology* **79**: 75–95.

Heady, H. F. (ed.) 1988. *The Vale Rangeland Rehabilitation Program: An Evaluation*. USDA Forest Service, Resource Bulletin PNW-RB-157, 151 pp.

Heady, H. F. and J. Bartolome. 1977. *The Vale Rangeland Rehabilitation Program: The Desert Repaired in Southeastern Oregon*. USDA Forest Service, Resource Bulletin PHW-70, 139 pp.

Heckman, D. S., D. M. Geiser, B. R. Eidell, R. L. Stauffer, N. L. Kardos, and S. B. Hedges. 2001. Molecular evidence for the early colonization of land by fungi and plants. *Science* **293**: 1129–1133.

Heinselman, M. L. 1973. Fire in the virgin forests of the Boundary Waters Canoe Area, Minnesota. *Quaternary Research* **3**: 329–382.

Heinselman, M. L. 1981. Fire and succession in the conifer forests of northern North America. pp. 374–405. In D. C. West, H. H. Shugart, and D. B. Botkin (eds.) *Forest Succession: Concepts and Applications*. New York: Springer-Verlag.

Hemphill, N. and S. D. Cooper. 1983. The effect of physical disturbance on the relative abundances of two filter-feeding insects in a small stream. *Oecologia* **58**: 378–382.

Higgs, E. S. 1997. What is good ecological restoration? *Conservation Biology* **11**: 338–348.

Hill, N. M. and P. A. Keddy. 1992. Predicting numbers of rarities from habitat variables: coastal plain plants of Nova Scotian lakeshores. *Ecology* **73**: 1852–1859.

Hills, G. A. 1961. *The Ecological Basis for Land-Use Planning*. Report No. 46. Ontario: Ontario Department of Lands and Forests, Research Branch.

Hoagland, B. W. and S. L. Collins. 1997. Gradient models, gradient analysis, and hierarchical structure in plant communities. *Oikos* **78**: 23–30.

Hoffman, T. M., G. F. Midgley, and R. M. Cowling. 1994. Plant richness is negatively related to energy availability in semi-arid southern Africa. *Biodiversity Letters* **2**: 35–38.

Hogenbirk, J. C. and R. W. Wein. 1991. Fire and drought experiments in northern wetlands: a climate change analogue. *Canadian Journal of Botany* **69**: 1991–1997.

Hogg, E. H., V. J. Lieffers, and R. W. Wein. 1992. Potential carbon losses from peat profiles: effects of temperature, drought cycles, and fire. *Ecological Applications* **2**: 298–306.

Holechek, J. L., M. Vavra, and R. D. Pieper. 1982. Botanical composition determination of herbivore diets: a review. *Journal of Range Management* **31**: 309–315.

Holling, C. S. 1959. The components of predation as revealed by a study of small-mammal predation of the European pine sawfly. *Canadian Entomologist* **91**: 293–320.

Holling, C. S. (ed.) 1978a. *Adaptive Environmental Assessment and Management*. New York: John Wiley and Sons.

Holling, C. S. 1978b. The spruce-budworm/forest-management problem. pp. 143–182. In C. S. Holling (ed.) *Adaptive Environmental Assessment and Management*. New York: John Wiley and Sons.

Holt, R. D. and J. H. Lawton. 1993. Apparent competition and enemy-free space in insect host-parasitoid communities. *The American Naturalist* **142**: 623–645.

Holt, R. D. and J. H. Lawton. 1994. The ecological consequences of shared natural enemies. *Annual Review of Ecology and Systematics* **25**: 495–520.

Hook, D. D. 1984. Adaptations to flooding with fresh water. pp. 265–294. In T. T. Kozlowski (ed.) *Flooding and Plant Growth*. Orlando: Academic Press.

Hopkins, D. M. (ed.) 1967. *The Bering Land Bridge*. Stanford: Stanford University Press.

Horn, H. S. 1971. *The Adaptive Geometry of Trees*. Princeton: Princeton University Press.

Horn, H. 1976. Succession. pp. 187–204. In R. M. May (ed.) *Theoretical Ecology: Principles and Applications*. Philadelphia: W. B. Saunders.

Horn, H. S. 1981. Some causes of variety of patterns of secondary succession. pp. 24–35. In D. C. West, H. H. Shugart, and D. B. Botkin (eds.) *Forest Succession: Concepts and Application*. New York: Springer-Verlag.

Horn, H. S. and R. H. MacArthur. 1972. Competition among fugitive species in a harlequin environment. *Ecology* **53**: 749–752.

Houck, O. 2006. Can we save New Orleans? *Tulane Environmental Law Journal* **19**: 1–68.

Hubbell, S. P. and R. B. Foster. 1986. Biology, chance and history and the structure of the tropical rain forest tree communities. pp. 314–329. In J. Diamond and T. J. Case (eds.) *Community Ecology*. New York: Harper and Row.

Huber, H., S. Lukács, and M. A. Watson. 1999. Spatial structure of stoloniferous herbs: an interplay between structural blue-print, ontogeny and phenotypic plasticity. *Plant Ecology* **141**: 107–115.

Hughes, J. D. 1982. Deforestation, erosion, and forest management in ancient Greece and Rome. *Journal of Forest History* **26**: 60–75.

Humphries, C. J. 1981. Biogeographical methods and the southern beeches. pp. 283–297. In P. L. Forey (ed.) *The Evolving Biosphere*. British Museum (Natural History). Cambridge: London and Cambridge University Press.

Hunt, R., D. W. Hand, M. A. Hannah, and A. M. Neal. 1991. Response to CO_2 enrichment in 27 herbaceous species. *Functional Ecology* **5**: 410–421.

Hunter, M. D. and P. W. Price. 1992. Playing chutes and ladders: heterogeneity and the relative roles of bottom-up and top-down forces in natural communities. *Ecology* **73**: 724–732.

Huntley, B. 1990. European post-glacial forests: compositional changes in response to climatic change. *Journal of Vegetation Science* **1**: 507–518.

Hurlbert, S.H. 1984. Pseudoreplication and the design of ecological field experiments. *Ecological Monographs* **54**: 187–211.

Hurlbert, S.H. 1990. Spatial distribution of the montane unicorn. *Oikos* **58**: 257–271.

Huston, M.A. 1979. A general hypothesis of species diversity. *The American Naturalist* **113**: 81–101.

Huston, M.A. 1994. *Biological Diversity. The Coexistence of Species on Changing Landscapes.* Cambridge: Cambridge University Press.

Huston, M.A. 1997. Hidden treatments in ecological experiments: re-evaluating the ecosystem function of biodiversity. *Oecologia* **110**: 449–460.

Hutchinson, G.E. 1959. Homage to Santa Rosalia; or, why are there so many kinds of animals? *The American Naturalist* **93**: 145–159.

Hutchinson, G.E. 1970. The biosphere. pp. 194–203. In E.O. Wilson (ed.) 1974. *Ecology, Evolution, and Population Biology.* Readings from Scientific American. San Francisco: W.H. Freeman and Company.

Hutchinson, G.E. 1975. *A Treatise on Limnology*, Vol. 3. Limnological Botany. New York: John Wiley and Sons.

Huxley, C.R. 1980. Symbiosis between plants and epiphytes. *Biological Reviews* **55**: 321–340.

Imbrie, J., et al. 1992. On the structure and origin of major glaciation cycles 2. The 100 000-year cycle. *Paleoceanography* **8**: 699–736.

International Joint Commission. 1980. *Pollution in the Great Lakes Basin from Land Use Activities.* Washington, D.C.: International Joint Commission.

Irion, G.M., J. Müller, J.N. de Mello, and W.J. Junk. 1995. Quaternary geology of the Amazon lowland. *Geo-Marine Letters* **15**: 172–178.

Jackson, J.B.C. 1981. Interspecific competition and species distributions: the ghosts of theories and data past. *American Zoologist* **21**: 889–901.

Jackson, J.B.C., L.W. Buss, and R.E. Cook. 1985. *Population Biology and Evolution of Clonal Organisms.* New Haven: Yale University Press.

Jackson, M.B. and M.C. Drew. 1984. Effects of flooding on growth and metabolism of herbaceous plants. pp. 47–128. In T.T. Kozlowski (ed.) *Flooding and Plant Growth.* Orlando: Academic Press.

Jaksic, F.M. and E.R. Fuentes. 1980. Why are native herbs in the Chilean matorral more abundant beneath bushes: microclimate or grazing? *Journal of Ecology* **68**: 665–669.

James, W. 1907. *Pragmatism.* Reprinted pp. xv–xvii, 1–89. In M.J. Adler (ed.) 1990. *Great Books of the Western World.* Vol. 55. Chicago: Encyclopaedia Britannica.

Janis, C. 1976. The evolutionary strategy of the Equidae and the origins of rumen and cecal digestion. *Evolution* **30**: 757–774.

Janssens, F., A. Peeters, J.R.B. Tallowin, J.P. Bakker, F. Fillat, and M.J.M. Oomes. 1998. Relationship between soil chemical factors and grassland diversity. *Plant and Soil* **202**: 69–78.

Janzen, D.H. 1966. Coevolution of mutualism between ants and acacias in Central America. *Evolution* **20**: 249–275.

Janzen, D.H. 1967. Interaction of the bull's-horn acacia (*Acacia cornigera* L.) with an ant inhabitant (*Pseudomyrmex ferruginea* F. Smith) in eastern Mexico. *The University of Kansas Science Bulletin* **XLVII**: 315–558.

Janzen, D.H. 1971. Seed predation by animals. *Annual Review of Ecology and Systematics* **2**: 465–492.

Janzen, D. H. 1974. Epiphytic myrmecophytes in Sarawak: mutualism through the feeding of plants by ants. *Biotropica* **6**: 237–259.

Janzen, D. H. 1976. Why bamboos wait so long to flower. *Annual Review of Ecology and Systematics* **7**: 347–391.

Janzen, D. H. 1983. Dispersal of seeds by vertebrate guts. pp. 232–262. In D. J. Futuyma and M. Slatkin (eds.) *Coevolution*. Sunderland: Sinauer.

Janzen, D. H. 1985. The natural history of mutualisms. pp. 40–99. In D. H. Boucher (ed.) *The Biology of Mutualism: Ecology and Evolution*. New York: Oxford University Press.

Janzen, D. H. and P. S. Martin. 1982. Neotropical anachronisms: the fruits the gomphotheres ate. *Science* **215**: 19–27.

Janzen, D. H., G. A. Miller, J. Hackforth-Jones, C. M. Pond, K. Hooper, and D. P. Janos. 1976. Two Costa Rican bat-generated seed shadows of *Andira inermis* (Leguminosae). *Ecology* **57**: 1068–1075.

Jarvis, P. G. 1964. Interference by *Deschampsia flexuosa* (L.) Trin. *Oikos* **15**: 56–78.

Jefferies, R. L. 1977. The vegetation of salt marshes at some coastal sites in arctic North America. *Journal of Ecology* **65**: 661–672.

Jeglum, J. K. 1983. Changes in tree species composition in naturally regenerating strip clearcuts in shallow-soil upland black spruce. pp. 180–193. In R. W. Wein, R. R. Riewe, and I. R. Methven (eds.) *Resources and Dynamics of the Boreal Zone*. Ottawa: Association of Canadian Universities for Northern Studies.

Jensen, T. S. 1985. Seed–seed predator interactions of European beech, *Fagus silvatica* and forest rodents, *Clethrionomys glareolus* and *Apodemus flavicollis*. *Oikos* **44**: 149–156.

Jickells, T. D., S. Dorling, W. G. Deuser, T. M. Church, R. Arimoto, and J. M. Propsero. 1998. Air-borne dust fluxes to a deep water sediment trap in the Sargasso Sea. *Global Biogeochemical Cycles* **12**: 311–320.

Johansson, M. E. and P. A. Keddy. 1991. Intensity and asymmetry of competition between plant pairs of different degrees of similarity: an experimental study on two guilds of wetland plants. *Oikos* **60**: 27–34.

Johnson, P. L. and W. D. Billings. 1962. The alpine vegetation of the Beartooth Plateau in relation to cryopedogenic processes and patterns. *Ecological Monographs* **32**: 105–135.

Johnston, A. E. 1994. The Rothamsted classical experiments. pp. 9–35. In R. A. Leigh and A. E. Johnston (eds.) *Long-term Experiments in Agricultural and Ecological Sciences*. Proceedings of a conference to celebrate the 150th anniversary of Rothamsted Experimental Station, held at Rothamsted, July 14–17, 1993. Wallingford: CAB International.

Johnston, C. A. and R. J. Naiman. 1990. Aquatic patch creation in relation to beaver population trends. *Ecology* **71**: 1617–1621.

Jones, C. G., J. H. Lawton, and M. Shachak. 1994. Organisms as ecosystem engineers. *Oikos* **69**: 373–386.

Jones, R. K., G. Pierpoint, G. M. Wickware, and J. K. Jeglum. 1983a. A classification and ordination of forest ecosystems in the Great Claybelt of northeastern Ontario. pp. 83–96. In R. W. Wein, R. R. Riewe, and I. R. Methven (eds.) *Resources and Dynamics of the Boreal Zone*. Proceedings of a Conference held at Thunder Bay, Ontario, August 1982. Ottawa: Association of Canadian Universities for Northern Studies.

Jones, R. K., G. Pierpoint, G. M. Wickware, J. K. Jeglum, R. W. Arnup, and J. M. Bowles. 1983b. *Field Guide to Forest Classification for the Clay Belt, Site Region 3E*. Toronto: Queen's Printer for Ontario.

Jones, W. G., K. D. Hill, and J. M. Allen. 1995. *Wollemia nobilis*, a new living Australian genus and species in the Araucariaceae. *Telopea* **6**: 173–176.

Jordan, C. F., F. B. Golley, J. D. Hall, and J. Hall. 1980. Nutrient scavenging of rainfall by the canopy of an Amazonian rain forest. *Biotropica* **12**: 61–66.

Jordan, W. R. III, M. E. Gilpin, and J. D. Aber. 1987. *Restoration Ecology: A Synthetic Approach to Ecological Research.* Cambridge: Cambridge University Press.

Judd, W. S., C. S. Campbell, E. A. Kellogg, P. F. Stevens, and M. J. Donoghue. 2002. *Plant Systematics: A Phylogenetic Approach.* 2nd edn. Sunderland: Sinauer.

Judson, S. 1968. Erosion of the land, or what's happening to our continents? *American Scientist* **56**: 356–374.

Junk, W. J. 1983. Ecology of swamps on the Middle Amazon. pp. 269–294. In A. J. P. Gore. (ed.) *Ecosystems of the World 4B: Mires: Swamp, Bog, Fen, and Moor.* Amsterdam: Elsevier Science.

Jutila, H. M. and J. B. Grace. 2002. Effects of disturbance on germination and seedling establishment in a coastal prairie grassland: a test of the competitive release hypothesis. *Journal of Ecology* **90**: 291–302.

Kalamees, K. 1982. The composition and seasonal dynamics of fungal cover on peat soils. pp. 12–29. In V. Masing (ed.) *Peatland Ecosystems: Researches into the Plant Cover of Estonian Bogs and Their Productivity.* Tallinn: Academy of Sciences of the Estonian S.S.R.

Kalliola, R., J. Salo, M. Puhakka, and M. Rajasilta. 1991. New site formation and colonizing vegetation in primary succession on the western Amazon floodplains. *Journal of Ecology* **79**: 877–901.

Kaminski, R. M. and H. H. Prince. 1981. Dabbling duck and aquatic macroinvertebrate responses to manipulated wetland habitat. *Journal of Wildlife Management* **45**: 1–15.

Kaplan, D. R. and T. J. Cooke. 1996. The genius of Wilhelm Hofmeister: The origin of causal-analytical research in plant development. *American Journal of Botany* **83**: 1647–1660.

Kastner, T. P., and M. A. Goñi. 2003. Constancy in the vegetation of the Amazon Basin during the late Pleistocene: evidence from the organic matter composition of Amazon deep sea fan sediments. *Geology* **31**: 291–294.

Kay, S. 1993. Factors affecting severity of deer browsing damage within coppiced woodlands in the south of England. *Biological Conservation* **63**: 524–532.

Kearney, T. H. and H. L. Shantz. 1912. The water economy of dry-land crops. pp. 351–362. *Yearbook of the United States Department of Agriculture-1911.* Washington: Department of Agriculture.

Keddy, P. A. 1980. Population ecology in an environmental mosaic: *Cakile edentula* on a gravel bar. *Canadian Journal of Botany* **58**: 1095–1100.

Keddy, P. A. 1981a. Why gametophytes and sporophytes are different: form and function in a terrestrial environment. *The American Naturalist* **118**: 452–454.

Keddy, P. A. 1981b. Vegetation with Atlantic coastal plain affinities in Axe Lake, near Georgian Bay, Ontario. *The Canadian Field Naturalist* **95**: 241–248.

Keddy, P. A. 1981c. Experimental demography of the sand dune annual, *Cakile edentula*, growing along an environmental gradient in Nova Scotia. *Journal of Ecology* **69**: 615–630.

Keddy, P. A. 1982. Population ecology on an environmental gradient: *Cakile edentula* on a sand dune. *Oecologia* **52**: 348–355.

Keddy, P. A. 1983. Shoreline vegetation in Axe Lake, Ontario: effects of exposure on zonation patterns. *Ecology* **64**: 331–344.

Keddy, P. A. 1987. Beyond reductionism and scholasticism in plant community ecology. *Vegetatio* **69**: 209–211.

Keddy, P. A. 1989. *Competition.* London: Chapman and Hall.

Keddy, P. A. 1990a. The use of functional as opposed to phylogenetic systematics: a first step in predictive community ecology. pp. 387–406. In S. Kawano (ed.) *Biological Approaches and Evolutionary Trends in Plants.* London: Academic Press.

Keddy, P. A. 1990b. Competitive hierarchies and centrifugal organization in plant communities. pp. 265–289. In J. B. Grace and D. Tilman (eds.) *Perspectives on Plant Competition.* San Diego: Academic Press.

Keddy, P. A. 1991. Biological monitoring and ecological prediction: from nature reserve management to national state of environment indicators. pp. 249–267. In F. B. Goldsmith (ed.) *Biological Monitoring for Conservation.* London: Chapman and Hall.

Keddy, P. A. 1992. Assembly and response rules: two goals for predictive community ecology. *Journal of Vegetation Science* **3**: 157–164.

Keddy, P. 1994. Reflections on the 21st birthday of MacArthur's Geographical Ecology – applications of the Hertzprung-Russel star diagram to ecology. *Trends in Ecology and Evolution* **9**: 231–234.

Keddy, P. 1998. Review of *Null Models in Ecology* (N. J. Gotelli and G. R. Graves, 1996, Smithsonian Institution Press, Washington). *The Canadian Field-Naturalist* **112**: 752–754.

Keddy, P. A. 2000. *Wetland Ecology: Principles and Conservation.* Cambridge: Cambridge University Press.

Keddy, P. A. 2001. *Competition.* 2nd edn. Dordrecht: Kluwer.

Keddy, P. A. 2004. Plants matter. Review of *The Ecology Of Plants* (J. Gurevitch, S. Scheiner and G. A. Fox. 2002. Sinauer Associates, Sunderland, Massachusetts). *The Quarterly Review of Biology* **79**: 55–59.

Keddy, P. A. 2005a. Milestones in ecological thought – a canon for plant ecology. *Journal of Vegetation Science* **16**: 145–150.

Keddy, P. A. 2005b. Putting the plants back into plant ecology: six pragmatic models for understanding, conserving and restoring plant diversity. *Annals of Botany* **96**: 177–189.

Keddy, P. A. and P. Constabel. 1986. Germination of ten shoreline plants in relation to seed size, soil particle size and water level: an experimental study. *Journal of Ecology* **74**: 122–141.

Keddy, P. A. and C. G. Drummond. 1996. Ecological properties for the evaluation, management, and restoration of temperate deciduous forest ecosystems. *Ecological Applications* **6**: 748–762.

Keddy, P. A. and L. H. Fraser. 2005. Introduction: big is beautiful. pp. 1–10. In L. H. Fraser and P. A. Keddy (eds.) *The World's Largest Wetlands: Ecology and Conservation.* Cambridge: Cambridge University Press.

Keddy, P. A. and P. MacLellan 1990. Centrifugal organization in forests. *Oikos* **59**: 75–84.

Keddy, P. A. and A. A. Reznicek. 1982. The role of seed banks in the persistence of Ontario's coastal plain flora. *American Journal of Botany* **69**: 13–22.

Keddy, P. A. and A. A. Reznicek. 1986. Great Lakes vegetation dynamics: the role of fluctuating water levels and buried seeds. *Journal of Great Lakes Research* **12**: 25–36.

Keddy, P. A. and B. Shipley. 1989. Competitive hierarchies in plant communities. *Oikos* **49**: 234–241.

Keddy, P. A. and I. C. Wisheu. 1989. Ecology, biogeography, and conservation of coastal plain plants: some general principles from the study of Nova Scotian wetlands. *Rhodora* **91**: 72–94.

Keddy, P. A., H. T. Lee, and I. C. Wisheu. 1993. Choosing indicators of ecosystem integrity: wetlands as a model system. pp. 61–79. In S. Woodley, J. Kay, and G. Francis (eds.) *Ecological Integrity and the Management of Ecosystems.* Ottawa: St-Lucie Press.

Keddy, P. A., L. Twolan-Strutt, and I. C. Wisheu. 1994. Competitive effect and response rankings in 20 wetland plants: are they consistent across three enivronments? *Journal of Ecology* **82**: 635–643.

Keddy, P. A., K. Nielsen, E. Weiher, and L. R. Lawson. 2002. Relative competitive performance of 63 species of terrestrial herbaceous plants. *Journal of Vegetation Science* **13**: 5–16.

Keeler, K. H. 1985. Cost:benefit models of mutualism. pp. 100–127. In D. H. Boucher (ed.) *The Biology of Mutualism: Ecology and Evolution.* New York: Oxford University Press.

Keeley, J. E. 1998. CAM photosynthesis in submerged aquatic plants. *The Botanical Review* **64**: 121–175.

Keeley, J. E. and P. W. Rundel. 2003. Evolution of CAM and C_4 carbon-concentrating mechanisms. *International Journal of Plant Science* **164** (Supplement): S55–S77.

Keeley, J. E., D. A. DeMason, R. Gonzalez, and K. R. Markham. 1994. Sediment-based carbon nutrition in tropical alpine *Isoetes.* pp. 167–194. In P. W. Rundel, A. P. Smith, and F. C. Meinzer (eds.) *Tropical Alpine Environments Plant Form and Function.* Cambridge: Cambridge University Press.

Keeling, C. D. and T. P. Whorf. 2005. Atmospheric CO_2 records from sites in the SIO air sampling network. In *Trends: A Compendium of Data on Global Change.* Carbon Dioxide Information Analysis Center, Oak Ridge National Laboratory, U.S. Department of Energy, Oak Ridge, TN.

Keller, G., T. Adatte, W. Stinnesbeck et al. 2004. Chicxulub impact predates the K-T boundary mass extinction. *Proceedings of the National Academy of Sciences (of the United States of America)* **101**: 3753–3758.

Kellman, M. 1985. Forest seedling establishment in Neotropical savannas: transplant experiments with *Xylopia frutescens* and *Calophyllum brasiliense. Journal of Biogeography* **12**: 373–379.

Kellman, M. and B. Delfosse. 1993. Effect of the red land crab (*Gecarcinus lateralis*) on leaf litter in a tropical dry forest in Vera Cruz, Mexico. *Journal of Tropical Ecology* **9**: 55–65.

Kellman, M. and M. Kading. 1992. Facilitation of tree seedling establishment in a sand dune succession. *Journal of Vegetation Science* **3**: 679–688.

Kellman, M. and N. Roulet. 1990. Nutrient flux and retention in a tropical sand-dune succession. *Journal of Ecology* **78**: 664–676.

Kellner, L. 1963. *Alexander von Humboldt.* London: Oxford University Press.

Kenrick, P. and P. R. Crane. 1997. The origin and early evolution of plants on land. *Nature* **389**: 33–39.

Kershaw, K. A. 1962. Quantitative ecological studies from Landmannahellir, Iceland. *Journal of Ecology* **50**: 171–179.

Kershaw, K. A. 1973. *Quantitative and Dynamic Plant Ecology.* 2nd edn. London: Edward Arnold.

Kershaw, K. A. and J. H. H. Looney. 1985. *Quantitative and Dynamic Plant Ecology.* 3rd edn. Victoria: Edward Arnold.

Kevan, P. G. 1975. Sun-tracking solar furnaces in high arctic flowers: significance for pollination and insects. *Science* **189**: 723–726.

Kidston, R. and W. H. Lang. 1921. *Transactions of the Royal Society Edinburgh* **LII(IV)**: 855–902.

Killingbeck, K. T. 1996. Nutrients in senesced leaves: keys to the search for potential resorption and resorption efficiency. *Ecology* **77**: 1716–1727.

King, J. 1997. *Reaching for the Sun: How Plants Work.* New York: Cambridge University Press.

Kinzig, A. P., S. Pacala, and G. D. Tilman (eds.) 2002. *The Functional Consequences of Biodiversity: Empirical Progress and Theoretical Extensions.* Princeton: Princeton University Press.

Knoll, A. H. 1992. The early evolution of eukaryotes: a geological perspective. *Science* **256**: 622–627.

Koerselman, W. and A. F. M. Meulman. 1996. The vegetation N:P ratio: a new tool to detect the nature of nutrient limitation. *Journal of Applied Ecology* **33**: 1441–1450.

Koyama, H. and T. Kira. 1956. Intraspecific competition among higher plants. VIII. Frequency distributions of individual plant weight as affected by the interaction between plants. *Journal of the Institute of Polytechnics, Osaka City University Series D* **7**: 73–94.

Kozlowski, T. T. (ed.) 1984. *Flooding and Plant Growth.* Orlando: Academic Press.

Kozlowski, T. T. and S. G. Pallardy. 1984. Effect of flooding on water, carbohydrate, and mineral relations. pp. 165–193. In T. T. Kozlowski (ed.) *Flooding and Plant Growth.* Orlando: Academic Press.

Kramer, P. J. 1983. *Water Relations of Plants.* Orlando: Academic Press.

Krebs, C. J. 1978. *Ecology: The Experimental Analysis of Distribution and Abundance.* New York: Harper and Row.

Krebs, C. J. 1989. *Ecological Methodology.* New York: Harper and Row.

Kruckeberg, A. R. 1954. The ecology of serpentine soils. III. Plant species in relation to serpentine soils. *Ecology* **35**: 267–274.

Küchler, A. W. 1949. A physiognomic classification of vegetation. *Annals of the Association of American Geographers* **39**: 201–210.

Küchler, A. W. 1966. Analyzing the physiognomy and structure of vegetation. *Annals of the Association of American Geographers* **56**: 112–127.

Kuhry, P. 1994. The role of fire in the development of *Sphagnum*-dominated peatlands in western boreal Canada. *Journal of Ecology* **82**: 899–910.

Kuijt, J. 1969. *The Biology of Parasitic Flowering Plants.* Berkeley: University of California Press.

Kyte, F. T. 1998. A meteorite from the Cretaceous/Tertiary boundary. *Nature* **396**: 237–239.

Lack, D. 1947. *Darwin's Finches: An Essay on the General Biological Theory of Evolution.* New York: Harper and Row.

Laing, H. E. 1940. Respiration of the rhizomes of *Nuphar advenum* and other water plants. *The American Journal of Botany* **27**: 574–581.

Laing, H. E. 1941. Effect of concentration of oxygen and pressure of water upon growth of rhizomes of semi-submerged water plants. *Botanical Gazette* **102**: 712–724.

Langer, P. 1974. Stomach evolution in the artiodactyla. *Mammalia* **38**: 295–314.

Larcher, W. 1995. *Physiological Plant Ecology: Ecophysiology and Stress Physiology of Functional Groups.* 3rd edn. New York: Springer-Verlag.

Larcher, W. 2003. *Physiological Plant Ecology: Ecophysiology and Stress Physiology of Functional Groups.* 4th edn. Berlin: Springer-Verlag.

Larcher, W. and H. Bauer. 1981. Ecological significance of resistance to low temperature. pp. 403–437. In O. L. Lange, P. S. Nobel, C. B. Osmond, and H. Ziegler (eds.) *Physiological Plant Ecology I: Responses to the Physical*

Environment. Encyclopedia of Plant Physiology: New Series, Vol. 12A. Berlin: Springer-Verlag.

Larson, D. W. 1980. Patterns of species distribution in an *Umbilicaria*-dominated community. *Canadian Journal of Botany* **58**: 1269–1279.

Larson, D. W. 1982. Environmental stress and *Umbilicaria* lichens: the effect of subzero temperature pretreatments. *Oecologia* **55**: 268–278.

Larson, D. W. 1989. The impact of ten years at −20 °C on gas exchange in five lichen species. *Oecologia* **78**: 87–92.

Larson, D. W. 1996. Brown's Woods: an early gravel pit forest restoration project, Ontario, Canada. *Society for Ecological Restoration* **4**: 11–18.

Larson, D. W. 2001. The paradox of great longevity in a short-lived tree species. *Experimental Gerontology* **36**: 651–673.

Latham, P. J., L. G. Pearlstine, and W. M. Kitchens. 1994. Species association changes across a gradient of freshwater, oligohaline, and mesohaline tidal marshes along the lower Savanna River. *Wetlands* **14**: 174–183.

Latham, R. E. and R. E. Ricklefs. 1993a. Global patterns of tree species richness in moist forests: energy-diversity theory does not account for variation in species richness. *Oikos* **67**: 325–333.

Latham, R. E. and R. E. Ricklefs. 1993b. Continental comparisons of temperate-zone tree species diversity. pp. 294–314. In R. E. Ricklefs and D. Schluter (eds.) *Species Diversity in Ecological Communities: Historical and Geographical Perspectives*. Chicago: The University of Chicago Press.

Latham, R. E., J. Beyea, M. Benner, C. A. Dunn, M. A. Fajvan, R. R. Freed, M. Grund, S. B. Horsley, A. F. Rhoads, and B. P. Shissler. 2005. *Managing White-tailed Deer in Forest Habitat from an Ecosystem Perspective: Pennsylvania Case Study*. Harrisburg: Audubon Pennsylvania and Pennsylvania Habitat Alliance.

Lavoisier, A. L. 1789. *Elements of Chemistry*. Translated by R. Kerr and reprinted in xi, xii and pp. 1–60. In M. J. Adler (ed.) 1990. *Great Books of the Western World*. 2nd edn., Vol. 42. Chicago: Encyclopaedia Britannica.

Lechowicz, M. J. 1981. The effects of climatic pattern on lichen productivity: *Cetraria cucullata* (Bell.) Ach. in the arctic tundra of northern Alaska. *Oecologia* **50**: 210–216.

Leck, M. A. and K. J. Graveline. 1979. The seed bank of a freshwater tidal marsh. *American Journal of Botany* **66**: 1006–1015.

Leck, M. A., V. T. Parker, and R. L. Simpson (eds.) 1989 *Ecology of Soil Seed Banks*. San Diego: Academic Press.

Lee, K. E. 1985. *Earthworms: Their Ecology and Relationships with Soils and Land Use*. Sydney: Academic Press.

Legendre, L. and P. Legendre. 1983. *Numerical Ecology*. Amsterdam: Elsevier.

Leopold, A. 1949. *A Sand County Almanac*. London: Oxford University Press.

Le Page, C. and P. A. Keddy. 1988. Reserves of buried seeds in beaver ponds. *Wetlands* **18**: 242–248.

Le Page, C. and P. A. Keddy. 1998. Reserves of buried seeds in beaver ponds. *Wetlands* **18**: 242–248.

Levin, H. L. 1994. *The Earth Through Time*. 4th edn., updated. Fort Worth: Saunders College Publishing; Harcourt Brace College Publishers.

Levins, R. 1968. *Evolution in Changing Environments*. Princeton: Princeton University Press.

Levitt, J. 1977. The nature of stress injury and resistance. pp. 11–21. In J. Levitt (ed.) *Responses of Plants to Environmental Stress*. New York: Academic Press.

Levitt, J. 1980. *Responses of Plants to Environmental Stresses*, Vols. I and II. 2nd edn. New York: Academic Press.

Lewis, D. H. 1987. Evolutionary aspects of mutualistic associations between fungi and photosynthetic organisms. pp. 161–178. In A. D. M. Rayner, C. M. Brasier, and D. Moore (eds.) *Evolutionary Biology of the Fungi*. Symposium of the British Mycological Society, held at the University of Bristol, April 1986. Cambridge: Cambridge University Press.

Lewis, III, R. R. (ed.) 1982. *Creation and Restoration of Coastal Plant Communities*. Boca Raton: CRC Press.

Leyser, O. and Fitter, A. 1998. Roots are branching out in patches. *Trends in Plant Science* **3**: 203–204.

Li, X.-L., E. George, and H. Marschner. 1991. Phosphorus depletion and pH decrease at the root-soil and hyphae-soil interfaces of VA mycorrhizal white clover fertilized with ammonium. *New Phytologist* **119**: 397–404.

Lieth, H. 1975. Historical survey of primary productivity research. pp. 7–16. In H. Leith and R. H. Whittaker (eds.) *Primary Productivity of the Biosphere*. New York: Springer-Verlag.

Likens, G. E., F. H. Bormann, R. S. Pierce, J. S. Eaton, and N. M. Johnson. 1977. *Biogeochemistry of a Forested Ecosystem*. New York: Springer-Verlag.

Little, C. E. 1995. *The Dying of the Trees: The Pandemic in America's Forests*. New York: Penguin Books.

Llewellyn, D. W., G. P. Shaffer, N. J. Craig, L. Creasman, D. Pashley, M. Swan, and C. Brown. 1996. A decision-support system for prioritizing restoration sites on the Mississippi River alluvial plain. *Conservation Biology* **10**: 1446–1455.

Lloyd, D. G. and S. C. H. Barrett (eds.) 1996. *Floral Biology: Studies on Floral Evolution in Animal-Pollinated Plants*. London: Chapman and Hall.

Lodge, D. M. 1991. Herbivory on freshwater macrophytes. *Aquatic Botany* **41**: 195–224.

Loehle, C. 1998a. Height growth rate tradeoffs determine northern and southern range limits for trees. *Journal of Biogeography* **25**: 735–742.

Loehle, C. 1988b. Problems with the triangular model for representing plant strategies. *Ecology* **69**: 284–286.

Loehle, C. 1995. Anomalous responses of plants to CO_2 enrichment. *Oikos* **73**: 181–187.

Lopoukhine, N. 1983. Parks Canada in the boreal forest ecosystem (a pilgrim's progress). pp. 167–179. In R. W. Wein, R. R. Riewe, and I. R. Methven (eds.) *Resources and Dynamics of the Boreal Zone*. Proceedings of a Conference held at Thunder Bay, Ontario, August 1982. Ottawa: Association of Canadian Universities for Northern Studies.

Loreau, M. L. 2000. Biodiversity and ecosystem functioning: recent theoretical advances. *Oikos* **91**: 3–17.

Louda, S. M. and S. Mole. 1991. Glucosinolates: chemistry and ecology. pp. 124–164. In G. A. Rosenthal and M. R. Berenbaum (eds.) *Herbivores: Their Interactions with Secondary Plant Metabolites*. San Diego: Academic Press.

Louda, S. M., K. H. Keller, and R. D. Holt. 1990. Herbivore influence on plant performance and competitive interactions. pp. 413–444. In J. B. Grace and D. Tilman (eds.) *Perspectives on Plant Competiton*. San Diego: Academic Press.

Lovejoy, T. E., R. O. Bierregaard, Jr., A. B. Rylands, J. R. Malcolm, C. E. Quintela, L. H. Harper, K. S. Brown, Jr., A. H. Powell, G. V. N. Powell, H. O. R. Schubart, and M. B. Hays. 1986. Edge and other effects of isolation on Amazon forest fragments. pp. 257–285. In M. E. Soulé (ed.) *Conservation Biology; the Science of Scarcity and Diversity*. Sunderland: Sinauer Associates.

Loveless, C. M. 1959. A study of the vegetation in the Florida Everglades. *Ecology* **40**: 1–9.

Lowman, M.D. 1992. Leaf growth dynamics and herbivory in five species of Australian rain-forest canopy trees. *Journal of Ecology* **80**: 433–447.

Lowman, M.D. and H.B. Rinker (eds). 2004. *Forest Canopies*. 2nd edn. Burlington: Elsevier Academic Press.

Ludwig, D., D.D. Jones, and C.S. Holling. 1978. Qualitative analysis of insect outbreak systems: the spruce budworm and forest. *Journal of Animal Ecology* **47**: 315–332.

Lugo, A.E. and S.C. Snedaker. 1974. The ecology of mangroves. *Annual Review of Ecology and Systematics* **5**: 39–64.

Lutman, J. 1978. The role of slugs in an *Agrostis–Festuca* grassland. pp. 332–347. In O.W. Heal and D.F. Perkins (eds.) *Production Ecology of British Moors and Montane Grasslands*. Ecological Studies, Vol. 27. Berlin: Springer-Verlag.

Mabry, C.M. 2004. The number and size of seeds in common versus restricted woodland herbaceous species in central Iowa, USA. *Oikos* **107**: 497–504.

MacArthur, R.H. 1957. On the relative abundance of bird species. *Proceedings of the National Academy of Sciences of the USA* **43**: 293–295.

MacArthur, R.H. 1972. *Geographical Ecology*. New York: Harper and Row.

MacArthur, R.H. and E.O. Wilson. 1967. *The Theory of Island Biogeography*. Monographs in Population Biology, No. 1. Princeton: Princeton University Press.

MacDonald, P. (ed.) 1989. *The Solar System. The World of Science*, Vol. 7. Oxford: Equinox (Oxford) Ltd.

MacFarland, C.G., J. Villa, and B. Toro. 1974. The Galápagos giant tortoises (*Geochelone elephantopus*). Part I: Status of the surviving populations. *Biological Conservation* **6**: 118–133.

MacGillivray, C.W., J.P. Grime and the Integrated Screening Programme (ISP) team. 1995. Testing predictions of the resistance and resilience of vegetation subjected to extreme events. *Functional Ecology* **9**: 640–649.

MacMahon, J.A. 1981. Successional processes: comparisons among biomes with special reference to probable roles of and influence on animals. pp. 277–305. In D.C. West, H.H. Shugart, and D.B. Botkin (eds.) *Forest Succession: Concepts and Application*. New York: Springer-Verlag.

Magnuson, J.J., H.A. Regier, W.J. Christie, and W.C. Sonzongi. 1980. To rehabilitate and restore Great Lakes ecosystems. pp. 95–122. In J. Cairns Jr. (ed.) *The Recovery Process in Damaged Ecosystmens*. Ann Arbour: Ann Arbour Science Publishers.

Magnusson, M. (ed.) 1990. *Chambers Biographical Dictionary*. 5th edn. Edinburgh: W & R Chambers.

Mains, G. 1972. *The Oxygen Revolution*. London: David and Charles.

Major, J. 1988. Endemism: a botanical perspective. pp. 117–146. In A.A. Myers and P.S. Giller (eds.) *Analytical Biogeography*. London: Chapman and Hall.

Margulis, L. 1970. *Origin of Eukaryotic Cells*. New Haven: Yale University Press.

Margulis, L. 1993. *Symbiosis in Cell Evolution*. 2nd edn. New York: W.H. Freeman.

Margulis, L. and D. Sagan. 1986. *Microcosmos: Four Billion Years of Evolution from Our Microbial Ancestors*. Reprinted in 1997 in paperback. Berkeley: University of California Press.

Marquis, R. 1991. Evolution of resistance in plants to herbivores. *Evolutionary Trends in Plants* **5**: 23–29.

Marquis, R. and C. Whelan. 1994. Insectivorous birds increase growth of white oak through consumption of leaf-chewing insects. *Ecology* **75**: 2007–2014.

Marschner, H. 1995. *Mineral Nutrition of Higher Plants*. 2nd edn. London: Academic Press.

Martin, J.H. *et al.* 1994. Testing the iron hypothesis in ecosystems of the equatorial Pacific Ocean. *Nature* **371**: 123–129.

Martin, P.S. and R.J. Klein. 1984. *Quaternary Extinctions: A Prehistoric Revolution*. Tucson: The University of Arizona Press.

Marx, K. 1867. In F. Engles (ed.) *Capital*. Translated from 3rd German edition by S. Moore and E. Aveling. Revised from 4th edition by M. Sachey and H. Lamm. pp. 1–411. In M.J. Adler (ed.) *Great Books of the Western World*. 2nd edn. 1990. Vol. 50. Chicago: Encyclopaedia Britannica.

Matson, P.A., K. Lohse, and S. Hall. 2002. The globalization of nitrogen deposition: consequences for terrestrial ecosystems. *Ambio* **31**: 113–119.

Matthes-Sears, U., J. Gerrath, and D. Larson. 1997. Abundance, biomass, and productivity of endolithic and epilithic lower plants on the temperate-zone cliffs of the Niagara Escarpment, Canada. *International Journal of Plant Science* **158**: 451–460.

Maun, M.A. and J. Lapierre. 1986. Effects of burial by sand on seed germination and seedling emergence of four dune species. *American Journal of Botany* **73**: 450–455.

May, E. 1982. *Budworm Battles: The Fight to Stop the Aerial Insecticide Spraying of the Forests of Eastern Canada*. Halifax: Four East Publications Ltd.

May, R.M. 1973. *Stability and Complexity in Model Ecosystems*. Princeton: Princeton University Press.

May, R.M. 1977. Thresholds and breakpoints in ecosystems with a multiplicity of stable states. *Nature* **269**: 471–477.

May, R.M. 1981. Patterns in multi-species communities. pp. 197–227. In R.M. May (ed.) *Theoretical Ecology*. Oxford: Blackwell.

May, R.M. 1988. How many species are there on Earth? *Science* **241**: 1441–1449.

Maynard Smith, J. 1978. *The Evolution of Sex*. Cambridge: Cambridge University Press.

Mayr, E. 1982. *The Growth of Biological Thought: Diversity, Evolution, and Inheritance*. Cambridge: Belknap Press of Harvard University Press.

McCanny, S.J., P.A. Keddy, T.J. Arnason, C.L. Gaudet, D.R.J. Moore, and B. Shipley. 1990. Fertility and the food quality of wetland plants: a test of the resource availability hypothesis. *Oikos* **59**: 373–381.

McCarthy, K.A. 1987. Spatial and temporal distributions of species in two intermittent-tent ponds in Atlantic county, N.J. MSc thesis. New Brunswick: Rutgers University.

McClaran, M.P. 2003. A century of vegetation change on the Santa Rita Experimental Range. pp. 16–33. In *USDA Forest Service Proceedings RMRS-P-30*. US Department of Agriculture.

McClure, J.W. 1970. Secondary constituents of aquatic angiosperms. pp. 233–265. In J.B. Harborne (ed.) *Phytochemical Phylogeny*. New York: Academic Press.

McComb, W.C. and R.N. Muller. 1983. Snag management in old growth and second-growth Appalachian forests. *Journal of Wildlife Management* **47**: 376–382.

McGraw, J.B. 2001. Evidence for decline in stature of American ginseng plants from herbarium specimens. *Biological Conservation* **98**: 25–32.

McGraw, J.B. and M.A. Furedi. 2005. Deer browsing and population viability of a forest understory plant. *Science* **307**: 920–922.

McIntosh, R. P. 1967. The continuum concept of vegetation. *The Botanical Review* **33**: 130–187.

McIntosh, R. P. 1981. Succession and ecological theory. pp. 10–23. In D. C. West, H. H. Shugart, and D. B. Botkin (eds.) *Forest Succession: Concepts and Application*. New York: Springer-Verlag.

McIntosh, R. P. 1985. *The Background of Ecology: Concept and Theory*. Cambridge: Cambridge University Press.

McKenzie, D. H., D. E. Hyatt, and V. J. McDonald. 1992. *Ecological Indicators*, Vols. 1 and 2. London: Elsevier.

McNaughton, S. J. 1985. Ecology of a grazing ecosystem: the Serengeti. *Ecological Monographs* **55**: 259–294.

McNaughton, S. J., R. W. Ruess, and S. W. Seagle. 1988. Large mammal and process dynamics in African ecosystems. *Bioscience* **38**: 794–800.

McNeill, J. R. and V. Winiwarter. 2004. Breaking the sod: humankind, history and soil. *Science* **304**: 1627–1629.

McShea, W. J. and J. H. Rappole. 2000. Managing the abundance and diversity of breeding bird populations through manipulation of deer populations. *Conservation Biology* **14**: 1161–1170.

McVaugh, R. 1943. The vegetation of the granitic flat-rocks of the southeastern United States. *Ecological Monographs* **13**: 119–166.

Meadows, D. H., D. L. Meadows, J. Randers, and W. W. Behrens III. 1974. *The Limits to Growth: A Report for the Club of Rome's Project on the Predicament of Mankind*. 2nd edn. New York: The New American Library.

Meave, J. and M. Kellman. 1994. Maintenance of rain forest diversity in riparian forest of tropical savannas: implications for species conservation during Pleistocene drought. *Journal of Biogeography* **21**: 121–135.

Merrens, E. J. and D. R. Peart. 1992. Effects of hurricane damage on individual growth and stand structure in a hardwood forest in New Hampshire, USA. *Journal of Ecology* **80**: 787–795.

Milchunas, D. G. and W. K. Lauenroth. 1993. Quantitative effects of grazing on vegetation and soils over a global range of environments. *Ecological Monographs* **63**: 327–366.

Milchunas, D. G., W. K. Laurenroth, and I. C. Burk. 1998. Livestock grazing: animal and plant biodiversity of shortgrass steppe and the relationship to ecosystem function. *Oikos* **83**: 65–74.

Miller, G. R. and A. Watson. 1978. Heather productivity and its relevance to the regulation of red grouse populations. pp. 277–285. In O. W. Heal, D. F. Perkins and W. M. Brown (eds.) *Production Ecology of British Moors and Montaine Grasslands*. Berlin: Springer-Verlag.

Miller, G. R. and A. Watson. 1983. Heather moorland in northern Britain. pp. 101–117. In A. Warren and F. B. Goldsmith (eds.) *Conservation in Perspective*. Chichester: John Wiley and Sons Ltd.

Miller, K. G., M. A. Kominz, J. V. Browning, J. D. Wright, G. S. Mountain, M. E. Katz, P. J. Sugarman, B. S. Cramer, N. Christie-Blick, and S. F. Pekar. 2005. The Phanerozoic record of global sea-level changes. *Science* **310**: 1293–1298.

Miller, R. S. 1967. Pattern and process in competition. *Advances in Ecological Research* **4**: 1–74.

Miller, S. L. 1953. A production of amino acids under possible primitive earth conditions. *Science* **117**: 528–529.

Milliman, J. D. and R. H. Meade. 1983. World-wide delivery of river sediment to the oceans. *Journal of Geology* **91**: 1–21.

Milton, S. J., W. R. J. Dean, M. A. du Plessis, and W. R. Siegfried. 1994. A conceptual model of arid rangeland degradation. *Bioscience* **44**: 70–76.

Mitchley, J. 1988. Control of relative abundance of perennials in chalk grassland in southern England. II. Vertical canopy structure. *Journal of Ecology* **76**: 341–350.

Mitchley, J. and P. J. Grubb. 1986. Control of relative abundance of perennials in chalk grassland in southern England. I. Constancy of rank order and results of pot- and field-experiments on the role of interference. *Journal of Ecology* **74**: 1139–1166.

Mitsch, W. J. and J. G. Gosselink. 1986. *Wetlands*. New York: Van Nostrand Reinhold.

Mitsch, W. J. and J. G. Gosselink. 2000. *Wetlands*. 3rd edn. New York: John Wiley & Sons.

Mitsch, W. J. and S. E. Jørgensen. 1990. Modelling and management. pp. 727–744. In B. C. Patten (ed.) *Wetlands and Shallow Continental Water Bodies*, Vol. 1. The Hague: SPB Academic Publishing.

Moffett, M. W. 1994. *The High Frontier: Exploring the Tropical Rainforest Canopy*. Cambridge: Harvard University Press.

Moles, A. T., D. D. Ackerly, C. O. Webb, J. C. Tweddle, J. B. Dickie, and M. Westoby. 2005. A brief history of seed size. *Science* **307**: 576–580.

Molisch, H. 1937. *Der Einfluss einer Pflanze auf die andere. Allelopathie*. Jena: Gustav Fischer.

Moolman, H. J. and R. M. Cowling. 1994. The impact of elephant and goat grazing on the endemic flora of South African succulent thicket. *Biological Conservation* **68**: 53–61.

Mooney, H. A. and E. L. Dunn. 1970. Convergent evolution of mediterranean-climate evergreen sclerophyll shrubs. *Evolution* **24**: 292–303.

Mooney, H. A., B. G. Drake, R. J. Luxmoore, W. C. Oechel, and L. F. Pitelka. 1991. Predicting ecosystem responses to elevated CO_2 concentrations. *Bioscience* **41**: 96–104.

Moore, B. and B. Bolin. 1987. The oceans, carbon dioxide and global climate change. *Oceanus* **29**: 9–15.

Moore, D. R. J. 1990. Pattern and process in wetlands of varying standing crop: the importance of scale. PhD thesis. Ottawa: University of Ottawa.

Moore, D. R. J. 1998. The ecological component of ecological risk assessment: lessons from a field experiment. *Human and Ecological Risk Assessment* **4**: 1103–1123.

Moore, D. R. J. and P. A. Keddy. 1989a. The relationship between species richness and standing crop in wetlands: the importance of scale. *Vegetatio* **79**: 99–106.

Moore, D. R. J. and P. A. Keddy. 1989b. Infertile wetlands: conservation priorities and management. pp. 391–397. In M. J. Bardecki and N. Patterson (eds.) *Wetlands: Inertia or Momentum*. Proceedings of a Conference held in Toronto, Ontario, October 21–22, 1988. Federation of Ontario Naturalists.

Moore, D. R. J. and R. W. Wein. 1977. Viable seed populations by soil depth and potential site recolonization after disturbance. *Canadian Journal of Botany* **55**: 2408–2412.

Moore, D. R. J., P. A. Keddy, C. L. Gaudet, and I. C. Wisheu. 1989. Conservation of wetlands: do infertile wetlands deserve a higher priority? *Biological Conservation* **47**: 203–217.

Moore, P. D., J. A. Webb, and M. E. Collinson. 1991. *Pollen Analysis*. London: Blackwell Scientific.

Moreno, M. T., J. I Cubero, D. Berner, D. Joel, L. J. Musselman, and C. Parker (eds.) 1996. *Advances in Parasitic Plant Research.* Cordoba: Junta de Andalucia, Dirección General de Investigación Agraria.

Morgan, R. and B. Whitaker 1986. *Rainbow Warrior: The French Attempt to Sink Greenpeace.* London: Arrow Books Ltd.

Morowitz, H. J. 1968. *Energy Flow in Biology: Biological Organization as a Problem in Thermal Physics.* New York: Academic Press.

Morris, E. C. and P. J. Myerscough. 1991. Self-thinning and competition intensity over a gradient of nutrient availability. *Journal of Ecology* **79**: 903–923.

Moss, B. 1983. The Norfolk Broadland: experiments in the restoration of a complex wetland. *Biological Reviews of the Cambridge Philosophical Society* **58**: 521–561.

Moss, B. 1984. Medieval man-made lakes: progeny and casualties of English social history, patients of twentieth century ecology. *Transactions of the Royal Society of South Africa* **45**: 115–128.

Mueller-Dombois, D. 1987. Natural dieback in forests. *Bioscience* **37**: 575–583.

Mueller-Dombois, D. and H. Ellenberg. 1974. *Aims and Methods of Vegetation Ecology.* New York: John Wiley and Sons.

Muller, C. H. 1966. The role of chemical inhibition (allelopathy) in vegetational composition. *Bulletin of the Torrey Botanical Club* **93**: 332–351.

Muller, C. H. 1969. Allelopathy as a factor in ecological process. *Vegetatio* **18**: 348–357.

Müller, J., G. Irion, J. N. de Mello, and W. J. Junk. 1995. Hydrological changes of the Amazon during the last glacial-interglacial cycle in Central Amazonia (Brazil). *Naturwissenschaften* **82**: 232–235.

Muller, R. A. and G. J. MacDonald. 1997. Glacial cycles and astronomical forcing. *Science* **277**: 215–218.

Musselman, L. J. and W. F. Mann, Jr. 1978. *Root Parasites of Southern Forests.* Southern Forest Experiment Station, Forest Service, U.S. Department of Agriculture.

Myers, C. W. and M. A. Donnelly. 1997. A tepui herpetofauna on a granitic mountain (Tamacuari) in the borderland between Venezuela and Brazil: report from the Phipps Tapirapecó expedition. *American Museum Novitates* **3213**: 1–71.

Myers, N. 1988. Threatened biotas: "hotspots" in tropical forests. *Environmentalist* **8**: 1–20.

Myers, N., R. A. Mittermeier, C. G. Mittermeier, G. A. B. da Fonseca, and J. Kent. 2000. Biodiversity hotspots for conservation priorities. *Nature* **403**: 853–858.

Myers, R., J. O'Brien, and S. Morrison. 2006. *Fire Management Overview of the Caribbean Pine (*Pinus caribaea*) Savannas of the Mosquitia, Honduras.* GFI Technical Report 2006-1b. Arlington: The Nature Conservancy.

Nabokov, P. 1993. Long threads. pp. 301–383. In B. Ballantine and I. Ballantine (eds.) *The Native Americans: An Illustrated History.* Atlanta: Turner Publishing Inc.

Naeem, S. 2002. Ecosystem consequences of biodiversity loss: the evolution of a paradigm. *Ecology* **83**: 1537–1552.

Naeem, S. L., J. Thompson, S. P. Lawler, J. H. Lawton, and R. M. Woodfin. 1994. Declining biodiversity can alter the performance of ecosystems. *Nature* **368**: 734–737.

Naiman, R. J., C. A. Johnston, and J. C. Kelley. 1988. Alteration of North American streams by beaver. *Bioscience* **38**: 753–762.

Nakamura, R. P. 1980. Plant kin selection. *Evolutionary Theory* **5**: 113–117.

Nanson, G. C. and H. F. Beach. 1977. Forest succession and sedimentation on a meandering-river floodplain, northeast British Columbia, Canada. *Journal of Biogeography* **4**: 229–251.

Nantel, P. and P. Neuman. 1992. Ecology of ectomycorrhizal-basidiomycete communities on a local vegetation gradient. *Ecology* **73**: 99–117.

Nantel, P., D. Gagnon, and A. Nault. 1996. Population viability analysis of American ginseng and wild leek harvested in stochastic environments. *Conservation Biology* **10**: 608–621.

National Parks and Wildlife Service. 1998. *Wollemi Pine Recovery Plan*. Sydney: NPWS.

Newman, E. I. 1988. Mycorrhizal links between plants: their functioning and ecological significance. *Advances in Ecological Research* **18**: 243–270.

Newman, E. I. 1993. *Applied Ecology*. Oxford: Blackwell Scientific Publications.

Newman, S., J. B. Grace, and J. W. Koebel. 1996. Effects of nutrients and hydroperiod on *Typha*, *Cladium* and *Eleocharis*: implications of Everglades restoration. *Ecological Applications* **6**: 774–783.

Nicholson, A. and P. A. Keddy. 1983. The depth profile of a shoreline seed bank in Matchedash Lake, Ontario. *Canadian Journal of Botany* **61**: 3293–3296.

Nickrent, D. L. 2006. The parasitic plant connection. (http://www.parasitic plants.siu/index.htm) accessed 10 Nov. 2006.

Nicolson, M. and R. P. McIntosh. 2002. H. A. Gleason and the individualistic hypothesis revisited. *Bulletin of the Ecological Society of America* (April 2002): 133–142.

Niering, W. A. and R. S. Warren. 1980. Vegetation patterns and processes in New England salt marshes. *Bioscience* **30**: 301–307.

Niklas, K. J. 1994. Predicting the height of fossil plant remains: an allometric approach to an old problem. *American Journal of Botany* **81**: 1235–1242.

Niklas, K. J., B. H. Tiffney, and A. H. Knoll. 1983. Patterns in vascular land plant diversification. *Nature* **303**: 614–616.

Niklas, K. J., B. H. Tiffney, and A. H. Knoll. 1985. Patterns in vascular plant diversification: an analysis at the species level. pp. 97–128. In J. W. Valentine (ed.) *Phanerozoic Diversity Pattern: Profiles in Macroevolution*. Princeton: Princeton University Press.

Nilsson, L. A. 1992. Orchid pollination biology. *Trends in Ecology and Evolution* **7**: 255–259.

Nobel, P. S. 1976. Water relations and photosynthesis of a desert CAM plant, *Agave deserti*. *Plant Physiology* **58**: 576–582.

Nobel, P. S. 1977. Water relations and photosynthesis of a barrel cactus, *Ferocactus acanthodes*, in the Colorado Desert. *Oecologia* **27**: 117–133.

Nobel, P. S. 1985. Desert succulents. pp. 181–197. In B. F. Chabot and H. A. Mooney (eds.) *Physiological Ecology of North American Plant Communities*. London: Chapman and Hall.

Noble, I. R. and R. O. Slatyer. 1980. The use of vital attributes to predict successional changes in plant communities subject to recurrent disturbances. *Vegetatio* **43**: 5–21.

Noss, R. 1995. *Maintaining Ecological Integrity in Representative Reserve Networks*. A World Wildlife Fund Canada/United States Discussion Paper, WWF.

Noss, R. F. and A. Y. Cooperrider. 1994. *Saving Nature's Legacy*. Washington, D.C.: Island Press.

Noy-Meir, I. 1973. Desert ecosystems: environment and producers. *Annual Review of Ecology and Systematics* **4**: 25–51.

Noy-Meir, L. 1975. Stability of grazing systems: an application of predator–prey graphs. *Journal of Ecology* **63**: 459–481.

Oakes, E. H. 2002. *Notable Scientists. A to Z of Chemists*. New York: Facts on File.

Ocampo, J. A. 1986. Vesicular-arbuscular mycorrhizal infection of "host" and "non-host" plants: effect on the growth responses of the plants and competition between them. *Soil Biology and Biochemistry* **18**: 607–610.

Ochoa, J. G., C. Molina, and S. Giner. 1993. Inventario y estudio comunitario de los mamiferos del Parque National Canaima, con una lista de las especies registradas para la Guayana Venezolana. *Ecologia Acta Científica Venezolana* **44**: 245–262.

Okihana, H. and C. Ponnamperuma. 1982. A protective function of the coacervates against UV light on the primitive Earth. *Nature* **299**: 347–349.

Oksanen, L. 1990. Predation, herbivory, and plant strategies along gradients of primary production. pp. 445–474. In J. B. Grace and D. Tilman (eds.) *Perspectives on Plant Competition*. San Diego: Academic Press.

Oksanen, L., S. D. Fretwell, J. Arruda, and P. Niemelä. 1981. Exploitation ecosystems in gradients of primary productivity. *The American Naturalist* **118**: 240–261.

Oksanen, L., M. Aunapuu, T. Oksanen, M. Schneider, P. Ekerholm, P. A. Lundberg, T. Armulik, V. Aruoja, and L. Bondestad. 1997. Outlines of food webs in a low arctic tundra landscape in relation to three theories on trophic dynamics. pp. 351–373. In A. C. Gange and V. K. Brown (eds.) *Multitrophic Interactions in Terrestrial Systems*. The 36th Symposium of The British Ecological Society. Oxford: Blackwell Science.

Olson, D. M. *et al.* 2001. Terrestrial ecoregions of the world: a new map of life on Earth. *Bioscience* **51**: 933–938.

Ondok, J. P. 1990. Modelling ecological processes. pp. 659–89. In B. C. Patten (ed.) *Wetlands and Shallow Continental Water Bodies*, Vol. 1. The Hague: SPB Academic Publishing.

Oosting, H. J. 1956. *The Study of Plant Communities*, 2nd edn. San Francisco: W. H. Freeman.

Oparin, A. I. 1938. *The Origin of Life*. New York: The Macmillan Company. Translated by S. Morgulis.

Orloci, L. 1978. *Multivariate Analysis in Vegetation Research*. 2nd edn. The Hague: Junk.

Orson, R. A., R. L. Simpson, and R. E. Good. 1990. Rates of sediment accumulation in a tidal freshwater marsh. *Journal of Sedimentary Petrology* **60**: 859–869.

Ostrofsky, M. L. and E. R. Zettler. 1986. Chemical defenses in aquatic plants. *Journal of Ecology* **74**: 279–287.

Oxford Atlas of the World. 1997. New York: Oxford University Press.

Parkinson, C. L., K. L. Adams, and J. D. Palmer. 1999. Multigene analyses identify the three earliest lineages of extant flowering plants. *Current Biology* **9**: 1485–1491.

Parks, J. C. and C. R. Werth. 1993. A study of spatial features of clones in a population of bracken fern, *Pteridium aquilinum* (Dennstaedtiaceae). *American Journal of Botany* **80**: 537–544.

Pärtel, M., M. Zobel, K. Zobel, and E. van der Maarel. 1996. The species pool and its relationship to species richness: evidence from Estonia plant communities. *Oikos* **75**: 111–117.

Pearce, C. M. 1993. Coping with forest fragmentation in southwestern Ontario. pp. 100–113. In S. F. Poser, W. J. Crins, and T. J. Beechey (eds.) *Size and Integrity Standards for Natural Heritage Areas in Ontario*. Proceedings of a Seminar. Parks and Natural Heritage Policy Branch, Ontario Ministry of Natural Resources, Queen's Printer, Toronto.

Pearsall, W. H. 1920. The aquatic vegetation of the English Lakes. *Journal of Ecology* **8**: 163–201.

Peat, H. J. and A. H. Fitter. 1993. The distribution of arbuscular mycorrhizas in the British flora. *New Phytologist* **125**: 845–854.

Peattie, D. C. 1922. The Atlantic coastal plain element in the flora of the Great Lakes. *Rhodora* **24**: 50–70, 80–88.

Pedersen, O., K. Sand-Jensen, and N. P. Revsbech. 1995. Diel pulses of O_2 and CO_2 in sandy lake sediments inhabited by *Lobelia dortmanna*. *Ecology* **76**: 1536–1545.

Peet, R. K. 1974. The measurement of species diversity. *Annual Review of Ecology and Systematics* **5**: 285–307.

Peet, R. K. 1978. Forest vegetation of the Colorado Front Range: patterns of species diversity. *Vegetatio* **37**: 65–78.

Peet, R. K. 1992. Community structure and ecosystem function. pp. 103–151. In D. C. Glenn-Lewin, R. K. Peet, and T. T. Veblen (eds.) *Plant Succession: Theory and Prediction. Population and Community Biology*, Vol. 11. London: Chapman and Hall.

Peet, R. K. and D. J Allard. 1993. Longleaf pine vegetation of the southern Atlantic and eastern Gulf coast regions: a preliminary classification. pp. 45–81. In S. M. Hermann (ed.) *Proceedings of the Tall Timbers Fire Ecology Conference*. No. 18. *The Longleaf Pine Ecosystem: Ecology, Restoration, and Management*. Florida: Tall Timbers Research Station.

Pennings, S. C. and R. M. Callaway. 1996. Impact of a parasitic plant on the structure and dynamics of salt marsh vegetation. *Ecology* **77**: 1410–1419.

Pennings, S. C., T. H. Carefoot, E. L. Siska, M. E. Chase, and T. A. Page. 1998. Feeding preferences of a generalist salt-marsh crab: relative importance of multiple plant traits. *Ecology* **79**: 1968–1979.

Percival, M. S. 1965. *Floral Diversity*. Oxford: Pergamon Press.

Perry, D. 1986. *Life Above the Jungle Floor*. San José: Don Perro Press.

Peters, R. H. 1992. *A Critique for Ecology*. Cambridge: Cambridge University Press.

Petit, J. R. et al. 1999. Climate and atmospheric history of the past 420 000 years from the Vostok ice core, Antarctica. *Nature* **399**: 429–436.

Petterson, B. 1965. Gotland and Öland: two limestone islands compared. *Acta Phytogeographic Suecica* **50**: 131–140.

Phillips, D. L. and D. J. Shure. 1990. Patch-size effects on early succession in southern Appalachian forest. *Ecology* **71**: 204–212.

Phipps, R. W. 1883. *On the Necessity of Preserving and Replanting Forests*. Toronto: Blackett and Robinson.

Pianka, E. R. 1981. Competition and niche theory. pp. 167–196. In R. M. May (ed.) *Theoretical Ecology*. Oxford: Blackwell.

Pianka, E. R. 1983. *Evolutionary Ecology*. 3rd edn. New York: Harper and Row.

Pickett, S. T. A. 1980. Non-equilibrium coexistence of plants. *Bulletin of the Torrey Botanical Club* **107**: 238–248.

Pickett, S. T. A. and P. S. White. 1985. *The Ecology of Natural Disturbance and Patch Dynamics*. Orlando: Academic Press.

Pielou, E. C. 1975. *Ecological Diversity*. New York: John Wiley and Sons.

Pielou, E. C. 1977. *Mathematical Ecology*. New York: John Wiley and Sons.

Pielou, E. C. 1979. *Biogeography*. New York: John Wiley and Sons.

Pielou, E. C. 1984. *The Interpretation of Ecological Data: A Primer on Classification and Ordination*. New York: Wiley.

Pielou, E. C. and R. D. Routledge. 1976. Salt marsh vegetation: latitudinal gradients in the zonation patterns. *Oecologia* **24**: 311–321.

Pietropaolo, J. and P. Pietropaolo. 1986. *Carnivorous Plants of the World.* Portland: Timber Press.

Pimm, S. L. 2001. *The World According to Pimm: A Scientist Audits the Earth.* New York: McGraw-Hill.

Pirozynski, D. W. and D. W. Malloch. 1988. Seeds, spores and stomachs: coevolution in seed dispersal mutualisms. pp. 228–244. In K. A. Pirozynski and D. L. Hawksworth (eds.) *Coevolution of Fungi with Plants and Animals.* London: Academic Press.

Pirozynski, K. A. and Y. Dalpé. 1989. Geological history of the Glomaceae with particular reference to mycorrhizal symbiosis. *Symbiosis* **7**: 1–36.

Pitman, N. C. A. and P. M. Jørgensen. 2002. Estimating the size of the world's threatened flora. *Science* **298**: 989.

Platt, W. J. 1999. Southeastern pine savannas. pp. 23–51. In R. C. Anderson, J. S. Fralish, and J. M. Baskin (eds.) *Savannas, Barrens and Rock Outcrop Communities of North America.* Cambridge: Cambridge University Press.

Poljakoff-Mayber, A. and J. Gale. (eds.) 1975. *Plants in Saline Environments.* Berlin: Springer-Verlag.

Ponnamperuma, F. N. 1984. Effects of flooding on soils. pp. 9–45. In T. T. Kozlowski (ed.) *Flooding and Plant Growth.* Orlando: Academic Press.

Poole, R. W. and B. J. Rathcke. 1979. Regularity, randomness, and aggregation in flowering phenologies. *Science* **203**: 470–471.

Porter, C. L. 1967. *Taxonomy of Flowering Plants.* 2nd edn. San Francisco: W. H. Freeman.

Porter, H. 1993. Interspecific variation in the growth response of plants to an elevated ambient CO_2 concentration. *Vegetatio* **104/105**: 77–97.

Postel, S. L., G. C. Daily, and P. R. Ehrlich. 1996. Human appropriation of renewable fresh water. *Science* **271**: 785–788.

Pound, R. 1893. Symbiosis and mutualism. *The American Naturalist* **27**: 509–520.

Power, M. E. 1992. Top-down and bottom-up forces in food webs: do plants have primacy? *Ecology* **73**: 733–746.

Prance, G. T. and D. M. Johnson. 1991. Plant collections from the plateau of Serra do Aracá (Amazonas, Brazil) and their phytogeographic affinities. *Kew Bulletin* **47**: 1–24.

Press, M. C. and J. D. Graves (eds.) 1995. *Parasitic Plants.* London: Chapman and Hall.

Pressey, R. L., C. J. Humphries, C. R. Margules, R. I. Vane-Wright, and P. H. Williams. 1993. Beyond opportunism: key principles for systematic reserve selection. *Trends in Ecology and Evolution* **8**: 124–128.

Preston, F. W. 1962a. The canonical distribution of commonness and rarity: Part I. *Ecology* **43**: 185–215.

Preston, F. W. 1962b. The canonical distribution of commonness and rarity: Part II. *Ecology* **43**: 410–432.

Price, M. V. 1983. Ecological consequences of body size: a model for patch choice in desert rodents. *Oecologia* **59**: 384–392.

Price, M. V. 1984. Alternative paradigms in community ecology. pp. 354–383. In P. W. Price, C. N. Slobodchikoff, and W. S. A. Gaud (eds.) *A New Ecology: Novel Approaches to Interactive Systems.* New York: John Wiley and Sons.

Price, M. V. and O. J. Reichman. 1987. Distribution of seeds in Sonoran Desert soils: implications for heteromyid rodent foraging. *Ecology* **68**: 1797–1811.

Pringle, H. 1996. *In Search of Ancient North America*. New York: John Wiley and Sons.

Pritchard, P. C. H. 1996. *The Galápagos Tortoises: Nomenclatural and Survival Status*. Chelonian Research Monographs No. 1. Lunenbug: Chelonian Research Foundation.

Puckett, L. J. 1994. *Nonpoint and Point Sources of Nitrogen in Major Watersheds of the United States*. U.S. Geological Survey Water-Resources Investigations Report 94–4001.

Puerto, A., M. Rico, M. D. Matias, and J. A. García. 1990. Variation in structure and diversity in Mediterranean grasslands related to trophic status and grazing intensity. *Journal of Vegetation Science* **1**: 445–452.

Pusey, A. and M. Wolf. 1996. Inbreeding avoidance in animals. *Trends in Ecology and Evolution* **11**: 201–206.

Putwain, P. D. and J. L. Harper. 1970. Studies in the dynamics of plant populations. III. The influence of associated species on populations of *Rumex acetosa* L. and *R. acetosella* L. in grassland. *Journal of Ecology* **58**: 251–264.

Putz, F. E. and C. D. Canham. 1992. Mechanisms of arrested succession in shrublands: root and shoot competition between shrubs and tree seedlings. *Forest Ecology and Management* **49**: 267–275.

Quinn, C. J. and R. A. Price. 2003. Phylogeny of the southern hemisphere conifers. pp. 129–136. In R. R. Mill (ed.) *Proceedings of the 4th International Conifer Conference*. ISHS Acta Horticulturae 615.

Radford, A. E., H. E. Ahles and C. R. Bell. 1968. *Manual of the Vascular Flora of the Carolinas*. Chapel Hill: The University of North Carolina Press.

Rapport, D. J. 1989. What constitutes ecosystem health? *Perspectives in Biology and Medicine* **33**: 120–132.

Rapport D. J., C. Thorpe, and T. C. Hutchinson. 1985. Ecosystem behaviour under stress. *The American Naturalist* **125**: 617–640.

Rasker, R. and A. Hackman. 1996. Economic development and the conservation of large carnivores. *Conservation Biology* **10**: 991–1002.

Raunkiaer, C. 1907. The life-forms of plants and their bearing on geography. Translated from Danish and republished in 1934. In *The Life Forms of Plants and Statistical Plant Geography*. pp. 2–104. Oxford: Clarendon Press.

Raunkiaer, C. 1908. The statistics of life-forms as a basis for biological plant geography. Translated from Danish and republished in 1934. In *The Life Forms of Plants and Statistical Plant Geography*. pp. 111–147. Oxford: Clarendon Press.

Raunkiaer, C. 1918. On the biological normal spectrum. Translated from German and republished in 1934 in *The Life Forms of Plants and Statistical Plant Geography*. pp. 425–434. Oxford: Clarendon Press.

Raunkiaer, C. 1934. *The Life Forms of Plants and Statistical Plant Geography: Being the Collected Papers of Raunkiaer*. Translated from the Danish, French and German. Preface by A. G. Tansley. Oxford: Clarendon Press.

Raven, P. H., R. F. Evert, and S. E. Eichhorn. 1999. *Biology of Plants*. 6th edn. New York: W. H. Freeman and Company/Worth Publishers.

Raven, P. H., R. F. Evert, and S. E. Eichhorn. 2005. *Biology of Plants*. 7th edn. New York: W. H. Freeman and Company Publishers.

Ravera, O. 1989. Lake ecosystem degradation and recovery studied by the enclosure method. pp. 217–243. In O. Ravera (ed.) *Ecological Assessment of Environmental Degradation, Pollution and Recovery*. Amsterdam: Elsevier Science Publishers.

Rawes, M. and O. W. Heal. 1978. The blanket bog as part of a Pennine moorland. pp. 224–243. In O. W. Heal and D. F. Perkins (eds.) *Production Ecology of British Moors and Montane Grasslands*. Ecological Studies, Vol. 27. Berlin: Springer-Verlag.

Read, D. J., H. K. Koucheki, and J. Hodgson. 1976. Vesicular-arbuscular mycorrhizae in natural vegetation systems. 1. The occurrence of infection. *New Phytologist* **77**: 641–653.

Reader, R. J. and B. J. Best. 1989. Variation in competition along an environmental gradient: *Hieracium floribundum* in an abandoned pasture. *Journal of Ecology* **77**: 673–684.

Rees, W. E. and M. Wackernagel. 1994. Ecological footprints and appropriated carrying capacity: measuring the natural capital requirements of the human economy. pp. 362–390. In A. Jansson, M. Hammer, C. Folke, and R. Costanza (eds.) *Investing in Natural Capital: The Ecological Economics Approach to Sustainability*. Washington, D.C.: Island Press.

Regal, P. J. 1977. Ecology and evolution of flowering plant dominance. *Science* **196**: 622–629.

Reid, D. M. and K. J. Bradford. 1984. Effect of flooding on hormone relations. pp. 195–219. In T. T. Kozlowski (ed.) *Flooding and Plant Growth*. Orlando: Academic Press.

Reid, W. V., J. A. McNeely, D. B. Tunstall, D. A. Bryant, and M. Winograd. 1993. *Biodiversity Indicators for Policymakers*. Washington, D.C.: World Resources Institute.

Richards, P. W. 1952. *The Tropical Rain Forest: An Ecological Study*. Paperback edition 1979. Cambridge: Cambridge University Press.

Richardson, C. J. (ed.) 1981. *Pocosin Wetlands: An Integrated Analysis of Coastal Plain Freshwater Bogs in North Carolina*. Stroudsburg: Hutchinson Ross Publishing Company.

Richardson, S. J., D. A. Peltzer, R. B. Allen, and M. S. McGlone. 2005. Resorption proficiency along a chronosequence: responses among communities and within species. *Ecology* **80**: 20–25.

Rickerl, D. H., F. O. Sancho, and S. Ananth. 1994. Vesicular-arbuscular endomycorrhizal colonization of wetland plants. *Journal of Environmental Quality* **23**: 913–916.

Rigler, F. H. 1982. Recognition of the possible: an advantage of empiricism in ecology. *Canadian Journal of Fisheries and Aquatic Sciences* **39**: 1323–1331.

Rigler, F. H. and R. H. Peters. 1995. *Science and Limnology*. Oldendorf/Lutie: Ecology Institute.

Ritchie, J. C. 1987. *Postglacial Vegetation of Canada*. New York: Cambridge University Press.

Roberts, B. A. 1992. The serpentinized areas of Newfoundland, Canada: a brief review of their soils and vegetation. pp. 53–66. In A. J. M. Baker, J. Proctor, and R. D. Reeves (eds.) *The Vegetation of Ultramafic (Serpentine) Soils*. Andover: Intercept.

Roberts, J. and J. A. Ludwig. 1991. Riparian vegetation along current-exposure gradients in floodplain wetlands of the River Murray, Australia. *Journal of Ecology* **79**: 117–127.

Robinson, A. R. 1973. Sediment, our greatest pollutant? In R. W. Tank (ed.) *Focus on Environmental Geology*. London: University Press.

Robinson, D. 1996. Resource capture by localised root proliferation: why do plants bother? *Annals of Botany* **77**: 179–185.

Robinson, J. M. 1990. Lignin, land plants, and fungi: biological evolution affecting phanerozoic oxygen balance. *Geology* **18**: 607–610.

Rodman, J. E. 1974. Systematics and evolution of the genus *Cakile* (Cruciferae). *Contributions from the Gray Herbarium* **205**: 3–146.

Rodrigues, A. S. L. *et al.* 2004. Effectiveness of the global protected areas network in representing species diversity. *Nature* **428**: 640–643.

Roger, A. J. 1999. Reconstructing early events in eukaryotic evolution. *The American Naturalist* **154** (Suppl.): S146–S163.

Rohde, K. 1997. The larger area of tropics does not explain latitudinal gradients in species diversity. *Oikos* **79**: 169–172.

Rolston, H. 1994. Foreword. pp. xi–xiii. In L. Westra (ed.) *An Environmental Proposal for Ethics: The Principle of Integrity.* Lanham: Rowman and Littlefield. In R. Noss (ed.) 1995. *Maintaining Ecological Integrity in Representative Reserve Networks.* A World Wildlife Fund Canada/World Wildlife Fund/United States Discussion Paper, WWF.

Rose, R. 1924. Man and the Galapagos Islands. pp. 332–417. In W. Beebe (ed.) *Galapagos: World's End.* New York: Putnam's Sons.

Rosenthal, G. A. and M. R. Berenbaum. (eds.) 1991. *Herbivores: Their Interactions with Secondary Plant Metabolites.* San Diego: Academic Press.

Rosenzweig, M. L. 1995. *Species Diversity in Space and Time.* Cambridge: Cambridge University Press.

Rosgen, D. L. 1995. River restoration utilizing natural stability concepts. pp. 55–62. In J. A. Kusler, D. E. Willard, and H. C. Hull Jr. (eds.) *Wetlands and Watershed Management: Science Applications and Public Policy.* A collection of papers from a national symposium and several workshops at Tampa, Florida, April 23–26. New York: The Association of State Wetland Managers.

Rowe, J. S. and G. W. Scotter. 1973. Fire in the boreal forest. *Quaternary Research* **3**: 444–464.

Rozan, T. F., K. S. Hunter, and G. Benoit. 1994. Industrialization as recorded in floodplain deposits of the Quinnipiac River, Connecticut. *Marine Pollution Bulletin* **28**: 564–569.

Rundel, P. W., R. M. Cowling, K. J. Esler, P. M. Mustart, E. van Jaarsveld, and H. Bezuidenhout. 1995. Winter growth phenology and leaf orientation in *Pachypodium namaquanum* (Apocynaceae) in the succulent karoo of the Richtersveld, South Africa. *Oecologia* **101**: 472–477.

Russell, F. L., D. B. Zippin, and N. L. Fowler. 2001. Effects of white-tailed deer (*Odocoileus virginianus*) on plants, plant populations and communities: a review. *The American Midland Naturalist* **146**: 1–26.

Rybicki, N. B. and V. Carter. 1986. Effect of sediment depth and sediment type on the survival of *Vallisneria americana* Michx. grown from tubers. *Aquatic Botany* **24**: 233–240.

Salisbury, E. J. 1942. *The Reproductive Capacity of Plants. Studies in Quantitative Biology.* London: G. Bell and Sons Ltd.

Salisbury, F. B. and C. W. Ross. 1988. *Plant Physiology.* 3rd edn. Belmont: Wadsworth Publishers.

Salisbury, S. E. 1970. The pioneer vegetation of exposed muds and its biological features. *Royal Society of London, Philosophical Transactions, Series B,* **259**: 207–255.

Salo, J., R. Kalliola, I. Hakkinen, Y. Makinen, P. Niemela, M. Puhakka, and P. D. Coley. 1986. River dynamics and the diversity of Amazon lowland forest. *Nature* **322**: 254–258.

Salzman, A. G. and M. A. Parker. 1985. Neighbours ameliorate local salinity stress for a rhizomatous plant in a heterogeneous environment. *Oecologia* **65**: 273–277.

Sandars, N. K. 1972. *The Epic of Gilgamesh*. An English version with an introduction by N. K. Sanders. Revised edition. London: Penguin Books.

Sarthou, C. and J-F. Villiers. 1998. Epilithic plant communities on inselbergs in French Guiana. *Journal of Vegetation Science* **9**: 847–860.

Sather, J. H. and R. D. Smith. 1984. *An Overview of Major Wetland Functions*. U. S. Fish and Wildlife Service. FWS/OBS-84/18.

Saunders, D. A., R. J. Hobbs, and P. R. Ehrlich (eds.) 1993. *Nature Conservation 3: Reconstruction of Fragmented Ecosystems – Global and Regional Perspectives*. Chipping Norton: Surrey Beatty and Sons Pty Limited.

Savile, D. B. O. 1956. Known dispersal rates and migratory potentials as clues to the origin of the North American biota. *The American Midland Naturalist* **56**: 434–453.

Savile, D. B. O. 1972. *Arctic Adaptations in Plants*. Monograph No. 6. Ottawa: Canada Department of Agriculture.

Sayre, N. F. 2003. Recognizing history in range ecology: 100 years of science and management on the Santa Rita Experimental Range. pp. 1–15. In *USDA Forest Service Proceedings RMRS-P-30*. US Department of Agriculture.

Scagel, R. F., G. E. Rouse, J. R. Stein, R. J. Bandoni, W. B. Schofield, and T. M. C. Taylor. 1965. *An Evolutionary Survey of the Plant Kingdom*. Belmont: Wadsworth Publishing Company.

Scagel, R. F., R. J. Bandoni, G. E. Rouse, W. B. Schofield, J. R. Stein, and T. M. C. Taylor. 1969. *Plant Diversity: An Evolutionary Approach*. Belmont: Wadsworth Publishing Company.

Schaal, B. A. 1984. Life-history variation, natural selection, and maternal effects in plant populations. pp. 188–206. In R. Dirzo and J. Sarukhán (eds.) *Perspectives on Plant Population Ecology*. Sunderland: Sinauer Associates.

Schell, J. 1982. *The Fate of the Earth*. New York: Alfred A. Knopf.

Schnitzler A. 1995. Successional status of trees in gallery forest along the river Rhine. *Journal of Vegetation Science* **6**: 479–486.

Scholander, P. F., H. T. Hammel, B. D. Bradstreet, and E. A. Hemmingsen. 1965. Sap pressure in vascular plants. *Science* **148**: 339–346.

Schopf, J. W. and E. S. Barghoorn. 1967. Alga-like fossils from the early Precambrian of South Africa. *Science* **156**: 508–512.

Schwinning, S. and O. E. Sala. 2004. Hierarchy of responses to resource pulses in arid and semi-arid ecosystems. *Oecologia* **141**: 211–220.

Scott, J. M., B. Csuti, J. D. Jacobi, and J. E. Estes. 1987. Species richness: a geographic approach to protecting future biological diversity. *Bioscience* **37**: 782–788.

Scott, M. G. and D. W. Larson. 1985. The effect of winter field conditions on the distribution of two species of *Umbilicaria*. I. CO_2 exchange in reciprocally transplanted thalli. *New Phytologist* **101**: 89–101.

Sculthorpe, C. D. 1967. *The Biology of Aquatic Vascular Plants*. Reprinted in 1985. London: Edward Arnold.

Seischab, F. K. and D. Orwig. 1991. Catastrophic disturbances in the presettlement forests of western New York. *Bulletin of the Torrey Botanical Club* **118**: 117–122.

Shaffer, G. P., C. E. Sasser, J. G. Gosselink, and M. Rejmanek. 1992. Vegetation dynamics in the emerging Atchafalaya Delta, Louisiana, USA. *Journal of Ecology* **80**: 677–687.

Shaffer, G. P., J. G. Gosselink, and S. S. Hoeppner. 2005. The Mississippi River alluvial plain. pp. 272–315. In L. H. Fraser and P. A. Keddy (eds.) *The World's Largest Wetlands: Ecology and Conservation*. Cambridge: Cambridge University Press.

Shannon, C. E. and W. Weaver. 1949. *The Mathematical Theory of Communication.* Urbana: University of Illinois Press.

Sheail, J. and T. C. E. Wells. 1983. The fenlands of Huntingdonshire, England: a case study in catastrophic change. pp. 375–393. In A. J. P. Gore (ed.) *Ecosystems of the World 4B. Mires: Swamp, Bog, Fen and Moor.* Amsterdam: Elsevier Scientific Publishing Company.

Shimwell, D. W. 1971. *The Description and Classification of Vegetation.* Seattle: University of Washington Press.

Shipley, B. 1993. A null model for competitive hierarchies in competition matrices. *Ecology* **74**: 1693–1699.

Shipley, B. and J. Dion. 1992. The allometry of seed production in herbaceous angiosperms. *The American Naturalist* **139**: 467–483.

Shipley, B. and P. A. Keddy. 1987. The individualistic and community-unit concepts as falsifiable hypotheses. *Vegetatio* **69**: 47–55.

Shipley, B. and P. A. Keddy. 1994. Evaluating the evidence for competitive hierarchies in plant communities. *Oikos* **69**: 340–345.

Shipley, B. and R. H. Peters. 1990. A test of the Tilman model of plant strategies: relative growth rate and biomass partioning. *The American Naturalist* **136**: 139–153.

Shipley, B., P. A. Keddy, and L. P. Lefkovitch. 1991. Mechanisms producing plant zonation along a water depth gradient: a comparison with the exposure gradient. *Canadian Journal of Botany* **69**: 1420–1424.

Shrader-Frechette, K. S. and E. D. McCoy. 1993. *Method in Ecology: Strategies for Conservation.* Cambridge: Cambridge University Press.

Shugart, H. H., D. C. West, and W. R. Emanuel. 1981. Patterns and dynamics of forests: an application of simulation models. pp. 74–106. In D. C., West, H. H. Shugart, and D. B. Botkin (eds.) *Forest Succession Concepts and Applications.* New York: Springer-Verlag.

Shure, D. J. 1999. Granite outcrops of the southeastern United States. pp. 99–118. In R. C. Anderson, J. S. Fralish, and J. M. Baskin (eds.) *Savannas, Barrens, and Rock Outcrop Plant Communities of North America.* Cambridge: Cambridge University Press.

Silliman, B. R. and M. D. Bertness. 2002. A trophic cascade regulates salt marsh primary production. *Proceedings of the National Academy of Sciences USA* **99**: 10500–10505.

Silver, T. 1990. *A New Face on the Countryside. Indians, Colonists and Slaves in the South Atlantic Forests, 1500–1800.* Cambridge: Cambridge University Press.

Silvertown, J. 1980. The dynamics of a grassland ecosystem: botanical equilibrium in the Park Grass Experiment. *Journal of Applied Ecology* **17**: 491–504.

Silvertown, J. 1987. *Introduction to Plant Population Ecology.* 2nd edn. London: Longman.

Silvertown, J. and D. Charlesworth. 2001. *Introduction to Plant Population Biology.* 4th edn. Oxford: Blackwell Science.

Silvertown, J., M. E. Dodd, K. McConway, J. Potts, and M. Crawley. 1994. Rainfall, biomass variation, and community composition in the Park Grass Experiment. *Ecology* **75**: 2430–2437.

Silvertown, J., P. Poulton, E. Johnston, G. Edwards, M. Heard and P. M. Biss. 2006. The Park Grass experiment 1856–2006: its contribution to ecology. *Journal of Ecology* **94**: 801–814.

Simon, L., J. Bousquet, R. C. Lévesque, and M. Lalonde. 1993. Origin and diversification of endomycorrhizal fungi and coincidence with vascular land plants. *Nature* **363**: 67–69.

Simpson, E. H. 1949. Measurement of diversity. *Nature* **163**: 688.

Sinclair, A. R. E. 1983. The adaptations of African ungulates and their effects on community function. pp. 401–425. In F. Bouliere (ed.) *Tropical Savannas*. Amsterdam: Elsevier.

Sinclair, A. R. E. and J. M. Fryxell. 1985. The Sahel of Africa: ecology of a disaster. *Canadian Journal of Zoology* **63**: 987–994.

Sinclair, A. R. E., D. S. Hik, O. J. Schmitz, G. G. E. Scudder, D. H. Turpin, and N. C. Larter. 1995. Biodiversity and the need for habitat renewal. *Ecological Applications* **5**: 579–587.

Sinclair, A. R. E., C. J. Krebs, J. M. Fryxell, R. Turkington, S. Boutin, R. Boonstra, P. Seccombe-Hett, P. Lundberg, and L. Oksanen. 2000. Testing hypotheses of trophic level interactions: a boreal forest ecosystem. *Oikos* **89**: 313–328.

Sinclair, A. R. E. and C. J. Krebs. 2001. Trophic interactions, community organization, and the Kluane ecosystem. pp. 25–48. In C. J. Krebs, S. Boutin, and R. Boonstra (eds.) *Ecosystem Dynamics of the Boreal Forest. The Kluane Project*. New York: Oxford University Press.

Sioli, H. 1964. General features of the limnology of Amazonia. *Verhandlungen/ Internationale Vereinigung für theoretische und angewandte Limnologie* **15**: 1053–1058.

Sklar, F. H., R. Costanza, and J. W. Day Jr. 1990. Model conceptualization. pp. 625–658. In B. C. Patten (ed.) *Wetlands and Shallow Continental Water Bodies*, Vol. 1. The Hague: SPB Academic Publishing.

Sklar, F. H. *et al.* 2005. The ecological–societal underpinnings of Everglades restoration. *Frontiers in Ecology and the Environment* **3**: 161–169.

Slade, A. J. and M. J. Hutchings. 1987. The effects of nutrient availability on foraging in the clonal herb *Glechoma hederacea*. *Journal of Ecology* **75**: 95–112.

Sletvold, N. 2002. Effects of plant size on reproductive output and offspring performance in the facultative biennial *Digitalis purpurea*. *Journal of Ecology* **90**: 958–996.

Small, E. 1972a. Water relations of plants in raised *Sphagnum* peat bogs. *Ecology* **53**: 726–728.

Small, E. 1972b. Photosynthetic rates in relation to nitrogen recycling as an adaptation to nutrient deficiency in peat bogs. *Canadian Journal of Botany* **50**: 2227–2233.

Smart, R. M. and J. W. Barko. 1978. Influence of sediment salinity and nutrients on the physiological ecology of selected salt marsh plants. *Estuarine and Coastal Marine Science* **7**: 487–495.

Smith, A. 1776. An enquiry into the nature and causes of the wealth of nations. In M. J. Adler (ed.) 1990. *Great Books of the Western World*, Vol. 36. Chicago: Encyclopaedia Britannica.

Smith, C. C. 1970. The coevolution of pine squirrels (*Tamiasciurus*) and conifers. *Ecological Monographs* **40**: 349–371.

Smith, C. C. and D. Follmer. 1972. Food preference of squirrels. *Ecology* **53**: 82–91.

Smith, D. C. 1980. Mechanisms of nutrient movement between lichen symbionts. pp. 197–227. In C. B. Cook, P. W. Pappas, and E. D. Rudolph (eds.) *Cellular Interactions in Symbiosis and Parasitism*. Columbus: Ohio State University Press.

Smith, D. C. and A. E. Douglas. 1987. *The Biology of Symbiosis*. London: Edward Arnold.

Smith, L. M. and J. A. Kadlec. 1983. Seed banks and their role during the drawdown of a North American marsh. *Journal of Applied Ecology* **20**: 673–684.

Smith, L. M. and J. A. Kadlec. 1985a. Fire and herbivory in a Great Salt Lake marsh. *Ecology* **66**: 259–265.

Smith, L. M. and J. A. Kadlec. 1985b. Comparisons of prescribed burning and cutting of Utah marsh plants. *Great Basin Naturalist* **45**: 463–466.

Smith, R. L. 1986. *Elements of Ecology*. New York: Harper and Row.

Smith, V. H. 1982. The nitrogen and phosphorus dependence of algal biomass in lakes: an empirical and theoretical analysis. *Limnology and Oceanography* **27**: 1101–1112.

Smith, V. H. 1983. Low nitrogen to phosphorus ratios favor dominance by blue-green algae in lake phytoplankton. *Science* **221**: 669–671.

Smol, J. P. and B. F. Cumming. 2000. Tracking long-term changes in climate using algal indicators in lake sediments. *Journal of Phycology* **36**: 986–1011.

Sneath, P. H. A. and R. R. Sokal. 1973. *Numerical Taxonomy*. San Francisco: W. H. Freeman.

Snell, T. W. and D. G. Burch. 1975. The effects of density on resource partitioning in *Chamaesyce hirta* (Euphorbiaceae). *Ecology* **56**: 742–746.

Snow, A. A. and S. W. Vince. 1984. Plant zonation in an Alaskan salt marsh. II: an experimental study of the role of edaphic conditions. *Journal of Ecology* **72**: 669–684.

Sobel, D. 1995. *Longitude: The True Story of a Lone Genius Who Solved the Greatest Scientific Problem of His Time*. New York: Penguin Books.

Soper, J. H. and P. F. Maycock. 1963. A community of arctic-alpine plants on the east shore of Lake Superior. *Canadian Journal of Botany* **41**: 183–198.

Sorrie, B. A. 1994. Coastal plain ponds in New England. *Biological Conservation* **68**: 225–233.

Soulé, M. and R. Noss. 1998. Rewilding and biodiversity: complementary goals for continental conservation. *Wild Earth* **8**(3): 18–28.

Sousa, W. P. 1984. The role of disturbance in natural communities. *Annual Review of Ecology and Systematics* **15**: 353–391.

Southwood, T. R. E. 1977. Habitat, the templet for ecological strategies? *Journal of Animal Ecology* **46**: 337–365.

Southwood, T. R. E. 1985. Interactions of plants and animals: patterns and processes. *Oikos* **44**: 5–11.

Southwood, T. R. E. 1988. Tactics, strategies, and templets. *Oikos* **52**: 3–18.

Specht, A. and R. Specht. 1993. Species richness and canopy productivity of Australian plant communities. *Biodiversity and Conservation* **2**: 152–167.

Specht, R. L. and A. Specht. 1989. Species richness of overstorey strata in Australian plant communities – the influence of overstorey growth rates. *Australian Journal of Botany* **37**: 321–336.

Spence, D. H. N. 1982. The zonation of plants in freshwater lakes. *Advances in Ecological Research* **12**: 37–125.

Spencer, D. F. and G. G. Ksander. 1997. Influence of anoxia on sprouting of vegetative propagules of three species of aquatic plant propagules. *Wetlands* **17**: 55–64.

Sporne, K. R. 1956. The phylogenetic classification of the angiosperms. *Biological Reviews* **31**: 1–29.

Sporne, K. R. 1970. *The Morphology of Pteridophytes: The Structure of Ferns and Allied Plants*. 3rd edn. London: Hutchinson and Co.

Sprengel, C. K. 1793. Discovery of the secret of nature in the structure and fertilization of flowers. Vieweq, Berlin. Translation of title and first chapter by P. Haase. pp. 3–43. In D. G. Lloyd and S. C. H. Barrett (eds.) *Floral Biology. Studies on Floral Evolution in Animal-Pollinated Plants*. London: Chapman and Hall.

Starfield, A. M. and A. L. Bleloch. 1986. *Building Models for Conservation and Wildlife Management*. New York: Macmillan.

Starfield, A. M. and A. L. Bleloch. 1991. *Building Models for Conservation and Wildlife Management*. 2nd edn. Edina: MN Burgers International Group.

Stearn, W. T. 1979. Linnaean classification. pp. 96–101. In D. Black (ed.) 1979. *Carl Linnaeus: Travels*. New York: Scribner's Sons.

Steedman, R. J. 1988. Modification and assessment of an index of biotic integrity to quantify stream quality in southern Ontario. *Canadian Journal of Fisheries and Aquatic Sciences* **45**: 492–501.

Steenbergh, W. F. and C. H. Lowe. 1969. Critical factors during the first years of life of the saguaro (*Cereus giganteus*) at Saguaro National Monument, Arizona. *Ecology* **50**: 825–834.

Steila, D. 1993. Soils. pp. 47–54. *In Flora of North America*, Vol. 1. *Introduction*. New York: Oxford University Press.

Stein, B. A., L. S. Kutner, and J. S. Adams (eds.) 2000. *Precious Heritage. The Status of Biodiversity in the United States*. Oxford: Oxford University Press.

Steneck, R. S. and M. N. Dethier. 1994. A functional group approach to the structure of algal-dominated communities. *Oikos* **69**: 476–498.

Stephenson, N. L. 1990. Climatic control of vegetation distribution: the role of the water balance. *The American Naturalist* **135**: 649–680.

Stephenson, S. N. and P. S. Herendeen. 1986. Short-term drought effects on the alvar communities of Drummond Island, Michigan. *The Michigan Botanist* **25**: 16–27.

Stevenson, J. C., L. G. Ward, and M. S. Kearney. 1986. Vertical accretion in marshes with varying rates of sea level rise. pp. 241–259. In D. A. Wolfe (ed.) *Estuarine Variability*. San Diego: Academic Press.

Stewart, W. N. and G. W. Rothwell. 1993. *Paleobotany and the Evolution of Plants*. 2nd edn. Cambridge: Cambridge University Press.

Steyermark, J. A. 1982. Relationships of some Venezuelan forest refuges with lowland tropical floras. pp. 182–220. In G. T. Prance (ed.) *Biological Diversification in the Tropics*. New York: Columbia University Press.

Stoltzenberg, D. 2004. *Fritz Haber. Chemist, Nobel Laureate, German, Jew*. Philadelphia: Chemical Heritage Press.

Strahler, A. N. 1971. *The Earth Sciences*. 2nd edn. New York: Harper and Row.

Street, F. A. and A. T. Grove. 1979. Global maps of lake-level fluctuations since 30,000 yr B.P. *Quaternary Research* **12**: 83–118.

Strong, D. R. Jr., D. Simberloff, L. G. Abele, and A. B. Thistle (eds). 1984. *Ecological Communities. Conceptual Issues and the Evidence*. Princeton: Princeton University Press.

Stupka, A. 1964. *Trees, Shrubs and Woody Vines of Great Smoky National Park*. Knoxville: The University of Tennessee Press.

Suffling, R., C. Lihou, and Y. Morand. 1988. Control of landscape diversity by catastrophic disturbance: a theory and case study of fire in a Canadian boreal forest. *Environmental Management* **12**: 73–78.

Sun, G., Q. Ji, D. L. Dilcher, S. Zheng, K. C. Nixon, and X. Wang. 2002. Archaefructaceae, a new basal angiosperm family. *Science* **296**: 899–904.

Sutter, R. D. and R. Kral. 1994. The ecology, status, and conservation of two non-alluvial wetland communities in the south Atlantic and eastern Gulf coastal plain, USA. *Biological Conservation* **68**: 235–243.

Szarek, S. R. and I. P. Ting. 1975. Photosynthetic efficiency of CAM plants in relation to C_3 and C_4 plants. pp. 289–297. In R. Marcelle (ed.) *Environmental and Biological Control of Photosynthesis*. The Hague: W. Junk.

Tabachnick, B. G. and L. S. Fidell. 2001. *Using Multivariate Statistics*. 4th edn. Boston: Allyn and Bacon.

Taiz, L. and E. Zeiger. 1991. *Plant Physiology*. San Francisco: Benjamin-Cummings.

Takhtajan, A. 1969. *Flowering Plants: Origin and Dispersal*. Edinburgh: Oliver and Boyd. Translated and revised from a Russian second edition published in Moscow in 1961.

Takhtajan, A. 1986. *Floristic Regions of the World*. Berkeley: University of California Press. Translated by T. J. Crovello.

Tansley, A. G. 1939. *The British Islands and their Vegetation*. Cambridge: Cambridge University Press.

Tansley, A. 1987. What is ecology? *Biological Journal of the Linnean Society* **32**: 5–16.

Tansley, A. G. and R. S. Adamson. 1925. Studies of the vegetation of the English chalk. Part III. The chalk grasslands of the Hampshire-Sussex border. *Journal of Ecology* **XIII**: 177–223.

Tansley, A. G. and T. F. Chipp (eds.) 1926. *Aims and Methods in the Study of Vegetation*. London: The British Empire Vegetation Committee and Crown Agents for Colonies.

Taylor, D. R., L. W. Aarssen, and C. Loehle. 1990. On the relationship between r/K selection and environmental carrying capacity: a new habitat template for life history strategies. *Oikos* **58**: 239–250.

Taylor, T. N., H. Kerp, and H. Hass. 2005. Life history biology of early land plants: deciphering the gametophyte phase. *Proceedings of the National Academy of Sciences* **102**: 5892–5897.

Taylor, J. G. 1984. *Louisiana: A History*. New York: W. W. Norton & Company.

Taylor, K. L. and J. B. Grace. 1995. The effects of vertebrate herbivory on plant community structure in the coastal marshes of the Pearl River, Louisiana, USA. *Wetlands* **15**: 68–73.

Taylor, T. N. 1988. The origin of land plants: some answers, more questions. *Taxon* **37**: 805–833.

Taylor, T. N. 1990. Fungal associations in the terrestrial paleoecosystem. *Trends in Ecology and Evolution* **5**: 21–25.

Temple, S. A. 1977. Plant–animal mutualism: coevolution with dodo leads to near extinction of plant. *Science* **197**: 886–887.

Terborgh, J. 1989. *Where Have All the Birds Gone?* Princeton: Princeton University Press.

Terborgh, J. *et al.* 2001. Ecological meltdown in predator-free forest fragments. *Science* **294**: 1923–1926.

Thirgood, J. V. 1981. *Man and the Mediterranean Forest: A History of Resource Depletion*. London: Academic Press.

Thompson, D. J. and J. M. Shay. 1988. First-year response of a *Phragmites* marsh community to seasonal burning. *Canadian Journal of Botany* **67**: 1448–1455.

Thorne, R. F. 1963. Some problems and guiding principles of angiosperm phylogeny. *The American Naturalist* **97**: 287–305.

Tilghman, N. G. 1989. Impacts of white-tailed deer on forest regeneration in northwestern Pennsylvania. *Journal of Wildlife Management* **53**: 524–532.

Tilman, D. 1982. *Resource Competition and Community Structure*. Princeton: Princeton University Press.

Tilman, D. and S. Pacala. 1993. The maintenance of species richness in plant communities. pp. 13–25. In R. E. Ricklefs and D. Schluter (eds.) *Species Diversity in Ecological Communities*, Chicago: University of Chicago Press.

Tilman, D., D. Wedin, and J. Knops. 1996. Productivity and sustainability influenced by biodiversity in grassland ecosystems. *Nature* **379**: 718–720.

Tinker, P. B., M. D. Jones, and D. M. Durall. 1992. A functional comparison of ecto- and endomycorrhizas. pp. 303–310. In D. J. Read, D. H. Lewis, A. H. Fitter, and I. J. Alexander (eds.) *Mycorrhizas in Ecosystems*. Wallingford: CAB International.

Tomlinson, P. B. 1986. *The Botany of Mangroves*. Cambridge: Cambridge University Press.

Tschudy, R. H., C. L. Pillmore, C. J. Orth, J. S. Gilmore, and J. D. Knight. 1984. Disruption of the terrestrial plant ecosystem at the Cretaceous-Tertiary boundary, Western Interior. *Science* **225**: 1030–1032.

Tubbs, C. H., R. M. DeGraff, M. Yamasaki, and W. M. Healy. 1987. Guide to wildlife tree management in New England northern hardwoods. United States Department of Agriculture and Forestry Service General Technical Report NE-118.

Turner, F. 1994. *Beyond Geography. The Western Spirit Against the Wilderness*. Fifth printing, first edition in 1983. New Brunswick: Rutgers University Press.

Turner, R. E. 1977. Intertidal vegetation and commercial yields of penaeid shrimp. *Transactions of the American Fisheries Society* **106**: 411–416.

Turner, R. M. 1990. Long-term vegetation change at a fully protected Sonoran Desert site. *Ecology* **71**: 464–477.

Turner, R. M., S. M. Alcorn, G. Olin, and J. A. Booth. 1966. The influence of shade, soil, and water on saguaro seedling establishment. *Botanical Gazette* **127**: 95–102.

Twolan-Strutt, L. and P. Keddy. 1996. Above- and belowground competition intensity in two contrasting wetland plant communities. *Ecology* **77**: 259–270.

Udvardy, M. D. F. 1975. *A Classification of the Biogeographical Provinces of the World*. IUCN Occasional Paper No. 18. Morges: International Union for the Conservation of Nature and Natural Resources.

Uhl, C. and J. B. Kauffman. 1990. Deforestation, fire susceptibility and potential responses to fire in the eastern Amazon. *Ecology* **71**: 437–449.

Underwood, A. J. 1978. The detection of non-random patterns of distribution of species along a gradient. *Oecologia* **36**: 317–326.

Urban, D. L. and H. H. Shugart. 1992. Individual based models of forest succession. pp. 249–292. In D. C. Glenn-Lewin, R. K. Peet, and T. T. Veblen. (eds.) *Plant Succession*. London: Chapman and Hall.

U.S. Army Coastal Engineering Research Centre. 1977. *Shore Protection Manual*, Vol. 1, 3rd edn. Washington, D.C.: US Government Printing Office.

U.S. Army Corps of Engineers. 2004. *The Mississippi River and Tributaries Project*. New Orleans District Office Website (www.mvn.usace.army.mil/pao/bro/misstrib.htm) accessed 26 Mar. 2006.

U.S.D.A. 1975. *Soil Taxonomy: A Basic System of Soil Classification for Making and Interpreting Soil Surveys*. Agricultural Handbook 436, Washington, D.C.: U.S.D.A.

U.S.D.A. 2004. Emerald ash borer; the green menace. Animal and Plant Health Inspection Service. Program Aid No. 1769.

Vallentyne, J. R. 1974. *The Algal Bowl. Lakes and Man*. Miscellaneous Special Publication 22. Ottawa: Department of the Environment, Fisheries and Marine Service.

van Breemen, N. 1995. How *Sphagnum* bogs down other plants. *Trends in Ecology and Evolution* **10**: 270–275.

Vandermeer, J. B., B. A. Hazlett, and B. Rathcke. 1985. Indirect facilitation and mutualism. pp. 326–343. In D. H. Boucher (ed.) *The Ecology of Mutualism*. New York: Oxford University Press.

van der Valk, A. G. 1981. Succession in wetlands: a Gleasonian approach. *Ecology* **62**: 688–696.

van der Valk, A. G. and C. B. Davis. 1976. The seed banks of prairie glacial marshes. *Canadian Journal of Botany* **54**: 1832–1838.

van der Valk, A. G. and C. B. Davis. 1978. The role of seed banks in the vegetation dynamics of prairie glacial marshes. *Ecology* **59**: 322–335.

van der Werf, A., A. Welschen, R. Welschen, and H. Lambers. 1988. Respiratory energy costs for the maintenance of biomass, for growth and for iron uptake in roots of *Carex diandra* and *Carex acutiformis*. *Physiologia Plantarum* **72**: 483–491.

Venable, D. L. and C. E. Pake. 1999. Population ecology of Sonoran Desert annual plants. pp. 115–142. In R. H. Robichaux (ed.) *The Ecology of Sonoran Desert Plants and Plant Communities*. Tucson: University of Arizona Press.

Veneklaas, E. J., A. Fajardo, S. Obregon, and J. Lozano. 2005. Gallery forest types and their environmental correlates in a Colombian savanna landscape. *Ecography* **28**: 236–252.

Verhoeven, J. T. A. and W. M. Liefveld. 1997. The ecological significance of organochemical compounds in *Sphagnum*. *Acta Botanica Neerlandica* **46**: 117–130.

Verhoeven, J. T. A. and M. B. Schmitz. 1991. Control of plant growth by nitrogen and phosphorus in mesotrophic fens. *Biogeochemistry* **12**: 135–148.

Verhoeven, J. T. A., R. H. Kemmers, and W. Koerselman. 1993. Nutrient enrichment of freshwater wetlands. pp. 33–59. In C. C. Vos and P. Opdam. *Landscape Ecology of a Stressed Environment*. London: Chapman and Hall.

Verhoeven, J. T. A., W. Koerselman, and A. F. M. Meuleman. 1996. Nitrogen- or phosphorus-limited growth in herbaceous, wet vegetation: relations with atmospheric inputs and management regimes. *Trends in Ecology and Evolution* **11**: 494–497.

Vernadsky, V. 1929. *La Biosphère*. Paris: Felix Alcan.

Vernadsky, V. I. 1998. *The Biosphere*. New York: Copernicus, Springer-Verlag. Translated from the French and Russian, including a new foreword, introduction and appendices.

Vesey-FitzGerald, D. F. 1960. Grazing succession among East African game animals. *Journal of Mammalogy* **41**: 161–172.

Vince, S. W. and A. A. Snow. 1984. Plant zonation in an Alaskan salt marsh I: Distribution, abundance, and environmental factors. *Journal of Ecology* **72**: 651–667.

Vitousek, P. M. 1982. Nutrient cycling and nitrogen use efficiency. *The American Naturalist* **119**: 553–572.

Vitousek, P., P. R. Ehrlich, A. H. Ehrlich, and P. Matson. 1986. Human appropriation of the products of photosynthesis. *Bioscience* **36**: 368–373.

Vitousek, P. M. *et al.* 1997. Human alteration of the global nitrogen cycle: causes and consequences. *Ecological Applications* **7**: 737–750.

Vitt, D. H. and W. Chee. 1990. The relationship of vegetation to surface water chemistry and peat chemistry in fens of Alberta, Canada. *Vegetatio* **89**: 87–106.

Vivian-Smith, G. 1997. Microtopographic heterogeneity and floristic diversity in experimental wetland communities. *Journal of Ecology* **85**: 71–82.

Vogel, S. 1996. Christian Konrad Sprengel's theory of the flower: the cradle of floral ecology. pp. 44–62. In D. G. Lloyd and S. C. H. Barrett (eds.) *Floral Biology. Studies on Floral Evolution in Animal-Pollinated Plants*. London: Chapman and Hall.

Vogl, R. 1969. One hundred and thirty years of plant succession in a southeastern Wisconsin lowland. *Ecology* **50**: 248–255.

von Humboldt, A. 1845. *Cosmos: A Sketch of the Physical Description of the Universe*, Vol. 1. Translated by E. C. Otté. Foundations of Natural History. Baltimore: Johns Hopkins University Press. 1997. (Originally produced in five volumes: 1845, 1847, 1850–51, 1858, and 1862.)

Waggoner, P. E. and G. R. Stephens. 1970. Transition probabilities for a forest. *Nature* **225**: 1160–1161.

Walker, D. 1970. Direction and rate in some British post-glacial hydroseres. pp. 117–139. In D. Walker and R. G. West (eds.) *Studies in the Vegetational History of the British Isles*. Cambridge: Cambridge University Press.

Walker, J., C. H. Thompson, I. F. Fergus, and B. R. Tunstall. 1981. Plant succession and soil development in coastal sand dunes of subtropical eastern Australia. pp. 107–131. In D. C. West, H. H. Shugart, and D. B. Botkin (eds.) *Forest Succession. Concepts and Application*. New York: Springer-Verlag.

Wallin, I. E. 1927. *Symbioticism and the Origin of Species*. Baltimore: Williams and Wilkins.

Wardle, D. A. 1995. Impact of disturbance on detritus food-webs in agro-ecosystems of contrasting tillage and weed management practices. *Advances in Ecological Research* **26**: 105–185.

Wardle, D. A. 2002. *Communities and Ecosystems: Linking the Aboveground and Belowground Components*. Princeton: Princeton University Press.

Wardle, D. A., M. A. Huston, J. P. Grime, F. Berendse, E. Garnier, W. K. Laurenroth, H. Setala, and S. D. Wilson. 2000. Biodiversity and ecosystem function: an issue in ecology. *Bulletin of the Ecological Society of America* **81**: 235–239.

Wardle, D. A., R. D. Bardgett, J. N. Klironomos, H. Setälä, W. H. van der Putten, and D. H. Wall. 2004. Ecological linkages between aboveground and belowground biota. *Science* **304**: 1629–1633.

Watkinson, A. R. 1985a. Plant responses to crowding. pp. 275–289. In J. White (ed.) *Studies in Plant Demography: A Festschrift for John L. Harper*. London: Academic Press.

Watkinson, A. R. 1985b. On the abundance of plants along an environmental gradient. *Journal of Ecology* **73**: 569–578.

Watkinson, A. R. and R. P. Freckleton. 1997. Quantifying the impact of arbuscular mycorrhizae on plant competition. *Journal of Ecology* **85**: 541–545.

Watkinson, A. R. and C. C. Gibson. 1988. Plant parasitism: the population dynamics of parasitic plants and their effects upon plant community structure. pp. 393–411. In A. J. Davy, M. J. Hutchings, and A. R. Watkinson. *Plant Population Biology*. Oxford: Blackwell Scientific Publications.

Watt, A. S. 1919. On the causes of failure of natural regeneration in British oakwoods. *Journal of Ecology* **7**: 173–203.

Watt, A. S. 1923. On the ecology of British beechwoods with special reference to their regeneration. Part I. The causes of failure of natural regeneration of the beech. *Journal of Ecology* **11**: 1–48.

Weaver, J. E. and F. E. Clements. 1929. *Plant Ecology*. New York: McGraw-Hill.

Weaver, J. E. and F. E. Clements. 1938. *Plant Ecology*. 2nd edn. New York: McGraw-Hill Book Company.

Weber, W. and A. Rabinowitz. 1996. A global perspective on large carnivore conservation. *Conservation Biology* **10**: 1046–1054.

Weetman, G. F. 1983. Forestry practices and stress on Canadian forest land. pp. 260–301. In W. Simpson-Lewis, R. McKechnie, and V. Neimanis (eds.) *Stress on Land in Canada*. Ottawa: Lands Directorate, Environment Canada.

Weiher, E. and P. A. Keddy. 1995a. The assembly of experimental wetland plant communities. *Oikos* **73**: 323–335.

Weiher, E. and P. A. Keddy. 1995b. Assembly rules, null models, and trait dispersion: new questions from old patterns. *Oikos* **74**: 159–165.

Weiher, E. and P. A. Keddy (eds.). 1999. *Ecological Assembly Rules: Perspectives, Advances, Retreats*. Cambridge: Cambridge University Press.

Weiher, E., A. van der Werf, K. Thompson, M. Roderick, E. Garnier, and O. Eriksson. 1999. Challenging Theophrastus: a common core list of plant traits for functional ecology. *Journal of Vegetation Science* **10**: 609–620.

Wein, R. W. 1983. Fire behaviour and ecological effects in organic terrain. pp. 81–95. In R. W. Wein and D. A. MacLean (eds.) *The Role of Fire in Northern Circumpolar Ecosystems*. New York: John Wiley and Sons Ltd.

Wein, R. W. and J. M. Moore. 1977. Fire history and rotations in the New Brunswick Acadian forest. *Canadian Journal of Forest Research* **7**: 285–294.

Weiner, J. 1985. Size hierarchies in experimental populations of annual plants. *Ecology* **66**: 743–752.

Weiner, J. 1986. How competition for light and nutrients affects size variablility in *Ipomea tricolor* populations. *Ecology* **67**: 1425–1427.

Weiner, J. and S. C. Thomas. 1986. Size variability and competition in plant monocultures. *Oikos* **47**: 221–222.

Weisner, S. E. B. 1990. Emergent Vegetation in Eutrophic Lakes: Distributional Patterns and Ecophysiological Constraints. Sweden: Grahns Boktryckeri.

Welcomme, R. L. 1976. Some general and theoretical considerations on the fish yield of African rivers. *Journal of Fish Biology* **8**: 351–364.

Welcomme, R. L. 1979. *Fisheries Ecology of Floodplain Rivers*. London: Longman.

Weldon, C. W. and W. L. Slauson. 1986. The intensity of competition versus its importance: an overlooked distinction and some implications. *The Quarterly Review of Biology* **61**: 23–44.

Weller, D. E. 1990. Will the real self-thinning rule please stand up? A reply to Osawa and Sugita. *Ecology* **71**: 1204–1207.

Weller, M. W. 1978. Management of freshwater marshes for wildlife. pp. 267–284. In R. E. Good, D. F. Whigham, and R. L. Simpson (eds.) *Freshwater Wetlands: Ecological Processes and Management Potential*. New York: Academic Press.

Weller, M. W. 1994. *Freshwater Marshes: Ecology and Wildlife Management*. 3rd edn. Minneapolis: University of Minnesota.

Wells, H. G. 1956. *The Outline of History: Being a Plain History of Life and Mankind*. Garden City, NY: Garden City Books. Revised and brought up to the end of the Second World War by Raymond Postgate.

West, D. C., H. H. Shugart, and D. B. Botkin (eds.) 1981. *Forest Succession: Concepts and Application*. New York: Springer-Verlag.

Westhoff, V. and E. van der Maarel. 1973. The Braun–Blanquet approach. pp. 617–707. In R. H. Whittaker (ed.) *Ordination and Classification of Communities*. The Hague: Junk.

Westoby, M. 1984. The self-thinning rule. *Advances in Ecological Research* **14**: 167–225.

Westoby, M. 1998. Leaf–height–seed (LHS) plant ecology strategy scheme. *Plant and Soil* **199**: 213–227.

Westoby, M., M. Leishman, and J. Lord. 1997. Comparative ecology of seed size and dispersal. pp. 143–162. In J. Silvertown, M. Franco, and J. L. Harper (eds.) *Plant Life Histories: Ecology, Phylogeny and Evolution*. Cambridge: Cambridge University Press.

Wheeler, B. D. and K. E. Giller. 1982. Species richness of herbaceous fen vegetation in Broadland, Norfolk in relation to the quantity of aboveground plant material. *Journal of Ecology* **70**: 179–200.

Whelan, P. M. and O. Hamann. 1989. Vegetation regrowth on Isla Pinta: a success story. *Noticias de Galápagos* **48**: 11–13.

Whelan, R. J. 1995. *The Ecology of Fire*. Cambridge: Cambridge University Press.

Whisenant, S. G. 1999. *Repairing Damaged Wildlands*. Cambridge: Cambridge University Press.

White, I. D., D. N. Mottershead, and S. J. Harrison. 1992. *Environmental Systems: An Introductory Text*. 2nd edn. London: Chapman and Hall.

White, P. S. 1979. Pattern, process and natural disturbance in vegetation. *The Botanical Review* **45**: 229–299.

White, P. S. 1994. Synthesis: vegetation pattern and process in the Everglades ecosystem. pp. 445–460. In S. Davis and J. Ogden (eds.) *Everglades: The Ecosystem and its Restoration*. Delray Beach: St. Lucie Press.

White, P. S., S. P. Wilds, and G. A. Thunhorst. 1998. Southeast. pp. 255–314. In M. J. Mac, P. A. Opler, C. E. Puckett Haecker, and P. D. Doran. (eds.) *Status and Trends of the Nation's Biological Resources*, 2 Vols. Reston: U.S. Department of the Interior, U.S. Geological Survey.

White, T. C. R. 1993. *The Inadequate Environment: Nitrogen and the Abundance of Animals*. Berlin: Springer-Verlag.

Whittaker, R. H. 1952. A study of summer foliage insect communities in the Great Smoky Mountains. *Ecological Monographs* **22**: 1–44.

Whittaker, R. H. 1954a. The ecology of serpentine soils. I. Introduction. *Ecology* **35**: 258–259.

Whittaker, R. H. 1954b. The ecology of serpentine soils. IV. The vegetational response to serpentine soils. *Ecology* **35**: 275–288.

Whittaker, R. H. 1956. Vegetation of the Great Smoky Mountains. *Ecological Monographs* **26**: 1–79.

Whittaker, R. H. 1960. Vegetation of the Siskiyou Mountains, Oregon and California. *Ecological Monographs* **30**: 279–338.

Whittaker, R. H. 1962. Classification of natural communities. *The Botanical Review* **28**: 1–239.

Whittaker, R. H. 1965. Dominance and diversity in land plant communities. *Science* **147**: 250–260.

Whittaker, R. H. 1967. Gradient analysis of vegetation. *Biological Reviews* **42**: 207–264.

Whittaker, R. H. 1972. Evolution and measurement of species diversity. *Taxon* **21**: 213–251.

Whittaker, R. H. 1973a. Direct gradient analysis: techniques. pp. 9–31. In R. H. Whittaker (ed.) *Ordination and Classification of Communities*. Part V. The Hague: W. Junk.

Whittaker, R. H. (ed.) 1973b. *Ordination and Classification of Communities*. Part V. The Hague: W. Junk.

Whittaker, R. H. 1975. *Communities and Ecosystems*. 2nd edn. London: Macmillan.

Wiens, J. A. 1977. On competition and variable environments. *American Scientist* **65**: 590–597.

Wilcove, D. S., C. H. McLellan, and A. P. Dobson. 1986. Habitat fragmentation in the temperate zone. pp. 237–256. In M. E. Soulé (ed.) *Conservation B; the Science of Scarcity and Diversity*. Sunderland: Sinauer Associates.

Wilde, S. A. 1958. *Forest Soils: Their Properties and Relation to Silviculture*. New York: The Ronald Press Company.

Wilf, P., N. R. Cúneo, K. R. Johnson, J. F. Hicks, S. L. Wing, and J. D. Obradovich. 2003. High plant diversity in Eocene South America: evidence from Patagonia. *Science* **300**: 122–125.

Williams, C. B. 1964. *Patterns in the Balance of Nature*. London: Academic Press.

Williams, E. J. 1962. The analysis of competition experiments. *Australian Journal of Biological Science* **15**: 509–525.

Williams, G. C. 1975. *Sex and Evolution*. Monographs in Population Biology. No. 8. Princeton: Princeton University Press.

Williams, M. 1989. The lumberman's assault on the southern forest, 1880–1920. pp. 238–288. In M. Williams. *Americans and Their Forests: A Historical Geography*. Cambridge: Cambridge University Press.

Williamson, G. B. 1990. Allelopathy, Koch's Postulates and the neck riddle. pp. 143–162. In J. B. Grace and D. Tilman (eds.) *Perspectives on Plant Competition*. San Diego: Academic Press.

Willig, M. R., D. M. Kaufman, and R. D. Stevens. 2003. Latitudinal gradients of biodiversity: pattern, process, scale and synthesis. *Annual Review of Ecology, Evolution and Systematics* **34**: 273–309.

Willis, A. J. 1963. Braunton Burrows: the effects on the vegetation of the addition of mineral nutrients to the dune soils. *Journal of Ecology* **51**: 353–374.

Willson, M. F. 1984. Mating patterns in plants. pp. 261–276. In R. Dirzo and J. Sarukhán (eds.) *Perspectives on Plant Population Ecology*. Sunderland: Sinauer Associates.

Wilson, E. O. 1993. *The Diversity of Life*. New York: W. W. Norton.

Wilson, E. O. and W. H. Bossert. 1971. *A Primer of Population Biology*. Sunderland: Sinauer Associates.

Wilson, J. B. 1988. Shoot competition and root competition. *Journal of Applied Ecology* **25**: 279–296.

Wilson, J. B., T. C. E. Wells, I. C. Trueman, G. Jones, M. D. Atkinson, M. J. Crawley, M. E. Dodds, and J. Silvertown. 1996. Are there assembly rules for plant species abundance? An investigation in relation to soil resources and successional trends. *Journal of Ecology* **84**: 527–538.

Wilson, S. D. 1993. Competition and resource availability in heath and grassland in the Snowy Mountains of Australia. *Journal of Ecology* **81**: 445–451.

Wilson, S. D. 1999. Plant interactions during secondary succession. pp. 629–650. In L. R. Walker (ed.) *Ecosystems of Disturbed Ground*. Amsterdam: Elsevier.

Wilson, S. D. and P. A. Keddy. 1986a. Measuring diffuse competition along an environmental gradient: results from a shoreline plant community. *The American Naturalist* **127**: 862–869.

Wilson, S. D. and P. A. Keddy. 1986b. Species competitive ability and position along a natural stress/disturbance gradient. *Ecology* **67**: 1236–1242.

Wimsatt, W. C. 1982. Reductionistic research strategies and their biases in the units of selection controversy. pp. 155–201. In E. Saarinen (ed.) *Conceptual Issues in Ecology*. Dordrecht: D. Reidel.

Wing, S. L. 1997. Global warming and plant species richness: a case study of the Paleocene/Eocene boundary. pp. 163–185. In M. L. Reaka-Kudla, D. E. Wilson, and E. O. Wilson (eds.) *Biodiversity II: Understanding and Protecting Our Biological Resources*. Washington, D.C.: Joseph Henry Press.

Wing, S. L. and B. H. Tiffney. 1987. Interactions of angiosperms and herbivorous tetrapods through time. pp. 203–224. In E. Friis, W. G. Chaloner, and P. R. Crane (eds.) *The Origins of Angiosperms and Their Biological Consequences*. Cambridge: Cambridge University Press.

Wiser, S. K., R. K. Peet, and P. S. White. 1996. High-elevation rock outcrop vegetation of the southern Appalachian Mountains. *Journal of Vegetation Science* **7**: 703–722.

Wisheu, I. C. and P. A. Keddy. 1989a. Species richness – standing crop relationships along four lakeshore gradients: constraints on the general model. *Canadian Journal of Botany* **67**: 1609–1617.

Wisheu, I. C. and P. A. Keddy. 1989b. The conservation and management of a threatened coastal plain plant community in eastern North America (Nova Scotia, Canada). *Biological Conservation* **48**: 229–238.

Wisheu, I. C. and P. A. Keddy. 1991. Seed banks of a rare wetland plant community: distribution patterns and effects of human induced disturbance. *Journal of Vegetation Science* **2**: 181–188.

Wisheu, I. C. and P. A. Keddy. 1992. Competition and centrifugal organization of plant communities: theory and tests. *Journal of Vegetation Science* **3**: 147–156.

Wisheu, I. C. and P. A. Keddy. 1996. Three competing models for predicting the size of species pools: a test using eastern North American wetlands. *Oikos* **76**: 253–258.

Wisheu, I. C., P. A. Keddy, D. R. J. Moore, S. J. McCanny, and C. L. Gaudet. 1991. Effects of eutrophication on wetland vegetation. pp. 112–121. In J. Kusler and R. Smardon (eds.) *Wetlands of the Great Lakes: Protection and Restoration Policies; Status of the Science*. New York: Managers Inc.

Witmer, M. C. and A. S. Cheke. 1991. The dodo and the tambalacoque tree: an obligate mutualism reconsidered. *Oikos* **61**: 133–137.

Wium-Anderson, S. 1971. Photosynthetic uptake of free CO_2 by the roots of *Lobelia dortmanna*. *Plantarum* **25**: 245–248.

Wolbach, W. S., R. S. Lewis, and E. Anders. 1985. Cretaceous extinctions: evidence for wildfires and search for meteoritic material. *Science* **230**: 167–170.

Wolfe, J. A. 1991. Palaeobotanical evidence for a June "impact winter" at the Cretaceous/Tertiary boundary. *Nature* **352**: 420–423.

Wolff, W. J. 1993. Netherlands-wetlands. *Hydrobiologia* **265**: 1–14.

Wolin, C. L. 1985. The population dynamics of mutualistic systems. pp. 248–269. In D. H. Boucher (ed.) *The Biology of Mutualism: Ecology and Evolution*. New York: Oxford University Press.

Woodbury, A. M. 1947. Distribution of pigmy conifers in Utah and northeastern Arizona. *Ecology* **28**: 113–126.

Woodley, S., J. Kay, and G. Francis. (eds.) 1993. *Ecological Integrity and the Management of Ecosystems*. Delray Beach: St. Lucie Press.

Woods, K. D. and R. H. Whittaker. 1981. Canopy–understory interaction and the internal dynamics of mature hardwood and hemlock-hardwood forests. pp. 305–323. In D. C. West, H. H. Shugart, and D. B. Botkin (eds.) *Forest Succession: Concepts and Applications*. New York: Springer-Verlag.

Woodward, F. I. 1987. *Climate and Plant Distribution*. Cambridge: Cambridge University Press.

Woodward, F. I. 1992. Predicting plant responses to global environmental change. *New Phytologist* **122**: 239–251.

Woodward, F. I. and C. K. Kelly. 1997. Plant functional types: towards a definition by environmental constraints. pp. 47–65. In T. M. Smith, H. H. Shugart, and F. I. Woodward (eds.) *Plant Functional Types*. Cambridge: Cambridge University Press.

Woodwell, G. M. 1962. Effects of ionizing radiation on terrestrial ecosystems. *Science* **138**: 572–577.

Woodwell, G. M. 1963. The ecological effects of radiation. *Scientific American* **208**: 42–47.

World Commission on Environment and Development. 1987. *Our Common Future*. Oxford: Oxford University Press.

Wright, D. H. and J. H. Reeves. 1992. On the meaning and measurement of nestedness of species assemblage. *Oecologia* **92**: 416–428.

Wright, H. A. and A. W. Bailey. 1982. *Fire Ecology*. New York: Wiley.

Wright, J. P., C. G. Jones, and A. S. Flecker. 2002. An ecosystem engineer, the beaver, increases species richness at the landscape scale. *Oecologia* **132**: 96–101.

Wright, R. 2004. *A Short History of Progress*. Toronto: Anansi Press.

Yoda, K., T. Kira, H. Ogawa, and K. Hozumi. 1963. Self-thinning in overcrowded pure stands under cultivated and natural conditions. *Journal of Biology/Osaka City University* **14**: 107–129.

Yodzis, P. 1986. Competition, mortality, and community structure. pp. 480–492. In J. Diamond and T. J. Case (eds.) *Community Ecology*. New York: Harper and Row.

Yodzis, P. 1989. *Introduction to Theoretical Ecology*. New York: Harper and Row.

Young, E. 2006. Easter Island: a monumental collapse? *New Scientist* **2562**: 30–34.

Young, K., C. U. Ulloa, J. L. Luteyn, and S. Knapp. 2002. Plant evolution and endemism in Andean South America: an introduction. *The Botanical Review* **68**: 4–21.

Young, T. P. and C. K. Augspruger. 1991. Ecology and evolution of long-lived semelparous plants. *Trends in Ecology and Evolution* **6**: 285–289.

Yu, Z., J. H. McAndrews, and D. Siddiqi. 1996. Influences of Holocene climate and water levels on vegetation dynamics of a lakeside wetland. *Canadian Journal of Botany* **74**: 1602–1615.

Zachos, J., M. Pagani, L. Sloan, E. Thomas, and K. Billups. 2001. Trends, rhythms, and aberrations in global climate 65 Ma to present. *Science* **292**: 686–693.

Zedler, J. B. and P. A. Beare. 1986. Temporal variability of salt marsh vegetation: the role of low-salinity gaps and environmental stress. pp. 295–306. In D. A. Wolfe (ed.) *Estuarine Variability*. San Diego: Academic Press.

Zedler, J. B. and C. P. Onuf. 1984. Biological and physical filtering in arid-region estuaries: seasonality, extreme events, and effects of watershed modification. pp. 415–432. In V. S. Kennedy (ed.) *The Estuary as a Filter*. New York: Academic Press.

Zobel, M. 1997. The relative role of species pools in determining plant species richness: an alternative explanation of species coexistence? *Trends in Ecology and Evolution* **12**: 266–269.

Index

Page numbers given for main entries which have subheadings refer to general aspects of that topic.
Page numbers given in *italics* represent *figures*. Page numbers given in **bold** represent **tables**.

abrasion stress, wind-driven snow 170
abundance, relative *see* relative
    abundance
Acacia/ant mutualism 387–389,
    388, **389**
Acadian Forest 442, **444**
adaptations to stress *see also*
    arctic–alpine vegetation;
    deserts; flooding; peat bogs;
    salinity
  climatic extremes, morphological
    changes 132
  costs/cost-benefit trade-offs 131–133
  evolutionary costs 132–134
  fire adaptations, gymnosperm
    cones 295, **296**
  growth rate reductions 133–134
  limestone versus productive
    grassland comparison 134, *134*
  natural selection 131, *133*
  production and operating costs 133
  risk-aversive strategy 133
  short-term versus long-term 131
adaptive ecosystem management 602
aerenchyma 176, *177*, 343
Africa, grassland mammals 286–289,
    287, *288*
  evolutionary adaptations 286–289
agriculture, effects *see*
    eutrophication;
    fragmentation of natural
    landscapes; habitat
    destruction; humans
    ecological impact; introduced
    species; logging/paper
    industry; overgrazing; sheep,
    herbivory
Agriolimax reticulatus 292
air pollution stress *179*, 179–180
Alaska, Glacier Bay *432*, 432–434,
    433, 434
Aldabra atoll Indian Ocean 290,
    292, 306
algae, *see also* cyanobacteria, lichens,
    phytoplankton
  functional groups 281
  land plant ancestor 22

alkaloids 149
allelopathy/interference
    competition 194
alligator holes 242–243, *243*
allogenic burial 244–246, *246 see also*
    disturbance
alluvial deposition 274
Algonquin Provincial Park,
    Ontario 506
alternation of generations/
    gametophytes
  Hofmeister, W. 416, *417*
  plant life cycle evolution 415
  seed and pollen origin 415, *417*
altitude/competition intensity
    gradients 220–223
altitudinal range, and species
    diversity 506–507, *507*
alvars 154, *155*, 218–220
Amazon
  basin 507–508, *508*
  forest floodplains 237–238, *239*
  ice age in 423–425, *423*
Amborellaceae 42
American ginseng (*Panax*
    quinquefolius) 315
amino acid structure 65, *65*
anaerobic
  gut organisms *see* gut symbiont
    micro-organisms
  respiration/fermentation 178–179
Andes
  biodiversity hotspot 573–574,
    574, **575**
  temperate evergreen forest 410
Andira inermis dispersal by bats 370–371
angiosperms *see also* classification,
    phylogenetic
  evolution *see* angiosperms,
    origin/evolution *40, 41*, 508,
    514, 515–516
  insect pollination 515
  life cycle 515
  secondary metabolites 515
angiosperms, origin/evolution *40, 41*,
    405–409, *406, 408*, 508, 514,
    515–516

Australia 414
  and continental drift 405, 409, *410*,
    412–413
  deserts 411–412
  fossil 423
  and gymnosperm diversity
    405–408
  Nothofagus 410, 411
  Proteaceae 413, *414*
  Restionaceae 413, *414*
  tropical floras 412–414, *413*
animal–plant associations *see* gut
    symbiont micro-organisms;
    pollination; seed dispersal
animals
  defense of plants by, *Acacia*/ant
    example 387–389, *388*, **389**
  disturbance by 238–243 *see also*
    burial; disturbance; herbivory
    alligator holes 242–243, *243*
    beaver ponds 238–242, *240*,
    241, **241**
annuals 102
Antarctica, Vostok ice core *30, 31*
Antennaria parvifolia 385
anthocyanin pigmentation 169
Anthoxanthum odoratum 381–382, *382*
anti-freezing compounds 169
ants
  /*Acacia* mutualism 387–389,
    388, **389**
  colonies 109–110, *110*
  seed dispersal 371–373, *372*
aphid–rotifer model, clonal
    reproduction 142
apomixis 385–386
Appalachian Mountains, North
    America 522
  regeneration in deciduous forests
    272–273, *273*
Arecaceae 40
Araucariaceae 411
architecture, plant 70–73
  height, selection pressures 77–78
  mechanical ideal 70–71, *72*
  net primary production and plant
    size 78, *78*–79

architecture, plant (cont.)
redundancy hypothesis 72
selection for small leaves 72–73
arctic–alpine vegetation 167,
167–171, 169, 170, 171, 172
abrasion by wind-driven snow 170
anthocyanin pigmentation 169
cliffs simulating arctic conditions
170–171
effects of low temperatures 168
frost tolerance 162, 168, 169
lichens, cold/drought tolerance
173–174, **174**
stress avoidance 169
stress tolerance through anti-
freezing compounds 169
sun tracking 169
temperature limits 169
Argentina 307, 308, **308**
arid conditions see drought stress
aridisols 119
Arion intermedius 292
Aristolochia genus 364–365
Asclepidiaceae 365
asexual reproduction 385–386 see also
clonal reproduction
Assyria, ancient 550–551
Asteraceae 43–46
asymmetric competition 195,
198–200, 202–203, 211
atmosphere, origins 1–2, 5, **5**, 20
see also biosphere; carbon
dioxide/carbon; oxygen
revolution
Cambrian 21
historical viewpoints 66–67
oxygen 21, 22, **33**
ozone 19, 20–21, 22, **33**
photosynthesis, role in creation
of 1–2, **33**
planetary comparisons, Earth/
Mars/Venus 26, **27**
atomic number, CHNOPS life forms
64, 65
ATP, phosphorus importance 67
Australia
angiosperm evolution 414
diversity, species 508–511, 518
New South Wales 289
River Murray 252
succession, sand-dunes 437
Tasmanian rainforest 444–446, 445
autogenic burial 244, 246 see also
disturbance

banded iron formations 19
barrel cactus 111, 339
Bartram, William 243
bats, seed dispersal 370–371
beaver ponds 238–242, 240, 241, **241**
Beltian bodies 387
Bentham, George 36, 37–38
Bernard, Frank 348
Bessey, C. E. 39–41
biennials 102–105
biodiversity maintenance 590, 592–593
biogenic accumulation 244, 246
see also burial; disturbance
biogeographic world regions 37
see also ecoregions; world
floristic regions
biosphere, genesis 1–4, 3–4, 33
see also energy flow
atmosphere, origins 1–2, 5, **5**
concept of term 2, 3–4
early characteristics/conditions 5, 9
experimental work 7–9, 8
photosynthesis, role in creation of
1–2, **33**
water/hydrological cycle 4, 7
Biosphère, La (Vladimir Vernadsky) 2, 3–4
biotic disturbance see animals,
disturbance by; see also
herbivory
birds
pollination (ornithophily) 359–361,
360, 361, 362
predation of insects, and tree
growth 305
bituminous shale cliffs 179, 179–180
block diagrams, vegetation
patterns 458
blue-green algae see cyanobacteria
boreal forests see forests, boreal,
conservation/management
bottom-up control see top-down/
bottom-up control, plant
communities
Boundary Waters Canoe Area, North
America 440–442, **441**
Acadian Forest 442, **444**
fire-dependent species 442
shade-tolerant species 442
broken stick model 534
Budworm Battles 331
burial 243–249, 246 see also
disturbance
adaptations of wetland plants to
248, 248

allogenic 244–246, 246
autogenic 244, 246
deposition rates 247, 247–248
recovery from 248–249
sedimentation by rivers 243–249,
244, 246
butternut (Juglans cinerea) 584

cacti (Opuntia fragilis) study 218
barrel cactus 111, 339
Cakile edentula
density dependence 200–202
seed dispersal 367–369, 368, 370
California, species diversity 518
Calluna vulgaris 292
CAM (crassulacean acid metabolism)
46, 74–75, 147, 149, 150
Cambrian explosion, multicellular
organisms 21
and atmospheric oxygen 21
and atmospheric ozone 21
fossil record 21
Canada see also Ontario
Algonquin Provincial Park 506
boreal forests, conservation/
management 569
Ottawa River 268–269, 269
canopy
architecture see architecture, plant
ecology, epiphytes 109–110
Cape Province, South Africa 307, 307
carbon dioxide/carbon 26–28, 27, 29, **33**
atmospheric foraging 68–69
C3/C4 plants 73–74
coal/oil sequestration 27–28, **33**
distribution in plants and
animals 35
/drought trade-off 74
greenhouse effect 26–27, 31, 32
limiting/suboptimal levels 69, **69**
local depletion 69
planetary comparisons, Earth/
Mars/Venus 26, **27**
root uptake 75–76
Caribbean, tropical forest 423, 425, 583
carnivores, large
conservation research study
580–581
as indicators of ecological
health 603
carnivorous plants 111–112, 112,
134–135, 138, 162,
520–521, **521**
Darwin's discovery 136-138, 138

carrion mimicry, by flowers 363, *364*, 365
carrying capacity, global 595
Carson, Rachel *Silent Spring* 331
Carthaginian civilization 121–122
Castanea dentata 584, **586**
catastrophes, high intensity 254
 see also disturbance
 landslides 254–255, *256*
 meteor impacts 259–264, *260*, *261*, **262**
 nuclear war 264
 volcanic eruptions 255–259, *257*
cell membranes, origins/evolution 10–11 *see also* eukaryotic cells, origins/evolution; prokaryotic cells
 clay particles hypothesis 11
 coacervate droplets 10
 lipid bilayer hypothesis 10–11, *11*
cellulose
 degradation, by gut micro-organisms 390, *391*
 versus chitin as structural molecule 92
centrifugal model, species diversity *273*, 529–531, *530*
change, inevitability/working with 592–593, *594*
 dynamic nature of plant communities 590, 592–593
 resource bottlenecks 106
 resource fluctuations 105–108, *106*, *107*
chemical warfare/poison gas 87
chernozems 119
chestnut tree disease (*Castanea dentata*) 584, **586**
Chile, diversity 518
chlorophyll, evolution 17–18
chloroplasts 14–15, 22
CHNOPS perspective 63–67, **64** *see also* carbon dioxide/carbon; nitrogen; oxygen; phosphorus
 amino acid structure 65, *65*
 ATP 67
 chemical properties 64
 hydrogen 79
 ionization energy/atomic number *64*, *65*
 micro/macronutrients 67
 natural selection, molecules 64
 relative abundance in biomass/organisms 63, **64**

chromosome volume, and radiosensitivity 181
Churchill, Winston 324
cities, human 593–595
 ecological footprints 595, *596*
cladograms 42, 42–43
classification of vegetation 59–61
 see also gradients/local patterns
 cladograms 42, 42–43
 climatic 56–58
 ecoregions 37, 61, *61*
 Field Guide to Forest Ecosystem Classification 480–484, *481*, *482*, *483*, *484*
 functional 35, 50–51
 and land management 457, 474, 476–484
 molecular systematics 35, 41–43, *45*
 phylogenetic *see below*
 phytosociology 475, **476**, 477
 recent developments 42, 43
 value/limitations 48–50, 58–59, 457, 474–475
 world floristic regions 46–48, *47*, **48**
classification, phylogenetic 35, *36*, **49**
 Amborellaceae 42
 Arecaceae 40
 Asteraceae 43–46
 Illiciaceae 42, 43
 Magnoliales 39–40
 Nymphaeaceae 42
 Orchidaceae 40, 43, 46
 Poaceae 40
clay particles hypothesis 11
Clements, Frederick 450–451, 485–486, 488–490 *see also* community-unit concept/hypothesis
climate
 classification, vegetation types 56–58
 extreme, morphological changes 132
 warmth/moisture *see* rainfall/climatic warmth
climate change 28–33, 428
 carbon dioxide levels 30, 31, *32*
 ice core, Antarctica *30*
 plant-climate linkages 31
 Milankovitch cycles 31
 sediment cores 30, *31*
climax vegetation 431, 450–451
 see also succession
clonal reproduction 140–144, *141*
 aphid-rotifer model 142

elm-oyster model 142–144
 and foraging 143
 strawberry-coral model 142
 wetland species 140–141, 143
coacervate droplets 10
coal/oil, carbon sequestration 27–28, **33**
coevolution *see* evolution
cold environments *see* arctic-alpine vegetation
Coleochaete 22
commensalism 336, 338, 355
 see also mutualism; mycorrhizae
communities, plant *see* classification of vegetation; discrete communities debate; ecosystems; gradients/local patterns, vegetation; zoned communities
community-unit concept/hypothesis 491, *492*, 496, *498*, 499
competition, apparent 398–399
 parable from Darwin's observations 398, 402
competition, intraspecific 188–190, 197, 215, 223 *see also* competitive (various entries); CSR synthesis
 above/below-ground 135
 asymmetric 195, 198–200, 202–203, *203*, 211
 between cell lines 194
 between genotypes 194
 coniferous forests 159
 costs, stress/strain 187–188, *188*
 definition 187
 density dependence 188–190, 197, 200–202
 diffuse 216
 and diversity 517
 economics analogy 215
 equation 190
 importance 186–187
 intensity 191–193, **193**, 202–203 *see also* competition intensity gradients
 intra/interspecific, distinction 190–191
 and mycorrhizae 214–215, *215*
 self-thinning *197*, 197–198, *198*
 stressed environments 129, 131, 341–342, *344*
 and succession 453, *454*

competition intensity gradients
216–223
altitudinal 220–223
cacti (*Opuntia fragilis*) study 218
exemplary experimental study
222, 222–223
hawkweed (*Hierachium floribundum*)
study 216, 217–218
measuring 216, 216–217
and mutualistic interactions
341–342, 343, 344
soil depth, alvar vegetation type
218–220, 219
in wetlands 220, 222
competitive dominance 194–197,
195, 196
asymmetric competition 195
and dominance 196–197
and interference competition/
allelopathy 194
and species diversity, field
experiments 542, 542
competitive effect/response 193–194
competitive exclusion, and species
diversity 546
competitive hierarchies 204–214
asymmetric competition
198–200, 211
consistency 206–209, 209, 210
contingent competition 206
de Wit replacement series 204
establishing 204–207, 207, **208**
intraspecific size hierarchies 207
light patches, foraging 212–214,
213, 214
light and shoot size 209–215, 212
mechanisms 199–200, 199
monocultures 198–200
resource depletion models
198–200
resource foraging, soil nutrients
212–214
resource pre-emption models
198–200
and species diversity 526–527
Compton experiment 535, **535**
computer modeling/simulation,
succession 446–448, 447
FORET 447
JABOWA 447, 448
conservation 549–550, 604–608 *see also*
fragmentation of natural
landscapes; Galapagos Islands;
habitat destruction; humans,

ecological impact; indicators,
ecological; management
perspectives; nature reserves;
restoration, habitat
Assyria, ancient 550–551
boreal forests 569–570
carnivore conservation research
study 580–581
carrying capacity, global 595
change, working with 592–593, 594
deciduous forests, agricultural
areas 584–585, 585
degradation 598–599
dynamic nature of plant
communities 590, 592–593
Easter Island 564, 564
economic growth/human welfare
580–581, 581
extinctions/ecosystem losses
549, 553
fens, English 582–584
goals 587–588
Guyana highlands 578–579, 579
habitat renewal 587
and intermediate disturbance
model 528
optimism 550
overgrazing 545–546, 595–598
primary forests 574–576, 577
priority locations 544, 544 *see also*
hot spots, diversity
Rome/Mediterranean, ancient
551–553, 552
safety margins, species/habitat
loss 592
and species diversity 543–546,
544, 546
strategies 584
thresholds, critical 550,
595–599, 598
tropical forest, Caribbean 583
vegetation types at risk 553
wetlands 576, **578**, 578
consumer pressure 606
continental drift 405, 409, 410,
412–413, 514
Gondwana 405, 409, 514
Laurasia 405, 409, 514
continuum model *see* community-
unit concept/hypothesis
Cook, Captain 403
*Cooperation Among Animals with
Human Implications* (Warder
Allee) 337

cost-benefit models
mutualism 396–398
mycorrhizae 347, 354–355, 355
coypu (nutria), impact on fringing
reed/marsh vegetation
316–317, **317**
crabs, herbivory in tropical forests
305–306
crassulacean acid metabolism (CAM)
46, 74–75, 147, 149, 150
Cretaceous/Tertiary boundary
260–262
cryptophytes 51, 513
CSR (competition, disturbance, stress)
synthesis 276–280, 279
botanical (Philip Grime,
University of Sheffield)
277–279, **278**, 280
Raunkiaer system 280
zoological 277
cyanophytes *see* cyanobacteria
cyanobacteria
abundance with N:P ratio 82
heterocysts 82
origin of plant cell 11–15, 14
cypress swamps, Louisiana
559–564
cypress regeneration 560, 562
drainage ditches 560
pull boat logging 559, 561
salt water intrusion 560
water table lowering 560

Darwin, Charles 186, 565
buried seed banks 453
carnivorous plants 136–138
collaboration with Hooker 38
collaboration with Wallace 36,
38–39
*Descent of Man and Selection in Relation
to Sex, The* 186
Expression of the Emotions 136
Insectivorous Plants 136–138
Origin of Species, The 136
outcrossing 381
parable, apparent competition
398, 402
plant demography 104
sundews 136-138, 138
data matrices 465–466, 466
Dawkins, Richard *The Selfish Gene* 9
Day, W. *Genesis on Planet Earth* 10
DCA (detrended correspondence
analysis) 471

deciduous
  forests *see* forests, deciduous
  plants, resource acquisition 114–116
decomposition 602
deer herbivory
  American ginseng 315
  impact on deciduous forest
      313–316, *314*, **314**
defense of plants by animals, *Acacia/*
      ant example 387–389, *388*, **389**
      see also mutualism
defenses, plant 149, 293–303 *see also*
      herbivory; secondary
      metabolites
  coevolution 302–303, *303*
  dilemma, pollen/seed distribution
      versus herbivory
      deterrence 302
  evolutionary context 293, *293*
  interpretation of anti-herbivore
      traits 299
  morphological 293
  nitrogen content and food quality
      300–302, **301**, 323
  present-day defenses protecting
      from extinct herbivores 295,
      300, *301*
  Salvinia molesta example 301–302
  seed-protecting structures
      293–295, 303
  strobili in gymnosperms *294*,
      294–295, **296**
  toughness 302
De Luc, J. A. *Geologic Travels* 450
demography, Darwinian approach 104
deposition 243–246, *244–246*, 274
      see also burial; disturbance
  Pleistocene glaciations 419, *421*
  rates *247*, 247–248
  and resource gradients 94
*Descent of Man and Selection in Relation
      to Sex, The* (Charles Darwin) 186
deserts
  angiosperms 411–412
  geographical data 144
  rainfall 144
deserts, plant adaptations 144–149,
      145, **146**, *146*
  anti-herbivory 149
  CAM (crassulean acid metabolism)
      photosynthesis 147, *149*, *150*
  drought escaping/evading/enduring
      classification 145, *146*
  epidermal/stomatal 146–147

leaf surface area 147, *147*, *148*, *149*
  reproductive 514
  seed dispersal 372–373
  spines 148–149
  water absorption/storage 147–148
detrended correspondence analysis
      (DCA) 471
de Wit replacement series 204
diffuse competition 216 *see also*
      competition intensity
      gradients
Dionaea muscipula (venus fly trap) 521,
      522, *522*
direct gradient analysis 458 *see also*
      gradients/local patterns,
      vegetation
discrete communities debate
      485–486, 491 *see also* gradients/
      local patterns, vegetation
      cover types/templates
  community-unit concept/
      hypothesis 491, *492*, 496,
      498, 499
  critique/discussion of 486–487
  individualistic concept/hypothesis
      486–487, 491, *492*, **492**, 496
  pragmatic method (James) 487
  superorganisms, communities as
      437, 485–486
  synthesis, Gleason/Clements 497
diseases/pest introductions,
      deciduous forest fragments
      584, **586** *see also* introduced
      species
  butternut (*Juglans cinerea*) 584
  chestnut (*Castanea dentata*) 584, **586**
  elm (*Ulmus americana*) 584, **586**
  waldsterben 585
disturbance 225–226, 282 *see also*
      burial; catastrophes, high
      intensity; CSR synthesis; fire;
      gap dynamics; herbivory;
      intermediate disturbance
      model; water erosion
  area (property) 228, *282*
  biotic *see* animals, disturbance by;
      see also herbivory
  definition 225–226
  duration (property) 226
  Everglades, Florida 275–276, *276*
  frequency (property) 227, *227*
  Hubbard Brook, White Mountains,
      New Hampshire 264–268, *265*,
      266, *267*

ice 249, *250*, **250**
  intensity (property) *226*,
      226–227, *282*
  measuring effects 264
  Ottawa River, Canada, herbaceous
      marshes 268–269, *269*
  storms 252–254, *253*, *254*
  stressed environments 134, 184
  and succession 447, 452
  waves 249–252, *251*
diversity 502, 546–547, **547**
      see also centrifugal model,
      species diversity; hot spots,
      diversity; humped-back
      model; intermediate
      disturbance model; relative
      abundance
  and altitudinal range 506–507, *507*
  angiosperms 508
  artificial grassland communities
      539
  artificial wetland communities
      539–540, *541*
  climatic warmth/moisture
      relationship 57, 508–513
  and competitive exclusion 546
  and competitive hierarchies
      526–527
  conservation implications
      543–546, **544**, 546
  deciduous forests 522
  endemism 522–523, *523*
  and environmental factors 546
  equatorial areas 508–513,
      509, **509**
  eutrophication, effects of 525, 531
  evolution *see* evolution
  and fertility 537, 542, *542*, *543*
  field experiments 541–543, *543*
  fugitive/interstitial/peripheral
      species 506
  gymnosperms 508
  and habitat diversity 505–508
  historical factors 522
  laboratory experiments 539–540,
      540, *540*
  and life form 513
  local versus larger scale 545,
      546, **547**
  lowland tropical forest
      507–508, *508*
  mangrove swamps 517
  Mediterranean climate 518–520, **520**
  microcosms 539

diversity (cont.)
  models, small scale 523–524
    see also centrifugal model,
      species diversity; humped-
      back model
  New Jersey experiment, USA
    542–543
  overstorey 509–510, *510*, *511*, *512*
  Park Grass experiment 535, **535**,
    536–538, 541–542
  physiological constraints, additive
    effects 516–518, *518*
  Pleistocene glaciations 423
  primary forests 574
  pteridophytes 508
  and radiation 181
  and speciation rates 518, *519*
  species-area model 502–505, *503*,
    504, 506, *519*
  species flocks 508
  species pools 516, **516**
  stressed environments 134, 135
  understorey 510
DNA based classification *see*
  molecular systematics
dodo 377–379
domatia/ant colonies 109–110, *110*
dominance, definitions 196–197
    see also competitive dominance
drought stress *see also* deserts; forests,
    coniferous; Mediterranean
    shrublands; rock barrens
  escaping/evading/enduring
    classification 145, *146*
  lichens, cold/drought tolerance
    173–174, **174**
  Pleistocene glaciations 423
  and salinity 163, *164*
Dutch elm disease 584, **586**

earthworms, soil formation 120
Easter Island 564, *564*
ecological footprints 595, *596*
    see also humans, ecological
    impact
ecological meltdown 587 *see also*
    conservation; humans,
    ecological impact
ecological research *see* research,
    ecological
economic growth, and conservation
    580–581, *581*
  carnivore conservation research
    study 580–581

ecoregions 61 *see also* floristic regions,
    world
  world map 37, *61*
ecosystems *see also* classification;
    discrete communities debate;
    gradients/local patterns
  engineers 238–242 *see also*
    disturbance
  integrity, preservation 599–600
    see also restoration, habitat
  losses *see* habitat destruction;
    see also conservation; humans,
    ecological impact
  management, adaptive 602 *see also*
    management, land/ecosystem;
    restoration, habitat
  as superorganisms 437, 485–486
ectomycorrhizae *see* mycorrhizae
electromagnetic spectrum, selection
    for exploitation *16*, 16–17, **17**
eliasomes 371
elm-oyster model, clonal
    reproduction 142–144
elm tree (*Ulmus americana*) disease
    584, **586**
endemism 522–523, *523*
  causal variables 522–523
endolithic communities 174–176, *175*
endomycorrhizae *see* mycorrhizae
endosymbiosis, serial 12–15, *14*
energy flow 4–9
  and biological systems 4–5
  ionization energy/atomic number
    64, *65*
  and molecular complexity 5–6, **6**, *8*
  replication/reproduction of
    molecules 9
  stability/natural selection of
    molecules 7, 9, 64
  synthesis, evolutionary
    possibilities 16, **17**
  thermodynamics, second law 5–6, *7*
England, fens 582–584
Engler, Adolf 39
entisols 119
Epic of Gilgamesh, The 550–551
epidemics *see* disease/pest
    introductions
Epidendrum ciliare 382–385, *383*
epiphytes 109–110
Erie, Pennsylvania 158, *158*
erosion
  ice 419, *421*
  rivers *see* water erosion

eukaryotic cells, origins/evolution
    11–15, **33**
  chloroplasts 14–15
  extant example 15, *15*
  flagella 15
  mitochondria 13–14
  serial endosymbiosis theory
    12–15, *14*
eutrophication, effects on species
    diversity 525, 531 *see also*
    fertility; humans, ecological
    impact
evaporative coefficient equation 509
evapotranspiration 79–80, *80*
Everglades, disturbance 275–276, *276*
evergreen foliage 114–116, 160
evolution *see also* selection, natural
  angiosperms *see* angiosperms,
    origins/evolution
  chlorophyll 17–18
  chloroplasts 22
  and continental drift 514
  defenses, plant 302–303, *303*
  drought, reproductive adaptations
    to 514
  fungal–plant associations 22, *23*
  gymnosperms 405–408
  insect pollination 515
  key events 514
  land living, adaptations 514
  life cycle simplification 515
  mammals, African grassland
    286–289
  parasitism 113
  passerine birds 423
  photosynthesis *see* photosynthesis,
    origins/evolution
  plant defenses 293, *293*, 302–303, *303*
  plant/fungal symbiosis 22, *23*
  secondary metabolites 515
  seed dispersal by animals 365, 366,
    373–374, 377–378
  sexual reproduction 22, 23–24
  and species diversity 513, *514*,
    515–516
  succession 24, 24–26, *25*, **33**
  tree masting 373–374
  trends in vascular plants *26*
evolutionary trees *see* cladograms
Expression of the Emotions (Charles
    Darwin) 136
extinctions 549, 553 *see also* habitat
    destruction
  large mammals 429

fens, English 582–584
fermentation 15
  as adaptation to flooding 178–179
  foregut 390–393, **392**, *393*, *394*
  hindgut 393–395, **394**
ferralsol 119
fertility *see also* eutrophication
  and competitive dominance
    542, *542*
  and diversity 537
  gradients 250, *252*
  natural/man-made sources 85–86
  stressed environments 135
Field Guide to Forest Ecosystem
  Classification for the Clay Belt, Site
  Region 3E 480–484, *481*, *482*,
  483, *484*
fields, limestone versus productive
  comparison 134, *134*
fire 228–236 *see also* disturbance
  critical temperature 228
  dependent species 442
  and meteor impacts 261–262
  and plant diversity in boreal forests
    528–529, *529*
  and prairie/savanna vegetation
    types 230–232, *231*
  Sphagnum peat communities
    232–236, *236*
  tree bark insulation 228–230, *229*,
    230, 230, *231*
  in wetlands 232, **234**, *235*
Fisher, Sir R. A. *488*, 536
flagelli 15
Flagstaff, Arizona 158
flooding *see also* water erosion
  aerenchyma 176, *177*
  anaerobic respiration/
    fermentation 178–179
  and diversity 517
  Epic of Gilgamesh, The 550–551
  Pleistocene glaciations 430
  pneumatophores 176–177, *178*
  tolerance 176–179
floristic regions, world 46–48, *47*, **48**
flowers, pollination *see* pollination
fly pollination 363–365
  Aristolochia genus 364–365
  Asclepidiaceae 365
  carrion mimicry 363, *364*, 365
  Rafflesia genus 363–364
footprints, ecological 595, *596*
  see also humans, ecological
  impact

foraging *see also* resource acquisition
  atmosphere/soil 63, 68–69
  and clonal reproduction 143
  light patches 212–214, *213*, *214*
  root proliferation, transitory
    nutrient patches *100*,
    100–101, *101*
  soil nutrients 212–214
Forest Ecosystem Classification for the
  Clay Belt, Field Guide 480–484,
  481, *482*, *483*, *484*
forest site types 460, *461 see also*
  gradients/local patterns,
  vegetation
forests, alluvial *see* Louisiana, alluvial
  forest destruction
forests, boreal, conservation/
  management 569–570
  clear-cutting 569
  fire vs. clear-cutting 569–570
  fire and plant diversity in
    528–529, *529*
  logging/paper industry 569
forests, coniferous 156–159, *157*, *159*
  see also Boundary Waters
    Canoe Area; gymnosperms;
    strobili in gymnosperms
  affected by fire 439–440
  and competition 159
  water/temperature interactions
    156–157
forests, deciduous
  in agricultural areas,
    fragmentation 584–585, *585*
  climatic conditions 157–158
  conservation strategies 584
  deer herbivory 313–316, *314*, **314**
  disease/pest introductions 584, **586**
  indicators 603
  insect herbivory 304–305, *305*
  regeneration 272–273, *273*
  species diversity 522
forests, primary 574–576, *577*
  and diversity 574
forests, temperate evergreen
  410, *411*
forests, tropical
  Caribbean 583
  habitat/species diversity
    correlation 507–508, *508*
  insects, canopy 289–290, **291**
  land crab herbivory 305–306
  overstorey diversity 509–510, *510*,
    511, *512*

rhinoceros herbivory 313
secondary metabolites 297–298, **299**
FORET 447
fossil record
  multicellular organisms 21
  plant defensive morphology
    293, *293*
  prokaryotic cells 11
  studying 404
fragmentation of natural landscapes
  581, 583
  conservation strategies 584
  deciduous forests in agricultural
    areas 584–585, *585*
  diseases/pests 584, **586**
  fens, English 582–584
  tropical forest, Caribbean,
    history 583
Frank, Bernard 348
frontier forests *see* forests, primary
frost tolerance *162*, *168*, 169
  see also arctic–alpine
    vegetation
fruit production 365, *366 see also* seed
  dispersal, by animals
  ripening 366
fugitive species 506
functional
  classification 35, 50–51
  perspective, land management
    588–592, *589*, **591**
fungal–plant associations *see also*
  lichens; mycorrhizae
  difficulties in studying 350
  evolution 22, *23*
fynbos 151, 518

Galapagos Islands 290, 306,
  565–568, *566*
  goat introduction/overgrazing
    567–568, *569*
  tortoise grazing 566–567,
    567, 568, *568*
gametophyte *see also* sporophyte
  alternation of generations 415–418
  apomixis 385
  description 415
  fossil *417*
  phylogeny 42
  plant colonization of land 22, 415
  pollinators 382
  size in terrestrial plants 77–78,
    415–417
  taxonomic classification 49

Ganges-Brahmaputra River 244
gap colonization 527–529
gap dynamics 269–270, 527
  alluvial deposition 274
  freshwater marshes 274–275, *275*
  regeneration from buried seed
    banks 270–272, **271**
  regeneration in deciduous forests
    272–273, *273*
gene-based classification *see*
    molecular systematics
Genera Plantarum (George Bentham/Sir
    Joseph Hooker) 37
Genesis on Planet Earth (W. Day) 10
geographic regions *see* floristic
    regions, world
Geologic Travels (J. A. De Luc) 450
geological record, Cretaceous/
    Tertiary boundary 260–262
geometric ranked abundance
    model 534
geophytes 513
Gilgamesh, Epic of 550–551
Ginkgo biloba/Ginkgoales 406
Glacier Bay, Alaska *432*, 432–434,
    433, *434*
glaciations *see* Pleistocene glaciations
Gleason, Henry 451–452, 485–487,
    488–490 *see also* individualistic
    concept/hypothesis
Glossopteris/Glossopteridales
    405–406
goats, overgrazing by 567–568, *569*
Gondwana 405, 409, 514
gradients/local patterns, vegetation
    457–458, 500–501 *see also*
    classification of vegetation;
    competition intensity
    gradients; discrete
    communities debate; resource
    gradients; zoned communities
  aggregation, statistical tests
    498–499
  block diagrams 458
  direct gradient analysis 458
  empirical studies 491–499, *492*, *492*
  exposure gradients, measuring
    251–252
  fertility gradients 250, *252*
  forest site types *460*, *461*
  freshwater marsh example
    495–496, *496*
  importance of pattern analysis as
    research tool 496

lakeshore example 493–494, *494*, *495*
  measurable properties 457
  Morisita's index *498*, *499*
  natural gradients 458–464
  nested patterns 498–499
  null model 487–490
  patterns 458
  profile diagrams 458, *460*
  quantitative studies 491
  salt marsh example 163–165,
    492–493, *493*
  searching for patterns *see*
    multivariate methodology
  statistical tests 498–499
  summary displays *463*, *463*
  vegetation cover types *460*, *461*
  vegetation templates *462*, *462*
  wetland vegetation analysis
    496–499, **499**
grazing *see* herbivory
Great Lakes, development *421*, *430*
greenhouse effect 26–27, 31, *32*
Grime, Philip, (University of
    Sheffield)
  artificial grassland
    communities 539
  CSR synthesis 277–279, **278**, *280*
  humped-back model *524*,
    524–526, *526*
  limestone versus productive
    grassland comparison
    134, *134*
Grisebach, A. H. R. *Die Vegetation der
    Erde* 51
growth rates, and resource capture
    100–101, *101*
growth rates, in stressed
    environments 133–134
  above/below-ground competition
    135
  anti-grazing strategies 135
  consequences of low 134–135
  and disturbance/management
    strategies 134, 184
  ecological interest 135, 184
  and fertilization 135
  mycorrhizae 135
  and plant diversity 134, 135
  RGR screening 162
  symbiotic interactions 135, 138
gut symbiont micro-organisms 15, *15*
  cellulose degradation 390, *391*
  foregut fermentation 390–393,
    392, *393*, *394*

hindgut fermentation 393–395
  Myxotricha paradoxa 15, *15*
  nitrogen economy, host species 392
Guyana highlands 578–579
gymnosperms
  and angiosperm evolution 405–408
  species diversity 508
  strobili *see* strobili in gymnosperms
  taxonomic divisions included **49**

Haber, Fritz 87–88, *87*, 605
habitat destruction 549, 553, *588*
    see also conservation; humans,
    ecological impact; logging/
    paper industry
  critical thresholds 598–599
  historical 550–553, *552*, 583 *see also*
    Louisiana, alluvial forest
    destruction
habitat/species diversity correlation
    505–508
  altitudinal range 506–507, *507*
  fugitive/interstitial/peripheral
    species 506
  lowland tropical forest, e.g.
    Amazon basin 507–508, *508*
  Saxifraga aizoon, Algonquin
    Provincial Park, Ontario 506
  species flocks/redundancy 508
Harrison, John 403
hawkweed (*Hieracium floribundum*)
    study *216*, 217–218
heather moorlands 292
herbivory 284–286, 332–334 *see also*
    defenses, plant; disturbance;
    species composition, top-
    down/bottom-up control
  aquatic macrophytes/algae/
    terrestrial plants comparison
    320–322
  coypu/nutria, impact on fringing
    reed/marsh vegetation
    experiment 316–317, **317**
  deer, impact on deciduous forest
    experiment 313–316, *314*, **314**
  demographic study, deer grazing
    on American ginseng (*Panax
    quinquefolius*) 315
  and ecosystem management 334
  experimental design, enclosure
    experiments 312–313
  experimental meta-analyses/
    multiple regression analyses
    318–322, **319**

field experiments 303–304, *304*, *321*, *322*
field observations, wildlife diets 286
giant tortoises, island 290, **292**, 566–567, *567*, 568, *568*
grassland herbivores experiments 306–313
impact on plant communities 285–286, *333*, 334
insects, impact on deciduous forests experiment 304–305, *305*
insects, tropical forest canopy 289–290, **291**
land crabs in tropical forests experiment 305–306
mammals, African grassland 286–289, **287**, *288*
man-made landscapes 292
modeling *see* mathematical modeling
and mowing 325
plant–herbivore interactions 284–285, *285*
rhinoceros, tropical floodplain forests experiment 313
selective 290, 324–325
sheep 292
slugs 292
squirrel herbivory, gymnosperm cones 295, *296*
heterocysts 82
Hieracium floribundum (hawkweed) study 217–218
history, habitat destruction 550–553, *552*, 583 *see also* Louisiana, alluvial forest destruction
histosols 119
Hofmeister, W. 416, *417*
Holland 37
Holocene 418
hominids/*Homo sapiens* 426, 428–430 *see also* humans, ecological impact
extinction of large mammals 429
Hooker, Sir Joseph 36, 37–38
hot spots, diversity 544, *544*, **572**, 573–574, *574*, **576**
conservation value 573
degree of risk 573
Indo-Burma 573
Philippines 573
protected status 574
vegetation cover losses 573

Hubbard Brook, White Mountains, New Hampshire 264–268, *265*, *266*, *266*, *267*
humans, ecological impact 549 *see also* conservation; eutrophication, effects on species diversity; fragmentation of natural landscapes; habitat destruction; introduced species; management, land/ ecosystem
Assyria, ancient 550–551
Carthaginian example 121–122
cities 593–595
ecological footprints 595, *596*
ecological meltdown 587
economic growth and conservation 580–581, *581*
Europeans, impact 557–558
extinction of large mammals 429
global appropriation of primary production/water supplies 553
habitat loss *588*
man-made landscapes 292
Mayan example 122, *123*
overgrazing 545–546, 549, 567–568, *569*, 595–598
perspectives, American/ European 601
Rome/Mediterranean, ancient 551–553, *552*
soil erosion 121–122, 555
humming birds, pollination 360, **360**
humped-back model *524*, 524–526, *525*, 525, 526
Huntingdonshire fen 582–584
hybrid vigor 381, 385
hydrogen 79 *see also* CHNOPS perspective
hydrological cycle 4, 7
early experimental work 7–9, *8*
hydroseres 450

ice
abrasion 170
ages *see* Pleistocene glaciations
erosion 249, *250*, **250**
Illiciaceae 42, 43, *45*
inbreeding depression 381, 385
indicators, ecological 602–603, **604**
adaptive ecosystem management 602
biological properties 602

critical values 602
deciduous forest 603
decomposition 602
keystone species 603
large carnivores 603
monitoring 571, 602, 603
physical factors 602
primary production 602
snags (dead trees) 603
individualistic concept/hypothesis 486–487, 491, 492, *492*, 496
Indo-Burma 573
Insectivorous Plants (Charles Darwin) 136–138
insects
bird predation, and tree growth 305
impact on deciduous forests 304–305, *305*
pollination 359, **359**, 515 *see also* fly pollination
inselbergs/tepui *579*
intensity, competition 191–193, **193**
asymmetric 202–203
gradients *see* competition intensity gradients
interference competition/allelopathy 194
intermediate biomass, Grime's humped-back model *524*, 524–526, *525*, 525, 526
intermediate disturbance model *527*, 527–529, 546
boreal forests, fire and plant diversity in 528–529, *529*, 529
conservation implications 528
contingency factors 528
gap dynamics 527
interspecific competition 190–191, 191, 215 *see also* competition
interstitial species 506
intraspecific
competition *see* competition, intraspecific
size hierarchies 207
introduced species *see also* diseases/ pest introductions
goats, overgrazing by 567–568, *569*
nutria (coypu), impact on fringing reed/marsh vegetation 316–317, **317**
ion capture 100
ionizing radiation *see* radiation, ionizing
Isoëtes 75–76

JABOWA 447, 448
James, W. philosopher 487
Juglans cinerea (butternut) 584

keystone species 603
Köppen, W. 57–58, *58*
Ksudach volcano, Kamchatka
    Peninsula, Russia 255–258, **257**
Küchler, A. W. 37, 55–56, **56**
kwongan, southwestern Australia,
    diversity 518

land, colonization 21–26, **33**
    adaptations 514
    and atmospheric oxygen
        22, **33**
    and atmospheric ozone 22, **33**
    and chloroplast evolution 22
    evolutionary succession *24*, 24–26,
        25, **33**
    and oceanic nutrient depletion
        22, **33**
    and plant/fungal symbiosis
        evolution 22, *23*
    selection pressures 23
    and sexual reproduction, evolution
        22, 23–24
land management *see* conservation;
    management land/
    ecosystems
landslides 254–255, *256 see also*
    disturbance
Lapland 37
Laurasia 405, 409, 514
Lavoisier, Antoine 66–67
leaves
    epidermal/stomatal adaptations
        to drought 146–147
    lobed/toothed and climate
        171–173, *172*
    selection for small size 72–73
    surface area 147, *147, 148, 149*
Lepidodendron trees 24, *25*
Les Commensaux et les Parasites (Pierre
    van Benden) 337
lichens 355–358, *356*, **357**
    cold/drought tolerance 173–174, **174**
    mycobionts 356
    as parasitism 356, 358
    phycobionts 355
    relative benefit to partners 356
Liebig's Law of the Minimum 536
life-form classification (C. Raunkiaer)
    513

life history, and succession 444, *444*
life/living organisms
    energy needs 4–5
    resource needs 5
light acquisition *see also*
        photosynthesis
    photon harvesting measures 70
    and plant architecture 70–73
    root uptake of carbon dioxide
        75–76
    selection for visible light
        exploitation *16*, 16–17, **17**
limestone versus productive
        grassland comparison 134, *134*
Linnaeus, Carolus 36–37, 508
    botanical pornography 37
    Systema Naturae 36, 37–38
lipid bilayer membrane hypothesis
    10–11, *11*
Lithops (stone plants) 149
Lobelia dortmanna 345, 354
local patterns, vegetation *see* gradients/
    local patterns, vegetation
loess 419–421, *422*
log-normal relative abundance
    model 534
logging/paper industry 569
    pull boat logging, Louisiana
        559, 561
    and succession 446
Long Island forest experiment *180*,
    180–181, *181*
Lotka–Volterra models,
    mutualism 395
Louisiana, alluvial forest destruction
    553–557, **563** *see also*
        conservation; cypress swamps,
        Louisiana
    European human influences
        557–558
    Mississippi delta 553–557, *554,
        556, 557*
    pull boat logging *559, 561*
    soil erosion 555
    sugar cane/cotton plantations
        558–559
Lupinus texensis 381
Luquillo Mountains, Puerto Rico
    254–255

Magnoliales, classification 39–40
Malthus, Thomas 186
    An Essay on the Principle of
        Population 187

mammals, African grassland
    286–289, **287**, *288*
    evolutionary adaptations 286–289
management, land/ecosystem *see also*
        conservation; restoration,
        habitat
    adaptive ecosystem
        management 602
    and herbivory 334
    rehabilitation programs 546
    stressed environments 134, 184
    and succession 446
    and vegetation classification/
        description 457, 474, 476–484
management perspectives 588–592,
    589 see also conservation
    biodiversity maintenance 590,
        592–593
    functional redundancy 592
    service of humans/functional
        perspective 588–592,
        589, **591**
    structural/community perspective
        589–592
man-made landscapes, herbivory 292
    see also humans, ecological
        impact
mangrove swamps, diversity 517
maquis 151
Marat, Jean Paul 67
Mars, atmosphere 26, **27**
marshes, freshwater
    gap dynamics 274–275, *275*
    vegetation patterns 495–496, *496*
marshes, salt *see* salinity, salt marsh
    studies
mast years 373–375, **374**
    coevolution 373–374
    pig dispersal 374
    squirrel dispersal 375
    zoological perspective 375
mathematical modeling, herbivory
    325–327, *326*
    critical herbivore density *328*,
        329–331
    extended models 327–332,
        329, 330
    spruce budworm population
        dynamics 331–332, *332*
mathematical modeling, mutualism
    cost-benefit models 396–398
    facultative/obligate *395, 396*
    Lotka–Volterra models 395
    population dynamics 395–396

mathematical modeling, relative abundance *see* ranked abundance models

Maximilliana maripa dispersal by tapir 370

Mayan civilization 122, *123*

meanders, river 236–237, *237*, 243–249, *244*, *246 see also* burial; disturbance

Mediterranean climate, and species diversity 518–520, **520**

California 518

central Chile 518

Mediterranean basin 518

South Africa (fynbos) 518

southwestern Australia (kwongan) 518

Mediterranean shrublands *150*, 150–152, *152*

fynbos (South Africa) 151

kwongan (southwestern Australia) 518

life-form spectra **151**

maquis 151

plant community/soil characteristics **153**

meiosis, cost 379–381, 382

membranes, cell *see* cell membranes

meteor impacts 259–264, *260*, *261*, **262** *see also* catastrophes, high intensity

disturbance fires 261–262

study through geological record discontinuities, Cretaceous/ Tertiary boundary 260–262

Tunguska event, Siberia 264

micro-organisms, digestive *see* gut symbiont micro-organisms

migration, ice-age 426–428, *428*, *429*

mineral nutrients *see* nutrients; resource acquisition

Mississippi delta 553–557, *554*, *556*, *557*

mitochondria 13–14

models *see* computer modeling/ simulation; mathematical modeling

moisture/climatic warmth, and diversity 508–513

molecular systematics 35, 41–43, *45*

cladograms *42*, 42–43

molecules

amino acid structure 65, *65*

complexity 5–6, **6**, *8*

replication/reproduction of 9

stability/natural selection 7, 9, 64

mollisols 119

Monks Wood experiment 534, **535**

monocultures 197–200

moorlands 292

Moosonee, Ontario 158

Morisita's index 498, 499

mosaics, successional 237–238

Mount St. Helens, US 258–259, *259*

multicellular organisms, evolution *see* Cambrian explosion, multicellular organisms; *see also* eukaryotic cells, origins/evolution

multivariate methodology 464–465, 500–501 *see also* gradients/local patterns, vegetation

abundance data 467

correlations 470

data matrices 465–466, *466*

detrended correspondence analysis (DCA) 471

factor analysis 470

functional simplification, ordination 471–474, *474*

measuring similarity 466–468

ordination techniques 468

presence/absence data 466–467, *467*

principal components analysis (PCA) 468

species data ordinations 468–470, *469*

species/environmental data ordinations 470–471, *472*

TWINSPAN classification 471

Murray River, Australia 252

mutualism 399–402 *see also* gut symbiont micro-organisms; lichens; mycorrhizae; pollination; seed dispersal, by animals

animal-plant, *Acacia*/ant example 387–389, *388*, **389**

asymmetric 336

commensalism 336, 338, 355

and competition, apparent 398–399

definitions 336–337

divine order, confusion with 400

facilitation 338

facultative/obligate *395*, 396

fungal–plant associations, difficulties in studying 350

history of research into/use of term **337**, 337–338

measuring, importance of 400, *401*

modeling *see* mathematical modeling

parable from Darwin's observations 398

plant–plant *see* nurse plants; plant–plant associations

stressed environments 135, 138

and symbiosis 336

mycobionts 356

mycorrhizae

and commensalism 355

and competition 214–215

cost-benefits 347, 354–355, *355*

discovery 348

economics analogy 215

ectomycorrhizae/ endomycorrhizae 346

ectomycorrhizae in forests **337**, 349–350, **351–352**

infection rates/commonality 352, *353*, 353–354

and nitrogen uptake *347*

oxygen availability 350, 354

and parasitism 355

phosphorus uptake 347–349

and resource capture 83–85, 347–349

and resource gradients 95, *97*

and soil fertility 352

stressed environments 135

in wetlands 350–354, *353*

myrmecochory 371–373, *372*

Myxotricha paradoxa 15, *15*

Narrative of Travels on the Amazon and Rio Negro, A (Alfred Wallace) 38

natural selection *see* selection, natural; *see also* evolution

nature reserves 550

buffer zones 572

designing 570–573, *571*

and diversity 546 *see also* hot spots, diversity

ecological interest of stressed communities 135, 184

gap analysis 573

representativeness of habitat type 573

nature reserves (cont.)
size 505, 571–572, 586–588 *see also* species-area model
steps to follow 570–571
wildlife corridors 584
nature study, and biology 399
nectar, availability 108
Netherlands *596, 597*
New Jersey, USA, species diversity 542–543, *545*
New South Wales, Australia 289
nitrogen 65, *82*, 85–86 *see also* fertility
content and food quality 300–302, **301**, 323
cycle/Fritz Haber's work 87–88, 605
limitation 83–85, 86–91, *90*, 91–93, *93*
natural/man-made sources 85–86
secondary metabolites 297
uptake, and mutualism *347*, 392
Nothofagus 410, *411*
nuclear testing 606–607
nuclear war/nuclear winter 264, 604 *see also* catastrophes, high intensity; disturbance; radiation, ionizing
null model 487–490, 488–490
nurse plants 338–341 *see also* plant–plant associations
Barrel cactus/perennial bunch grass mutualism 339
competition from 340, 341
during primary succession 341
effects on physical environment 340
Saguaro cactus/creosote bush mutualism 338–339, *339*, *340*, 341
nutria (coypu), impact on fringing reed/marsh vegetation 316–317, **317**
nutrient/s *see also* resource acquisition
conservation 114–116
cyanophyte single cell model 81–83, *82*
gradient studies 116, *116*
resorption/resorption efficiency/ proficiency 115–116
soil 212–214
uptake components **83**
Nymphaeaceae 42, 43, *44*

oceanic
chemistry 18–19, **33**
nutrient depletion 22, **33**

oil sequestration 27–28, **33**
Ontario
Algonquin Provincial Park 506
Moosonee 158
Oparin, Aleksandr 5, 10
Opuntia fragilis study 218
orchid (*Epidendrum ciliare*) 382–385, *383*
Orchidaceae 40, 43, 46
Origin of Species, The (Charles Darwin) 136
ornithophily (bird pollination) 359–361, **360**, *361, 362*
Ottawa River, Canada, marshes 268–269, *269 see also* disturbance
overgrazing 545–546, 549, 567–568, *569*, 595–598
oxisols 120
oxygen
release, *Lobelia dortmanna* 345
uptake, and mycorrhizae 350, 354
oxygen revolution 15, 18–21, **33** *see also* atmosphere, origins; photosynthesis
and atmospheric composition 20, **33**
and ocean chemistry 18–19, **33**
ozone layer formation 19, 20–21, **33**
ozone layer 21, 22
formation *19*, 20–21, **33**

palynology 31, 404
Amazon 424
evergreen forests 410–411
fire history 232
plant succession 450
Pampas, South America 307–309
Panax quinquefolius (American ginseng) 315
paper industry 569 *see also* logging/ paper industry
parasitism 112–114, *113*
aerial parasites 114
documentation, historical 113
evolution 113
hemiparasites/holoparasites 113
influence on host species 114
limitation to dicotyledons 112
and mutualism 355, 356, 358 *see also* fly pollination
Park Grass experiment, Rothamsted, England 534, 535, **535**, 536–538, 541–542

patches, resource *see also* resource gradients
resource patches other than water 108
small-scale heterogeneity 93–94, *94*
transitory patches *100*, 100–101, *101*
patterns, vegetation *see* classification of vegetation; gradients/local patterns vegetation
peat bogs 160–161
carnivory 162
evergreen foliage 160
pH gradients 161
Sphagnum moss 160–161, *161*, 232–236, *236*, 434
succession *434*, 434–437, *435*, *436*, 454
Pereira, Ferdinand, conservationist 606
perennials/biennials 102–105
peripheral species 506
pesticide use, conifer timber plantations 331
pests *see* disease/pest introductions; *see also* defenses, plant; secondary metabolites
phanerophytes 513
phenolics 297
Philippines 573
phosphorus 67, 83–85
levels, lake 602
limitation 83–85, 86–91, *90*, 91–93, *93*
uptake, and mycorrhizae 347–349
photon harvesting 70
photosynthesis **71**
C3/C4 73–74
CAM (crassulacean acid metabolism) 46, 74–75, 147, *149, 150*
carbon dioxide/drought trade-off 74
origins/evolution *see below*
sciophytes 76–77
type classification 73–75, *76, 77*
photosynthesis, origins/evolution 15–18
chlorophyll evolution 17–18
electromagnetic spectrum, selection of visible light exploitation *16*, 16–17, **17**
energy synthesis, evolutionary possibilities 16, **17**
and fermentation 15

role in creation of atmosphere
1–2, **33**
selection for 16
phycobionts 355
phylogenetic classification *see*
classification, phylogenetic
phytoplankton
nitrogen and phosphorus 81–83,
81, 82
phytosociology 475, **476**, 477 *see also*
classification of vegetation
pine cones *see* strobili in
gymnosperms
plant–animal mutualism *see*
animal–plant associations
plant architecture *see* architecture,
plant
plant communities *see* classification,
phylogenetic; discrete
communities debate;
ecosystems; gradients/local
patterns, vegetation
plant defenses *see* defenses, plant
plant–plant associations 338,
342–346, *346 see also* nurse
plants
aerenchyma oxygen transport by
Typha latifolia 343
beach/bay study 341–342
and competition/stress gradients
341–342, *343, 344*
marsh elder seedling
recruitment 342
oxygen release by roots of *Lobelia
dortmanna* 345
salt marsh study mutualistic
interactions 342
Plants and Vegetation, overview/
scope 605
Pleistocene glaciations 418–419
drought 423
erosion/deposition 419, *421*
extinction of large mammals 429
flooding 430
Great Lakes development
421, 430
Hominids/*Homo sapiens* 426,
428–430
ice cores, Vostok *30*
ice sheet advances/retreats
418–419, 430
loess 419–421, *422*
migration 426–428, *428, 429*
passerine birds, evolution 423

pluvial lakes 422, *422*
refuge model, tropical forests
423, *423*
sea level changes 425–426,
426, 430
sediment cores, deep sea *30*, 31
species diversity 423
pneumatophores 176–177, *178*
Poaceae 40
Podocarpaceae 237, 410–411, **412**
podsols 119
pollination 515
birds (ornithophily) 359–361, **360**,
361, 362
ecology 362–363, **363**
efficiency 382–385
and herbivory deterrence
dilemma 302
insects 359, **359** *see also* fly
pollination
and nectar supply 358–361
population dynamics, mathematical
models 331–332, *332*,
395–396
Portland, Oregon 158, *159*
positive topography 95, *95*
prairie/savanna vegetation types, and
fire 230–232, *231*
Prantl, Karl 39
precipitation/temperature *see* rainfall/
climatic warmth
primary forests *see* forests, primary
primary production 602
gradients 323–324
and plant size *78*, 78–79
principal components analysis
(PCA) 468
Principles of Animal Ecology (Warder
Allee) 337
profile diagrams 458, *460*
prokaryotic cells 11, 12, *12, 13*
see also gut symbiont micro-
organisms
fossils 11
Proteaceae 413, *414*
protest, active 606
pteridophytes, diversity 508
Puerto Rico, Luquillo Mountains
254–255
pull boat logging *559, 561*
pyroclastic flows 255, **257**, 259

Quaternary 418–419
Queensland, Australia 437

radiation, ionizing
Long Island forest experiment *180*,
180–181, *181*
and plant diversity 181
radiosensitivity and chromosome
volume 181
Rafflesia genus 363–364
Rainbow Warrior, sinking 606–607
rainfall/climatic warmth
and diversity 508–513
interactions 156–157
ratios 57
ranked abundance models 532–539,
533, 535, **535**
broken stick model 534
Compton experiment 535, **535**
geometric model 534
log-normal model 534
Monks Wood experiment
534, **535**
Zipf–Mandelbrot model 534, 535
Raunkiaer, C. *51*, 51–55, **54**
life-form classification 280, 513
null model 488–490
red grouse 292
redundancy hypothesis, leaf
architecture 72
refuge model, tropical forests
423, *423*
regeneration *see also* restoration,
habitat; succession
from buried seed banks
270–272, **271**
cypress swamp 560, 562
deciduous forests, Appalachian
Mountains 272–273, *273*
relative abundance 532–539, *535*
see also diversity
evenness 532
ranked abundance models
532–539, *533*, **535**
Shannon–Weaver index 533
Simpson's index 533
relative growth rates (RGR) screening
162 *see also* growth rates
reproduction *see* clonal reproduction;
sexual reproduction
research, ecological *see also* science
locations 544, *545*
projects/careers 605, *608*
reading monographs/papers,
cautionary advice 592
role in conservation 606
reserves *see* nature reserves

resource acquisition 123–125 *see also* carbon dioxide/carbon; CHNOPS perspective; foraging; light acquisition; photosynthesis, origins/evolution; resource gradients
acquisition costs 67–68
availability patterns 93–99, 101–105, *102, 103* see also below
bottlenecks 105–108, *106, 107*
commodity concept 67–68
depletion models 198–200
energetic costs 68
ion capture 100
and life span 102–105
limitation **91**, 108–109
mineral nutrients, cyanobacteria single cell model 81–83, *82*
needs 5
nutrient conservation 114–116
nutrient uptake components **83**
pre-emption models 198–200
resorption/resorption efficiency/proficiency 115–116
small-scale heterogeneity 93–94, *94*
stress-tolerant plant attributes **109**
symbiotic mycorrhizae 83–85
transitory patches *100,* 100–101, *101*
water/evapotranspiration process 79–80, *80*
resource fluctuations, study complications 105–108, *106, 107*
resource gradients 94–99, *95, 96,* **99**
biogeographical (long term) approach 106
examples 97, *98,* 129–131, *132, 252*
forest-soil treatise 95
mycorrhizal associations 95, *97*
nutrient gradient studies 116, *116*
scales 97–99
terminology 95
water erosion/deposition 94
Restionaceae 413, *414*
restoration, habitat 599–601, *600*
history 600–601
integrity of community, preservation 599–600
objectives/targets 599
perspectives, American/European 601

rehabilitation programs 546
reversing changes 600
safety margins 592
thresholds, critical 550, 595–599, *598*
RGR (relative growth rates) screening 162 *see also* growth rates, in stressed environments
Rhine, River 274
rhinoceros, in tropical floodplain forests 313
Richards, P. W. 55, **55**
risk-aversive strategies 133
rivers
erosion *see* water erosion
meanders, river 236–237, *237,* 243–249, *244, 246 see also* burial; disturbance
sedimentation *see* deposition
valleys/floodplains 236–238
rock barrens 152–156
alvars 154, *155*
serpentine rock communities 155–156
tepui 154
rock domes 154
Rome/Mediterranean, ancient 551–553, *552*
deforestation/erosion 551–553
Rothamsted, England, Park Grass Experiment 535, **535**, 536–538, *538,* 541–542
ruderals
life history 102
strategy *see* CSR synthesis
ruminants *see* gut symbiont micro-organisms
Russia
boreal forests, conservation/management 569
Ksudach volcano, Kamchatka Peninsula 255–258, **257**

Saguaro cactus/creosote bush mutualism 338–339
salinity 162–165, *163*
and diversity 517
and drought 163, *164*
and plant distribution 163–165
salt marsh studies 164–165, 342, 492–493, *493*
soils (solonchaks) 119

Salvinia molesta 301–302
sand dunes, succession 437–439, *438, 439*
savanna vegetation types, and fire 230–232, *231*
Saxifraga aizoon, Algonquin Provincial Park, Ontario 506
scale effects, species distribution 182–183, *183*
science *see also* research, ecological importance of 400, *401*
nature study, and biology 399
sciophytes 76–77
sea level changes, Pleistocene glaciations 425–426, *426, 430*
secondary metabolites 149, 297, 297–299, *298,* 323 *see also* defenses, plant
angiosperms 515
nitrogen containing 297
phenolics 297
terpenes 297
tropical forest example 297–298, **299**
wetland plants 298–299, *300*
sedimentation by rivers *see* deposition
seed banks 102
Darwin's observations 453
regeneration from 270–272, **271**
and succession 453
seed dispersal, by animals 365–367 *see also* mutualism; mast years
Andira inermis dispersal by bats 370–371
Cakile edentula on sand dunes 367–369, *368, 370*
coevolution 366
cost benefits 366–367
evolution 365, 366, 373–374, 377–379
fruit production 365, 366
Maximilliana maripa dispersal by tapir 370
myrmecochory 371–373, *372, 372–373*
obligate (single-species) dependence 377–379
quantitative studies **376,** 376–377, *377*
seed distribution versus herbivory deterrence dilemma 302
tambalacoque (*Sideroxylon*) and dodo 377–379

seed production/output 386–387
  number/size relationship 386, *387*
  and shoot size 386–387
  stressed environments 135–140,
    139, *140*
seed-protecting structures 293–295
  hard coats 303
  strobili in gymnosperms *294*,
    294–295, **296**
seedling
  mortality, stressed environments
    140–141, 143
  recruitment, marsh elder 342
selection, natural *see also* evolution
  cellulose versus chitin as structural
    molecule 92
  height 77–78
  land, colonization 23
  of molecules 7, 9, 64
  photosynthesis 16
  for small leaves 72–73
  stress adaptations 131, 133
  visible light exploitation,
    electromagnetic spectrum
    16, 16–17, **17**
Selfish Gene, The (Richard Dawkins) 9
self-thinning 197–198
Serengeti National Park, Tanzania
  289, 309–313, **310**
seres 431, 450, *451*
serial endosymbiosis theory 12–15, *14*
serotinous cones *see* strobili in
  gymnosperms
serpentine rock communities
  155–156
sexual reproduction
  Antennaria parvifolia 385
  Anthoxanthum odoratum
    381–382, *382*
  and apomixis 385–386
  cost benefits 379–381, **380**
  evolution 22, 23–24
  inbreeding depression 381, 385
  Lupinus texensis 381
  meiosis, cost 379–381, 382
  orchid (*Epidendrum ciliare*)
    382–385, *383*
  out-crossing, experimental
    measures 381–382
  pollination efficiency 382–385
shade-tolerant species 442
shading, and shoot size 209–215, *213*
Shannon–Weaver index 533
sheep, herbivory 292

shorelines, succession 448–450, *449*,
  454–455
Siberia, Tunguska event 264
Sideroxylon see tambalacoque
Silent Spring (Rachel Carson) 331
Simpson's index 533
slugs, herbivory 292
smoking hills *179*, 179–180
snags (dead trees) 603
snow abrasion, wind-driven 170
soils 116–120
  classification *118*, 118–120
  earthworms, role 120
  electrical charge 117
  erosion 121–122, 555
  fertility, and mycorrhizae 352
  forest-soil treatise 95
  formation, factors driving 117
  surface area 117
solonchaks 119
South Africa
  Cape Province 307, *307*
  fynbos 151, 518
South America, Pampas 307–309
speciation rates, and diversity
  518, *519*
species-area model 502–505, *503*,
  504, 506, *519*, 571
  conservation implications 505,
    586–588
  equation 503
  extinction rates 505, 547
species composition
  grazed/ungrazed vegetation
    318–320, *320*
  top-down/bottom-up control 305,
    322–324
species data ordinations 468–470,
  469, 470–471, *472*
species diversity *see* diversity
species flocks 508
species pools 516, **516**
Sphagnum peat communities 160–161,
  161, 232–236, *236*, 434
spines, desert plants 148–149
spodosols 119
sporophyte *see also* gametophyte
  alternation of generations
    415–418
  description 415
  phylogeny 42
  plant colonization of land 22, 415
  size in terrestrial plants 77–78,
    415–417

Sphagnum 161
  taxonomic classification 49
Sprengel, C. K. 362–363
spruce budworm population
    dynamics 331–332, *332*
squirrels
  dispersal, tree seeds 375
  herbivory 295, *296*
statistical tests for species
    aggregation 498–499
  Morisita's index 498
  nestedness 498–499
stone plants (*Lithops*) 149
strawberry-coral, model clonal
  reproduction 142
stress 182–183, 184–185 *see also*
    adaptations to stress;
    arctic–alpine vegetation;
    CSR synthesis; drought,
    definitions; flooding; growth
    rates; peat bogs; radiation,
    ionizing; salinity
  air pollution stress *179*, 179–180
  categorization/classification
    184–185
  competition, role of 129, 131,
    341–342, *344*
  ecological interest of communities
    135, 184
  ecological/physiological responses
    129, *130*
  endolithic communities
    174–176, *175*
  experimental examples
    129–131, *132*
  importance of accurate definitions/
    terminology 126
  lichens, cold/drought tolerance
    173–174, **174**
  plant attributes **109**
  regulators, stress 160–161, 162–179
  resource unavailability 159–162
  RGR screening 162
  scale effects, moisture and
    temperature 182–183, *183*
  scope of chapter 127
  seed size 135–140, *139*, *140*
  seedling mortality 140–141, 143
  short-term metabolic costs
    128–131
  strain, definition 127
  stress avoidance 127, 169
  stress, definition 126, 127, 128
  stress factor/stressor, definition 127

stress (cont.)
stress response/state of stress, definition 127
stress tolerance 124, 127, 169
strobili in gymnosperms 294, 294–295, **296**
fire adaptations, gymnosperm cones 295, **296**
squirrel herbivory on 295, 296
structural perspective, land management 589–592
succession 431–432, 454–455
Acadian Forest 442, **444**
barrens 446
Boundary Waters Canoe Area, North America 440–442, **441**
buried seed banks 453
climax 431, 450–451
and competition 453, 454
conifer forests affected by fire 439–440
controversy/synthesis 431, 448, 452–454, 455
and disturbance 447, 452
facilitation 453
fire-dependent species 442
historical views 454
hydroseres 450
and landscape management 446
and life-history 444, 444
mechanisms of change 452–453
mosaics, successional 237–238
peat bogs 434, 434–437, 435, 436, 454
and plant size 78, 78–79
post-glacial, Glacier Bay, Alaska 432, 432–434, 434
predictive models 446–448, 447
primary 431
progressive/retrogressive 437
sand dunes 437–439, 438, 439
secondary 431
seres 431, 450, 451
shade-tolerant species 442
shorelines 448–450, 449, 454–455
Tasmanian rainforest 444–446, 445
usefulness of concept 455
vegetation dynamics approach 452, 455
zoned communities 403, 448–450, 453
succulents 110–111, 111
sugar cane/cotton plantations 558–559
sulfur see CHNOPS perspective

summary displays 463, 463
sun tracking 169
sundews 136–138, 138
superorganisms 437, 485–486
Sweden 37
symbiosis 336–337 see also gut symbiont micro-organisms; mutualism
Systema Naturae (Linnaeus) 36, 37–38

Takhtajan, A. regional floristic classification 46–48, 47, **48**
tambalacoque (Sideroxylon) and dodo coevolution 377–379
re-evaluation 378
Tanzania, Serengeti National Park **289**, 309–313, **310**
tapir, Maximilliana maripa dispersal by 370
temperature/rainfall see rainfall/climatic warmth
tephra deposits 255, **257**, 259
tepui 154, 579
terpenes 297
terrestrial species see land colonization
Tertiary/Cretaceous boundary 260–262
thermodynamics, second law 5–6, 7
Thornthwaite, C. W. 57
thresholds, critical 550, 595–599, 598
degradation 598–599
overgrazing 595–598
reversing changes 600
time/timescales 403–405, 404 see also succession
climate change 428
ecological 403–405
fossils, studying 404
historical research 404
measurement 403
Titus Smith Jr. 121
top-down/bottom-up control, plant communities 322–324
other plant–animal interactions 324
primary productivity gradients 323–324
trophic cascades/effects of carnivorous predators 323
tortoises, giant 290, **292**, 566–567, 567, 568, 568
tragedy of the commons 331
tree/s see also canopy; forests (various)
bark insulation, from fire 228–230, 229, 230, 231

mast see mast years
overstorey diversity 509–510, 510, 511, 512
trophic cascades/effects of carnivorous predators 323
tropical floras 412–414, 413 see also forests, tropical
Australia 414
New-World vertebrates 413–414
Tunguska event, Siberia 264
TWINSPAN classification 471
Typha latifolia 343

Ulmus americana 584, **586**
ultisols 120
Umbilicaria species, cold/drought tolerance 173–174, **174**

van Helmont, J. B. 120–121
vascular plants, evolutionary trends 26
vegetation cover types 460, 461
vegetation dynamics 452, 455
vegetation templates 462, 462
vegetative reproduction see clonal reproduction
Venus, atmosphere 26, **27**
venus fly trap (Dionaea muscipula) 521, 522, 522
Vernadsky, Vladimir La Biosphère 2, 3, 3–4
volcanic eruptions 255–259, 257 see also catastrophes; disturbance
distribution, western US 255
Ksudach volcano, Kamchatka Peninsula, Russia 255–258, **257**
Mount St. Helens, US 258–259, 259
tephra deposits 255, **257**, 259 air borne pyroclastic material
von Humboldt, A. 51, 52, 52–54

waldsterben 585
Wallace, Alfred 36, 37, 38–39, 186
A Narrative of Travels on the Amazon and Rio Negro 38
warfare
chemical 87
nuclear 264, 604 see also catastrophes; disturbance; radiation, ionizing
warmth, climatic see rainfall/climatic warmth

water absorption/storage, desert
plants 147–148
water erosion 236–238
Amazon forest floodplains
237–238, *239*
meanders, river 236–237, *237*,
243–249, *244*, *246 see also*
burial; disturbance
mosaics, successional 237–238
podocarp forests 237
and resource gradients 94
river valleys/floodplains 236–238
water evapotranspiration 79–80, *80*
water table lowering 560
waves 249–252, *251*

exposure gradients, measuring
251–252
fertility gradients created by
250, *252*
and vegetation types, River Murray,
Australia 252
wetland/s
clonal reproduction 140–141, 143
competition intensity gradients
220, *221*
conservation 576, **578**
ecological role 576
fire in 232, **234**, *235*
largest in the world 576, **578**, *578*
mycorrhizae 350–354, *353*

resource gradient experimental
example 130–131, *132*
secondary metabolites
298–299, *300*
vegetation analysis 496–499, **499**
wildlife corridors 584
world floristic regions 46–48, *47*, **48**
see also ecoregions

Zipf-Mandelbrot relative abundance
model 534, 535
zonation *see* gradients/local patterns,
vegetation
zoned communities 403, 448–450,
453